A HANDBOOK OF
ENGLISH LITERATURE

A HANDBOOK OF
ENGLISH LITERATURE

HOMER A. WATT
Late Chairman Department of English
New York University

WILLIAM W. WATT
Late Professor of English
Lafayette College

BARNES & NOBLE, INC. · NEW YORK
PUBLISHERS · BOOKSELLERS · SINCE 1873
AN EVERYDAY HANDBOOK

©

Copyright, 1945, 1946
By BARNES & NOBLE, INC.

Ninth Printing, 1959

All rights reserved

L.C. Catalogue Card Number: 55–12383
Formerly published under the title:
A DICTIONARY OF ENGLISH LITERATURE

PR1- * 68-0221 PB
W343h

PREFACE

This book was written to fill the need for a general reference work in English literature which would be usable, readable, portable, and inexpensive. It is designed for all who would appreciate a concise cyclopedia of literary facts and terminology, biographical data, and brief critical evaluations. It is designed also as a supplementary textbook and review book for students—especially college undergraduates—who are seeking a comprehensive knowledge of the entire field. It is intended as a stimulus and guide to reading and an aid to appreciation and understanding.

The book is divided into five parts: 1. *Dictionary of Authors;* 2. *List of Anonymous Works;* 3. *Glossary of Literary Terms;* 4. *Note on Versification;* and 5. *Chronological Chart.*

The first and longest part, *Dictionary of Authors,* contains biographical and critical notes on about nine hundred writers—including a few pseudonymous authors—from the Old English period down to the present day. We have made our selections according to the following principles:

1. We have tried to include all authors of the very first rank and all secondary figures with whom—if only for their historical importance—the student of English literature should be moderately familiar. In addition, we have entered a large number of more obscure writers, not because of their intrinsic importance but because their names appear with some frequency. Finally, we have made room for a few where tradition has established a hypothetical author, or where an anonymous writer or group of writers is generally known by some epithet (Junius, William Langland, Martin Marprelate, Pearl Poet, Smectymnuus, Wakefield Master).

2. Although we have made no formal classification of "major" and "minor" figures, the amount of space devoted to a writer is usually a fair indication of his relative importance. Of course, a prolific poet with a flair for making headlines demands more space than a highly selective artist who spent his uneventful years in comfortable obscurity. We would not imply, for example, by the comparative length of the entries that Lord Byron is twice as good a poet as Thomas Gray.

3. Because of the compression demanded in a general reference

book of this sort, we have had to be scrupulously selective in choosing the biographical and bibliographical data for the author entries. We have tried not to give a complete biographical sketch of every author but only to select highlights to illuminate his personality and his work. With some major figures—Shakespeare, for example—we have summarized the known facts at considerable length; with many of the minor figures—like Martin Tupper—we have omitted biographical material entirely.

4. Since we have used the word *literature* in a broad sense, we have included a number of figures—Charles Darwin, William Harvey, Sir Isaac Newton, and Adam Smith, for example—who, although their works may not belong in the restricted realm of *belles-lettres,* made important contributions to human knowledge.

5. We have included not only writers from the British Isles but a few outstanding figures from Australia, Canada, and South Africa, as well as several—like Joseph Conrad, Henry James, W. H. Hudson, and T. S. Eliot—who were born elsewhere but who became British subjects.

6. Writers are listed under the names by which they are best known. Thus Lewis Carroll is entered under CARROLL, with a cross-reference under Dodgson; George Villiers, second duke of Buckingham, under BUCKINGHAM, with a cross-reference under Villiers. We have also entered such well-known pseudonyms and epithets as Isaac BICKERSTAFF and the ETTRICK SHEPHERD, with appropriate cross-references.

The second part of the book, *List of Anonymous Works,* supplements the first part by listing alphabetically some works for which no author has been suggested and others for which none of several possible authors has a clear enough claim to justify his inclusion in Part One. Since the roster of anonymous works in English literature, especially before the middle of the seventeenth century, is almost endless, only a few of the most significant items could be included.

In the third part, *Glossary of Literary Terms,* we have undertaken the difficult task of defining the terms usually encountered in the study of English literature. This glossary includes in alphabetical order brief definitions of literary types (ballad, novel, etc.), historical movements and periods (Renaissance, Restoration, etc.), "schools" (Pre-Raphaelite Brotherhood, Metaphysical Poets, etc.), and a large number of the "isms" and other abstractions which are tossed about so loosely in literary criticism. Obviously the meanings of these terms vary widely with the context. In some entries we have merely indicated the broad area of meaning encompassed by a single term, with special emphasis on the sense in which we have used it elsewhere in the book. In our glossary we have not included rhetorical terms like *irony, metaphor, metonymy,* or any of the terminology of versification which is covered in Part Four.

Part Four, *Note on Versification,* is a concise treatment of the traditional approach to English prosody, including definitions of the most common terms. We have not considered any of the less orthodox theories of versification.

Part Five, *Chronological Chart,* is designed to place the major English authors in their chronological relationship one with another and with some of the principal historical and literary events in England and on the Continent. It should be used in connection with Parts One, Two, and Three. In preparing the Chart the authors acknowledge their indebtedness to the content and form of the *Chronological Table of History and Literature,* in Woods, Watt, and Anderson's *The Literature of England* (Scott, Foresman, and Company, second edition 1941).

Since we have intended from the beginning to make this book as readable as possible, we have tried hard to avoid some of the characteristics that make too many other reference books of this sort conspicuously unreadable. We have escaped as far as possible from the monotonous biographical pattern of birth-schooling-marriage-works-and-deathbed gasp. We have assiduously eschewed shorthand and telegrammatic fragments—(b. 1852, 3 child. by 1st wife, wks. met cold recep., d. 1903 boots on, etc.). We have proceeded throughout on the principle that the mere mention of a minor biographical fact (attended the Puddleby Grammar School) or a list of titles without comment (His works are:) is meaningless to the average reader. Frankly critical, we have made no pretense of concealing our opinion that Chaucer is a greater poet than Erasmus Darwin. In brief, although our arrangement is alphabetical and not chronological, we hope that this book will prove as readable as a good short history of English literature.

At the same time we have tried to be meticulously accurate and consistent. Dates and other details have been checked and re-checked many times in standard sources. Whenever authorities disagreed, we either made our own investigation or indicated the uncertainty by using a *c.* or a question mark. In spite of our care to be accurate, we are under no illusion that the book will be without error; that it may be more correct in subsequent reprintings and revisions, we shall be very grateful to readers who point out to us any slips or misprints that they may detect.

Some special obligations demand acknowledgment. For the dates of plays before 1700 we have relied largely on Alfred Harbage's admirable *Annals of English Drama* (University of Pennsylvania Press, 1940); for the dates of later plays on the valuable surveys of Allardyce Nicoll, *History of Early Eighteenth Century Drama, 1700–1750, History of Late Eighteenth Century Drama, 1750–1800, History of Early Nineteenth Century Drama, 1800–1850,* and *History of Late Nineteenth Century Drama, 1850–1900* (Macmillan, 1925, 1927, 1930, and 1942, respectively). Unless otherwise noted in the text, all dates of plays are those of the first *performance*. Publication dates of other works, birth and death dates, and the wording of titles have been checked, wherever possible, against *The Cambridge Bibliography of English Literature* (F. W. Bateson, editor, The Macmillan Company and the Cambridge University Press, 1941). Excepting where specifically stated, dates of non-dramatic works are those of first *publication;* dates of composition have been included only when a work was never published or when several years elapsed between writing and publication. We have modernized the spelling of titles, excepting in a few instances where we have retained the original spelling for flavor or because it was an intentional device on the part of the author.

We can list here only a few of the many other sources to which we are indebted: *The Dictionary of National Biography; The Cambridge History of English Literature* (G. P. Putnam's Sons, 1907–1917); *Webster's Biographical Dictionary* (1943); *The Oxford Companion to English Literature* (editor, Sir Paul Harvey, Oxford, 1932); E. A. Baker's *History of the English Novel* (Barnes & Noble, New York, 1950); *Introductions to English Literature* (general editor, Bonamy Dobrée, The Cresset Press, London, 1939, etc.); and Fred B. Millett's *Contemporary British Literature* (Harcourt Brace, New York, 1935).

Finally we owe a special personal debt to Virginia H. Lederer and May Goldberg, who carefully and conscientiously typed the final manuscript.

H. A. W.
W. W. W.

CONTENTS

CONTENTS

DICTIONARY OF AUTHORS

I

DICTIONARY OF AUTHORS

A

ABERCROMBIE, Lascelles (1881–1938) was a poet and critic. His poetry (*Collected Poems,* 1930) is philosophical in content, traditional in form. *The Sale of St. Thomas* (1911, 1930) is the best known of his several ventures in the field of poetic drama. Among his provocative critical works are *An Essay towards a Theory of Art* (1922), *The Idea of Great Poetry* (1925), and *Romanticism* (1926).

ADDISON, Joseph (1672–1719) was born in the same year as his famous collaborator, Sir Richard Steele. They attended the same school, Charterhouse, and the same university, Oxford. But whereas the erratic Steele left without a degree to sow wild oats in the King's Life Guards, Addison stayed on at the university after taking his first degree and won distinction as a classical scholar and a writer of Latin verses. He left the university in 1699 to enter upon four years of travel on the Continent. The literary fruits of this journey were two unpromising prose works: *Dialogues upon the Usefulness of Ancient Medals* (probably written 1703–5; published 1721), a piece of recondite research in numismatics; and *Remarks on Several Parts of Italy* (1705), a travel diary. But on his return Addison also published *The Campaign* (1705), a declamatory poem in heroic couplets celebrating Marlborough's victory at the battle of Blenheim. Like most patriotic war poems, its popularity far exceeded its artistic merit, and Addison's political fortune was made. From then until his death he held one post after another. He served twice as chief secretary to the Lord Lieutenant in Ireland, became Secretary of State in 1717, and retired in 1718 with a pension of £1500. Even when his Whig party was out of favor, Addison did not go begging like Dick Steele; he was returned to Parliament regularly from 1708 until his death.

In addition to the works already mentioned, Addison wrote a number of majestic hymns, the best known of which, "The spacious firmament on high," is still widely sung. Of his three dramatic pieces—an opera, *Rosamund* (1707), a tragedy, *Cato* (1713), and a comedy, *The Drummer* (1716)—only the tragedy is well

known. Partly because of political implications, *Cato* was enor-
mously popular when it first appeared; most readers today find it
static and platitudinous and, by conceding that it is one of the
best of the *classical* tragedies in English, damn it with faint
praise. To the world at large, Addison is the great essayist who
collaborated with Steele on the *Tatler* (April 12, 1709–January 2,
1711) and the *Spectator* (March 1, 1711–December 6, 1712).
Steele began the first of these famous periodicals by himself, and
Addison's first contribution was the eighteenth of its thrice-weekly
numbers. Although the *Tatler* improved as the two essayists
learned their craft, it remained little more than an aimless miscellany of news and gossip. The *Spectator* was different. Addison
was in from the beginning, and he seems to have been the guiding
spirit. From the first two of its daily numbers, the *Spectator* obviously had a plan. The Spectator himself, introduced by Addison
in the first paper, was a mellow philosopher who was to comment with a sort of Olympian detachment on the follies of the
world. The members of his club, four of whom Steele introduced
in the second number, were to serve as representatives of social
types from various walks of life: Sir Andrew Freeport, the city
merchant; Captain Sentry, a soldier; Will Honeycomb, a man of
fashion; and—"the first of our society"—Sir Roger de Coverley,
the immortal country gentleman.

The acid portrait of "Atticus" which Pope included in his
Epistle to Dr. Arbuthnot (1735) is not a true index to Addison's
reputation among his contemporaries, for he was one of the most
popular men of his time. Few men have come closer to observing
the golden mean in their lives and in their writing. Although he
was not, like the Spectator, a complete neutral in the quarrels
between Whig and Tory, he wrote, in an age which knew the
savagery of Swift and Pope, with a remarkable degree of serenity,
restraint, and objectivity. As a moralist, he showed his middle-
class readers a way of moderation between the excesses of the
Restoration and the crabbed Puritanism of Jeremy Collier. As a
stylist, he found a happy medium between the conversational garrulity which often characterized the prose of Steele and the frigid
pedantry which one might have expected of a university don.
Johnson wrote: "Whoever wishes to attain an English style, familiar but not coarse, and elegant but not ostentatious, must
give his days and nights to the volumes of Addison."

Æ was the pseudonym of **George William Russell** (1867–1935),
one of the major figures of the Irish Renaissance. In a series of

books of verse—from *Homeward; Songs by the Way* in 1894 to
The House of the Titans in the year before his death—he revealed
himself as a mystical lyric poet with a rare gift for capturing the
magic of the Irish countryside. At the same time, he was pursuing
active careers in journalism and politics, editing the *Irish Home-
stead* (1904–23) and the *Irish Statesman* (1923–30) and issuing
numerous pamphlets on such subjects as Irish foreign policy, labor
conditions in Dublin, and—his favorite theme—agricultural reform.

AELFRIC (c. 955–c. 1020). The earliest writers in English literature were churchmen who composed more often in Latin than in
Old English. Of these one of the most notable was Aelfric, called
"Grammaticus." After a training in a monastery at Winchester,
he left in 987 to teach the brothers of the Cernel monastery in
Dorsetshire. This experience led him to devote his life to religious
teaching and writing. He seems to have begun with the composition of a series of homilies in 989; a second series followed in 993–
4. He also wrote tracts on church policy and Bible commentaries,
some of which contain scraps of actual translation from the Old
Testament. But his most important works were his alliterative
Lives of the Saints (996) and his *Colloquy on the Occupations*.
The latter is a didactic Latin dialogue between a master and a
pupil in which various craftsmen—the farmer, the fisher, the
hunter, the smith, the carpenter, and others—discourse about their
labors. It was translated early and by an unknown hand into Old
English.

AINSWORTH, William Harrison (1805–82) was a conceited,
over-dressed magazine editor whose thirty-nine novels were chiefly
historical romances. He specialized in Gothic horrors (*Rookwood,*
1834, *The Tower of London,* 1840) and in romantic crime (*Jack
Sheppard,* 1839). When Thomas Hardy was a boy, Ainsworth was
his favorite novelist.

AKENSIDE, Mark (1721–70) was a minor poet who stopped writing at twenty-five and became a very successful physician and hospital superintendent. His *Pleasures of the Imagination* (1744) is a
heavy, didactic poem, based largely on Addison's essays from the
Spectator. Of this labored work Johnson said to Boswell: "Sir, I
could not read it through." Johnson also remarked that Akenside's
Odes (1745) made him sick.

ALCUIN (735–804). The debt of Anglo-Saxon England to the
numerous missionary scholars and teachers from Ireland and the
Continent was heavy. Part of the debt was repaid when the theo-

logian, philosopher, and writer, Alcuin, left the ecclesiastical school at York in 782 to become the cultural adviser of Charlemagne (742–814), King of the Franks and Emperor of the West. In 796 Alcuin became Abbot of the French monastery of Tours. He was one of the most industrious of the early scholars and writers, but all his writings are in Latin, and he left to later authors the task of composition in the vernacular. In addition to numerous theological and philosophical tracts, he wrote a life of Willibrord (657?–738?), a missionary in the Netherlands, and over three hundred letters, which contain valuable historical materials. His poem *On the Mutability of All Human Affairs* is a Latin elegy on the destruction by Danish raiders in 793 of Lindisfarne Abbey, famous seat of culture and learning in northern England.

ALDHELM, ST. (640?–709) was Bishop of Sherborne. Although he composed some English songs which have not survived, he is remembered, like the later clerics, Bede and Alcuin, for his writings in Latin. Among those extant are a collection of letters, a series of riddles, and a learned treatise in praise of virginity. He wrote in an artificial style full of rare words and intricate circumlocutions.

ALDINGTON, Richard (1892–   ), novelist, poet, critic, translator, and anthologist, is probably best known as the author of *Death of a Hero* (1929), one of the bitterest novels produced by the First World War. When he was editor of the *Egoist* (1914–17), he was one of the leaders of the "imagist" poets, but many of the verses in his *Collected Poems* (1934) reveal that he has since transcended the narrow limits of imagism.

ALEXANDER, Sir William, Earl of Stirling (1567?–1640), Scottish poet and dramatist, was a friend of William Drummond of Hawthornden. His works include: *Aurora* (1604), containing 106 sonnets and other poetical "first fancies of the Author's youth"; and *The Monarchic Tragedies* (published 1603–7), four dreary classical tragedies on the lives of Darius, Croesus, Alexander, and Julius Caesar.

ALFRED (849–901). By far the most notable of the early kings of England was Alfred, King of Wessex from 871 to 901. For services to his country both in peace and in war, he well earned the title of "the Great." His father, the noble Ethelwulf, had the wisdom to send his son to Rome for his early education. Here Alfred acquired that enthusiasm for learning and culture which was so marked a characteristic of his later activities. When he came to the throne of the West Saxons, the invading Danes had already overrun the northern part of England and were pressing against the borders of Wessex. The brilliant young king beat them back by military force and astute statecraft until by the Treaty of Wedmore in 886 he restricted them to the northeastern part of England known as the Danelagh. Thus King Alfred saved England for the English and got for his people a period of peace during which he could encourage learning. To his court flocked a notable group of scholars, including Asser, a Welsh cleric who became Bishop of Sherborne. Asser wrote the biography of his royal master (about 894) and helped him make numerous translations from Latin into West Saxon. Among these translations are Pope Gregory's *Pastoral Care,* a guide for the clergy; Orosius' *Universal History;* Boethius' *Concerning the Consolation of Philosophy,* a dialogue of the early fifth century; and—perhaps most important—Bede's *Ecclesiastical History of the English Nation* (731). Although to modern readers the translations seem Latinized and stiff, they are astonishing evidence of the great king's desire to revive and maintain learning among his people, and they have brought him the title of "Father of English Prose." Alfred does not seem to have written any original prose, but he did much to encourage the continuation of that long series of historical records known as *The Anglo-Saxon Chronicle.* The *Chronicle* began long before Alfred's time and continued until that of Henry II, King of England from 1154 to 1189.

ALLINGHAM, William (1824–89), an Irish poet, was a friend of D. G. Rossetti and Carlyle. He is remembered chiefly by a single fanciful lyric, *The Fairies* ("Up the airy mountain"). It appeared in his *Day and Night Songs* (1854).

AMORY, Thomas (1691?–1788) was an obscure Irishman who wrote two eccentric books which can hardly be called novels: *Memoirs of Several Ladies of Great Britain* (1755) and *The Life of John Buncle* (1756, 1766). The first is a baffling memoir of one lady; the second, and more readable, a rollicking picaresque narrative of a hero with eight successive wives. Like *Tristram Shandy,* both are bizarre scrapbooks of the author's opinions on every subject which entered his head.

ANSTEY, Christopher (1724–1805) wrote one popular work, *The New Bath Guide* (1766), a series of "poetical epistles" in which he travestied the manners of the famous watering place by narrating the adventures of the "Blunderhead Family."

ANSTEY, F. was the pseudonym of **Thomas Anstey Guthrie** (1856–1934). He wrote a great deal of miscellaneous work in which serious satire is often hidden under a cloak of trivial jesting. Much of it first appeared in *Punch*. It includes the satirical novel *Vice Versa, or a Lesson to Fathers* (1882), *Mr. Punch's Pocket Ibsen* (1893), and a once-popular play, *The Man from Blankley's* (1901).

ARBUTHNOT, John (1667–1735). The "good John" to whom Pope addressed his *Epistle to Dr. Arbuthnot* (1735) was physician to Queen Anne and a close friend of Pope, Swift, and Gay. In 1712 he published *The History of John Bull,* a group of five allegorical pamphlets in which he derided the Duke of Marlborough and urged cessation of the war with France. The work is one of the best political satires in English. Although each of three other nations is exemplified in a central character—Lewis Baboon (the French king), Lord Strutt (Philip of Spain), and Nicholas Frog (the Dutch)—only John Bull (Britain) has survived as a national symbol. In addition to his major work, Dr. Arbuthnot collaborated with Pope and Gay on the farce *Three Hours after Marriage* (1717) and wrote at least part of the *Memoirs of . . . Martinus Scriblerus* (1741), a satire on false taste in learning.

ARMIN, Robert (1565?–1610) was an actor who played comic rôles in Shakespeare's plays. He was the author of a curious play called *The History of the Two Maids of More-clacke* (printed 1609) and a jesting prose pamphlet entitled *A Nest of Ninnies* (1608).

ARMSTRONG, John (1709–79) was a Scotsman who practiced medicine in London. He wrote poetry under the influence of his friend James Thomson, to whose *Castle of Indolence* (1748) he contributed four stanzas. Armstrong's most celebrated work is an artificial blank-verse essay, *The Art of Preserving Health* (1744), in which he called a "cold bath" a "gelid cistern."

ARNOLD, Matthew (1822–88) was the son of Thomas Arnold, famous headmaster of Rugby. He was educated at his father's school and was graduated from Oxford with honors in classical studies. After he had served for a time as secretary to Lord Lansdowne, an appointment in 1851 as government inspector of schools enabled him to marry Frances Lucy Wightman. Eight years later, as foreign commissioner of education, he surveyed the school systems of Europe and wrote reports that were of immense value to his government. From 1857 to 1867 he was professor of poetry at Oxford. In 1883, five years before his death, he made the customary American tour, during which he delivered the series of lectures that were collected as *Discourses in America* (1885).

At the beginning of his literary career Arnold devoted most of his attention to poetry. Some of his poems—for example, the famous sonnet on Shakespeare in his first collection (1849)—are literary criticism. Others, like the pompous narrative *Sohrab and Rustum* (1853) and the prosy "Greek" tragedy *Merope* (1858), reveal Arnold practising his own doctrine that criticism should precede creation and playing the too-sedulous ape to his beloved classics. Still other poems—the sonnets *Quiet Work* (1849) and *To an Independent Preacher* (1849), for example—reflect ethical tenets which are familiar to readers of Arnold's later prose. The dominant mood of Arnold's poetry is melancholy, a melancholy profoundly colored by religious doubt. This is the mood of the beautiful *Dover Beach* (1867), in which Arnold reflects on the withdrawal of the Sea of Faith, which leaves the poet and his love

> ". . . as on a darkling plain
> Swept with confused alarms of struggle and flight,
> Where ignorant armies clash by night."

A similar mood pervades many of his best poems, including *The Strayed Reveler* (1849); *The Forsaken Merman* (1849); the dramatic poem *Empedocles on Etna* (1852); *The Scholar-Gipsy* (1853), a poem of Oxford; and *Thyrsis* (1866), the pastoral elegy on Arthur Hugh Clough. At his worst Arnold could write notoriously inane lines like "A prop gave way! crash fell a platform! lo"; at his best he was a great lyric poet.

Arnold's prose has been classified, somewhat arbitrarily, into groups which include literary criticism, social and political criticism, works on education, and works on religion. His literary criticism includes useful essays on general principles, among them the prefaces to the 1853 and 1854 editions of his poems; *The Function of Criticism at the Present Time* and *The Literary Influence of Academies*—both published in *Essays in Criticism* (first series, 1865); and *The Study of Poetry* (1880). Among his many critical estimates on more specific subjects are the three lectures *On Translating Homer* (1861), the essay *On the Study of Celtic Literature* (1867), the celebrated critique on *Shelley* (1888), and essays on *Joubert* (1863), *Sainte-Beuve* (1869), and other French writers whom he especially admired. Arnold's reverence for the ancient Greeks and their exacting rules has made much of his literary criticism unfashionable today, but he deserves respect as a critic who was not afraid to tell his readers, in clear, orderly language, exactly where he stood. Many of his favorite phrases—"the grand style," poetry as "the criticism of life," "high seriousness," "touchstones of taste"—still survive as testimony to his *usefulness* as a critic of literature.

9

The keystone of Arnold's social criticism is *Culture and Anarchy* (1869). In this book he enshrined his faith in "culture" as a cure for the brutality and ugliness, the materialism and "machinery" of Victorian civilization. "Culture" he defined as a compound of "sweetness and light"—or reasonableness and intelligence. It became effective through knowledge of "the best that has been thought and said in the world." He argued for a rebirth of "Hellenism"—with its emphasis on clear thinking—to offset the Victorian type of "Hebraism"—which stressed conduct and action. Although he stigmatized the members of the great British middle class as "Philistines," "the strong, dogged, unenlightened opponents of light," he believed, nevertheless, that the salvation of England lay in the reformation of this group through culture. So he continued to preach to them, steadily if somewhat hopelessly, and, for his curious mixture of intellectual and personal dandyism with persistent pessimism, earned himself the epithet "the kid-glove Jeremiah."

Since Arnold found in Greek civilization many aspects of the "culture" which he preached, it is natural that his educational works should reflect his devotion to the classics. His special studies of Continental education are not so well known today as *A Speech at Eton* (1879), an ingenious argument for a broad-minded classical training, and *Literature and Science* (1882), a somewhat shortsighted defense of the classical curriculum against the encroachments of the pure sciences so vigorously advocated by Thomas Henry Huxley. *Literature and Science* might also be classified as literary criticism. The same is true of *Literature and Dogma* (1873) and *God and the Bible* (1875), two of Arnold's major works in religious controversy. For in them he urged his readers to approach the Bible with the objective analysis of careful literary critics.

When Matthew Arnold died after a life of crusading against things as they were, one of his friends is reported to have remarked, "Poor Mat, he won't like God." But whatever his dissatisfaction in Heaven may have been, it is to be hoped that he was rewarded there for honesty, courage, and idealism not surpassed among Victorian authors.

ASCHAM, Roger (1515–68). Of the numerous English humanists of the sixteenth century who served the Tudor rulers, one of the most individual and distinguished was the Yorkshire educator Roger Ascham. He was tutor to the Princess Elizabeth in 1548, when she was a girl of fifteen. Then he taught Greek and Latin to the unfortunate Lady Jane Grey, beheaded in 1554 as pretender to the crown. He was Latin secretary to Mary Tudor, queen from 1553 to 1558—an extraordinary position for him to hold, since he was as ardent a Protestant as the queen was a Catholic. Under Mary's successor, Elizabeth, Ascham became Greek preceptor at the Royal Court. In his writing the teacher—and too often, perhaps, the pedant—appears. *Toxophilus* (1545) is a treatise on archery, in which he supports the traditional English theory that manly sports should always be a part of education. His more famous treatise is *The Schoolmaster* (1570), on which he was still working at the time of his death. In this book on education—subtitled a "Plain and Perfite Way of teachyng Children the Latin tong"—he protests against brutal corporal punishments in the schools, attacks the influence of Italy on young men who travel to that country, and praises the scholarship of the learned Queen Elizabeth. In spite of his own profound interest in Greek and Latin learning, Ascham championed the English language against the Latin as a literary medium. By so doing he did much to destroy the conception among English scholars that all serious prose should be composed in the language of the Church. He was a fearless and outspoken scholar, and there is a polemical flavor in most of his work. Nevertheless, he wrote easily and smoothly and, at times, even brilliantly and entertainingly, as where, for example, he describes how the gentle and accomplished Lady Jane Grey studied Plato's *Phaedo*.

ASHMOLE, Elias (1617–92), antiquarian and scientist, was one of the first members of the Royal Society. His *Antiquities of Berkshire* was published posthumously in 1719.

ASHTON, Winifred. See **DANE, Clemence.**

ASSER (d. 910) was a Welsh cleric who later became Bishop of Sherborne. After 886, according to his own story, he spent six months of each year in Alfred's household helping the king on numerous Latin translations. His Latin life of King Alfred (c. 894) is called "the earliest biography of an English layman." There is, however, some suspicion that it may be a forgery.

ATTERBURY, Francis (1662–1732), Bishop of Rochester, was a member of the Scriblerus Club along with Pope, Swift, Gay, and Arbuthnot. His works include, besides sermons and letters, a number of trenchant pamphlets which testify to his leadership in the literary, religious, and political disputes of his time. In the 1690's he participated in the famous "Phalaris Controversy," collaborating with Charles Boyle against Richard Bentley. In 1720 he was imprisoned, accused of a plot to overthrow the Hanoverian dynasty. Three years later he was banished to France for life.

AUBREY, John (1626–97). In his *Lives of Eminent Men* (first published 1813) this good-natured antiquarian jotted down ill-considered trifles about the appearances and idiosyncrasies of such worthies as Milton and Hobbes in his own day, Shakespeare and Jonson from a previous era. His friend Anthony à Wood called him "credulous" and "magotie-headed," but through his honest efforts to dissect personality, Aubrey earned a place in the history of English biography.

AUDEN, W(ystan) H(ugh) (1907–   ) belongs—with Stephen Spender, C. Day Lewis, and others—to the widely discussed group of young English poets who were contemporaries at Oxford. He has been an active radical on the international political scene, and his social consciousness is mirrored in his writing. His work reflects a range of influences extending from the earliest poetry to the latest street-corner slang; his mood varies from sentimentality to bitterness, his medium from the swinging rhythms of free verse to the exacting confines of the *Don Juan* stanza. In his eagerness to try almost everything lie both his strength and weakness. Among his works are three collections of verse, *Poems* (1930), *Look Stranger* (1936), and *Selected Poems* (1940); two experiments in drama (with Christopher Isherwood), *The Dog beneath the Skin* (1935) and *The Ascent of F.6* (1936); a witty travel-diary in verse and prose (with Louis MacNeice), *Letters from Iceland* (1937); and three anthologies, *Oxford Poetry* (with Charles Plumb) (1926), *The Poet's Tongue* (with John Garrett) (1935), and *The Oxford Book of Light Verse* (1938).

AUSTEN, Jane (1775–1817). When this daughter of a country rector began to write novels, Anne Radcliffe and "Monk" Lewis were England's favorite fictioneers. She mocked (see *Northanger Abbey*) their extravagant claptrap, choosing instead to depict the people of the upper middle class and minor gentry with whom she had grown up. She had lived since birth in the country town of Steventon, and although her uneventful life later took her to Bath, Southampton, Chawton, and Winchester, the little world of her novels did not expand. Her fame rests on six: *Sense and Sensibility* (1811, begun about 1795); *Pride and Prejudice* (1813, begun 1796); *Mansfield Park* (1814); *Emma* (1816); *Northanger Abbey* (1818, begun 1797); and *Persuasion* (1818). Her characters are real gentlefolk who take walks for exercise, pay calls, play backgammon, attend teas, garden parties, and balls, worry about the weather, and talk endlessly. A coquette's glance is news, and an elopement makes the headlines—but Jane Austen had, as Sir

Walter Scott observed, "the exquisite touch which renders ordinary commonplace things and characters interesting. . . ." Relegating men to the back seats, she specializes in the folly of women and the giddiness of girls. With delicate, detached irony she unmasks their flirting, gossiping, match-making, social-climbing, and sentimental day-dreaming. In contrast to the pale, swooning paragons of Gothic Romance, her most popular heroines, Elizabeth Bennet (*Pride and Prejudice*) and Emma Woodhouse (*Emma*), are human, lively, and fundamentally sensible, but by no means immune to feminine failings. Dialogue, sometimes artificial but often arrestingly authentic, is her natural medium. Common sense in courtship is her persistent theme. She herself never married.

AUSTIN, Alfred (1835–1913) succeeded Tennyson as poet laureate in 1896. He had written editorials for the conservative *Standard* (1866–96), edited the *National Review* (1887–95), and cheered ardently for Disraeli's foreign policy. His poetic works include verse satires (*The Golden Age,* 1871), verse dramas (*Savonarola,* 1881), and, as might be expected, patriotic poems (*England's Darling,* 1896; *Songs of England,* 1898). Most modern critics prefer his simple prose work, *The Garden that I Love* (1894), to his pretentious moralizings in verse. Austin is often held up as an illustration of how an inferior poet can win the laureateship.

AYTOUN, William Edmonstoune (1813–65) collaborated with Sir Theodore Martin (1816–1909) on the *Bon Gaultier Ballads* (1845), a brilliant collection of light verse in which appear parodies of Tennyson, Macaulay, and Mrs. Browning. Aytoun also wrote the serious *Lays of the Scottish Cavaliers* (1849) and *Firmilian* (1854), a dramatic burlesque of the writings of P. J. Bailey, Dobell, Alexander Smith, and other members of the group which he christened the "Spasmodic School" of poetry.

B

BACON, Sir Francis (1561–1626). The most intellectually daring thinker of the reigns of Elizabeth and James I was he who said, "I hold all knowledge to be my province," and who prepared the seed-bed for the philosophical and scientific advancements of the modern world. Francis Bacon was born in London, son of Sir Nicholas Bacon, lord keeper of the great seal. He was educated at Cambridge, admitted to the bar in 1582, and elected to Parliament two years later. Although he was made Queen's Counsel in 1598, Elizabeth does not seem to have trusted him completely, and his advancement during her reign was relatively slow. Under the reign of her successor, however, honors and responsibilities were heaped upon him. He became successively solicitor-general (1607), attorney-general (1613), privy councilor (1616), lord keeper (1617), and lord chancellor (1618). In 1603 he was knighted; in 1618 he was created Baron Verulam; in 1621, Viscount St. Albans. But in that very year when he seemed to be touching the button on Fortune's cap, he was charged with corruption in his high office, confessed his guilt, and was deprived of the chancellorship, fined, and imprisoned. He lived five years longer, dying, according to the tradition, as the result of a chill brought on by gathering snow that he might try its preservative qualities on the flesh of a fowl.

Bacon was so titanic in his powers that all of his service to the king did not check his labors on the most pretentious program of thinking and writing ever conceived. His plan was no less than that of studying all existing sciences, developing a new method of scientific investigation, and ultimately reconstructing all knowledge by the application of this new method. No one mortal could complete such a labor, but Bacon went far enough with it to make for himself a leading place among the philosophers of the world. His completed writings—mainly in Latin—were divided into *The Advancement of Learning* (1605), *Novum Organum* (1620), and *De Augumentis Scientiarum* (1623). *The New Atlantis,* written in 1624, was left unfinished at his death and published in 1627. Standing at the threshold of the modern world, Bacon did more than any of his contemporaries to introduce and develop the "new philosophy." He was an anti-Aristotelian and an ardent proponent of the inductive approach to knowledge. In his labors on his great "instauration" or renewal of science he defined with the most penetrating insight and logic the fogs that keep men from seeing truth clearly, and proposed methods for sounder thinking. In *The New Atlantis* he presented, in an allegory, a plan for the creation of a learned society of scientific workers which actually forecast the establishment of the Royal Society in 1662.

Few laymen read Bacon's philosophical treatises; many more, however, know him as the wise author of "Bacon's Essays." These he wrote in English for his own diversion, developing most of them out of the jottings of his memoranda books. The earliest group to be published (1597) reveals the influence of the French essayist Montaigne; the two later groups (1612 and 1625) are more independent. The essays are brief, blunt, aphoristic; they contain more worldly wisdom than any similar writings in English and have something of the epigrammatic quality of Solomon's proverbs. They provide rare guides to commonplace living.

Bacon's contribution to English thought has been so undeniably genuine that certain of his admirers have done him no kindness in putting him forward as the "real author" of Shakespeare's plays. The "Baconians" have been composed mainly of mystics who are willing to base their claims for Bacon on manufactured evidence of a subjective and cryptic sort. The best reply to these persons is the reminder that their faith in Bacon (their "evidence of things not seen") is matched by that of the adherents of other claimants to the crown, and that too much is known about Shakespeare's life and work to make his position in any way unsafe.

BACON, Roger (1214?–94), was a Franciscan friar who spent several years of his life studying and teaching at Oxford. He enshrined some of his immense learning in three Latin treatises: *Opus Majus, Opus Minus,* and *Opus Tertium.* He was more than once imprisoned for heresy and had a widespread reputation as a necromancer. His contemporaries credited him with having invented a talking head of brass, and Robert Greene later played with that legend in his comedy, *Friar Bacon and Friar Bungay* (printed 1594). Modern scholars hail Bacon as "the founder of English philosophy," "the father of experimental science," and the inventor of spectacles.

BAGE, Robert (1728–1801) was a successful paper-maker who turned novelist when past middle life. His six novels, like those of Godwin and Holcroft, reflect the spirit of radical reform which the French Revolution helped to spread in England. The last and best is *Hermsprong, or Man as he is Not* (1796), in which the hero, after spending his first twenty years among the noble Indians of America, returns to chafe at civilization in England.

BAGEHOT, Walter (1826–77). Banker, economist, journalist, and literary critic—Bagehot had one of the most versatile minds in his century. His *English Constitution* (1867) is an excellent analysis of government, *Physics and Politics* (1872) one of the best attempts to apply the newly discovered principles of evolution, *Lombard Street* (1873) a keen introduction to finance. In his *Literary Studies* (1879), collected from essays published in the *National Review,* are sane treatments of Shakespeare, Wordsworth, Scott, Dickens, Tennyson, and Browning.

BAILEY, Philip James (1816–1902) published, at the tender age of twenty-three, a long philosophical poem called *Festus* (1839), a treatment of the Faust legend. Victorian readers gobbled it up, and for all its turgidness, it did have some fair purple passages. But in the next half century, Bailey continued to bring out new and enlarged editions of his masterpiece until in the eleventh edition (1889), bloated with great gobbets of *The Angel World* (1850), *The Mystic* (1855), and *The Universal Hymn* (1867)—works which the public had snubbed in the meantime—*Festus* was swollen to twice the original 20,000 words. Today it is regarded as a literary monstrosity, and its author is traditionally mocked as the father of what Aytoun loosely called the "Spasmodic School" of poetry. Among Bailey's "followers" were Sydney Dobell and Alexander Smith.

BAILLIE, Joanna (1762–1851) was a naïve, moralizing Scottish poetess and dramatist whose work was praised by Scott. In *A Series of Plays in which it is attempted to delineate the Stronger Passions* (3 vols., 1798, 1802, 1812), she tried to develop a single ruling passion in each central character. *De Montfort* (printed 1798, acted 1800), for example, is a sensational Gothic play on Hate. Miss Baillie also wrote pleasant, conventional songs and ballads, both in Scots and in English.

BALE, John (1495–1563), Bishop of Ossory, wrote many pamphlets and plays to advance the cause of the Reformation. His *King John* (c. 1530–36) is an incoherent, polemical interlude which is sometimes called the first chronicle play in English.

BANIM, John (1798–1842) and **Michael** (1796–1874). Although these Irish brothers wrote separate works, they are best known for a work on which they collaborated, *Tales by the O'Hara Family* (1825–6), a group of authentic stories of Irish life.

BARBAULD, Anna Letitia, née Aikin (1743–1825) was a pious woman of letters who did a good deal of industrious editing, including William Collins' poetry (1794), Richardson's letters (1804), and a fifty-volume series of *British Novelists* (1810). Her original works include the conventional lyric "Life! I know not what thou art" and two children's books, *Lessons for Children* (1778) and *Hymns in Prose for Children* (1781). Many know her only for her naïve objections to Coleridge about *The Rime of the Ancient Mariner,* that it was improbable and had no moral.

BARBOUR, John (1316?–95) was archdeacon of Aberdeen and auditor of the exchequer under Robert II of Scotland. He is famous as the author of *The Bruce* (c. 1375), a rugged epic of 13,615 octosyllabic lines in praise of the hero of Scottish independence, who had been dead only fifty years when the poem was written. Although Barbour promised to "say nocht but suthfast thing," he freely mixed legend with history, chauvinism with objective chronicling. The best-known passages are an outburst on freedom (I, 226–246) and the clanging tale of Bannockburn (XII, 407–XIII, 408).

BARCLAY, Alexander (1475?–1552) was a divine who is remembered for two contributions to English poetry. In *The Ship of Fools* (1509), a free translation of Sebastian Brandt's well-known *Narrenschiff,* he inveighed against the evils of his England. His satirical eclogues (written 1515) are interesting chiefly as the first appearance in English of the classical pastoral type which Spenser later followed in *The Shepheardes Calender* (1579).

BARHAM, Richard Harris (1788–1845) was a clergyman who is remembered as the author of *The Ingoldsby Legends* (1840–7), a collection of ingenious light-verse narratives on many subjects in many meters. Although such irreverent rhymes as *The Jackdaw of Rheims* disturbed some of England's higher high-churchmen, these verses were among the most popular in a century of excellent light verse.

BARNES, Barnabe (1569?–1609). Although he wrote other works, including a tragedy, *The Devil's Charter* (1607), Barnes is known chiefly as a sonneteer. His *Parthenophil and Parthenophe* (1593) contains, in addition to "madrigals, elegies, and odes," 105 sonnets. They are full of conventional borrowings, especially from classical sources, but the originality of some of Barnes' conceits has led critics to name him as a forerunner of the metaphysical poets. On the whole, however, his sonnets are ranked far below those of Sidney, Daniel, and Drayton, which appeared in the same golden decade.

BARNES, William (1801–86) was a Dorsetshire clergyman who wrote *Poems of Rural Life in the Dorset Dialect* (1844). Readers who have not been balked by such lines as "I'll zit me in the lwonesome pleäce" find in Barnes' simple verse an unaffected charm. The poet taught school in Dorchester next door to the office in which Thomas Hardy studied architecture, and his work helped to fire the young apprentice with literary aspirations.

BARNFIELD, Richard (1574–1627) was the author of *The Affectionate Shepherd* (1594), a pastoral poem based on Vergil's second eclogue; *Cynthia* (1595), a classical allegory professedly in imitation of the verse of *The Faerie Queene;* and *The Encomium of Lady Pecunia* (1598), a satirical poem on "the praise of money." Commonly ascribed to Barnfield are the sonnet "If music and sweet poetry agree" and the plaintive lyric "As it fell upon a day"

—both originally published in *The Passionate Pilgrim* (1599) and once assigned to Shakespeare.

BARRETT, Eaton Stannard (1786–1820) was a satirist who is remembered for his novel *The Heroine, or Adventures of a Fair Romance Reader* (1813), a more thorough travesty of the craze for Gothic fiction than Jane Austen's *Northanger Abbey*. In grooming herself for the rôle of a heroine, Barrett's Cherry changed her name to Cherubina and "practised tripping, gliding, flitting, and tottering with great success."

BARRIE, Sir James Matthew (1860–1937) was born in Kirriemuir, Scotland, the "Thrums" which he made famous in his early writing. Both in the short sketches of *Auld Licht Idylls* (1888) and *A Window in Thrums* (1889) and in his two most popular novels, *The Little Minister* (1891) and *Sentimental Tommy* (1896), he treated the quaint humors of his fellow villagers in a manner which blends authentic regionalism with romantic sentimentality. With these stories he earned his title as the father of the Kailyard (or Kitchen garden) School of Scottish fiction. In the present century he confined his attention largely to the drama. Among his successes are: *The Admirable Crichton* (1902), a comedy of manners in a romantic setting; *Peter Pan* (1904), the dramatization of his sentimental fantasy about "the boy who wouldn't grow up"; *What Every Woman Knows* (1908), a spirited comedy of life in Scotland; *The Old Lady Shows Her Medals* (1917), a sentimental piece of war propaganda; and *Dear Brutus* (1917), a moral fantasy. In his insistence on the reality of the world of day-dreams, Barrie was a literary descendant of Robert Louis Stevenson, but, unlike this friend of his youth, he was more at home in the airy region of sentimental whimsy than in the land of robust, red-blooded romance. It is highly probable that *Peter Pan* will outlive all his more substantial creations.

BARROW, Isaac (1630–77), who taught both Greek and mathematics at Cambridge, was one of the best preachers in a period which has been called "the golden age of the English pulpit." His lengthy sermons were published in 1678. He also wrote controversial religious works, including a treatise against the papacy, *On the Pope's Supremacy* (1680).

BARRY CORNWALL. See **CORNWALL**, Barry.

BAXTER, Richard (1615–91) was a Presbyterian divine who wrote unceasingly in a simple, conversational prose style. His *Saint's Everlasting Rest* (1650) is one of the classics of the literature of dissent, and his autobiography, *Reliquiae Baxterianae* (1696), is a valuable commentary on the religious upheavals of his time.

BAYLY, Thomas Haynes (1797–1839) was the author of some novels and numerous dramatic pieces, including the farce *Perfection* (1830). He is better known as a prolific writer of popular songs. Such bygone twitterings as "She wore a wreath of roses" and "I'd be a butterfly" have met with much ridicule.

BEACONSFIELD. See DISRAELI.

BEATTIE, James (1735–1803). This Scottish professor of moral philosophy survives as the author of *The Minstrel* (Book I, 1771; II, 1774), an unfinished poem in Spenserian stanzas. In it he proposed "to trace the progress of a poetical genius . . . from the first dawning of fancy and reason, till that period at which he may be supposed capable of appearing in the world as a minstrel" and to imitate Spenser's "harmony, simplicity, and variety" without resorting to his archaic vocabulary. Beattie's verse is turgid and artificial, but in his enthusiasm for Nature and nostalgia for "Gothic days" he anticipated the romantic poets of the next century.

BEAUMONT, Francis (1584–1616). In Elizabethan and Jacobean playmaking the collaboration of two or more writers was frequent and has provided numerous puzzles for scholars. Of these collaborations none is so famous as the partnership of Francis Beaumont and John Fletcher. It is a popular error, in fact, to give their linked names to all of the fifty-odd plays with which either was associated. Actually the two dramatists do not appear to have become intimately acquainted until about 1606, and Beaumont— the younger by five years—died nine years before his friend. Their literary partnership, therefore, could not have covered all of the plays connected with the name of one or the other; and it is certain that both wrote plays alone and plays also composed in collaboration with dramatists not in the dual partnership. Just how the labor on the joint plays was divided, it is impossible to tell. From a study of the independent plays, it has become possible, however, to make some estimate of the literary characteristics of each playwright. Beaumont seems to have been the more serious of the two, and the one more concerned, therefore, with tragic scenes. Fletcher was the coarser and the more comic, but, at the same time, the more poetic both in his blank verse and in his incidental lyrics. Both were distinguished dramatists whose names, taken individually or together, stand high in the roster of Jacobean playwrights. Although their plays are marred occasionally by

Jacobean decadence, they are well constructed and are marked by magnificent single scenes and excellent characterizations.

Of the plays that Beaumont seems to have written alone, *The Woman Hater* (1606) is less effective than several that he did with Fletcher. Of these partnership plays the most famous is the lively burlesque *The Knight of the Burning Pestle* (1607–c. 1610), a satirical attack on bourgeois literary taste with an incidental presentation of the popular stage in action. *The Maid's Tragedy* (c. 1608–11) is a stirring, heartbreaking play, melodramatic in parts, but dignified by some of the most powerful and restrained tragic scenes in the period. *Philaster, or Love lies a-Bleeding* (1608–10) is a melodrama best described by its subtitle. It runs the gamut of heart-throbs and tense situations, and is Jacobean rather than Elizabethan in its content and mood.

BECKFORD, William (1759–1844) is remembered today as the author of *Vathek* (written in French, 1782, printed in English, 1786), the mad tale of a caliph's futile search for knowledge and power. It combines the ingredients of Gothic horror, Oriental exoticism, and Voltairian irony into a unique romantic brew. To his contemporaries Beckford was a tireless traveller, a princely connoisseur of books and paintings, the creator of Gargantuan pseudo-Gothic Fonthill Abbey, and an indifferent M. P.

BEDDOES, Thomas Lovell (1803–49) was a brooding, eccentric admirer of Keats and Shelley. He spent many of his post-Oxford years on the Continent, where he eventually went mad and apparently took his own life. In a time when interest in Elizabethan drama was being revived, he wrote two plays in the harrowing manner of Webster and Tourneur: *The Bride's Tragedy* (1822) and, his chief work, *Death's Jest Book, or The Fool's Tragedy* (begun in 1825, printed 1850). A bad playwright, he is remembered for a handful of simple, dreamy songs. Two of the best are Wolfram's dirge (from *Death's Jest Book*) and *Dream-Pedlary*. Lytton Strachey called Beddoes "the last Elizabethan."

BEDE (673–735), called "The Venerable," and also alluded to as "Father of English Learning," and "Father of English History," was the outstanding scholar of the Old English period. He spent his life in the Northumbrian monasteries of Wearmouth and Jarrow, where his labors resulted in a production of forty books on theological, historical, and scientific subjects. These are all in Latin, but a lost translation of the Gospel of St. John was in Old English. Bede wrote homilies, commentaries on the Latin church fathers, Latin hymns, and two biographies of St. Cuthbert, an

English bishop who died in 687. But his most famous works are his *De Natura Rerum* (*Concerning the Nature of Things*), and his *Historia Ecclesiastica Gentis Anglorum* (*Ecclesiastical History of the English Nation*). The *History* was completed (in Latin) in 731 and was translated into Old English by Alfred, King of the West Saxons, at the end of the following century. It is an extraordinarily important document, which tells in five books of the early history of England, of the struggle between the Irish and the Roman churches in the island, and of the conversion, step by step, of the Anglo-Saxons. Of the incidental narratives in this history the most vivid are that of the conversion of King Edwin of Northumbria through the preaching of the missionary Paulinus, Bishop of York, and that of the miraculous coming of the divine gift of song to the herdsman Caedmon, the earliest English poet who is known by name.

BEDE, Cuthbert, was the pseudonym of **Edward Bradley** (1827–89), a popular mid-Victorian contributor to *Punch, All the Year Round,* and other magazines. He is remembered as the author and illustrator of *The Adventures of Mr. Verdant Green, an Oxford Freshman* (1853), *The Further Adventures of Mr. Verdant Green, an Oxford Undergraduate* (1854), and *Mr. Verdant Green married and done for* (1857).

BEERBOHM, Sir Max (1872–1956). When *The Works of Max Beerbohm* appeared in 1896, he was one of the clever young men who were puncturing Victorian illusions for the *Yellow Book*. In the previous year he had vowed to write no more. He has been writing off and on ever since. His best-known work is *Zuleika Dobson* (1911), an impudent satire on Oxford traditions. Although Max Beerbohm in his impish irreverence lacks the tenderness and delicacy of Charles Lamb, his work is in the best tradition of the English informal essay. He has shown that the informal essay—when penned by a man of thorough culture, not by a garrulous schoolboy—can be elegantly trivial without being pointless, pleasantly rambling without being utterly aimless. The same sharp wit and careful craftsmanship which distinguish his writing have made him even more celebrated as a cartoonist and caricaturist.

BEHN, Aphra (1640–89) is believed to be the first English woman to earn a living by writing. She had little title to her pen name "Divine Astraea." Inspired by an acute commercial instinct, she fashioned her novels, plays, and poems to suit the depraved taste of the Restoration. Although her novels are full of the amorous intrigue familiar to readers of Italian *novelle,* she spared no pains to make them credible. Her most famous "history" is *Oroonoko, or The Royal Slave* (1688), an early plea for the oppressed Negro. It is permeated with "eye-witness" details, and only recently has scholarship cast grave doubts on the long-accepted tradition that the author had actually spent her girlhood in the Surinam of the novel. Mrs. Behn knew the theater and specialized in renovating purloined plots with fresh farcical situations (*The Rover,* two parts, 1677, 1681; *The City-Heiress,* 1682). Even her contemporaries found her plays immoral, ironically dubbing her "The Chaste Aphra." Sneered Pope later:

> The stage how loosely does Astraea tread
> Who fairly puts all characters to bed.

BELL, Currer, Ellis, and **Acton.** Pseudonyms respectively of **Charlotte, Emily,** and **Anne Brontë.**

BELLOC (Joseph Hilary Pierre), pseud. Hilaire (1870–1953) was born of French parents near Paris but became a British subject in 1903. He is commonly linked with his friend and collaborator, G. K. Chesterton—Shaw has spoken of the four-legged animal called "The Chesterbelloc." The two men shared a passionate faith in Roman Catholicism, a hatred of socialism, and the energy to write prolifically in multitudinous fields. Belloc's versatile achievement includes *The Bad Child's Book of Beasts* (1896), a nursery classic; *The Path to Rome* (1902), a book of travel sketches; *A Companion to Mr. Wells' "Outline of History"* (1926), an objection to the historian's treatment of the Catholic church; *Wolsey* (1930), a biography; and *The Crisis of Civilization* (1937), a politico-sociological study—in addition to several books of poems and numerous novels.

BENNETT, (Enoch) Arnold (1867–1931). From 1900, when he resigned as editor of *Woman,* down to the end of his life, Arnold Bennett was an exceedingly prolific writer of novels, short stories, plays, and magazine articles. By many readers, however, he is remembered today as the author of a single novel, *The Old Wives' Tale* (1908). It is a long novel about two sisters, Constance and Sophia Baines. Both were born in Bennett's native Staffordshire, in one of the "Five Towns" which he often chose as the locale for his fiction. Constance, the younger, married a local bore, and spent her drab life in the provincial atmosphere of her father's clothing shop; but impetuous Sophia eloped to Paris with a worthless traveling salesman, saw the Revolution of 1870, and struggled alone through poverty to material success. Their reunion in old age, when Sophia returns to England, heightens the contrast between their bitter lives. Although the book is not without flashes of romantic melodrama and humor, the dominant tone, as in most of Bennett's novels, is one of somber naturalism. More recent novelists, notably Virginia Woolf, have revolted against his painstaking documentation and called his novels pedestrian and artless, but many readers consider *The Old Wives' Tale* one of the classics of the twentieth century. Among the best of Bennett's other novels are *Buried Alive* (1908), *Riceyman Steps* (1923), and the "Clayhanger Trilogy": *Clayhanger* (1910), *Hilda Lessways* (1911), and *These Twain* (1916). *The Journal of Arnold Bennett* (1932–3) gives a frank, worldly account of the author's literary career, with special emphasis on the commercial aspects of the writing game.

BENSON, E(dward) F(rederic) (1867–1940), novelist and biographer, wrote *Dodo* (1893), a novel about high society which was popular in the nineties; *As We Were* (1930), "a Victorian peep show"; and an intelligent life of Charlotte Brontë (1932). His brother, **Arthur Christopher Benson** (1862–1925), was also a miscellaneous writer.

BENSON, Stella (1892–1933) was a novelist and short-story writer whose work was enriched by her extensive travels. Among her novels are *I Pose* (1915), her first published work; *Living Alone* (1919), a fantasy of London in wartime; and *Tobit Transplanted* (1931) (American edition *The Far-away Bride,* 1930), a novel about China, where the author lived from 1921 until her death.

BENTHAM, Jeremy (1748–1832) did not originate the popular system of social philosophy which is variously called *Utilitarianism, Benthamism,* and *Philosophical Radicalism.* But he developed it in infinite detail. In the preface to his first book, *A Fragment on Government* (1776), he announced his famous principle that "the greatest happiness of the greatest number . . . is the measure of right and wrong," and in *An Introduction to the Principles of Morals and Legislation* (1789), he elaborated upon it at considerable length. Bentham's chief disciple and also his guide was James Mill (1773–1836), father of the even more famous John Stuart Mill (1806–73). Both Mills accepted the doctrine of Utilitarianism, the son with some modifications, and both were active in promulgating the theory. Utilitarianism had a widespread vogue throughout the first half of the century, and, for many people, the invariable test of an act or object became "Is it useful?"

BENTLEY, Richard (1662–1742) was a distinguished classical scholar who has two significant connections with English literature. In his *Dissertation upon the Epistles of Phalaris* (1697) he took sides in a famous teapot-tempest, and thereby earned himself a prominent place in Swift's *Battle of the Books* (written 1697, published 1704). In his edition of *Paradise Lost* (1732), he undertook to emend Milton, and thus earned himself the eternal enmity of Milton scholars.

BERKELEY, George (1685–1753). The leading philosopher and one of the most polished prose writers of the age of Pope was a Kilkenny Irishman who came to England in 1713 by way of the University of Dublin, where he had studied Greek, mathematics, and metaphysics. Before leaving Dublin for London, George Berkeley had already acquired a wide reputation as a brilliant metaphysician. His *Essay towards a New Theory of Vision* (1709), his *Treatise Concerning the Principles of Human Knowledge* (1710), and his three *Dialogues between Hylas and Philonous* (1713) all promulgated the new and startling theory of the non-existence of matter. In London his personal charm and high intelligence endeared him to Pope, Swift, Addison, Steele, and other prominent authors of widely diverse temperaments, who came to regard him as possessed of "every virtue under heaven." After extensive travel in France and Italy, he returned to England in 1720. A year later, on the bursting of the South Sea Bubble and the ruination of numerous speculators, he wrote an economic treatise entitled *An Essay towards Preventing the Ruin of Great Britain* (1721). His receipt in 1723 of a legacy of four thousand pounds from Esther Vanhomrigh (Swift's "Vanessa"), who does not appear to have known him personally, and in 1725 of a government charter to found a missionary college in the Bermudas were two strange episodes in his career. When he sailed from England in 1728, however, it was not to go to the Bermudas—that scheme having fallen through—but to Rhode Island. In America he wrote one book, *Alciphron* (1732). In 1733, two years after his return to London, he was made Bishop of Cloyne. His last writings reveal an odd eccentricity. Convinced of the medicinal value of tar-water, he published in 1744 *A Chain of Philosophical Reflections and Inquiries concerning the Virtues of Tar-Water*. In spite of the subject of this tract, it contains some of his most brilliant prose. *Farther Thoughts on Tar-Water* appeared in 1752, and in the same year Bishop Berkeley established a residence in Oxford. It was his intention to continue his philosophical writings in this learned atmosphere, but he died the following year.

BERNERS, John Bourchier, second baron (1467–1533) was a statesman in the courts of Henry VII and VIII who earned a place in English literary history as a translator. His best-known work is an excellent translation of the Chronicles of Jean Froissart (1337?–1410). Froissart's work is a romantic survey of fourteenth-century English and European history. Lord Berners' translation appeared in 1523–5.

BESANT, Sir Walter (1836–1901) published a great quantity of fiction, mostly historical, and a number of non-fiction studies of early, medieval, and modern London. His most celebrated novel, *All Sorts and Conditions of Men* (1882), is a study of the slums of London's East End. It reflects the interest in lower-class life which was flooding into English literature at the end of the nineteenth century.

BICKERSTAFF, Isaac. Pseudonym used by Swift in the "Bickerstaff papers," and by Steele in the *Tatler*.

BICKERSTAFFE, Isaac (d. 1812?) was a clever Irishman who, before he fled to the Continent under a cloud in 1772, was popular in London as a playwright. He was particularly successful at turning others' plots into opera libretti. Some of his comic opera hits were: *Love in a Village* (1762), *The Maid of the Mill* (1765, based on Richardson's *Pamela*), *The Padlock* (1768), and *Lionel and Clarissa* (1768, later altered as *The School for Fathers,* 1770).

BINYON, (Robert) Laurence (1869–1943) won the Newdigate poetry prize at Oxford in 1890 and continued to write and publish poetry until his death. His *Collected Poems* appeared in 1931. Among his best-known works are *For the Fallen* (1917), a poem of the First World War, and *The Sirens, an Ode* (1924). Binyon also published a handful of plays and numerous studies of art. Employed for thirty-eight years (1895–1933) in the Department of Prints and Drawings at the British Museum, he was an authority on Oriental art and on the drawings and engravings of William Blake.

BIRRELL, Augustine (1850–1933) was a liberal statesman who wrote graceful informal essays (*Obiter Dicta,* 1884, etc.) and pleasant studies of William Hazlitt (1902) and Andrew Marvell (1905) for the *English Men of Letters* series.

BLACK, William (1841–98) wrote a number of once-popular novels, most of them about his native Scotland. They include *A Daughter of Heth* (1871), in which he brought a French heroine into the Scottish domestic setting; and *A Princess of Thule* (1874), a romance of the Hebrides.

BLACKMORE, Sir Richard (d. 1729), physician to Queen Anne, was the author of a number of long poems, including: *Prince Arthur* (1695) and *King Arthur* (1697), a pair of "heroick" poems; *A Paraphrase on the Book of Job, etc.* (1700); and *Creation: A Philosophical Poem* (1712). The last of these, generally considered Blackmore's best, was praised by both Addison and Johnson. In the preface to *Prince Arthur,* Blackmore anticipated Jeremy Collier with an attack on the immorality of the stage, and he later tangled with Dryden on the same issue.

BLACKMORE, Richard Doddridge (1825–1900) is remembered today as the author of *Lorna Doone* (1869), a charming historical romance of the seventeenth century. The story centers in the love of John Ridd, a high-minded peasant youth, for Lorna, a Scottish nobleman's daughter, who has been stolen away in childhood by the robber band of Doones. Blackmore also wrote *Clara Vaughan* (1864), a sensational mystery story in the Wilkie Collins manner, and *Springhaven* (1887), a historical novel of the Napoleonic Wars. Although he relied strongly on the conventional motifs of romance and melodrama, his best work displays a genuine charm and a deep feeling for the English countryside.

BLACKSTONE, Sir William (1723–80) is the classic authority on English law. His *Commentaries on the Laws of England* (1765–9), written when he was a professor of law at Oxford, has been censured from the legal point of view, but survives as a reminder that some lawyers write clear, comprehensible prose.

BLAIR, Robert (1699–1746). This Scottish clergyman is remembered as the author of *The Grave* (1743), a poem which was later illustrated by William Blake. Blair ranges through 767 lines of uneven blank verse from a Gothic depiction of "the gloomy horrors of the tomb" to a happy promise of immortality. The poem shares with Edward Young's *Night Thoughts* (1742–5) much of the responsibility for the rash of eighteenth-century funereal verse by poets usually dignified as the "Graveyard School." Hence Blair is a remote ancestor of nineteenth-century Romanticism.

BLAKE, Nicholas. Pseudonym of **C(ecil) Day Lewis.**

BLAKE, William (1757–1827). To be equally famous in the fields of poetry and engraving is a distinction that has come to William Blake alone. And both engraving tool and pen were the instruments with which this extraordinarily sensitive mystic expressed his soul. He was born in London, the son of a hosier, and apparently had little or no formal education. At fourteen he was apprenticed to Basire, an engraver, and began to work in the schools of the Royal Academy. During his teens he must also have written poetry, for his first volume, *Poetical Sketches,* although published in 1783, was certainly written before 1777. During the three years from 1784 to 1787 Blake was a seller of prints. With *Songs of Innocence* (1789) he issued the first important work in his long and amazing series of engraved books. The charming lyrics of this little collection were not type-set but were cut on copper plates, together with the delicate colored pictures that illustrate them. This was followed by several made after the same manner: the prose *Marriage of Heaven and Hell* (c. 1793), *Visions of the Daughters of Albion* (1793), *America, a Prophecy* (1793), *Songs of Experience* (1794)—printed with the earlier *Songs of Innocence* as "shewing Two Contrary States of the Human Soul," *Europe, a Prophecy* (1794), *The First Book of Urizen* (1794), *The Book of Ahania* (1795), and *The Book of Los* (1795). Blake left London for Felpham but returned to the city in 1803 after a false charge of sedition had been brought against him. *Milton* was completed c. 1808, *Jerusalem, The Emanation of the Giant Albion* c. 1820, and *The Ghost of Abel* in 1822.

Blake's love of the symbolic, the mystic, and the macabre is revealed not only in his poems but in his engravings. He chose, for example, to illustrate Young's *Night Thoughts* (1797) and Blair's *Grave* (1808). His engravings for the book of *Job* (c. 1825) and Dante's *Divine Comedy* (1826–27) have an apocalyptic grandeur that is breath-taking. His cavalcade of the pilgrims for Chaucer's *Canterbury Tales* (1809) is a famous group. Naturally Blake's skill in illustration affected his verse-writing. His poems have not only the form and color of his engravings, but most of them have the same mystic, rhapsodical quality. Many, indeed, like *The Book of Thel,* are cryptic and allegorical to the point of unintelligibility. For most readers Blake's simple songs are worth in lyrical quality a bookful of his vague and cloudy rhapsodical visions. The piper song that introduces the *Songs of Innocence,* and "The Lamb," "The Little Black Boy," and the "Cradle Song" in that collection have a naïve and restrained charm; and "The Fly," "The Tiger," "A Poison Tree" and "The Chimney-Sweeper" of the *Songs of Experience*—presenting the bitter side of human life—are extraordinarily poignant and moving.

BLIND HARRY (fl. 1470–92), or Henry the Minstrel, probably wrote *The Wallace* (c. 1460), a poem of 11,858 unwieldy decasyllabic lines about Scotland's hero. Sir William Wallace spent his life fighting the English, who finally executed him in 1305. John Barbour's *Bruce* (c. 1375) has some historical accuracy and objectivity; *The Wallace* is largely a tissue of legends, an exercise in Anglophobia. For example, in the opening legend, the hero single-handed dispatches three of the five English knights who try to steal his fish.

BLOOMFIELD, Robert (1766–1823) was a poor farm laborer whose first publication, *The Farmer's Boy, a Rural Poem* (1800), met popular acclaim. He is traditionally compared with John Clare (1793–1864), a "farmer's boy" whose verse is better than Bloomfield's.

BLUNDEN, Edmund (Charles) (1896–   ), Fellow and Tutor in English Literature at Merton College, Oxford, is a poet, critic, and scholar. His poetry is often on pastoral themes, the mood varying from realistic depiction of nature to a mystical, more imaginative approach. Among his literary studies are *Leigh Hunt and his Circle* (1930), *Charles Lamb and his Contemporaries* (1933), and *Thomas Hardy, a Literary Biography* (1941).

BLUNT, Wilfrid Scawen (1840–1922) has left behind a number of prose works which reflect his stormy career in the government service. He was a staunch defender of Irish, Indian, and Egyptian nationalism. As a poet, he is best known for the stately, conventional sonnets of *The Love Sonnets of Proteus* (1880) and *Esther* (1892).

BOETHIUS or BOECE, Hector (1465?–1536) was a Scotsman who studied and taught at the University of Paris, where he was a friend of Erasmus. His *Lives of the Bishops of Mortlach and Aberdeen* (1522) and his *History of the Scottish People* (1526) were both written in Latin under the influence of the Roman historian Livy. The history includes the story of Macbeth and Duncan, which later found its way through Holinshed's chronicles into Shakespeare's tragedy.

BOLINGBROKE, Henry St. John, first viscount (1678–1751) had a long and stormy life. He reached the political heights early while the Tories were in power, fled to the Continent in 1715, shortly after the accession of George I, returned in 1723 to fight the Walpole government, and finally retired to France in 1735. His vast output of prose on political, historical, and philosophical matters is marked, on the whole, by lucidity, but marred by frequent spasms of invective and flights of the sort of declamation which made him a famous orator. Among his best-known works are the *Letter to Sir William Wyndham* (written 1717, published 1753), a defense of the author's conduct before his exile; and *The Idea of a Patriotic King* (written 1738, published 1749), a famous treatise on the limitations of monarchy. Bolingbroke's deistic philosophy was retailed at second hand by his friend and admirer, Pope, notably in the *Essay on Man*.

BORROW, George Henry (1803–81) may have got from his recruiting officer father the gypsy foot that led him for years over highways and byways of Europe and brought him the materials for his travel books. From his native East Dereham, he went at twenty-one to London, where he tried his hand at literary hack work. But he soon became a wanderer and tramp, fell in with various bands of gypsies, and apparently adopted their attitudes and their manner of living. In 1833 the Bible Society recognized Borrow's peculiar qualifications by appointing him as its agent, and for years he carried on the work of the Society in Russia, Spain, and Morocco, becoming a skilled linguist and translator. He returned to England in 1840, settled in a home of his own in Oulton, and wrote there the amazing series of volumes that have given him a place in English literature. *The Zincali* (1841) was followed by *The Bible in Spain* (1843). *Lavengro* (1851), *The Romany Rye* (1857), and *Wild Wales* (1862). Just how much of the stirring and exotic materials in these books is fact and how much fiction no reader will ever know. But unless the reader is a pedant, he will be satisfied with the descriptions and episodes for their own sake and with the peculiar flavor of a series of travel and personal adventure books that are definitely different from others.

BOSWELL, James (1740–95) met Samuel Johnson for the first time on May 16, 1763. Between this meeting and Johnson's death in 1784, Boswell studied and travelled in Europe (1763–66); wrote two books growing out of his friendship with the Corsican patriot, Paoli (*An Account of Corsica,* 1768, *British Essays in Favor of the Brave Corsicans,* 1769); and practised law in his native Edinburgh, where his father had been a judge. He visited Johnson frequently in London, and in 1773 made with him the journey which he later celebrated in *The Journal of a Tour to the Hebrides* (1785). But whether they were together or apart, the shadow of Boswell's awesome idol never left him. *The Life of Samuel Johnson, LL.D.* (1791) was the fulfillment of almost thirty years' devotion to the task. It is generally considered the greatest biography in the language. Despite Boswell's idolatry, the *Life* is not the panegyric which usually passed for biography before his day; despite his scrupulous attention to intimate details, it is not the debunking exposé which often serves in ours. It depicts the living Johnson, with many of his virtues and his vices, growling his pontifical opinions in countless conversations at The Mitre Tavern and "The Club" or penning them in letters couched in matchless eloquence. Opinions on Boswell have differed widely. Some readers, amazed by the humanity of the biography, have hailed its author as an unquestionable genius; others, annoyed by "Bozzy's" shameless toadying, have scorned him as a persistent fool. Recent publication of parts of his revealing correspondence and journals has helped to solve the riddle. Genius or fool, Boswell was certainly endowed with an insatiable interest in personality and gave himself a remarkable training in observing, recollecting, and recording. If he was not a great literary artist, he was surely a magnificent reporter.

BOUCICAULT, Dion(ysius Lardner) (1822–90) was a prolific playwright. Counting adaptations and collaborations, he had a hand in over a hundred plays. His artificial *London Assurance,* which caused a sensation at Covent Garden in 1841, showed him at nineteen already a master of all the timeworn tricks in the book of comedy. The melodrama *After Dark* (1868) was successfully revived in 1928 at Christopher Morley's short-lived Hoboken playhouse. Boucicault also wrote a number of Irish melodramas, including *The Colleen Bawn* (1859), *Arragh-na-Pogue* (1864), and *The Shaughraun* (1875).

BOWDLER, Thomas (1754–1825) was an Edinburgh physician who, by editing *The Family Shakespeare* (1807), a collection of twenty expurgated plays, begat the verb "bowdlerize," a synonym for prudish expurgation.

BOWLES, William Lisle (1762–1850). The melancholy *Fourteen Sonnets* (1789) of this scholarly clergyman started a sonnet revival and drew a seventeen-year-old enthusiast named Coleridge away from metaphysics and theology (alas temporarily) to an interest in romantic poetry. In his edition of Pope (1806) Bowles questioned the supremacy of the great couplet-maker, and frowned on his choice of "unpoetical" subjects. The work set the whole generation aquibble trying to pigeon-hole Pope. Among the editor's adversaries in the "Bowles controversy" over Pope's merits, were Byron and Campbell.

BOYLE, Charles, fourth earl of Orrery (1676–1731) edited *The Epistles of Phalaris* (1695), which Richard Bentley later proved to be spurious. Echoes of the "Phalaris Controversy" are heard in Swift's *Battle of the Books* (written 1697, published 1704), where Boyle is one of the warriors on the side of the Ancients.

BOYLE, Roger, first earl of Orrery (1621–79) wrote *Parthenissa, a Romance in Six Tomes* (1654–5), most famous of the English imitations of the interminable French romances of La Calprenède (c. 1610–63) and Mlle. de Scudéry (1607–1701). Orrery's heroic drama, *Henry V* (1664), may have been the first regular stage play to be written completely in heroic couplets.

BRADDON, Mary Elizabeth (1837–1915) wrote over seventy novels, most of them thrillers and many of them best-sellers. Her most celebrated novel is *Lady Audley's Secret* (1862), a mystery thriller in the manner of Wilkie Collins.

BRADLEY, Edward. See **BEDE, Cuthbert.**

BRETON, Nicholas (1545?–1626?) was a persistent poetaster who scribbled with more facility than real art under both Elizabeth and James. He was the son of a London tradesman of good ancestry. He returned to his birthplace with an Oxford degree and sought a literary patron after the fashion of the times. He was in service of Sir Philip Sidney until that nobleman's death in 1586; then he served Sidney's sister, the Countess of Pembroke. Meanwhile he courted the Muse of literature as diligently as he did his patrons and produced many separate collections of prose and verse, some of which have been lost. His facile and artless verses also found their way into several of the anthologies of the period. His best-known collection is *The Passionate Shepherd* (1604), the title of which reveals Breton's conventional interest in pastoral themes. *Wit's Trenchmour* (1597) is an angling idyll which anticipates Izaak Walton's much greater *Compleat Angler* of 1653.

BRIDGES, Robert (Seymour) (1844–1930) was a learned scholar as well as a poet. He was a purist in matters of diction and a conscientious student of the niceties of versification. He patterned much of his verse on classical models, experimenting with the use of quantitative meters. Although he wrote many good short lyrics, especially during the last thirty years of the nineteenth century, he is best known for *The Testament of Beauty* (1927–9), a ponderous long poem in which, towards the end of his life, he enshrined his philosophy of living. Bridges was made poet laureate in 1913, but his work has never been widely read. Many readers have condemned him for aloofness and pedantry. But if he had never written any original poetry, he would deserve gratitude for editing that of his friends D. M. Dolben, R. W. Dixon, and, most important of all, Gerard Manley Hopkins.

BROME, Richard (d. 1652?) was a servant of Ben Jonson and imitated the dramatic technique of his master. Fifteen of his plays have survived. The best known of these are *A Jovial Crew* (1641), a merry comedy of gypsy life, and *The City Wit, or the Woman Wears the Breeches* (1623–37), a farcical comedy of intrigue.

BRONTË, Anne (1820–49), **Charlotte** (1816–55), and **Emily (Jane)** (1818–48). The tragedy of this ill-starred family of genius has hypnotized novelists and biographers for a century. Patrick Brunty, an irritable Irish curate and second-rate writer, settled with his family at Haworth on the lonely moors in 1820. A year later his wife died of cancer. In 1824 the two oldest daughters, followed her in death. Charlotte became the family mother before her ninth birthday. Restricted largely to the solitary life of the parsonage, the four remaining children escaped into a unique land of dreams, the mysteries of which they divulged in a fantastic series of stories, poems, and pictures. As the years crept by, the father retired into his shell of eccentricity. The only brother, Branwell, deadened his talents for painting and writing in drugs and drink. The three sisters struggled on, counting the years as governesses and schoolteachers while Charlotte dreamed of their day of literary triumph. The dream was not fulfilled by the appearance in 1846 of *Poems by Currer, Ellis, and Acton Bell,* the pseudonymous collaboration of Charlotte, Emily, and Anne. But in the next year all three published novels. Then in 1848 Tragedy came back. Branwell died in the fall, grief-stricken Emily went in December, Anne in the following May—all of them victims of consumption. Finally in 1855 Charlotte died of childbirth complications only nine months after her marriage to Mr. A. B. Nicholls, her father's curate.

Quiet, religious Anne might well be forgotten if she had not been born a Brontë. Her characteristic melancholy is mirrored in two novels, *Agnes Grey* (1847), the story of a lonely governess like herself, and *The Tenant of Wildfell Hall* (1848), the morbid, moralizing tale of a drunkard like Branwell.

Charlotte's best-known novel, *Jane Eyre* (1847), is an uneven mixture of real autobiography, Cinderella, and Mrs. Radcliffe.

The melodramatic hokum (centering in a mad wife whose husband has concealed her in an attic from which she pops periodically to scare his second-bride-to-be) fascinated and shocked Victorian England. Today's readers find more lasting value in the book's authentic social backgrounds and precise poetic descriptions. Charlotte's other novels are semi-autobiographical. The heroine of *Shirley* (1849) is an idealized Emily, while *Villette* (1853) and *The Professor* (written 1847, published 1857) reflect the author's interest in M. Héger, the married director of a school in Brussels where she and Emily had studied in 1842.

Emily concealed beneath an unattractive manly exterior strange depths of secret power which her sisters could not begin to fathom. Whether or not she died, as the story goes, standing resolutely in the parlor with her hand on the mantel-piece, she had an inflexible will and relentless courage. Wrote Charlotte: "I have never seen her parallel in anything. Stronger than a man, simpler than a child, her nature stood alone." The same combination of manly strength and childish simplicity has left many readers of her only novel, *Wuthering Heights* (1847), at a loss to find its parallel. The tale of the moorland madness of Heathcliffe and Cathy was unappreciated at first; some Victorians, hearing only the creaking of the story-within-story machinery, called it a crude *Jane Eyre,* while others found it so somber and haunting and breathing with death that they cried out for a glimpse of sunshine. But the book has bewitched more recent critics into wild conjectures about Emily's mystical inner self, her untold love and dark despair. It was her poems in manuscript which inspired the collaboration of the "Bells," and, by Charlotte's own admission, hers are the only ones worth remembering. The best of them, *Remembrance* and *The Prisoner,* for example, are mystical love lyrics in the same sad minor key as the novel. They deserve to be better known.

BROOKE, Henry (1703?–83) was an Irishman who wrote plays, poems, political treatises, and two novels. His famous novel, *The Fool of Quality* (1764–70), is one of the many eighteenth-century dilutions of Rousseau's thesis that the sins of man result from his abandoning the natural state for the corruptions of civilization. Like Thomas Day's *Sandford and Merton* (1783–9), this sentimental sermon in fiction presents contrasting characters from the two environments. It also reflects Brooke's absorption in two eighteenth-century religious movements, the Mysticism of William Law and the Methodism of the Wesleys. John Wesley, in revising the novel for the edification of his followers (1781), wrote: "I know not who can survey it with tearless eyes, unless he has a heart of stone."

BROOKE, Lord. See **GREVILLE.**

BROOKE, Rupert (Chawner) (1887–1915). This brilliant scholar and athlete was one of the significant English poets of the First World War. War is the theme of his best-known work, *1914* (1915), a sequence of five conventional sonnets pervaded by the romantic idealism of youth. In the fifth and most famous of these, "If I should die, think only this of me," Brooke expressed the English soldier's fervent love for his homeland. Almost as popular as these sonnets is his lyric *The Great Lover*. He died of blood-poisoning while serving in the Dardanelles and is buried on the Island of Skyros.

BROUGHAM, Henry Peter, Baron Brougham (1778–1868). Lord Brougham (pronounced Broom) had a long career in Parliament and from 1830 to 1834 was Lord Chancellor of England. He is remembered by students of literature as a co-founder, with Lord Jeffrey and Sydney Smith, of the *Edinburgh Review* (1802). His contemptuous review of Byron's youthful *Hours of Idleness* (1807) appeared in the *Edinburgh* in January 1808, and provoked the young lord's Popeian satire, *English Bards and Scotch Reviewers* (1809).

BROUGHTON, Rhoda (1840–1920) was a minor Victorian novelist. Among her novels are *Not Wisely, but Too Well* (1867), *Belinda* (1883), and *Doctor Cupid* (1886). Her friend Anthony Trollope objected that she made her characters "speak as men and women do speak." Victorian England found her daring. But she lived to know a generation which regarded her books as tame.

BROWN, Dr. John (1810–82) was an Edinburgh physician who occasionally did some writing. He composed mellow personal essays which were collected under the title *Horae Subsecivae* (1858–82). One of the best of these is a sketch of Marjorie Fleming, the "Pet Marjorie" upon whom Sir Walter Scott doted. But the doctor's masterpiece is *Rab and his Friends* (1859), a moving dog story which is still widely read.

BROWN, Thomas (1663–1704) wrote an immense amount of miscellaneous prose and verse, most of it satirical, and not a little of it bawdy. His *Amusements, Serious and Comical* (1700) is a series of sketches of London manners which anticipate those in the *Tatler* and *Spectator*. He has also been credited with *The Stage Beaux Tossed in a Blanket* (printed 1704), an obscene farce on the play-damning divine, Jeremy Collier. Most people know the classic quatrain, "I do not love thee, Dr. Fell," but few are aware that Tom Brown wrote it.

BROWN, Thomas Edward (1830–97) was a schoolmaster who published most of his verse after he was fifty. His poems include swiftly moving narratives and mystical lyrics. The best known are the "fo'c'sle yarn" *Betsy Lee* (1873) and the much-quoted lyric "A garden is a lovesome thing, God wot!" Many of Brown's poems are in his native Manx dialect; he has been called "the poet of Manxland."

BROWNE, Sir Thomas (1605–82). "The world that I regard is my self . . . for the other, I use it but like my Globe, and turn it round sometimes for my recreation." Browne wrote that in his first book, *Religio Medici,* about 1635. When the book was published against his will in 1642, he was quietly practicing medicine in Norwich. He still lived there when Charles II knighted him in 1671. Through years of civil war, while Milton pamphleteered in the Puritan cause, Browne, though of Royalist sympathies, chose to contemplate the miracle of himself. He examined the mysteries and played with the riddle of the "other world" but shunned its transient turmoils.

The *Religio* shows him as one who did not let the religious dogma of others direct his own personal beliefs. He compromised carefully between faith and skepticism: "Therefore that Miracles have been I do believe; that they may yet be wrought by the living, I do not deny; but have no confidence in those which are fathered on the dead." In *Pseudodoxia Epidemica* (1646), he drew on his recondite learning to disprove such "vulgar errors" as the belief that the salamander is impervious to flames; yet in testifying at a trial as late as 1664 he reasserted his early belief in witchcraft. Despite his confession in the *Religio* of the "slender and doubtful respect" he had "always held unto antiquities," both *Hydriotaphia* (or *Urn Burial*) and *The Garden of Cyrus* (published together 1658) are ostensibly antiquarian research—the first on certain "sepulchral urns" exhumed in Norfolk, the second on ancient gardens. *Hydriotaphia,* however, turns out to be a rumination on the vanity of earthly greatness, climaxed by a gorgeous chapter on "Time which antiquates Antiquities" and Death. In its companion piece Browne quibbles quaintly on the mystical properties of the "quincuncial lozenge" (:.:). The best known of his posthumous works, *Christian Morals* (1716), was edited by Samuel Johnson in 1756.

Browne's famous style has the natural rhythm of the King
James Bible rather than the more cumbrous, symmetrical balance
popularized by Johnson. His sentences are carefully built, but his
meaning is sometimes clouded by obscure allusions and rare Latin
derivatives. As Charles Lamb has shown, certain tricks of his
style are artificial and imitable. The prose poetry of Chapter V
in *Hydriotaphia* and the keen intellect are not.

BROWNE, William, of Tavistock (1591–1643) was a prolific poet
who depended heavily on the pastoral legacy. *The Shepherd's
Pipe* (1614), written in collaboration with George Wither, is a
series of eclogues in the tradition of Spenser's *Shepheardes Calender* (1579). *Britannia's Pastorals* (3 books, 1613, 1616, 1852) is
an endless and complex verse romance dotted with occasional
lyrics—a poem similar in many respects to Sidney's prose *Arcadia*
(1590). Both these works display some real nature poetry in the
midst of much conventional pastoral imagery. Browne is usually
named as the author of the famous six-line epitaph *On the Countess Dowager of Pembroke* ("Underneath this sable hearse").

BROWNING, Elizabeth Barrett (1806–61). It is difficult for a
twentieth-century reader to think of Elizabeth Barrett Browning
as ever having had an identity apart from that of her more famous
husband. Nevertheless, at the time of her marriage to Robert
Browning in 1846, the delicate, forty-year-old poetess was much
better known than he and was rather widely regarded as the
logical rival of Alfred Tennyson. She was a shy, sensitive creature,
one of the "Barretts of Wimpole Street" (in London), living
with her sisters under the domination of an unbalanced father who
kept his daughters virtual prisoners. An injury to her spine when
she was fifteen and the shock of her brother Edward's drowning
in 1840 added to her father's tyranny to make her a semi-invalid.
But in her confinement in the gloomy house in Wimpole Street
she studied seriously and wrote poems industriously. Her sound
scholarship appeared early in her *Essay on Mind, with Other
Poems* (1826) and in her translation of the *Prometheus Bound*
of Aeschylus (1833). *The Seraphim and Other Poems* (1838) was
followed by *Poems* (1844). In this slender volume the social sympathy that was one of her deepest characteristics emerged in *The
Cry of the Children* and *The Cry of the Human*. It was this volume, moreover, that introduced her to Robert Browning, for her
Lady Geraldine's Courtship contains a flattering allusion to his
poetry. Two years later he rescued the gentle lady from her dark
home and took her off to the sunshine of Casa Guidi in Italy to

spend the rest of her life in an ideal intellectual companionship.

In the new and happier life in Italy Mrs. Browning blossomed into her best work. Her *Sonnets from the Portuguese* (1850) are beautiful love poems addressed to Robert. They take their name from the circumstance that in allusion to her dark complexion he called her playfully his "little Portuguese." The Italian struggle for freedom, which stirred her greatly, produced *Casa Guidi Windows* (1851) and *Poems before Congress* (1860). Her longest poem was *Aurora Leigh* (1857), a blank-verse romance overloaded with social comment. *Last Poems* (1862) was published the year after her death.

As a poet Elizabeth Barrett Browning no longer has the rating that she enjoyed among her contemporaries. Even if she did not suffer by comparison with her much greater husband, there are certain qualities in her work that have operated against its permanence. She was too intellectual, too sentimental, too feminine—too Victorian, one may almost say. Moreover she lacked in her art the sense of compression and economy that marks all truly great poetry; she never learned to omit thoughts, lines, words, and so her poetry suffered from excesses. It is for this reason that her sonnets are really her best poems; not only do they have unity of feeling, but their very narrowness of form has forced their author into a restraint that she did not inherently possess. But if Elizabeth Barrett Browning cannot be listed with the great Victorian poets, she can hardly be spared. Elizabeth Barrett of Wimpole Street was a poem herself—and so was Mrs. Robert Browning of Casa Guidi.

BROWNING, Robert (1812–89) was the most intellectual and erudite of Victorian poets. His verse was the trenchant instrument by which he expressed his profound interest in men and women. He was always curious about their habits, their motives, their thoughts and feelings, their social patterns, and the effects upon them of their backgrounds and human associates. Browning was never unsympathetic, but essentially he was coolly analytical in tendencies and habits. This attitude and his unwillingness to write down to his readers made most of his poetry seem profound, recondite, and difficult for the average man immediately to understand. Browning was never a popular poet and never can become one. He was and still is the poet of the intelligentsia, the high priest of the "Browning clubs," of the bluestockings who love to read and pretend to pluck out the meaning of his profundities. There glows about him an aura of the cultured aristocrat, living in his ivory tower of art and safely protected from the unscholarly populace.

Browning was the over-privileged son of a well-to-do clerk in the Bank of England. He was educated mostly by private tutors and thus belongs to that very small group of English poets who were not university trained. He read voluminously and wisely, not only in his *lehrjahre* but throughout his lifetime, and he was a connoisseur of music and of art. Early travels to Russia and Italy helped to broaden his vision and make him less of an Englishman and more of a European. His first poem, published in 1833 through the benevolence of a wealthy aunt, was *Pauline,* done clearly under the influence of the intellectual romanticist Shelley. It created not a ripple of public interest. Two years later, however, the appearance of *Paracelsus,* a dramatic poem dealing with the life and character of a fifteenth-century alchemist, revealed that a new—and somewhat strange—poetic star was ascending. The poem disclosed also that the new poet was interested in the Renaissance and in the study of human souls. *Strafford* (printed 1837), his first play, failed completely on the stage; so, also, it may be added, did his other dramas, including *The Return of the Druses* (printed 1843), *A Blot in the 'Scutcheon* (printed 1843), and *Colombe's Birthday* (printed 1844). Browning was too much of a psychologist to be a good dramatist, and in most of his plays there is too much talking and self-analysis and not enough dramatic action. The most discussed of his early poems—and one of the most satirized—is *Sordello* (1840), another medieval characterization so detailed, so involute, so erudite and profound that Tennyson, on reading it, is reported to have thought himself going insane. Such a poem could not be widely read, and Browning's publishers tried to increase his popularity by issuing some of his poems and poetic dramas in a series of pamphlets (1841–6) called *Bells and Pomegranates;* among other items these include the sentimental play *Pippa Passes* and the dramatic monologues *My Last Duchess* and *The Bishop Orders His Tomb.*

In 1846 occurred the most important single event in Browning's life, his marriage to the popular poetess Elizabeth Barrett. He rescued this semi-invalid from a tyrannical father and spirited her off to Italy, where from 1848 until her death thirteen years later, they lived in almost perfect domestic and intellectual companionship at Casa Guidi in Florence. Under her influence he wrote *Christmas Eve and Easter-Day* (1850) and *Men and Women* (1855), an amazing series of poems in which he lets his subjects

reveal their own souls through the device of the "dramatic monologue." Among these profound studies of human character, *Fra
Lippo Lippi* and *Andrea del Sarto* are but two evidences of his
constant interest in Renaissance art.

On the death of his wife Browning returned to London, where
he allowed his grief to make him a semi-recluse for a number of
years before he emerged again into society. To this period belong *Dramatis Personae* (1864) and his most ambitious poem,
The Ring and the Book (1868–9). This astounding work in four
volumes is the dramatic retelling of an old Italian murder trial
which he had found recorded in the "Old Yellow Book"; the
"Ring" is the perfect circle of the truth—with some alloy of himself—that resulted from his repeating the story of the murder and
the trial from ten points of view. These include that of the
criminal count, Guido Franceschini, on trial for murdering his
base-born wife; Pompilia, the murdered girl; Giuseppe Capon-
sacchi, a young canon who befriended her; and ultimately the
Pope, who takes a divinely detached view of the crimes and
sorrows of all. The vividness of each section of the poem keeps
the ten retellings from becoming monotonous. *The Ring and the
Book* was the capstone of Browning's poetic achievement. His
last long poems, save for some magnificent translations—or rather
transcriptions—of Greek tragedies, tend to be grotesque, fantastic,
and at times prosaic. In 1878 Browning returned to his beloved
Italy, and there he died eleven years later.

Robert Browning and Alfred Tennyson are traditionally brack-
eted together as the two foremost Victorian poets. Of the two,
Browning is undoubtedly the more unconventional and original.
In spite of the erudition that prevented his becoming popular, he
is far from being pedantic or heavily didactic. His love of humanity kept him from becoming too completely analytical in
his study of human souls. His "men and women" are not subjects for post-mortems; they live, breathe, act, and reveal their
inner motives by what they say. There is in Browning a sturdy
British optimism and faith in essential humanity. As a craftsman
of verse he introduced a new realism of phrase, and although
his lines do not always have the lightness and movement that they
possess in *The Pied Piper of Hamelin* and *How They Brought the
Good News from Ghent to Aix,* he is always potentially versatile
and facile. And above all, his poems have strength and fibre, with
seldom an unsubstantial or mawkish line. All in all, for universality of content and qualities that are permanent Browning
is among the best of English poets.

BRUNTON, Mary (1778–1818) was a Scottish pastor's wife whose once-popular novels are in the didactic tradition of Maria Edgeworth and Hannah More. Their titles, *Self Control* (1811) and *Discipline* (1814), make no secret of their moral objectives.

BUCHANAN, George (1506–82) was a Scottish scholar who spent many years of his life in France, where he taught Montaigne. In 1560 he returned to Scotland and for seven years read the classics and wrote poetry for Queen Mary. After the murder of Darnley, however, he became her bitter enemy. From 1570 to 1578 he tutored the young Scottish prince who was later to become James I of England. Before turning Protestant in middle life, Buchanan freely satirized the Roman Catholic clergy; afterwards he was an important figure in the Scottish reformation. Like most Renaissance scholars, he wrote largely in Latin, including *De Maria Scotorum Regina,* etc. (1571?), an attack on the queen, *De Jure Regni apud Scotos* (1579), a treatise on Protestant political policy, and *Rerum Scoticarum Historia* (1582), long regarded as the foremost history of Scotland. His two major prose works in vernacular Scots are *The Chamaeleon* (1570), a personal satire, and *An Admonition Direct to the True Lords* (1571), a pamphlet on political strategy.

BUCHANAN, Robert Williams (1841–1901). Although this Scot wrote novels and poetry, he is remembered chiefly as the author of a single piece of criticism, "The Fleshly School of Poetry," published under the pseudonym "Robert Maitland" in the *Contemporary Review* for October, 1871. In it he attacked the Pre-Raphaelites, especially D. G. Rossetti. He characterized their medievalism as grotesque affectation and dismissed their love poetry with a shudder at its sensuality and an outburst of bewilderment "at the kind of women whom it seems the unhappy lot of these gentlemen to encounter."

BUCKHURST, Lord and **Baron.** See **SACKVILLE, Charles** and **Thomas.**

BUCKINGHAM, George Villiers, second duke of (1628–97). Influential figure in the reign of Charles II, vicious political schemer and turncoat, ribald rhymester, hard-drinking, duelling debaucher of women—Buckingham was called by Scott "the most lively, mercurial, ambitious, and licentious genius who ever lived." He is remembered as the chief author of *The Rehearsal* (1671), a brilliant burlesque of heroic drama. Beside its hero, Drawcansir, athletic Almanzor of Dryden's *Conquest of Granada* dwindles to a pygmy. But Buckingham was later deftly damned for posterity as Zimri in the laureate's *Absalom and Achitophel* (1681).

BUDGELL, Eustace (1686–1737). In his happier days he was a respected member of the "little senate" of his cousin Addison, and a contributor to the *Spectator*. But after Addison's death he went from bad to worse, and finally, in the words of Macaulay, "closed a wicked and unhappy life by self-murder." Budgell was damned by Pope in both the *Epistle to Dr. Arbuthnot* and the *Dunciad*.

BULWER–LYTTON, Edward Lytton, first baron (1803–73) was one of England's statesman-authors. In a long career of bickering both with the public and with his wife, he found time to edit the *New Monthly Magazine,* sit in Parliament, and write voluminously in almost every form. He is best known for historical novels more lavish, sensational, and footnote-ridden than Scott's. Posterity's favorite is *The Last Days of Pompeii* (1834). Keeping his finger on the public pulse, he also turned out tales of fashionable society (*Pelham,* 1828), sympathetic studies of crime (*Paul Clifford,* 1830), pseudo-scientific Gothic thrillers (*Zanoni,* 1842), and humorous domestic stories (*The Caxtons,* 1849). Much of his fiction is pervaded by melodramatic rhetoric and secondhand philosophy. His romantic comedy, *The Lady of Lyons* (1838), was long popular, and his cloak-and-sword drama, *Richelieu* (1839), still thunders occasionally from the boards.

BUNYAN, John (1628–88) presents the strange phenomenon of a Bedfordshire tinker who was inspired by the Bible to write the greatest sacred allegory in English prose. He was born at Elstow, Bedfordshire, entered the Parliamentary army at sixteen, and returned home to mend pots and pans and to get his education out of the Bible. In 1653 he became a member of the Baptist Church in Bedford and three years later published the first of his religious prose writings, *Some Gospel Truths Opened* (1656). With the restoration of Charles II in 1660 Bunyan was clapped into the Bedford jail for non-conformist preaching. Here he remained for twelve years, still meditating on holy writ and writing what the Spirit moved him to set down. *The Holy City, or The New Jerusalem* (1665) followed his reading of *Revelation*. *Grace Abounding to the Chief of Sinners* (1666) is the record of his sins and conversion. On his release in 1672 he became pastor of the Bedford Church, but three years later he was back in prison for another six months. It was during this period that he wrote "the book that followed the Bible," *The Pilgrim's Progress from this world to That which is to come* (1678).

41

This allegory of a Christian's salvation is an extraordinarily powerful and vivid narrative which has been universally read. Of it Dr. Johnson said: "This is the great merit of the book, that the most cultivated man cannot find anything to praise more highly, and the child knows nothing more amusing." So fascinating were the episodes of Christian's fight with Apollyon, his escape from Giant Despair, his temptations in Vanity Fair, and his arrival at the Celestial City that *Pilgrim's Progress* came almost to be thought of as Bunyan's only book. But the merits of his greatest work appear also in his last two: *The Life and Death of Mr. Badman* (1680), an allegory of a vicious sinner's downfall, and *The Holy War* (1682), an allegory of the siege of the city of Mansoul. Bunyan's literary purpose was essentially didactic. He would certainly be surprised at the extent of his influence on the course of realism in secular fiction.

BURGOYNE, John (1722–92). Few students of American history know that the British general who lost the battle of Saratoga in 1777 also wrote plays and poetry. Burgoyne is credited with four plays. His masterpiece, *The Heiress* (1786), was an immense success on the stage. It contains the mixture of sentimentality and manners-comedy which was popular at the time.

BURKE, Edmund (1729–97). By most Americans Burke is thought of solely as defender of the colonies in their war for freedom from British oppression. Thus his interests and activities are forced into a narrow channel. Actually, his plea for appeasement with the American colonials was only one, and perhaps not the most famous, of his numerous attacks on injustice and corruption. Burke was born in Dublin and had a good education and professional training at the University of Dublin and the Middle Temple in London, but he chose not to practice law. After an early, and rather astonishing excursion into the field of aesthetics, which led him to write *A Philosophical Enquiry into the Origin of our Ideas of the Sublime and the Beautiful* (1757), he became private secretary (1761–3) to "Single-speech" Hamilton, Secretary for Ireland, an official whom he came to despise heartily. In 1765 he was elected to Parliament, and in the same year became secretary to the Marquis of Rockingham, a statesman whom he served faithfully for seventeen years. During this period he became agent to the Province of New York.

In America, Burke's most significant articles and speeches are, of course, his *Thoughts on the Cause of the Present Discontents* (1770), *On American Taxation* (1774), *On Reconcilia-*

tion with America (1775), and *A Letter to the Sheriffs of Bristol* (1777). In England, however, his speeches against Warren Hastings, Governor-General of India, and his *Reflections on the Revolution in France* (1790) are more important. Hastings was impeached in 1787, some time after Burke's initial charges against him for malfeasance in office; and although he was ultimately acquitted, the system which he represented was slain by the honesty and vigor of the Irish orator's attacks. Burke's incoherent pamphlet on the Revolution contains a casuistical defense of the inherited rights of kings and noblemen, denial of the "natural rights" of the people, a panicky picture of the horrors of mob violence in France, and a sentimental lament for the dying glory of "the age of chivalry." Burke did not bother to account for the Revolution with any pretense at historical objectivity, and Thomas Paine, in *The Rights of Man* (1791-2) was quick to make this clear. Only two important publications followed Burke's retirement in 1794, his burning but dignified *Letter to a Noble Lord* (1796) in defense of his own public record, and his series of four *Thoughts on the Prospect of a Regicide Peace* (1796-7).

Although Burke's contemporaries hailed him as a great orator, they also called him—because of his reputation for clearing the benches—"the dinner-bell of the house." Macaulay warned that the prose of Burke's last years was "ungracefully gorgeous" and ridiculed his fondness for discussing "treaties and tariffs in the most fervid and brilliant language of romance." Matthew Arnold called him "our greatest English prose-writer" but found him guilty of passages of "Asiatic prose . . . barbarously rich and overloaded." The truth is that Burke's style varied considerably with the occasion and that an oration intended to arouse a dozing Parliament to action in 1775 should not be studied as a model for today's high-school compositions.

BURKE, Thomas (1887-1945), short-story writer, novelist, poet, and essayist, is best known for his studies of life in East London. His works include *Limehouse Nights* (1916), a collection of short-stories about Chinatown; *The Wind and the Rain* (1924), an autobiographical novel; and *Night Pieces* (1935), a group of tales. His sobbing drama, *Broken Blossoms* (1919), was once popular.

BURNAND, Sir Francis Cowley (1836-1917), editor of *Punch* from 1880 to 1906, was the author of *Happy Thoughts* (1866), *The Incompleat Angler* (1887), and numerous pieces for the stage. His short operetta, *Cox and Box* (1867), based on J. M.

Morton's farce *Box and Cox* and set to music by Sir Arthur Sullivan, is still popular.

BURNET, Gilbert (1643–1715), Bishop of Salisbury, was a prominent churchman and historian. His three-part *History of the Reformation of the Church* (1679, 1681, 1715) is marked, in view of the author's strong Protestant convictions and the contemporary terror of the Popish Plot, by a surprising amount of scholarly objectivity. Better known is Bishop Burnet's *History of His Own Time* (published 1724, 1734). Despite his high ideals as a historian, this work is colored by Whig prejudices and is neither as artistic or as dignified as the more famous history of his contemporary Clarendon. It is still, however, a readable and valuable guide to the period.

BURNET, Thomas (1635?–1715), Master of Charterhouse, wrote *The Sacred Theory of the Earth,* the English version of which, translated from the original Latin, was published in 1684. The work is a mixture of scientific knowledge and romance. It has been praised by Addison and others for its eloquent prose.

BURNEY, Frances (Mme. D'Arblay) (1752–1840). This daughter of Charles Burney, the eminent music historian, was the little lioness of Dr. Johnson's circle. Her first published novel, *Evelina* (1778), made her famous. Its well-bred heroine scoffs at the vulgar manners of London in a series of humorous, satirical letters to her guardian in the country. Despite a tinge of Richardsonian sentimentality and a parcel of melodramatic tricks, the book displays a real presentation of ordinary events which anticipates Jane Austen. *Cecilia* (1782), more complex and tragic, shows some of this skill, but pompous *Camilla* (1796) and *The Wanderer* (1814) are not in the same class. "Fanny" Burney's *Early Diary* (1768–78, published 1889) throws light on her beginnings as a writer and on her friendship with Garrick and Johnson. Her *Diary and Letters* (1778–1840, published 1842–6) gives the inside story of life at court, where for five years (1786–91) she was Second Keeper of the Robes to Queen Charlotte.

BURNS, Robert (1759–96), Scotland's greatest poet, was born in a clay cot in Ayrshire. He spent his youth behind the plough and received only a humble education. When, in 1786, the first modest edition of his poems was published at Kilmarnock, his local reputation as a poet spread to Edinburgh. After the Edinburgh edition of the following year, he was the literary lion of the hour. Blessed by sudden fortune, he married Jean Armour in

1788 and settled on a farm near Dumfries. But this farming
venture failed, and he had to depend upon a government job as
a wine gauger. Early privations and too frequent carousals un-
dermined his health, and he died in poverty long before his
time.

As Carlyle never tired of repeating, Robert Burns was a sincere man. Like his fellow-Scotsman, Burns hated shams—the
sham-learning which he ridiculed in *The Epistle to J. Lapraik*
(1786), the sham-righteousness which he satirized in *Address to
the Unco Guid* (1787), the sham of rank which he exposed in
A Man's a Man for A' That (1795). He loved honest humanity—
whether he found it in the person of the god-fearing cottager of
The Cotter's Saturday Night (1786), the demon-haunted boozer
of his lusty narrative poem, *Tam O'Shanter* (1791), or the bawdy,
thirsty revelers of his cantata, *The Jolly Beggars* (1799, written
1785). He was sincerely moved by God's world as he showed
tenderly in *To a Mouse* (1786) and *To a Mountain Daisy* (1786).
And he sang sincere songs of love, good fellowship, and patriotism: *Auld Lang Syne, John Anderson My Jo, Comin' Thro
the Rye, The Banks of Doon, Sweet Afton, Mary Morison,* "Scots
Wha Hae"—the list is almost endless. To the student of English
literary history, Burns is important because he deserted the
artificial tradition of eighteenth-century poetry, replacing poetic
diction with the pungent vernacular, false sentiment with true
tenderness, shams with realities. He taught the Romantics, in
Wordsworth's words,

> How Verse may build a princely throne
> On humble truth.

To the world at large he is merely a singer of timeless songs.

BURTON, Sir Richard Francis (1821–90) was the most colorful
of Victorian travelers and travel-writers. In his *Pilgrimage to
El-Medinah and Mecca* (1855–6) he wrote about his secret entrance into the Holy City disguised as a Moslem. In subsequent
works, he told of his travels and explorations in Africa and
South America. Like a later adventurer in Arabia, T. E. Lawrence, Burton was also a scholar. He made a famous translation
of *The Arabian Nights* (1885–8).

BURTON, Robert (1577–1640). Of the group of early seventeenth-
century writers of heavy, learned, Latinized prose, one of the
most eccentric was Robert Burton. After graduation from Oxford
with degrees in both letters and theology, Burton became vicar

of St. Thomas there and continued to live and write in the university precincts. He wrote *Philosophaster,* curious satirical poems in Latin which were published in various places but not collected and edited until 1862. But his most important work and the only one by which he became widely known is *The Anatomy of Melancholy* (1621). Starting out as a medical treatise on the disease with which the hypochondriacal Burton was himself unhappily afflicted, it developed into an extended analysis of the symptoms and the cures of all kinds of melancholic insanity—religious, erotic, scholarly, etc. For his illustrations and "evidences" the author drew heavily upon Greek and Latin writers, and the curious treatise is stuffed with abstruse learning. In spite of its content and style, it had a definite influence on many subsequent poets and prose writers, including John Milton and Charles Lamb. Burton's lengthy and exhaustive study of melancholy does not seem to have relieved him of his own black depression of spirits, for when he was found dead in his room, there was considerable suspicion that he had perished by his own hand.

BURY, Richard d'Aungerville de (1281–1345) founded a library at Durham, where he was Bishop, and wrote in Latin *Philobiblon* (printed in Cologne, 1473), the autobiography of a book-lover.

BUTLER, Joseph (1692–1752), Bishop of Bristol (1738–50) and Durham (1750–2), was the author of *Fifteen Sermons* (1726) and *The Analogy of Religion, Natural and Revealed to the Constitution and Course of Nature* (1736). *The Analogy* has been called the final word in the "deistical controversy" which loomed large in English philosophy at the beginning of the eighteenth century.

BUTLER, Samuel (1612–80). The restoration of Charles II in 1660 released a storm of literary abuse upon the Puritans who had controlled England for two decades. Of these attacks the most popular and witty was Butler's *Hudibras* (1663, 1664, 1678), a mock-heroic poem after the satirical manner of Cervantes' *Don Quixote* (1605). The first part of the poem was printed in 1663, and additional parts appeared in 1664 and 1678, but it was never completed. By temperament and experience Butler was well equipped to vilify the Puritans. He was a disappointed and irascible wit whose royalist inclinations had been strengthened by his association with non-conformists in the household of Sir Samuel Luke of Bedfordshire. This fanatical colonel in Crom-

well's army was probably the original of Butler's hero. Hudibras is a "Presbyterian true blue" knight whose

> "trenchant blade, Toledo trusty,
> For want of fighting was grown rusty."

He and his grotesque squire, Ralpho, set out to put down amusements in England and succeeded only in providing amusement
for others. The rough tetrameter couplets of the poem are stuffed
with the most absurd grotesqueries—mock erudition, oddly
twisted phrases, and outlandish rhymes elbowing for place in a
mad helter-skelter. The diarist Pepys found the first part of
Hudibras "so silly an abuse of the Presbyter Knight going to
the wars" that he sold his copy at a loss the same day he bought
it. But King Charles liked Butler's wit so well that he gave the
poet a present of three hundred pounds. For *Paradise Lost,* published in the same decade, the Puritan Milton received eighteen.

BUTLER, Samuel (1835–1902) was born in Nottinghamshire.
His grandfather was the famous Dr. Samuel Butler, head master
of Shrewsbury School and Bishop of Lichfield. After graduation
from Cambridge he spent five years as a sheep-rancher in New
Zealand. Here he began the first of a series of attacks on the
natural scientists, whose rational processes he opposed. *Darwin
on the Origin of Species* appeared in 1862 and *Darwin among the
Machines* the year following. In 1864 Butler returned to England
and settled down to an active life as journalist, satirist, essayist,
and novelist. While on a visit to Canada he composed the famous
Psalm of Montreal (written 1875, published 1884), a short poem
ridiculing Victorian prudery and Philistinism. A journey to Italy
produced *Alps and Sanctuaries of Piedmont and the Canton
Ticino* (1882), a sparkling travel book. Meanwhile his battle with
the professional scientists continued. In *Life and Habit* (1878),
Evolution Old and New (1879), *God the Known and God the
Unknown* (1879), and *The Deadlock in Darwinism* (1890) he
continued his arguments against a plan of life that omits the intellectual and spiritual elements and reduces the vital pattern to
a mechanism. At the same time he branched out into other
fields. His study of musical composition led indirectly to an interest in the Homeric epics. He translated the *Iliad* (1898) and
the *Odyssey* (1900), and in *The Authoress of the Odyssey* (1897)
expressed the startling theory that the poem was written by a
woman. In *Shakespeare's Sonnets Reconsidered* (1899) his ideas
were unconventional but not so eccentric as in his pamphlet on
Homer.

Of all Butler's works, the best known and the most important are *Erewhon* (1872) and *The Way of All Flesh* (1903). *Erewhon* —the word is an anagram for *Nowhere* and is divided into three syllables—is a satirical Utopia in which Butler attacks the frozen patterns of Victorian society, particularly those of education and religion. Its most famous analogue in English literature is Swift's *Gulliver's Travels,* and it is almost equally fantastic and bitter. *Erewhon Revisited* (1900) is a less successful sequel in which Butler makes a brilliant assault on theological thinking and hypocrisy. *The Way of All Flesh* had a curious history. Although Butler began it in 1872 and worked at it intermittently until 1885, it was not actually published until a year after his death. In the history of successive generations of the Pontifex family Butler presented his own theory of the continuity of development from father to son and vigorously attacked the educational system under which he had suffered in his own family. The entire tribe of the Pontifex, except for the hero's aunt Alithea, is depicted bitterly in a style bristling with barbed epigrams. The book is not a coherent novel but a tissue of remorseless comments on the petrified life of the Victorian middle-class family.

Butler enjoyed little fame while he lived, but his stock rose steadily after his death. Today he is widely recognized both as a founder of the modern genealogical novel and as a harbinger of twentieth-century thought. He called himself, with characteristic bitterness, "the *enfant terrible* of literature." G. B. Shaw, in admitting his own substantial debt to Butler, called him "in his own department the greatest English writer of the latter half of the nineteenth century."

BYROM, John (1692–1763) was a successful teacher of his own system of shorthand and a facile versifier with a taste for religious mysticism. He idolized William Law, the English mystic; his *Epistle to a Gentleman of the Temple* (1749) and *Enthusiasm* (1751) are both verse paraphrases of Law's prose works, and his *Private Journal* (published 1854–7) gives a glowing account of his reverence for Law. But the only poem of Byrom's which is at all well known today is the humorous four-line toast beginning, "God bless the King!—I mean the Faith's defender." The author of the quatrain was a Jacobite.

BYRON, George Gordon Noel, sixth baron (1788–1824) was born with what he called an "inheritance of storms." He was the grandson of Admiral ("Foulweather Jack") Byron, who "never went to sea without encountering a storm," and the son of Captain

("Mad Jack") Byron, a notorious profligate, and Catherine Gordon, a foolish, fiery woman who pampered and maltreated little George to suit her moods. At ten he succeeded to the family estate of Newstead Abbey in Nottinghamshire as sixth baron Byron. After preparing at Harrow (1801–5), where, despite a deformed foot, he excelled in swimming, boxing, and cricket, he entered Trinity College, Cambridge (1805–8), where he distinguished himself in numerous unrecognized extra-curricular activities. While still an undergraduate, he published two slight collections of verse. When the second, *Hours of Idleness* (1807), was ridiculed in the Whig *Edinburgh Review,* "the noble minor" responded with a youthful *Dunciad* called *English Bards and Scotch Reviewers* (1809). In it he attacked, among others, Francis Jeffrey, whom he had mistaken as the guilty reviewer, Wordsworth, Coleridge, and Southey. From 1809 to 1811 Byron traveled in the Mediterranean countries, particularly in the Near East, where he courted the maids of Athens, swam the Hellespont, and finished the first two cantos of his narrative poem *Childe Harold* (1812; III, 1816; IV, 1818). Shortly after his return they were published. "I awoke one morning," wrote Byron, "to find myself famous."

The Byron fever in England during the next four years is not hard to explain. In his early narrative poems the poet gave new life to a type of hero which was already immensely popular. "The Byronic hero," the passionate, pale-browed misanthrope who wanders forever on the fringe of civilized society wrapped in the gloom of a mysterious past, had previously scowled at English readers from the pages of Mrs. Radcliffe's novels and Scott's poetry. Childe Harold, who travels over Europe in flight from disillusionment over a misspent youth, is this familiar figure of romance brought closer to the contemporary scene and endowed with nobler hopes for the future of mankind. The dark heroes of *The Giaour* (1813), *The Bride of Abydos* (1813), *The Corsair* (1814) and its sequel, *Lara* (1814), are Harold's not-too-distant Oriental relatives. And each was a tough self-portrait of a poet who in person was even more compelling—a poet who had swum the Hellespont, a member of the House of Lords who talked of revolution, a cynic full of passionate idealism, a great lover who loved no one so much as himself. In the wild, pleasure-loving age of the Regency, men found Lord Byron a good companion at the ringside and around the gaming table. Women eyed the cluster of curls on his pale brow and whispered eagerly about his scandalous reputation. "Mad, bad, and dangerous to know," gasped Lady Caroline Lamb, and she was only one of many women who learned this truth at first hand.

Although the romantic picture still fascinates the world, the first fever of adulation in England soon subsided. On January 3, 1815, Byron married Anne Isabella Milbanke, and a year later she walked out with their five-weeks-old daughter. This scandal, linked with gossip about his relations with his half-sister, Augusta, made Byron a social outcast. In April, 1816, Childe Harold set out "once more upon the waters," never to return alive to England. After wandering on the Continent, he settled in Italy. During his exile he saw much of the Shelleys and carried on a notorious liaison with an Italian countess, Teresa Guiccioli. In 1823 he sailed from Italy to help the Greeks in their fight for freedom from the Turks, and after a heroic effort to unify the Greek tribes, he died, probably of meningitis, at Missolonghi, on April 19, 1824. He was buried in England.

Lord Byron was the most versatile of the Romantic poets. He wrote numerous narrative poems, long and short, including, in addition to those already mentioned, such favorites as *The Destruction of Sennacherib* (from *Hebrew Melodies,* 1815), *The Prisoner of Chillon* (1816), and *Mazeppa* (1819). He composed some of the most perfect English lyrics: "Maid of Athens, ere we part," "When we two parted," "She walks in beauty," "There be none of Beauty's daughters," "So we'll go no more a-roving," *Stanzas Written on the Road between Florence and Pisa,* and *On This Day I Complete My Thirty-Sixth Year.* He tried various dramatic forms: romantic closet dramas—*Manfred* (1817), *Cain* (1821), *Heaven and Earth* (1823), *Werner* (1823), and *The Deformer Transformed* (unfinished, 1824); classical tragedies—*Marino Faliero* (acted against his will at Drury Lane, 1820), *The Two Foscari* (1821), and *Sardanapalus* (1821); dramatic soliloquies—*The Lament of Tasso* (1817) and *The Prophecy of Dante* (1821). In the best known of these, *Manfred* and *Cain,* he presented further variations on the theme of the Byronic hero. In *Manfred* he told a Faust-like story of man's bondage to the powers of evil, and in *Cain* he audaciously used for his hero the first murderer from the Bible.

Towards the end of his life Byron turned again to satire, this time employing, not the classical heroic couplet of *English Bards and Scotch Reviewers,* but an English adaptation of the Italian stanzaic form, *ottava rima.* He used this stanza in *Beppo* (1818), a gay narrative of adultery in Italy, and in *The Vision of Judgment* (1822), a travesty of Southey's *A Vision of Judgment*

(1821) and an attack on both the Tory laureate and the late King George III. But to many readers *ottava rima* will always be the "Don Juan stanza" in honor of Byron's long unfinished epic satire, *Don Juan,* the sixteen cantos of which he poured out fitfully between 1819 and 1824. The ribald story of the wanderings of its unprincipled hero (Byron rhymes his name with "new one") is merely a framework for the poet's prolific observations on wine and women, poetry and politics. Like Sterne in *Tristram Shandy,* Byron followed his moods at will, placing eccentric polysyllabic rhymes side by side with beautiful lyrical passages like *The Isles of Greece* (Canto III). The facility and ebulliency which had made his verse so uneven in the past were now combined as positive virtues. Most readers acclaim *Don Juan* as Byron's masterpiece.

C

CAEDMON (fl. 670). In Book IV, Chapter 24, of the Venerable Bede's *Ecclesiastical History of the English Nation* (731) is the story of how a lay brother at the Abbey at Whitby, unable to sing when the harp was passed around the table, retired in embarrassment to a stable, and there fell asleep. As he slumbered, there came to him in a vision a person who said: "Caedmon, sing some song." And lo, there came to the simple herdsman the divine gift of song, and he sang of "the Maker of the heavenly kingdom, the power of the Creator, and his counsel, the deeds of the Father of glory." Bede's narrative is the only account of the first known English poet. The figure of the poet is vague and uncertain, and there exists of his authentic work only a single nine-line fragment in praise of his Creator. A number of poems on biblical themes, formerly attributed to him, are now thought to be the work of a group of imitators sometimes called "the Caedmonian School." These poems include two from *Genesis,* one from *Exodus,* and a very dramatic and vigorous epic paraphrase from the apocryphal story of Judith, the Hebrew heroine who slew Holofernes, leader of the Assyrian army encamped against her people. All of these poems that have become attached to the shadowy figure of Caedmon are in Old English and are of uncertain date.

CAINE, (Sir Thomas Henry) Hall (1853–1931) was a writer of exciting escapist fiction whose novels were extremely popular at the turn of the century. The list includes *The Shadow of a Crime* (1885), *The Deemster* (1887), *The Bondman* (1890), and *The*

Manxman (1894). The scenes of several of Hall Caine's books are laid in the Isle of Man. He lived with D. G. Rossetti for the last two years of the poet's life and wrote *Recollections of D. G. Rossetti* (1882).

CALVERLEY, Charles Stuart (1831–84) was a lawyer who translated the classics and wrote facile light verse. His books include *Verses and Translations* (1862), *Translations into English and Latin* (1866), *Theocritus Translated into English Verse* (1869), and *Fly Leaves* (1872). Among his many parodies of the Victorian poetry is the nonsense ballad "The auld wife sat at her ivied door," a take-off on the literary ballads of Rossetti and his fellow Pre-Raphaelites.

CAMDEN, William (1551–1623) was an antiquarian and historian. His chief work, *Britannia* (1586, etc.), was, according to the title page, "a chorographical description of the flourishing Kingdoms of England, Scotland, and Ireland from the earliest antiquity." It is still valuable to scholars. He also wrote *Annals of England and Ireland in the Reign of Elizabeth* (pt. 1, 1615; pts. 1 and 2, 1625). Both are in Latin. The Camden Society, founded in 1838, was named in his honor.

CAMPBELL, (Ignatius) Roy (Dunnachie) (1902–1957) was a South African of Scottish parentage who spent part of his adventurous life in Spain. His poetry reflects a rebellious energy that has led some critics to compare him with Byron. Among his longer works are *The Flaming Terrapin* (1924), a vigorous poem expressing the wild grandeur of nature, and *The Georgiad* (1931), "a satirical fantasy" on his contemporaries in literature. His best-known short poem is *The Zebras,* published in the collection called *Adamastor* (1931).

CAMPBELL, Thomas (1777–1844) was a Scot who became a popular poet early with *The Pleasures of Hope* (1799), a work of some five hundred heroic couplets. It is choked with the allegorical rhetoric of the dying century, but pleased the public with certain topical passages like that on the partition of Poland ("And Freedom shrieked when Kosciusko fell"). Although subsequent long poems like the sentimental *Gertrude of Wyoming* (1809) deserve oblivion, England worships Campbell as the author of some of her favorite martial odes and ballads: "Ye Mariners of England," *Hohenlinden,* and *The Battle of the Baltic.* Campbell was also a magazine editor, an anthologist, and a critic. He defended the old order in poetry against the experiments of the "Lakers"; in the

"Bowles Controversy" he seconded Byron in defense of Pope's merit as a poet.

CAMPION, Thomas (1567–1620). The extraordinary variety of interests which marked the lives of most Elizabethan writers is exemplified in the activities of Thomas Campion. The circumstance that he was a physician with an active and apparently successful practice did not prevent him from being equally successful in the strangely remote fields of poetry, music, and literary criticism. His first publication was *Poemata* (1595), a collection of original Latin poems in which he revealed his interest in metrical experimentation. This concern appears also in his critical treatise, *Observations in the Art of English Poesie* (1602). Here he followed Sidney, Gabriel Harvey, and other contemporary critics in assailing rhyme. His musical skill both as a composer and as a lutanist qualified him to write court masques, and in this field he is second only to Ben Jonson. One of his best known is *The Lord's Masque* (1613). As might be expected, his poems are filled with musical allusions. Moreover, he apparently expressed himself with equal facility in words and in music, for he is probably the only lyrist of the period who set his own poems to melodies. Most of his lyrics, with the musical accompaniments, appear in his four *Books of Airs* (Books 1 and 2, 1610; Books 3 and 4, 1617?). Among them is the lovely song "There is a garden in her face."

CANNING, George (1770–1827). This faithful follower of William Pitt the Younger is known to students of literature as the founder of the *Anti-Jacobin* (1797–8), a magazine calculated to counteract the political influences of the French Revolution. In its pages appeared such memorable mimicry as *The Loves of the Triangles,* a parody of Erasmus Darwin's *Loves of the Plants; The Rovers,* a burlesque of German drama; and *The Friend of Humanity and the Knife Grinder,* a parody of one of Southey's Sapphics. Canning collaborated on these with John Hookham Frere. George Ellis also contributed to the *Anti-Jacobin.* It was edited by William Gifford.

CAPGRAVE, John (1393–1464) was a prolific friar who wrote more in Latin than in English. In Latin he wrote commentaries on the Bible, saints' lives, and lives of "the illustrious Henries." His best-known English work is a plain prose *Chronicle of England,* which is valuable for the light it throws on Capgrave's own time.

CAREW, Thomas (1598?-1639?). Wine, women, and song was the formula for the devil-may-care Cavalier poets of the early Stuart period, and Thomas Carew lived up to the formula without questioning it. His father, Sir Matthew Carew (sometimes pronounced and often spelled Carey), Master in Chancery, gave him a training at Oxford and at the Middle Temple, but the boy took seriously neither to learning nor to law. He became early an attaché at the English embassy at Venice, and in 1619 was in France with Lord Herbert of Cherbury. At the court of Charles I he became one of the gentlemen of the privy-chamber and a sewer-in-ordinary, or taster of royal dishes, to his majesty. Besides the gay irresponsibles at the court, Carew numbered among his intimate acquaintances the learned Dr. John Donne, Ben Jonson, literary senator for a score of young poets, John Suckling, Cavalier versifier, and Davenant, the dramatist. Like other Cavalier poets he wrote sophisticated, clever, and irresponsible verses. These were gathered into a collection of *Poems* and published in 1640, just after his death. His *Coelum Britannicum* (1634) is a beautiful court masque, one of the last of its type, and his *Elegy upon the Death of Dr. Donne* (1631) is a graceful tribute to the character and genius of his older friend.

CAREY, Henry (1687?-1743) wrote *The Dragon of Wantley* (1737), a burlesque opera, and *The Tragedy of Chrononhotonthologos, being the most Tragical Tragedy that ever was Tragedized by any Company of Tragedians* (1734). The latter is a burlesque of the drama not unlike Fielding's *Tom Thumb* (1730). It contains one character whose name fills out an entire iambic pentameter line, Aldiborontiphoscophornio. Carey's most popular work, however, is the playful song *Sally in our Alley,* of which he wrote both words and music.

CARLETON, William (1794-1869) was the youngest of fourteen children of an Irish peasant. He made his reputation with a series of authentic sketches about the people whom he knew: *Traits and Stories of the Irish Peasantry* (1830-3). He followed them with a number of successful novels, including *Fardorougha the Miser* (1839), the study of a man torn between his love of money and love of his only son; *The Black Prophet* (1847), a tale of the Irish famine; and *Valentine McClutchy, the Irish Agent* (1845), an exposé of the evils of absentee landlordism. Carleton combined Celtic humor and mysticism with the burning indignation of the social reformer.

CARLYLE, Thomas (1795–1881) was the son of a Scottish stone-mason. He wavered in the choice of a career, studying for both Church and Bench, even teaching mathematics before settling definitely upon literature. In 1826 he married Jane Welsh. Their life together, first on the lonely farm of Craigenputtock in Scotland (1826–34), later in Chelsea, London (1834–66), is partly revealed in Jane's lively letters and has been mercilessly X-rayed since the disclosures of Carlyle's frank biographer, James Anthony Froude. It was the troubled life of an irascible, dyspeptic man and a brilliant woman who, although she appreciated his genius, still retained a shrewd individuality of her own.

Carlyle's early work consisted largely of reviews, translations, and biographical essays and was dominated by his effort to introduce German literature to England. Among his early essays are three on English literature—*Burns* (1828), *Boswell's Johnson* (1832), and *Scott* (1838)—and two ventures into social criticism—*Signs of the Times* (1829) and *Characteristics* (1831). His first work to cause a real stir in England was *Sartor Resartus* (1833–4), in which, disguised as a fictitious German sage, Diogenes Teufelsdröckh, he told the story of his own spiritual conversion and advocated his "clothes-philosophy" as a cure for England's social ills. In 1837 he published his sulphuric *French Revolution*, a didactic and subjective history. During the next fifteen years he preached incessantly against the evils of his day. In the lectures *On Heroes, Hero-Worship, and the Heroic in History* (1841), he exhorted his audience to seek out Great Men to lead them. In *Past and Present* (1843) he extolled the simple, sincere spirituality of the medieval monastery in contrast to the shams and machinery of Victorian England. In *Chartism* (1839) and *Latter-Day Pamphlets* (1850) he dealt more directly with the political problems of his own day. During the same period he edited Cromwell's *Letters and Speeches* (1845) and wrote an excellent biography of his friend, John Sterling (1851). His last major work was the monumental, ten-volume *Frederick the Great* (1858–65), over which he struggled for years in his famous sound-proof room.

Although Carlyle actually had several "styles," it is the eccentric manner of *Sartor Resartus* with which most readers associate his name: an explosive style strongly colored by both Scottish and German influences and marked by the omission of non-essential words and the profusion of concrete images, exclamations, rhetorical questions, compound coinages, and capitalized nouns.

Carlyle's favorite texts can be briefly summarized: Man is

clothed with shams—false creeds, symbols, and trappings. Victorian England is corrupt with fox-hunting dilettantes and Mammon-worshipers. She should learn the gospel of hard Work, learn to seek, not happiness, but blessedness. She should renew her reverence for the past—for history, and, since history is only "the essence of innumerable biographies," for the heroes of history, the sincere men free from sham, the silent men of action. In spite of Carlyle's deep respect for the potentialities of every human soul, however humble, he distrusted the masses, scorned the machinery of democracy, and defended the strong man as the maker of history. In many respects, he was a forerunner of twentieth-century fascism.

CARROLL, Lewis (1832–98). **Charles Lutwidge Dodgson** lectured in mathematics at Oxford from 1855 to 1881 and wrote several treatises in his field. But the world knows him best as Lewis Carroll, the author of *Alice's Adventures in Wonderland* (1865). Composed originally for the amusement of a little real-life Alice, it soon grew into a nursery classic and has since become one of the most commonly quoted works in the whole gamut of English literature. For the mathematician not only projected himself into the whimsical nonsense land of childhood but brought along with him an endowment of adult logic and adult wit. The illustrations which Sir John Tenniel drew for this book and for its sequel, *Through the Looking Glass* (1872), are classics in their own right. The same is true of the verses which are sprinkled throughout the two books: *Alice in Wonderland* contains *The Crocodile* and *Father William,* irreverent parodies respectively of poems by Isaac Watts and Robert Southey; *Through the Looking Glass* includes the tearful tale of *The Walrus and the Carpenter* and the inspired epic of nonsense, *Jabberwocky*. Lewis Carroll also wrote, in verse, *The Hunting of the Snark* (1876) and, in prose, *Sylvie and Bruno* (1889–93). He has recently been "re-discovered" as a surrealist and a forerunner of James Joyce.

CARTER, Elizabeth (1717–1806) was a member of the original "Bluestockings," the ladies' intellectual circle which also included Hester Chapone and Elizabeth Montagu. She published poetry (1738, 1762), a translation of *Epictetus* (1758), and two essays, numbers 44 and 100, in Johnson's *Rambler*.

CARTWRIGHT, William (1611–43) was one of the lesser singers of the "tribe of Ben" Jonson. Before taking orders in 1638 he wrote a handful of comedies and tragi-comedies, including *The*

Royal Slave (1636). He was adept at fashioning occasional verses of the type that in later years were expected of the poets laureate. In *To Chloe, Who Wished Herself Young Enough For Me,* he bridged the chronological gap with a pretty conceit. In the lines *On His Majesty's Recovery from the Small-Pox,* the conceit of comparing the ravages of the disease to "stars fixed in a Milky-way" is hardly happy.

CAVENDISH, George (1500–61?) was a gentleman usher in the household of Thomas Wolsey (1475?–1530). His *Life of Cardinal Wolsey* was written during the reign of Mary Tudor (1553–8) but was passed around in manuscript for almost a century before publication in 1641. Cavendish described the cardinal's tragic rise and fall with genuine, if unconscious, literary art. The work has been called the first "artistic biography" in English.

CAVENDISH, Margaret. See **NEWCASTLE.**

CAXTON, William (1421–91). Some five hundred years ago a German named John Gutenberg (1398–1468) developed a process of multiplying books through the use of movable metal type. Printing, thus invented, was brought to England a generation later by a retired merchant named William Caxton, who thereby made to English literature a contribution of inestimable value. Caxton had lived in Bruges, in Flanders, apparently as a mercer, from 1441 to 1470. Then he retired from business and engaged in literary pursuits with the encouragement of Margaret, Duchess of Burgundy, sister of King Edward IV of England. His translation from the French of Raoul de Fèvres's *Recuyell of the Histories of Troy,* a series of Trojan stories, he completed in 1471; and when this translation was printed, in Bruges four years later, it became the first book ever printed in the English language. Returning to England in 1476 Caxton set up a printing press in Westminster, and from then until his death fifteen years later he issued more than eighty books. The first printed on English soil was *Dictes or Sayings of the Philosophers* (1477). In the decade and a half that followed, Caxton printed Chaucer's *Canterbury Tales,* Gower's *Confessio Amantis,* Malory's *Morte Darthur,* and many others, including some twenty of his own translations. That the first printer was no mere reproducer of the works of others, but an author in his own right, is revealed by the series of prefaces and epilogues which he added to the books printed. Most of these have distinct literary merit. The most famous of them is the Preface to the *Morte Darthur,* Malory's great series of the tales of Arthur and the Table Round, "by me [Caxton] divided into twenty-one books, chaptered and imprinted, and finished in the Abbey Westminster the last day of July the year of our Lord MCCCCLXXXV."

CENTLIVRE, Susanna (1667?–1723). This wife of a cook in Queen Anne's court (husband No. 3) became a popular dramatist by seasoning borrowed plays with a spice of her own. In *The Busybody* (1709), *The Wonder: A Woman Keeps a Secret* (1714), and *A Bold Stroke for a Wife* (1718), containing the original Simon Pure, she preserved the robustness and salaciousness of her Restoration forerunner, Aphra Behn, in an age of sentimental comedy, and gave the stage three "acting" plays which were favorites for more than a century. Said Hazlitt: "She could do nothing without a stratagem; but she could do everything with one."

CHAMBERLAYNE, William (1619–89), a Cavalier physician, was the author of *Pharonnida* (1659), a long romance in heroic couplets.

CHAPMAN, George (1559?–1634) is better known from a single sonnet by John Keats, *On First Looking into Chapman's Homer,* than from all his melodramatic tragedies. His translation of the *Iliad* he began in 1598, when he was nearly forty years old; he completed it about 1610, just a year or two before the death of the scholarly young Prince Henry Stuart, to whom he had been server-in-ordinary. The translation of the *Odyssey* he completed about 1615. The first of the great translations is in rhyming lines of fourteen syllables, the second in rhyming ten-syllable lines. The metrical power which Chapman displayed in his epics he had revealed earlier in his courageous completion (1598) of Marlowe's *Hero and Leander,* left unfinished at Marlowe's death in 1593.

In his plays Chapman is more of a poet and translator of epics than a dramatist. There are in the dramas some fine poetic passages, but he had little sense of dramatic construction, and the epic quality tends constantly to elbow the dramatic out of the way. His comedies—*All Fools* (printed 1605), *Monsieur d'Olive* (1604), and *May-Day* (printed 1611)—are inferior, and his tragi-comedy, *The Gentleman Usher* (printed 1606), is undistinguished. As a dramatist he is best in the four melodramatic tragedies of contemporary French history, *Bussy D'Ambois* (printed 1607), *The Revenge of Bussy D'Ambois* (printed 1613), and the two parts of *The Conspiracy and Tragedy of Charles, Duke of Byron* (printed 1608). All of these have as their theme the rise and fall of an upstart at the French court, and all are heavily melodramatic. The plots are rambling and not infrequently confusing, the episodes are often absurd, and the characters are quite unnatural. For example, the report to the king of the fight of Bussy and two friends against three courtiers who had insulted him is definitely epic-narrative and not drama. Similarly, Chapman blows reality to the winds when, in *Bussy D'Ambois,* the friar who has acted as go-between for the adventurer and his married mistress continues to function even more effectively after the abused husband has made a ghost of him. In spite of occasional good poetry and vivid passages that disclose the hand of Chapman the poet, these melodramas often descend into ridiculous burlesques of genuine and restrained tragedy.

CHAPONE, Hester (1727–1801). Like Elizabeth Carter, and Elizabeth Montagu, Mrs. Chapone was one of the original "Bluestockings" of the middle of the eighteenth century. She was a friend of Richardson and wrote part of number ten of Johnson's *Rambler.* Her most popular work was *Letters on the Improvement of the Mind* (1773).

CHATTERTON, Thomas (1752–70) dreamt romantic dreams beneath the Gothic cathedral towers of his native Bristol and embarked upon a fantastic career of trying to palm off home-made documents as genuine literary antiques. He had some success in fooling local antiquarians, but fame and fortune came slowly, and after a desperate four-month struggle to write for a living in London, he took his life with poison. Chatterton's most famous forgeries are the "Rowley Poems," most of them ascribed to an imaginary fifteenth-century priest named Thomas Rowley. Only one of them, *Elinoure and Juga* (1769), appeared in the poet's lifetime. Thomas Tyrwhitt edited a collection in 1777 and in the next year added an appendix in which he exposed the hoax. The poems betray their precocious author as a real poet, steeped in the Middle Ages but with a command of verse forms which were unknown in the fifteenth century. Chatterton had considerable influence upon the Romantic poets of the nineteenth century. Wordsworth, in *Resolution and Independence,* wrote of

> ". . . the marvelous boy,
> The sleepless Soul that perished in his pride."

Keats sang in a sonnet: "O Chatterton, how sweetly sad thy fate!" Shelley, in *Adonais,* conjured up his pale shadow at the tomb of Keats.

CHAUCER, Geoffrey (1340?–1400). England's first major poet, "the morning star of song," as Tennyson called him, was a government official who wrote poems for diversion a century before the printing press came to England. He was an aristocrat whose kindly regard for all classes of society filled his pages, especially those of his greatest poem, with a cavalcade of medieval characters. He was a medievalist in learning and in philosophy, but his attitude toward mankind was so universal that his work is timeless.

Chaucer was the London-born son of a wine-merchant; his association with the court began when he became in 1357 page to the Countess of Ulster, daughter-in-law of King Edward III. In 1359–60 he was with the English army in France, was taken prisoner, and was ransomed with the help of the king. In 1366 or thereabouts he married the sister of the future wife of John of Gaunt, Duke of Lancaster, who became his patron. Government missions took him often abroad. In 1372 he went to Italy to negotiate a commercial treaty with Genoa, and so came under the influence of Italian life and art. Later embassies brought him a similar knowledge of French culture. He held many important government posts, including that of comptroller of customs, wools, and wines. When in 1386 he gave up his appointments and his house in London to become a country gentleman in Kent, honors pursued him. He became successively justice of the peace, knight of the shire, member of Parliament, and, in 1389, Clerk of the King's Works with supervision over the royal palaces. Two years later he was appointed Deputy Forester of the royal forest of North Petherton. From both Richard II and Henry IV he received grants and royal pensions. During the whole of this active life he read assiduously Ovid, Vergil, Petrarch, Dante, and other poets, and wrote industriously, apparently for his own delight and that of his patrons and friends.

In terms of his literary output Chaucer's career as a writer has been divided into three major periods: the French period, which extends roughly from 1355 to 1370; the Italian period, continuing to 1385; and the English period covering the last fifteen years of his life. In the first period the major poems are the fragmentary *Romaunt of the Rose,* a translation of a French allegory, and *The Book of the Duchess* (1369–70), an elegy for Blanche, the first wife of John of Gaunt. The second, or Italian, period is more important. Besides some brief lyrics it includes *The Parliament of Fowls* (c. 1380–86), a satire on Parliament and popular representation; *The House of Fame* (c. 1372–80), a love-vision symbolizing the union of Richard II and Anne of Bohemia; *The Legend of Good Women* (c. 1380–86), a dream-poem in which nine famous women—out of twenty contemplated—are eulogized in verse; and, finally, *Troilus and Criseyde* (c. 1380–86), which has been variously characterized as the first great poem and the first psychological novel in English. Next to *The Canterbury Tales*, Chaucer's story of the warrior and the coquette is his finest poem. That it was based on the formal medieval system of courtly love has not kept it from being a moving love-story in which Chaucer's analyses of the characters of the hero and heroine, as well as those of Pandarus and others, are startlingly complex and fascinating.

The poet's English period includes a curious prose *Treatise on the Astrolabe* (c. 1391–2), written for his ten-year-old son; a number of lyrics such as his good-natured *Complaint of Chaucer to his Empty Purse* (c. 1393–1400)—which brought him an increase in his royal pension; and *The Canterbury Tales* (c. 1387–1400). *The Canterbury Tales* is a series of stories told, like *The Arabian Nights* and Boccaccio's *Decameron,* in a framework. A group of pilgrims going from the Tabard Inn in Southwark, London, to the shrine of St. Thomas à Becket at Canterbury, agree to pass the time away by telling two stories each on the outward journey and two more on the return. Thus Chaucer projected about one hundred and twenty tales. Actually he wrote only twenty-four, and several of these are unfinished. Here are the extant parts arranged in the order followed by Professor F. N. Robinson in his admirable edition of Chaucer: *The General Prologue,* where the pilgrims are introduced in a famous gallery of thumbnail portraits; *The Knight's Tale,* the chivalric romance of Palamon and Arcite; *The Miller's Tale, Reeve's Tale,* and fragmentary *Cook's Tale*—all of them earthy *fabliaux; The Man of Law's Prologue* and his *Tale of Constance,* the "calumniated wife"; *The Wife of Bath's Prologue*—a lusty defense of wedded women by one who has had five "housbondes at chirche dore"— and the *Tale* of the "Loathly Lady" which illustrates her thesis; *The Friar's Tale* and *The Summoner's Tale*—two more *fabliaux; The Clerk's Tale* of Patient Griselda; *The Merchant's Tale* of January and May; *The Squire's Tale,* the unfinished romance of "Cambuscan bold"; *The Franklin's Tale,* the "Breton lay" of Arviragus and Dorigen; *The Physician's Tale,* the classical story of Appius and Virginia; *The Pardoner's Prologue*—the inside story of his trade—and his *Tale* of the "riotoures thre" who go in search of Death; *The Shipman's Tale,* the *fabliau* of a merchant cuckolded by a monk; *The Prioress's Tale,* the tender legend of a murdered schoolboy; the unfinished *Rime of Sir Thopas,* told by Chaucer himself, a doggerel burlesque of the medieval romances; *The Tale of Melibee,* a tedious moral tale in prose; *The Monk's Tale,* a series of brief "tragedies"; *The Nun's Priest's Tale,* a spirited fable featured by the barnyard disputation of the learned cock, Chauntecleer, and the practical hen, Pertelote; *The Second Nun's Tale,* the life of the martyred Saint Cecilia; *The Canon's Yeoman's Tale* of a rascally alchemist; *The Manciple's Prologue* and his *Tale* of the "tell-tale bird"; and *The Parson's Prologue* and his so-called *Tale,* a ponderous prose treatise on the Seven Deadly Sins.

Since the pilgrims come from all walks of life and all occupations, from knight to cook and miller, the company represents the whole range of medieval English society. And as each tale told—with one or two exceptions—suits the character and taste of the teller, the stories cover all possible medieval literary types from stately romance to salty *fabliau.* Not the least entertaining parts of *The Canterbury Tales* are the links between the stories, in which the narrators introduce themselves or have their squabbles settled by the jolly host of the Tabard, who makes the pilgrimage to act as master of ceremonies and to see to it that such a goodly company stops at no other inn on the return voyage.

Chaucer's language is the East Midland dialect of Middle English. To a modern reader with a modicum of intelligence and diligence it presents no very great difficulty, and the slight labor involved is repaid by the satisfaction of reading the famous tales as Chaucer wrote them.

CHEKE, Sir John (1514–57), who tutored Edward VI and later taught Greek at Cambridge, was one of the leaders of the classical renaissance. Almost all his works are in Latin, many of them translations from the Greek. He made efforts to revise both Greek pronunciation and English spelling.

CHESTERFIELD, Philip Dormer Stanhope, fourth earl of (1694–1773) had a distinguished career as member of both houses, Ambassador to Holland, Lord Lieutenant of Ireland, and Secretary of State. But many know him as the recipient of a single letter—the masterpiece (1755) in which Samuel Johnson, after waiting seven years in vain for expected aid on the *Dictionary,* greeted his Lordship's tardy puffs with eloquent disdain. Lord Chesterfield is equally famous for his own letters, especially the series (written 1737–68, published 1774) in which he tried to teach his illegitimate son, Philip Stanhope, how to succeed like father. Although never intended for publication, they are as elegant and polished as the fashion plate who penned them. The Chesterfield curriculum balanced Greek with night life, mixed basic rules for living with the veneer of ballroom etiquette. He admitted that good breeding was a "lesser talent" than honor, virtue, and learning, but he preached often from the worldly text: "Manner is all, in everything." Lord Chesterfield also addressed a series of letters to his godson, another Philip Stanhope (written 1763–70, published 1890).

CHESTERTON, G(ilbert) K(eith) (1874–1936). Journalist, critic, story-teller, biographer, dramatist, poet, and illustrator—G. K. Chesterton was a man of amazing gusto and versatility. His achievement in prose includes countless essays (*Orthodoxy,* 1908: *Tremendous Trifles,* 1909); several books of literary criticism (*Charles Dickens,* 1906; *George Bernard Shaw,* 1909; *The Victorian Age in Literature,* 1913); and the series of detective stories popularizing the clerical sleuth Father Brown (1911–35). In verse Chesterton wrote satires like the epigrammatic *Elegy in a Country Churchyard* and the rollicking, anti-prohibitionist *Wine and Water,* as well as stirring narrative poems like *The Ballad of the White Horse* (1911) and *Lepanto* (1915). He was a crusader all his life. He entered the Roman Catholic Church in 1922, and, like his friend and collaborator Hilaire Belloc, wrote vigorously in defense of Catholic doctrines. An extreme conservative in religion and politics, he fought against the modern trends towards agnosticism and socialism. Whether he was writing criticism or detective fiction, Chesterton was a brilliant ironist and a master of surprise and paradox. Paradoxically enough, the brilliance of his manner often gave the appearance of dazzling newness to the most orthodox ideas.

CHETTLE, Henry (1560?–1607?) was an Elizabethan printer and minor playwright. He wrote prolifically, both on his own and in collaboration with Dekker, Jonson, Day, and Munday, but few of his plays have survived. The only extant play which is attributed to him alone is *The Tragedy of Hoffman* (1602–3). In this coarse melodrama of a son's revenge for the execution of his pirate-father, Chettle shows skill in developing an atmosphere of horror.

CHILLINGWORTH, William (1602–44) wrote *The Religion of Protestants a Safe Way to Salvation* (1638), a controversial treatise containing arguments against papal infallibility. It is notable, in parts at least, for its clear, forceful prose.

CHURCH, Richard William (1815–90), Dean of St. Paul's, was distinguished as preacher, religious historian, and literary critic. He wrote the definitive history of the Oxford Movement (1891) and excellent studies of Dante (1850), Spenser (1879), and Sir Francis Bacon (1884).

CHURCHILL, Charles (1731–64) was a clergyman's son who was true to the tradition. He married below his station at eighteen, matriculated at Cambridge and never attended, and after taking orders himself at twenty-five, spent most of the rest of his days in reckless living, dying, as the story goes, with "What a fool I have been" on his lips. In three last years of intense productivity he showed a remarkable facility for grinding out satires in vigorous, venomous heroic couplets. His most famous, *The Rosciad* (1761), a bitter roll-call of the actors of his day, spawned a whole school of "iads" by inferior imitators. *An Epistle to W. Hogarth* (1763) is a reply to the artist's caricature of the poet. *The Ghost* (1762–3) is remembered for the portrait which misrepresents Samuel "Pomposo" Johnson as one of the believers in the story of the ghost of Cock Lane. A rabid follower of the people's hero, John Wilkes, Churchill bombarded the *North Briton* with political verse satires. *The Prophecy of Famine* (1763), for example, is an attack on Lord Bute and the Scots. Churchill's work is little read today. He "blazed," as Byron later wrote, "the comet of a season."

CHURCHYARD, Thomas (1520?–1604) was a wandering soldier and courtier who wrote verse during the whole of his adult life. Like Surrey, whom he at one time served, Churchyard is represented in *Tottel's Miscellany* (1557). His *Shore's Wife,* a poem on the tragic career of Jane Shore (d. 1527?), mistress of Edward IV, was, in its day, the most popular contribution to *A Mirror for Magistrates*. It appeared in the second part, which came out in 1563.

CIBBER, Colley (1671–1757). For his official odes as poet laureate (1730–57) Cibber earned his election as King of Dullness in the 1743 revision of Pope's *Dunciad*. But he himself confessed that his appointment was purely political, and, however dull, he was certainly a faithful royal anniversifier. He deserves a better name as actor, playwright and play-adapter, co-manager of Drury Lane Theater, and dramatic historian. Sir Novelty Fashion in his first play, sentimental *Love's Last Shift* (1696), modified the tradi-

tional stage-fop type. Later, Cibber responded good-naturedly to
Collier's condemnation of the theater's immorality, and *The
Careless Husband* (1704), with its sickening fifth-act conversion,
was admittedly a reform move. His frank and amusing *Apology
for the Life of Colley Cibber, Comedian* (1740) is a portrait-
studded record of two generations of theatrical history.

CIBBER, Theophilus (1703-58). Like his father, Colley Cibber,
he was a comedian, a playwright, and a historian of the theater.
Although he has come down to posterity as the chief editor of
*The Lives of the Poets of Great Britain and Ireland to the Time
of Dean Swift* (1753), the work was compiled mainly by one
Robert Shiels.

CLARE, John (1793-1864) spent some of his early years at farm
labor and published four volumes of rural poetry: *Poems Descriptive of Rural Life and Scenery* (1820); *The Village Minstrel*
(1821); *The Shepherd's Calendar* (1827); and *The Rural Muse*
(1835). He went insane in 1841. The fascinating poems written
during his madness have never been completely collected. He is
best known for the three pathetic stanzas *Written in Northampton
County Asylum* ("I am! yet what I am who cares, or knows?").
Clare's life and works are often compared with those of a lesser
rural poet, Robert Bloomfield (1766-1823).

CLARENDON, Edward Hyde, first earl of (1609-74) began his
great history in exile in 1646 and finished it, again in exile, just
before his death. Between those two periods he helped to engineer
Charles II's restoration and saw his daughter wed the Duke of
York, who later became James II. His masterpiece was called
*The History of the Rebellion and Civil Wars in England, Begun
in the Year 1641* (published 1702-4). It is actually an incoherent
memoir in defense of the old order. Yet Clarendon has fixed for
posterity many of the conflict's great moments, and has left—
in his pictures of such figures as Charles I, Cromwell, and
Hampden—excellent samples of that unique seventeenth-century
type, the character.

CLARKE, Charles Cowden (1787-1877) was the schoolmaster
who introduced Keats into the realm of poetry, guiding him
through Spenser's *Faerie Queene* and Chapman's *Homer*. He
edited numerous authors and collaborated with his wife Mary
on *Recollections of Writers* (1878).

CLEVELAND, John (1613-58). This metaphysical poet was extremely popular in his day but is now remembered largely for

the extravagance of his conceits. When his Phillis goes walking, the trees quiver with "religious paulsie" to "divest their bliss" and bestrew her footsteps. Cleveland also wrote *The Rebel Scot* (1647)—a vicious satire on the Scots for betraying Charles I— and a curiously awkward little *Elegy on Ben Jonson.*

CLOUGH, Arthur Hugh (1819–61) was graduated in 1837 from Rugby, where he had been one of Dr. Thomas Arnold's most brilliant scholar-athletes. He took his A.B. with second honors at Balliol College, Oxford, in 1841, and two years later was elected a fellow of Oriel College. But although he had been a friend of the Oxford Movement, grave religious doubts began to crowd in upon his scrupulous conscience. In 1848, feeling that he no longer believed in the Articles of the Church of England, he resigned his fellowship. The remainder of his short life was marked by mental and physical troubles. He spent a year (1852) writing and teaching in America and later served as examiner in the Education Office, London, and as amanuensis to the dynamic Florence Nightingale. He died in Italy, where he had gone in search of health. His intimate friend, Matthew Arnold, commemorated his death in *Thyrsis* (1866), a moving pastoral elegy.

Clough's longer poems are not well known today. *The Bothie of Tober-na-Vuolich* (1848) is a pleasant tale about love on an Oxford vacation. *Amours de Voyage* (1853–62) is another love story, told in a series of rambling verse-letters. Both of these are written in prosy hexameters. Among Clough's shorter poems are *The Latest Decalogue* (written 1847, published 1862), a bitter epigrammatic satire on the ten commandments of Victorian England; *Qua Cursum Ventus* (1849) and "Say Not the Struggle Nought Availeth," (1849–62), two rugged lyrics expressing a note of hope amid despair; and *Songs of Absence* (published 1862), a series of fourteen simple love lyrics written either *en route* to or in America.

COBBETT, William (1762–1835). As editor of the *Weekly Political Register* (1802–35), this impulsive laborer's son was one of the most influential journalists of his time. When he began it in 1802, he wrote as an ultra-Tory, but he later swung around to lead the fight for the emancipation of the working classes through legislation. He survived imprisonment and exile to win a seat in Parliament in 1832, the year in which the famous Reform Bill finally went through. Cobbett's *Rural Rides* (collected 1830) combine unaffected observation of nature with vigorous social protest. His sensible *Advice to Young Men* (1829) is still read.

COLERIDGE, Hartley (1796–1849). The "babe so beautiful" whom Samuel Taylor Coleridge pictures in the cradle in *Frost at Midnight* grew up to display a share of his father's talents for intemperance and poetry. He wrote a number of graceful but conventional lyrics, including "She is not fair to outward view," "I have lived, and I have loved," and sonnets on Shakespeare, Homer, and prayer.

COLERIDGE, Samuel Taylor (1772–1834) was a slave to two opiates, laudanum and indolence. In a life saddened by private misery and public disgrace, he planned much, began less, and finished almost nothing. His adult years can be divided into four periods. The first (1793–95), a period of youthful restlessness, is high-lighted by his elopement from Cambridge to join the Dragoons (1793), his discussions with Southey on the glories of the French Revolution (1794–5), their abortive plan for a Utopian "Pantisocracy" in Pennsylvania, and his foolish marriage to Sara Fricker (1795). In the second period (1796–1803), encouraged by the intimate friendship with Wordsworth and his sister Dorothy, he wrote almost all his important poetry. In the third (1804–15), a period of drug-addiction and despair, marked by two dreary years in Malta (1804–6) and estrangement from his wife and from Wordsworth, he gave his spasmodic lectures and wrote his major prose work. During the fourth (1816–34), partly saved from himself at the home of James Gillman, he "sat on the brow of Highgate Hill" and talked in wondrous circles to the awed Boswells who, like Carlyle, came to pay him homage.

Coleridge wrote a handful of great poems. In *The Rime of the Ancient Mariner,* his chief contribution to the first edition of *Lyrical Ballads* (1798), he tried successfully to treat the supernatural so realistically as to induce in the reader "that willing suspension of disbelief for the moment, which constitutes poetic faith." Drawing his materials from a score of weird travel books, he produced a perfect fusion of the simplicity of the folk ballad and the subtlety of the sophisticated poem. There is the same colorful, musical rendering of a world of mystery in unfinished *Christabel* (written 1797–1800, published 1816), a haunting tale of medieval witchery, and in *Kubla Khan* (written 1797, published 1816), a shadowy fragment resurrected from a dream. Coleridge also wrote two noble odes: *France* (1798), in which he retracted his earlier faith in the Revolution, and *Dejection* (1802), which foreshadowed his darkest period.

His prose is not remarkable for its lucidity; he loved long

words for their own sake and often wandered confusedly in his own word-jungle. This is especially true of the political philosophy in his short-lived magazine, *The Friend* (1809, book form, 1818) and in the abstruse German metaphysics of certain chapters of the *Biographia Literaria* (1817). His more concrete literary criticism is better known. The Shakespeare lectures, although disorganized and badly reported, mark him as the leader of the new school of romantic critics who idolized Shakespeare as a supreme genius. More famous are the central chapters of the *Biographia* (XIV–XXII), which are remarkable for their provoking discussion of the language of poetry in general and their eminently fair judgment of Wordsworth's in particular.

COLLIER, Jeremy (1650–1726). The learned divine's *Short View of the Profaneness and Immorality of the English Stage* (1698) is neither short nor concerned solely with profaneness and immorality. Coming, however, as the climax to a flurry of lesser blows by other reformers, it landed with some force. Although Dryden and Cibber pleaded guilty to certain of Collier's charges, Vanbrugh and Congreve, both of whom had been singled out for special dishonorable mention, fought back in defense of their art. When Collier answered them in *A Defense of the Short View* (1699), a long pamphlet war was on. The grounds of controversy shifted from such special issues as oaths and stage-clergymen to the broader questions of whether the theater as an institution was the Devil's work and whether comedy could teach morality. Some arrests were made, some fines assessed, some lewd plays left unproduced. While the fight raged, the specter of Sentimental Comedy sneaked in to rule supreme for three-quarters of a century. It is an error, however, to ascribe a far-flung revolution in taste to one embattled parson.

COLLINS, (William) Wilkie (1824–89). "Make 'em laugh, make 'em cry, make 'em wait." Charles Reade's *Recipe for a Successful Novel* is frequently ascribed to this sometime painter and lawyer who became one of Victorian England's most popular storytellers. It is the last of these three admonitions that really dominates Wilkie Collins' two most popular novels. *The Woman in White* (1860) is a suspense-jammed tale of mystery and revenge with hero and heroine sniffing out the dark deeds of two full-fledged villains, one of whom, fat Fosco, is as astoundingly versatile as any in fiction. *The Moonstone* (1868) introduces the famous detective, Sergeant Cuff, who, although he would rather raise roses than trail jewel thieves, finds time to help in solving the mysterious theft of the sacred Indian diamond. According to an eminent crime-fancier, Alexander Woollcott, *The Moonstone* is "the first full-length detective story and still the best." Collins is significant, not only as a forerunner of Conan Doyle, but as a novelist of social protest, and as a conscientious master of plotting unknown in the straggling serials of most of his contemporaries. Some of this skill in plotting he imparted to his friend and collaborator, Charles Dickens. Dickens is said to have begun *The Mystery of Edwin Drood* (1870) as an effort to out-Collins Collins.

COLLINS, William (1721–59). The genius of this short-lived forerunner of the Romantic Movement was touched with a profound melancholy that terminated during the last nine years of his life in outright insanity. Like several other English poets with romantic inclinations he wrote verses while a boy. His first volume of poetry, *Persian Eclogues* (1742), was published anonymously when he was twenty-one; the second edition was issued under the title *Oriental Eclogues* the year of his death. The appearance of Sir Thomas Hanmer's edition of Shakespeare's plays in 1743 led to Collins' writing tributary verses to the editor and the lovely and moving *Dirge in Cymbeline*. But Collins' most famous poems are the magnificent *Odes on Several Descriptive and Allegorical Subjects* (1746–7). Among these are his contemplative *Ode to Evening*, in unrhymed lines, his "How Sleep the Brave," and his *Ode to a Lady*. His *Ode Occasion'd by the Death of Mr. Thomson* and his *Ode on the Popular Superstitions of the Highlands of Scotland* were probably composed in 1749. *The Passions, an Ode,* appeared in 1750. The indolence and irresolution of the poet, which led to his being quite unable to manage his own financial affairs or to carry through any of the "vast projects" that his friend Samuel Johnson declared he kept making, may have been the result of his growing emotional instability. He is one of the slightest of the genuine poets in English literature, but his contribution is important. In the eighteenth century he is one of the links between the neo-classicists of the age of Pope and the romanticists of the age of Wordsworth. In his contemplative pastoral odes particularly he echoes Milton and foreshadows Wordsworth.

COLMAN, George, the elder (1732–94). As manager of the Covent Garden (1767–74) and Haymarket (1777–89) theaters, Colman exerted a profound influence on the drama of his time. Both as a producer of Goldsmith's two comedies and as a playwright himself, he helped to divorce comedy from sentimentality after sixty dreary years. His first play, *Polly Honeycombe* (1760), was a farce mocking the sentimental novel. *The Jealous Wife* (1761) was based partly on Fielding's *Tom Jones,* and *The Clandestine Marriage* (1766, in collaboration with Garrick) was inspired by Hogarth's series of caricatures, *Marriage à la Mode.* Despite generous helpings of syrup, both preserve some of the broad comic spirit of these sources. Colman also contributed to the drama by translating Terence (1765), editing Beaumont and Fletcher (1778), and writing numerous prologues and epilogues.

COLMAN, George, the younger (1762–1836), son of Colman the elder, first attracted attention for his *Inkle and Yarico* (1787), a humanitarian comic opera in the romantic "Noble Savage" tradition. Two of his non-operatic works are kept alive by individual characters. Pedantic, degree-laden Dr. Pangloss, whose humor is misquoting literature with a self-satisfied "Hem," saved *The Heir at Law* (1797) from drowning in tears. Honest, generous, gruff Job Thornberry in *John Bull* (1803) is supposed to represent the English character. Colman succeeded his father as manager of the Haymarket Theater in 1789.

COLUM, Padraic (1881–   ) was born in Ireland but has lived part of his life in the United States. He is married to Mary (Maguire) Colum, the reviewer. With James Stephens and Thomas MacDonagh he founded the *Irish Review.* He helped Yeats and Lady Gregory during the early years of the Abbey Theater. Among his plays are *The Land* (1905), *The Fiddler's House* (1907), and *Thomas Muskerry* (1910). Colum has also published poetry (*Collected Poems,* 1932), travel books, and numerous stories for children.

COLVIN, Sir Sidney (1845–1927) taught fine arts at Cambridge from 1873 to 1885 and was keeper of the prints and drawings at the British Museum from 1884 to 1912. He was a close friend of Robert Louis Stevenson and a capable literary critic in his own right. His works include short lives of Landor (1881) and Keats (1887) in the *English Men of Letters* series and *John Keats: his Life and Poetry, his Friends, Critics, and After-Fame* (1917).

COMBE, William (1741–1823) was a disreputable hack who could stoop to forgery and slander and sometimes rise to the level of first-rate verse satire. He is best known for the doggerel which he composed in debtors' prison to accompany Thomas Rowlandson's drawings for *The Tour of Dr. Syntax in Search of the*

Picturesque (*Poetical Magazine,* 1809; book, 1812). This parody of contemporary travel books was an immense success, and Combe and Rowlandson later collaborated on *Dr. Syntax in Search of Consolation* (1820) and *Dr. Syntax in Search of a Wife* (1821).

CONGREVE, William (1670–1729) was the greatest comic dramatist of the Restoration. *The Old Bachelor* (1693) was his first play. He had absorbed a good education at Trinity College, Dublin, and stabbed tentatively at the law in London. He had dabbled in verse and published anonymously a slight, artificial romance called *Incognita* (1692). But he was still an unknown youth of twenty-three when Betterton first played his surly Heartwell, and entrancing Anne Bracegirdle gave flesh to Araminta. After that, Congreve was hailed as the savior of fainting comedy. *The Double Dealer* (1693) was a relative failure, partly because of the unconvincing soliloquies of black-blooded Maskwell. But bawdy, bustling *Love for Love* (1695) was even more successful than *The Old Bachelor.* And although few moderns know that those two proverbial lines, "Nor Hell a fury like a woman scorned" and "Music has charms to soothe a savage breast" were once buried in the declamation of *The Mourning Bride* (1697), Congreve's bombastic tragedy was an immediate hit and survived for years as a hardy perennial. When he returned to comedy after barking back spitefully at Jeremy Collier's attack on the stage, he wrote *The Way of the World* (1700). But the public was apathetic, and he never finished another play. Except for an occasional Pindaric ode, he virtually retired at thirty from active literary work. Comfortable in political sinecures, he sank rapidly into old-bachelordom, the gouty but good-natured coffee-house crony of Pope, Swift, and Gay, and the particular friend of Anne Bracegirdle and the Duchess of Marlborough.

Although Congreve never totally abandoned the farcical stage business of his predecessors, he learned to write dialogue which neither Etherege, with his frothy jesting, nor Wycherley, with his rough-hewn satire, could have touched. He fashioned his brittle sentences with the delicate precision of a jeweller. The world of *The Way of the World* never existed, but readers still attend while the plot stands still, to the verbal fencing of its philandering Mirabel and tantalizing Millamant. That failure is his masterpiece.

CONRAD, Joseph (1857–1924). Teodor Józef Konrad Korzeniowski was born of Polish parents in the Ukraine. He spent his boyhood in northern Russia, where his father had been exiled for revolutionary activities, and at a school in Cracow. In 1874 he signed aboard a French vessel and began twenty years of wandering at sea. Ten years later he became a British subject and got his certificate as a master seaman. In 1894 he left the sea for good, although he did not know it yet, and settled in England. For five years he had been nursing the manuscript of an unfinished novel. The completed story appeared in 1895 under the title *Almayer's Folly*. Conrad drew heavily on his experiences at sea for his first novel and for most of the novels and long shortstories that followed, including *The Outcast of the Islands* (1896), *The Nigger of the "Narcissus"* (1898), *Lord Jim* (1900), *Youth* (1902), *Typhoon* (1903), *Nostromo* (1904), *Chance* (1913), *Victory* (1915), and *The Shadow Line* (1917). The tropical jungle, which looms large in several of these, is the setting for *The Heart of Darkness* (1902), a long short-story about a white man's degeneration in the Belgian Congo. Only occasionally— as in *The Secret Agent* (1907) and *Under Western Eyes* (1911) —did he set his story on the European continent.

Conrad is an acknowledged master of atmosphere, whether he is conjuring up a typhoon at sea or evoking the sultry mystery of the Malay jungle. Beyond that, he is difficult to pin down. In his love of distant lands and melodramatic action, in his emphasis on the point of honor which makes Lord Jim's single act of cowardice the mainspring of a whole novel, he might be loosely classified as a "romantic." But no writer ever strained more intensely to *realize* a scene. "My task. . . ," he once wrote, "is, by the power of the written word, to make you hear, to make you feel, it is—before all—to make you *see*." The knots which tangle the web of his narrative—the exasperating use of story within story and the interminable digressions and irrelevancies— grew out of his honest struggle to achieve verisimilitude in the handling of point of view. Conrad was not a facile romancer, escaping, as Scott and Stevenson often did, to a world of mingled history, legend, and dreams; he was a sensitive artist striving to realize what he had seen. If he painted it in unbelievable colors, it was because in him—to use his own words—"the romantic feeling of reality was . . . an inborn faculty."

CONSTABLE, Henry (1562–1613). To the golden decade of Elizabethan sonnet sequences belongs Constable's *Diana* (1592–4). These twenty-eight sonnets, many of them derived from the French, are not so well known as those of Sidney's *Astrophel and Stella* (1591), Daniel's *Delia* (1592–4), and Drayton's *Idea* (1593), but they were popular in their author's time. Constable's best-known sonnets are the four "to Sir P. Sidney's Soul," prefixed to the 1595 edition of Sidney's *Defense of Poesy*.

COPPARD, A(lfred) E(dgar) (1878–   ). Although Coppard's short-stories vary widely in mood and material, they are usually written in a rhythmical, lyrical prose which borders on poetry. His best-known tale is the title-story of his first collection, *Adam and Eve and Pinch Me* (1921). He has also published many poems, which were gathered together in *Collected Poems* (1928).

CORNWALL, Barry was the pseudonym of **Bryan Waller Procter** (1787–1874). He was once well known as the author of a successful verse tragedy, *Mirandola* (1821), and a popular book of verse, *English Songs* (1832). Today he is better known as a friend of Lamb, Hazlitt, Beddoes, and other literary men of more talent than he. His daughter, **Adelaide Anne Procter** (1825–64), was the minor songstress who wrote the words to Sir Arthur Sullivan's *Lost Chord*.

CORY, William Johnson (1823–92) changed his last name from Johnson to Cory in 1872. He was an assistant master at Eton with a gift for lyric poetry. His *Ionica* (1858, enlarged 1891) includes the two quatrains beginning: "They told me, Heraclitus, they told me you were dead," a translation from the Greek of Callimachus (c. 260–240 B.C.). The lyric is known to many who do not know the author's name.

CORYAT, Thomas (1577?–1617) was an eccentric scholar and traveler. His best-known work, *Coryat's Crudities* (1611), is a fantastic collection of observations "hastily gobled up in five moneths travells" in Europe. Because of the extravagance of its language, it is considered today largely as a literary freak.

COTTON, Charles (1630–87) was the "hearty, cheerful Mr. Cotton" whose poem *The New Year* Charles Lamb reprinted and recommended in his essay *New Year's Eve*. He also wrote part of the fifth edition of Izaak Walton's *Compleat Angler* (1676), burlesques of Vergil and Lucian, and a fairly faithful translation of Montaigne's essays (1685–6). Landor, in his *Imaginary Conversations,* presents Cotton in a leisurely talk with Walton and an imaginary character, William Oldways.

COVENTRY, Francis (d. 1759?) is remembered as the author of *The History of Pompey the Little* (1751), a satirical novel centering in "the life and adventures of a lap-dog."

COVERDALE, Miles (1488–1568). On October 4, 1935, the English-speaking world celebrated the four-hundredth anniversary of the publication of the first complete Bible to be printed in English. The man responsible for this publication was Miles Coverdale, a "Bible man" throughout his long and active life. Coverdale was not as good a scholar as his friend William Tyndale, the first of the Tudor Bible translators, for he did not know Greek and Hebrew. But his knowledge of Latin and his patient study of Wycliffe's translation of the Bible into English (1382–89) and of Luther's into German (1522) gave him a basis for a translation that was substantial and sound if not as inspired as was that of Tyndale. Furthermore, he did not meet in his work quite that stern opposition that Tyndale had encountered. In 1535 the pressure that Coverdale had been making toward a publication "by royal authority" had not yet brought full results. He was soon invited by Thomas Cromwell, however, to assist in the preparation of another issue, and in 1539 appeared "the Great Bible," the first translation "appointed to the use of the churches." Coverdale became Bishop of Exeter in 1551, but with the coming to the English throne of the Catholic queen, Mary Tudor, he joined other Protestant refugees in Geneva. Here in 1558 he apparently labored with William Whittingham, Anthony Gilby, Thomas Sampson, and others on a new translation. In April, 1560, this Calvinist version was published, a novelty in small-size, Roman type, instead of black letter, with divided and numbered verses. Next to the King James version of 1611 the Geneva Bible is the most famous of the early translations. It was not entirely replaced, in fact, by the so-called "authorized" version until nearly a century after its first appearance.

COWARD, Noel (Pierce) (1899–   ). Actor, playwright, composer, director, and producer—Noel Coward has been indispensable in the stage and movie worlds on both sides of the Atlantic. A series of sparkling comedies—including *Hay Fever* (1925), *Private Lives* (1930), *Design for Living* (1933), and *Blithe Spirit* (1941)—have given him a reputation as a master of the sudden sallies of sophisticated dialogue. But his repertoire is by no means limited to repartee. Among his other achievements are *The Vortex* (1921), a serious drama; *Bitter Sweet* (1929), a musical show for which he wrote both music and lyrics; *Cavalcade* (1931), an effective cinema pageant of recent English history; *Present Indicative* (1937), a witty autobiography; and *In Which We Serve* (1943), a stirring movie celebrating the British seamen of the Second World War.

COWLEY, Abraham (1618–67), who pronounced his name Cooley, was a Royalist spy in the Civil War, later a charter member of the Royal Society. As an essayist he moralized gracefully on himself, gardens, and solitude. As a poet, he belongs generally to the "metaphysical" school of Donne. His contemporaries called him a great poet, but seventy years after his death Pope asked: "Who now reads Cowley?" Today, although Donne's conceits intrigue us still, Cowley's lover writing in lemon juice so that his secrets will come to light only under the fire of his mistress' eyes leaves us cold (*The Mistress,* 1647, a collection of love poems). He is at his best in the *Hymn to Light, Lines on the Death of William Hervey,* and the playful "anacreontic," *Drinking. Poetical Blossoms,* published at fourteen, contains amazing juvenilia. *Davideis* (1656) is an unfinished sacred epic in heroic couplets. In *Pindarique Odes* (1656), Cowley tried to imitate the odes of the Greek poet Pindar (c. 522–442 B.C.) and instead popularized the looser ode form which is common in subsequent English literature.

COWLEY, Hannah (1743–1809), who wrote verse under the pseudonym "Anna Matilda," was the author of several plays, the best known of which are *The Runaway* (1776), *The Belle's Stratagem* (1780), and *A Bold Stroke for a Husband* (1783). The first of these is a sentimental comedy; the other two are busy comedies of intrigue.

COWPER, William (1731–1800) (pronounced Cooper) was too gentle for this world. Several times the hair-spring mechanism of his mind broke down. In 1763 he was seized by a suicidal mania; ten years later he was deep in religious melancholia; towards the end he gave in utterly to fear of eternal damnation. In 1765 he found sanctuary in the home of Mrs. Unwin. She urged him to write poetry, and in middle life he collaborated with John Newton on *Olney Hymns* (1779) and published his first collection of secular poems (1782–5). When another close friend, Lady Reynolds, challenged him to write about a sofa, he produced *The Task,* wherein he charmingly proved that "God made the country, and man made the town." When she also told him a funny story about a man at a horse's mercy, he turned out *The Diverting History of John Gilpin.* The two poems were published together in 1785. Later writings include the robust lament *On the Loss of the Royal George* (1803), the tender tribute *To Mary* [Unwin] (1803), an unpopular translation of Homer (1791), and his agonized swansong, *The Castaway* (1803). Cowper best portrays himself in *The Task* and in his letters—a kindly soul despite habitual depression, alert to the quiet beauties of the rural scene, acutely sensitive to man's inhumanity to man, and able to express his thoughts in a language as simple, direct, and unaffected as he himself was.

CRABBE, George (1754–1832). This son of a Suffolk tax-collector knew poverty in his youth. He felt its pinch when he practiced medicine in his home town and again when he sought his literary fortune in London. No wonder then that in *The Village* (1783), his best-known poem, he chose

> . . . to paint the cot
> As Truth will paint it, and as bards will not.

Although he later found some contentment in the ministry, Crabbe continued in *The Newspaper* (1785), *The Parish Register* (1807), and *The Borough* (1810) to write narrative verse in the same dark, grimly humorous vein. Not for him to loll in the genial Arcadianism of Goldsmith, exalt, like Cowper and Wordsworth, the humble rural virtues, or blind his eyes to squalid ugliness while he searched "poetic" beauties. He was not a sweet singer; he was a reformer and a realist.

CRAIK, Mrs. See **MULOCK, Dinah Maria.**

CRANMER, Thomas (1489–1556) was appointed Archbishop of Canterbury in 1533 after helping Henry VIII to divorce Catherine of Aragon. He was condemned as a heretic under Catholic Queen Mary and burned at the stake. Although he wrote theological treatises in both Latin and English, he is best known as the chief author of the Anglican liturgy. Cranmer probably composed all of the Litany which appeared in Henry VIII's *Primer* of 1545, and he certainly played the leading rôle in the writing of the Prayer Books published under Edward VI in 1549 and 1552. There have been revisions since then—under Elizabeth, James I, and Charles II—but the *Book of Common Prayer,* as it stands today, is, for the most part, the work of Archbishop Cranmer. He also supervised the preparation of the *Great Bible* (1539) and wrote a preface for the second edition (1540). This edition is called *Cranmer's Bible.*

CRASHAW, Richard (1612?–49) was the son of a Puritan clergyman. He turned Catholic in his early thirties and was made a canon in Italy just before he died there. The title of his important collection, *Steps to the Temple* (1646), was inspired by

The Temple of another "sacred metaphysical" poet, George Herbert. Crashaw's poetry is an uneven mixture of clumsiness and grace, conventional imagery and original fancy. For example, *Love's Horoscope* is a tissue of time-worn conceits, and *The Weeper*—wherein the eyes of Mary Magdalene are metamorphosed into

> Two walking baths; two weeping motions,
> Portable and compendious oceans—

reveals the metaphysical conceit at its most ludicrous. Yet *Wishes to his Supposed Mistress* is a delightfully fanciful love poem, and *The Flaming Heart,* addressed to St. Theresa, is a masterpiece of passionate religious lyricism.

CROCKETT, Samuel Rutherford (1860–1914) was one of the "Kailyard School" of Scottish fiction writers. His best-known story is *The Stickit Minister,* a sentimental tale of an older brother's self-sacrifice for a selfish younger one. He also wrote some romantic novels, including *Mad Uchtred* (1894) and *Man of the Mountain* (1909).

CROKER, John Wilson (1780–1857). This Tory politician has a black record in the annals of English literature. Shelley and Byron blamed his review of *Endymion* (1818)—groundlessly, to be sure—for the death of Keats. Carlyle and Macaulay condemned his bulky edition of Boswell's *Johnson* (1831). Disraeli caricatured him in *Coningsby* (1844) as Rigby, a despicable political opportunist. Croker entered Parliament in 1807 and from 1810 to 1830 was secretary to the Admiralty. Having vowed never to sit in a reformed Parliament, he abandoned his parliamentary career when the Reform Bill passed in 1832.

CRONIN, A(rchibald) J(oseph) (1896–   ) gave up medicine for literature in 1930 and almost instantly became one of England's most popular novelists. Among his best-sellers are *Hatter's Castle* (1931), *The Citadel* (1937), and *The Keys to the Kingdom* (1941).

CROWNE, John (1640?–1703) was a prolific Restoration dramatist. His tragedies are all but forgotten. In his best-known comedy, *Sir Courtly Nice* (1685), he depicted the familiar Restoration stage fop against a background of religious and political bickering. Topical satire forms the basis of *The City Politics* (1683), a violent assault on Shaftesbury, and *The English Friar* (1689), an attack on the Catholic priests in the court of James II.

CUDWORTH, Ralph (1617–88), Professor of Hebrew at Cambridge, belonged, like Henry More, to the school of philosophers called "the Cambridge Platonists." In his masterpiece, *The True Intellectual System of the Universe* (1678), he attacked the materialism of Thomas Hobbes.

CUMBERLAND, Richard (1732–1811) was a versatile man of letters—poet, novelist, journalist, classical scholar, and prolific playwright. After the furor over Hugh Kelly's *False Delicacy* (1768) had died down, Cumberland became the acknowledged leader in the field of sentimental drama. Both in *The Brothers* (1769) and in his masterpiece, *The West Indian* (1771), he introduced to the *genre* scenes of robust, outdoor action quite different from the delicate drawing-room colloquies of his predecessors. Sheridan's caricature of Cumberland is Sir Fretful Plagiary of *The Critic* (1779). Cumberland's more flattering picture of himself is in his *Memoirs* (1806–7).

CUNNINGHAM, Allan (1784–1842) was a native of Dumfriesshire, Scotland, who was first a stonemason and later secretary to the sculptor Sir Francis Chantrey. In his *Songs of Scotland Ancient and Modern* (1825), he published original poems as well as resurrecting many of the old Scottish ballads and lyrics. Among his own are *Hame, Hame, Hame; My Nannie O; The Spring of the Year;* and, best known of all, the swinging saltwater lyric *A Wet Sheet and a Flowing Sea.*

CUNNINGHAME GRAHAM, R(obert) B(ontine) (1852–1936), son of a Scottish laird, spent part of his life in politics as an ardent supporter of labor, part of it in travel and adventure in North Africa and South America. His essays, short-stories, and biographies reveal him as an independent individual with a flair for irony and an eye for the exotic. Some of his best work may be found in *Thirteen Stories* (1900), *Scottish Stories* (1914), and *Thirty Tales and Sketches* (1929).

CYNEWULF (fl. 750) was an Old English poet, probably a Northumbrian, about whom much has been guessed, little proved. Among many pieces ascribed to him, including *The Dream of the Rood,* scholars agree on four religious poems which bear his signature in runes: *The Ascension* (or second part of a confused three-part work called *The Christ*), *The Fates of the Apostles,* and two saints' legends, *Juliana* and *Elene.* In the last and best the poet tells with some imaginative vigor the story of how St. Helena, mother of Constantine, found the true Cross.

D

DANE, Clemence (fl. 1917–   ) is the pseudonym of the novelist and playwright **Winifred Ashton**. She drew on her experience as a schoolteacher in Ireland for her first novel, *Regiment of Women* (1917), a study of a girls' school, and on her brief career as a professional actress for *Broome Stages* (with Helen Simpson, 1931), a novel about several generations of a theatrical family. Her most popular play, *A Bill of Divorcement* (1921), provided a vehicle for early triumphs of Katharine Cornell, on the stage, and Katharine Hepburn, on the screen.

DANIEL, Samuel (1562–1619) began his career by tutoring in noble households and ended it a respected manager of entertainment in the court of James I. His story lacks the colorful patriotism of Sidney's and Raleigh's, but he worked hard to glorify his country's history and literature. He took years to put the Wars of the Roses into *ottava rima* (*Civil Wars,* 1595–1609). He argued boldly for his native tongue in the verse dialogue *Musophilus* (1598) and for English verse forms in the prose *Defence of Rhyme* (1603). His varied poetic work includes *The Complaint of Rosamond* (mistress of Henry II) (1592), stately epistles to the Countesses of Bedford and Pembroke, "Senecan" tragedies, court masques, and the sonnet sequence, *Delia* (1592–4). To most readers, "well-languaged" Daniel lives only as the "sweet, honey-dropping" artificer of such imitative sonnets as "Care-charmer Sleep, son of the sable Night."

D'ARBLAY, MME. See **BURNEY, Frances.**

DARLEY, George (1795–1846) was an Irishman who wrote literary criticism, plays, poetry, and, of all things, mathematics textbooks. Buried in *The Errors of Ecstasie, a Dramatic Poem* (1822), *Sylvia . . . a Lyrical Drama* (1827), and the cantos on Joy and Melancholy called *Nepenthe* (1835) are passages of lyric gold. The "dramatic chronicles," *Thomas à Becket* (printed 1840) and *Ethelstan* (printed 1841), are usually regarded as pure dross.

DARWIN, Charles (Robert) (1809–82). The Victorian period presents no man as famous and at the same time as persistently modest as Charles Darwin. He seems to have been almost totally indifferent to the storm which his theories created and to the renown which they brought him. Except for the extended travels of his early years, he led an uneventful life. He was the son of a Shrewsbury physician and the grandson of the biologist and poetaster Erasmus Darwin. After completing his education at the University of Edinburgh and at Cambridge, he received an appointment as traveling naturalist on H.M.S. *Beagle*. This was in 1831, and it was not until after five years of wandering and note-taking in South America and elsewhere that he finally returned to England. Here he was elected a member of the Royal Society, published *The Voyage of H.M.S. Beagle* (1839), and settled in London to continue his scientific study and writing. In 1842 he moved to Orpington, Kent, where he made his home for the rest of his life. With amazing persistence he fought down ill-health that may have resulted from his hard life on the *Beagle* and produced a series of treatises that revolutionized men's thinking in science and theology. The earliest of these, *Coral Reefs* (1842) and *Volcanic Islands* (1844), created no stir. His *On the Origin of Species,* however, published in 1859 after prolonged study and labor, upset the intellectual world and caused a battle of which the echoes are still reverberating. Darwin's biological theory, which earlier scientists had suggested but not elaborated, was that the animate world grew gradually by slow evolution from lower to higher forms, by natural selection, and by adaptation to environment. To certain "clerical minds," as Huxley called them, these ideas were blasphemous. With the storms of controversy raging around him, Darwin continued unmoved to other important if less famous books. *Fertilization of Orchids* (1862) and *The Variation of Animals and Plants under Domestication* (1868) were followed by *The Descent of Man* (1871). This last book continued to expound the doctrine of evolution but caused less resentment than had *The Origin of Species*. In the decade before his death Darwin completed his arduous scientific labors with *The Expression of the Emotions* (1872), *Insectivorous Plants* (1875), and *The Formation of Vegetable Mold through the Action of Worms* (1881).

DARWIN, Erasmus (1731–1802) is respected by scientists as the author of *Zoönamia, or the Laws of Organic Life* (1794–6), a treatise in which he foreshadowed the evolutionary principles of his grandson, Charles Darwin. He is ridiculed by literary scholars as the author of *The Botanic Garden,* Part II of which, *The Loves of the Plants,* appeared in 1789, and Part I, *The Economy of Vegetation,* in 1791. An excruciating effort to romanticize the laws of botany in heroic couplets, it is frequently cited to show how the eighteenth-century tradition in poetry had gone to seed. It received its just due in Canning and Frere's parody, *The Loves of the Triangles.*

DAVENANT or **D'AVENANT, Sir William** (1606–68) was prominent as a playwright and manager during two generations of the theater. His pre-war plays include a popular comedy called *The Wits* (1634) and *Love and Honor* (1634), an early effort in the heroic drama, which Dryden credited him with founding. After the war he helped remove the Puritan padlock from the theater with his two-part *Siege of Rhodes* (1656, 1658?), an experiment in dressing up the love-and-honor dilemma as an opera with elaborate scenic effects. It is traditionally called the first English opera. He was later guilty of operatic alterations of *Macbeth* (1663) and *The Tempest* (with Dryden, 1667). Between the two periods he fought for Charles I, spent two years in the Tower, and wrote his unfinished epic of chivalry, *Gondibert* (1651).

DAVIDSON, John (1857–1909) labored at various tasks in Scotland from 1872 to 1890, spent two poverty-stricken decades in London writing, and finally drowned himself. Like James (*Dreadful Night*) Thomson, he was a poet of despair. He expounded his bitter philosophy in a series of blank-verse *Testaments* (1901–8) and in the two parts of his unfinished dramatic trilogy, *God and Mammon* (1907–8). There is melancholy and bitterness in such short poems as *The Last Rose, Waiting,* and *A Ballad of Heaven.* The last-named, a melodramatic tale of a violinist whose wife and child starve to death as he completes his symphony, is the best-known example of the type with which Davidson was most successful.

DAVIES, Sir John (1569–1626) was a successful statesman and jurist who, in the year of his death, was appointed Lord Chief Justice under Charles I. His work in poetry dates back to the closing years of Elizabeth's reign. It includes *Orchestra* (1596), a philosophical poem on the order of the universe disguised under a whimsical dialogue on the subject of dancing; *Hymns of Astraea* (1599), a series of twenty-six ingenious acrostics on the name *Elizabeth Regina;* and *Nosce Teipsum* (1599), a long philosophical poem on man and immortality. The last is Davies' masterpiece. The two stately quatrains beginning "I know my soul hath power to know all things" are the best known.

DAVIES, John, of Hereford (1565?–1618?) spent most of his life at Oxford as a writing-master. He wrote dreary verse arguments on philosophical and theological questions: *Mirum in Modum* (1602), *Microcosmos* (1603), *Summa Totalis* (1607), the first and third based on the *Nosce Teipsum* of Sir John Davies (1569–1626). The love of paradox and conceit which characterizes these is also apparent in a quite different work, *The Scourge of Folly* (1611?), a series of epigrams on bad manners.

DAVIES, W(illiam) H(enry) (1871–1940). Before he published his first collection of verse, *The Soul's Destroyer and Other Poems* (1905), and thereby attracted the interest of George Bernard Shaw, Davies had lived the life of a vagabond, both in England and in America. The story of how he wandered the highways and rode the rails, eventually losing his right leg in a fall from a train, is told in *The Autobiography of a Super-Tramp* (1908). The dominant note of his poetry is tender sympathy with nature, expressed with extreme simplicity. Like Wordsworth, with whom he suggests inevitable comparison, Davies has been ridiculed and parodied for sometimes crossing the thin line which separates the childlike from the childish.

DAY, John (c. 1574–c. 1640). Most of what is known about Day appears in the diary of Philip Henslowe, the theatrical manager for whom he worked. He was a prolific journeyman playwright who collaborated with Dekker and Rowley, among others, and who seems to have done his best writing in the first decade of the seventeenth century. His best-known work is *The Parliament of Bees* (printed 1607?), an airy, allegorical fantasy.

DAY, Thomas (1748–89) is remembered as the author of *Sandford and Merton* (1783–9). Like Henry Brooke's *Fool of Quality* (1765–70) and Elizabeth Inchbald's *Nature and Art* (1796), it is an attempt to express Rousseau's summons "back to Nature" in a didactic novel. The sentimental story of Tommy Merton, spoiled son of a rich Jamaica planter, and Harry Sandford, virtuous offspring of a poor but honest farmer, was required reading in the nursery for many years.

DAY–LEWIS, C(ecil) (1904–   ), was born in Ireland and was at Oxford with W. H. Auden and Stephen Spender. His works include *Collected Poems, 1929–33* (1935); *The Friendly Tree* (1936), a novel; and *A Hope for Poetry* (1934), a critical essay in which he defends the use of poetry as an instrument of political action. Under the pseudonym of "Nicholas Blake" he has also written ten or a dozen mystery and detective stories.

DEFOE, Daniel (1659-1731). It falls to the lot of few authors to write a story that is universally known, read, translated, and imitated. All of these recognitions came to *Robinson Crusoe* (1719), one of the most famous tales in English literature. Its author, Daniel Defoe, was a Puritan and a moralist, a soldier, pamphleteer, journalist, and realistic novelist. He was born in London of middle-class parents and was still in his teens when the anti-Catholic rebellion forced King James II from the throne of England and brought in William of Orange. Defoe's earliest pamphlets favored the change. So did his satirical poem, *The True-Born Englishman* (1701), directed against those who objected to King William's foreign birth. His *Shortest Way with Dissenters* (1702) was such a bitter verse attack on the Church of England party that it brought its author fine and imprisonment. Released in 1704, Defoe started the *Review,* a political and social paper that forecast the more famous periodicals of Addison and Steele. His greatest work has already been mentioned. *Robinson Crusoe* (1719) was followed by *Memoirs of a Cavalier* and *Captain Singleton,* both published in 1720. Two years later appeared *The Fortunes and Misfortunes of the Famous Moll Flanders,* the story of a girl pickpocket, and *The History of Colonel Jack.* But Defoe's best-known narrative of 1722 was his truly remarkable *Journal of the Plague Year* (1722), an account of London in 1665, when the "Great Plague" swept away a large part of the population. Defoe was only five or six at the time and could hardly have remembered much of the catastrophe, but so realistic is his amazing reconstruction of the events of those terrible months that no eye-witness could have done better. *Roxana, or the Fortunate Mistress* was published in 1724.

Defoe's great power was that of the accurate, subtle journalist. By introducing specific and well-chosen details into his fictions he created the illusion of exact truth, tricking the reader into suspension of disbelief. Defoe's wild tales of misadventure and roguery —*Captain Singleton, Moll Flanders,* and *Colonel Jack*—provide an important literary link between Thomas Nashe's story of the wanderings of Jack Wilton and the novels of Tobias Smollett. They are essentially picaresque; the heroes are rogues who survive kidnapping, deportation to Virginia, and adventures by land and sea, to become repentant at a time when their wealth does not make repentance inconvenient.

DEKKER, Thomas (1572?–1632). The few facts known about Thomas Dekker indicate that during much of his life he wrestled out an uncertain living, harassed by debt and threatened with imprisonment. He seems to have had the support of no patron, but apparently had to depend upon his own efforts as miscellaneous writer in a London that offered thin support to its free-lance scribblers. In spite of these hardships, he earned a distinct position for himself as poet, pamphleteer, and dramatist. Dekker was a city-man, and save for an occasional excursion into conventional romance he wrote always of the city and almost always of its middle-class. He was an admirable reporter, and realism and human understanding are characteristics of his work. He was often satirical but never bitter; perhaps his own hardships mellowed his sympathies. As pamphleteer Dekker would have earned a place in literature even if he had never written a play. *The Wonderful Year* (1603) is the vivid and detailed account of the London plague upon which Daniel Defoe later drew for his *Journal of the Plague Year* (1722), and *The Seven Deadly Sins of London* (1606) is a chilling allegory of God's punishment of the wicked metropolis. *The Bellman of London* (1608) and its sequel, *Lanthorne and Candle-light* (1608), are his contributions to the literature of roguery, unoriginal revivals of the thieves' tricks and jargon made popular by Robert Greene and others in the preceding century. *The Gull's Hornbook* (1609), much more original, is a delightfully satirical primer for London fops of the time and presents these gulls at the theater, in the ordinary, and elsewhere.

As dramatist, Dekker sometimes worked alone but just as often with collaborators. Collaborating, apparently, with John Marston, he attacked Ben Jonson in *Satiromastix, or the Untrussing of the Humorous Poet* (1601), a dramatic riposte to Jonson's *Poetaster*, in which both Marston and Dekker had been assailed. With Middleton, Dekker wrote *The Roaring Girl* (printed 1611), in which a contemporary gun-moll is transformed into a female Robin Hood; and with Ford and Rowley he demonstrated in the domestic tragedy of *The Witch of Edmonton* (1621) that crime never pays. *Patient Grissel* (1600) was an early comedy on the patient wife theme, written in 1598 with Chettle and Haughton. *Old Fortunatus* (1599) is a folklore play on the theme of the miraculous purse. Dekker's best plays are the two-part *Honest Whore* (1604-1605) and the justly famous *Shoemakers' Holiday* (1599). The first may owe its sentimental main plot to the labor of Middleton, but Dekker certainly was responsible for the secondary plot of the "patient man and the longing wife" and for the vivid London scenes. Elizabethan life is even better presented in the craftsmen's comedy of the shoemakers. The plot, borrowed partly from Deloney's *Gentle Craft* (1597), is episodic, sprawling, and not always dramatic, but the antics of the madcap shoemaker Simon Eyre and his frolicsome journeyman Firk make up for this lack of dramatic structure. The comedy shows the journalist-dramatist at his best, and that best is excellent.

DELAFIELD, E. M. (1890–1943) is the pseudonym of Mrs. Edmée Elizabeth Monica de la Pasture Dashwood, prolific novelist, short-story writer, and playwright. Her work is marked by amusing satire of the contemporary scene. It includes *The War-Workers* (1918), a satirical novel about the fighting females of the First World War; *Consequences* (1919), a novel portraying the humors of domesticity; *Women are Like That* (1929), a volume of short-stories; *To See Ourselves* (1932), a domestic comedy; and a series of "Provincial Lady" diaries including *The Provincial Lady in America* (1934), her notes on an American lecture tour, and *The Provincial Lady in Wartime* (1940).

DE LA MARE, Walter (1873–1956) has published poems, plays, essays, and fiction for forty years. He is remembered by most readers for a single poem, *The Listeners* (1912), and a single novel, *Memoirs of a Midget* (1921). In the poem he clothed a simple narrative with the haunting magic of a dream. In choosing a midget as the heroine of his unique novel, he ran the risk of producing a grotesque *tour de force;* but he succeeded in endowing her life with exquisite beauty. De la Mare has also written some excellent children's stories and verses, as in his *Peacock Pie* (1913) and *The Lord Fish and Other Stories* (1933).

DE LA RAMÉE, Marie Louise. See **OUIDA.**

DELONEY, Thomas (1543?–1607?) was a Norwich silk-weaver who made his London literary début as a maker of broadside ballads. More notable are three prose narratives, each celebrating a craft: *Jack of Newbury* (the weavers), *Thomas of Reading* (the clothiers), and *The Gentle Craft* (the shoemakers), all licensed in 1597. The heroes of all three are historical, but Deloney, in a style ranging from the euphuistic to the vernacular, freely combined the world of romantic legends with the real, workaday life of Elizabethan London. Thus the first two parts of *The Gentle Craft* glorify patron saints of shoemakers, while the third tells the lively tale of "how Sir Simon Eyre, being at first a shoemaker, became in the end Mayor of London, through the counsel of his wife." This story inspired that rollicking comedy, Dekker's *Shoemakers' Holiday* (1599).

DE MORGAN, William Frend (1839–1917). After a long and successful career as a potter, during part of which he was associated with William Morris, De Morgan started to write fiction in his middle sixties. *Joseph Vance* (1906), his first novel and his masterpiece, and *Alice-for-Short* (1907) are reminiscent of Dickens and Thackeray, whom the author had admired years before; hence his work represents a sort of Indian summer of Victorian fiction.

DENHAM, Sir John (1615–69). A line from Pope links "Denham's strength and Waller's sweetness." Although Waller was a far better poet, the two are traditionally paired as pioneers in the closed couplet. Such works as *The Sophy,* a tragedy (printed 1642), *The Destruction of Troy,* a translation from the *Aeneid* (1656), and the *Elegy on Cowley's Death* (1667) are all but forgotten. Better known is *Cooper's Hill* (1642), a long poem in which Denham describes the scenery from a hill near Windsor Forest and meditates on the history of the neighborhood. Amid its often prosaic, sometimes ungrammatical passages, the classic quatrain on the Thames ("Oh, could I flow like thee," etc.) stands out in lonely splendor. *Cooper's Hill* inspired Pope's *Windsor Forest* (1713).

DENNIS, John (1657–1734) was a Cambridge graduate and customs-house officer who gloried in the smoke of literary battle. Despite persistent abuse from his most formidable enemy, Pope, he was a reputable critic if a poor playwright. His best-known works are: *The Advancement and Reformation of Modern Poetry* (1701), *The Grounds of Criticism in Poetry* (1704), *An Essay on the Genius and Writings of Shakespeare* (1712). True he insisted dogmatically that stage business was the essence of true comedy, preferred the Falstaff of *The Merry Wives* to the fat knight of *Henry IV,* and asserted that the Moderns could not approach the Ancients until they adopted the unities and shot their plays full of religion and poetic justice. But in the dark age of Collier and Rymer, to speak favorably of the Modern stage, even of Shakespeare, was progressive criticism.

DE QUINCEY, Thomas (1785–1859) was a child prodigy. And while he grew mentally from an introspective schoolboy who daily translated the newspaper into Greek at sight to an eccentric little man who took almost all knowledge for his province, he remained, in the ways of the world, a child. In earliest boyhood he escaped from the playground to a dream world "peopled with solemn imagery," and he never came back for long. At sixteen he ran away from school in his native Manchester. Six years later he ran away from Oxford on the eve of his honors examinations. In 1804, shortly after entering college, he had sought relief in opium—at first from the pain of a toothache. By 1812 the habit was on him for good. Like his early friend and "rival" addict, Coleridge, he was tempest-tossed through life, swearing off and surrendering, dreading deadlines, promising editors and procrastinating.

He published nothing of importance until *Blackwood's Magazine* appeared in 1821 with his *Confessions of an English Opium Eater*. It was a wildfire success. Here was no humble apology for a misspent life, no sober warning to growing boys—but a lurid, unrepentant story of the author's own vagrant youth, and a candid analysis of the pleasures and pains of opium, including an amazing series of actual opium dreams. The *Confessions* forecast most of the later tendencies in De Quincey's writing: the malicious gossip which crops up later in *Reminiscences of the English Lake Poets* (1834, etc.); the digressions and witticisms of the first part of *Murder Considered as one of the Fine Arts* (1827 and 1839); the subtle analysis displayed again in his critique *On the Knocking at the Gate in Macbeth* (1823); most important, vivid dream fantasies like those to be unfolded in *Suspiria de Profundis* (1845) and in the third section of *The English Mail Coach* (1849). The style of the dreams is an ornate poetic prose, woven of rich Latin words, sensuous imagery, and swelling periodic sentences. Although De Quincey wrote widely in the fields of biography, history, literary criticism, philosophy, theology, and politics, most people read him for the purple patches of his gorgeous style. And although he was a timid, gentle little man who dearly loved his six children, many remember him only as a connoisseur of opium and murder.

DE VERE, Aubrey Thomas (1814–1902) was the son of the poet **Sir Aubrey de Vere** (1788–1846). Among his collections of poems are *The Waldenses and Other Poems* (1842) and *The Legends of St. Patrick* (1872). His most popular poem is probably the pious sonnet on *Sorrow* ("Count each affliction, whether light or grave"). He wrote in prose *Essays, chiefly on Poetry* (1887) and *Essays, chiefly Literary and Ethical* (1889). Because of the unusual length of his life, his *Recollections* (1897) are valuable to students of literary history.

DICKENS, Charles (1812–70) was the most popular, the most bustling, the most voluminous of Victorian novelists. He was a journalist, a dramatist, a humorist, a satirist, and a sentimentalist rolled into one very busy story-teller. But his chief interest was in creating a great gallery of human animals, who lived and moved and had their eccentric beings against the background of Victorian England and particularly Victorian London.

The hardships that Dickens suffered as a boy are reflected in

Oliver Twist, David Copperfield, and *Great Expectations*. He was
born in Landport, but was moved to Chatham when he was
four and to London when he was nine. His father, an irresponsible
and underpaid clerk, who more than once saw the inside of the
debtors' prison of Marshalsea, was the original of Wilkins Mi-
cawber of *David Copperfield;* his mother appears as the erratic
mother of the hero in *Nicholas Nickleby*. Dickens' drudgery in
a blacking warehouse is echoed in young Copperfield's slavery
at Murdstone and Grinby's.

He began his journalistic career as a self-taught shorthand reporter in Doctors' Commons. In 1834 he became reporter on the
Morning Chronicle and began there the studies of London types
that bore their first fruits in *Sketches by Boz* (1835–6). *The
Posthumous Papers of the Pickwick Club* (1836–7) originated
as a series of literary sketches to accompany drawings depicting
the adventures of a ludicrous quartette of London sportsmen, but
they soon went beyond their original intention and made their
author famous. *Pickwick Papers* was followed by a long train
of successful novels, serialized first in the magazines before publication in book form. *Oliver Twist* (1837–9) deals with London
crime, *Nicholas Nickleby* (1838–9) with the brutal Yorkshire
schools. *Old Curiosity Shop* (1840–1) is the tale of an unhappy
girl and her gambling grandfather. *Barnaby Rudge* (1841), a
story of the Lord Gordon riots in London, and *A Tale of Two
Cities* (1859), a story of the French Revolution, are Dickens' two
excursions into the historical novel. Dickens' first journey to
America resulted in his unkind and unfair *American Notes*
(1842) and in his novel *Martin Chuzzlewit* (1843–4); on his
second journey, made in 1868 to deliver a popular series of readings, he did much to heal the wounds which these books had
made. His sentimental eagerness to build up a Christmas cult
found expression in the perennially popular *Christmas Carol*
(1843), *The Chimes* (1844), *The Cricket on the Hearth* (1845),
and other less entertaining Christmas stories. His later novels are
Dombey and Son (1846–8), *David Copperfield* (1849–50)—fictionized autobiography which introduces the novelist's "child-
wife" as Dora—, *Bleak House* (1852–3), *Hard Times* (1854),
Little Dorrit (1855–7), *Great Expectations* (1860–1), *Our Mutual
Friend* (1864–5), and the unfinished *Mystery of Edwin Drood*
(1870).

Although Dickens' work was extensive and varied, a number
of characteristic traits predominate. First, the novels are journalistic; they reveal Dickens the reporter at work, especially in the

tales with a London background. Again, they are dramatic—often melodramatic. One of Dickens' chief enthusiasms was the theater; at one time he managed a company of amateur actors, and he loved to play parts himself and to give dramatic readings from his own books. His favorite dramatist was Ben Jonson, the Elizabethan creator of the "comedy of humors," and the affinity between seventeenth-century playwright and nineteenth-century novelist is readily apparent. As a humorist—a master of unrestrained hyperbole, an expert in building infinite variations on a single theme of human eccentricity, a deft manipulator of farcical situations—Dickens is at his best in *Pickwick Papers*. As he grew older, his mood darkened, and in *Bleak House* and *Hard Times* the more genial humor is overshadowed by a bitter, didactic satire on man's inhumanity to man.

Dickens' major faults are a tendency to let pathos slop over into bathos, a preference for caricature rather than characterization, and an annoying lack of concern for either form or economy. He is interested, like an actor, in creating impressions upon a contemporary audience, and too often he moulded his amorphous serials to suit his whims. He got his reward in an immense popularity during his lifetime; but he is paying the price in a dying fame among readers to whom his Victorian characters seem strange, and his Victorian moods outmoded.

DILLON, Wentworth. See **ROSCOMMON.**

DISRAELI, Benjamin, first earl of Beaconsfield (1804–81) is famous as the prime minister who bought England's controlling interest in the Suez Canal and elevated Victoria to Empress of India. He was also a talented novelist. His first novel was *Vivian Gray* (1826–7), a romantic story of a precocious youth in fashionable society. Three novels reflect the "Tory democracy" of his Young England party in the forties: *Coningsby* (1844) narrates the struggle of a young man against the reaction of his grandfather and the corruption of unprincipled politicians; *Sybil* (1845) presents a shocking contrast between the "two nations" of England, the rich, fox-hunting idlers and the poor, starving workers in industry and agriculture; the more mystical *Tancred* (1847) urges a spiritual remedy effected by fresh contact with the home of the author's ancestors, Palestine. The novels often betray, in their false rhetoric, the love of sham and glitter which made "Dizzy" England's number one dude and ladies' man; but they also display the mastery of irony and genuine sympathy for humanity which made him one of her greatest statesmen.

DIXON, Richard Watson (1833–1900), poet and religious historian, was for many years a canon of Carlisle. His six-volume *History of the Church of England from the Abolition of the Roman Jurisdiction* (1878–1902) is still highly regarded by scholars. His poems, although not widely read, have been treasured by a few discerning critics. The most ambitious is *Mano* (1883), a "poetical history" in *terza rima* laid in the tenth and eleventh centuries. Better known are a few lyrics—*Fallen Rain, The Feathers of the Willow, Ode on Advancing Age*—which have led critics to compare Dixon with such a goodly company as Blake, Wordsworth, Coleridge, and Keats. He was a friend of William Morris, Robert Bridges, and Gerard Manley Hopkins. Bridges edited three volumes of his poems (1896, 1905, 1909). His correspondence with Hopkins was published in 1935.

DOBELL, Sydney Thompson (1824–74) wrote two drawing-room verse dramas, *The Roman* (printed 1850) and the unfinished *Balder* (printed 1853); and two books of verse on the Crimean War, *Sonnets on the War* (with Alexander Smith, 1855) and *England in Time of War* (1856). He is at his best in the eerie ballad of Keith of Ravelston (from *A Nuptial Song*) and in the pathetic lament *Tommy's Dead*. At his worst, he betrays the strenuous struggle towards strangeness in language and subject matter which is the trademark of the "Spasmodic School," the group in which W. E. Aytoun loosely classified Dobell, Alexander Smith, and P. J. Bailey.

DOBSON, Henry Austin (1840–1921). Although this pleasant poet, essayist, critic, and biographer served the London Board of Trade for forty-five years (1856–1901), he was steeped in the literature of the eighteenth century. Austin Dobson was a master of a kind of pretty poetic trifle which is commonly classified as *vers de société*. Like Henley, Swinburne, and other late Victorians he experimented widely with French forms. His miniature masterpiece, "Rose kissed me today," is one of the few successful triolets in English.

DODGSON, Charles Lutwidge. See **CARROLL, Lewis.**

DODSLEY, Robert (1703–64) is known among students of the English drama chiefly as the editor and publisher of an anthology entitled *Select Collection of Old Plays* (1744), popularly called *Dodsley's Old Plays*. He also wrote some dramas of his own, notably *The Toyshop, a Dramatic Satire* (1735) and *The Blind Beggar of Bethnal Green* (1741), a musical play. In partnership with Edmund Burke he founded in London in 1758 the *Annual Register,* a digest of the principal events of the preceding year. It is still being published.

DOLBEN, Digby Mackworth (1848–67) was drowned at the age of nineteen before he could fulfill his promise as a poet. Although he was never actually received into the Church, his work belongs in spirit with that of the Roman Catholic Victorians, Alice Meynell, Francis Thompson, Coventry Patmore, and Lionel Johnson. His poems were edited by his friend Robert Bridges in 1911.

DONNE, John (1573–1631). The early life of John Donne (pronounced Dun) followed a familiar pattern for young gentlemen: Oxford and Cambridge, a journey on the Continent, Lincoln's Inn, two expeditions with the dashing Essex (1596–7), a position as private secretary to Sir Thomas Egerton, Keeper of the Great Seal (1596–1601). When in 1601 he secretly married Sir Thomas' niece, Anne More, he was dismissed and spent a time in prison. Then followed years in which Donne sought favors in vain at court and wondered if, born a Catholic, he ought to seek a career in the Church of England. After a prolonged spiritual struggle, he finally took Anglican orders in 1615. In 1621 he was made Dean of St. Paul's. When he died, he was one of England's greatest preachers.

The best known of the prose works published during Donne's lifetime is *Devotions upon Emergent Occasions* (1624), a series of melodious, melancholy reflections written when the author believed himself at death's door. Most of his sermons were published at intervals after his death (1634–60). Despite elaborate theological reasoning and quaint, learned diction, they are remarkable for their sonorous music. The bulk of Donne's poetry was also published posthumously, the first collected edition appearing in 1633. In his gay youth he wrote love poems in a variety of moods—"Go and catch a falling star," *The Ecstasy, The Sun Rising, The Funeral,* and *The Relic,* to mention but a few. In his more sober later years he wrote numerous divine poems, including *Good Friday, 1613; To God, my God, in my Sickness; To God the Father* (with the refrain "When thou hast done, thou hast not done"); and, best known of his *Holy Sonnets,* "Death, be not proud." He also wrote satires, dwelling on such subjects as religious freedom, the frivolousness of court and city life and the miseries of petitioners; elegies (*His Picture, On His Mistress*); verse-letters (*To Sir H. W. at his Going Ambassador to Venice, To the Countess of Bedford*); and an unfinished long poem called *The*

Progress of the Soul, an ambitious effort to trace the migration of the soul of Eve's apple through the bodies of all the great heretics.

Although much of Donne's poetry is chronologically Elizabethan it seems to come from another age. In both his secular and his religious verse, he replaced the artificial surface feelings of the Elizabethans with intense personal passion. Conventional fancies gave way to astounding intellectual conceits; smooth, honeyed verse compounded of "poetic" diction was replaced by jerky stanzas full of blunt colloquialisms and strange "metaphysical" language. Instead of taking love for granted as a pleasant plaything, he dissected it like a trained scientist. Instead of writing of religion objectively and didactically, he turned inward to his own individual experience.

Although he inspired a host of imitators, a whole "school" of "metaphysical poets,"—including Crashaw, Herbert, Vaughan, and Cowley—Donne was not entirely appreciated in his day. Ben Jonson, who thought him "the first poet in the world in some things," asserted that "for not keeping of accent he deserved hanging." In the next century Addison and Samuel Johnson dismissed him as a dealer in eccentricities. Today, however, when most poets prefer intellectual subtleties to commonplace fancies, startling rhythms to smooth cadences, Donne's influence is everywhere apparent.

DORSET. See SACKVILLE.

DOUGHTY, Charles Montagu (1843–1926) wrote a long epic, *The Dawn in Britain* (1906), and other long poems. The obscurity of his poetry is produced partly by his deliberate use of archaic words, many of them from Chaucer and Spenser. Similar archaisms jostle with Arabic words in Doughty's prose masterpiece, *Travels in Arabia Deserta* (1888). This epic of a two years' journey (1876–8) is, for all its strangeness, one of the most magnificent travel books in English.

DOUGLAS, Gavin or Gawin (1474?–1522). This Scottish bishop wrote two conventional allegorical poems: *The Palace of Honor* (written 1501), a museum-piece for students of the aureate dream-allegory; and *King Hart* (first printed 1786), in which the human heart, seconded by his servants, the senses, throbs through adventures with a number of personified abstractions. But he is best known for his translation into ten-syllable couplets of Vergil's *Aeneid* (written 1513). Although many find the elaborate personal prologues which he tied to each book more interesting than the epic itself, Douglas deserves recognition as the first translator of the classics into an English dialect, hence as a forerunner of the Renaissance.

DOUGLAS, (George) Norman (1868–1952) spent most of his life away from the Scotland of his ancestry. His works include fiction, books of travel, and serious scientific essays. He is best known for his first novel, *South Wind* (1917). In it he traced the degeneration of an English bishop during a visit to a Mediterranean island, where the bishop falls beneath the spell of the sirocco and the seductive escapism of the English and American intellectuals who have made their homes there. This lotos-land of "Nepenthe" is supposed to be the Isle of Capri, where Douglas himself lived for years. The novel is a carefree satire on the conventional *mores* of civilized society, a fantastic mélange of brilliant paradoxes, sensuous description, and strange scientific lore.

DOWDEN, Edward (1843–1913), Professor of English Literature at Trinity College, Dublin, was the author of *Shakspere, a Critical Study of his Mind and Art* (1875) and other distinguished volumes of Shakespearean criticism. His *Life of Shelley* (1886) was for many years the standard biography of the poet.

DOWSON, Ernest Christopher (1867–1900) was a poet whose life and work reflect the "decadence" which tinged English literature at the end of the nineteenth century. A French scholar, he published several translations from that tongue and frequently employed French forms in his verse. His poems (*Verses*, 1896) include the fragile song "They are not long, the weeping and the laughter" and *Non Sum Qualis Eram Bonae sub Regno Cynarae*. The Latin title disguises the lyric with the refrain "I have been faithful to thee, Cynara! in my fashion." This poem, with its strange blend of cynicism and pathos, has haunted many who do not remember its author's name.

DOYLE, Sir Arthur Conan (1859–1930). Sherlock Holmes was not the first detective in fiction. He had been preceded in France by Gaboriau's Lecoq, in America by Poe's Dupin, and in England by Sergeant Cuff of Wilkie Collins' *Moonstone* (1868). But in the popular imagination Conan Doyle's sleuth is the father of them all. In the breadth of their legal and scientific knowledge, in the profusion of their hobbies and eccentricities, some of Sherlock's many descendants may have outdone him, but for universality of appeal he is unsurpassed. And no detective has ever had a more delightful stooge than Dr. Watson. *A Study in Scarlet* (1887), *The Sign of the Four* (1890), and *The Hound*

of the Baskervilles (1902) are among the most popular of the
longer stories; *The Red-headed League* and *A Scandal in Bohemia*
stand out among the shorter tales. Although the adventures of
Sherlock Holmes have overshadowed Conan Doyle's work as a
historical novelist, *The White Company* (1891) remains a popular book for boys. His *History of Spiritualism* (1926) reveals the
consuming interest of his last years.

DRAYTON, Michael (1563–1631) was a prolific, versatile poet.
He began with a volume of religious verse, *The Harmony of the
Church* (1591). Then he wrote a string of nine pastoral eclogues
entitled *The Shepherd's Garland* (1593) and a sonnet sequence,
Idea's Mirror (1594), both, apparently, praising the same girl.
Later he turned to history—composing fancied verse letters for
famous historical couples (*England's Heroical Epistles*, 1597);
surveying entire periods (*The Barons' Wars*, 1596, 1603); singing the glorious single achievements of past and present (*Ballad
of Agincourt, Ode to the Virginian Voyage*, 1606). Moved by the
same spirit, he worked a quarter century on *Polyolbion* (1612–
22, begun 1598), a "description of all the tracts, rivers, mountains, forests, and other parts of this renowned isle of Great
Britain, with intermixture of the most remarkable stories, antiquities, wonders, rarities, pleasures, and commodities of the
same." The whole was dutifully chronicled in 15,000 twelve-
foot lines—an appalling patriotic sacrifice, not a poem. In contrast with this *magnum opus* is whimsical *Nymphidia* (1627),
where he created an exquisite miniature fairyland like that in
A Midsummer Night's Dream. Obviously with such a repertoire
Drayton could write real poetry only in flashes. For one of these,
the sonnet beginning "Since there's no help, come let us kiss
and part," most readers would gladly trade the entire *Polyolbion*.

DRINKWATER, John (1882–1937) was a versatile man of letters who published poems, plays, biographies, and critical essays.
He is remembered chiefly for his plays, most of them written while
he was manager of the Birmingham Repertory Theater. The historical drama *Abraham Lincoln* (printed 1918) is the work by
which he is best known. He also wrote the highly popular comedy
Bird-in-Hand (printed 1927).

DRUMMOND, William, of Hawthornden (1585–1649). His
name is inseparable from the sumptuous manor-house near Edinburgh in which he was born. After early education and travel,
he settled down there among his books, a true amateur of letters.
And there, having pamphleteered in vain for Charles I, he died.

Among his poems are sonnets which reflect the sadness occasioned by the death of his fiancée on the eve of the wedding (*Poems*, 1616); panegyrics which show his respect for royalty (*Forth Feasting*, 1617); religious sonnets (*Flowers of Sion*, 1623); and many songs ("Phoebus, arise, And paint the sable skies."). Two prose works are more famous: *The Cypress Grove* (1623), a meditation on death which deserves comparison with Sir Thomas Browne's *Hydriotaphia* (1658); and *Conversations*, based on talks with Ben Jonson at Hawthornden in 1619, although not published until 1833. The *Conversations*, frank and not entirely complimentary, is the fullest personal record of Jonson.

DRYDEN, John (1631–1700). Dryden was the outstanding writer of the Restoration period—poet, dramatist, critic, satirist, pamphleteer, and dictator of literary taste. He was born in Northamptonshire of Puritan parents and educated at Cambridge University. He began his literary career before the end of the Puritan Protectorate, and his *Heroic Stanzas* (1659) was "consecrated to the glorious memory" of Oliver Cromwell. In the very next year, however, he turned his political and literary coat in *Astraea Redux*, "a poem on the happy restoration and return of his sacred majesty, Charles the second." *Annus Mirabilis* (1667) commemorates the Great Fire, the Great Plague, and the Dutch War of 1665–6. In 1668 appeared his most famous literary criticism, *An Essay of Dramatic Poesy*, in the form of a discussion among Neander (Dryden), and Crites, Eugenius, and Lisideius (respectively, Sir Robert Howard, Lord Buckhurst, and Sir Charles Sedley) on the comparative merits of French and English drama and on other literary themes.

Dryden became poet laureate in 1670, and many of his subsequent poems are sharply polemical. *Absalom and Achitophel* (1681) is an attack upon Lord Shaftesbury (Achitophel), whose party was attempting to establish the succession of the Duke of Monmouth (Absalom), bastard son of Charles II (David), in place of the king's brother James; the allegorical basis for the satire is in the first Book of Kings. To a second part of this poem (1682), written mainly by Nahum Tate, Dryden contributed some two hundred lines, in which he aimed a shaft at Thomas Shadwell, a contemporary poet and dramatist, who had called him an atheist. In the same year he took the full measure of Shadwell in *Mac Flecknoe, or a Satyr upon the True-Blew-Protestant Poet, T. S.* (1682), thereby creating one of the most famous of personal satires in literature and a worthy ancestor of Pope's *Dunciad*. With no apparent fear of reprisal Dryden vented all of his spleen against the "Son of Flecknoe," who was the heir and the crowned king of dullness:

> "The rest to some faint meaning make pretence
> But Shadwell never deviates into sense."

With the accession of James II in 1685 Dryden became a Roman Catholic convert, and his earlier *Religio Laici* (1682), a poem in defense of the Church of England, was eclipsed in brilliance by *The Hind and the Panther* (1687), in which the "milk-white hind" (the Roman Catholic Church) is contrasted with the sleek panther (the Church of England) and various other beasts (the dissenting creeds). Outside the field of satire Dryden's best-known poems are the two songs that he wrote for the celebrations of St. Cecilia's Day: *A Song for St. Cecilia's Day* (1687) and the more famous *Alexander's Feast* (1697), in which the lines and the words interpret a succession of musical moods. Dryden's *Fables, Ancient and Modern,* with a critical *Preface* in which he pays tribute to Chaucer, was published in the year of his death.

It is inconceivable that, in a period in which the drama flourished, the literary dictator should not write plays as well as satirical verse and criticism. Dryden composed many, some independently, and others in collaboration with lesser dramatists. He was a pioneer in the rhymed heroic play. *The Indian Queen* (with Sir Robert Howard, 1664), *The Conquest of Granada* (two parts, 1670–1), and *Aureng-Zebe* (1675) are three successful dramas in the bombastic *genre* that was famously satirized in Buckingham's *Rehearsal* (1671). Dryden's best tragedy, *All for Love* (1677), is in blank verse like its original, Shakespeare's *Antony and Cleopatra;* but, unlike Shakespeare, Dryden observed the dramatic unities of time, place, and action. His best comedy is *Marriage-à-la-Mode* (1671–2), a medley of amorous intrigue.

Matthew Arnold called Dryden "the inaugurator of an age of prose and reason." He was one of the most witty, brilliant, penetrating—and merciless—of satirists. He was a keen and rational literary critic. He was one of the ablest of Restoration dramatists. In verse he established the heroic couplet as an instrument of satiric expression. In prose he was direct, lucid, vigorous. He dictated the literary taste in his own lifetime, and in the following century he had a literary reincarnation in the waspish satirist, Alexander Pope.

DUNBAR, William (1460?–1520?) was a Franciscan friar who later became an unofficial laureate in the court of James IV of Scotland. A virtuoso in metrics and rhetorical ornaments (especially alliteration), he was the most versatile if not the greatest of the Scottish Chaucerians. Most of his poems belong to the first decade of the sixteenth century. *The Thistle and the Rose,* modelled on Chaucer's *Parliament of Fowls,* and *The Golden Targe* are conventional dream allegories. Contrasting with their aureate artificiality is the simplicity of the *Lament for the Makers,* an elegy on the British poets from Chaucer to Dunbar's day—with the well-known refrain "Timor Mortis conturbat me." *The Dance of the Seven Deadly Sins,* despite its artificial form, has the grotesque realism of Burns' *Tam O'Shanter,* while *The Two Married Women and the Widow,* a coarse fabliau, and *The Ballad of Kind Kittok,* the rollicking rhyme of an alewife's thirst in Heaven, would have delighted Chaucer's Wife of Bath.

DUNSANY, Lord (Edward John Moreton Drax Plunkett, eighteenth baron Dunsany) (1878–1958) was an Irish playwright and short-story writer who dwelt often in the realm of mystery and romance, drawing heavily on Celtic and Oriental mythology. Such popular plays as *The Gods of the Mountain* (1911) and *A Night at an Inn* (1916) are effective theater. Some of the best of his stories appear in *A Dreamer's Tales* (1910) and *Tales of Wonder* (1916).

D'URFEY, Thomas (1653–1723) was a carefree denizen of Grub Street, familiarly known to king and commoner alike as plain Tom D'Urfey. He spawned every conceivable kind of composition, bombastic tragedies (*The Siege of Memphis,* 1676); bawdy comedies (*Madam Fickle,* 1676; *The Virtuous Wife,* 1679); political satires; fawning panegyrics of royalty; and multitudinous songs and ballads. The most prolific and popular ballad-writer of his time, he compiled a valuable song-book, *Wit and Mirth, or Pills to Purge Melancholy* (1719–20).

DYER, Sir Edward (d. 1607) was a courtier and diplomat, a favorite of the Earl of Leicester and a great friend of Sir Philip Sidney. He is remembered as the author of a single lyric of contentment, "My mind to me a kingdom is."

DYER, John (1700?–58) was a Welshman who turned from painting to the ministry. In two slight early poems, *Grongar Hill* and *The Country Walk,* both published in 1726, he described natural scenery with a freshness and accuracy uncommon in his time. In two later, more ambitious poems, *The Ruins of Rome* (1740) and *The Fleece* (1757), he was less successful. *The Fleece* is a didactic poem in four books on the wool industry, a subject which Dr. Johnson found singularly unpoetic.

E

EADMER (d. 1124?), a Canterbury monk, wrote a Latin history of his own times down to 1122, *Historia Novorum in Anglia,* and a Latin life of his intimate friend St. Anselm. The history is notable among early chronicles for its author's decision to limit himself to contemporary events.

EARLE, John (1601?–65), Bishop of Salisbury, was the chief author of *Microcosmography, or a Piece of the World Discovered* (1628). Like earlier works by Joseph Hall and Sir Thomas Overbury, this was a collection of "characters," or thumbnail portraits of social types, in the manner of the Greek philosopher, Theophrastus (d. 287? B.C.). In general, Earle's characters have more in common with the sober moralizings of Hall than with the lighter, homelier sketches of Overbury.

EDGEWORTH, Maria (1767–1849) was the daughter of Richard Lovell Edgeworth, Irish educational expert. He inspired most of her work and collaborated in some. After helping him with *Practical Education* (1798), she turned naturally to teaching through novel and short-story. While many of the characters in her novels are lessons on legs, the fascinating Irish figures in *Castle Rackrent* (1800), *The Absentee* (1812), and *Ormond* (1817) are genuine. *Castle Rackrent,* usually called her best, depicts the degeneration of a late eighteenth-century Irish household under several different squires. The didactic short-stories of *The Parent's Assistant* (1795) and *Early Lessons* (1801–15), with their simple, black-and-white contrasts between good and evil, established her as a guide for the nursery.

EDWARDS, Richard (1523?–66). This musician and playwright was "master of the children of the chapel royal" in the reign of Elizabeth. He wrote *Damon and Pythias* (1564?), a rhymed "tragical comedy" on the classical legend of friendship, and edited *The Paradise of Dainty Devices* (1576), a popular Elizabethan anthology that contains ninety-nine poems.

EGAN, Pierce, the elder (1772–1849) was the author of *Tom and Jerry, Life in London, or the Day and Night Scenes of Jerry Hawthorn Esq. and his elegant friend Corinthian Tom* (1821–3). This immensely popular guide to the sporting life of the metropolis was illustrated by the brothers Cruikshank; on the stage the characters became popular in a play by William Thomas Moncrieff. *Tom and Jerry* is no longer widely read, but its heroes,

Tom and Jerry, survive as the name of a rum drink, a verb meaning "to indulge in drunken roistering," and an adjective "designating a low tavern." As an authentic depicter of London lowlife, Egan is a forerunner of Dickens. His son, **Pierce Egan, the younger** (1814–80), wrote cheap novels.

ELIA. Pseudonym of **Charles Lamb.**

ELIOT, George (1819–80) was born **Mary Ann Evans.** Her early education was conventional; laced in the strict Calvinism of her father, she believed that theater-going was wicked. In her twenties, however, her narrow world widened to include certain unorthodox Coventry intellectuals. Under their influence she travelled far from the safe harbor of her childhood religion. She translated from the German Strauss' unconventional *Life of Jesus* (1846) and wrote skeptical essays for the radical *Westminster Review,* a journal which she served for a time as assistant editor (1851–3). In 1854 she consented to live with the philosopher-journalist, George Henry Lewes. After his death in 1879, George Eliot married J. W. Cross, who later wrote her biography.

Although her poetic drama, *The Spanish Gypsy* (1868), and her last essays, *Impressions of Theophrastus Such* (1879), still have some readers, her real fame depends on her fiction. Inspired by Lewes, she made her début as George Eliot with *Amos Barton* (*Blackwood's,* 1857), the first of her *Scenes from Clerical Life* (1858). Three full-length novels followed rapidly: *Adam Bede* (1859), *The Mill on the Floss* (1860), and *Silas Marner* (1861). In these and in the later *Middlemarch* (1871–2) she drew naturally on her early life; for example, Adam Bede is a partial portrait of her father, Dinah Morris in the same novel is her aunt, and the troubled childhood of Maggie and Tom Tulliver is that of the author and her brother. In seeking material farther afield she was less successful. Although she grew old digging for *Romola* (1863), her historical novel of fifteenth-century Florence does not come to life. In the political novel *Felix Holt, the Radical* (1866) and the Zionist plea *Daniel Deronda* (1876), the sermon swallows the story.

As widely cultured as any woman of her age, George Eliot saw clearly the pettiness of rural life in her native Warwickshire. Yet beneath her realistic satire lie deep veins of humor and sympathy. She was a stern moralist, earnestly preaching Carlylean resignation to duty and the purifying effect of sorrow. Since storytelling is incidental to her main purpose, she regularly neglects her narrative to moralize and sometimes cannot manage her plot without calling on Providence. But in the searching analysis of the minds of her characters she was far ahead of her time.

ELIOT, T(homas) S(tearns) (1888–   ) was born in St. Louis, Missouri, and took an A.B. and an M.A. at Harvard (1909, 1910). But since 1915 he has made his home in England, where he has served as schoolteacher, bank-clerk, assistant editor of the *Egoist,* co-founder and editor of the *Criterion,* and a director of the publishing firm of Faber and Faber. He became a British subject in 1927. T. S. Eliot's first important poem, *The Love Song of J. Alfred Prufrock,* was conceived when he was still an undergraduate and published in the magazine *Poetry* in 1915. His first collection, *Prufrock and Other Observations,* followed in 1917. In *Poems* (1919) appeared *Gerontian,* the soliloquy of "an old man in a dry month," along with such shorter pieces as the satirical *Hippopotamus* and the bizarre *Sweeney among the Nightingales.* In *The Waste Land* (1922) and *The Hollow Men* (1925) Eliot expressed his despair over the utter emptiness of contemporary civilization. In *Ash-Wednesday* (1930) he struck a more affirmative note, in tune with his conversion to Anglo-Catholicism. His *Murder in the Cathedral,* a highly original verse drama on the life of Thomas à Becket, was produced successfully in 1935. *Four Quartets* (1943), a book of four long poems in a new form, showed that he has lost neither his poetic power nor his zest for experimentation.

Eliot is a complex product of diverse literary influences—the French symbolists, Ezra Pound, the Elizabethans, John Donne—and the characteristics of his poetry, the symbolism, the allusiveness, the sudden shifts in key, have made him a "difficult" poet for most readers. Through the mysterious allusion-jungle of *The Waste Land,* few have followed him, although his fondest admirers have liberally provided them with maps. On the other hand, many have felt the horror and humor and grotesque beauty of his shorter poems, and no one can deny his importance as a major influence on modern poetry. In addition to his poetry, Eliot has also published some of the most distinguished criticism of our time. A self-confessed "classicist in literature," he has written re-evaluations of such diverse figures as Dante, Shakespeare, Donne, Dryden, and Kipling. His *Selected Essays* appeared in 1932.

ELLIOTT, Ebenezer (1781–1849) was a Sheffield iron-founder who helped to swell the chorus of protest which arose from the English working classes after Waterloo. In *Corn-Law Rhymes* (1831) he protested bitterly against the celebrated series of tariff acts which, by limiting the importation of foreign wheat under the pretext of protecting agriculture at home, caused widespread distress among the poor of England. Carlyle praised him for his courage and sincerity but cautioned him for imitating the verse of George Crabbe and Felicia Hemans. Although Elliott wrote other poems, he is permanently classified as the "Corn-Law-Rhymer."

ELLIS, George (1753–1815) was one of the collaborators in *Criticisms on the Rolliad, a Poem* (1784–90), a series of Whig verse satires on Tory politicians. Ellis later changed sides and collaborated with George Canning and J. H. Frere in the Tory *Anti-Jacobin* (1797–8), a magazine famous for its parodies.

ELLIS, (Henry) Havelock (1859–1939) began his career as a literary critic. He edited Landor's *Imaginary Conversations* (1886), Ibsen's plays (1887), and some of the volumes in the useful *Mermaid* series of Elizabethan and Restoration dramatists (1887–9). He is best known, however, for his *Studies in the Psychology of Sex* (1897–1928), a monumental life work which has had an immeasurable influence in liberating modern life and literature from Victorian taboos.

ELYOT, Sir Thomas (1499?–1546). His fame now rests on *The Book named the Governor* (1531), one of the earliest educational treatises following the classical renaissance in Europe. Planned specifically to mold youths into statesmen, it has more in common with *The Courtier* (1528) of the Italian Castiglione than with later educational treatises of Ascham and Mulcaster. Elyot plans the ideal curriculum, specifically tabooing football, and discourses, with ample classical allusions, on politics and morals. Whether or not the book made any governors, it was apparently the author's ticket of admission to a diplomatic career.

ERVINE, St. John (Greer) (1883–   ) is an Irish playwright, critic, and novelist. During the early part of his career he was associated with the Abbey Theater in Dublin. There in 1915 appeared *John Ferguson,* a fatalistic tragedy of an old man's blind faith in God. Its revival in New York in 1919 saved the Theater Guild from dissolution. Among his other plays are *Jane Clegg* (1912), a domestic tragedy, and *The First Mrs. Fraser* (1929), a drawing-room comedy. His best-known novel is *Changing Winds* (1917).

ETHEREGE, Sir George (1635?–91) was the earliest of the major figures of Restoration Comedy. *The Comical Revenge, or Love* *in a Tub* (1664) is a hybrid play—a prose jumble of drunkenness and disguise mixed with a clumsy verse sub-plot on the love-and-honor theme. But in *She Would if She Could* (1668) farce has yielded ground to wit; verse has given way entirely to prose; the unreal world of false heroics has been replaced by genuine Restoration London, where honor is a joke, not the horn of a persistent dilemma. *The Man of Mode, or Sir Fopling Flutter* (1676), relying even less on situation, more on effervescent dialogue playfully mocking the follies of the town, is the closest of the three to the temper of Congreve's *Way of the World* (1700). The little that is known about the life of "Gentle George"—much of it gathered from personal records of an experience as envoy to Ratisbon—indicates that his interest in the carefree rakes and flirts of his comedies was not purely academic.

ETTRICK SHEPHERD, THE. Epithet applied to James Hogg.

EUSDEN, Laurence (1688–1730) was one of the obscurest of England's obscure poets laureate. The Duke of Newcastle appointed him on the death of Nicholas Rowe in 1718. In the previous year Eusden had written *A Poem on the Marriage of His Grace the Duke of Newcastle,* thereby demonstrating his fitness as an anniversifier.

EVANS, Mary Ann. See **ELIOT, George.**

EVELYN, John (1620–1706). An early member of the Royal Society, Evelyn wrote treatises on a diversity of subjects—smoke abatement, engraving, arboriculture, navigation, numismatics—to mention but a few. He also wrote an affectionate life of his friend Mrs. Godolphin (published 1847). But he is best known for his *Diary.* In this famous work, first published in incomplete form in 1818, Evelyn recorded impressions of his travels in Europe and events and personalities of seventeenth-century England. His chronicle of over sixty years (1641–1706) is valuable but far less readable than the nine-year diary (1660–9) of his friend, Samuel Pepys. Pepys wrote as an individual harassed by most of the frailties to which the flesh is heir, Evelyn as a cultivated gentleman with an inquiring mind.

F

FABYAN, Robert (d. 1513) was one of the earliest English chroniclers. In his *Concordance of Histories* (1516), usually called *Fabyan's Chronicle,* he traced English history from the time of Brutus, legendary founder of the British race, down to the accession of Henry VII in 1485. The early parts, borrowed from other historians, are sketchy and untrustworthy, but, since the author had once been Sheriff of London, the sections dealing with the London of his own day are valuable.

FAIRCHILD, Cicily Isabel. See **WEST, Rebecca.**

FALCONER, William (1732–69), a mariner, wrote *The Shipwreck* (1762), a narrative poem which went through an incredible number of editions in its first half century. There is little reality in the poem to support the tradition that its author actually experienced the wreck he narrates. He was, however, drowned in a shipwreck.

FARADAY, Michael (1791–1867) was a great physicist whose experiments, particularly his discovery of magneto-electricity, paved the way for revolutionary changes in the industrial world. He was an excellent lecturer, and his *Experimental Researches in Electricity* (1839–55) and *Experimental Researches in Chemistry and Physics* (1859) are written in a clear, readable prose.

FARQUHAR, George (1678–1707). After failing in his native Ireland both as a college student and as an actor, Farquhar began a brief career of play-writing in London with a comedy distinguished mainly by its name, *Love and a Bottle* (1698). The remaining seven show an improvement that culminated in *The Recruiting Officer* (1706) and *The Beaux' Stratagem* (1707), two plays which took comedy out of the lovers' lanes and drawing rooms of London to the taverns and highways of rural England. The swaggering recruiting officers Captain Plume and Sergeant Kite were probably drawn from Farquhar's own army experience. *The Beaux' Stratagem,* in which Aimwell and Archer go a-fortune-hunting, was penned in six weeks of poverty and sickness. Its author lived only long enough to hear the first burst of approval. Generally acclaimed as his masterpiece, it is a fitting swan song to Restoration Comedy.

FELTHAM or **FELLTHAM, Owen** (1602?–68?). His *Resolves; Divine, Moral, and Political* (1628) is a collection of sententious moral essays, many of which show the influence of Bacon. Some of them are "characters." They enjoyed tremendous popularity in their day but are now almost as little read as Feltham's verse.

FERGUSON, Sir Samuel (1810–86) was an Irish poet with a love for early Irish folklore. He was one of the precursors of the Irish Renaissance which came in full glory at the end of his century.

Among his poems are *Thomas Davis* (1845), an elegy on the death of a famous nationalist leader; *Congal* (1872), an epic of the last stand of Celtic paganism against Christianity; and *Conary* (1880), a narrative poem based on an Irish folk tale.

FERGUSSON, Robert (1750–74) died in a madhouse at 24, only a year after the appearance of his first collection of poems. Like Burns, he wrote naturally in his native Scots dialect. Fergusson's *Farmer's Ingle* suggested the title and general plan of *The Cotter's Saturday Night.* Burns hailed him as his master, and, in the *Epistle to J. Lapraik,* called him "bauld an' slee"—bold and clever. Although such nature lyrics as *To the Bee* and *The Gowdspink* have been praised, Fergusson was primarily a city poet—the carefree bard of the "Auld Reekie" or old town of Edinburgh.

FERRIER, Susan Edmonstone (1782–1854) was one of the founders of a school of Scottish domestic fiction. Her three novels, *Marriage* (1818), *The Inheritance* (1824), and *Destiny, or the Chief's Daughter* (1831), reveal skill in depicting humble village types.

FIELD, Nathaniel (1587–1633) was a Jacobean actor and playwright. Ben Jonson spoke highly of Nat Field's acting, and Field's two racy comedies, *A Woman is a Weathercock* (1609–10) and *Amends for Ladies* (c. 1610–11), show a distinct debt to Jonson. Field also collaborated with Massinger on *The Fatal Dowry* (c. 1618–9) and may have had a hand in several plays of Beaumont and Fletcher.

FIELDING, Henry (1707–54). This great English novelist began his literary career as a playwright. Between 1728, when he settled in London, and 1737, when the Walpole government refused him a license to continue as manager of the Haymarket Theater, he wrote more than two dozen dramatic pieces, mostly comedies, farces, and burlesques. A few people today know *Pasquin* (1736) and *The Historical Register for 1736* (1737), two satirical medleys on the follies of the time. Most readers know only *The Tragedy of Tragedies, or the Life and Death of Tom Thumb the Great* (1730), an unrestrained burlesque of dramatic conventions, containing passing shots at no fewer than forty-two plays from Dryden to James Thomson.

When Fielding abandoned playwriting he resumed the study of law begun years earlier at the University of Leyden and was admitted to the bar in 1740. In that year appeared the first part of *Pamela, or Virtue Rewarded,* a first novel by an earnest, hard-working printer named Samuel Richardson. Fielding, whose robust, manly, Rabelaisian nature was hardly attuned to the delicate distresses of sentimental femininity, saw in *Pamela* a perfect target for burlesque. Whether he wrote the bawdy *Apology for the Life of Mrs. Shamela Andrews* (1741) is a matter of dispute. But he did write *The History of the Adventures of Joseph Andrews and his Friend Mr. Abraham Adams* (1742). This began as an obvious parody, with Pamela's tearful trials at the hands of Mr. B. metamorphosed into the temptations of her brother Joseph in the household of his employer, Lady Booby. But not long after Parson Adams entered the story in Chapter III the color began to change, and by Chapter X Fielding had cut himself adrift from *Pamela* and sailed off into an independent novel. In spite of a busy life in politics and journalism, Fielding wrote three more novels before his death. *Jonathan Wild* (1743) is a cynical commentary on sham greatness, imbedded in the mock-heroic "biography" of a notorious eighteenth-century outlaw. *Tom Jones* (1749), usually called his masterpiece, is the story of a thoroughly normal young man with a warm heart and feet of clay. *Amelia* (1751) is the somber tale of the marriage of a virtuous heroine and a penniless weakling; the story is the vehicle for attacks on social evils—the law courts, sponging-houses, prisons—which the author had encountered at first hand in his experience as Justice of the Peace for Westminster.

Both in theory, as expressed in the critical interchapters of *Tom Jones,* and in practice, Fielding made a momentous contribution to the development of the novel in England. He gave form to the novel by constructing, in *Tom Jones,* at least, a beautifully balanced dramatic plot. He gave it a definite purpose by using it as the vehicle for satire and reform, chastising with special zeal self-seekers and hypocrites. He helped to make the novel real by drawing living people; Square and Thwackum may be mouthpieces, Sophia Western and Amelia too untarnished, but Parson Adams, Tom Jones, Squire Western, and Molly Seagrim are alive. In his own century Fielding's novels were not so popular as those of the sentimental printer whom he parodied. Today the opposite is true.

FIELDING, Sarah (1710–68) was one of the earliest of Samuel Richardson's literary descendants. Her *Adventures of David Simple* (1744) is a sentimental novel about a delicate man of feeling who "Travels through London and Westminster in Search of a Real Friend," and, just when he is about to resign himself to utter disillusionment, finds three—one of whom, Camilla, he blissfully weds. An introduction to the first edition was written by the author's brother Henry, the greatest of Richardson's parodists.

FINCH, Anne. See **WINCHILSEA.**

FIONA MACLEOD. Pseudonym of **William Sharp.**

FISHER, John (1459?–1535), Bishop of Rochester and Chancellor of Cambridge University, was beheaded for refusing to recognize Henry VIII as supreme head of the Church. His English works, consisting mostly of sermons, include *A Sermon against the Pernicious Doctrine of Martin Luther* (1521?). His prose is full of artificial ornament, but as a conscious literary artist he was far ahead of his time.

FITZGERALD, Edward (1809–83). This country gentleman and amateur yachtsman was unhampered by worldly employment. He had time to render into English, plays of Calderon, Aeschylus, and Sophocles, time to talk books with his intimate friends, Tennyson and Thackeray. A single poem made him famous. *The Rubáiyát* (1859) is a coherent paraphrase (in quatrains rhyming *aaba*) of the isolated "rubā'īs" of Omar Khayyám, a Persian poet and astronomer who died in 1123. Fitzgerald molded the "tent-maker's" lines into an original meditation, mixing solemn thoughts on Time and Death with devil-may-care praise of the life of love, laughter, and wine. Few poems have appeared in as many de luxe editions, few are more supremely quotable. "A Book of Verses underneath the Bough . . . Ah, take the Cash, and let the Credit go . . . The Moving finger writes . . . Yet Ah, that Spring should vanish with the Rose"—such phrases still haunt the minds of many who have never heard of Edward Fitzgerald.

FLATMAN, Thomas (1637–88) was a poet and painter. He wrote funeral odes, hymns, and songs. His shorter poems were published in successive volumes under the title *Poems and Songs* (1674–86). One of his happiest productions is the half-serious lyric "O the sad day!"

FLECKER, James Elroy (1884–1915) was in government service in Turkey and Syria from 1910 to 1913, and much of his poetry has an Oriental flavor. Among his best-known works are *The Golden Journey to Samarkand* (1913), *The Old Ships* (1915), and *Hassan,* a play (1922). His collected poems were published in 1916.

FLECKNOE, Richard (c. 1620–78?) was a literary Irish priest. His own writings, including *A Short Discourse on the English Stage* (1664), appended to *Love's Kingdom,* a play, are less important than two works in which he was pilloried. Andrew Marvell wrote a lampoon about him in 1645, and it later suggested Dryden's *Mac Flecknoe* (1682), in which Flecknoe cedes his throne as ruler of "all the realms of nonsense" to Thomas Shadwell.

FLEMING, Marjorie (1803–11) was the precocious daughter of James Fleming of Kirkcaldy, Scotland. Under the loving and patient instruction of an older cousin, Isabel, she learned to read and write early, and before her death at eight years she had composed a quaint diary and numerous "poems"—most of them on historical themes. "Pet Marjorie," as she was called, was a favorite of Sir Walter Scott and the subject of a sentimental essay by Dr. John Brown (1810–82).

FLETCHER, Giles, the elder (1549?–1611) was the uncle of John Fletcher, the playwright, and the father of two poets, Giles the younger and Phineas. He wrote a book on Russia (*The Russ Commonwealth,* 1591), where he had served as envoy, and a sequence of fifty-two allegorical sonnets, *Licia, or Poems of Love* (1593).

FLETCHER, Giles, the younger (1588?–1623) was the son of Giles, the elder, and brother of Phineas. He was a follower of Spenser. His masterpiece, *Christ's Victory and Triumph in Heaven and Earth* (1610), applies the allegorical method of *The Faerie Queene* to a religious subject and is written in an eight-line abridgment of the Spenserian stanza. Although the dropping of the seventh line detracts somewhat from the sweep of the stanza, the poem is marked by majestic music. Despite metaphysical subtleties, it shows a strong religious fervor.

FLETCHER, John (1579–1625). The dramatic partnership of John Fletcher and his close friend Francis Beaumont (1585?–1616) is commented on in the entry under Beaumont's name. But both Beaumont and Fletcher wrote independently and are entitled to separate consideration as poets and playwrights. This is particularly true of John Fletcher, for he outlived his friend by nine years and continued to write until he died of the plague. His father was John Fletcher, Dean of Peterborough and afterwards Bishop of London, and he was the most famous of a family of distinguished scholars and poets. As a lyric poet he outshone Beaumont. In the plays in which he collaborated with his younger friend—several of which are commented on in the Beaumont entry—he was more flexible and musical in his blank verse, more humorous and more earthy in his plot-episodes, and more realistic in his characterizations. The best comedy which he wrote alone is *Rule a Wife and Have a Wife* (1624). *The Faithful Shepherdess* (1608–9) is probably the best of all Jacobean examples of the Arcadian tragi-comedy. It is fundamentally sweet and moral, but coarse almost to obscenity in some of the lustful episodes and characters. *The Wild Goose Chase* (1619–22), with a farcical plot in which a predatory lady finally traps a husband, belongs in its mood and hilarious unrestraint to the Restoration comedy of manners and formed the basis of Farquhar's *Inconstant* (1702). In writing *The Beggars' Bush* (c. 1615–22), a strange, romantic comedy filled with beggars' cant, Fletcher collaborated with Massinger. And, finally, he seems to have had a finger, at least, in *The Two Noble Kinsmen* (1613–6), which is usually *not* assigned to Shakespeare, and in *Henry VIII* (1613), which usually is.

FLETCHER, Phineas (1582–1650) like his brother Giles, the younger, imitated Spenser. His seven *Sylva Poetica* (1633) are an inferior *Shepheardes Calender* with fishermen instead of shepherds. In his ambitious, twelve-canto *Purple Island* (1633), he used a seven-line modification of the Spenserian stanza and borrowed allegorical hints from *The Faerie Queene*. Starting with the concept of the human body as a purple island whereon the virtues and vices are at war, he pushed the analogy between geography and anatomy to a bizarre extreme.

FLORIO, John (1553?–1625) was a London language teacher of Italian descent. He poured his passionate love of words into an Italian-English dictionary (1598) and a famous translation of Montaigne's *Essais* (1603). The translation is really a creative paraphrase, containing as much of the egotistic, ebullient phrase-maker, Florio, as of Montaigne. It marks the beginning of a major French influence on English literature and philosophy.

FOOTE, Samuel (1720–77) was a versatile man of the theater known to his contemporaries as "the English Aristophanes." He bought the Little Theater in the Haymarket in 1747 and built the new one there in 1767. Even after losing a leg in 1766, he carried on, displaying an amazing gift for mimicry in the rôles which he played himself and a prolific talent for burlesque in the many short after-pieces which he wrote. Among the subjects of his ridicule were: the Methodist preacher George Whitefield

(*The Minor,* 1760); Elizabeth Linley, the singer who later married Sheridan (*The Maid of Bath,* 1771); sentimental comedy (*The Handsome Housemaid, or Piety in Pattens,* 1773); and the letters of Lord Chesterfield (*The Cozeners,* 1774).

FORD, Ford Madox (1873–1939) changed his last name from Hueffer to Ford in 1919. At the turn of the century he joined with Joseph Conrad in a revolt against the artificial method of narration in the traditional nineteenth-century novel. He collaborated with Conrad in three novels: *The Inheritors* (1901), *Romance* (1903), and *The Nature of a Crime* (1924). The best known of his independent novels are those in the satirical series on the First World War, *Some Do Not* (1924), *No More Parades* (1925), *A Man Could Stand Up* (1926), and *Last Post* (1928). He also wrote poems, critical studies, and reminiscences, and, as editor of the *English Review,* "discovered" a number of promising writers.

FORD, John (1586–1639). Four of Ford's plays were "unluckily burned or put under pye bottoms" by Betsy Baker, antiquary Warburton's infamous cook. Those which have survived include: *The Witch of Edmonton* (1621), a domestic tragedy written in collaboration with Dekker and Rowley; *The Lover's Melancholy* (1628), a romantic comedy showing the influence of Burton's *Anatomy;* and *Perkin Warbeck* (c. 1629–34), a good historical play about the fifteenth-century impostor who masqueraded as a son of Edward IV. Violent, abnormal passion is the theme of each of Ford's three tragedies. *Love's Sacrifice* (c. 1625–33) deals with the incestuous love of Fernando for his sister, Bianca; *'Tis Pity She's a Whore* (c. 1625–33) with incest between Giovanni and his sister Arabella; *The Broken Heart* (c. 1625–33) with a brother (Ithocles) who forces his sister (Penthea) to marry against her will. Like many modern writers, Ford was a serious student of abnormal psychology; like few of them he had a rare sense of the melody of language. But he seems fatalistically to have regarded physical passion as a substitute for moral laws, and he portrayed it with painful horror. Hence he is traditionally regarded as the epitome of decadence in the Elizabethan drama.

FORSTER, E(dward) M(organ) (1879–   ). Although he has published only five novels over a period of nearly forty years, E. M. Forster is considered by many discriminating readers as England's greatest living novelist. Whether he is writing of England, as in *The Longest Journey* (1907) and *Howards End*

(1910), of Italy, as in *Where Angels Fear to Tread* (1905) and *A Room with a View* (1908), or of India, as in *A Passage to India* (1924), Forster dwells habitually in the delicate thought processes of sensitive individuals, studying their struggles to adjust to unfriendly environments. His most widely read novel, *A Passage to India,* is more than an amusing satire on British imperialism. It is a sympathetic analysis of the conflicting philos‹›ophies of human beings with totally different environments, a subtle sociological study of a complex inter-racial problem. Forster's *Aspects of the Novel* (1927) is based on a course of lectures given at Trinity College, Cambridge. *Abinger Harvest* (1926) is a collection of his critical essays. In 1943 Lionel Trilling published a brilliant study of Forster which has stimulated a recent revival of interest in the novels.

FORSTER, John (1812–76) was an energetic Victorian journalist who wrote a number of first-rate biographies, including lives of Goldsmith (1854), Landor (1869), Dickens (1872–4), and an unfinished life of Swift (1876). Because of Forster's close friendship with Dickens, his life of the novelist is especially valuable.

FORTESCUE, Sir John (1394?–1476?), Chief Justice of the King's Bench under Henry VI, has been called England's first constitutional lawyer. He wrote more in Latin than in English. His chief works are *De Natura Legis Naturae* (written 1461–3?) and *De Laudibus Legum Angliae* (written 1471?). These were not published until centuries after his death.

FOX, George (1624–91), founder of the Society of Friends (1648–50) was son of a poorly educated weaver. He had trouble with spelling and grammar, and a large part of his *Journal* was dictated to Thomas Ellwood and other Quakers, who edited it for publication in 1694. For the simple directness of its style and the sincerity of its message, it deserves comparison with a contemporary spiritual autobiography, Bunyan's *Grace Abounding* (1666).

FOXE, John (1516–87) was a Protestant clergyman and controversialist of Salisbury, who is known almost solely for a famous sermon, *On Christ Crucified* (1570), and a popular history of Christian martyrs. The lengthy title of this martyrology is *Acts and Monuments of these Latter and Perilous Times,* but it came to be universally known as *Foxe's Book of Martyrs.* Foxe wrote the book in Latin, but translated it into English. The first English edition appeared in 1563, just five years after the death of Mary Tudor, Catholic queen of England. Although the first sections of the book contain some account of martyrs of the early Christian Church, Foxe naturally devoted ample space to a dramatic series of tales of martyrdoms in Queen Mary's reign. The *Book of Martyrs* is much more sensational than accurate; it is, in fact, a narrative tractate against the Catholics. With Protestants who loved to suffer vicariously by reading accounts of Protestant martyrdoms it became very popular. Episodes paraphrased from it even found their way across the Atlantic and into *The New England Primer,* where they could strengthen the faith of young descendants of Protestant emigrants to America.

FRANCIS, Sir Philip (1740–1818). See **JUNIUS.**

FRAZER, Sir James George (1854–1941) was professor of social anthropology at the University of Liverpool from 1907 to 1922. His monumental masterpiece, *The Golden Bough* (1890–1915), a twelve-volume "study of comparative religion," is one of the classics of modern scholarship.

FREEMAN, Edward Augustus (1823–92), professor of history at Oxford, was one of the major historians of the Victorian era. In his major work, *The History of the Norman Conquest of England* (1867–79), he emphasized the Germanic nature of English institutions both before and after the Conquest. His style was undistinguished, and many of his conclusions have been altered.

FRERE, John Hookham (1769–1846) was a contributor, along with George Canning and George Ellis, to the *Anti-Jacobin* (1797–8), a short-lived anti-revolutionary magazine. In its pages he collaborated with Canning on *The Loves of the Triangles, The Friend of Humanity and the Knife Grinder,* and *The Rovers,* celebrated parodies respectively of Erasmus Darwin, Southey, and German drama. Frere also composed, under the double pseudonym of William and Robert Whistlecraft, an unfinished mock-epic poem on King Arthur (1817–18), the manner and form of which inspired Byron's *Beppo* and *Don Juan.* He is also known for his metrical translations of the most important comedies of Aristophanes.

FROUDE, James Anthony (1818–94) was a historian and biographer. His long career included the editorship of *Fraser's Magazine* (1860–74) and an Oxford professorship (1892–94). As a youth, he was influenced by John Henry Newman and studied for the Church. His change from orthodoxy to skepticism is reflected in his semi-autobiographical novel, *The Nemesis of Faith* (1849). In the same year he met Carlyle, who helped to direct his course as a historian. The imposing *History of England from the Fall of Wolsey to the Defeat of the Spanish Armada* (1856-70) is notable for its clear, readable prose and its dramatic picturization of the characters and incidents of the time; it is traditionally damned for inaccuracy and unfairness. As official executor of Carlyle's literary remains, Froude treated the domesticities of Cheyne Row with an openness which shocked his readers and began an endless controversy. But whatever the truth or ethics of his later disclosures, the central biography of Carlyle (1882-4) is one of the best biographies in the language.

FROUDE, Richard Hurrell (1803-36), older brother of J. A. Froude, was one of the leaders in the Oxford Movement, the great nineteenth-century reaction against growing rationalism in the Church of England. Along with Newman, Keble, and others, Froude contributed sacred poems and prose tracts respectively to *Lyra Apostolica* (1836) and *Tracts for the Times* (1833-5), two literary monuments to the early years of the movement. The publication of his *Literary Remains* (1837, 1839) turned many against the cause.

FULLER, Thomas (1608-61). Still in his early thirties at the outbreak of the Civil War between king and Parliament, Fuller was already a popular London preacher. During the war he was a chaplain in the Royalist army; after the Restoration he became chaplain to Charles II. That his pen flowed optimistically through the darkest years is shown by such good-natured titles as *Good Thoughts in Bad Times* (1645), *Good Thoughts in Worse Times* (1647), and *Mixed Contemplations in Better Times* (1660). He also wrote: *The Holy War* (1639), a history of the Crusades; *The Holy State and the Profane State* (1642), a study of good and bad characters in history; a *Church History of Britain* (1655-6); and the unfinished *History of the Worthies of England* (1662). The *Worthies* is his most famous and most characteristic work. In it he set out to extol the celebrities of England county by county, pausing at will to sprinkle the page with curious, often amusing anecdotes and unforgivable puns. He has more in common with the genial antiquary Sir Thomas Browne than with melancholy Burton or gloomy Jeremy Taylor. Coleridge admired him, and Lamb reverently aped his eccentric stylistic tricks.

G

GALSWORTHY, John (1867–1933) is widely known as the creator of the Forsyte clan. *The Man of Property,* first of the Forsyte novels, appeared in 1906. It was republished—together with *In Chancery* (1920), *To Let* (1921), and two short interludes—as part of *The Forsyte Saga* (1922). The family story had thus far been carried from 1886 to 1920. In *A Modern Comedy* (1929)—including *The White Monkey* (1924), *The Silver Spoon* (1926), and *Swan Song* (1928)—Galsworthy continued the story through the chaos of the middle-twenties, down to the eventual death of Soames Forsyte, the Man of Property. Most critics prefer the original *Forsyte Saga* to its sequel. As a work of art, *The Forsyte Saga* has its shortcomings; many readers are annoyed by the continual flitting from branch to branch on the family tree and bored by the interminable musings of such champion ruminators as Old Jolyon. But as "a narrative study of a class [the British upper-middle class], through the doings of a typically large clan within that class"—those are Galsworthy's own words—the book has undoubted sociological value. "Forsytism"—with its tribal instinct, its possessive love of property, its studied resistance to natural emotion and imperviousness to all artistic feeling—has become, like Sinclair Lewis' "Babbittry," a permanent symbol.

Galsworthy's first play, *The Silver Box,* appeared in the same year as *The Man of Property* (1906), and after that he turned out plays even more regularly than his novels. In his best plays he is a social reformer, generally sympathetic with the underdog, but too often sitting on the fence with a pair of scales earnestly trying to mete out equal justice to both sides. He wrote about the Law's predilection for the rich (*The Silver Box*), the struggle between capital and labor (*Strife,* 1909), and the injustice of the prison system (*Justice,* 1910). But in one of his most popular plays, *Escape* (1926), he began as if to treat injustice and ended by writing a genial, quasi-philosophical pursuit drama of the Bulldog Drummond stamp. To many Americans who have known the incisive novels of John Dos Passos, and the bitter, hard-hitting plays of Clifford Odets, Galsworthy's novels and plays are insufferably stuffy and genteel. But to others he fully deserved the Nobel prize which he received in 1932.

GALT, John (1779–1839) was the Scottish novelist who traveled part of the way with Byron on his early tour of the Mediterranean (1809–11). He was highly regarded by Byron, Carlyle, Coleridge, and Scott for his harsh, ironic novels of life in Scotland, *Annals* *of the Parish* (1821), *The Provost* (1822), and *The Entail* (1823). The last is usually considered his best.

GARNETT, David (1892–) is the son of the literary critic, **Edward Garnett** (1868–1937) and grandson of **Richard Garnett,** librarian and scholar (1835–1906). He is best known for his fantastic novels, *Lady into Fox* (1922) and *A Man in the Zoo* (1924). The first, generally considered as his masterpiece, is the story of a woman's metamorphosis into a red fox and of her husband's efforts to adjust to her vixenish temperament. His *War in the Air* (1941) is based on his experiences as a flight lieutenant and staff officer in the Intelligence at the Air Ministry in London.

GARRICK, David (1717–79). When Garrick first came up to London in 1737 with an unknown hack-writer named Samuel Johnson, he was merely one of three obscure youths who had made up the student body of Johnson's short-lived private school in Edial, Staffordshire. When he died, he was the most celebrated actor in England. As manager of Drury Lane from 1747 to 1776, Garrick did more to direct the course of the English drama than any other man in his century. A great performer in both tragic and comic rôles, he led the trend away from static declamation to mobile, relatively natural playing. At the same time his intimate friendship with distinguished men like Johnson, Burke, and Reynolds brought greater esteem to his profession. Moderns have trouble reconciling Garrick's idolatry of Shakespeare with the irreverent adaptations in which he performed; but his service as an interpreter and popularizer of *Richard III, Hamlet, King Lear,* and *Macbeth* far outweighed the evil of his editorial "improvements." Besides these butcheries he revamped many plays for his contemporaries, wrote several successful farces (*The Lying Valet,* 1741; *Miss in her Teens,* 1747; *Bon Ton, or High Life Above Stairs,* 1775), and collaborated with Colman the elder on a well-made, if conventional, comedy, *The Clandestine Marriage* (1766). He was a little man, only five feet four inches tall, but there are few bigger names in theatrical annals.

GARTH, Sir Samuel (1661–1719) was the personal physician of Dryden and a friend of the leading Queen Anne writers. His long poem, *The Dispensary* (1699), deals with an ephemeral quarrel between physicians and apothecaries over the distribution of drugs. It is of some significance as a skillful example of the mock-heroic manner and as a step in the development of the heroic couplet during the interval between Dryden and Pope.

GASCOIGNE, George (1525?–77) was a hard-living member of
Parliament and soldier of fortune. Scholars like to assign to him
several of the "firsts" in English literature. Thus *The Supposes*
(printed 1566), adapted from an Italian play, is traditionally
called the first prose comedy, *Certain Notes of Instruction concerning the Making of Verse or Rhyme in English* (1575) the
first treatise on prosody, and *The Steel Glass* (1576) the first
satire in blank verse. He also wrote *Jocasta* (printed 1566), an
early blank-verse tragedy borrowed from a classical original, and
The Glass of Government (printed 1575), an early prose comedy
on the prodigal son theme. He deserves to be remembered as a
pioneer in many of the fields which better Elizabethan writers
later exploited.

GASKELL, Elizabeth Cleghorn (1810–65) was a novelist who
knew two worlds. Before her marriage in 1832, to the Reverend
William Gaskell, a Unitarian minister, she lived in the charming
village of Knutsford in Cheshire; afterward in the tempestuous
manufacturing city of Manchester. She treated the petty problems
of the village in a series of sketches for Dickens' magazine,
Household Words (1851–3); in book form they became *Cranford* (1853), a "novel" which combines some of the rural felicity
of Goldsmith's *Vicar of Wakefield,* the calm satire of Jane Austen's *Emma,* and the restrained realism of Mary Mitford's *Our
Village*. She also grappled with the more vital problems of the
city. Better acquainted than either Disraeli or Dickens with industrial conditions in the "hungry forties," she shocked England
in *Mary Barton* (1848) with her depiction of Henry Carson, the
relentless employer. At the end of *North and South* (1855) employer John Thornton awakens to the need for better understanding of labor's problems—a theme which the author em-
phasizes in both books. In *Ruth* (1853) she pondered a different
problem, the struggle of a milliner's apprentice, once seduced, to
become respectable in Victorian society. Mrs. Gaskell's best-known
non-fiction work is a sympathetic biography of Charlotte Brontë
(1857).

GAY, John (1685–1732). Lazy, happy-go-lucky, self-indulgent,
Gay jested his way through a life of ups and downs; without the
prodding of Tory friends Swift, Pope, and Arbuthnot, and the
lure of social and political preferment, he would doubtless have
written little. His best-known works are satirical. In *The Shepherd's Week* (1714), a series of six pastorals, he mocked the
rustic pastorals of Ambrose ("Namby-Pamby") Philips by replac-

ing the artificial Colins and Rosalinds of classical tradition with coarse eighteenth-century country bumpkins. In a sort of city twin, *Trivia, or the Art of Walking the Streets of London* (1716), he offered a verse guide to strolling through a real city of slops and smells and ubiquitous mud. His sixty-six fables in four-foot couplets (1727, 1738) made the La Fontaine form popular in England. But *The Beggar's Opera* (1728), which ran uninterrupted for 63 nights on its first London appearance, has overshadowed his other plays and poems. Remembered today for a handful of airy songs and the exciting romance of Polly Peachum and high-wayman Macheath, it struck home originally as a satire on the Walpole government and the Italian opera craze. The production of its sequel *Polly* (printed 1729) was banned by the lord chamberlain.

GENEST, John (1764–1839) was the author of *Some Account of the English Stage from 1660 to 1830* (1832), a ten-volume record of performances which is indispensable to the scholar working on the drama of the period.

GEOFFREY of Monmouth (1100?–54) was a bishop, probably of Welsh descent. His *Historia Regum Britanniae* (c. 1135) is a Latin prose chronicle of the legendary British kings from Brutus, great-grandson of Aeneas, to Cadwallader, eighth successor to Arthur. Although the chronicler pretends to be following an ancient British source, he apparently owes much to legend-mongers like Gildas and Nennius and to his own imagination. The *Historia* is far less important as history than as a seed-bed for literature. In it lay seeds, not only of single works like *Gorboduc* and *King Lear,* but of the whole glorious tradition of Arthurian romance.

GIBBON, Edward (1737–94) went up to Magdalen College, Oxford, at the tender age of fifteen. At sixteen he was converted to Roman Catholicism, but his father deported him to Lausanne, Switzerland, where he was changed back to an undevout Protestantism. At Lausanne he fell in love with the girl who was later to become Madame Necker, wife of the famous French statesman, but at his father's request he broke off the engagement. He returned to England in 1758 and served for four years in the militia. In 1764 he toured Italy, and, while contemplating the ruins of Rome, conceived his masterpiece. *The History of the Decline and Fall of the Roman Empire* was finally begun in 1772. Progress was not seriously interrupted by Gibbon's election to Parliament two years later, and the first volume appeared in 1776. Volumes two and three followed in 1781 and the last three, completed at Lausanne, in 1788.

The Decline and Fall caused a sensation from the start. Numerous writers sprang up to attack Gibbon for his account of the early history of the Christian Church, especially for chapters 15 and 16, and the historian replied in 1779 with *A Vindication.* Since then, many writers have condemned Gibbon for his skepticism about Christianity. Another objection is that the causes assigned to Rome's fall are too entirely political. Moreover, Gibbon's style, however forceful and majestic, is somewhat overpompous and ornate for modern ears. But no history on such a scale had been attempted before his time and few have appeared since. As an exhaustive, scholarly, panoramic study of the period, *The Decline and Fall* is irreplaceable. Many consider it the greatest history in the English language. Gibbon's lesser works include *Essai sur l'Etude de la Littérature* (1761), written in French, and a series of autobiographical fragments which were collected after his death as *Memoirs* and published in 1796.

GIBSON, Wilfrid (Wilson) (1878–   ) has written poetry prolifically and consistently since the appearance of his first volumes, *Urlyn the Harper* and *The Queen's Vigil,* in 1902. His language is simple, both in the shorter lyrics and in the longer dramatic poems. He has dealt much with the beauty of nature and with the lives of the working poor, in country and in city. One of his best works is the verse drama *Daily Bread* **(1910).** His *Collected Poems* (1905–25) appeared in 1926.

GIFFORD, William (1756–1826) first achieved fame as the author of two verse satires, *The Baviad* (1791) and *The Maeviad* (1795). Later he turned to journalism, serving as editor of two Tory periodicals, the short-lived *Anti-Jacobin* (1797–8) and the *Quarterly Review* (1809–24). Founded as a political antidote to the Whig *Edinburgh Review,* the *Quarterly* was notorious, under Gifford's editorship, for confusing slander with criticism, politics with poetry. Reviewer Croker damned Keats the poet ("killed," wrote Byron) for associating with Leigh Hunt the radical, and blamed the experimental language of *Endymion* on its author's "Cockney" background. Gifford himself wrote abusive, pedantic reviews of Hazlitt's lectures and essays; and Hazlitt, in *A Letter to William Gifford* (1819) and *The Spirit of the Age* (1825), laid bare the speciousness of Gifford's criticism and reminded the public that the proud flatterer of lords was a glazier's son who had once been apprenticed to a shoemaker.

GILBERT, (Sir) W(illiam) S(chwenck) (1836–1911). Although Gilbert wrote some works independently, including the whimsical *Bab Ballads* (1869–73), his name is inseparable from the comic "Savoy Operas" on which he collaborated with the composer, Sir Arthur Sullivan. "Bab" brought to this unique collaboration a rare virtuosity in light verse and a talent for camouflaging his satire with airy nonsense. His topical thrusts—at the English courts (*Trial by Jury,* 1875) the "Queen's navee" (*H.M.S. Pinafore,* 1878), the aesthetic school of Oscar Wilde (*Patience,* 1881), and the embattled feminists (*Princess Ida,* 1884)—have lost some of their sting. But the disciples of Gilbert and Sullivan are as idolatrous as ever.

GILDAS (d. c. 570), called "the Wise," was the author of *De Excidio et Conquestu Britanniae* (before 547), a short Latin work which includes both a chronicle of British history and, in the words of a later editor, a "lamentable castigation uttered against the kings, princes, and priests thereof." Gildas was from the west of England. His sketchy chronicle, along with those of Nennius and Bede, seems to have been one of the chief sources of Geoffrey of Monmouth's *Historia Regum Britanniae* (c. 1135).

GILDON, Charles (1665–1724), a hack of all trades, wrote *The Lives and Characters of the English Dramatic Poets* (1699), the continuation of an earlier work by Gerald Langbaine; and *The Life and Strange Surprising Adventures of Mr. D—— De F——* (1719), an early commentary on Defoe's *Robinson Crusoe*. He also wrote plays and poems and did considerable editing and translating.

GIRALDUS DE BARRI, called **Cambrensis** (1146?–1220?), was a Norman-Welsh churchman who wrote, in Latin, *Topographia Hibernica* and *Itinerarium Cambriae,* topographical studies, respectively, of Ireland and Wales.

GISSING, George Robert (1857–1903). During the years of his early manhood, Gissing was a lonely exile, wandering in America, studying in Germany, tutoring and scribbling in London. He knew full well the bitterness of poverty. His early novels, *The Unclassed* (1884), *Demos* (1886), *Thyrza* (1887), and *The Nether World* (1889), are pessimistic studies of the effects of poverty on character. They are, for the most part, untouched by the sunny glints which light the darkest pages of Dickens or by the purposeful propaganda of Disraeli and Mrs. Gaskell. They have been compared to the novels of Zola and the French naturalists. In *The New Grub Street* (1891), Gissing's best-known novel, he wrote about the writer's struggle to succeed in the commercialized literary world of his day and drew heavily on his experiences in America. But Gissing is not remembered solely for his bitter novels. *The Private Papers of Henry Rye-croft* (1903) is the fictitious journal of a retired author who has found contentment among his memories and his books. Gissing called it "much more an aspiration than a memory." His monograph on Charles Dickens (1906) is a sympathetic study of a novelist whose humor he could not himself achieve. H. G. Wells, who stood at Gissing's death-bed in Paris, epitomized him thus: "He spent his big fine brain depreciating life, because he would not and perhaps could not look life squarely in the eyes."

GLANVILL, Joseph (1636–80) was a churchman who wrote several theological works in a prose style which has been compared to that of Sir Thomas Browne. His *Vanity of Dogmatizing* (1661) was the source of Matthew Arnold's *Scholar-Gipsy*.

GLOVER, Richard (1712–85) was a poet, playwright, and politician. His interminable blank-verse epics, *Leonidas* (1737) and *The Athenaid* (1787), were popular in an age of fustian but have today a reputation for insufferable dullness. In contrast to these, Glover's swiftly moving political ballad, *Admiral Hosier's Ghost* (1740), does not seem to be by the same hand.

GODWIN, Mary Wollstonecraft (1759–97) made her reputation as a daring feminist with the publication of *A Vindication of the Rights of Woman* in 1792. Shortly afterwards her enlightenment led her into a sordid affair with Gilbert Imlay, an unprincipled American who deserted her in 1795 after she had borne him an illegitimate daughter. Her subsequent relationship with William Godwin, the philosopher and reformer, was legalized in 1797. In the same year she died giving birth to a daughter Mary, who was to become the second wife of the poet Shelley.

GODWIN, William (1756–1836) was a leader of the English radicals whose social philosophy reflected the doctrines behind the French Revolution. In *An Enquiry concerning Political Justice* (1793) he scoffed at the aristocracy, preached equality, and projected a state of anarchy in which man's reason would make government and law superfluous. In the best known of his six novels, *Caleb Williams* (1794), he combined a thesis on social injustice with the pursuit *motif* of Gothic Romance. In 1797 he legalized his relationship with the feminist Mary Wollstonecraft; she died in the same year. Godwin made her the heroine of his novel of the supernatural, *St. Leon* (1799). Their daughter,

Mary, eloped with the most famous of Godwin's later disciples, Percy Bysshe Shelley.

GOLDING, Arthur (1536?–1605?) is remembered for his verse translation in 1565–7 of the *Metamorphoses* of the Latin poet Ovid (43 B.C.–A.D. 18?). This was one of the earliest of the important Elizabethan translations.

GOLDSMITH, Oliver (1728–74) was a village clergyman's son. He was born in Ireland and graduated from Trinity College, Dublin. After a period of restless vagabondage, during which he studied medicine in Edinburgh and on the Continent, he arrived in London in 1756 with a doubtful European medical degree. Failing in his medical practice, he soon took to school-teaching and hack-writing. In 1761 he met Johnson, and in 1764 became a charter member of "The Club," along with Johnson, Burke, and Sir Joshua Reynolds. With Johnson's help he rose to literary fame, but he squandered his earnings and died, beset by debts and worries, at the height of his career.

Dr. Goldsmith's early anonymous work includes a series of satirical essays in the popular Oriental vogue: *The Citizen of the World, or Letters from a Chinese Philosopher, Residing in London, to his Friends in the East* (1762). The first work under his own name was *The Traveller* (1764), a long poem in heroic couplets wherein he purported to show "a prospect of society" as he had viewed it while journeying on foot across Europe in search of happiness. In *The Deserted Village* (1770), similar in length and form, he painted an idyllic picture of "Sweet Auburn, loveliest village of the plain" and lamented its passing when "wealth accumulates, and men decay." Despite authentic features of the Irish village of his boyhood, the poem is an idealized pastel beside the bold etching of George Crabbe. Goldsmith's shorter poems include: two light occasional pieces, *Retaliation* (1774) and *The Haunch of Venison* (1776); two deft mock-elegies, *On Mrs. Mary Blaize* (1759) and *On the Death of a Mad Dog;* and the finished but artificial lyric "When Lovely Woman Stoops to Folly." The last two appeared in his novel, *The Vicar of Wakefield* (1766). This slim classic is the story of the appalling misfortunes of gentle Dr. Primrose, whose son Moses, a David Harum in reverse, trades a horse for a pair of green spectacles, and whose proud daughter Olivia "stoops to folly" with worldly Squire Thornhill. It is a mixture of true comedy and sentimentality, pure entertainment and humanitarian propaganda—in a plot full of incredible coincidences. In his two comedies, Goldsmith turned against the sentimentality which had monopolized the stage for three-quarters of a century. Both *The Good Natured Man* (1768), with its splenetic Croaker, and *She Stoops to Conquer* (1773), with its waggish Tony Lumpkin, represent a return to the bustling, laughing farce of George Farquhar.

"Noll" Goldsmith was a chinless, awkward, stammering little man who strutted about in "tyrian satin bloom" when he had money and sat desolate over a bottle of Madeira when he did not. Walpole called him "an inspired idiot," Garrick one "who wrote like an angel, and talked like Poor Poll." Boswell pictured him as a tender-hearted and generous human being but a grotesque *poseur* ridiculously envious of the success of others. "But let not his frailties be remembered," wrote Johnson after his death; "he was a very great man."

GOOGE, Barnabe (1540–94). The eight eclogues in Googe's *Eclogues, Epitaphs, and Sonnets* (1563) represent the second appearance (after Alexander Barclay's) of the pastoral eclogue in English. A more famous series, Spenser's *Shepheardes Calender,* followed in 1579.

GORE, Catherine Grace Frances (1799–1861), novelist, poetess, and dramatist, was one of the leading ladies of the "Silver Fork School" of fashionable fiction which flourished at the beginning of Victoria's reign. Her many novels include *Mothers and Daughters* (1831), *Mrs. Armitage, or Female Domination* (1836), and *Cecil, or the Adventures of a Coxcomb* (1841). In *Novels by Eminent Hands* (1847) Thackeray derisively represented Mrs. Gore as the authoress of *Lords and Liveries, Dukes and Déjeuners,* and *Marchionesses and Milliners.*

GOSSE, Sir Edmund William (1849–1928). During a long career this distinguished critic and biographer held the posts of Assistant Librarian in the British Museum (1867–75), Lecturer in English Literature at Cambridge (1884–9), and Librarian of the House of Lords (1904–14). He produced numerous critical studies of literature, including *English Literature, an Illustrated Record* (with Richard Garnett, 1903–4) and *French Profiles* (1905). His own literary masterpiece, *Father and Son* (1907), is "a study of two temperaments" and two generations. Like Samuel Butler in *The Way of All Flesh* (1903), but with less bitterness and brilliance, Gosse analyzed his own reaction against the Victorian world of his father. This book is one of the best autobiographies in English.

GOSSON, Stephen (1554–1624) began his literary life by writing plays and later turned Puritan censor. His *School of Abuse* (1579) contained "a pleasant invective against poets, pipers, players, jesters, and such like caterpillers of a commonwealth." He exposed the stage to special scorn—admitting only six good plays, one by Gosson—and thus earned an early place on the long list of Puritan play-damners which later included William Prynne and Jeremy Collier. The dedication of this and a subsequent tract to Sir Philip Sidney probably inspired the poet's noble *Defence of Poesy* (written c. 1580).

GOWER, John (1330?–1408?) was a wealthy follower of Richard II who later bolted to Bolingbroke. Chaucer, in choosing his friend and rival poet as one of the two dedicatees of *Troilus and Criseyde,* dubbed him "moral Gower." Gower's three best-known poems bear out this label. The French *Speculum Meditantis* (or *Mirour de L'Omme,* c. 1379) is a thirty-thousand-line sermon on the sins of the time. The Latin *Vox Clamantis* (1382), about a third as long, sharpens a similar sermon with direct allusions to the Peasants' Revolt of 1381. In the English *Confessio Amantis* (1390) a lover, confessing to Genius, priest of Venus, tells more than a hundred stories to exemplify the vices of love. Gower was a competent story-teller, but one has only to compare his *Tale of Florent* with its analogue, Chaucer's *Wife of Bath's Tale,* to see how far the jingling *Confessio* falls below the level of the *Canterbury Tales.* Nevertheless Gower's version of the old story of Apollonius of Tyre earned him the rôle of Chorus in Shakespeare's *Pericles, Prince of Tyre* (1607–8).

GRAHAM. See CUNNINGHAME GRAHAM.

GRANVILLE–BARKER, Harley (Granville) (1877–1946) pursued a distinguished career in the theater as actor, playwright, producer, and critic. In *The Marrying of Anne Leete* (1901), *The Voysey Inheritance* (1905), and *Waste* (1907)—published together as *Three Plays* in 1909—he dramatized the conflict between private and public morality. His series of *Prefaces* to Shakespeare (1923–37) reflects his long experience in practical production, an aspect of the drama which academic critics often overlook. His expositions of dramatic method are also important: *On Dramatic Method* (1931), *The Study of Drama* (1934), and *On Poetry in Drama* (1937).

GRAVES, Richard (1715–1804) was a country rector who composed novels, poems, essays, and translations from the classics. In his most celebrated work, a "comic romance" called *The*

Spiritual Quixote (1773), he burlesqued Methodist enthusiasm through the adventures of enthusiastic Geoffrey Wildgoose of Oxford and Jerry Tugwell, the village cobbler. The novel contains a sketch of Graves' good friend William Shenstone.

GRAVES, Robert (von Ranke) (1895–   ). Like his friend Siegfried Sassoon, Graves earned his reputation as a poet during the First World War. His verse varies from the genial whimsy of much of his early work to a more recent tone of metaphysical obscurity. He is the author, with Laura Riding, of *A Survey of Modernist Poetry* (1927) and is well known for his rebellious autobiography, *Good-bye to All That* (1929), and his unusual historical novel, *I, Claudius* (1934). In 1943, in collaboration with Alan Hodge (1915–   ), Graves published *The Reader over Your Shoulder,* a provocative handbook on English prose style which contains copious examples of bad writing by celebrated authors.

GRAY, Thomas (1716–71) was born in London, and his education at Eton and Cambridge was supplemented by a three-year tour of Europe (1739–41) with Horace Walpole. The rest of his placid life, save for a year at Stoke Poges, and brief visits to the English Lakes, Scotland, and elsewhere, he lived as a scholar at Cambridge, studying and writing so shyly and quietly that a single shift of residence from Peterhouse to Pembroke in 1756 was an event in his career.

A score of poems—none very long—a journal of the Lake Country trip, and a sheaf of charming letters form his literary output. His *Ode on Spring, Hymn to Adversity,* and *Hymn to Ignorance*—all published in 1742—were his first completed poems. *Ode on a Distant Prospect of Eton College* (1747), one of Gray's best-known works, shows his characteristic mixture of morality and melancholy, a mood of constant recurrence in all but his playful *Ode on the Death of a Favorite Cat Drowned in a Tub of Gold Fishes* (1748). The most famous of his poems, and one of the most quoted in English literature, is his polished *Elegy Written in a Country Church Yard*. This poem he began in 1742, completed in 1749, and published in 1751. Its popularity comes from its democratic quality, its simple philosophy of life and death, and its eminent quotability. It is the greatest achievement of the "Graveyard School" of reflective poetry. Gray's interest in medieval and Scandinavian themes produced four odes, the first two in imitation of Pindar, Greek lyric poet of the fifth century B.C.: *The Progress of Poesy, The Bard*—both published at Horace Walpole's Strawberry Hill press in 1757, *The Fatal*

Sisters (1761), and *The Descent of Odin* (1761). His collected poems were issued in 1768; his *Journal* of the English Lake trip and his *Letters* were published four years after his death. The *Letters* are among the best in English literature. Thomas Gray has the distinction of having declined the poet-laureateship (1757). He did, however, accept the post of professor of modern literature at Cambridge (1768), an honorary appointment that required no lecturing.

Gray received little praise from the literary dictator of his own day. "Sir," said Johnson to Boswell, "he was dull in company, dull in his closet, dull everywhere. He was dull in a new way, and that made people think him great." Johnson condemned the logic of the *Ode on . . . a Favorite Cat,* and said of the other odes, "They are forced plants raised in a hot-bed; and they are poor plants; they are but cucumbers after all." As Wordsworth also observed, Gray did have an unfortunate taste for affected, "poetic" diction. Nevertheless, he remains one of the major forerunners of English romanticism. At his best, as in the noblest passages of the *Elegy,* he is unsurpassed. As Johnson said, "Had Gray written often thus it had been vain to blame, and useless to praise him."

GREEN, John Richard (1837-83). Green's *Short History of the English People* (1874) is popular without being unscholarly, and concise without overlooking the "constitutional, intellectual, and social advance" of the nation in favor of battles, treaties, and dates. Hence although some of Green's statements have been since proved inaccurate, his work is still regarded as a classic.

GREEN, Matthew (1696-1737) was a customs-house clerk who is remembered for a single poem. *The Spleen* (1737) is a spirited ramble in four-foot couplets recommending the simple, carefree life as a cure for the blues.

GREENE, Robert (1558-92) was a "University Wit" who knew what the Elizabethan public wanted. He pandered to their taste for artificial romance by aping Lyly's *Euphues* (*Mamillia,* 1583) and Sidney's *Arcadia* (*Menaphon,* 1589). He appealed to their love of sensational realism with a series of playful pamphlets on the crooked tricks of the underworld (*Conny-catching Pamphlets,* 1591-2). He answered their growing demand for the drama with such plays as farcical *Friar Bacon and Friar Bungay* (c. 1589-92) and pseudo-historical *James IV* (c. 1590-91). A journalist to the end, he capitalized on his own misspent Bohemian life with a batch of last-gasp pamphlets. One of these, *Greene's Groat's*

Worth of Wit Bought with a Million of Repentance (1592), contains the earliest extant allusion to Shakespeare: "an upstart Crow . . . with his Tygers heart wrapt in a Players hide." Greene never lived to see his own romance, *Pandosto* (1588), blossom into Shakespeare's *Winter's Tale* (1610–11). He died young, succumbing—to swallow the traditional story—to a "surfeit of pickled herrings and Rhenish wine."

GREGORY, Lady (Isabella Augusta Persse) (1852–1932) was a leading figure in the Irish Renaissance and helped W. B. Yeats in the establishment of the Abbey Theater. She is best known for her sprightly one-act comedies of Irish village life. Among her successes in this kind are *Spreading the News* (printed 1904), *Hyacinth Halvey* (printed 1906), and *The Workhouse Ward* (printed 1909), all of which may be found in her collection, *Seven Short Plays* (1909).

GREVILLE, Sir Fulke, first baron Brooke (1554–1628). This favorite in the courts of both Elizabeth and James I is better known as a friend and patron of writers than as a writer himself. He was a close friend of Sir Philip Sidney and wrote a life of the poet which appeared in 1652. His works, most of them published posthumously, include *Caelica* (1633), one of many Elizabethan collections of songs and sonnets, and two unactable political tragedies, *Mustapha* (printed 1609) and *Alaham* (printed 1633).

GRIMALD, Nicholas (1519?–62) was a chaplain at Christ College, Cambridge, who collaborated with Richard Tottel in the publication of the famous verse anthology known popularly as *Tottel's Miscellany* (1557). He himself contributed some forty poems.

GROSSETESTE, Robert (d. 1253), Bishop of Lincoln, was one of the most learned men of his time. In his *Compendium Scientiarum* he attempted—like Sir Francis Bacon later—to classify all knowledge. He also wrote a French poem, *Château d'Amour,* an allegory in which the "castle of love" symbolizes the body of the Virgin Mary.

GUEDALLA, Philip (1889–1944) labored in the interdependent fields of history and biography. Primarily historical are *The Second Empire* (1922), a study of France under Louis Napoleon; *The Hundred Days* (1934), the story of Napoleon Bonaparte's brief struggle between Elba and St. Helena; and *The Hundred Years* (1936), a survey of the century between Waterloo and the First World War. Guedalla's biographical studies range from the miniatures of *Fathers of the Revolution* (1926) and *Bonnet and Shawl* (1928) to the full-dress studies, *Palmerston* (1926), *Wellington* (1931), and *Mr. Churchill* (1942). Whether he was concerned with one biography or with the innumerable biographies that make up history, Guedalla was forever occupied with painting backdrops and evoking atmosphere. He followed Lytton Strachey in the movement to replace the deadly Victorian chronicles with lively works of art, and, like Strachey, he sometimes overworked the tricks of rhetoric. He was less gifted in handling irony but less prone to debunkery, sometimes a more frivolous jester but usually a more dependable scholar.

GUTHRIE, Thomas Anstey. See ANSTEY, F.

H

HABINGTON, William (1605–54) published a tragi-comedy, *The Queen of Arragon* (1640), and a collection of verse, *Castara* (three parts, 1634–40). The title of the collection is the fanciful name which Habington gave his wife in numerous verses about their chaste, pure love: *To Roses in the Bosom of Castara; To Cupid, Upon a Dimple in Castara's Cheek; To Castara, in a Trance,* and many more. The collection also contains sacred poems and poems addressed to the poet's mistress.

HAGGARD, (Sir Henry) Rider (1856–1925) was one of the novelists—with Stevenson, Kipling, and others—who brought about the renaissance in romantic fiction at the end of the nineteenth century. While Kipling looked towards India for material, Rider Haggard turned to Africa. In such popular romances as *King Solomon's Mines* (1885), *Allan Quatermain* (1887), and *She* (1887), he exploited the weird mystery of the Dark Continent. He is linked with Kipling in the famous lines in which James K. Stephen yearned for the day—

"When the Rudyards cease from kipling
And the Haggards ride no more."

HAKLUYT, Richard (1552?–1616) devoted years to collecting stories of voyagers. His earliest work in this field was entitled *Divers Voyages touching the Discovery of America* (1582). His *magnum opus* covers the *Principal Navigations, Voyages, and Discoveries of the English Nation* within "these 1500 yeares." It was first published in 1589. The enlarged edition, appearing in three giant folio volumes between 1598 and 1600, includes exploits of the Hawkinses, Drake, Frobisher, Gilbert, Raleigh, and other

Elizabethan sea dogs. Hakluyt's work was continued after his death by Samuel Purchas in *Hakluytus Posthumus, or Purchas his Pilgrims* (1625).

HALIFAX, George Savile, Marquis of (1633–95). It was a versatile statesman who, amid the bitter struggles of Restoration politics, could write that tender guide to feminine conduct, *The Lady's New-Year's-Gift, or Advice to a Daughter* (1688). More worldly are Halifax's two well-known "characters." *A Character of King Charles II* (not published until 1750) is a frank but tolerant dissection of the vices and virtues of the merry monarch by one who knew him. *The Character of a Trimmer* (1688) is a defense of him who, like the author, is so sworn to moderate, middle-of-the-road principles that "he will neither be bawled, threatened, laughed, nor drunk out of them." To one who knows the essays of "the Great Trimmer," his gift for antithesis and aphorism, his "piercing wit and pregnant thought," it is not surprising that he was also a great orator.

HALL, Joseph (1574–1656) was Bishop of Exeter and Norwich. His *Virgidemiarum* (1597–8), a "harvest of rods" on contemporary manners, types, and individuals, has been called the first Juvenalian satire in English. Better known is a somewhat similar work in prose, *Characters of Virtues and Vices* (1608). These "characters," didactic sketches of human types in the general manner of the Greek philosopher, Theophrastus (d. 287? B.C.), were early examples of one of the favorite literary *genres* in the century. Bishop Hall was followed in the same field by Sir Thomas Overbury and John Earle. Taken together, the "character writers" influenced the development of characterization in the English novel and made a contribution to the essay which is readily apparent in the *Spectator* papers and the *Essays of Elia.* Hall's "characters" are pleasanter reading than his stubborn controversial pamphlets. In his defense of the episcopacy he attacked violently both the five Presbyterian divines who wrote under the pseudonym of "Smectymnuus" and John Milton, who came to their rescue.

HALLAM, Arthur Henry (1811–33) was the son of Henry Hallam, the historian. At Cambridge he exerted a great influence over a fellow-student and intimate friend, Alfred Tennyson. Grief-stricken by Hallam's death, Tennyson wrote *In Memoriam* (published 1850), one of the great elegies in English. Hallam's own *Remains in Verse and Prose* (1834) shows promise but has proved to be an ephemeral memorial.

HALLAM, Henry (1777–1859), father of A. H. Hallam (1811–33), was the first important historian in the nineteenth century. Despite his affiliation with the Whigs, his *View of the State of Europe during the Middle Ages* (1818) and the better-known *Constitutional History of England from the Accession of Henry VII to the Death of George II* (1827) have been much praised for their fairness. Hallam also wrote a four-volume *Introduction to the Literature of Europe, in the Fifteenth, Sixteenth, and Seventeenth Centuries* (1837–9).

HAMPOLE. See ROLLE, Richard.

HANKIN, St. John (Emile Clavering) (1869–1909). Although never a popular playwright, Hankin wrote a number of witty comedies which reveal him as a deft satirist of human foibles. Three of them, *The Return of the Prodigal* (1905), *The Charity that Began at Home* (1906), and *The Cassilis Engagement* (1907), are collected in the volume entitled *Three Plays with Happy Endings* (1907).

HARDY, Thomas (1840–1928) was born in Dorsetshire, the heart of that general region of southwestern England which his readers know as Wessex. His father was a builder, and after a time at school in Dorchester (Casterbridge) the boy was apprenticed to a local architect and helped to draw up plans for the restoration of several Dorset churches. In 1862 he obtained a position as assistant to a London architect, and in the following year he won two prizes in his field. In the meantime, however, he had continued his education at night and tried his hand at poetry and fiction. When George Meredith, a reader for the publishers Chapman and Hall, rejected a story with the suggestion that Hardy try something in the sensational vein of Wilkie Collins, he wrote his first novel, *Desperate Remedies* (1871), a tale of "mystery, entanglement, surprise, and moral obliquity."

During the next twenty-five years Hardy published thirteen more novels and three volumes of short-stories. Some of the novels he classified, with *Desperate Remedies,* as "novels of ingenuity." Others, *A Pair of Blue Eyes* (1873), for example, were "romances and fantasies." But he found his real vein in "novels of character and environment." In this category he included *Under the Greenwood Tree* (1872), *Far from the Madding Crowd* (1874), *The Return of the Native* (1878), *The Mayor of Casterbridge* (1886), *The Woodlanders* (1887), *Tess of the D'Urbervilles* (1891), and *Jude the Obscure* (1896). After the publication of *Jude,* he abandoned novel-writing for good and turned again to poetry. He wrote several volumes of shorter verses, including *Wessex Poems* (1898), *Poems of the Past and Present* (1902), *Time's Laughingstocks* (1909), *Satires of Circumstance* (1914), and *Winter Words* (1928). But his great achievement in poetry is *The Dynasts,* a gigantic epic-drama of the Napoleonic Wars (three parts, 1903–8).

Although Hardy is sometimes called "the last of the great Victorians," he is really a transition figure. Both *Tess* and *Jude* aroused storms of moral indignation in the nineties, and the prevailing mood of all his writing is the pessimism of a more recent generation. He saw man, not as the favorite of merciful Providence, but as the helpless plaything of a malevolent power—of the "President of the Immortals" who sports with Tess Durbeyfield, the "Immanent Will" who oversees the futile strivings of Napoleon, the unseen presence whom the reader feels behind the scenes of the miniature tragedies in *Satires of Circumstance.* In implementing this fatalistic philosophy in fiction, Hardy overworked the undelivered message, the unexpected meeting, the undivulged secret—all the little coincidences which make fiction stranger than truth. But if he never entirely dispensed with the sensationalism of his first novel, he did learn to use plot, not as an end in itself, but as a frame for the interweaving of character and environment. He took one corner of the English countryside —with its fairs and festivals, its songs and superstitions, its gloomy moors and sunny farms—and peopled it with real individuals. Hardy's characters are rooted like trees in their environment. It is next to impossible for the mind to separate Clym Yeobright, Eustacia Vye, and Diggory Venn from somber Egdon Heath, Tess Durbeyfield and Angel Clare from the magic twilight of Talbothays Dairy—or Thomas Hardy from his native Wessex.

HARINGTON, Sir John (1561–1612). At the request of his godmother, Queen Elizabeth, Harington made the first English translation (1591) of Ariosto's *Orlando Furioso* (1532), rendering it in undistinguished "heroical verse." In his critical introduction he praised the Italian epic poet for following Vergil, and in his notes he praised himself and his relatives. Harington's *Epigrams* (1615, 1618) throw light on the practices of contemporary writers. He also wrote bawdy satires.

HARRINGTON, James (1611–77) is remembered for his quaint *Commonwealth of Oceana* (1656), a Utopian romance answering Hobbes' *Leviathan* (1651). Politically the book is a strange hybrid.

Harrington envisions a condition of equality achieved through equal distribution of property. He pictures a government based on three orders, "the senate debating and proposing, the people resolving, and the magistracy executing." Yet he vests supreme power in one elected prince and retains the nobility to accomplish duties "peculiar only to the genius of a gentleman."

HARTLEY, David (1705-57) was a philosopher and physician who pioneered in the realm of psychology. In the first part of his *Observations on Man* (1749) he presented a physiological theory about the association of ideas which contradicted the central thesis of an earlier philosopher, Lord Shaftesbury, and greatly influenced the thought of a later one, James Mill.

HARVEY, Gabriel (1545?-1630?) has long had a black name in English literature for several reasons. (1) He could not resist the powder-smell of argument. He fought with his colleagues at Cambridge; he mixed in the "Martin Marprelate" attacks on the English bishops; he fumed against Robert Greene (*Four Letters,* 1592); and he waged, with Thomas Nashe, a notoriously venomous pamphlet squabble (*Pierce's Supererogation, or a New Praise of the Old Ass,* 1593). (2) He worked for the absurd introduction of classical hexameters into English verse. (3) He once pooh-poohed Spenser's *Faerie Queene.* Recent defenders have pointed out that Harvey, for all his pedantry and bellicosity, was a friend and guide of both Spenser and Sidney, that his metrical experiments were hardly serious, and that he liked Chaucer and, as early as 1600, recognized Shakespeare's genius.

HARVEY, William (1578-1657) was physician to Charles I. His discoveries about the circulation of the blood were first explained to the College of Physicians in 1618. The book on the subject, *Exercitatio Anatomica de Motu Cordis et Sanguinis in Animalibus,* appeared in 1628. Harvey's theory was complete in all significant details except for the omission of capillaries, the discovery of which had to await the invention of the compound microscope. He also published *Exercitationes de Generatione Animalium* (1651), a pioneering work in embryology.

HAWES, Stephen (1475?-1523?) was a verse-loving groom in the chamber of Henry VII who chose Lydgate as his literary master. More moralist than poet, he left behind two lengthy verse allegories, *The Example of Virtue* (1504?) and *The Pastime of Pleasure* (1509). The better-known *Pastime* traces in ragged doggerel "the Course of Man's Life in this World" through the history of the knight, Graunde Amoure, and his love, La Bel Pucel.

The knight learns the "Seven Sciences" in the "Tower of Doctrine," overcomes multiheaded monsters, marries the lady, and dies in old age still surrounded by allegorical abstractions. As a blend of allegory with the romance of chivalry *The Pastime* faintly foreshadows Spenser's *Faerie Queene*.

HAWKER, Robert Stephen (1803–75) was an eccentric clergyman, vicar of Morwenstow in Cornwall. He is best known for his *Song of the Western Men* (1825). The refrain, "And shall Trelawney die?" etc., was based on that of a seventeenth-century folk ballad, and Hawker's entire poem was published as an old one. Scott and Macaulay, among others, were taken in by the imposture. Hawker never finished his long poem, *The Quest of the Sangraal* (1864).

HAWKINS, Sir Anthony Hope. See **HOPE, Anthony.**

HAYLEY, William (1745–1820) was a tasteless poetaster whose *Triumphs of Temper* (1781) has been ranked even below Erasmus Darwin's *Botanic Garden* (1789–91) as an illustration of the decline of versifying at the close of the eighteenth century. Hayley also wrote a life of Milton (1796), a life of himself (1823), and *A Philosophical, Historical and Moral Essay on Old Maids* (1785).

HAYWARD, Sir John (1564?–1627) was a scholarly historian whose writing is full of sententious borrowings from the Ancients. His works include: *The First Part of the Life and Reign of King Henry IV* (1599), *The Lives of the Three Normans, Kings of England* (1613), and *The Life and Reign of King Edward VI* (1630).

HAYWOOD, Eliza (1693?–1756) wrote amorous tales of intrigue, scandalous "memoirs" of her contemporaries, and several novels in the manner of Richardson. The best of the novels, *The History of Miss Betsy Thoughtless* (1751), superficially resembles Fanny Burney's *Evelina* (1778).

HAZLITT, William (1778–1830). "I have not written a line that licks the dust." William Hazlitt's boast was bold but well-founded. Of all the English essayists of the early nineteenth century, he was the clearest, the most direct, the most virile. Moreover, he had considerable influence on later English essayists, notably on Robert Louis Stevenson, who said of him: "We are all mighty fine fellows, but none of us can write like Hazlitt." And yet Hazlitt the writer was not born, but self-made by constant imitation and practice. Early in his life when he was studying to be a painter but longed to be a powerful writer like Edmund Burke, he said of his weakness: "I was at that time dumb, inarticulate, helpless like a worm by the wayside." He developed his literary powers by studying Montaigne, visiting with Coleridge and Wordsworth, and conversing with Charles and Mary Lamb. Hazlitt's clarity and felicity of expression came from his self-imposed training. The richness and color of his style came from his knowledge of painting and from a love of nature that drove him to take long walks in the country with his father and alone through the hills of Shropshire and Wales. The vigor and contentiousness of his writing he inherited. His father was a Unitarian minister who suffered for his non-conformity by being driven from one post to another, even spending three years in America. Ultimately this dissenter settled for twenty-five years in Wem near Shrewsbury, and here young Hazlitt learned to fight that long series of battles against convention that roughened his temper and made him something of a quarrelsome individualist. An inveterate Whig and king-hater, he was pilloried by the Tory reviewers as a member of the "Cockney School." His famous *Letter to William Gifford* (1819), the reviewer who had attacked him, helps to explain why, of all his early friends, only Charles Lamb remained faithful to him.

In spite of his unpopularity, however, Hazlitt was admired by his contemporaries for the quality of his work. He was a good talker, who wrote as easily as he talked. He wrote readable comments on the older English drama, comments that were not ruined by too much scholarship and stodgy analysis. Of these the best known are *Characters of Shakespeare's Plays* (1817), *English Comic Writers* (1819), and *Dramatic Literature of the Age of Elizabeth* (1820). He was the first, and probably the most notable, of the nineteenth-century commentators on the contemporary stage. In his *View of the English Stage,* a series of dramatic criticisms written for the magazines between 1818 and 1821, the actors of his time continue to live and to perform. He criticized his contemporaries in *The Spirit of the Age* (1825), criticized them clearly but often unfairly. But the works that have had the widest influence are the miscellaneous essays of *Table Talk, or Original Essays on Men and Manners* (1821–22). "On Going a Journey," "On the Fear of Death," "The Fight," and "The Feeling of Immortality in Youth" contain some of the best of Hazlitt. When accused of not reading enough, he replied that if he read more, he would think less. Certainly he thought well, but certainly he also read so widely that his essays are tesselated with lines borrowed from his reading, lines not always quoted accurately but woven so skillfully into his own work that they seem to be an integral part of it.

HEAD, Richard (1637?–86?) collaborated with Francis Kirkman on *The English Rogue* (1665–71), "a complete history of the most eminent cheats." It helps to link Elizabethan rogue fiction with the journalistic novels of Defoe.

HEMANS, Felicia Dorothea (1793–1835). This prolific poetess was absurdly popular a century ago. Although her star has since fallen low, such schoolboy favorites as the melodramatic *Casabianca* ("The boy stood on the burning deck") and the high-sounding *Landing of the Pilgrim Fathers* ("The breaking waves dashed high") will survive as long as popular taste prefers sentimentality and false heroics to poetry.

HENLEY, William Ernest (1849–1903). In his boyhood Henley contracted a tubercular disease which eventually cost him the loss of a foot. His other foot was saved only after a struggle of twenty months in the Old Infirmary in Edinburgh. This experience inspired him to write the series of poems, *In Hospital,* which was later published in his best-known collection, *A Book of Verses* (1888). One poem, "Apparition," is a thumbnail portrait of "thin-legged, thin-chested" Robert Louis Stevenson, a fellow-tubercular who visited Henley at the infirmary, and with whom he later collaborated on several plays. Another poem, written in 1875 shortly after his discharge, is the popular and powerful *Invictus,* the lyric in which Henley cried out that, despite the horror he had undergone, he was still the captain of his soul. Henley was a bold experimenter with free verse, as in the tender memorial lyric *I. M. Margaritae Sorori* ("A late lark twitters from the quiet skies"). He was also a bold advocate of British imperialism; he struck this note often in the *National Observer* during his editorship, and it rings out in his chauvinistic song *England, My England.*

HENRY THE MINSTREL. See BLIND HARRY.

HENRYSON, Robert (1425?–1500?). Whoever this Scottish Chaucerian was, he has left behind some of the most interesting poems of his century. *The Testament of Cresseid* (published 1532) is a 616-line sequel to Chaucer's *Troilus and Criseyde*. Disliking his master's leniency with the Trojan heroine, Henryson called in Saturn and Cynthia to blast her with ugliness and leprosy. At the tragic climax Cresseid learns that she has begged by the roadside from her deserted lover, Troilus, neither one recognizing the other. *Moral Fables* (published 1570) is a collection of thirteen tales from Aesop in the same rhyme royal as *The Testament,* full of sly humor and close to the soil of Scotland. *Robyn and Makyn* (not published until 1765), a saucy dialogue between a vacillating shepherd and his impudent lass, is sometimes called the first English pastoral.

HERBERT, A(lan) P(atrick) (1890–   ) is a popular London jester and M. P. who has spent part of his life on a houseboat on the Thames carrying on a one-man campaign to give the river back to pleasure craft. His playful contributions to *Punch* (since 1910) are equaled in profusion only by his serious letters to the *Times.* His works include *Ballads for Broadbrows* (1930), a collection of light verse; *The Secret Battle* (1919), a serious war novel; and numerous plays, librettos, and miscellaneous articles.

HERBERT, Edward, first baron Herbert of Cherbury (1583–1648) was the older brother of George Herbert (1593–1633). In a busy career as courtier, diplomat, and soldier of fortune, he found time for various literary efforts. His philosophical prose works have earned him the title: "Father of English Deism." The greatest of these is the Latin treatise *De Veritate* (1624). Although his poetry is inferior to his brother's, he wrote some captivating love lyrics in the metaphysical manner. He also wrote *The Life and Reign of King Henry VIII* (1649) and an autobiography which Horace Walpole first published at Strawberry Hill in 1764.

HERBERT, George (1593–1633) was born to the purple, the younger brother of Lord Herbert of Cherbury. He was a favorite of James I and was Public Orator for eight years (1619–26) at Cambridge. Then he put away worldly things, took orders, and spent the last three years of his life as a humble rector in Wiltshire. His *Priest to the Temple* (published 1652) is a simple prose lesson growing out of his life as a country parson. *The Temple* (1633) is a miscellaneous collection of poems, some of which reveal the inner religious struggle which led to his conversion. For example, in *The Collar* the poet threatens to escape to the world but yields to the Lord; in *The Quip* he asks the Lord to answer the temptations of the world; in *The Pulley* he sings of the "repining restlessness" which pulls man, despite the world's riches, to the Lord. Herbert lacks the ecstasy of his Catholic follower, Crashaw, and the glowing mysticism of his disciple, Vaughan. Although his love for bizarre conceits led to his adjusting the meter and typography of each stanza of *Easter Wings* to represent a wing—he was, on the whole, the simplest and most direct of the sacred metaphysical poets.

HERRICK, Robert (1591–1674). To the Cavalier readers of the second quarter of the seventeenth century the spectacle of a clergyman's writing "pagan" poetry was not so startling as it would have been a hundred years later. Robert Herrick's life and writings were almost equally influenced by the court, the church, and the country. Under the influence of his friends of the court—and notably under the inspiration of Ben Jonson, to whose tribe of younger poets he belongs—he wrote early of "many stately mistresses." He wrote about Julia's silk dress and about Mistress Susanna Southwell's pretty feet. "Gather ye rosebuds while ye may," he wrote "to the virgins" in advising them to "make much of time." "Put on your foliage," he begged his Corinna, and "go a-Maying." But he had taken orders in the Anglican Church, and had served as chaplain for the Duke of Buckingham and as servant of God in Dean Prior of Devonshire. And so when his conscience smote him for his "unbaptized rhymes" written in his "wild, unhallowed times," he wrote, in *Noble Numbers* (1648), "A Prayer for Absolution" and other penitent verses. Herrick first went to Dean Prior in 1629 and came to love the country there and to write of the "maypoles, hock-carts, wassails, wakes" of his parishioners. In 1647, because he refused to subscribe to the Solemn League and Covenant of the Puritan government, he was ejected from his living. The following year he gathered his poetical rosebuds into the *Hesperides* (1648), an anthology of much variety. When in 1660 King Charles II came into his own again, Herrick went back to Devonshire. Probably no poet of the period has revealed in his verse so much freshness, spontaneity, and simple charm.

HERVEY, John, Baron Hervey of Ickworth (1696–1743), Vice-chamberlain in the court of George II, is remembered in literary annals for his bitter quarrel with Pope. The "wicked wasp of Twickenham" stung Hervey on several occasions, the most famous of which is the passage in the *Epistle to Dr. Arbuthnot* (1735) where the lord is caricatured as "Sporus, that mere white curd of ass's milk." At his death Hervey left posterity his spiteful, cynical *Memoirs of the Reign of George the Second*. They were finally edited a century later by John Wilson Croker (1848).

HEWLETT, Maurice (Henry) (1861–1923). Although Hewlett published several volumes of essays and poetry, he is remembered chiefly as a fiction-writer. He wrote numerous scholarly historical romances, including *The Life and Death of Richard Yea-and-Nay* (1900), a novel about Richard the Lion-hearted; *Little Novels of Italy* (1899), a group of five *novelle* set in the fourteenth century; and *The Queen's Quair* (1904), the tragic tale of Mary Queen of Scots. The time is the present in *Halfway House* (1908), *Open Country* (1909), and *Rest Harrow* (1910), the three volumes of Hewlett's trilogy about a wandering naturalist.

HEYWOOD, Jasper (1535?–98), son of John Heywood, distinguished himself in the reign of Elizabeth by making Seneca's *Troas* (1559), *Thyestes* (1560), and *Hercules Furens* (1561) into English closet dramas. His translations of these plays were included in the collected English Seneca of 1581.

HEYWOOD, John (1497?–1580?) was a director of entertainments in the courts of Henry VIII and Mary Tudor. Although he has left us a collection of proverbs and epigrams, he is more famous as the author of England's best-known dramatic "interludes." Of six usually attributed to him, three—*The Play of the Weather* (printed 1533), *A Play of Love* (printed 1533), and *A Dialogue concerning Witty and Witless* (c. 1520–1533)—are little more than moral disputations on set themes. The other three —*A Merry Play between John John the Husband, Tyb the Wife, and Sir John the Priest* (1520–33), *The Play called the Four PP* (c. 1520–22), and *A Merry Play between the Pardoner and the Friar* (1513–21)—have some dramatic value. Here there is more stage action, more real characterization, and more of the unabashed ribaldry of Chaucer's bawdier pilgrims. Although Heywood's interludes reveal the influences of the medieval morality, *débat*, and fabliau, they mark, nevertheless, a distinct advance toward the later Tudor realistic comedy.

HEYWOOD, Thomas (c. 1570–1641) was an actor who stoutly defended his calling (*An Apology for Actors*, 1612) and an amazingly prolific playwright. After almost forty years in the theater, he wrote of having had "either an entire hand, or at least a main finger" in two hundred and twenty pieces. He composed formless chronicle histories (*Edward IV*, two parts, 1592–9), melodramatic adventure plays (*The Fair Maid of the West*, two parts, 1607–31), dramas of classical mythology, pageants, and masques. But he is at his best as a pioneer in domestic melodrama. Both *A Woman Killed with Kindness* (1603) and *The English Traveller* (1620–33) are sentimental treatments of adultery and heartbreak. In *A Woman Killed*, where he substitutes charity and pathos for the cruelty and horror which his fellow playwrights loved, he comes closest to deserving Charles Lamb's epithet: "A sort of prose Shakespeare."

HIGDEN, Ranulf (d. 1364) was a monk of Chester. His *Polychronicon*, written about 1350, was a Latin survey of world history from the creation down to Higden's own time. The work is better known in the English translation of John de Trevisa (1387), which was printed by William Caxton in 1482.

HILL, Aaron (1685–1750). In a life dedicated to the strenuous pursuit of curious money-making schemes, Hill found time to write plays and poetry. Among his dramatic pieces are the opera *Rinaldo* (1711), to which Handel wrote the music, and four bombastic tragedies adapted from Voltaire: *Zara* (1736), *Alzira* (1736), *Merope* (1749), and *The Roman Revenge* (1753). Among his non-dramatic productions is *The Progress of Wit* (1730), an answer to Pope, who had attacked him in *The Dunciad* (1728).

HILTON, Arthur Clement (1851–77) was the editor of *The Light Green* (1872), a Cambridge University humorous magazine which survived for only two numbers. Because of some excellent light verse by Hilton, including *The Octopus,* a remarkable parody of Swinburne, the magazine has been treated with a respect which few similar publications either attain or deserve.

HOADLY, Benjamin (1676–1761) was a Whig churchman with one eye on God and the other on political preferment. As Bishop of Bangor and chaplain to King George I, he preached a sermon called *The Nature of the Kingdom or Church of Christ* (1717) which touched off the so-called "Bangorian Controversy" on the relative importance of Church and State. He was answered in three letters (1717–19) by William Law.

HOADLY, Benjamin (1706–57), son of Bishop Hoadly (1676–1761), was a physician who collaborated with his brother John on a popular comedy called *The Suspicious Husband* (1747). David Garrick was a success in the leading rôle of Ranger.

HOBBES, Thomas (1588–1679). This ambitious man—who worked with Bacon and talked with Galileo, tutored a prince (Charles II) in mathematics, wrote his autobiography in Latin verse, and translated Homer at eighty-six—is remembered today largely for a single work in political philosophy: *Leviathan, or the Matter, Form, and Power of a Commonwealth, Ecclesiastical and Civil* (1651). In it the cynical philosopher pictures natural man as selfish, lawless, unaltruistic—innately addicted to "contention, enmity, and war." Man's only hope of peace and freedom lies in complete surrender to an absolute civil authority (or "leviathan"), preferably a single dictator. Hobbes makes his deductions in a naked, precise, mathematical style far removed from the sonorous word-music of Browne or the quaintly decorated rhetoric of Fuller. The book set England by the ears. Harrington replied to it with his *Commonwealth of Oceana* (1656). Churchmen proscribed it, and Oxford burned it. Yet it lived to leave its mark on the philosophy of state.

HOCCLEVE. Variant spelling of **OCCLEVE.**

HODGSON, Ralph (1871–   ) has published an exceedingly small amount of poetry, but his work reveals conscientious craftsmanship. He is remembered by two long poems, *The Bull* (1913) and *The Song of Honor* (1913), and by a handful of delicate lyrics, including "Time, you old gipsy man," *The Bride,* and *Eve.* Other works include *Poems* (1917) and *Skylark* (1959).

HOGG, James (1770–1835). This Scottish poet, journalist, and novelist was called "the Ettrick Shepherd" because of his early home and occupation. Steeped, like his discoverer, Scott, in the folk ballads of his native land, he dubbed himself "King of the Mountain and Fairy School of Poetry." His poetry varies from simple lyrics like *A Boy's Song* to long, swinging narratives like *Kilmeny.* This poem, a delightful fairy tale of a girl who was carried away by spirits, is the best known of the songs sung to Mary of Scotland by the bards in *The Queen's Wake* (1813). Hogg was a leading contributor to *Blackwood's Magazine* and was co-author, and (as "the Ettrick Shepherd") a chief character, of the lively dialogues called *Noctes Ambrosianae* (*Blackwood's* 1822–35).

HOGG, Thomas Jefferson (1792–1862). While an undergraduate at Oxford, Hogg collaborated with his friend Shelley on a prose pamphlet called *The Necessity of Atheism* (1811), and both were expelled. Hogg's two-volume *Life of Shelley* appeared in 1858.

HOLCROFT, Thomas (1745–1809). In his autobiography Holcroft wrote with roguish gaiety of his early years as stable-boy, shoemaker, tutor, prompter, strolling-player, and hack-writer. His early privations helped later to direct him into William Godwin's footsteps as a serious advocate of revolutionary reforms. Two of his four novels, *Anna St. Ives* (1792) and *Hugh Trevor* (1794), present altruistic men of feeling combatting the greed and intolerance of England's ruling classes. His once-popular play,

The Road to Ruin (1792), is both a lesson against extravagance and a sentimental demonstration of man's innate goodness.

HOLINSHED, Raphael (d. 1580?) was the chief compiler of the *Chronicles of England, Scotland, and Ireland* (1577, 1587). This vast historical and geographical compendium, familiarly known as "Holinshed," was a favorite Elizabethan source book. Spenser drew on it for part of *The Faerie Queene*. Shakespeare went to it for *Macbeth, Cymbeline,* and many of his history plays.

HOLLAND, Philemon (1552–1637) was, in the words of Thomas Fuller, "the Translator General in his age." Going back directly to the original Greek and Latin, he rendered the classics faithfully in a rich and musical, if over-ornamental, prose. Among his translations are those of Livy's *Roman History* (1600), Pliny's *Natural History* (1601), Plutarch's *Morals* (1603), and Suetonius' *History of Twelve Caesars* (1606).

HOME, John (1722–1808) was a Scottish preacher turned playwright. His tragedy, *Douglas* (1756), was a hit in an age of bad tragedies. Legend has it that a fellow-countryman shouted in midperformance: "Weel, lods, hwar's yeer Wolly Shokspeer noo?" It is a romantic reworking of the theme of an old Scottish ballad and is cursed with a minimum of stage business and a number of interminable recitations. One of these ("My name is Norval; on the Grampian hills," Act II, Scene 1) is better known today than all the rest of the tragedy.

HOOD, Thomas (1799–1845) was a magazine editor, versatile poet, and prolific punster. As assistant sub-editor on the *London Magazine* (1821–23), he knew De Quincey, Hazlitt, and Lamb. He was later editor of two annuals—the *Germ* (1829) and the *Comic Annual* (1830–42)—, the *New Monthly Magazine* (1841–43), and *Hood's Magazine* (1844). He could write simple songs ("I remember, I remember," 1827), effective description (*The Haunted House*), exciting narrative (*The Dream of Eugene Aram*, 1829), and fantastic satire (*Miss Kilmansegg and her Precious Leg,* 1841). Fighting constantly against poverty, he pumped the magazines full of pun-laden verses, some no funnier than the practical jokes he played on his wife. But he sometimes wrote in bitter earnest. *The Song of the Shirt* (published in the Christmas number of *Punch,* 1843) is the chant of a real seven-shillings-a-week needlewoman to the stitch-stitch-stitch of the sweat shop. *The Bridge of Sighs* (*Hood's Magazine,* 1844) is a poem about a lost girl's suicide in the river; it tumbles along with helter-skelter polysyllabic rhymes, pathos flirting dangerously with nonsense. Neither is great poetry, but they bid fair to outlive Hood's sunnier pieces. As Lowell wrote when Tom Hood died of consumption:

> "If thou wouldst learn how truly great was he,
>   Go ask it of the poor."

On his monument is inscribed, "He sang the Song of the Shirt."

HOOK, Theodore Edward (1788–1841) was a celebrated practical joker who sang and jested his way into London society. then struggled to pay the debts of loose living by editing magazines and scribbling novels. The novels, such as *Sayings and Doings* (1824–29), *Maxwell* (1830), reveal him as a malicious gossip and a careless satirist who delighted particularly in snobbish ridicule of middle-class social-climbers. In his emphasis on caricature and his prodigal use of minute details, Hook is a forerunner of Dickens.

HOOKER, Richard (1554–1600). According to his biographer, Izaak Walton, this country rector had the meekness of Moses and the patience of Job. These qualities, besides helping Hooker to abide the shrew he married, served to make *Of the Laws of Ecclesiastical Polity* (1594, etc.) a monument of religious tolerance. In it he defended the middle road of Elizabethan Anglicanism against Puritan attacks and pleaded eloquently for a church government based on man's reason, not solely on scriptural authority. The argument is refreshingly free from the snake-bites of Elizabethan lampoons like Gabriel Harvey's. The style, although too heavy with Latinity for modern ears, shows an advance over the parlor tricks of euphuism.

HOPE, Anthony, was the pseudonym of **Sir Anthony Hope Hawkins** (1863–1933), author of *The Prisoner of Zenda* (1894) and its sequel *Rupert of Hentzau* (1898). During the renaissance of romantic fiction at the close of the nineteenth century, few novels were more popular than these breathless tales of the trials of resourceful Rudolf Rassendyl at the hands of the villain Rupert. And Ruritania, the never-never land where the scene was set, has since become a symbol of glamorous escapism. Anthony Hope also wrote the witty, once-popular *Dolly Dialogues* (1894).

HOPKINS, Gerard Manley (1844–89) studied at Oxford under Walter Pater. In 1866 he met Cardinal Newman and was converted to Roman Catholicism, entering the Jesuit priesthood two years later. He taught Greek at the University of Dublin from

1884 until his death. Although most of Hopkins' poems were written in the seventies and eighties, they were published post-humously. Robert Bridges, the friend to whom they had been consigned, released them gradually, a few appearing in A. H. Miles' *The Poets and Poetry of the Century* (vol. VIII) in 1893, several more in 1916, the first relatively complete collection in 1918, and an augmented collection in 1930. It is doubtful if Hopkins' fame would have come in the Victorian era, had his poems been published then. His favorite themes—pious love of nature, as in *Pied Beauty,* sympathy with laboring men, as in *Felix Randal* and *Harry Ploughman*—are conventional enough, and there is nothing puzzling about the form or content of an exquisite lyric like *Heaven-Haven*. But Hopkins' prevailing intel-lectualism and ceaseless technical experiment were alien to the calm, sweet Victorian tradition. Like Bridges, he was a patient student of prosody. He experimented with ellipsis, startling com-pound words, and the alliteration so vital to Old English poetry. He even coined his own terms; the meter of *The Windhover,* for example, he described as "falling paeonic rhythm, sprung and outriding." Hopkins, then, is not an exhumed Victorian; he is a modern poet. And since 1930, his name has been magic to many of the younger poets of both England and America.

HORNE, Richard Henry or **Hengist** (1803–84) was a playwright, poet, critic, and adventurer. His tragedies, *Cosmo de' Medici*—in verse—(1837) and *The Death of Marlowe*—in mixed prose and verse—(1837), contain some good passages but were never pro-duced. His epic poem, *Orion* (1843), which he cynically peddled for a farthing a copy, is, of course, often said to be worth con-siderably more. Elizabeth Barrett, not yet Mrs. Browning, helped him on his critical work, *A New Spirit of the Age* (1844). His *Australian Facts and Prospects* (1859) includes the spirited tale of his adventures "down under" as a gold-escort.

HOUSMAN, A(lfred) E(dward) (1859–1936). Like Thomas Gray and other English poets who loved quality in verse, A. E. Hous-man wrote exquisitely but meagerly. His first poems he hid modestly away for many years, and it was not until 1896 that *A Shropshire Lad* appeared. Then for a quarter of a century more he continued to write before publishing *Last Poems* in 1922. Finally, in the autumn following his death *More Poems* was issued by his brother Laurence. These three slender volumes have put their creator securely among the best of the modern lyric poets of England. Every poem in them has been written with such classical restraint in word and feeling that not a line can be spared—and this is a sound measure of high art.

Housman was born in Worcestershire, east of the Shropshire hills that were the inspiration of his first poems. The classical studies in which he excelled at Oxford he continued to follow even during his ten years of service as Higher Division clerk in the London Patent Office. This position he resigned in 1892 to become professor of Latin in University College, London; in 1911 he took a similar post at Cambridge University.

His saturation in the best poetry of the Latin lyrists is apparent in the compression and economy of his lines. He gets his effects almost as much by what he omits as by what he says, and his verses are filled with eloquent silences. There is, moreover, a mood of pagan melancholy in his poems. He denied that this poignancy has its source in pessimism. The mood, like Wordsworth's, comes from listening to "the still, sad music of humanity."

> "They say my verse is sad: no wonder;
>   Its narrow measure spans
> Tears of eternity, and sorrow,
>   Not mine, but man's."

In most of his poems he echoes Shakespeare's lament that

> "Golden lads and girls all must,
> As chimney-sweepers, come to dust."

Housman objected to being called "pure Latinist"; his inspiration came too, he said, from Shakespeare's songs and from the English and Scottish popular ballads. His debt to Shakespeare is readily apparent, and that to the ballads also appears frequently, as, for example, in the tragic echoes of *Edward* and *The Wife of Usher's Well* in the eighth of his Shropshire Lad series. But in spite of these English influences the Latin classics must be thought of as the first source of his literary inspiration.

HOUSMAN, Laurence (1865–   ), unlike his brother, A. E. Housman, has written prolifically in a number of fields. Among his numerous dramatic productions are thirty-six little plays on the life of St. Francis (1922–33) and *Victoria Regina* (1934), a successful "dramatic biography." His novels include *An Englishwoman's Love Letters,* published anonymously in 1900, and *Trimblerigg* (1924), a bitter political satire. His autobiography he called *The Unexpected Years* (1937).

HOWARD, Sir Robert (1626–98), Restoration playwright, historian, and politician, was John Dryden's brother-in-law. Dryden collaborated with him on *The Indian Queen* (1664), a bombastic work which is sometimes awarded the doubtful distinction of being the first heroic play in English. By himself Howard wrote *The Surprisal* (1662) and *The Committee* (1662)—comedies—and *The Duke of Lerma* (1668), a tragedy, as well as several historical studies. He is the Crites of Dryden's *Essay of Dramatic Poesy*. His brothers, **Edward** (1624–c. 1700) and **James** (b. 1630?), also wrote plays.

HOWELL, James (1594?–1666) is remembered chiefly as the author of *Epistolae Ho-Elianae* (1645–55), a collection of "familiar letters domestic and forren" on a wide variety of subjects. Some of them are essays written to imaginary correspondents. Many were composed in the Fleet prison, where Howell was imprisoned as a Royalist from 1643 to 1651.

HUCHOWN (fl. 14th cent.). The mysterious "Huchown of the Awle Ryale" is mentioned as a "maker" in Andrew of Wyntoun's *Orygynale Cronykle*, written about 1420. He is perhaps "the gude Syr Hew of Eglintoun," a Scottish statesman whom Dunbar mentions in his *Lament for the Makers*. To him has been ascribed a chain of alliterative romances, including an alliterative *Morte Arthure*, *The Pistyl of Susan*, *Gawain and the Green Knight*, *Patience*, *The Pearl*, and *Cleanness*. Of these the first two ascriptions are the most probable.

HUDSON, William Henry (1841–1922) was born of American parents on the pampas of Argentina but moved to England in 1869 and became a British subject in 1900. He was a semi-invalid from youth on and struggled against poverty most of his life. He did not taste fame until his middle sixties, when a second edition of *Green Mansions* (1904) appeared with a preface by Galsworthy. Had he not been blessed with greater gifts, Hudson would be remembered as a keen-eyed ornithologist, the author of numerous books on birds. But he was also a remarkable writer and a born romantic. Throughout the years in England he lived still in the magic continent of his boyhood. He wrote about it in *The Purple Land* (1885), a semi-autobiographical tale of revolution in Uruguay; *Green Mansions,* the romance of a man's hopeless love for Rima, the enchanting bird-girl of the Orinoco jungle; *A Little Boy Lost* (1905), the story of a South American Mowgli; and *Far Away and Long Ago* (1918), the nostalgic narrative of the author's early life. These four books, especially *Green Mansions,* have captivated hundreds of readers who are not responsive to the books of ordinary nature-lovers.

HUEFFER, Ford Madox. See FORD, Ford Madox.

HUGHES, Thomas (fl. 1587) was the author of one of the most elaborate of the Elizabethan classical tragedies, *The Misfortunes of Arthur,* presented by the "Gentlemen of Graye's Inne" before Her Majesty at Greenwich in 1588. Like the earlier *Gorboduc* (1562) of Norton and Sackville, Hughes' tragedy was drawn from early British legend but was heavily permeated with the mood and the devices of the Senecan tragedies. "The dumbe showes" which adorn the play were "partly devised" by other young gentlemen of Gray's Inn.

HUGHES, Thomas (1822–96) was, like Charles Kingsley, a follower of the "Christian Socialist" F. D. Maurice. Some of his reforming spirit is reflected in the two novels for which he is remembered today, *Tom Brown's Schooldays* (1857) and the less successful *Tom Brown at Oxford* (1861). In the first of these he gave a relatively authentic picture of Rugby under the headmastership of Dr. Thomas Arnold and awoke some Englishmen to the shortcomings of their fashionable public schools.

HUME, David (1711–76). One of the most restless Scottish writers of the eighteenth century was the philosopher and historian David Hume. He was born—like James Boswell, the son of a Scotch laird—at Ninewells, just over the English border, but he flitted about a good deal before finally settling in Edinburgh a few years before his death. He was secretary to General St. Clair and was with his chief in the Orient and later in Austria and Italy. In the sixties he was in Paris with Lord Hertford, and there made the acquaintance of the famous Frenchman Rousseau. And he shuttled between London and Edinburgh, living for considerable periods in both cities.

Wherever he was he kept writing. His *Treatise on Human Nature* was written during an early sojourn in France in 1734, but was not published until five years later. In his native town of Ninewells in 1737 he wrote *Essays, Moral and Political;* these were published anonymously in 1741–2. During his services to General St. Clair he wrote *Philosophical Essays concerning Human Understanding* (published 1748), and shortly after his return to England in 1749 published his *Enquiry concerning Morals* (1751) and his *Political Discourses* (1752). His *Dialogues concerning Natural Religion* were also written in the fifties but were not published until 1779, three years after his death. Hume's famous histories appeared while he was living in Edinburgh. The first volume of the *History of Great Britain* was issued in 1754, and the second volume three years later. The *Natural History of Religion* was published in 1757. Hume's essays on religion earned him a reputation for atheism, but he probably was not nearly so radical as his enemies made him out to be. He described himself as "a man of mild disposition, of command of temper, of an open, social, and cheerful humor." The prose of his histories makes up in vigor what it lacks in polish. His historical statements are often far from accurate, usually because he wrote with a Tory enthusiasm that led to his frequent distortion of Whig accomplishments.

HUNT, (James Henry) Leigh (1784–1859). In 1818 Tory *Blackwood's Magazine* called him "the meanest, the filthiest, and the most vulgar of Cockney poetasters." This judgment was not based entirely on aesthetic principles. As editor of the *Examiner* and the *Reflector,* Hunt had been a notable Tory-baiter, and for his attack on the fat, middle-aged Prince Regent—later George IV—he had already served a two-year prison term (1813–15). Certainly the King of the "Cockney School" was a better poet than his political enemies would admit. Although his long narrative poem, *The Story of Rimini* (1816), is seldom read today, it is worth remembering as a serious experiment in opening the closed couplet. His simple sermonette, *Abou ben Adhem,* and his fragile rondeau, "Jenny kissed me," have persistently escaped the winnowings of the anthologists. On the whole, however, his prose is better than his poetry. In addition to much capable routine journalism, he composed charming familiar essays, a graceful autobiography (1850), and some honest literary criticism. The critical clairvoyance which led him to take young John Keats under his wing was unhealthful for Endymion's poetry and reputation. But Leigh Hunt at least knew a true poet when he saw one.

HURD, Richard (1720–1808), Bishop of Lichfield and Worcester, was a literary critic. His *Letters on Chivalry and Romance* (1762) presents an early example of the interest in the Middle Ages which heralded the dawn of English Romanticism.

HUTCHINSON, Lucy (b. 1620) was the wife of Colonel John Hutchinson, the Puritan Governor of Nottingham who signed the death warrant of King Charles I. Her *Memoirs of the Life of Colonel Hutchinson* (published 1806) is both a fervid defense of the Puritan cause and a monument to marital devotion. It is a valuable eye-witness picture of the Civil War and a miniature landmark in English biography.

HUTTON, Richard Holt (1826–97). As co-editor with Walter Bagehot of the *National Review* from 1855 to 1864 and as co-editor of the *Spectator* from 1861 to 1897, Hutton exerted a signifi-cant influence on English thought. He was more interested in theology, however, than in literature proper. His books include *Essays, Theological and Literary* (1871) and *Aspects of Religious and Scientific Thought* (1899).

HUXLEY, Aldous (Leonard) (1894–   ) is the brother of the biologist Julian Huxley, the son of the writer Leonard Huxley, the grandson of Thomas Henry Huxley, and the grand-nephew of Matthew Arnold. He went to fashionable Eton, where eye trouble left him nearly sightless, and to Balliol College, Oxford. Since serving his journalistic apprenticeship in London, first as a staff-member of the *Athenaeum* (1919–20), and then as dramatic critic for the *Westminster Gazette* (1920–1), he has spent his life wandering and writing, traveling in Italy, Mexico, and the United States. Recently he has made his home in Southern California, where he has done some writing for the motion pictures.

Novel-writing, Huxley once said in an interview, is "like catch-as-catch-can wrestling. You can do what you can get away with." And as a novelist, he has shown little reverence for artistic form. For example, in his early novels, *Crome Yellow* (1921), *Antic Hay* (1923), and *These Barren Leaves* (1925), he pursued the simple formula of Thomas Love Peacock: introduce a mis-cellaneous collection of clever people to one another, and have them converse brilliantly on all conceivable subjects. Yet in *Point Counter Point* (1928), with its ingenious contrapuntal construc-tion, borrowed from the realm of music, and in *Eyeless in Gaza* (1936), with its confusing handling of the time element, Huxley revealed himself as a serious student of new techniques within the novel-form. Primarily Huxley is a satirist, a satirist with a gamut which extends from the playful intellectual wit of a Peacock or a Meredith to the dark savagery of a Swift. In his early novels, he scorched the wells of traditional values one by one and left behind the bitter dregs of disillusionment. Even faith in science, which his grandfather held so dear, is blasted in *Brave New World* (1932)—with its monstrous caricature of a future in which Ford-plant efficiency has replaced emotion, and babies are produced in test-tubes. Hence Huxley is generally considered as the epitome of the intellectual cynicism which per-vaded the intelligentsia of the 1920's. Some critics, however, re-fuse to discard him as an anachronism. They point to affirmative values in his books, particularly to the humanism of Mr. Propter in his novel *After Many a Summer* (1939). In addition to his novels, Huxley has published poems, short-stories (*Brief Candles,* 1930), travel books, a provocative outline of his personal philosophy (*Ends and Means,* 1937), and an excellent biography of Father Joseph, right-hand man of Cardinal Richelieu (*Grey Eminence,* 1941).

HUXLEY, Thomas Henry (1825–95) was the most dogged and effective of the Victorian scientists who crusaded in defense of Charles Darwin's evolutionary hypothesis. In his boyhood he had a brief period of formal schooling and spent long hours in self-education inspired by an "extraordinary attraction . . . towards the study of the intricacies of living structure." After completing his medical training at the Charing Cross School of Medicine, he spent four years (1846–50) in the South Seas as Assistant Surgeon on H.M.S. *Rattlesnake,* returning to find that one of the scientific papers which he had been sending home had actually been published by the Royal Society. In 1854 he accepted a post as Lecturer on Natural History in the Government School of Mines in London and was launched on a lifetime career of teaching and research. The extent of his scientific researches can be inferred from a glance at the list of 173 monographs mentioned by his son and biographer, Leonard Huxley. But, as he himself admitted in his genial, modest *Autobiography* (1889), it was for his teaching that he wanted most to be remembered—for his devotion "to the popularization of science; to the development and organization of scientific education; and to untiring opposition to that ecclesiastical spirit . . . which in England . . . is the deadly enemy of science." This "agnostic"—it was a word he coined himself to fit his form of skepticism—fought "battles and skirmishes" against Bishop Wilberforce on man's descent from the apes, against Matthew Arnold on the relative importance of science and literature in education, against Gladstone on the historical accuracy of the Bible in regard to the miracle of the Gadarene swine. A stubborn adversary, he called himself "Darwin's bulldog." Arnold, who battled against him persistently, called him "the very prince of debaters."

For the general reader the most important of Huxley's writings are his popular lectures, many of them originally delivered to audiences of workers. These include talks on science in general and on the place of science in education. To the first category belong the following: the famous exposition of the scientific method in Lecture III of the 1863 series *On Our Knowledge of the Causes of the Phenomena of Organic Nature;* and three of the *Lay Sermons* (published 1870), *On the Advisableness of Improving Natural Knowledge, On the Physical Basis of Life,* and *On a Piece of Chalk.* To the second category belong *A Liberal Education: and Where to Find it* (*Lay Sermons*), *Address on University Education* (delivered at the opening of Johns Hopkins University in 1876), and *Science and Culture* (delivered at the opening of Sir Josiah Mason's Science College at Birmingham in 1880). These lectures are gems of lucid expression and still appear perennially in the composition books as models of exposition. No writer on science has succeeded better in striking the tenuous balance between the ponderosity of technical jargon and the self-conscious breeziness which too often characterizes the popularizings of the science-for-the-millions school.

HYDE, Edward. See CLARENDON.

I

INCHBALD, Elizabeth (1753–1821) was a novelist, playwright, play-editor, actress, and well-known beauty. In her plays she combined comedy of manners with sentimental moralizing. Among them are *I'll Tell You What* (1785), *Such Things Are* (1787), and *Everyone has his Fault* (1793). Her novels are novels of purpose. In *A Simple Story* (1791) she admittedly set out to prove the importance of a proper education; in *Nature and Art* (1796) she used the *Sandford and Merton* formula, drawing the "instructive contrast" between an unspoiled child of nature and his unbearable cousin, who has been the victim of a "civilized" education.

INGELOW, Jean (1820–97) was a popular Victorian versifier who occasionally struck a note of real poetry. Her first series of *Poems* (1863) went through twenty-three editions by 1880. Among her best poems are *Divided* and *High Tide on the Coast of Lincolnshire, 1571.* She also wrote fiction.

IRELAND, William Henry (1777–1835) was a literary impostor. His forged Shakespeariana range from mere signatures to complete manuscripts of two plays, *Vortigern and Rowena* and *Henry II,* both published in 1799. Despite its obvious clumsy borrowings from Shakespeare's tragedies, *Vortigern* was actually produced at Drury Lane in 1796 before its teen-age author confessed his dishonesty.

J

JACOBS, W(illiam) W(ymark) (1863–1944), short-story writer and playwright, was the son of a London wharf-owner. As the titles of his short-story collections imply—*Many Cargoes* (1896), *Light Freights* (1901), *Deep Waters* (1919)—most of his tales have a background of shipping, and most of his characters are longshoremen and river sailors. His taste for humorous exaggeration is reflected in such nautical yarns as *The Skipper's Wooing* and *A Change of Treatment.* Neither humorous nor nautical is his most celebrated story, *The Monkey's Paw,* a classic of horror that has been converted into a successful one-act play.

JAMES I (1394–1437) was King of Scotland from 1424 until his violent death. He was the author (to all but a few skeptics) of *The King's Quair* (written c. 1424), a poem of 1379 lines about his love for Joan Beaufort, niece to Henry IV of England. The royal poet met and married her at the end of nineteen years' imprisonment in England (1405–24). Although used several times by Chaucer, the seven-line stanza (*ababbcc*) of the poem is called "rhyme royal" in James' honor. The story has many of the artificial trappings of the dream allegories spawned by the *Roman de la Rose.* It echoes Chaucer throughout, particularly *The Knight's Tale.* King James is the earliest of the "Scottish Chaucerians."

JAMES, George Payne Rainsford (1799–1860) was a popular imitator of Scott who concocted about sixty historical novels from a single recipe. One of these is *Richelieu, or A Tale of France* (1829). In *Novels by Eminent Hands* (1847) Thackeray ridiculed his stock beginnings.

JAMES, Henry (1843–1916) is one of the small group of Anglo-American writers who are entitled by their American birth and their British citizenship to a place in the literary history of both countries. He was born in New York City in a family in which good breeding, cultivation of the intellect, and social restraint were the normal way of life. His father—also a Henry James—was a philosopher with an enthusiasm for the teachings of Swedenborg. His older brother William became the brilliant professor of philosophy and pragmatist at Harvard University. It may be partly because of these family connections that the younger Henry is said, in a familiar critical cliché, to have employed fiction only as the vehicle for his psychological and philosophical ideas. James' literary ancestors in America were the New England thinkers and mystics, Emerson, Thoreau, and especially Hawthorne. But in spite of these spiritual ties with his native land, he became increasingly impatient with what he regarded as the almost total lack of literary and historical perspective in America. Ultimately, in 1876, he climaxed long periods of sojourning in England and on the Continent by establishing a permanent residence in London. Here, in the quiet atmosphere of late Victorian England, he lived the life of a cultivated man of letters, pouring out his novels for a public of the *intelligentsia* and renewing his spiritual enthusiasms for literature and art by communing with the monuments of the past and the creators of the present. Although before very many years he came to be regarded by many as more British than American, it was not until 1915, the year before his death, that he actually became a British subject. He was moved to take this step, it was said at the time, by his resentment at the slowness of the Americans in bringing aid to the British in their struggle against Germany. What the British thought of him appears in their giving him the "Order of Merit" on New Year's Day, 1916.

Henry James has sometimes been called "the American literary ambassador to England." The epithet is not entirely unjustified. Living in London for almost the whole of his professional life, he wrote, nevertheless, principally about the Americans, and usually about Americans abroad. Such novels as *Roderick Hudson* (1876), *The American* (1877), *Daisy Miller* (1879), and *The Portrait of a Lady* (1881) have to do with the impingement of the Old World culture upon the New World type of character. He was more successful in dealing with the American character than with the American scene and did not consider *Washington Square* (1881) and *The Bostonians* (1886) as among his best novels. Until the end of his life the novel was the principal channel of his artistic expression, but occasionally he varied his output with a collection of stories—*The Real Thing and Other Tales* (1893) and *The Two Magics* (1898)—with a biography—*Nathaniel Hawthorne* (1880)—or with autobiographical sketches—*A Small Boy and Others* (1913) and *Notes of a Son and Brother* (1914).

The narrative technique of Henry James is that of the psychoanalyst. He was more concerned with situations than with plots, with characters than with stories, with dialogue than with action. In dissecting his characters he is complete, careful, detailed. He writes with the painstaking care of a portrait—sometimes a miniature—painter, and his literary brush strokes are fine and delicate. As a result his writing is so involute, his mood so frequently cold, and his tempo so slow that readers who like compression, crispness, feeling, and rapid movement are often impatient with him. He was never a popular writer—a fact which did not, apparently, concern him in the least. Of all his novels the only one that approached popularity is *Daisy Miller* (1879), the story of a charming young American girl abroad, and this novel, significantly enough, contains tender sentiment that is exceedingly rare in the work of James. But that his usual unemotional treatment of his material is not ineffective is apparent, to illustrate, in such long short-stories as *The Real Thing* (1893) and that most terrible of psychological ghost stories, *The Turn of the Screw* (1898).

JAMESON, (Margaret) Storm (1897–   ) is one of the most talented of modern English novelists. Among her novels are *Three Kingdoms* (1926), in which she treats the familiar feminine problem of marriage vs. career; the three parts of a trilogy about a Victorian woman, *The Lovely Ship* (1927), *The Voyage Home* (1930), and *A Richer Dust* (1931); and *Cloudless May* (1944), a long, somber, well-documented novel about the fall of France. Storm Jameson has also published a historical essay, *The Decline of Merry England* (1930), and an autobiography, *No Time Like the Present* (1933).

JEFFERIES, Richard (1848–87) was an essayist and novelist who wrote, from intimate acquaintance, about the English countryside. His feeling for nature is dominant in *The Gamekeeper at Home* (1878), a collection of "sketches," *Wood Magic* (1881), a "fable," and *The Story of My Heart* (1883), a spiritual autobiography. He has been compared with Gilbert White, whose *Natural History of Selborne* he edited in 1887.

JEFFREY, Francis, Lord (1773–1850). Shortly after his admission to the bar, this versatile Scot became co-founder and editor (1802–29) of the Whig *Edinburgh Review*. He was soon hailed by Byron as "pertest of the train" of "Scotch reviewers." He wrote criticism like an attorney arguing a case; while he privately admired Wordsworth's poems, he posed in print as defense counsel for eighteenth-century conventions in poetry and relentless prosecutor of the experimenting "Lakers." His review of Wordsworth's *Excursion* (1814), beginning abruptly with "This will never do," has become a classic of critical damnation. Jeffrey was a brilliant phrase-maker and an important pioneer in the use of the review as a mere springboard into an essay on a broad aspect of literature. But he lacked intuitive feeling for poetry and was not untainted by the original sins of reviewers: name-calling, hair-splitting, quoting by the yard without comment, catch-all generalizing, and unabashed gushing.

JERROLD, Douglas William (1803–57). In addition to his celebrated play *Black-eyed Susan* (1829), Jerrold wrote a number of popular comedies, including *The Prisoner of War* (1842), *Time Works Wonders* (1845), and *The Catspaw* (1850). But his journalistic work is of more lasting importance. Under the pseudonym "Q" he contributed to *Punch* from the very first years of its life (1841), and such *jeux d'esprit* as *Punch's Letters to his Son* (1843), *Punch's Complete Letter-Writer* (1845), and, best known of all, *Mrs. Caudle's Curtain Lectures* (1846), set the characteristic tone of that inimitable, unextinguishable publication.

JEWSBURY, Geraldine Endsor (1812–80), and **Maria Jane** (1800–33). Geraldine was a homely, ninety-pound bluestocking who wrote novels (*Zoe,* 1845; *The Half-Sisters,* 1848) which in her day were considered naughty. She hero-worshipped Carlyle. When she visited Chelsea, she lay at the sage's feet looking up at him, and then went home and wrote spiteful letters to Jane Welsh Carlyle sympathizing with her for having to live with such a man. Her older sister, Maria, was a minor poetess who was much admired by Wordsworth.

JOCELIN of Brakelond (fl. 1200) was the monk of Bury St. Edmunds whose Latin chronicle about his monastery (1173–1202) was the source of the "past" which Carlyle depicted in *Past and Present* (1843).

JOHNSON, Lionel Pigot (1867–1902) was a Roman Catholic poet, critic, and scholar. Among his volumes of verse are *Poems* (1895), *Ireland, with Other Poems* (1897), and *Poetical Works* (1915). His prose works include a valuable essay on *The Art of Thomas Hardy* (1894) and *Post Liminium* (1911), a collection of "essays and critical papers."

JOHNSON, Richard (1573–1659?), an Elizabethan hack, was the author of *The Most Famous History of the Seven Champions of Christendom* (1596–7), a popular book of legends about St. George and the six knights whom he released from enchantment.

JOHNSON, Samuel (1709–84) was born in Lichfield, the older son of a melancholy bookseller. He entered Pembroke College, Oxford, in the fall of 1728, but three years later was forced by poverty to leave without a degree. Then followed a brief but tedious interval of teaching in the Market-Bosworth School, Leicestershire, and a period of hack-writing in Birmingham and

Lichfield. In 1735 Johnson married Elizabeth Porter, a fat Birmingham widow twenty-three years his senior. Down to the
moment of her death in 1752 he "proved a most affectionate and
indulgent husband." In 1736 he established a private academy
for "young gentlemen" at Edial in Staffordshire. It turned out
to be a *very* private academy, and in the following year Johnson
went up to London with one of his three pupils, a young gentleman named David Garrick. In London the pupil was to become
England's most celebrated actor, the teacher her most eminent
man of letters.

Only a year after his arrival, Johnson's anonymous poem *London* (1738) was well received. But he had to struggle against
poverty for a quarter of a century. For a time he shared the worst
privations of Grub Street with the poet Richard Savage (d. 1743),
being saved from utter destitution by occasional hack-work like
reporting the Parliamentary debates for the *Gentleman's Magazine.* Although his fame was established before *The Vanity of
Human Wishes* appeared in 1749, the poem brought him but
fifteen guineas, only five more than *London.* The age of patronage
was dying. Between 1747, when Johnson addressed the *Plan* for
his *Dictionary* to Lord Chesterfield, and February 7, 1755, when
he greeted His Lordship's tardy puffs with an immortal epistolary
snub, the lexicographer received exactly ten pounds from his
noble "patron." And in 1759 he composed *Rasselas* "in the eve-
nings of one week" to pay for his mother's funeral. But in 1762
Johnson's luck changed; he received a government pension of
three hundred pounds a year for life. On May 16 in the following year he met James Boswell, his biographer.

More than four-fifths of Boswell's *Life of Johnson* (1791) deals
with the twenty-one years of their friendship, and it is the
Johnson of this period whom all the world knows best. He was
a gigantic, misshapen caricature of a man, disfigured by scrofula
and blind in one eye—a man obsessed by prejudice, plagued by
indolence, and often steeped in melancholy—an amazing con-
versationalist, whether growling at "the Club" with Reynolds,
Burke, and Goldsmith, baiting "Bozzy" at the Mitre Tavern,
conversing with the Thrales at Streatham Park, dining with John
Wilkes at a London publisher's, or talking with King George
himself at Buckingham Palace. His friends called him "Ursa
Major," but Goldsmith observed that he had "nothing of the
bear but his skin." For he was as tender, generous, and human
as any figure in English literary history.

Although Johnson wrote unnumbered prefaces, prologues, book

reviews, prayers, sermons, translations, and occasional verses, the list of his major works is not long. His best-known poems are two imitations of verse satires by the Roman poet Juvenal (c. A.D. 60–c. 130). In *London* Johnson comments caustically on the degeneracy of the metropolis and alludes with gloomy self-pity to the slow rise of "worth, by poverty depressed." In *The Vanity of Human Wishes,* he soberly considers specific examples of thwarted ambition in various worldly walks and concludes that man should pray to Heaven for a healthful mind, obedient passions, love, patience, and faith. Although Johnson's heroic couplets are heavy with the circumlocutions and "poetic diction" of the time, the verse is smooth, dignified, and sometimes forceful. There is less to be said for the blank verse of the static tragedy *Irene* (written 1736–7), and Johnson's first and last play met a cool reception at Drury Lane in 1749. Shortly thereafter he began the *Rambler* (March 20, 1750–March 14, 1752), a series of didactic periodical essays on a wide variety of subjects. The *Rambler* belongs to the school of the *Spectator* and the *Tatler,* but there are obvious differences. As Boswell observed, "Addison writes with the ease of a gentleman. His readers fancy that a wise and accomplished companion is talking to them. . . . Johnson writes like a teacher. He dictates to his readers as if from an academical chair." And although Johnson's later periodical, the *Idler* (April 15, 1758–April 5, 1760), has "less body and more spirit," his humor is not the effervescent wit of Dick Steele. In the 1750's Johnson also wrote his only novel and completed his *Dictionary. Rasselas, Prince of Abyssinia* (1759) is a series of reflections on "the vanity of human wishes" tied together by a slender thread of narrative. The *Dictionary* (1755) was a monumental effort "to settle the orthography, display the analogy, regulate the strictures, and ascertain the signification of *English* words." To most readers its charm as a book lies in one of its most obvious shortcomings as a dictionary—Johnson's irrepressible tendency to color definitions with his whims and prejudices. In his famous entries under *Oats, Patron, Pension,* and *Willow,** he hardly conformed to his own definition of *Lexicographer:* "a writer of dictionaries, a harmless drudge."

---

* *Oats:* a grain which in England is generally given to horses, but in Scotland supports the people. *Patron:* one who countenances, supports, or protects. Commonly a wretch who supports with insolence, and is paid with flattery. *Pension:* an allowance made to anyone without an equivalent. In England it is generally understood to mean pay given to a state hireling for treason to his country. *Willow:* a tree worn by forlorn lovers.

Johnson's best-known contributions to literary criticism are his edition of Shakespeare (1765) and his *Lives of the Poets* (1779–81). The *Preface* to the Shakespeare contains a famous defense of the playwright's violations of the sacred unities of time, place, and action—a remarkable piece of forward-looking criticism in an age still enslaved by classical bonds. The *Lives* includes short critical biographies of fifty-two English poets from Cowley (1618–67) to Lyttleton (1709–73). Among them is the *Life of Richard Savage,* which had first appeared in 1744, a year after the Grub Street poet's death. Some of these short biographies, notably those of Milton and Gray, bristle with private prejudices. But, on the whole, Johnson shows in full measure the sanity and wisdom which made his contemporaries worship him as "the Great Cham of literature."

During his lifetime Johnson actually used several different styles, but like Carlyle he is remembered for a single one—eloquent and dignified, but freighted with ponderous Latinisms, mechanical antitheses, and tiresome tautologies. The shadow of this "great-whale" style falls across his time, and few of the prose writers of the next century could escape entirely from its baleful influence. Most modern readers prefer the direct, blunt speech of the man who thunders at Boswell in the *Life*.

JOHNSON–CORY, William. See CORY, William Johnson.

JOHNSTONE, Charles (1719?–1800) is remembered as the author of *Chrysal, or The Adventures of a Guinea* (1760–5), a satirical novel in which the guinea tells the story of its passing from owner to owner.

JONES, Henry Arthur (1851–1929). Although his plays are dated and all but forgotten, Jones deserves a place among the pioneers of the modern English drama. He worked valiantly to introduce a degree of naturalism into a theater which throughout the nineteenth century had been slumbering in a dream-world miles away from the everyday problems of everyday people. In this effort Jones was preceded by Tom Robertson and followed by Sir Arthur Wing Pinero. His first important play, *The Silver King* (1882), caused a minor revolution in the theater. Among the later plays are *The Masqueraders* (1894), *The Case of Rebellious Susan* (1894), and, often called his masterpiece, *The Liars* (1897). In addition to writing some sixty plays, Jones crusaded tirelessly in the cause of a "modern national drama" which would express "all that is vital and preservative and honourable in English life."

His struggle is recorded in *The Renascence of the English Drama* (based on essays and lectures, 1883–94, collected in 1895) and *Foundations of a National Drama* (essays and lectures collected 1913).

JONES, Sir William (1746–94), jurist, orientalist, philologist, and poet, pioneered in the study of Sanskrit and comparative philology. He published scholarly legal works, a *Grammar of the Persian Language* (1771), and numerous translations from Asiatic literature. His gift as a poet is shown in his *Ode in Imitation of Alcaeus* (1782) and the well-known epigram from the Persian, "On parent knees, a naked new-born child."

JONSON Ben(jamin) (1572–1637). No writer of the Elizabethan and Jacobean periods was such a bundle of inconsistencies as Ben Jonson. A thorough classical scholar, he was, nevertheless, the most vivid of contemporary realists. A bear-like personal satirist, he drew, however, the admiration and affection of younger poets. A composer of formal tragedies, he also composed the lovely song by which he is best known today, "Drink to me only with thine eyes." The more he is considered, the more astonishing does his character appear, and the more varied his attainments seem to be. Jonson's stepfather was a bricklayer, and he does not appear to have attended college; yet he educated himself so that his allusion to Shakespeare's "small Latin and less Greek" is not absurd. He was a soldier in the Dutch wars; he killed an actor in a duel; he wrote masques for the court and became court poet in 1616, the year of Shakespeare's death; in the same year he published in folio his "complete works"—a very bumptious procedure for the times. What he lost in royal favor on the death of James I in 1625, he made up in popularity with the young Cavalier poets who formed the "tribe of Ben" around his table at the Mermaid Tavern, where the conversation "outdid the frolic wine."

Of Ben Jonson's writings, his prose could best be dispensed with. *Underwoods* and *Timber, or Discoveries Made Upon Men and Matter,* both unpublished until three years after his death, are miscellanies of observation and comment. Too often, they reveal the result of Jonson's persistent habit of note-taking and paraphrasing. Except for their lyrics his court masques, detached from the pageantry of which they were the core, are as skeletal as so many opera librettos. In the creation of these extravagant court entertainments, Jonson collaborated with the painter and designer Inigo Jones—collaborated until they quarrelled violently

over the relative importance of their contributions. Of Jonson's
many masques perhaps the best are *The Masque of Queens*
(1609) and *Oberon* (1611). His construction of masques influenced some of his semi-dramatic writing, such as his unfinished *Hue and Cry after Cupid* (1608) and his *Sad Shepherd*
(printed 1641). Jonson was essentially a satirist. But, moved apparently by the popular success of Shakespeare's *Julius Caesar*
(1599), he wrote *Sejanus* (1603), a tragedy entirely in the classical
manner of Seneca. Although without action on the stage, it is,
on the whole, more actable than his *Catiline* (1611), a tragedy
for which he borrowed scores of lines from Cicero's orations
against the traitor.

Jonson's best dramas are his comedies. Of these a few make
hard reading today. This is especially true of *The Poetaster*
(1601) and *Cynthia's Revels* (1600–1), which embody personal
attacks on his rival dramatists Dekker and Marston. But *Eastward Ho* (1605)—in which he collaborated with Marston and
Chapman on a satire on the king's Scottish courtiers that landed
the three poets behind the bars—is still entertaining. Jonson's
greatest contribution to drama is his development of the comedy
of humors, a type in which he satirizes characters who are controlled by "humors," or ruling passions. *Every Man in His Humor*
(1598) is Jonson's first comedy of this type, and in the induction
of *Every Man out of His Humor* (1599) he defines the term.
All of his comedies of humor reveal the influence of the Latin
plays of Terence and Plautus. The action is restricted in time and
place, the plot is based on intrigue, the characters are contemporary types, the scene is local—or usually so. But within these
classical restrictions Jonson developed vivid satires of London life.
His chief interest was in characters, and his plots are often little
more than dramatic devices for presenting a parade of eccentric
types. But the satire is keen, the episodes are lusty, the characters
are clear and individual, and the comedy is definitely playable—
even before modern audiences. Of the remarkable series of
comedies which Jonson's satirical genius created, the best are:
Volpone, or the Fox (1605–6), a satire on greed; *Epicoene, or
The Silent Woman* (1609), a Jacobean *Charley's Aunt; The
Alchemist* (1610), which presents three London rogues and their
victims; and *Bartholomew Fair* (1614), which introduces the
audience to a congress of London fools and rascals on holiday.
Jonson's later comedies *The Devil is an Ass* (1616), *The Staple
of News* (1625–6), *The New Inn* (1629), *The Magnetic Lady*
(1632), and *A Tale of a Tub* (1633) are heavier, more com-

plicated, and marked by indications of the dramatist's declining power.

JOWETT, Benjamin (1817–93) taught Greek at Oxford for a lifetime and was one of the great classical scholars of the nineteenth century. His commentary on *The Epistles of St. Paul* (1855) is a landmark in the history of liberal theology, and his famous translations of *The Dialogues of Plato* (1871), *Thucydides* (1881), *The Politics of Aristotle* (1885) and *The Republic of Plato* (1894) have earned a place in English literature.

JOYCE, James (Augustine Aloysius) (1882–1941). The external facts in the life of the most amazing modern British novelist can be set down in a few simple sentences. James Joyce was born in Dublin of a "large, shabby-genteel" family. He was educated in the strict Catholic tradition first at the Jesuit "College" of Clongowes Wood, then at Belvedere, finally at the Royal University in Dublin. At seventeen, having already learned Norwegian that he might read the plays in the original, he published an essay on Ibsen in the *Fortnightly Review,* and at nineteen he and a fellow student at the university issued a pamphlet, *The Day of Rabblement,* in which they opposed the movement for a National Theater in Ireland. At twenty-one he took his degree and left for Paris, first to study medicine, then for a time to train his first-rate tenor voice for the concert stage. Upon the death of his mother in 1904, he went to London, where he married, and settled down to write. The short-stories collected in *Dubliners* were ready for the press in 1906 but were withheld until 1914 because of a passage that was supposed to be offensive to King Edward VII. *Chamber Music,* a collection of poems, appeared in 1907. After the publication of *Dubliners* he returned to Europe, and there he lived—at Trieste, Zurich, Rome, and Paris—until the end of his life.

Joyce's four major books reveal his gradual development from an objective observer writing naturalistic short-stories in an orthodox idiom to an introverted genius dwelling in a mysterious world of symbols and expressing himself in an obscure, polylingual medium of his own making. In *Dubliners* Joyce sketched a number of representative types in his native city. In *A Portrait of the Artist as a Young Man* (1916) he turned inward, expressing— with compression rare in autobiographical first novels—the strains and stresses of his own progress from childhood through young manhood. At the end of the novel Stephen Dedalus, liberated from his mother and from the religion in which he had been brought up, leaves Dublin for Paris to pursue a literary career; at the beginning of *Ulysses* (1922) he returns to Dublin to be present at his mother's deathbed. In *Ulysses* the time element is reduced to a single day, June 16, 1904, and Stephen's mental and physical wanderings through Dublin are interwoven with those of a Jewish advertisement canvasser named Leopold Bloom. What was originally projected as a short-story—*Mr. Bloom's Day in Dublin* —has been expanded—through seven years' labor—into an amazingly complex novel.

The intricate allegorical foundation of the novel—Stephen, for example, is Telemachus in search of a spiritual father (Ulysses or Bloom), and Mrs. Bloom is a lecherous, unfaithful Penelope —the subtlety with which Joyce penetrates into the stream of consciousness, and the virtuosity and allusiveness of the language make *Ulysses* one of the most difficult books of our time. Eighteen years after *Ulysses,* an interval marked by the occasional publication of scraps of *Work in Progress,* appeared Joyce's swan song, *Finnegans Wake* (1939). Here the novelist dwells less in the waking consciousness than in the mystic mid-region between waking and sleeping; he has all but abandoned realism for symbolism; and his language—a fascinating farrago of polylingual puns—presents so many difficulties that most critics greeted the book with an air of spellbound futility. Clifton Fadiman's review in the *New Yorker* was entitled, "Don't shoot the book reviewer; he's doing his best."

Joyce's works have brought him a number of reputations. The suppression of *Ulysses*—the American ban was not lifted until the famous decision of Judge Woolsey in 1933—has given him a reputation, both among prudes and students of the salacious, as a mere specialist in pornography. By some he has been accepted skeptically as a pedantic charlatan who devoted his later years to pulling both the public's legs. Among a loyal cult, members of which have supplied keys to both *Ulysses* and *Finnegans Wake,* he is the greatest of modern novelists. Other readers, while admitting his essential sincerity, his prodigious gifts, and his importance as an explorer of uncharted territory, question—at least in regard to *Finnegans Wake*—the ultimate value of a work of art so esoteric that most literate readers can apprehend it only in intermittent glimpses.

JUNIUS. The libels signed with this pseudonym were printed in the *Public Advertiser* between January, 1769, and November, 1771. Letters by the same writer under different disguises appeared both before and after those dates. Junius skillfully smeared George III and the Dukes of Grafton and Bedford while he defended radical John Wilkes. Although he was no mere newspaper crank, literary detectives have doubtless brought him more fame than he deserves. The leading suspect seems to be **Sir Philip Francis** (1740–1818), a secretary in the War Office who was an active anonymous journalist.

K

KAYE–SMITH, Sheila (1888–1956) made her reputation by writing novels—including *Sussex Gorse* (1916), *Green Apple Harvest* (1920), *Joanna Godden* (1921), and *The End of the House of Alard* (1923)—in which she stressed the influence of environment on character. To read them is to journey through the countryside of Sussex and Kent. The theme of religion, which appears in *Green Apple Harvest* and *The End of the House of Alard,* dominates *The Tramping Methodist* (1908), her first novel, and *Shepherds in Sackcloth* (1930). Her autobiography was published in 1937 under the title *Three Ways Home;* it stresses the spiritual elements in her character. In 1944 she collaborated with G. B. Stern on *Speaking of Jane Austen,* a book that reveals her intelligence as a biographer and her unabashed devotion to the nineteenth-century novelist.

KEATS, John (1795–1821) was the son of the keeper of a London livery-stable. When he was left an orphan at fifteen, his guardians apprenticed him to a surgeon in Edmonton. From 1814 to 1816 he was student assistant in a London hospital. But he found poetry more fascinating than "plasters, pills, and ointment boxes." His friend and teacher, Charles Cowden Clarke, introduced him to Vergil and Spenser; another friend, Leigh Hunt, published some of Keats' early efforts in his radical journal, the *Examiner.* The famous sonnet *On First Looking into Chapman's Homer* was written in 1815 after a night of reading at Clarke's home and published in Hunt's paper the following year. In 1817 appeared Keats' first volume of *Poems.* In 1818 he wrote *Endymion, Isabella or the Pot of Basil, The Eve of St. Agnes,* and *Hyperion.* The publication of the first of these—a promising but prolix narrative poem—was greeted with a storm of derision in the *Quarterly Review* and *Blackwood's Magazine*—the "Scotch reviewers" seizing on the young poet's connection with the "Cockney" radical, Hunt, to damn him as a member of the "Cockney School of Poetry." Although Keats himself protested that their sting was nothing com-

AUTHORS   [Kelly

pared to his own self-criticism, the attack was the foundation
for the romantic legend that the reviewers "killed John Keats."
Actually he was already ill from tuberculosis and in the sonnet,
"When I have fears that I may cease to be," had expressed a
premonition of his death and the hopelessness of his passion for
an unknown girl.

Eighteen-twenty saw the publication of *Isabella* and *The Eve of
St. Agnes*—two rich narratives in the Spenserian stanza; *Hyperion*
—a blank-verse fragment; four odes—*To Psyche, On a Grecian
Urn, On Melancholy,* and *To a Nightingale;* and the haunting
ballad of witchery, *La Belle Dame Sans Merci*. But this was the
last full year of the poet's life. In the fall he left England for the
drier climate of Italy, and on the boat wrote his last lines, the melancholy sonnet, "Bright star! would I were steadfast as thou art."
Four months later he died in Rome. He had composed his own
epitaph: "Here lies one whose name was writ in water." But his
friend Shelley gave him in *Adonais* as great a monument in verse
as any English poet has had.

Keats is linked always with Byron and Shelley as one of the
great trio of later romantic poets. Although he lacked the intellectual power of the other two, in lyrical phrasing and sheer
melody of words he often went beyond both. In his mature poems
there is nothing of the loose expansiveness of Byron or the vague
abstractness of Shelley. Like Spenser, in whom he found much
of his inspiration, Keats was a poet of the senses. He retained
until his death the capacity of an adolescent enthusiast for form,
color, and sound, and these enthusiasms he transmuted into pure
poetry, loading every rift with ore.

KEBLE, John (1792–1866) was the saintly professor of poetry at
Oxford whose sermon on "national apostasy" in 1833 touched off
the Oxford Movement. He also contributed to the *Tracts for the
Times* (1833–8), in which the leaders of the movement, including
his Oxford disciple, Newman, fought against the growing rationalism in the Church of England and insisted on more elaborate
ceremonies, more rigid dogma, and a greater reverence for the past.
Some years earlier he had blended his love of church ceremony
and nature in a collection of sacred poems, *The Christian Year*
(1827).

KELLY, Hugh (1739–77) was a pompous little Irish stay-maker
who came to London about 1760 and turned into a journalist
and play-maker. His "sentimental" comedy, *False Delicacy* (1768),
scored a big box-office victory over a contemporary "laughing"

161

comedy, Goldsmith's *Good Natured Man.* As the unscrupulous editor of the *Public Ledger,* Kelly made political enemies who pelted his second comedy, *A Word to the Wise* (1770), off the stage with oranges.

KEMP, William (fl. 1600), a famous comic actor in Shakespeare's company, wrote *Kemp's Nine Days Wonder, Performed in a Dance from London to Norwich* (1600). It was common in Elizabethan and Jacobean times for public figures to carry out wagers on such endurance tests and then publish accounts of them. A specialist in this field was John Taylor, the Water Poet.

KENNEDY, Margaret (1896–   ) is best known for her second novel, *The Constant Nymph* (1924), the story of the Bohemian life of a musician's family. She also wrote a sequel to it, *The Fool of the Family* (1930), and a popular comedy, *Escape Me Never!* (1934).

KILLIGREW, Thomas, the elder (1612–83) was a favorite in the courts of both Charles I and Charles II and a playwright of some note in both eras. His works include *The Prisoners* (1635–6), a romantic tragi-comedy, *The Parson's Wedding* (c. 1640), a notoriously bawdy comedy; and *Cecilia and Clorinda* (printed 1664), a tragi-comedy adapted from *Le Grand Cyrus,* a French romance by Madame de Scudéry. His son, **Thomas,** the younger (1657–1719), and his brothers, **Henry** (1613–1700) and **William** (1606–95), were all minor playwrights. His niece, **Anne** (1660–85), was the poetess and painter to whose memory Dryden addressed a famous ode.

KING, Henry (1592–1669), Bishop of Chichester, was a friend of Jonson, Walton, and Donne. Donne's influence is apparent in his *Poems, Elegies, Paradoxes, and Sonnets* (1657). Among his best pieces are the moving *Exequy* on his wife's death and the familiar lyric "Tell me no more how fair she is."

KING, William (1663–1712) was the author of a great deal of miscellaneous prose and verse, most of it humorous. His works include *Dialogues of the Dead* (1699), a pamphlet in which he sided with Charles Boyle in the "Phalaris Controversy"; *The Art of Cookery, In Imitation of Horace's Art of Poetry* (1708); and contributions to both the *Tatler* and the *Examiner.*

KINGLAKE, Alexander William (1809–91) was the author of *Eothen, or Traces of Travel Brought Home from the East* (1844). This delightful travel-classic is generally accorded far more merit as literature than its author's exhaustive eight-volume history, *The Invasion of the Crimea* (1863–87).

KINGSLEY, Charles (1819–75) was a country parson and Oxford history professor who was born to speak his mind in print. As a leader of the Broad Church Movement, he advocated for all England a rational religion which would compromise with science, a "muscular Christianity" which would stress the importance of physical culture. His struggle against the Roman Catholic tendencies of the Oxford Movement, reflected early in the dramatic poem, *The Saint's Tragedy* (1848), culminated in a personal attack which provoked Newman's *Apologia pro Vita Sua* in 1864. As a leader of the Christian Socialists, Kingsley plunged into the controversies of London in the "hungry forties," pamphleteering under the name "Parson Lot." He wrote two novels in defense of the oppressed workers in country (*Yeast,* 1851) and in city (*Alton Locke,* 1852). His *Water-Babies* (1863), too often thought of as only a fairy tale, is actually a tract on education and an attack on evolution. Even his historical novels, *Hypatia* (1853), *Westward Ho!* (1855), and *Hereward the Wake* (1866), contain thinly disguised lessons for Victorian England. Thousands, however, who do not know the controversial Kingsley, have read *Westward Ho!* as a gripping patriotic saga of Elizabethan sea-faring.

KINGSLEY, Henry (1830–76) was the younger brother of Charles Kingsley. In two of his novels, *The Recollections of Geoffrey Hamlyn* (1859) and *The Hillyars and the Burtons* (1865), the scene is laid in Australia, where Kingsley spent five years of his life (1853–8). In his best-known novel, *Ravenshoe* (1861), he mixed romantic melodrama with the social criticism and Catholic-baiting which are so prominent in his brother's work. He wrote too much too rapidly and has always been overshadowed by his brother.

KIPLING, Rudyard (1865–1936). During the twenty-five years before the First World War, Kipling was probably the most popular writer in the English-speaking world. Since 1920 his stock has fallen and today, in a tangle of contradictory opinions, it is hard to form a true picture of either his popularity or his merit. Into his verse he poured the ingredients which make for popular acclaim —the conventional inspirationalism of *When Earth's Last Picture is Painted* and of the inevitable *If;* the solemn pomp of the *Recessional;* the travel-folder exoticism of *Mandalay;* the drum-beat heroism of *Danny Deever, Gunga Din,* and *Fuzzy-Wuzzy.* He was a versifier of tremendous vigor and facility and, even when he lards the lines with Cockney vulgarisms, the movement seldom halts. At his best, as in *McAndrew's Hymn,* he wrote real poetry. But because *If* has been framed in too many bedrooms and *Mandalay* murdered in too many barrooms, many will deny this. Fewer deny Kipling's skill as a story-teller in prose. He was born in Bombay and spent most of his early life in India. On that complex land he drew for much of his fiction, treating his material partly with the authenticity of an honest journalist, partly with the mystery of a born romantic—mingling the gay humor of the British Tommy with the inscrutability of the dark-skinned native. These qualities mark Kipling's first collection of short-stories, *Plain Tales from the Hills* (1888), and the best of his novels, *Kim* (1901). Other short-stories appear in *Mine Own People* (1891), *The Day's Work* (1898), and *Traffics and Discoveries* (1904). Kipling was also a master of stories for children, as in *The Jungle Books* (1894–5), *Stalky and Co.* (1899), and *Just So Stories* (1902).

It has been fashionable during the last two decades to damn Kipling for his imperialism, and certainly he cannot be absolved of a share of the blame for propagating the gospel of "the White Man's Burden." Some apologists, however, have viewed his imperialism only as a sort of accidental medium through which he expressed his virile philosophy of action. One of his defenders is T. S. Eliot.

K(IRKE), E(dward) (1553–1613), a contemporary of Edmund Spenser at Pembroke Hall, Cambridge, was apparently the "E. K." who wrote the epistle dedicatory and notes to the *Shepheardes Calender* (1579). There has been some support, however, for the far-fetched theory that "E. K." is the poet himself.

KIRKMAN, Francis (fl. 1661–74.) This London bookseller collaborated with Richard Head in *The English Rogue,* "a complete history of the Most Eminent Cheats" (1665–88), and wrote *The Counterfeit Lady Unveiled* (1673), a fictitious biography of the famous Restoration cheat, Mary Carleton. They are memorable as links between the Elizabethan rogue stories and the more pretentious picaresque novels of Defoe. He also edited *The Wits, or Sport Upon Sport* (1672), a collection of farcical dramatic tidbits familiarly known as *Kirkman's Drolls.*

KNOLLES, Richard (1550?–1610) wrote *The General History of the Turks* (1603), a work which impressed Dr. Johnson, and which inspired the child Byron with a longing to visit the Orient.

KNOWLES, (James) Sheridan (1784–1862) was a playwright who attempted to reform the drama during a lean period. He wrote serious plays, including the verse tragedies *Caius Gracchus* (1815) and *Virginius* (1820), and comedies, including *The Hunchback* (1832) and *The Love-Chase* (1837). *Virginius,* a simple classical tragedy on the same theme as Chaucer's *Physician's Tale,* is usually called his masterpiece. Although the blank verse is often prosy, the play has a restraint and dignity which are lacking in the sensational Gothic melodramas of the author's time. After Knowles forsook the stage, he entered the Baptist ministry and published two polemical works against the Roman Catholics.

KNOX, John (1505–72) was the leader of the Protestant Reformation in Scotland. His works are almost entirely controversial, and most of them are of no importance as literature. Among the most famous are his *First Blast of the Trumpet against the Monstrous Regiment of Women* (1558) and his *History of the Reformation of Religion within the Realm in Scotland* (1586). The first is an attack on Mary Tudor, Queen of England, and Mary of Lorraine, Regent of Scotland. The second is more of a defense than an objective history of the Scottish reformation.

KYD, Thomas (1558–94). At about the time that the English beat off the Spanish Armada from their shores, there appeared on the public stage in London a tremendously popular, blood-and-thunder tragedy in blank verse in which a Spanish princeling was the villain. Kyd's *Spanish Tragedy* (printed 1594) was the first great dramatic thriller produced directly to entertain the London crowds. It is a revenge tragedy in which Hieronimo, the court marshal hero, avenges the murder of his son Horatio by Prince Lorenzo. Kyd was a "University Wit" who knew his Seneca well, and the play contains the chorus, the ghost, and the revenge motives of the ancient Latin tragedies. But Kyd was also an Elizabethan romanticist, and the tempo, the excitement, the Machiavellian villainies, and the accumulated horrors and bloodshed of his play break through the comparative restraint of Seneca's formal classical pieces. The popularity of *The Spanish Tragedy* is attested by its reissue in 1602, probably by Ben Jonson, with added scenes in which "Hieronimo goes mad again." Kyd was the author of only one great extant tragedy. But he is thought also to have written the lost revenge play of Hamlet, upon which Shakespeare based his most famous tragedy. In the fifteen-nineties, at any rate, appeared several allusions to a *Hamlet* much earlier than Shakespeare's play.

L

LAMB, Lady Caroline (1785–1828) was the victim of a hopeless passion for Lord Byron. A fictionized version of her infatuation for the poet appears in her novel, *Glenarvon,* published anonymously in 1816 and reprinted as *The Fatal Passion* in 1865. It was one of the first publications of the nineteenth-century "Silver Fork" school of fiction about fashionable life.

LAMB, Charles (1775–1834). In 1796–7 Lamb spent six weeks in an insane asylum. Shortly after his release, his sister Mary killed their mother in a fit of madness. After that he bore the family burden alone. Whenever Mary, who had been entrusted to his care, had a recurring attack, he took her tearfully back to the asylum. Meanwhile, he drudged on in the East India House at a dull, unstimulating job. Yet when in 1825 he "went home forever" from that job, he was one of England's greatest humorists.

His literary beginnings were not impressive. The melodramatic prose *Tale of Rosamund Gray* (1798), the pseudo-Elizabethan tragedy, *John Woodvil* (printed 1802), and the unsuccessful farce, *Mr. H.* (1806), are now seldom read. Of his poems, which he discussed seriously with his school friend, Coleridge, only the simple *Old Familiar Faces* (1798) is well known. More important are his contributions to the appreciation of Elizabethan drama. The *Tales from Shakespeare* (1807), written in collaboration with Mary, is a schoolboy classic; *Specimens of English Dramatic Poets Who Lived About the Time of Shakespeare* (1808) was work in an unplowed field; the *Essay on the Tragedies of Shakespeare* (1811) is a serious discussion of their actability, particularly that of *King Lear.*

But to most people Lamb means the *Essays of Elia* and *The Last Essays of Elia* (*London Magazine,* collected 1823, 1833, respectively). Their scope includes personal history (*Christ's Hospital Five and Thirty Years Ago*), literary criticism (*On the Artificial Comedy of the Last Century*), character sketches (*Mrs. Battle's Opinions on Whist*), and fantastic fictions (*A Dissertation on Roast Pig*). The tone ranges from the flippant ridicule of *A Bachelor's Complaint of the Behaviour of Married People* to the sentimental reverie of *Dream-Children.* The style frequently echoes Elia's reading in such seventeenth-century prose writers as Thomas Browne and Richard Fuller. But in a larger sense the strange mixture of epithets and epigrams, polysyllabic words, and recondite allusions, is peculiarly Lamb's own. To know him well one should also read his letters. He was a man of passionate enthusiasms. He preferred smoking and drinking to eating, old books to new, London's teeming Strand to Wordsworth's hills and lakes. He was small, with a chiseled face, a limp, and a stammer. And he liked, when the conversation grew most earnest, to break his own modest silence with a bad, blurted pun. But his friends still loved him.

LAMB, Mary Ann (1764–1847) was the sister of Charles Lamb, with whom she collaborated in *Tales from Shakespeare* (1807) and in a series of ten stories called *Mrs. Leicester's School* (1807).

LANDON, Letitia Elizabeth (1802–38), who wrote over the initials "L. E. L.," attained some success as a poetess during the lull between the Romantic and the Victorian periods. Her first collection, *The Fate of Adelaide . . . and Other Poems,* appeared in 1821, and *The Miscellaneous Poetical Works of L. E. L.* in 1835. No single piece of hers has stuck in posterity's memory like Mrs. Hemans' *Casabianca*. L. E. L. also published five novels, one of which is *Ethel Churchill, or The Two Brides* (1837). Shortly after marrying the governor of South Africa, she died mysteriously there, apparently from a dose of prussic acid.

LANDOR, Robert Eyres (1781–1869) was a retiring country parson whose work has been overshadowed by that of his more talented brother. Like the work of Walter Savage Landor, it savors too much of the Ivory Tower to attain wide popularity. It includes *The Count Arezzi* (printed 1824), an anonymous verse tragedy once attributed to Byron; *The Impious Feast* (1828), a long narrative poem on the biblical story of Belshazzar; *The Fawn of Sertorius* (1846), a prose fantasy once ascribed to Walter Savage Landor; and *The Fountain of Arethusa* (1848), a collection of imaginary prose dialogues.

LANDOR, Walter Savage (1775–1864). For nearly a third of his long life (1815–35, 1858–64) Landor lived in Italy. In his imagination he lived much of his life in ancient Rome and Greece. Hating "the crowd" and disdaining easy popularity, he worked carefully from ancient models. He wrote his long narrative poem, *Gebir* (1798), and his short narrative *Hellenics* (1847) in Latin as well as in English. His epigrams in verse have a true classical simplicity; such miniature masterpieces as the four lines *On his Seventy-fifth Birthday* and the eight-line *Rose Aylmer* have outlived his more ambitious poems. In prose he devoted years to a type little practised in England, the imaginary conversation, publishing a great number between 1824 and 1853. They vary from free dramatic renderings of historical crises, like the conversation between the Empress Catharine and Princess Dashkof at the assassination of Czar Peter III, to calm, undramatic discussions like that among Walton, Cotton, and Oldways. The characters, whether ancient warrior or modern philosopher, speak Landor's polished prose. Many of them parrot his opinions. And the proud, quarrelsome aristocrat who split with his college dons, his wife, and many of his friends was not without strong opinions. His irascibility earned him a place in Charles Dickens' portrait gallery as Boythorn of *Bleak House*.

LANG, Andrew (1844–1912). Few readers who were brought up on Lang's multicolored fairy-tale books appreciate the amazing versatility of the Scot who retold these tales. Andrew Lang's poems (*Poetical Works*, 1923) are not well known. The favorite of posterity is the sonnet prefixed to his translation of the *Odyssey* (1879). This translation, done in collaboration with S. H. Butcher, and the version of the *Iliad* (1883), on which Lang worked with Walter Leaf and Ernest Myers, are still considered by many scholars as the best prose translations of Homer's epics. In addition to this and other work in classical scholarship, Lang published pioneering works in anthropology and mythology (*Myth, Ritual, and Religion*, 1887), a biography of J. G. Lockhart (1897), a history of Scotland (1900–7), and a wide variety of miscellaneous writings on literature, art, and sports.

LANGLAND, William (1330?–1400?) is the poet who gradually emerged as scholars attempted to find the original of the mysterious "Long Will" of *The Vision of William Concerning Piers the Plowman*. This poem, extremely popular in Chaucer's day, has survived in three texts, traditionally labeled A, B, and C, and dated approximately 1362, 1377, and 1394. If a William Langland did write the A text, it is by no means certain that he also wrote the longer and more obscure B and C texts. The A is a 2500-line dream allegory in unrhymed alliterative verse. The main narrative of how Piers the Plowman offers to guide a group of penitent pilgrims from the "field of folk" in search of Saint Truth is chaotically confused with a digression on the marriage of "Lady Meed" and the inevitable shriving of the Seven Deadly Sins. The poem is both a sermon on the Gospel of Work and a satiric panorama of the corrupt society which led to the Peasants' Revolt in 1381. The vicious evils which Chaucer often surveyed with amused tolerance, Long Will attacked with the reformer's bludgeon.

LATIMER, Hugh (1485?–1555), Bishop of Worcester under Henry VIII, was clapped into the tower on Mary's accession in

1553 and burned as a heretic two years later. He was a famous preacher, fulminating against social wrongs in plain English words, driving home his message with blunt name-calling and homely story-telling. For his unaffected use of the vernacular, Latimer has been compared with John Bunyan and William Cobbett.

LAW, William (1686–1761) was a prose writer of considerable range and a religious thinker of profound importance. His works have been divided into three classes: (1) controversial treatises, including his three letters (1717–19) to Bishop Benjamin Hoadly in the "Bangorian Controversy," and his *Remarks upon . . . Mandeville's Fable of the Bees* (1724); (2) treatises on practical Christianity, including *A Practical Treatise upon Christian Perfection* (1726) and *A Serious Call to a Devout and Holy Life* (1728); (3) mystical writings, including *An Appeal to All that Doubt* (1740), which were influenced by the German Jacob Boehme (1575–1624), and which in turn influenced John Byrom and others. John Wesley remarked that *A Serious Call* sowed the seed of Methodism. And Dr. Johnson said, speaking of the surprise with which he read it at Oxford, "I found Law quite an over-match for me; and this was the first occasion of my thinking in earnest of religion."

LAWRENCE, D(avid) H(erbert) (1885–1930) was born in a small mining town in Nottinghamshire. His father was a black-bearded coal-miner who never read anything but newspapers; his mother was a quiet, cultured ex-schoolteacher who read and wrote poetry. In *Sons and Lovers* (1913), usually called his best novel, Lawrence revealed his boyhood distaste for his father's uncouth way of life and traced the growth of his mother-fixation, ending the story with her tragic death. She died in 1910. In the previous year Lawrence had already published a handful of poems in the *English Review,* and the publication of *The White Peacock* in 1911 encouraged him to abandon a teaching job in the elementary school at Croydon and devote the rest of his life to wandering and writing. *Sons and Lovers,* his third novel, was followed by a series of less orthodox creations, including *The Rainbow* (1915), *Women in Love* (1920), *Aaron's Rod* (1922), and *Lady Chatterley's Lover* (1928). Lawrence's novels are marked by passages of beautiful poetic prose and by experiment with the stream-of-consciousness technique. They reflect his intense preoccupation with the mystery of sex and his effort to conciliate the two worlds of conscious intelligence and unconscious instinct. *The Rainbow, Women in Love,* and *Lady Chatterley's Lover* have been suppressed at various times as pornography. But their author defended them as sincere expressions of his "great religion" that blood and flesh are wiser than the intellect, his belief "in the phallic consciousness, as against the irritable cerebral consciousness." During the far-flung travels of his last decade—he lived in Mexico, New Mexico, and Italy—Lawrence searched for a primitive society which would be more sympathetic to his rebellious philosophy. In addition to his novels, he published short-stories (*The Prussian Officer and other stories,* 1914), poems (*Collected Poems,* 1928), studies in psychoanalysis, travel books, and a volume of his paintings. The bickering over "the truth about D. H. Lawrence" appears interminable. Among the more intriguing solutions to the riddle of his personality is the character of Mark Rampion in Aldous Huxley's *Point Counter Point.* Lawrence once said this about himself: "I always say my motto is Art for my sake. One sheds one's sickness in books."

LAWRENCE, George Alfred (1827–76) was the anonymous author of *Guy Livingstone, or Thorough* (1857), a melodramatic novel which shocked Victorian England by its glorification of a protagonist with mighty muscles but questionable morals. The same ingredients can be found in the novels of "Ouida."

LAWRENCE, T(homas) E(dward) (1888–1935) was a soldier, adventurer, archaeologist, and classical scholar. He changed his name to Shaw in 1927. But it was as T. E. Lawrence that he became a legend during the First World War for his remarkable achievement in uniting the Arab tribes against the Turks. The complete account of that campaign, *The Seven Pillars of Wisdom,* appeared in a limited edition in 1926. An abridgment, *Revolt in the Desert,* followed in 1927, and a popular edition of the original appeared in 1935, after the author's death in a motorcycle accident. A well-written but scholarly blend of history and adventure, *The Seven Pillars* is a worthy descendant of Doughty's *Travels in Arabia Deserta* (1888). His translation of Homer's *Odyssey* appeared a year before his death.

LAYAMON (fl. 1200) was a Worcestershire priest who is famous as the author of a *Brut* or British history. He drew for much of his material on Wace's translation of Geoffrey of Monmouth's *Historia Regum Britanniae* but made appreciable improvements and additions. His additions to the legend of Arthur and the Table Round and his stories of Cymbeline and King Lear had an important bearing on later English literature. Layamon's *Brut,* written in alliterative verse, is the first extensive literary monument in Middle English and the first English narrative of England's legendary history. It has been of particular value to specialists in prosody and linguistics.

LEACOCK, Stephen (Butler) (1869–1944) was born in England, but came to Canada at the age of six and grew up to become head of the department of political economy at McGill University. He made his reputation as a humorist with such volumes as *Literary Lapses* (1910), *Nonsense Novels* (1911), *and Frenzied Fiction* (1918)—collections of parodies and informal essays from the borderland of lunacy. There is more sense in *Stephen Leacock's Plan to Relieve the Depression in Six Days, to Remove it in Six Months, to Eradicate it in Six Years* (1933), *Pursuit of Knowledge, a Discussion of Freedom and Compulsion in Education* (1934), and *How to Write* (1943). *My Discovery of England* (1922) contains some delightful satire on the land of his birth. His last collection of humorous stories was characteristically entitled *Happy Stories Just to Laugh At* (1943). Professor Leacock also wrote studies of *Mark Twain* (1932) and *Charles Dickens* (1933).

LEAR, Edward (1812–88) was a serious landscape painter who illustrated the poetry of his friend Tennyson and once tried to teach Queen Victoria how to paint. But to generations of children he has been the pleasant old man with a beard who, because he "loved to see little folks merry," wrote and illustrated *A Book of Nonsense* (1846) and four other immortal nonsense books (1871–7). In these collections Lear exploited, although he did not invent, the limerick, and his name is inseparable from that form. Into his longer verses he poured a blend of spontaneous nonsense, airy whimsy, and pure lyric beauty which neither Lewis Carroll nor A. A. Milne has surpassed. Today everybody knows that the owl and the pussy-cat went to sea in a beautiful, pea-green boat. But the Jumblies, the Yonghy-Bongy-Bò, and the Pobble Who Has no Toes have been largely replaced in the American nursery by Christopher Robin and Winnie-the-Pooh. On the other hand, some serious adults are now hailing Lear as a surrealist.

LEE, Harriet (1757–1851) and **Sophia** (1750–1824). The sisters Lee were novelists and playwrights. Sophia, the elder, wrote *The Recess* (1783–5), a Gothic novel with a background of sixteenth-century English history; and *The Chapter of Accidents* (printed 1780), a successful comedy. She and her sister collaborated on

The Canterbury Tales (1797–1805), a collection of short tales which included *Kruitzner,* the source of Byron's drama *Werner.*

LEE, Nathaniel (1649?–92). Mad, drunken Nat Lee spent five of his last years in Bedlam (1684–9), an ironic climax for one who made his name writing rant for actors. Today, although few read his *Nero* (1674) and *Sophonisba* (1675), many mock him as a horrible example of what was wrong with the rhymed heroic play. Lee was no match for his contemporary, Otway, but he was taken very seriously in his day. He had the honor of collaborating with Dryden on two tragedies, *Oedipus* (1678) and *The Duke of Guise* (1682), and his blank-verse tragedy, *The Rival Queens* (1677), has had, for all its bosom-beating—or perhaps because of it—a distinguished stage history. If he was guilty of incredible bawling, he was also capable at times of slipping strangely into real poetry.

LE FANU, Joseph Sheridan (1814–73) was an Irishman, the great grand-nephew of Richard Brinsley Sheridan. He was on the staff of the *Dublin University Magazine* from 1837 to 1872, and to it he contributed many of the short tales and novels which have given him a reputation with some as the greatest master of terror in his generation. Among his novels are *The House by the Church-yard* (1863), *Uncle Silas* (1864), and *In a Glass Darkly* (1872). He also wrote poems and plays.

L. E. L. Pseudonym of **Letitia Elizabeth Landon**.

LELAND, John (1506–52) was librarian and king's antiquary under Henry VIII. In a tour of several years up and down the island, he collected a mass of material for a projected work on English antiquities. *The Laborious Journey and Search of John Leland,* a pamphlet describing the results of his investigations, was presented to the king as a New Year's gift in 1546. It was his only finished work in English. Leland's nine-volume *Itinerary* was not published until 1710, his six-volume *Collectanea* following in 1715. Their intrinsic value as antiquarian research is not enhanced by their obvious lack of arrangement and selection. Leland has been named as the typical pedant who can project and collect but never organize.

LENNOX, Charlotte (1720–1804) was a friend of Dr. Johnson and a versatile woman of letters. She wrote a book of poems (1747), three plays, seven novels, eleven numbers of a magazine called the *Lady's Museum* (1760–1), and *Shakespear Illustrated, or the Novels and Histories, on which the Plays of Shakespear are founded* (1753–

4). Mrs Lennox's most celebrated novel is *The Female Quixote* (1752), in which the heroine, Arabella, like Catherine Morland in Jane Austen's *Northanger Abbey,* gets real life confused with the world of her favorite romances.

L'ESTRANGE, Sir Roger (1616–1704) was a politician, journalist, pamphleteer, and translator. As surveyor of the press under Charles II, he issued two periodicals, the *Intelligencer* (1663–6) and the *News* (1663–6). His *Observator* (1681–7) was one of a number of Restoration periodicals in question and answer form. In this and in a flurry of pamphlets he labored to quiet the popular fury against the Roman Catholics resulting from the discovery of the "Popish Plot." In a different world from these political labors are L'Estrange's numerous translations, the most celebrated of which is his version of *The Fables of Aesop* (1692, 1699).

LEVER, Charles (1806–72) was a Dublin physician and journalist whose many novels were extremely popular in Victorian England. He specialized in depicting military life, mixing the romance of war with an enormous amount of spirited farce and horseplay. The boisterous playboys of *The Confessions of Harry Lorrequer* (1839) and *Charles O'Malley* (1841) have more in common with the traditional eighteenth-century stage Irishmen than with the more authentic Hibernians of Maria Edgeworth's novels.

LEWES, George Henry (1817–78). Journalist, essayist, novelist, biographer, philosopher, and scientist—Lewes was a man so versatile that Thackeray once said he would not be surprised to see him riding a white elephant down Piccadilly. He wrote a scholarly *Life of Goethe* (1855) and a five-volume philosophical work, *Problems of Life and Mind* (1874–9). He showed his good sense as a literary critic when he told Charlotte Brontë on the publication of *Jane Eyre* to read Jane Austen and abandon melodrama. Much more important was his constant encouragement of a greater novelist, George Eliot, with whom he lived from 1854 until his death.

LEWIS, C(ecil) Day. See DAY–LEWIS, C(ecil).

LEWIS, Matthew Gregory (1775–1818) is remembered as the author of a single Gothic novel. *Ambrosio, or The Monk* (1796), finished at nineteen, is actually an incoherent reworking of familiar Gothic materials from French and German romance. But when to these horrors he added realistic seduction and a digression on the Bible's unsuitability for young readers, Britain revolted and the Society for the Suppression of Vice stepped in. The gentle, good-natured, boyish little M. P. was inflated into a monster of the circulating library with whom (wrote Byron, though "Mat" bored him terribly) "even Satan's self . . . might dread to dwell." His *Castle Spectre* (1797) was a successful Gothic play, and his terrifying ballads (*Tales of Terror,* 1799; *Tales of Wonder,* 1801) influenced an awed collaborator named Sir Walter Scott. But Lewis will always be tagged as one-book "Monk" Lewis.

LEWIS, (Percy) Wyndham (1884–1957) should not be confused with the columnist and biographer, D. B. Wyndham Lewis, of whom he was no relation. He was a painter as well as an author. Among his multifarious writings are several grotesque, satirical novels, including *Tarr* (1918) and *The Apes of God* (1930); numerous critical essays on literature, art, and politics, including *The Art of being Ruled* (1926) and *Time and Western Man* (1927); and an autobiography, *Blasting and Bombardiering* (1937). As a painter, Lewis was the leader of the "vorticists," a group of artists who attempted to reflect the complexity of modern industry. In his boisterous criticism he has been hostile both to the stream-of-consciousness technique of Joyce and the political propaganda of proletarian writers.

LILLO, George (1693–1739). In his once-popular tragedy, *The London Merchant, or the History of George Barnwell* (1731), Lillo dramatized an old ballad about how a harlot (Millwood) dragged an idle apprentice (George) swiftly along the downward path from robbery to murder to the gallows. It is a tabloid news-story twisted into a dramatic sermon and for years was produced at minor theaters on boxing nights for the express purpose of warning incipient Barnwells. Today it is historically important as a pioneering effort in domestic tragedy which had a profound influence in France and Germany, and as an early example of the use of prose as the chief medium in tragedy. The best known of Lillo's other plays is *Fatal Curiosity* (1736), a more conventional blank-verse tragedy which bears a superficial resemblance to *Macbeth.*

LINACRE, Thomas (1460?–1524) was a physician who, along with such men as Erasmus, Colet, and Sir Thomas More, contributed notably to the renaissance of the classics. He wrote a Latin primer, *The Rudiments of Grammar* (1524), and translated numerous medical works from the Greek and Latin.

LINDSAY, Sir David (1490?-1555). This courtier of James V of Scotland is called the last of the "Scottish Chaucerians." He was more of a reformer than a romancer, reflecting with especial zeal the spirit of the Protestant Reformation. Whether he framed his poetic complaints in the conventional dream allegory (*The Dream,* written 1528), ascribed them to the pen of a parrot (*The Testament and Complaint of our Soverign Lord's Papingo,* written c. 1530), or revealed them in dialogue between Experience and a courtier (*The Monarchy,* 1554?), he was a relentless compaigner against corruption in Church and State. His best-known poem, *A Pleasant Satire of the Three Estates* (1540), is a long and bawdy morality play lampooning nobility, burghers, and clergy. Of his major poems, only the romance, *Squire Meldrum* (written c. 1549), is relatively free from social protest.

LISTER, Thomas Henry (1800-42) is remembered as the author of *Granby* (1826), a novel which belongs to the "Silver Fork" school of fashionable fiction. It was an answer to Lady Caroline Lamb's *Glenarvon* (1816).

LOCKE, John (1632-1704) is considered by many as the greatest English philosopher. His *Essay concerning Human Understanding* (1690) was the first systematic study in England of the theory of knowledge. In it he advanced the thesis that man is born with a "tabula rasa" or clean-sheet mind free from any traces of innate ideas—that ideas come after birth through sensation and reflection. The practical philosopher led an active life as lecturer at Oxford, physician to Lord Shaftesbury, and political office-holder. His versatility is reflected in his other writings. In *Two Treatises on Government* (1690) he attacked the doctrine of divine right of kings. In *Some Thoughts concerning Education* (1693) he stressed the importance of character-training. In *The Reasonableness of Christianity* (1695) he emphasized the need for religious faith to supplement man's understanding.

LOCKER–LAMPSON, Frederick (1821-95) wrote graceful, polished lyrics, both sad and gay, in the *vers de société* tradition. He was an avowed literary descendant of Praed. His collection, *London Lyrics,* appeared first in 1857 and underwent numerous alterations before the definitive edition by Austin Dobson in 1904. Other pieces of his own are printed in his verse-anthology, *Lyra Elegantiarum* (1867), and his commonplace book of verse and prose, *Patchwork* (1879).

LOCKHART, John Gibson (1794-1854). In many ways this Scot's record resembles those of several versatile journalists of his day.

With the help of Wilson and Hogg he nourished the infant *Blackwood's Magazine* with gall (1817–25); and with more restraint he edited the *Quarterly Review* for nearly thirty years (1825–53). Although he brought to his task a training in law and in Continental literature, his reviews are not famous for logic or urbanity; whether or not he wrote the smug attack which told "Cockney" poet John Keats to go back to "plasters, pills, and ointment boxes," he certainly earned his soubriquet, "The Scorpion." Outside of his routine work, he wrote a series of Scottish sketches entitled *Peter's Letters to his Kinsfolk* (1819) and four novels, one of which, *Adam Blair* (1822), is still praised. But when Lockhart took to biography, he really soared above his fellow-journalists. His lives of Burns (1828) and Napoleon (1829) have been overshadowed by the masterpiece on his father-in-law, Sir Walter Scott (1837–38), the fruition of a fourteen-year intimacy. Lockhart's contemporaries damned its candor, and modern scholars have debunked its fictions, but it still ranks as one of the great English biographies. Many place it second only to Boswell's *Johnson*.

LODGE, Thomas (1558?–1625). Like most of the "University Wits," as the bright young university graduates who tried their hands at literature near the end of Queen Elizabeth's reign were called, Lodge was a miscellaneous writer, who turned out pamphlets, plays, and poetry with more facility than art. As a writer of plays he was entirely undistinguished; both his *Looking Glass for London and England* (with Robert Greene, 1587–91) and his *Wounds of Civil War* (1587–92) are rhetorical and soggy. His lyrics were more successful; although conventional, they are light and moving. Most of these poems he set in the matrix of his prose romances. Of the prose tales the most famous, principally because Shakespeare used it as the source of *As You Like It,* is *Rosalynde, Euphues' Golden Legacy* (1590). The plot of the story is by no means original; it is the old Robin Hood tale of the outlawed nobleman who, by turn of fortune and his own virtues, recovers his estates and marries the duke's daughter. Nor does the style have any more originality than the plot. As the subtitle indicates, Lodge copied directly the artificial literary manner that John Lyly had popularized in his two romances of Euphues. Euphuistic prose is highly artificial; it is marked by elaborate structural balance, labored figures of speech, and many "quaint conceits." Some of the best examples of this popular court style may be taken from Lodge's *Rosalynde.*

LOVELACE, Richard (1618–57?). In his glory Lovelace was the proud favorite of royalty, famously handsome, punctiliously mannered, dressed in "cloth of gold and silver." He died in rags at forty. He was wounded and twice imprisoned during England's Civil War, and when he was reported dead, his betrothed, "Lucasta," married another. With apparent abandon he tossed off songs (collected in *Lucasta*, 1649, and *Posthume Poems*, 1659). Many are strangled by ill-conceived conceits: a lady's glove becomes a snowy farm with five tenements. Some are almost meaningless. But, as if by accident, he wrote posterity's favorite "Cavalier lyrics": *To Althea, from Prison* ("Stone walls do not a prison make,") and *To Lucasta, Going to the Wars* ("I could not love thee, dear, so much"). They are the concentrated essence of storybook gallantry.

LOVER, Samuel (1797–1868) was an Irishman who wrote songs, novels, and plays. The title *Rory O'More* belongs to three of his works, his most popular song, and the novel (1837) and play (1837) which it suggested. The novel deals partly with the tragic Irish rebellion of 1798. Another novel, *Handy Andy* (1842), is the farcical saga of the blundering servant, Andy Rooney, who turns out in the end to be none other than Lord Scatterbrain.

LUCAS, E(dward) V(errall) (1868–1938) wrote essays, novels, poems, children's books, travel books, and biographies. His numerous volumes of essays, which appeared with almost annual regularity, belong generally to the tender, graceful tradition of Charles Lamb. Lucas wrote a standard *Life of Charles Lamb* (1905) and edited the *Works* (1903–5) and *Letters* (1935) of Charles and Mary Lamb.

LYDGATE, John (1370?–1451?). This monk of Bury St. Edmunds was, like Hoccleve, an early disciple of Chaucer. He was prolific and prosaic. Three of his verse marathons, all of them drawn from Continental sources, remind us of how tedious the Canterbury Pilgrims might have become without the good sense of their moderator, Harry Bailly. *The Story of Thebes* (c. 1420) is an amplification of Chaucer's *Knight's Tale; The Troy Book* (c. 1420) is a thirty-thousand-line rewriting of the medieval Homer-legend from which Chaucer had distilled *Troilus and Criseyde; The Fall of Princes* (c. 1430) is a thirty-six-thousand-line retelling of Boccaccio's *De Casibus Virorum Illustrium*, on which Chaucer had based his *Monk's Tale*. Although Lydgate seems to have had neither an ear for, nor a conscience about meter, he was, in his own day, a popular poet; Stephen Hawes, for example, idolized him. He is interesting today as a sort of one-man library of medieval types.

LYELL, Sir Charles (1797–1875) has been called "the father of modern geology." In his first great work, *The Principles of Geology* (1830–3), he prepared the way for the more startling revelations of Charles Darwin. After he read *On the Origin of Species* (1859), Lyell abandoned his previous skepticism about certain phases of evolution and became one of Darwin's leading advocates.

LYLY, John (1554?–1606). The influence of the royal court on literary art in the Elizabethan period is revealed clearly in the romances and plays of John Lyly. Lyly was protégé of two favorites of the Queen, Robert Dudley, Earl of Leicester, and Burleigh, Lord High Treasurer. He was also employed in the Office of the Revels, but neither his high connections nor his service in composing court romances and comedies brought him the Mastership of the Revels which he coveted, and he died an embittered man.

Although Lyly, like so many of his literary contemporaries, was a miscellaneous writer, his principal productions were romances and comedies, and in both forms of art he made highly influential contributions. His two "novels" of court etiquette, *Euphues, the Anatomy of Wit* (1579) and its sequel, *Euphues and his England* (1580), were extremely popular and produced a host of imitations, such as Lodge's *Rosalynde*. As stories they are almost totally lacking in life and movement, for their action is replaced by situations and by carefully constructed dialogues. Lyly was concerned, obviously, more with the manners and morals of his characters than with his plot; his Euphues was a "mirror" of court etiquette rather than a living man. Moreover, the literary style of the romances was more significant than the content. This *euphuistic* style, borrowed and popularized from Antonio de Guevara's *Dial of Princes* (1529), a Spanish etiquette romance that had been translated into English in 1557 by Sir Thomas North, was astonishingly ornate and artificial. Carefully balanced sentences, interwoven schemes of alliteration, assonance, and antithesis, labored metaphors and similes, and classical allusions—especially to Pliny's *Historia Naturalis*—drew so much attention to the manner of expression that the matter often seems secondary. It is hardly surprising that after a decade of enthusiastic imitation of such a style, Nashe, Shakespeare, and others began to ridicule and parody it. But to Lyly belongs the credit of bringing structure to prose.

Lyly's comedies, like his two romances, were of the court, courtly. In fact, most of the plays are euphuistic in content and language. Lyly was the first court dramatist to sublimate the earlier realistic comedies. His plays are structurally loose, but they are high comedy, with polish and intelligence. All of them are based on classical or medieval themes and are dramatic allegories of court situations and episodes. Like his romances they "mirror" Elizabethan court life and foreshadow, in a sense, the comedy of manners of a century later. The first of them, *Alexander and Campaspe* (1580–84) was followed by *Sapho and Phao* (1582–84), *Endimion* (1588), *Midas* (1589–90), and several others. All were novel and distinctive enough to influence the work of Lyly's dramatic contemporaries and followers, including even Shakespeare. The delightful songs which these comedies contain show that even if Lyly did write his dramas in euphuistic prose, he was also capable of composing lyrical poems of unusual merit.

LYND, Robert (1879–1949), born in Belfast, has been faithful to the tradition of the graceful, humorous informal essay—a tradition which, in America at least, has almost vanished before the flood of "articles" replete with factual "dope." Since his first volume, *Irish and English: Portraits and Impressions,* appeared in 1908, Lynd has published essays with the regularity of the late E. V. Lucas, another essayist in the same tradition.

LYNDSAY. Variant spelling of **LINDSAY.**

LYTTLETON, George, first baron Lyttleton (1709–73) was a politician who mixed with literary men and produced some minor literature himself. He was James Thomson's patron and literary executor and a friend of Pope, Fielding, and Shenstone. Among his works are a series of imaginary conversations called *Dialogues of the Dead* (1760–5) and *The History of the Life of King Henry the Second* (1767–71).

LYTTON. See **BULWER–LYTTON.**

M

MACAULAY, Rose (1895?–1958) has written poems, essays, and satirical novels. Her most celebrated novel, *Potterism, a tragifarcical tract* (1920), is a bitter attack on the unenlightened profiteers of the First World War. Among her other novels are *Told by an Idiot* (1923), the saga of an English family from the Victorian era through the War, and *Orphan Island* (1924), a satirical Utopia in the tradition of *Gulliver's Travels.*

MACAULAY, Thomas Babington, first baron Macaulay (1800–59), politician, poet, critic, and historian, was born in Rothley and educated at Trinity College, Cambridge, where his brilliance in classical studies and his extraordinary essay on Milton (1823) brought him a fellowship. In 1826 he was admitted to the bar, and in 1830 began his political career as a Whig member of Parliament. To better his financial condition he went to India in 1834 as legal adviser to the Supreme Council and remained there for four years. On returning to England he again became an M. P. and a member of the Cabinet as Secretary of War, but the fall of the Melbourne ministry in 1841 drove him out of politics and gave him much needed leisure for his writing.

The first fruits of this leisure were the highly popular narrative poems called *The Lays of Ancient Rome* (1842). Macaulay was by no means a great poet, but his verse was stirring, dramatic, and facile, and soon every schoolboy in England and America was fighting beside Horatius at the bridge or inveighing against Appius Claudius. Meanwhile Macaulay had begun his greatest work, his *History of England from the Accession of James II.* The first two volumes appeared in 1849, the third and fourth—eagerly awaited by thousands of readers—in 1855, two years before their author became Baron Macaulay of Rothley, and the fifth and last in 1861, edited by his sister after his death. A scholarly historian would hardly depend upon Macaulay's account, but the lay reader would prefer it to the work of Dr. Dryasdust. Although reflecting too often his marked Whig prejudices and his smug satisfaction with the material progress of the Victorians, Macaulay's history is vivid, detailed, dramatic, and as readable as are the historical novels of Sir Walter Scott, whom Macaulay greatly admired. "The perfect historian," said Macaulay, "is he in whose work the characters and spirit of an age is exhibited in miniature." The practice of such a theory resulted in a tremendous wealth of detail and in a sparkling story. It tended also to result, however, in a preference for narrative and dramatic effects rather than for accurate facts.

Macaulay wrote history as a novelist might write it. The same may be said of his biographical-historical essays, such as those on Lord Clive (1840) and Warren Hastings (1841), subjects in which his Indian experiences gave him a particular interest. These essays are brilliant but reveal sometimes the sacrifice of restraint and exactness to dramatic effects and color. Macaulay's tremendous energy carried him into other fields besides history; he wrote an extraordinary number of biographical and critical

essays. Many of these appeared in the current editions of the
Encyclopaedia Britannica, and others were published as book reviews in the contemporary literary journals and magazines. Such
famous essays as those on Addison and Boswell, for example, were
technically book reviews, although Macaulay took them far beyond the limits of the volumes under survey.

Macaulay's prose is notable for its smoothness, its lucidity, its
color, and its contrasts. His love of literary and dramatic effects,
and particularly of contrast, led him to write many balanced
sentences and to make much use of the less flamboyant figures of
speech. And his paragraphs are more richly illustrated by examples and details than those of most of his contemporaries.
Nevertheless, there is about his writing a footlight glitter that
reflects the superficiality of his thinking. Matthew Arnold called
him "the great apostle of the Philistines."

MACDONALD, George (1824–1905), a Scotsman, wrote a great
deal of prose and verse, much of it tinged with fantasy, mysticism,
and allegory. His works for adults include *Within and Without*
(1855), a narrative poem; *Phantastes* (1858), a "faerie romance"
chiefly in prose; *The Portent* (1864), "a story of the inner vision
of the highlanders, commonly called the second sight"; and
Robert Falconer (1868), a novel of Scottish life. Macdonald's
best-known work, however, is probably his fantasy for children,
At the Back of the North Wind (1871).

MACHEN, Arthur (1863–1947) is a Welsh novelist and essayist
who has written numerous tales dealing with the beauty and the
terror of the unseen world. Among his best stories are *The Great
God Pan and the Inmost Light* (1894), *The Hill of Dreams* (1907),
and the shorter tales appearing in *The Bowman, and other Legends
of the War* (1915).

MACKENZIE, (Edward Montagu) Compton (1883–   ) is a
prolific popular novelist. In *Sinister Street* (two vols., 1913–14) he
traced the adventures of his hero, Michael Fane, in school and at
Oxford. In the third and fourth volumes of the same series, *The
Early Life and Adventures of Sylvia Scarlett* (1918) and *Sylvia
and Michael* (1919), he dealt respectively with the world of the
theater and the problems of the First World War. Compton
Mackenzie has also written *The Altar Steps* (1922), *The Parson's
Progress* (1923), and *The Heavenly Ladder* (1924)—a trilogy on
ecclesiastical life—besides such single-volume satires as *Vestal Fire*
(1927) and *Water on the Brain* (1933). In *Mr. Roosevelt* (1944)

he has published a popular and sympathetic biography of the American president.

MACKENZIE, Henry (1745–1831). Although he wrote poems and plays and edited two periodicals, this Scot is remembered chiefly as a sentimental novelist. In his most celebrated novel, *The Man of Feeling* (1771), he depicted a hero, Harley, whose floodgates and purse strings are forever bursting with sympathy for suffering mankind. Harley's counterpart is the hypocritical seducer of Mackenzie's second novel, *The Man of the World* (1773). The "man of feeling" is a literary descendant of Sterne's Yorick, the "man of the world" of Richardson's Lovelace. Mackenzie wrote one other novel, *Julia de Roubigne* (1777), a senti- mental tragedy in a series of letters.

MACKINTOSH, Sir James (1765–1832), a Scottish professor of law and member of Parliament, wrote numerous works in prose on philosophy, history, and law. Among his productions are: *Vindiciae Gallicae* (1791), a defense of the French Revolution in answer to Burke's *Reflections; A Dissertation on the Progress of Ethical Philosophy* (1830), which provoked a bitter rejoinder by James Mill; and an unfinished *History of the Revolution in 1688* (1834), which was the subject of one of Macaulay's reviews (*Edinburgh Review,* LXI, 1835).

MACKLIN, Charles (1697?–1797), an Irishman, was one of the most celebrated actors on the eighteenth-century stage. He is remembered especially for his performance of Shylock in *The Merchant of Venice,* a play which he resurrected at Drury Lane in 1741. The contemporary compliment—"This is the Jew that Shakespeare drew"—has been attributed to Pope. Macklin wrote two popular plays, *Love à la Mode* (1759), a farce, and *The Man of the World* (1781), a comedy.

MACLAREN, Ian. Pseudonym of **John Watson** (1850–1907), clergyman and writer who contributed *Beside the Bonnie Brier Bush* (1894), sketches of humble life in Scotland, to the senti- mental "Kailyard School" before turning his attention to the writ- ing of religious books.

MACLEOD, Fiona. Pseudonym of **William Sharp.**

MACPHERSON, James (1736–96). In 1760 this Scottish school- master intrigued the literary world with his *Fragments of An- cient Poetry collected in the Highlands of Scotland and translated from the Gaelic or Erse Language.* He followed this success with two epics, *Fingal* (1762) and *Temora* (1763), ascribing both to

the third-century Gaelic bard, Ossian. It was soon revealed that
all these productions contained much Macpherson mixed with
little Erse. But Europe, on the eve of the Romantic Revival,
eagerly parroted his melancholy biblical cadences. And Macpherson did not, like another forger, Chatterton, drink poison.
He became a successful politician instead.

MAGINN, William (1793–1842), an Irishman, was one of the
early contributors to *Blackwood's Magazine* and the founder of
Fraser's Magazine (1830). He is said to have suggested the famous
dialogues of *Blackwood's* called *Noctes Ambrosianae* (1822–35),
and, although John Wilson was the chief author, he composed
several of them. He also wrote *The Maxims of Sir Morgan
O'Doherty* (1849), in imitation of La Rochefoucauld's famous
Réflexions, Sentences, et Maximes Morales (1665); and a great
many miscellaneous verses and short tales. Maginn was the original
of Captain Shandon in Thackeray's *Pendennis.*

MAITLAND, Robert. Pseudonym of **Robert William Buchanan.**

MALLET or **MALLOCH, David** (1705?–65), poet and playwright, is remembered chiefly as the author of *William and
Margaret* (1723?), a literary ballad which anticipated the general
revival of interest in the ballad form later in the century. He collaborated with James Thomson on *Alfred, a Masque* (1740) and
is thus a candidate for the honor of having written the patriotic
song, *Rule Britannia!*, which made its bow in that production.

MALLOCK, William Hurrell (1849–1923) wrote *The New Republic, or Culture, Faith and Philosophy in an English Country
House* (1877), a satiric symposium in which such celebrated Victorians as Ruskin, Arnold, Pater, and Huxley appear in disguise
and spout their favorite doctrines.

MALONE, Edmond (1741–1812) was one of the most careful and
painstaking of the eighteenth-century Shakespearean scholars.
His *Essay on the Chronology of Shakespeare's Plays,* contributed
to the Johnson-Steevens edition of 1778, is one of the first scholarly attempts to determine the dates of the dramas. His own
edition of the plays in 1790 was based on an honest, if sometimes
dull, study of the early folios and quartos. In these labors he
served Shakespeare better than he did when he whitewashed
the poet's bust in the Stratford Church—a bit of vandalism which
one would gladly forget. Malone was a member of Johnson's
"Club" and a friend of James Boswell. On the biographer's death
in 1795 he saw the *Life of Johnson* through its third edition.

MALORY, Sir Thomas (fl. 1470) wrote *Morte Darthur,* a work which was finished in prison in 1469 and printed by Caxton in 1485. "It treateth," wrote the first English printer, "of the birth, life, and acts of . . . King Arthur, of his noble knights of the Round Table, their marvellous enquests and adventures, the achieving of the Sangreal, and in the end the dolorous death and departing out of the world of them all." The book is actually a selection and condensation of familiar medieval legends, most of them translated from the French. But the obscure knight was a creative artist, and there is more poetry in his simple, homely prose than in all the earlier poetic versions of the story of Arthur. Both Spenser in *The Faerie Queene* and Tennyson in *Idylls of the King* were greatly indebted to Sir Thomas Malory.

MALTHUS, Thomas Robert (1766–1834) was a country curate who transformed himself almost overnight into an influential economist. In *An Essay on the Principle of Population* (1798) he pictured the population as expanding geometrically until it eventually outgrew the means of subsistence. Although Malthus cushioned the shock somewhat in his edition of 1803, "Malthusianism," spread far and wide by the Utilitarians, cast a shadow over nineteenth-century economic thinking.

MANDEVILLE, Barnard (1670–1733) was a cynical Dutchman who practised medicine and philosophy in London. His chief work began as a 400-line piece of doggerel called *The Grumbling Hive, or Knaves Turned Honest* (1705). It was later printed with copious prose additions as *The Fable of the Bees, or Private Vices Public Benefits* (1714, 1723). Mandeville assumed, like Hobbes, the innate selfishness of mankind and paradoxically argued that whatever virtue does exist in society depends on the conflicting vices of individuals. Since followers of his contemporary, Shaftesbury, were sworn defenders of man's innate goodness, *The Fable* caused much grumbling in the philosophic hive.

MANDEVILLE, Sir John (fl. 14th cent.?). *The Voiage and Travaile of Sir John Maundevile, Knight* purports to be a guide to the Holy Land based on actual travels. It is really a mixture of pilfered travel stories and marvelous fables of the Far East. The earliest known of many versions was printed in French at Liège in 1371. Whether it was by a John of Outremeuse or a Dr. John of Bourgogne, alias Sir John Mandeville, alias the Bearded, or by neither—is a time-honored puzzle. It is more important that, three and a half centuries before *Robinson Crusoe,* there appeared in English a travel tale told so convincingly that readers for years swallowed its Munchausen-marvels as facts.

MANLEY, Mary de la Rivière (1663–1724) is remembered for her amorous "key novels." Her once-popular *New Atalantis* (1709), for example, concealed beneath a romantic veil "secret memoirs and manners of several persons of quality of both sexes."

MANNYNG of Brunne, Robert (fl. 1288–1338) was a monk of Bourne in Lincolnshire. His chief work, *Handlyng Synne* (begun after 1303), is a free translation of the Anglo-Norman *Manuel des Pechiez* of William of Waddington. Here in a poem of over six thousand couplets, Mannyng issued a comprehensive compendium of sin to warn his unlearned contemporaries. Although the framework of the poem is based partly on the Ten Commandments, partly on the Seven Deadly Sins, the poet runs the complete gamut from "kyssing" to "karolles, wrastlynges, or somour games . . . yn cherche" and enhances the beauty of evil with sixty-five entertaining, illustrative tales. Less important from a literary standpoint is Mannyng's *Story of England* (c. 1338), a verse chronicle based partly on Wace's *Brut,* partly on the French of Pierre de Langtoft.

MANSFIELD, Katherine (1888–1923) was born Kathleen Beauchamp in Wellington, New Zealand. She studied at Queen's College, London, from 1902 to 1905 and returned to London from Wellington in 1908 to study music and literature. While convalescing from a breakdown in Germany, she wrote the short-stories which were published in her first collection, *In a German Pension* (1911). Ill-health pursued her for the rest of her life, and she died of tuberculosis at thirty-four. In the seven volumes which succeeded her first collection, among them *Bliss* (1920), *The Garden Party* (1922), and *The Doves' Nest* (1923), she was gradually revealed as a master of the short-story. She worked fastidiously with a fine brush on a small canvas, and in such miniature classics as *The Doll's House* and *A Cup of Tea* (both from *The Doves' Nest*) she realized the exquisite emotions of commonplace incidents. Her *Journal* (1927) and *Letters* (1928) were edited by her husband, J. Middleton Murry.

MAP or MAPES, Walter (fl. 1190). This scholar and wit was an itinerant judge under Henry II and in 1197 was appointed archdeacon of Oxford. He wrote *De Nugis Curialium* (c. 1180–93), a Latin miscellany which includes numerous satirical anecdotes about monks and courtiers. He has been credited also with a number of "Goliardic verses"—bawdy, satirical Latin poems on the dissolute Bishop Golias—and with a lost Latin source of the French prose romance, *Lancelot du Lac.*

MARKHAM, Gervase (1568?–1637). Although he made some minor contributions to *belles lettres,* including *The Most Honorable Tragedy of Sir Richard Grinvile, Knight* (1595)—a poem about the last fight of the *Revenge*—and *The Dumb Knight, a Pleasant Comedy* (1607–8), Markham is best known for his numerous prose works on country life in general and on horses in particular. His works include *A Discourse of Horsemanship* (1593), *Cavelarice, or the English Horseman* (1607), *A Cure for All Diseases in Horses* (1610), and *Country Contentments* (1615).

MARLOWE, Christopher (1564–93) was the greatest English dramatist before Shakespeare. His father was a shoemaker of Canterbury. Christopher took a degree at Cambridge University, apparently not because of any high attainments as a scholar but because of a government order which suggests that he had been serving at court. For a time he was a member of the Earl of Nottingham's players. He wrote poems and plays, and translated beautifully from the classics. And then, just before he was thirty, he was killed by a dagger thrust in a Deptford tavern. Whether Ingram Frisar, who killed him, was quarreling with the poet over a drinking score or was acting as a secret agent for the government, research has not yet discovered. But Kit Marlowe, born the same year as William Shakespeare, completed his work and his life when his great contemporary was writing his first plays.

If Marlowe had never written a play, his name would stand high among those of the English poets. There is a lyrical simplicity in his pastoral *The Passionate Shepherd to His Love* that gave the poem a place in *England's Helicon* (1600) and a romantic quality that drew Raleigh to write the realistic *Nymph's Reply to the Shepherd.* His translation of Ovid's *Amores* was published about 1599, and his narrative poem, *Hero and Leander,* left unfinished at his death, was completed by George Chapman in 1598. But Marlowe's greatest metrical contribution is the "mighty line" of his dramatic blank verse. He took the stiff iambic pentameter of earlier plays and made of it a flexible, varied, unrestrained, and powerful vehicle for his tragedies. And the tragedies are worthy of the poetry. They are essentially classical in their presentation of a single mighty hero who rises to a great height and crashes to a terrible fall. Marlowe's aim was always lofty. He condemned the "jigging veins of rhyming mother wits, and such conceits as clownage keeps in pay." Only his

Faustus contains farcical scenes, and for these he may not have been responsible. Titanic heroes, filled with the lust for power—these are his chief characters, not clowns, servants, or even women. And the plots, too, are on an epic scale, with the actions thrown against sweeping backgrounds.

Marlowe's first tragedy, the two-part *Tamburlane* (1587-8), presents a shepherd warrior of Scythia who drives emperors and kings before his unconquerable sword until he is himself conquered by Death. In *The Jew of Malta* (c. 1589-90) the hero is a Jew moved to atrocious acts of insane cruelty by the injustices that Christians have heaped upon him. Young Mortimer of the historical tragedy of *Edward II* (1591-3) rises to political heights until he has touched the very button on Fortune's cap and can scorn the order for his execution. But the most famous of Marlowe's plays is *The Tragical History of Doctor Faustus* (1588-92). Marlowe took the plot from a German chapbook account of a scholar-magician who sold his soul to the devil for twenty-four years of power. In all Marlowe's tragedies, with the possible exception of *The Jew of Malta,* the sheer strength of the dramatist and the lyrical quality of the poet save the play from inflation and rant. Exaggerated as characters and episodes frequently are, Marlowe's power keeps them from seeming unnatural and banal.

MARMION, Shakerley (1603-39), a friend of Suckling, was the author of a narrative poem, *Cupid and Psyche* (1637), and of three extant comedies, the best known of which is *The Antiquary* (1635-6).

MARPRELATE. See MARTIN MARPRELATE.

MARRYAT, Frederick (1792-1848) was a sea captain whose novels reflect his twenty-four years in the Royal Navy and his admiration for Smollett. *Peter Simple* (1834), *Jacob Faithful* (1834), and *Mr. Midshipman Easy* (1836) combine first-hand naval history with broad farce. *Snarleyyow, or the Dog Fiend* (1837) is a pseudo-historical farce-fantasy, *Masterman Ready* (1841-2) an excellent sea-tale for boys.

MARSTON, John (1575?-1634). The race of playwrights and players who helped make the Elizabethan and Jacobean periods great were for the most part a quarrelsome, temperamental lot. John Marston especially seems to have had a reputation for satirical bitterness. He was born at Coventry of an Italian mother, graduated from Oxford, and, in 1616, the year of Shakespeare's death, became rector of Christ Church, Hampshire, whereupon he stopped writing plays and devoted himself for the rest of his life to his parish work. Until this radical change, however, he wrote vigorously, realistically, and often coarsely—some poetry, and at least half a dozen important plays. His *Scourge of Villainy* (1598) was an early satirical poem, and *The Metamorphosis of Pygmalion's Image: and Certain Satires,* written in the same year, gave him a further outlet for his coarse bitterness. *The History of Antonio and Mellida* (two parts, 1599–1601) is a blood-revenge tragedy with so much inflation and ranting that Ben Jonson attacked it and its author in *The Poetaster* (1601), a satirical comedy. In collaboration with Thomas Dekker, another victim of Jonson's vitriolic pen, Marston retaliated with *Satiromastix, or the Untrussing of the Humorous Poet* (1601). But he and his gruff opponent seem to have made up their differences, because three years later Marston collaborated with Jonson and Chapman in *Eastward Ho* (1605), an assault on the king's Scots followers so naked in its satire that the three poets were jailed for libel. In 1603–4 appeared Marston's *Dutch Courtezan,* an earthy comedy. His best-known play, however, is *The Malcontent* (1604), a tragedy of court intrigue in which the bitter hero, Malevole, is given every opportunity to vent his misanthropic distaste for society.

MARSTON, John Westland (1819–90) and **MARSTON, Philip Bourke** (1850–87). The first was a dramatist and poet. *The Patrician's Daughter* (1842), *Strathmore* (1849), and *Philip of France and Marie de Méranie* (1850) are among the last appreciable verse tragedies in the nineteenth century. His best comedy is *The Favorite of Fortune* (1866). His blind son, **Philip,** author of *Song-Tide and other Poems* (1871), was one of the lesser Pre-Raphaelites.

MARTIN MARPRELATE was the screen from behind which a group of anonymous Elizabethan Puritans shot satirical shafts at their Church of England opponents. The "Martin Marprelate Controversy" began with a Star Chamber order of 1586 that put control of the printing presses completely into the hands of Archbishop Whitgift and the Bishop of London. This action drove the Puritan press underground, but with the help of one Robert Waldegrave and other printers the Puritan satirists replied to their Church of England opponents in a series of seven pamphlets that are among the most vigorous religious satires in English literature. From late 1588 to the end of 1589 appeared the following: 1. *The Epistle,* 2. *The Epitome,* 3. *Minerall Conclusions,* 4. *Hay* [have ye] *any Worke for Cooper?*—an attack on Bishop Cooper under the figure of a barrel-maker, 5. *Theses Martinianae or Martin Junior*, 6. *The Just Censure and Reproofe of Martin Junior*, and 7. *The Protestation of Martin Marprelat*. Shortly after the emergence of this last pamphlet three Puritans suspected of playing the rôle of Martin were arrested. John Penry, a Welshman, was condemned and hanged, John Udall was condemned to death but pardoned, and Job Throckmorton cleared himself, although he probably wrote most of the pamphlets. The paper battles involved many other writers, including John Lyly, Thomas Nashe, and Gabriel and Richard Harvey, all of whom attacked Martin Marprelate with more scurrility than skill. Indeed, the pamphlets on the side of the established Church had little of the satirical vigor of those issued by the rebel Puritans.

MARTIN, Sir Theodore (1816–1909) collaborated with W. E. Aytoun on the celebrated light-verse collection commonly called *Bon Gaultier Ballads* (1845). He also composed a *Memoir of W. E. Aytoun* (1867), the official biography of Prince Albert (1875–80), a life of his actress wife, Helena Faucit (1900), and numerous translations.

MARTINEAU, Harriet (1802–76) was a versatile reformer and skeptic, one of the bold Victorian women who would not stay put in the parlor. She taught the principles of economics through fiction (*Illustrations of Political Economy*, 1832–4); wrote a pair of novels (*Deerbrook*, 1839, *The Hour and the Man*, 1841), a successful collection of children's tales (*The Playfellow*, 1841), and a Whiggish *History of England during the Thirty Years' Peace, 1816–46* (1849–50). The religious doubt which led her to dismiss Christianity in her frank autobiography (1877) as a "monstrous superstition" was also reflected in her condensed translation of Comte's *Positive Philosophy* (1853). This translation helped to spread a movement which influenced both George Eliot and George Henry Lewes.

MARVELL, Andrew (1621–78). As a young man, this Calvinist minister's son spent two idyllic years (1650–2) in a Yorkshire manor house tutoring a nobleman's daughter. Later he entered politics; he served under his friend Milton as Assistant Latin Secretary of the Council of State and spent his last nineteen years as a member of Parliament. The work of Marvell's calmer youth has outlived the savage satires of his struggle against Restoration corruption. His lyrics, most of them in the metaphysical manner, include *The Garden*, a contented hymn to Nature; *The Bermudas*, which expresses the faith and hope of a group of religious exiles in the New World; *The Coronet,* a devout religious conceit; and *A Horatian Ode upon Cromwell's Return from Ireland.* But the embattled Puritan is known to many as the author of a single worldly love lyric, *To His Coy Mistress* (c. 1650). Here in forty-six lines he ranges from flirtatious flippancy to searing passion.

MASEFIELD, John (1878–   ). It is not unfitting that a man who is best known for his songs and tales of the sea should be poet laureate of England. Masefield ran away to sea at fourteen and followed the whale's way for a number of years. The experience is reflected in his first collection of poems, *Salt Water Ballads* (1902), in one of his most popular narrative poems, *The Dauber* (1913), and in the two lyrics most often reprinted, *Sea-Fever* (1902) and *Cargoes* (1910). But Masefield's gamut is by no means limited to nautical themes. To many mature critics, his best narrative poem is *Reynard the Fox* (1920), the tumbling tale of an English hunt, redolent with the flavor of the English countryside. In a recent narrative poem, *Wonderings* (1943), he reminisces in a mood half nostalgic, half critical, about the charming but backward England of his childhood. There are other fine lyrics besides the most popular anthology favorites; for example, the sonnet "Go, spend your penny, Beauty, when you will" and the mellow lines *On Growing Old* ("Be with me, Beauty, for the fire is dying"). Moreover, the laureate has also written novels and short-stories, dramatic verse (*The Everlasting Mercy,* 1911), and plays (*The Tragedy of Nan,* 1909). Masefield's work is notably uneven, but at his best he is a narrative poet of compelling vigor and a lyricist of rare beauty.

MASSINGER, Philip (1583–1640) was technically one of the best of the Jacobean dramatists. He was born in Salisbury and developed his dramatic art under the patronage of the Earl of Pembroke. Many of the fifteen plays attributed to him he did in collaboration with Fletcher, Dekker, Field, and other playwrights. One of his first plays, *The Maid of Honour* (printed 1632), is a typical romantic drama. His two early tragedies, *The Duke of Milan* (c. 1620–2) and *The Roman Actor* (1626), are not so good as *The Fatal Dowry* (1618–9), which he wrote in collaboration with Nathaniel Field (1587–1633). Although *The Great Duke of Florence* (1627) is a conventional Jacobean comedy, Massinger usually foreshadowed, as did other Jacobean dramatists, the comedy of manners of the Restoration period. This tendency appears especially in *The City Madam* (1632) and in *A New Way to Pay*

Old Debts (1621–5). The second of these is his best comedy. The intrigue plot he imitated from Middleton's *A Trick to Catch the Old One* (1604–7), but Massinger's play is better knit and much more original and vigorous in its episodes and characters. The villain of the piece is the unscrupulous and scheming Sir Giles Overreach, whom Massinger staged from Sir Giles Mompesson, a rackrent extortioner of the period. This comedy, like all of Massinger's dramas, is characterized by a morality that is vigorous but never mawkish.

MASSON, David (1822–1907) was Professor of English at Edinburgh University (1865–95) and founder and editor of *Macmillan's Magazine* (1859–67). He is known best for his ambitious and scholarly *Life of John Milton, narrated in Connexion with the Political, Ecclesiastical, and Literary History of his Time* (1859–94).

MATURIN, Charles Robert (1782–1824) was an Irish clergyman who trafficked in literary terror. Encouraged by Scott and Byron, he produced three melodramatic tragedies at Drury Lane, one of which, *Bertram* (1816), although damned by both Coleridge and Hazlitt, was a popular success. His best novel is *Melmoth the Wanderer* (1820), a late Gothic tale in which the hero, after selling his soul to Satan for wealth and eternal youth, wanders through the world seeking vainly for someone with whom to trade lots. It is a work of unbridled imagination, having more in common with Lewis' *Monk* than with the mechanical thrillers of Mrs. Radcliffe. Many call it the best of the Gothic romances.

MAUGHAM, W(illiam) Somerset (1874–   ) has written plays, short-stories, and novels. Typical of his numerous plays is *The Circle* (1921), a witty and sophisticated drawing-room comedy in the manner of Oscar Wilde. Two of his exotic short-stories, *Rain* (from *The Trembling of a Leaf,* 1921) and *The Letter* (from *The Casuarina Tree,* 1926), have been successfully adapted for stage and screen. His masterpiece is *Of Human Bondage* (1915), a solid autobiographical novel. In it he told how Philip Carey, handicapped at birth by a club foot and cloistered throughout his boyhood in the oppressive atmosphere of a Victorian vicarage and a snobbish school, struggled through young manhood to find a philosophy for living in the outside world. Three other novels are *The Moon and Sixpence* (1919), adapted from the life of the French painter, Paul Gauguin; *Cakes and Ale* (1930), in which Edward Driffield, the "grand old man of English letters," is evidently a caricature of Thomas Hardy; and *The*

Razor's Edge (1944), widely hailed as Maugham's best novel in recent years. *The Summing Up* (1938) is an informal summary of the author's literary career, including some shrewd observations on how to write readable English prose.

MAURICE, John Frederick Denison (1805–72) wrote *The Religions of the World* (1847) and *Theological Essays* (1853), works which many Victorians considered dangerously unorthodox. He found an outlet for his passion for social justice in what he called "Christian Socialism." This gospel, founded on the assumption that Christianity and Socialism are inseparable, was widely preached by Maurice's most celebrated follower, Charles Kingsley.

MAY, Thomas (1595–1650), a friend and imitator of Ben Jonson, composed two comedies, *The Heir* (1620) and *The Old Couple* (1636); classical tragedies on *Antigone, the Theban Princess* (1627–31), *Cleopatra, Queen of Egypt* (1626), and *Julia Agrippina, Empress of Rome* (1628); a history of the Long Parliament (1647); and translations of Lucan's *Pharsalia* (1626–7) and Vergil's *Georgics* (1628).

MEDWALL, Henry (fl. 1486) was chaplain to Cardinal Morton, in whose household Sir Thomas More was reared. He was the author of *Fulgens and Lucres* (c. 1490–c. 1501), a romantic interlude, which is remembered as the first purely secular play in English. He also wrote a moral interlude called *Nature* (c. 1490–c. 1501).

MEREDITH, George (1828–1909) was one of the most intellectual of Victorian poets and novelists. He was born in Portsmouth of Welsh and Irish ancestry and was trained for a time in a Moravian school at Neuwied, Germany. Like so many other British authors, he abandoned law to take up journalism and literature. His early connections in these fields were with the *Ipswich Journal, Once a Week,* and the *Morning Post,* his later with the *Fortnightly Review.* His longest unbroken professional relationship was a thirty-five-year service as reader for the publishing firm of Chapman and Hall; his work here began in 1860. Meredith's marriage in 1849 to Mary Ellen Nicolls, the widowed daughter of Thomas Love Peacock, novelist and poet, gave him an excellent opportunity to experience at first hand some of those problems of adjustment between man and woman that appear so often in his novels. After a ten-year struggle to reconcile their temperamental differences, the Merediths gave up the effort and were divorced. From a literary point of view only was their union fruitful; it resulted in Meredith's writing *Modern Love* (1862), a sequence of fifty sixteen-line poems that interpret the marital interlude of the two individualists. Meredith's marriage two years after his divorce to Marie Vulliamy resulted in a union that was smoother—but less interesting to his readers.

When Meredith wrote *Modern Love* he was already a seasoned poet; he had begun early to send his verses to the magazines and his *Poems* had appeared in 1851. Meredith never allowed his interest in writing poetry to be permanently eclipsed by his activity as a novelist. In his last years particularly he wrote much poetry—*Ballads and Poems of Tragic Life* (1887), *A Reading of Earth* (1888), *The Empty Purse and Other Poems* (1892), *Odes in Contribution to the Song of French History* (1898), *A Reading of Life, with Other Poems* (1901), and *Last Poems* (1909). The solid, intellectual quality of all his work appears strongly in his poems. Like Tennyson, he was fond of metrical experiment, but unlike Tennyson he had a sense of artistic compression.

Meredith's first novels were the exotic stories *The Shaving of Shagpat* (1856) and *Farina* (1857). The remarkable series of social studies that followed deals with problems of various sorts. In *The Ordeal of Richard Feverel* (1859) and *Evan Harrington* (1861) he was concerned with the induction of well-born youth into adult life. *Vittoria* (1867) and *Beauchamp's Career* (1876) deal with politics in England and Europe. *Rhoda Fleming* (1865) is one of his few novels in which the characters are not aristocrats. *The Egoist* (1879) is his best psychological study. *Diana of the Crossways* (1885) and *The Amazing Marriage* (1895) have to do with women under male domination. In all of these novels Meredith is less concerned with the story than with the psychology of the characters and the social problems in which they find themselves involved. He is less a satirist than a jester. At the beck of the "comic spirit" which he characterized in his brilliant lecture *On the Idea of Comedy* (1877), he centers the folly of mankind in the spotlight of common sense. His style is exceedingly individual. At its most exasperating, as in *The Ordeal of Richard Feverel*, the mood varies from cynical jesting to sentimental poetizing; the story line is now double-inked with melodrama, now severed by a swift transition, now buried in a heap of epigrams and aphorisms.

MERES, Francis (1565–1647). His *Palladis Tamia, Wit's Treasury* (1598) is both an anthology of quotations and a survey of English literary history from Chaucer to Elizabethan times. Meres' notes and comments, especially on the Elizabethans, have been invaluable to scholars. His book contains an incomplete account of Marlowe's death and a list of Shakespeare's works down to 1598 which has helped scholars to arrange their order of composition. It is from Meres, for example, that we learn that some of Shakespeare's sonnets, although not published until 1609, were in existence before 1598.

MEYNELL, Alice (1847–1922) belongs, with Gerard Manley Hopkins, Coventry Patmore, and Francis Thompson, to the group of distinguished nineteenth-century Catholic poets. Her first book of verse, *Preludes,* appeared in 1875 and her *Last Poems* in 1923. Her poems are few—partly because she was the mother of eight children—but they are marked by technical perfection and exquisite restraint. Among the best known are *The Shepherdess* ("She walks—the lady of my delight") and the sonnet, *Renouncement.* Mrs. Meynell also wrote finely fashioned critical essays, as in *Hearts of Controversy* (1917).

MIDDLETON, Thomas (1570?–1627) belongs to that important group of Jacobean dramatists in whom modern interest was revived by the comments of Charles Lamb. In 1808 Lamb alluded to Middleton's "exquisiteness of moral sensibility," a true enough statement of one element in the dramatist's plays. Regarding Middleton's early life very little is known. He was apparently born in London and made that city the center of his career, serving it as city chronologer during the last seven years of his life. He seems to have had many acquaintances among the dramatists of the period and collaborated in his dramatic writing with Munday, Dekker, Jonson, Fletcher, Webster, and notably William Rowley. Whether Ben Jonson's characterization of him as "a base fellow" alludes to his character or to the pedestrian nature of his dramatic art is hard to say, for Ben was a harsh fellow himself, who might have been guilty of either type of attack.

Middleton's best plays—selected from a list of many good, bad, and indifferent—are: *A Trick to Catch the Old One* (printed 1604–7); *The Roaring Girl* (1604–10), with Thomas Dekker; *The Witch* (c. 1613–c. 1616); *A Fair Quarrel* (1615–17), with William Rowley; *The Changeling* (1622), also with Rowley; and, finally, the popular *Game of Chess* (1624). *A Trick to Catch the Old One* is a "prodigal son" comedy on the same pattern as Massinger's *New Way to Pay Old Debts,* but inferior except for one or two realistic scenes. *The Roaring Girl* makes a popular female Robin Hood of Mary Frith, or Moll Cutpurse, a notorious woman bandit. *The Witch* is a romantic play notable for excellent witch scenes and songs that have been compared with those in *Macbeth*. Both of the plays done with Rowley are characterized by striking figures and melodramatic scenes. Captain Ager of *A Fair Quarrel* is neatly suspended between the horns of an ethical dilemma involving his honor. In the magnificent tragedy of *The Changeling* appear the titanic figures of Beatrice, the "fair murderess," and her rugged paramour De Flores. Middleton's most immediately popular play is his satirical *Game of Chess,* which Swinburne has called "the only work of English poetry that may properly be called Aristophanic." The drama is an attack upon the Spanish Court and especially upon the Spanish ambassador to England, Gondomar, who had plotted unsuccessfully to bring about a marriage between Prince Charles of England and the Infanta of Spain. The satire was immensely popular in London, but resulted in prison terms and fines for the actors and the playwright.

As a dramatic poet Middleton mixed romanticism and realism. Although he never made sin attractive, he dealt with it openly, grossly, and often brutally. His stage world is a Jacobean world of sex, vice, and knavery. His plots and passions are mean, and his characters are mainly gallants, wantons, and cozeners. Alone or in collaboration he wrote many plays—too many, perhaps. He wrote, on the whole, too easily and too hastily, with the result that only rarely did he reach the elevation of some of his best scenes in *A Fair Quarrel* and *The Changeling*.

MILL, James (1773-1836), economist and philosopher, was co-founder with Jeremy Bentham of the *Westminster Review* (1824), where he helped to spread Benthamite Utilitarianism. His chief works are *Elements of Political Economy* (1821) and *Analysis of the Phenomena of the Human Mind* (1829). His skeptical character is well displayed in Chapter II of the autobiography of his son, John Stuart Mill.

MILL, John Stuart (1806-73). Although his essays are primarily on philosophical, social, economic, and political subjects, John Stuart Mill wrote so well that most belletrists have admitted him to the gallery of nineteenth-century "prose masters." His father was James Mill (1773-1836), a philosopher who was almost as famous as his brilliant son. As J. S. Mill recounts in his frank *Autobiography* (1874), the elder Mill trained the younger by a rigid system that disciplined the boy intellectually at the same time that it came perilously near to ruining him physically and emotionally. At the age of three the child knew the Greek alphabet, at ten he could read Greek fluently, at fourteen he was in France studying economics, logic, mathematics—and more Greek. Three years later he found a living as junior clerk in the India Office, and although his intellectual interests lay outside his routine occupation, he advanced steadily until in 1856 he became chief of the office.

Meanwhile he was tremendously active in his study of economics, politics, and philosophy. The year of his entrance upon his clerkship he founded the Utilitarian Society, a group organized to study and promulgate the theories—somewhat modified—of Jeremy Bentham (1748–1832). Seven years later he founded the Speculative Society and was soon editor and writer for several radical journals. His first book, *A System of Logic,* was published in 1843, and his *Principles of Political Economy* in 1848. *On Liberty,* the most famous of his essays, and his *Thoughts on Parliamentary Government* were published in 1859. *Considerations on Representative Government* (1861) and *Utilitarianism* (1863) preceded his election to Parliament (1865); the office was not of his seeking, but he did not decline it. At the end of an apathetic three-year service he retired. In this year he issued *England and Ireland* (1868), a history and analysis of the relations of the two countries. One of his most remarkable essays—stimulated, perhaps, by a wife who was less intelligent than he thought her to be—is his *On the Subjection of Women* (1869). His last essay, *Nature and Theism,* did not appear until the year after his death. Mill's literary style is clear, cold, and direct. As might have been expected from his training and interests, he lived in a world of thought; his emotions were undeveloped, and his social instincts immature.

MILLER, Hugh (1802–56). In addition to works on geology, including *The Old Red Sandstone* (1841) and *The Testimony of the Rocks* (1857), Miller wrote *My Schools and Schoolmasters* (1852), a book which has been called "one of the best autobiographies in English."

MILNE, A(lan) A(lexander) (1882–1956). The works of A. A. Milne and Sir James Barrie have much in common. As playwrights, both have dealt successfully with fantasy and sentimental whimsy. Milne's *Mr. Pim Passes By* (1919) and *The Dover Road* (1922) are of such stuff as dreams are made on. And like the creator of Peter Pan, Milne has added an immortal to the nursery; Christopher Robin, named after Milne's own son, is a hero to the thousands who have enjoyed such childhood classics as *When We Were Very Young* (1924), *Winnie-the-Pooh* (1926), *Now We Are Six* (1927), and *The House at Pooh Corner* (1928). Trained as a writer of light verse, both as editor of the *Granta* at Cambridge and later as assistant editor of *Punch* (1906–14), Milne filled these books with delightful nonsense verses which give him a serious claim to the mantles of Edward Lear and Lewis Carroll. He has also written informal essays and a pleasant autobiography (1939).

MILTON, John (1608–74). The "organ-toned" poet of England's only important literary epic did much more than write *Paradise Lost.* He was also a government official, a powerful pamphleteer, a philosopher and moralist, and the creator of some of the best short lyrics and sonnets in English literature. Milton was born in London, the son of a lawyer who was a widely-known musician. He was educated at Christ's College, Cambridge, where his delicate features earned him the name of "The Lady of Christ's." For some years after his graduation he lived in scholarly retirement on his father's estate at Horton, twenty miles north of London. To his so-called "Horton period," which ended when he took a Continental tour in 1638, belong—probably—*L'Allegro* and *Il Penseroso,* lyrical descriptions of the happy man and the thoughtful man; *Comus* (1634), one of the last of the Jacobean masques; and *Lycidas* (1638), an elegy in memory of Edward King, a young poet whom Milton had known at Cambridge. In *Lycidas* Milton digressed from his subject to attack the Church of England clergy for their indolence and lack of spirituality.

With his return from Italy in 1639 begins his so-called second period, two decades of government service and pamphleteering that extended to the Restoration in 1660. Leaving Horton he took up private teaching in London, but became increasingly interested in the rebellion that was brewing. The attack on the Church of England clergy that had emerged as an incidental element in *Lycidas* was renewed in a fuller assault in his prose treatise *Of Reformation Touching Church Discipline in England* (1641). The outbreak of the Civil War in the year following found his sympathies on the side of Parliament. In 1643 he married Mary Powell, a seventeen-year-old girl who found living with an austere scholar twice her age so little to her taste that she left him within a month. Milton expressed himself on marriage in his *Doctrine and Discipline of Divorce* (1643); nevertheless, he was reunited to her two years later after her loyalist parents had become impoverished by the war; and she bore him three daughters. In this same year he published *Poems . . . both English and Latin, composed at several times.* His second period was marked, however, not by poetry but by prose. In 1649 he became Latin secretary to the commissioner of foreign affairs and wrote and translated Latin correspondence with European governments. He stood by the regicides who put Charles I to death in 1649 and defended them vigorously in two pamphlets, *Eikonoklastes* (1649), "the image-breaker," a reply to the anonymous *Eikon Basilike,* "the royal image"—a sentimental defense of the king—and *Defensio pro Populo Anglicano* (1651). These heavy pamphlets are neither so general in interest nor so well written as his deservedly famous *Areopagitica* (1644), an argument before Parliament for the freedom of the press. A decade of study and of slavery for the Commonwealth wore out Milton's vision, and in 1652—the year also of his wife's death—he became totally blind, an affliction that he faced courageously in his sonnet "On his blindness." His second wife, Catherine Woodcock, the "late espoused saint" of one of his finest sonnets, and his third wife, Elizabeth Minshull, who survived him by many years, he never saw.

With the restoration of King Charles II, the stubborn Puritan rebel retired to a house in Bunhill Fields, London, and so began his "third period," which lasted until his death fourteen years later. This is the period of his greatest work. It saw the publication of the religious epic *Paradise Lost* (1667), its inferior complementary poem *Paradise Regained* (1671), and the dramatic tragedy *Samson Agonistes* (1671). Milton had long contemplated the writing of an epic and had discarded several subjects before choosing finally the fall of man through the temptation of Satan. Milton was at once a classical and a biblical scholar, and the influences of Homer, Vergil, Dante, and the Bible are paramount in the poem. The epic ranges from Heaven to Hell and is magnificent in its scope. Curiously enough, however, it is not only a religious but a sectarian poem; even in his greatest work Milton could not forget that he was a Puritan—and a rebel. The poem is written in blank verse so free and full that it constantly overflows the line endings and sweeps on into metrical paragraphs. Just as *Paradise Lost* deals with the theme of man's destruction through yielding to sin, so its sequel *Paradise Regained* deals with man's salvation through resistance to temptation, Christ's "get thee behind me, Satan" contrasting with our first parents' pliant wel-

AUTHORS [Montagu

coming of sin that allured. *Samson Agonistes* is the story, in imitation of Greek tragedy, of the last day and triumphant death of the Hebrew Samson. It is impossible not to see in this hero, blinded, chained, and made the sport of his enemies, and yet stiff-necked and unyielding, a prototype of the blind, stubborn, Puritan hero-poet. Perhaps, like Samson, he would have wished to destroy more of his enemies at his death than he overthrew during his life. About such a poetic figure there must cling a tragic grandeur that is intensely moving. What seems in the twentieth century to have been a stubborn political and religious narrowness must have been grounded in a grandeur of vision and an intensity and steadfastness of purpose that have no equal in English literature.

MINOT, Laurence (1300?–1352?) was an obscure fourteenth-century poet, apparently a northerner, who wrote a handful of rugged war songs about Halidon Hill, Crécy, the Siege of Calais, and other historical events of the reign of Edward III.

MITFORD, Mary Russell (1787–1855). Although Mrs. Mitford wrote poems, plays, letters, and *Recollections of a Literary Life* (1852), she is best known for *Our Village* (1824–32), a series of graceful, detailed "sketches of rural character and scenery." She is sometimes credited with having invented the "sketch" as a literary form.

MOIR, David Macbeth (1798–1851) was a Scot whose *Life of Mansie Waugh, Tailor in Dalkeith, Written by Himself* (1828) is one of a number of Scottish domestic novels which followed Scott's success in picturing humble folk.

MONKHOUSE, Allan (Noble) (1858–1936) was a journalist, playwright, novelist, and dramatic critic. Among his best plays are *Mary Broome* (1911) and *The Conquering Hero* (1924).

MONRO, Harold (Edward) (1879–1932). In 1912 Monro founded the Poetry Bookshop in London. It became a famous rendezvous for the Georgian poets. *The Collected Poems of Harold Monro,* with a critical note by T. S. Eliot, appeared in 1933. Many of his carefully wrought lyrics have philosophical implications which the simple, almost conversational manner does not at first reveal.

MONTAGU, Elizabeth (1720–1800). In the middle of the eighteenth century this wealthy intellectual prodigy sat in the Chinese Room of her lavish London house and ruled over the "Blue-stockings"—Elizabeth Carter, Hester Chapone, and others—who came thither for cultural conversation. She wrote *An Essay on*

199

the Writings and Genius of Shakespeare . . . with some re-marks upon the misrepresentations of Mons. de Voltaire (1769) and the last three dialogues of Lord Lyttleton's *Dialogues of the Dead* (1760). Dr. Johnson christened her, with unintentional ambiguity, "Queen of the Blues."

MONTAGU, Lady Mary Wortley (1689–1762) was one of the celebrated eighteenth-century letter-writers. Her "Turkish Letters" (written May, 1716—November, 1718) grew out of her voyage to the Far East when her husband, Edward Wortley Montagu, was ambassador to Constantinople. Like Lady Hester Stanhope (1776–1839), she became enamored of Oriental culture—studied Turkish, wore Turkish garb, and strove to dispel the common Western illusions about Turkish women. The letters, however, were not published until 1763. The other large group of letters, written mostly to her daughter, Lady Bute, covers the period of twenty-one years (1739–60) during which Lady Mary lived in self-imposed exile in southern Europe. They are especially interesting for her spirited comments on the new novels which her daughter mailed from home. In her youth Lady Mary was a friend of Pope. Under his influence she wrote a batch of *Town Eclogues* (pirated by Edmund Curll in 1716) which are more interesting to the social historian than to the student of poetry. Later she quarreled with the satirist, and in his verse he called her a "furious Sappho." Even if Lady Mary had acquired no literary fame, she would still be recognized for having introduced into England from Turkey the practice of vaccination for smallpox.

MONTAGUE, Charles Edward (1867–1928) was an Irishman who served on the *Manchester Guardian* from 1890 to 1925 and then retired to devote more time to creative writing. Two of his novels, *Rough Justice* (1926) and *Right off the Map* (1927), reflect his experiences at the front during the First World War. *A Writer's Notes on his Trade* (1930) is an interesting study of the business of writing.

MONTGOMERIE, Alexander (1556?–1610), a Scottish court poet, is chiefly known as the author of *The Cherry and the Slae* (1597), a long poem in which the obscure allegory turns on the contrast between the sweet cherry growing on a high tree and the bitter sloe on a lowly bush. It is written in a curious fourteen-line stanza.

MONTGOMERY, Robert (1807–55) wrote religious poems, all of which would be mercifully forgotten were it not for Macaulay's bitter review of two of them—*The Omnipresence of the Deity* (1828) and *Satan* (1830)—in the *Edinburgh Review* (1830). *The Omnipresence* includes the inane couplet—

> The soul aspiring pants its source to mount
> As streams meander level with their fount—

which Macaulay called "the worst similitude in the world."

MOORE, Edward (1712–57) edited a periodical called the *World* (1753–6) and wrote *Fables for the Female Sex* (1744) and three plays: *The Foundling* (1748) and *Gil Blas* (1751)—comedies—and *The Gamester* (1753), a sentimental tragedy. *The Gamester,* in which a devoted wife struggles in vain to rescue her husband, Beverley, from the clutches of the vicious gambler, Stukeley, is the most famous of many eighteenth-century plays on the gambling evil and had a widespread vogue both in England and on the Continent.

MOORE, George (1852–1933) was born in Ireland, the son of a well-to-do country gentleman who kept a stable of race horses. In 1870 he went to Paris to study painting and there came to know the famous Impressionist painters. After his return to London in 1882, he wrote a series of novels in which the influence of several French naturalists—Balzac, Flaubert, the Goncourts, and Zola—has been often traced. *A Mummer's Wife* (1885) is the shabby tragedy of a sentimental woman who abandons a sick husband for the manager of a traveling opera company. *Esther Waters* (1894), often called Moore's best novel, is the sordid tale of the seduction and subsequent career of a poor servant girl, portrayed against the background of race-track gambling which the author knew so well. Moore's interest in the Irish Renaissance is reflected in his novel *Evelyn Innes* (1898). From 1901 to 1910 he lived in Dublin and participated in that famous movement. Not long after his return to London, he went to Palestine to gather material for *The Brook Kerith* (1916), an unusual novel about the life of Christ. His own life was one long apprenticeship to Art, and he kept the record up to date in a series of autobiographies. In *Confessions of a Young Man* (1888) and *Memoirs of My Dead Life* (1906), he wrote roguishly about his own Bohemian experience in Europe and mocked with self-conscious iconoclasm the life and literature of respectable Victorian England; in the trilogy *Hail and Farewell* (1911–14) he pictured the brilliant personalities of the Irish Renaissance. For his emphatic reaction against the Victorian respectability and for his serious preoccupation with art, Moore belongs among the rebels of the last two decades of the nineteenth century. But he had in him a strain of poetry and religion which hardly blends with the prosaic naturalism of his early novels.

MOORE, Dr. John (1729–1802) is remembered chiefly as the author of *Zeluco* (1786), a once-popular novel in which the Sicilian protagonist is a double-dyed villain.

MOORE, Thomas (1779–1852). This son of an Irish grocer was a friend and biographer of Byron. In his own day he was not far behind Scott and Byron as a popular poet. But both his *Twopenny Postbag* (1813), in which he attacked political reaction, and *The Fudge Family in Paris* (1818), wherein he playfully disclosed the folly of English innocents abroad, were too topical to last. The Oriental verse-tales which make up the once-famous *Lalla Rookh* (1817) are no longer in style. Today Moore's fame depends largely on the *Irish Melodies* (1808–34), for which he wrote both words and music. Analyzed from a textbook page, *The Minstrel Boy, Oft in the Stilly Night,* and *The Last Rose of Summer* seem mawkish and affected. But a century of popularity has not killed them.

MORE, Hannah (1745–1833) was a schoolteacher and Bluestocking, a friend of Garrick and Johnson. She had some success with an ethical tragedy called *Percy* (1777), a collection of *Sacred Dramas* (1782), and a novel, *Coelebs in Search of a Wife* (1808), in which the self-righteous hero goes about like a census-taker systematically eliminating possible in-laws. But her real life work was a prodigious effort to reclaim the masses with a shower of didactic tracts on religion, manners, education, and politics. The narrowness of her moral outlook can be inferred from the fact that she found in Shakespeare "so much indecent levity, false wit, and gross description, that he should only be read in parcels, and with the nicest selection."

MORE, Henry (1614–87). Like Ralph Cudworth, More was one of the leaders of the group of seventeenth-century philosophers called "Cambridge Platonists." Among his voluminous writings on philosophical and theological questions are *Platonica, or a Platonical Song of the Soul* (1642), in prosy Spenserian stanzas, and *Divine Dialogues* (1668), in prose.

MORE, Sir Thomas (1478–1535). The English works of this great humanist, many of them dealing with religious controversy, are no longer well known. His masterpiece, *Utopia,* was published in Latin in 1516, Ralph Robinson's English translation appearing in 1551. It describes the ideal socialist state of "Nowhere," free from war, poverty, and religious intolerance. It is a literary descendant of Plato's *Republic* and the ancestor of a long line of English Utopias, including Bacon's *New Atlantis* (1627). More's interest in humanity was progressive in un-utopian Tudor England. After a distinguished career as lawyer, diplomat, and Lord Chancellor he was beheaded by Henry VIII for refusing to accept the king's authority as head of the Church. Pius XI canonized him in 1935.

MORGAN, Charles (Langbridge) (1894–   ), a dramatic critic of the *London Times,* is the author of several novels, including *Portrait in a Mirror* (1929), *The Fountain* (1932), *Sparkenbroke* (1936), and *The Empty Room* (1941). The second of these, a study in mysticism, has been one of the most widely discussed best-sellers in recent years.

MORGANN, Maurice (1726–1802) wrote *An Essay on the Dramatic Character of Sir John Falstaff* (1777), one of the most famous contributions to eighteenth-century Shakespeare criticism. "I do not conceive," wrote Morgann of the fat knight, "Shakespeare ever meant to make Cowardice an essential part of his constitution." Dr. Johnson was unconvinced: "Why, Sir, we shall have the man come forth again; and as he has proved Falstaff to be no coward, he may prove Iago to be a very good character."

MORIER, James Justinian (1780–1849) was born in Smyrna, son of the British consul at Constantinople. His experiences during two diplomatic journeys to Persia were narrated in two travel books (1812, 1818). He is best known as the author of *The Adventures of Hajji Baba of Ispahan* (1824), a picaresque romance which was realistic enough to elicit a protest from the Persian minister in London. In his sequel, *The Adventures of Hajji Baba . . . in England* (1828), Morier made his hero comment satirically on Western civilization after the manner of Lien Chi Altangi in Goldsmith's *Citizen of the World.*

MORLEY, John, first viscount Morley of Blackburn (1838–1923), politician, literary critic, journalist, and biographer, edited the *Fortnightly Review* (1867–82) and *Pall Mall Gazette* (1881–3) and was general editor of the original *English Men of Letters* series. Among his best critical works are three studies of eighteenth-century French thought: *Voltaire* (1872), *Rousseau* (1873), *Diderot and the Encyclopaedists* (1878). He also wrote distinguished biographies of Richard Cobden (1881) and William Gladstone (1903).

MORRIS, Sir Lewis (1833–1907) was a poetaster whose work reveals the influence of Tennyson. Because of his genius for expressing the tritest commonplaces in the smoothest verse, his *Songs of Two Worlds* (1871–5) and *Epic of Hades* (1876–7) were once exceedingly popular.

MORRIS, William (1834–96) was a man of many talents. In his twenties he tried both architecture and painting. In 1861 he helped to establish the manufacturing and decorating firm of Morris, Marshall, Faulkner, and Company. He himself designed and executed tapestries, wallpaper, stained glass, and other house furnishings which revolutionized interior decorating in England. Although he did not actually invent the Morris chair, it still bears his name. During the 1880's he was a pamphleteer and stump-orator striving to spread the doctrine of socialism. In 1890 he took up printing and type designing and turned out beautiful de luxe editions at his Kelmscott Press. And through all those forty years he found the time to write both poetry and prose.

His first book of poetry, *The Defence of Guenevere and Other Poems* (1858), revealed him as a romantic lyric and narrative poet who, although he was partly influenced by his friend D. G. Rossetti, needed no nineteenth-century guide to the magic of the Middle Ages. The volume includes, besides the title poem, the ballad *Shameful Death* and *The Haystack in the Floods,* two models of compression and simplicity in narrative. Less popular today are the more elaborate narrative poems which followed. *The Life and Death of Jason,* a version of the classical story of the quest for the Golden Fleece, was published separately in 1867 when it grew too long for inclusion in *The Earthly Paradise* (1868–70). In the 42,000 lines of *The Earthly Paradise* Morris retells twenty-four stories from classical, Norse, and medieval sources. They are set in a frame similar to that of *The Canterbury Tales,* and the poet acknowledges his general indebtedness to Chaucer. The epic *Sigurd the Volsung and the Fall of the Niblungs* (1876) is the most impressive single monument to Morris' intense interest in Scandinavian literature. He also made verse translations of the *Aeneid* (1875), the *Odyssey* (1887), and *Beowulf* (1895). His prose works include the romance of a socialist Utopia, *News from Nowhere* (1891), and a number of "pure" romances written during his last years.

However various Morris' achievements were, they had a fundamental unity. Like Keats and Rossetti, he loved beauty for its own sake and found it in the distant past. Like Carlyle and

Ruskin, he worked to restore that beauty to drab Victorian England. One way was to give factory workers a new dignity, a real artistic pride in their creations. For this he saw no hope under Victorian capitalism. William Morris may have been, as he called himself, "a dreamer of dreams born out of his due time." But he was certainly no *idle* dreamer.

MORTON, John Maddison (1811–91), son of Thomas Morton, was a successful writer of farces. His *Box and Cox* (1847), adapted, like most of his farces, from the French, was the source of *Cox and Box* (1867), the popular musical burlesque by Sir F. C. Burnand and Sir Arthur Sullivan.

MORTON, Thomas (1764?–1838), father of J. M. Morton, was the author of a number of successful comedies, including *The Way to Get Married* (1796), *A Cure for the Heart-Ache* (1797), and *Speed the Plough* (1800). The last-named is full of allusions to the proper Mrs. Grundy who, although she never appears on the stage, has survived in the language as a symbol of the insidious female prude.

MULCASTER, Richard (1530?–1611). As head master of the Merchant Tailors' School (1561–86), where he taught Edmund Spenser, and later as high master of St. Paul's (1596–1608), Mulcaster was a significant figure in Elizabethan education. In two forward-looking treatises, *Positions* (1581) and *The Elementary* (1582), he championed the cause of the English language. He addressed his message, however, not, like his more famous predecessor Roger Ascham, to the sons of lords, but to the offspring of the middle classes.

MULGRAVE, John Sheffield, third earl of (1648–1721), was one of the lesser lights among the verse-writing courtiers of the Restoration. His best-known works are two uninspired verse essays, *An Essay on Satire* (published anonymously 1680) and *An Essay upon Poetry* (1682). Lord Rochester, angered at a personal attack in *An Essay on Satire,* had the supposed author, John Dryden, waylaid by ruffians and badly beaten. The evidence that Dryden had a hand in the poem is slight.

MULOCK, Dinah Maria (1826–87), whose married name was Craik, was a pious novelist chiefly remembered as the author of *John Halifax, Gentleman* (1856). This novel of a gentlemanly orphan who makes good by honest and persistent virtue reflects an optimistic attitude towards early Victorian middle-class life.

MUNDAY, Anthony (1553–1633) was a prolific hack—playwright, pamphleteer, translater, and, rarely, a poet. He collaborated with Drayton and others on a two-part history play, *The Life of Sir John Oldcastle* (1599–1600), and with Henry Chettle on two plays about Robin Hood, *The Downfall* (1598) and *The Death* (1598) *of Robert, Earl of Huntington.* He specialized in translating popular romances from the French, Italian, and Spanish, including *Palmerin D'Oliva* (1588, 1597) and *Amadis de Gaul* (1590). He probably wrote the delightful lyric "Beauty sat bathing by a spring," printed in 1600 in *England's Helicon.*

MUNRO, H(ector) H(ugh). See **SAKI.**

MURPHY, Arthur (1727–1805) was a competent playwright with a talent for refurbishing the wares of others. He adapted plays from both Voltaire and Molière. Among his more successful works are *The Way to Keep Him,* a comedy (1760), *The Grecian Daughter,* a tragedy (1772), and *Three Weeks after Marriage,* a farce (1776).

MURRAY, (George) Gilbert (Aimé) (1866–   ), Professor of Greek at Oxford, is noted for his verse translations of the Greek dramatists—including Aeschylus, Sophocles, Euripides, and Aristophanes. In 1926 he served as the Charles Eliot Norton Professor of Poetry at Harvard; in his *Classical Tradition in Poetry* (1927) are collected the lectures given under this appointment. His service as chairman of the League of Nations Union from 1923 to 1938 reveals that his interests are social and humanitarian as well as scholarly.

MURRY, John Middleton (1889–1957) was best known as a literary critic. Among his works are *Keats and Shakespeare, a study of Keats' poetic life from 1816 to 1820* (1925) and *Son of Woman, the story of D. H. Lawrence* (1931). In 1913 he married the short-story writer, Katherine Mansfield (1888–1923); after her death he edited her journal (1927) and letters (1928) and wrote her biography, with Ruth E. Mantz (1933). His own autobiography appeared in 1935 under the title of *Between Two Worlds.*

N

NAIRNE, Caroline Oliphant, Baroness (1766–1845). Under the influence of her fellow-countryman, Robert Burns, Lady Nairne wrote a number of excellent Scottish songs. Among the best are *The Land o' the Leal,* the humorous *Laird o' Cockpen,* and the Jacobite song, *The Hundred Pipers.* The first collected edition did not appear until the year after her death.

NAPIER, Sir William Francis Patrick (1785–1860). As a soldier in Spain, Napier was a participant in many of the events which he narrated in his famous *History of the War in the Peninsula* (1828–40). This classic was written partly to vindicate Sir John Moore, the martyr of the retreat to Coruña (1808–9), and partly as a radical counterblast to Southey's Tory *History of the Peninsular War* (1823–32). It is one of the best military histories in English.

NASHE or NASH, Thomas (1567–1601?). The man who wrote the happy, jingling lyric, "Spring, the sweet spring," first made his name as a name-caller. He pilloried the Puritan Martinists in the Martin Marprelate Controversy and had the better of a long pamphlet war with Gabriel Harvey. He satirized the sinners of his time humorously in *Pierce Penniless* (1592) and with more seriousness in *Christ's Tears over Jerusalem* (1593). Restraint was not in him. When writing in *Nashe's Lenten Stuff* (1599) on so trivial a subject as Yarmouth red herring, he shoveled on superlatives of praise with the same Rabelaisian gusto which he had shown in abusing his enemies. Nashe also tried his hand at plays, collaborating with Marlowe on *The Tragedy of Dido, Queen of Carthage* (c. 1587–93) and writing independently *A pleasant Comedy, called Summer's Last Will and Testament* (1592–3). But his novel of roguery, *The Unfortunate Traveller, or the Life of Jack Wilton* (1594), has outlived both his pamphlets and his plays. It is important historically as the first of a long line of picaresque romances in English, and is written with a brutal directness which makes it still highly readable.

NEALE, John Mason (1818–66) wrote a learned *History of the Holy Eastern Church* (1847–73) and a number of historical novels, some of them for children. But he is best known as one of England's most distinguished hymn-writers. Among the famous hymns which he either originated or translated are "Jerusalem the golden"; "The day is past and over"; "Art thou weary, art thou languid"; and "All glory, laud, and honor."

NENNIUS (fl. 796) was a Welshman who compiled, from various sources, a collection of notes on British history and geography which bears the name *Historia Britonum* (c. 796). This Latin work, more complete than the sixth-century chronicle by Gildas, is notable for the emphasis which it places on King Arthur as a leader in twelve battles. Geoffrey of Monmouth apparently drew on Nennius, as well as on Gildas and Bede, for his *Historia Regum Britanniae*.

NEWBOLT, Sir Henry John (1862–1938) was pre-eminently the proud singer of the glory of the British Empire. A naval historian as well as a versifier, he wrote much popular chauvinistic verse about Britain's sea might, including the narrative poem *Drake's Drum* (1914) and the ballad *San Stefano.* At his best he was a capable ballad-writer, but in such conventional inspirational verse as *Vitaï Lampada* ("Play up! play up! and play the game!") he did not rise far above the level of the syndicated sentimentalists.

NEWCASTLE, Margaret Cavendish, Duchess of (1624?–74) was an eccentric socialite with a passion for expressing herself on paper. She published plays, poems, *A True Relation of My Birth, Breeding, and Life* (1656), and *CCXI Sociable Letters* (1664). Like her contemporary, Lucy Hutchinson, she wrote a biography of her husband, *The Life of William Cavendish, Duke of Newcastle* (1667). He was still alive at the time. The title-page of her first collection of plays calls her "the Thrice, Noble, Illustrious and Excellent Princess," and Charles Lamb echoed that praise a century and a half later. Pepys, who called her "a mad, conceited, ridiculous woman," seems to have been closer to the truth.

NEWMAN, John Henry (1801–90). Not many who join in singing the favorite hymn "Lead, kindly Light" know that it was written as a prayer by a young clergyman returning from Italy to England to begin a long battle for his faith. Its famous author, John Henry Newman, was the brilliant young vicar of St. Mary's, Oxford. He had come to this post in 1828, eight years after his graduation from Oxford and four years after his ordination. In 1832 he had traveled to Italy with his friend Hurrell Froude, and it was while he was journeying home the following year that he wrote his lyrical prayer for guidance. Even as he wrote, the battle for church reform known as the Oxford Movement was beginning; in his sermons at St. Mary's (*Parochial Sermons,* 1824–42) and in his twenty-four contributions to *Tracts for the Times* (1834–41), Newman—with Pusey, Keble, Hurrell Froude and others—entered deep into the conflict. These works reveal a clear drift away from the Church of England toward Roman Catholicism, but it was not until after the publication of the critical Tract XC in 1842 that Newman crossed his ecclesiastical Rubicon, resigned his charge at St. Mary's, and retired to Littlemore. Three years later he became a Roman Catholic.

After two years in Italy Newman returned to England in 1848, and in the same year issued *Loss and Gain,* a fictionized account of his own conversion. *Discourses Addressed to Mixed Congregations* was published the following year, and *Lectures on the Present Position of Catholics in England* in 1851. His appointment as rector of the new Roman Catholic University in Dublin produced part of the famous series of educational lectures later called *The Idea of a University* (1852). Taken together these essays are a systematic analysis of the meaning and value of a classical training. Newman's second novel, *Callista* (1854), is a religious tale of a Christian hero of the third century and has little distinction as a narrative. The same cannot be said of Newman's marvelous autobiography, written ten years later. Charles Kingsley, a clergyman of the Church of England, had the bad taste to make a sordid assault on Newman's intellectual honesty. Newman's reply was the *Apologia pro Vita Sua* (1864), a moving account of his spiritual life, and one of the finest pieces of restrained classical prose in the nineteenth century. His apocalyptic poem *The Dream of Gerontius* (1866) was followed two years later by his *Verses on Various Occasions,* and by *An Essay in Aid of a Grammar of Assent.* His distinguished services to the church of his adoption were recognized in 1879 when he was created cardinal.

During the last decade of his long life Cardinal Newman was the most benign and revered of English authors. He would probably have attained this position without the dignity of the red cap, for he knew how to write. To be heard he did not need to shout like Carlyle nor dramatize like Macaulay. He won his distinction by quiet power expressed in prose that was lucid, graceful, polished, eloquent, and dignified.

NEWTON, Sir Isaac (1642–1727) was president of the Royal Society from 1703 until his death. His world-shaking "law of gravitation" was announced in 1687 in a Latin treatise entitled *Philosophiae Naturalis Principia Mathematica,* familiarly known as *Principia.*

NICOLSON, Harold (George) (1886–   ) is a diplomat, a journalist, and one of the most witty and versatile of modern English biographers. In *Tennyson* (1923), *Byron, the last Journey* (1924), and *Swinburne* (1926) he combined biography and literary criticism. In *Sir Arthur Nicolson* (1930), a portrait of his father, *Peacemaking, 1919* (1933), and *Curzon, the Last Phase, 1919–1925* (1934) he produced three related studies in diplomacy. His *Some People* (1927) is a unique autobiography; *The Development of English Biography* (1927) is a series of lectures.

NORTH, Christopher. Pseudonym of John Wilson.

NORTH, Roger (1652–1734) was the youngest of six brothers, three of whom he celebrated in slangy, chatty biographies. The so-called *Lives of the Norths* (1742, 1744)—memories of Francis, Keeper of the Great Seal, Dudley, the Turkey merchant, and John, master of Trinity College, Cambridge—are unique in English biography. Roger North also wrote *A Discourse of Fish and Fish-Ponds* (1713), *Examen,* a defense of Charles II (1740), and the life of a fourth North, himself (not published until 1887).

NORTH, Sir Thomas (1535?–1601?) was the author of *The Lives of the Noble Grecians and Romans* (1579), a dramatic and picturesque rendering of Amyot's French translation of Plutarch's *Lives.* It was one of the greatest in an age of great translations. Shakespeare, in drawing from it freely for his Roman plays (*Julius Caesar, Anthony and Cleopatra, Coriolanus*), frequently complimented the translator by retaining his original phrases. North also translated *The Dial of Princes* (1557) from the Spanish of Guevara. This was the main source of Lyly's *Euphues* (1579).

NORTON, Thomas (1532–84) was a lawyer and member of Parliament who collaborated with Thomas Sackville on *Gorboduc, or Ferrex and Porrex* (1562), the first English classical tragedy, which is essentially a political allegory written under Senecan influence. Norton probably wrote the first three acts. His contribution is noticeably inferior to that of his collaborator.

NOYES, Alfred (1880–1958) was a writer whose great popularity was based largely on two anthology favorites. *The Highwayman,* the more popular of the two, is a romantic literary ballad marked by a skillful blending of the narrative with the galloping meter. *The Barrel-organ* is a lyrical narrative poem dealing with the effects of street music on a group of London listeners. One of Noyes' most ambitious poems is *Drake, an English Epic* (1906–8). He was Professor of English Literature at Princeton from 1914–23 and lectured widely in America. In both his creative work and his critical pronouncements he has resisted contemporary trends in literature.

O

O'CASEY, Sean (1884–   ) was born and bred in the slums of Dublin. During his early struggle he was a "general laborer" and labor organizer. In 1916 he helped to organize the Irish Citizen

Army which instigated the famous Easter Rebellion in the streets of Dublin. He later turned to playwriting, achieving sudden fame when the Abbey Players produced his melodrama, *The Shadow of a Gunman,* in 1923. Two subsequent successes clinched his reputation as the most gifted of the Irish playwrights in the decades immediately after the First World War: *Juno and the Paycock* (1924), a tragi-comedy about the Dublin working class which has become indispensable in the Abbey Players' unique repertory; and *The Plough and the Stars* (1926), a militant, satirical tragedy about the Easter Rebellion. These two plays are likely to survive after the more literary, more mystical *Within the Gates* (1933) has been forgotten.

OCCLEVE or **HOCCLEVE, Thomas** (1368?–1450?). If this government clerk's own verse admission, *La Male Regle de T. Hoccleve* (written 1406), can be trusted, he was a sickly, stoop-shouldered, cowardly bar-fly. More plaintive confessions like the *Complaint* (written c. 1421) and the *Dialogue* (written c. 1421) substantiate one point at least—that he was an ingenuous chatterbox in verse, hardly a poet. His longest work, the five-thousand-line *De Regimine Principum* (written c. 1411–12), is a paraphrase from the Latin containing much advice to Prince Hal—who became Henry V—and some revealing satire on contemporary manners. Its most famous passage is the lament for the poet whose "lyknesse" Occleve has drawn in the manuscript margin, Geoffrey Chaucer. Today Occleve himself is little more than a handy measuring stick for the superiority of his acknowledged master.

O'FLAHERTY, Liam (1896–   ) was born in the Arran Islands off the coast of Ireland. He fought in both the First World War and the Irish Revolution. He has wandered the world over, laboring on various jobs and passionately preaching the cause of labor. And he has earned a reputation as a writer of short-stories (*Short Stories of Liam O'Flaherty,* 1937) and powerful, naturalistic novels (*The Informer,* 1925; *Mr. Gilhooley,* 1926; *The Assassin,* 1928). *The Informer,* the story of the mental torture of a hulking Dublin ex-policeman who betrays a comrade in a secret revolutionary society, was made into one of the best motion-pictures ever produced in Hollywood.

O'KEEFFE, John (1747–1833) was an Irish actor and playwright who wrote over fifty dramatic pieces between 1767 and 1798. In such comic operas as *The Castle of Andalusia* (1782), *The*

Poor Soldier (1783), and *The Highland Reel* (1788), O'Keeffe displayed an agreeable talent for song-writing.

OLDHAM, John (1653–83) is best known for his imitations of the Roman satirist, Juvenal. The polemics of his sneering *Satires Against the Jesuits* (1681), although of some historical interest as expressions of the bitterness which followed the Popish Plot of 1679, are crude in meter and in matter. When Oldham died young of smallpox, Dryden, who had not yet turned Catholic, wrote a flowery eulogy. Posterity has not confirmed that verdict.

OLDMIXON, John (1673–1742) began his literary career in the 1690's as a poet and playwright but later confined most of his attention to writing Whig pamphlets and histories for hire. *An Essay on Criticism,* issued with the third edition (1727) of his *Critical History of England* (1724–6), offended Pope and earned Oldmixon an eight-line attack in *The Dunciad*.

OLDYS, William (1696–1761), antiquary and literary historian, wrote a *Life of Sir Walter Raleigh* (1736) and numerous short lives for the *Biographia Britannica*. He is better known, however, for the simple twelve-line lyric *On a Fly Drinking Out of His Cup.*

OLIPHANT, Laurence (1829–88) was an eccentric adventurer whose work reflects his wandering life. Among his books are *A Journey to Katmandu* (1852), a story of travel in India; *Piccadilly* (1866), a satirical novel; *The Autobiography of a Joint-Stock Company* (1876), an exposé of American business methods; and *Episodes in a Life of Adventure* (1887), an autobiography.

OLIPHANT, Margaret (1828–97) was an industrious and prolific woman of letters. In the long list of her novels are *Merkland* (1851), one of several stories of her native Scotland; *The Chronicles of Carlingford* (1863–76), a series of five satirical novels on ecclesiastical life which have been favorably compared with Trollope's *Chronicles of Barset;* and *A Beleaguered City* (1880), a tale of the supernatural. Mrs. Oliphant also wrote short-stories, biography, and literary criticism.

OPIE, Amelia (1769–1853), wife of the painter John Opie, was a novelist and poetess. Her *Adelina Mowbray* (1804), a satirical novel about a mother who neglects her own daughter to pursue revolutionary political and philosophical doctrines, was based on the life of Mary Wollstonecraft Godwin.

ORINDA, The Matchless. Epithet for **Katherine Philips.**

ORM (fl. 1200?) was an Augustinian monk who apparently lived in the east of England. His *Ormulum,* written about 1200 by Orm or his disciples, represents a scheme to paraphrase in English verse a part of the Gospels for each day of the year, with an appropriate homily for every paraphrase. The work, as we have it, is incomplete, but runs to some 10,000 lines. Orm was certainly no poet, but the versification of *Ormulum*—fifteen-syllable unrhymed, unalliterative lines divided into couplets of eight and seven—is interesting. Even more interesting is the spelling. Orm was a purist. He spelled according to his own system, doubling letters at will, and he warned the scribes who followed him to copy his words correctly. Hence he has been called the first conscious orthographer and the first phonetician in English.

ORRERY. See BOYLE.

OSBORNE, Dorothy, Lady Temple, (1627–95) married Sir William Temple in 1655. Between 1652 and 1654 she wrote him a series of facile, witty, intelligent letters which are among the most delightful in English literature. They reveal her both as a sensible critic of the art of letter-writing and as an insatiable devourer of French heroic romances.

OTWAY, Thomas (1652–85). Like his contemporary, Nathaniel Lee, Otway failed as an actor before he succeeded as a playwright. And like mad Nat, he lived hard, drank deep, and died miserably in his thirties. Today his comedies are forgotten, and neither his rhymed heroic play, *Don Carlos* (1676), nor his irreverent adaptation of *Romeo and Juliet—Caius Marius* (1679)—is well known. But two blank-verse tragedies have earned him a place as a leading tragic playwright of the Restoration. *The Orphan* (1680) is an improbable domestic tale of the love of twin brothers, Castalio and Polydore, for their father's ward, Monimia. *Venice Preserved, or A Plot Discovered* (1682) presents the conventional love-and-honor dilemma against a background of seventeenth-century Venice—Jaffier torn between his duty to his fellow conspirators and his love for Belvidera, a senator's daughter. It also contains an allusion to the Popish Plot of 1679 and an indecent caricature of the lascivious Earl of Shaftesbury. Neither tragedy, despite obvious echoes of Shakespeare, rises often to the heights of poetry, but both are filled with stirring dramatic crises and were favorites in the theater for generations. Elizabeth Barry—whom Otway, in his own private tragedy, loved in vain—was but the first of many passionate Monimias and Belvideras.

OUIDA was the pseudonym of the Victorian novelist **Marie Louise De La Ramée** (1839–1908). Her contemporaries ridiculed her for writing boldly about a fashionable masculine world of which she was blissfully ignorant; she once wrote of an athlete so powerful that he stroked his crew at a higher beat than his fellow-oarsmen. But thousands once read her, and her "daring" treatment of the facts of life—though strangely tame today—helped to rescue English *mores* from the Victorian straitjacket. Still popular are *Under Two Flags* (1867), the battle-field thriller starring the immortal French heroine Cigarette, *A Dog of Flanders* (1872), a sentimental animal story, and *Bimbi* (1882), a collection of children's stories.

OVERBURY, Sir Thomas (1581–1613) was poisoned mysteriously in the Tower for opposing the marriage of his patron, Lord Rochester, to Lady Essex. He is best known for the *Characters,* the first twenty-one of which—some of them contributed by "other learned Gentlemen his Friends"—were published in 1614. They hit off contemporary types—"A Courtier," "A Fair and Happy Milkmaid," "An Excellent Actor"—pithy, often sarcastic, thumbnail sketches marked by the antithesis and artificial imagery of euphuism. The "character," as used by Overbury and other early English followers of Theophrastus (died 287? B.C.), like Joseph Hall and John Earle, influenced the course of the essay and novel in England.

OWEN, John (1560–1622) made his name as a creator of witty Latin epigrams. His *Epigrammata* appeared in several volumes between 1606 and 1612 and was translated into English in 1619. The epigrams had an extraordinary vogue in Germany during the seventeenth century.

OWEN, Robert (1771–1858) was a Welsh mill-owner who, after setting an excellent example of enlightened ownership in his own mills in Manchester, labored to secure the passing of the Factory Act of 1819. He was an ardent advocate of small coöperative villages and a leader in the fight for trade unions and popular education. His works include *A New View of Society* (1813–14) and *The Revolution in the Mind and Practice of the Human Race* (1849).

OWEN, Wilfred (1893–1918) was one of the soldier-poets of the First World War. He wrote a handful of sad lyrics about the pity and horror of the conflict, including *Arms and the Boy, Greater Love,* and *Anthem for Doomed Youth.* Like some of the later poems of Keats, whom Owen loved, several are prophetic of his own untimely death. He died in action exactly a week before the

Armistice. His *Poems* were published in 1920, with an introduction by his friend and fellow war-poet, Siegfried Sassoon. A new edition appeared in 1931.

P

PAINE, Thomas (1737–1809) is claimed for both English and American literature. He was born in England, the son of a stay-maker, and there worked at various occupations—staymaker, seaman, schoolteacher, tobacconist, and exciseman. After dismissal from the last of these jobs, he emigrated to America in 1774, bringing with him a questionable reputation and a letter of introduction to Benjamin Franklin. Here he published the two works which have made his name inseparable from the history of the American Revolution. In January, 1776, appeared *Common Sense,* a pamphlet which converted hundreds of skeptics to the cause of American independence. In December, Paine issued the first number of *The Crisis,* a series of sixteen papers on the struggle, which appeared periodically until the end of 1783. General Washington, in critical retreat across New Jersey, ordered the first paper—beginning with the ringing sentence "These are the times that try men's souls"—read to every soldier in his army.

After returning to England in 1787, Paine wrote the two parts of his *Rights of Man* (1791–2), dedicating them respectively to Washington and Lafayette. In this work he defended the French Revolution against the indictment of Burke's *Reflections* (1790), bitterly ridiculed the hereditary aristocracy of England, and set forth a constructive program for political and social reforms. In 1792, hounded as a dangerous revolutionary, he fled to France. There he published *The Age of Reason* (1794), a defence of deism, and narrowly escaped the guillotine for his opposition to the execution of Louis XVI. He returned to America in 1802 and died in New York seven years later. Although ignorant of history, Paine was a practical politician, a hard-headed controversialist, and a born journalist. His plain style, studded with sardonic metaphors and homely anecdotes, presents a strange contrast to the studied eloquence of Edmund Burke.

PAINTER, William (1540?–94) was the compiler of *The Palace of Pleasure* (1566–67), an anthology of a hundred and one simply told tales taken mainly from Greek, Latin, and Italian sources. It was a paradise of plots for Elizabethan dramatists. For example, Shakespeare borrowed the bare bones of *All's Well that Ends Well* from Painter's translation of Boccaccio's *novella.*

PALEY, William (1743–1805) was a philosopher whose works had a considerable influence on nineteenth-century thought. His four major writings—*The Principles of Moral and Political Philosophy* (1785), *Horae Paulinae* (1790), *A View of the Evidences of Christianity* (1794), and *Natural Theology* (1802)—are marked by clear reasoning expressed in a plain style. In the first he argued that man's actions are entirely motivated by his desire for happiness, a doctrine which has been called "theological utilitarianism."

PALTOCK, Robert (1697–1767) is remembered as the author of *The Life and Adventures of Peter Wilkins* (1751), a weird romance in which the hero is shipwrecked in the Antarctic and has remarkable experiences with flying people in the land of the Glums and Gawries.

PARIS, Matthew (d. 1259) succeeded Roger of Wendover as historiographer at the monastery of St. Albans in 1236 and continued Roger's Latin chronicle from 1235 down to 1259. A favorite of Henry III, Paris was in close touch with the court, and his *Chronica Majora* is a valuable history of affairs both in England and in Europe. He also wrote a *Historia Anglorum,* a chronicle of events between 1067 and 1253.

PARNELL, Thomas (1679–1718) was an Irish churchman who preferred the literary world of London, where he enjoyed the friendship of Pope and Swift. Although Gray once called him "the dunghill of Irish Grub Street," both Johnson and Goldsmith praised his verse. Pope had Parnell's works published posthumously in 1722. *The Hermit* is a moralizing Oriental tale in heroic couplets. Two odes in four-foot couplets, *A Night Piece on Death* and *A Hymn to Contentment,* contain pleasant hints of the simple, direct nature poetry which was to replace the artificial effusions of the Augustans.

PASTON, John and **Margaret** (fl. 1440–86). Among the most illuminating historical, social, and economic documents of the fifteenth century is the series of letters, reports, and accounts (known as *The Paston Letters*) written by John and Margaret Paston, members of a wealthy Norfolk family, and their sons. These documents were written between 1440 and 1486, during the reigns of Henry VI, Edward IV, Edward V, and Richard III. They deal in large part with the long legal struggles of the Pastons to keep in the family the Fastolf estates which they possessed, but they throw much light also on English life and manners during the rough and violent decades of the Wars of the Roses. Thus they provide for the English literature of this period a better background than do many documents more professedly literary. The first selection of *The Paston Letters* was published in 1787; other parts of the collection have been printed since then.

PATER, Walter Horatio (1839–94). In the "Conclusion" to his *Studies in the History of the Renaissance* (1873), Pater preached the gospel of living intensely for each fleeting moment: "To burn always with this hard, gem-like flame, to maintain this ecstasy, is success in life." He found this ecstasy, not in worldly pleasures —for he lived the quiet life of a timid Oxford tutor—but in a passionate study of the arts and a patient re-creation of the past. He became a passive leader in the aesthetic movement which was variously reflected in the lives and writings of D. G. Rossetti, Swinburne, Ruskin, and Wilde. *Marius the Epicurean* (1885), a philosophical romance tracing the "sensations and ideas" of a second-century Roman, is the best known of his more purely creative works, although the *Imaginary Portraits* (1887) and the exquisite autobiographical sketch called *The Child in the House* (1894) still have some readers. Except for the "Conclusion," the most famous passage from *Studies in the Renaissance* is a vivid appreciation of Da Vinci's *Mona Lisa*. Pater's miscellaneous critical works include two useful essays on general principles. In "Romanticism" (1876), he contrasts the "curiosity and the love of beauty" which characterize Romanticism with the "comely order" of Classicism. In "Style" (from *Appreciations,* 1889), he advises the reader to write "in the simplest, the most direct and exact manner possible, with no surplusage." Pater himself did not always heed this counsel. In love with "art for art's sake," he was often so absorbed in fashioning gem-like phrases that he overlooked such dull matters as sentence structure. Yesterday he was studied as a famous stylist. Today, in an age less mindful of aesthetic values, many regard his purple passages as lifeless curiosities—like glass flowers in a museum show-case.

PATMORE, Coventry (Kersey Dighton) (1823–96) published his first volume of poems in 1844. In 1850 he contributed to the *Germ,* the short-lived magazine of the *Pre-Raphaelites*. In 1854 appeared *The Betrothal,* the first part of his long poem on married love, *The Angel in the House*. Other parts followed at intervals: *The Espousals* in 1856, *Faithful for Ever* in 1860, and *The Victories of Love* in 1863. *The Angel in the House,* especially in the final section, contains flashes of true beauty and pathos, but the work has been condemned for the banality of its subject matter and diction. Swinburne referred to the separate parts as "idylls of the dining-room and deanery" and Edmund Gosse called them "humdrum stories of girls who smell of bread and butter." Patmore turned Roman Catholic in 1864, and his religious experience gave depth to his later work. *The Unknown Eros* (1877), a collection of dignified odes on human and divine love, is markedly different both in language and in content from *The Angel in the House*. Patmore's prose criticism appears in two collections of essays, *Principle in Art* (1889) and *Religio Poetae* (1893).

PATTISON, Mark (1813–84), rector of Lincoln College, Oxford, was a productive scholar. He wrote excellent biographies of the French Huguenot theologian, Isaac Casaubon (1875), and of John Milton (*English Men of Letters* series, 1879). His frank *Memoirs* (1885) reveals his early interest in and eventual reaction against the Oxford Movement. Pattison was the original of the forbidding Professor Forth of Rhoda Broughton's *Belinda*.

PEACOCK, Thomas Love (1785–1866). Satirist, poet, scholar, epicure, and business man—Peacock ran the gamut from talking poetry with his friend Shelley to drawing blueprints for steamships at the East India Company. Five of his seven novels— *Headlong Hall* (1816), *Melincourt* (1817), *Nightmare Abbey* (1818), *Crotchet Castle* (1831), *Gryll Grange* (1861)—follow the same formula. He gathers a miscellaneous crew of crotcheteers at a mad house-party, many of them obvious caricatures of contemporary celebrities. Here they muddle through certain farcical dilemmas and choose partners for the finale of wholesale matrimony. But most of the time they just talk—brilliant, unreal, satirical talk, every man in his humor and all together presenting a cross-section of the folly of their time. Two other novels— *Maid Marian* (1822), and *The Misfortunes of Elphin* (1829)— are extravagant romances, the former a burlesque Robin Hood full of lively songs, the latter a more serious political allegory woven into a texture of Welsh legends. The best known of Peacock's essays is *The Four Ages of Poetry* (1820), a half-serious survey notable for inspiring Shelley's famous *Defense of Poetry* (1821).

PEARL POET (fl. late 14th cent.) is the name given to an anonymous author usually thought to have been the composer of all four of the poems that appear in the same Cottonian manuscript in the British Museum. These are: *The Pearl, Patience, Cleanness,* and *Sir Gawayne and the Grene Knight. The Pearl* is a dream allegory in one hundred and one twelve-line stanzas; it presents the poet as lamenting for his little dead daughter (the

AUTHORS [*Peele*

pearl) and being comforted by a vision of her in Paradise. *Patience* is an alliterative poem of five hundred lines dealing with the biblical story of Jonah. *Cleanness* is an eighteen-hundred-line exaltation of Purity set forth by recounting the sins that brought about Noah's Flood, the destruction of Sodom and Gomorrah, and the fall of Babylon. *Sir Gawayne and the Grene Knight* might almost have been subtitled *Chastity,* for it is the beautifully told tale of an Arthurian knight's resistance to the lure of a lovely lady. The romance is filled with magic episodes, with hardships overcome, and with realistic details of living among the English nobles of the fourteenth century. It is by far the most entertaining of the four poems ascribed to the Pearl Poet. Although the author of the four poems is unknown, their dialect indicates that he came from the north of England, and their content reveals that he was a cultivated gentleman, probably of noble birth and breeding.

PEARSON, John (1613–86), Bishop of Chester, is remembered for his *Exposition of the Creed* (1659), a scholarly theological treatise based on a series of sermons which he preached in London in 1654.

PECOCK, Reginald (1395?–1460?). After a stormy career of religious controversy, Pecock was arraigned for heresy and compelled to abandon his post as Bishop of Chichester in 1458. His best-known work, *The Repressor of Overmuch Blaming of the Clergy* (1455), is an attack on the Lollards, or followers of John Wycliffe, in which he advocated converting them instead of burning them. As one of the earliest efforts to adapt the vernacular to the needs of scholastic argument it is a milestone in the history of the English language.

PEELE, George (1557?–96), Oxford graduate, "University Wit," and writer for the court, was a poet turned playwright. Most of his plays had little real structure, but he was one of the earliest to develop dramatic blank verse out of its stiff original form, and his dramas are filled with songs and lyrical passages. This is true not only of *Polyhymnia* (1590), a court pageant, and *The Arraignment of Paris* (1581–4), a court comedy seasoned with classical and pastoral devices, but also of his other pieces. *Edward the First* (1590–3) is a romanticized historical play, and *The Battle of Alcazar* (1588–9) is a verse play in which he imitated Greene and Marlowe. Peele's two most original and important plays, however, are *The Love of King David and Fair Bethsabe* (c. 1581–94) and *The Old Wives' Tale* (c. 1588–94). The first of these has no division into acts but is only a succession of scenes dramatized from the biblical stories of King David, in which the poetry is good, but the situations are often absurd. The second has the distinction of being the first dramatic burlesque in English literature. In it Peele satirized in the liveliest manner the contents, episodes, and characters of the romantic court dramas of his period. *The Old Wives' Tale* was the source of Milton's *Comus* (1634). Peele was not himself a great dramatist, but his plays had, nevertheless, a marked influence on the work of better playwrights.

PENN, William (1644–1718). The Quaker founder of Pennsylvania wrote a number of controversial pamphlets, including *The Sandy Foundation Shaken* (1668), an attack on certain Christian tenets which earned him a sentence in the Tower, and *No Cross No Crown* (1669), a treatise on self-denial written during his sojourn there. Of a more purely literary nature are the pithy, well-phrased maxims of *Some Fruits of Solitude* (1693).

PEPYS, Samuel (1633–1703). The six-volume manuscript of the most famous diary ever written contains about 1,300,000 words, mostly in shorthand. Although it was transcribed in 1819 and has gone through several editions, it has not yet been printed in its entirety. Pepys began it on January 1, 1660, when he was a poor clerk and gave it up for fear of blindness on May 31, 1669, a prosperous bigwig in the Royal Navy. In it he wrote about the coronation of Charles II, the Plague, the Great Fire, and the War with the Dutch. But he wrote more about himself. Whether between "up betimes" and "so to bed" he had collected money for the Fleet, enjoyed his first shave, set fire to his periwig, or sported with a kitchenmaid, he told all with unaffected directness and incredible candor. He left behind the picture of a shrewd business man and politician, a lover of books, music, and the theater, a wine-drinking, woman-chasing, wife-nagging libertine with a tinge of Puritan conscience—vain, snobbish, selfish, sometimes brutal, but seldom boring—a man as intimately revealed to posterity as any figure in English literature.

PERCY, Thomas (1729–1811). Bishop Percy's name is inseparable from his *Reliques of Ancient English Poetry* (1765). This miscellany, although it contained learned essays by the editor and poems of several kinds, is memorable chiefly for its popular ballads. Many of these Percy had found in a seventeenth-century manuscript which he had rescued from an acquaintance. Although he "improved" upon them freely, he was not, like Macpherson, a literary cheat. The *Reliques* inspired in Sir Walter Scott and others a passion for ballad-collecting which is characteristic of the Romantic Movement.

PET MARJORIE. See **FLEMING, Marjorie.**

PETTIE, George (1548–89). *A Petite Palace of Pettie his Pleasure* (1576) is not so important a source-book for literature as Painter's *Palace of Pleasure* (1566–7). But Pettie embroidered his twelve borrowed tales so prettily that some scholars have called him the instigator of euphuism. Although he did not invent the various rhetorical tricks which are gathered under that term, he was their chief exploiter before Lyly's *Euphues* appeared in 1579.

PHILIPS, Ambrose (1675?–1749). In 1709, when Philips' pastorals were published in the same volume of Tonson's *Miscellany* which contained Pope's, a literary war was in the making. Philips' Whig friends, Addison and Tickell, hailed him as a worthy successor to Spenser. Pope, in the *Guardian* (April 15, 1713), artfully proved how much better his own pastorals were by pretending to praise his rival's. Later, in *The Shepherd's Week* (1714), Gay guffawed at the rusticity of Philips' swains by peopling his parody with sweating country louts. When Philips' tender little verse compliments to his contemporaries appeared, Henry Carey converted "Ambrose" into "Namby-Pamby." And that sugary epithet has since stuck both to Philips and to the English language.

PHILIPS, John (1676–1709) wrote *Blenheim* (1705), a piece of Tory propaganda in verse answering Addison's *Campaign,* and *Cider* (1708), a blank-verse essay in honor of that beverage. But his most popular poem is *The Splendid Shilling* (1705), an amusing blank-verse burlesque of the grand style of Milton.

PHILIPS, Katherine (1632–64) called herself "Orinda" in the literary coterie over which she reigned. Her contemporaries added the adjective "matchless." And today, although her works are seldom read, "the Matchless Orinda" is still a memorable name. In addition to a successful translation (1663) of Corneille's tragedy *Pompée,* she wrote numerous short poems, many of them addressed to her friends in the coterie. The first authorized edition, *Poems, by the most deservedly Admired Mrs. Katherine Philips, the Matchless Orinda,* appeared in 1667. Among them are the verses beginning "Come, my Lucasia, since we see" and "Forbear, bold youth; all's heaven here."

PHILLPOTTS, Eden (1862–   ) has been a prolific creator of fiction, plays, and poetry for more than half a century. He is probably best known for his series of novels about Dartmoor in Devonshire, works which belong to the regional tradition of Thomas Hardy. Among them are *Children of the Mist* (1898), *Sons of the Morning* (1900), and *The Secret Woman* (1905).

PINDAR, Peter, was the pseudonym of **John Wolcot** (1738–1819), a verse satirist who enjoyed a considerable vogue at the end of the eighteenth century. Among his many titles are *The Lousiad* (1785–95), a prolix "heroic-comic poem" directed against George III; *Bozzy and Piozzi* (1786), a satire on Johnson's biographers, Boswell and Hester Thrale Piozzi; and *Ode upon Ode* (1787), an attack on the king in imitation of the laureate's annual New Year's Day offering.

PINERO, Sir Arthur Wing (1855–1934). In a series of social dramas, beginning with *The Second Mrs. Tanqueray* in 1893, Pinero carried on in England the revolutionary movement which the Norwegian dramatist, Henrik Ibsen, had initiated two decades earlier on the Continent. Breaking boldly away from the escapist tradition of the Victorian theater, he dared to present unpleasant social problems on the stage and to create characters whose talk is not unlike human conversation. *The Second Mrs. Tanqueray,* still Pinero's most popular play, is a problem tragedy of a woman's unsuccessful efforts to live down her past. Among his other plays are *Trelawny of the Wells* (1898), *The Thunderbolt* (1908), and *Mid-Channel* (1909). Pinero was not a great playwright, but he ranks with Henry Arthur Jones among the pioneers of the modern drama.

PIOZZI, Hester Lynch. See THRALE.

POMFRET, John (1667–1702) is remembered as the author of *The Choice, or Wish* (1700), a pleasant poem on a conventional theme, the ingredients of a happy life. During the eighteenth century the work enjoyed a popularity far out of proportion to its worth.

POOLE, John (1786–1872). During the first half of the nineteenth century Poole was one of the best of many popular writers of short comic pieces for the stage. His efforts include *Hamlet Travestie,* a burlesque (1811); *Paul Pry,* a comedy (1825); and *Lodgings for Single Gentlemen,* a farce (1829).

POPE, Alexander (1688–1744) was born in London, the son of a Roman Catholic linen draper. Following a short period of formal education, he went, at the age of eleven, to live at Binfield on the edge of Windsor Forest. After that he was largely self-educated. While still a child, he "lisp'd in numbers, for the

numbers came." His *Pastorals* (written 1704, published 1709)
revealed that at sixteen he was already a master of versification.
But these frigid eclogues and the subsequent *Windsor Forest*
(1713), a conventional descriptive poem inspired by Denham's
Cooper's Hill (1642), also indicated that Pope was not a spontaneous nature-poet. Moreover, that his genius was not essentially
lyrical was displayed upon the publication in 1717 of *Verses to
the Memory of an Unfortunate Lady* and *Eloisa to Abelard*, two
popular but artificial love lyrics.

Two other early poems revealed more definitely the direction in
which his work was headed. In *An Essay on Criticism* (1711) he
foretold his own future as a classical poet by summoning his
contemporaries to be faithful to ancient models. In *The Rape of
the Lock* (1712, 1714) he gave a brilliant demonstration of his
genius for satire. A certain Lord Petre had started a family feud
in London by snipping a lock from the precious tresses of Miss
Arabella Fermor, and Pope ridiculed the incident in 1712 with
a mock-epic treatment of the artificialities of London society. In
the 1714 version he expanded the poem from two to five cantos
by adding the "filigree fairyland" of sylphs and gnomes. Meanwhile, in 1713, he had begun to translate Homer's *Iliad* into
heroic couplets. The first volume was out in 1715 and the complete work in 1720. Richard Bentley remarked at the time: "A
fine poem, Mr. Pope, but you must not call it Homer," and
posterity has confirmed at least the second part of that verdict.
Pope later lost interest in a translation of the *Odyssey* (1725-6) and
deputed a large part of the work to two collaborators.

The proceeds from the *Iliad* enabled him to purchase "Pope's
Villa" on the Thames at Twickenham in 1719, and there he lived,
in moderate luxury, for the rest of his life. Not that he ever lived
in comfort. Pope's frail body had been distorted by illness in
childhood, and his life was "a long disease." His personality
too was warped. He was childish and deceitful, proud of his
moderate fortune and disdainful of poverty in others, thirsty for
praise and hypersensitive to censure. His contemporaries called
him "the wicked wasp of Twickenham." From the beginning
he had fought literary battles—tangling with John Dennis over
the *Essay on Criticism* and with Ambrose Philips over the relative merits of their pastorals. And although he had a few close
friends like Swift, Gay, Arbuthnot, and Martha Blount, his enemies
multiplied with the years.

The prevailing tone of Pope's later verse is satire far more bitter than the delicate ridicule of *The Rape of the Lock*. His

most ambitious satire is *The Dunciad* (1728–43). In the first edition of 1728 Pope enthroned his rival Shakespeare-critic, Lewis Theobald, as King of Dulness; in the 1743 revision he gave the honor to the actor and playwright, Colley Cibber. But in its final form *The Dunciad* is not, like Dryden's *Mac Flecknoe* (1682), a lampoon on an individual, but a massive, obscene judgment book in which, amid some general literary criticism, Pope paid off long-standing scores with all sorts and conditions of enemies.

Pope's miscellaneous *Satires* in imitation of Horace (1733–8) are in the savage manner commonly associated with Juvenal; in the first, for example, he made a vicious attack on his onetime friend, Lady Mary Wortley Montagu. His later verse, however, is not entirely satirical. Although his *Epistle to Dr. Arbuthnot* (1735) contains a gallery of satirical portraits, the most famous of which is that of "Atticus" (Addison, lines 193–214), the poem also includes a defense of the poet's own career and a tender tribute to his mother. His four *Moral Essays* (1731–5), although studded with thinly veiled caricatures of his contemporaries, are primarily disquisitions on ethical subjects suggested by his friend Bolingbroke. This politician and philosopher also supplied some of the material for the famous *Essay on Man* (1733–4). Pope himself was hardly a philosopher, and the work is fragmentary and unfinished. But his effort "to vindicate the ways of God to man"—with its basic thesis that "whatever is, is right"—has survived as a classic example of the optimism which pervaded much of the thinking in Pope's day.

No poet in the history of English literature owes more than Pope to the mastery of a single verse form. He was not the first to "close" the heroic couplet; Denham and Waller and Dryden had done it before him. But no one had ever used the closed couplet so consistently or wrought within it such gems of antithesis and anticlimax. Pope's verse, in general, yields to Dryden's in cumulative sweep, but surpasses it in quotability and epigrammatic brilliance. His influence was widespread. His classicism set the keynote of eighteenth-century English literature, and the closed heroic couplet became its favorite instrument. Although there were signs of early revolt against Pope's domination—in the works of James Thomson, for example—it was not until near the end of the century that the spell was definitely broken. Among the Romantics, Byron and Campbell stood almost alone in refuting the aspersions cast on Pope by one of his editors, William Lisle Bowles (1806), and it became a commonplace of criticism to argue that Pope was not a poet at all. Today, when his high rank

AUTHORS   *[Preston*

as a satirist is generally conceded, that argument seems unduly academic.

PORSON, Richard (1759–1808), Professor of Greek at Cambridge, was the greatest classical scholar of his time. In his edition of four plays of Euripides—*Hecuba* (1797), *Orestes* (1798), *Phoenissae* (1799), and *Medea* (1801)—he made a momentous contribution to Greek scholarship, particularly in regard to the problem of prosody.

PORTER, Jane (1776–1850) and **Anna Maria** (1780–1832). The sisters Porter labored in the field of the historical novel before Scott. His "Waverley Novels" dimmed their lights but did not totally eclipse Jane's *Thaddeus of Warsaw* (1803) and *Scottish Chiefs* (1810). The latter, for all its quasi-historical hokum, has survived as a popular monument to Wallace and Bruce.

POWYS, John Cowper (1872–   ), **Llewelyn** (1884–1939), and **T(heodore) F(rancis)** (1875–1953) are three brothers from a remarkable literary family. John Cowper, the eldest, is well known in America as a critic and popular lecturer on literature. He is the author of *The Meaning of Culture* (1929) and *Wolf Solent* (1929), a long novel about a frustrated artist. The miscellaneous achievement of Llewelyn includes *Black Laughter* (1924), a book of autobiographical sketches, and *Impassioned Clay* (1931), a collection of essays. T. F. is known as a writer of naturalistic fiction about rural life in southern England. His works include *The Left Leg* (1923), a collection of short-stories, and *Mr. Weston's Good Wine* (1927), a novel.

PRAED, Winthrop Mackworth (1802–39) was a member of Parliament who wrote a large amount of miscellaneous verse. He is commonly compared with Thomas Hood. Although it is generally agreed that Praed's serious poetry is inferior to Hood's, some maintain that, in light verse, he excelled his more famous contemporary. Two of Praed's best-known pieces are *The Red Fisherman,* a fantastic narrative poem, and *The Vicar,* a graceful character sketch.

PRESTON, Thomas (1537–98) was the author of *A Lamentable Tragedy, mixed full of pleasant mirth, containing the life of Cambises, King of Persia* (c. 1558–70). The "lamentable tragedy" includes four bloody murders on the stage; the "pleasant mirth" consists largely of horseplay between the vice and a number of rustic clowns. The title-page does not mention the obvious didactic elements surviving from the morality plays. Before the end of the

225

century, King Cambises had already become a symbol of theatrical rant. Says Falstaff to Prince Hal in *1 Henry IV* (1597–8): "I must speak in passion, and I will do it in King Cambises' vein."

PRICE, Richard (1723–91) was a Welshman and a Unitarian minister. His first book was entitled *A Review of the Principal Questions . . . in Morals* (1757). Later he became famous as a defender of both the American and French revolutions. *Observations on the Nature of Civil Liberty, the Principles of Government, and the Justice and Policy of the War with America* (1776) was an indictment of the British colonial policy. *A Discourse on the Love of our Country* (1789), a sermon in which Price compared the French Revolution with the Glorious Revolution of 1688, provoked Edmund Burke's famous *Reflections on the Revolution in France* (1790).

PRIESTLEY, J(ohn) B(oynton) (1894–   ) is a popular writer who has ventured into many fields. His varied achievements include novels (*The Good Companions,* 1929; *Angel Pavement,* 1930); plays (*Laburnum Grove,* 1933); travel books (*Midnight on the Desert,* 1937); literary studies (*George Meredith,* 1926); and several collections of informal essays. *The Good Companions,* the saga of a troupe of traveling actors, was popular in America, both in the original and in the stage adaptation.

PRIESTLEY, Joseph (1733–1804) was a Unitarian minister and a chemist who published important works in several fields. His philosophical writings include *The Doctrine of Philosophical Necessity Illustrated* (1777) and *A Free Discussion on the Doctrines of Materialism* (1778). To the realm of science belong *The History and Present State of Electricity* (1767) and *Experiments and Observations on Different Kinds of Air* (1774–86). Priestley's revolutionary political thought is reflected in *An Essay on the First Principles of Government* (1768), in which he enunciated the "greatest happiness" principle that formed the basis of Jeremy Bentham's utilitarianism, and *Observations on the Importance of the American Revolution* (1784). This versatile thinker is best known today as the discoverer, in 1774, of what he called "dephlogistated air"; Lavoisier later called it "oxygen."

PRIOR, Matthew (1664–1721) called his own life "parti-coloured, half pleasure, half care." The verse which he wrote for pleasure seldom betrays the cares of the diplomat who helped contrive the Treaty of Utrecht (1713), and who was later imprisoned for two years (1715–17) by his political enemies. Among his more ambitious poems are: *The Hind and the Panther Transversed to* the Story of the Country Mouse and the City Mouse (1687), a verse parody of Dryden's satirical poem on which he collaborated with Charles Montague; Alma, or the Progress of the Mind—written in prison 1715–17—a half-serious allegory in the manner of Butler's Hudibras; and Henry and Emma, a paraphrase of the fifteenth-century Nut-brown Maid. In prose he wrote a series of imaginary conversations, Four Dialogues of the Dead. He is best known, however, as a master of vers de société. Like Robert Herrick of an earlier day, he sang gaily of himself and tossed off simple verses for children and teasing songs and epigrams for imaginary Chloes, Euphelias, and Lisettas. Thackeray, who tried similar trifles, found Prior's "among the easiest, the richest, the most charmingly humorous of English lyrical poems."

PROCTER, Bryan Waller. See **CORNWALL, Barry.**

PRYNNE, William (1600–1669) was a fanatical Puritan pamphleteer who earned himself eternal damnation in the annals of English literature by his Histriomastix: The Players' Scourge, or Actors' Tragedy (1633). In this labor of seven years and eleven hundred pages, Prynne summarized with monstrous pedantry the indictment which the Puritans had been bringing regularly against the theater since the days of Gosson's School of Abuse (1579) and Stubbes' Anatomy of Abuses (1583). It is not known whether Prynne's definition of actresses as "notorious whores" was an intentional allusion to the rehearsal of a pastoral in which Queen Henrietta herself was to take part. But this insult was certainly a major reason for the terrible sentence which the Star Chamber pronounced upon him in 1634: the loss of both ears, the brand S. L. (seditious libeller) on both cheeks, a £5,000 fine, and life imprisonment. Prynne was released from prison by the Long Parliament in 1640. In 1642 he had the satisfaction of seeing the theaters closed by Puritan edict.

PURCHAS, Samuel (1575?–1626) carried on the labor of Richard Hakluyt in collecting stories of famous voyagers. His best-known work is Hakluytus Posthumus, or Purchas his Pilgrims, containing a History of the World in Sea Voyages and Land Travels by Englishmen and others (1625).

PUSEY, Edward Bouverie (1800–82) was a young professor of Hebrew at Oxford when he joined Newman, Keble, Hurrell Froude, and others in the Oxford Movement. After Newman seceded to the Church of Rome in 1845, Pusey became the nominal leader of the movement, and "Puseyism" became a common synonym for "Tractarianism." Pusey wrote at least eight of the

Tracts for the Times (1833–41) and published numerous subsequent theological works, including *The Doctrine of the Real Presence* (1855) and several volumes of sermons.

PUTTENHAM, George (d. 1590) and **Richard** (1520?–1601?). One of these two brothers probably wrote *The Art of English Poesy* (1589). A section of it includes some apt judgments on the poets of England; another displays the practical craft of moulding poems into pretty shapes—eggs, lozenges, and pyramids—like so many Christmas cookies—a craft which later invaded the sanctity of George Herbert's *Temple* (1633). Yet this treatise for all its eccentricities, remains the most comprehensive and scholarly of the Elizabethan treatments of prosody.

PYE, Henry James (1745–1813). The uninspired author of many weak patriotic poems and one epic, *Alfred* (1801). His elevation to the laureateship in 1790 through the influence of William Pitt the younger did not make a poet out of a poetaster.

Q

Q. Pseudonym of **Douglas William Jerrold** and of **Sir Arthur Quiller-Couch.**

QUARLES, Francis (1592–1644) is now remembered chiefly for his *Emblems* (1635), a collection of didactic verses on scriptural texts, illustrated with appropriate engravings.

QUILLER–COUCH, Sir Arthur (Thomas) (1863–1944) was King Edward the Seventh Professor of English Literature at Cambridge. He is well known as the editor of *The Oxford Book of English Verse* (1900) and of several comedies in the *New Cambridge Shakespeare,* as well as for such sane and amusing criticism as the popular lecture *On Jargon*—reprinted in countless textbooks. He was better known yesterday than today as "Q," the author of numerous light verses and of many novels and short-stories in the romantic tradition of Robert Louis Stevenson. One of his best tales is the patriotic ghost-story, *The Roll-call of the Reef.*

R

RADCLIFFE, Ann (1764–1823). This was the basic recipe for Mrs. Radcliffe's five Gothic romances: a super-sensitive heroine weeping and swooning her way to wedlock amid the mazes of mystery and the machinations of brooding villains. Her best novels are *The Romance of the Forest* (1791), *The Mysteries of Udolpho* (1794), and *The Italian* (1797). For sheer horror "Monk" Lewis could outshock her, but in the creation of mood and suspense she was unequaled. She could paint a melancholy Gothic ruin without missing an owl and postpone indefinitely the disappointing revelation of the "horror" behind a black veil. She was the acknowledged queen of a school of fiction which, however absurd, has left its mark on much subsequent writing, from the poetry of the Romantics to the modern mystery thriller.

RALEIGH or RALEGH, Sir Walter (1552?–1618). The courtier, soldier, and explorer who "discovered" Virginia and tobacco and who may have becloaked a puddle that his queen might cross dry-shod—was also a writer. His poems include: a sonnet to the *Faerie Queene* of his close friend, Spenser ("Methought I saw the grave where Laura lay"); a reply to Marlowe's *Passionate Shepherd* ("If all the world and love were young"); an allegorical prayer called *The Pilgrimage;* a ringing challenge to his enemies called *The Lie;* and the perfect eight-line supplication penned the night before he died ("Even such is time, that takes in trust"). In prose he preceded Tennyson with an account of the last fight of the *Revenge* (1591), and in *The Discovery of Guiana* (1596) anticipated Othello's tall tale of "men whose heads do grow beneath their shoulders." Sentenced under Elizabeth for falling in love and under James I on false charges of conspiring against the throne, he spent most of the last third of his life in the Tower before he was finally beheaded for piracy in 1618. In prison he optimistically projected a *History of the World* (1614) from the creation to his own time. Of the three-quarters of a million words which carried him down as far as 130 B.C., posterity remembers one final paragraph ("O eloquent, just, and mighty Death")—a classic example of balanced expression.

RAMSAY, Allan (1686–1758) was an Edinburgh wig-maker who turned to making poems and collections of poems. His own work includes a number of mock-elegies, two additional cantos (1718) for the old Scottish classic, *Christ's Kirk on the Green,* and a pastoral drama, *The Gentle Shepherd* (1725). More important historically are his two anthologies, *The Tea-Table Miscellany* (1724–37) and *The Evergreen* (1724). In these he not only published some verse of his own but revived many of the old Scottish songs, thus leading a renaissance in Scottish poetry which culminated, at the end of the century, in the achievements of Robert Burns.

RANDOLPH, Thomas (1605–35) was a poet and playwright who was influenced by his older friend, Ben Jonson. His best two plays reveal his characteristic interest in the classics. *The Muses' Looking-Glass* (1630) is a didactic comedy based on Aristotle's *Ethics*. *Amyntas* (1630), a humorous pastoral drama, has been ranked behind Jonson's *Sad Shepherd* and Fletcher's *Faithful Shepherdess* as the third best pastoral play in English.

RANDS, William Brighty (1823–82) wrote under several pseudonyms, including Henry Holbeach, Matthew Browne, and Thomas Talker. He preceded Stevenson as a favorite author of children's verse and, like his successor, has been called the Laureate of the Nursery. His work for children, both verse and prose, appears in a series of "Lilliput" books: *Lilliput Levee* (1864), *Lilliput Lectures* (1871–2), *Lilliput Revels* (1871), and *Lilliput Legends* (1872). For adults he wrote, as Matthew Browne, *Chaucer's England* (1869).

RASTELL, John (1470?–1536), London printer and brother-in-law of Sir Thomas More, was the author of *A New Interlude and a Merry of the Nature of the Four Elements,* a work which he himself printed in 1519. In the form of a morality, Rastell advocates the study of geography and urges the English to assume the lead in the discovery of new lands.

READE, Charles (1814–84). Dramatist, novelist, journalist—Reade wanted them on his monument in that order. He began as a dramatist, and in 1852 he and Tom Taylor scored a hit with *Masks and Faces,* a play about the theater. In the next year he turned it into his first novel, *Peg Woffington*. From then on, although he continued to write plays, he was more popular as a novelist. He wrote novels of purpose, crusading against abuses in the prisons (*It Is Never too Late to Mend,* 1856), insane asylums (*Hard Cash,* 1863), and labor unions (*Put Yourself in His Place,* 1870). Although he turned one-man clipping bureau in documenting these books, the taint of tabloid journalism permeates his truest revelations. When he applied the same conscientious industry to the historical novel, he was more successful. *The Cloister and the Hearth* (1861) is an authentic fifteenth-century romance about the parents of Erasmus. An age which has forgotten the quarrelsome Reade, a notorious copyright violater, remembers him as the author of one of the best historical novels in the language.

REDFORD, John (d. 1547), an early Tudor schoolmaster, is known principally for his authorship of *Wit and Science* (1538–

46), a morality of the conventional humanist pattern which presents the struggle of natural intelligence (Wit) to form a union with formal learning (Lady Science). Redford's allegorical playlet is saved from dullness by several lively scenes, such as the one that represents the vain efforts of the hoyden Idleness to teach Ignorance how to spell his name.

REEVE, Clara (1729–1807) is remembered chiefly as a pioneer Gothic novelist. In *The Old English Baron* (1777) she attempted to improve on Walpole's *Castle of Otranto* with an authentic picture of "Gothic times." Except for the introduction of one *bona fide* ghost, she explained away her supernatural horrors. In this practice she anticipated Mrs. Radcliffe. *The Progress of Romance through Times, Countries, and Manners* (1785) is an absurd dialogue in which Miss Reeve's mouthpiece applies a moral yardstick to a jumble of prose and poetry.

REID, Thomas (1710–96), a Scot, was the founder of the "commonsense school" of Scottish philosophy. His works include: *An Inquiry into the Human Mind on the Principles of Common Sense* (1763), *Essays on the Intellectual Powers of Man* (1785), and *Essays on the Active Powers of Man* (1788). In opposition to Locke, Berkeley, and Hume, Reid denied the existence of ideas.

RICARDO, David (1772–1823). After making a fortune as a stockbroker, Ricardo retired from business early to devote himself to the study of economics. In *Principles of Political Economy and Taxation* (1817) he refuted Adam Smith's belief in the essential harmony between the interests of the landowner and the masses by maintaining that the landowner's rent rises as the people are driven to cultivating less fertile soils for food.

RICH, Barnabe (1540?–1617) spent his early years as a soldier and the rest of his life as a miscellaneous writer. His *Farewell to the Military Profession* (1581), a collection of romances adapted from the French and Italian, includes the story of Apolonius and Silla, which may have been the source of Shakespeare's *Twelfth Night*. His *Honesty of this Age* (1614) is full of interesting sidelights on the England of his time.

RICHARDS, I(vor) A(rmstrong) (1893–   ) is one of the most original of modern English critics. He has taught and lectured widely in America. In a series of widely discussed studies—including *The Meaning of Meaning* (with C. K. Ogden, 1923), *Principles of Literary Criticism* (1924), *Practical Criticism* (1929), and *How to Read a Page* (1942)—he has been chiefly concerned, not with establishing arbitrary aesthetic rules, but with analyzing the processes by which people read and judge poetry and prose—delving into the mysterious world which lies between the reader and the printed page. Richards has been one of the leaders in the movement to popularize the simplified vocabulary known as "Basic English." He is also the author of *Coleridge on Imagination* (1934).

RICHARDSON, Dorothy M. (1882–   ) is a novelist who, like James Joyce and Virginia Woolf, has experimented widely with the interior monologue or stream-of-consciousness technique—to use a term she deplores. In her *magnum opus, Pilgrimage,* she traces the unexciting life of a sensitive English girl, Miriam Henderson, through a whole series of novels, dwelling almost entirely in the heroine's thought processes. The first volume, *Pointed Roofs,* was published in 1915, and the twelfth, *Dimple Hill* (along with the *Pilgrimage* Omnibus Edition) in 1938. For obvious reasons Miss Richardson has not been a popular novelist, but her work has had considerable influence on her fellow-craftsmen.

RICHARDSON, Henry Handel is the pseudonym of **Henrietta Richardson,** later **Robertson** (1880?–1946), a distinguished Australian novelist. Her first novel, *Maurice Gest,* the love-story of a musician, appeared under the masculine disguise in 1908. It was followed in 1910 by *The Getting of Wisdom,* and at widely separated intervals by *Australia Felix* (1917), *The Way Home* (1925), and *Ultima Thule* (1929)—the three parts of her great trilogy. This saga of a restless failure was published in one volume in 1930 as *The Fortunes of Richard Mahoney.* She has since published *The End of a Childhood* (1934), a slender sequel, and *The Young Cosima* (1939) a biographical novel of twelve years in the life of Franz Liszt's daughter. Fame did not come to Miss Richardson until the publication of *Ultima Thule,* but many today consider *Maurice Gest* and the trilogy among the most powerful novels of the twentieth century.

RICHARDSON, Samuel (1689–1761). The first and most influential of the major mid-eighteenth-century novelists was born in Derbyshire. His apprenticeship to a printer led to a slow but substantial rise in his craft until he became King's Printer and Master of the Stationers' Company. But apparently it did not occur to him to write a book until, when he was fifty, a publisher commissioned him to prepare a collection of model letters as a guide to the illiterate. The book appeared in 1741 as *Letters writ-*

ten to and for Particular Friends, on the most Important Occasions. In this form of composition Richardson had already had much unprofessional experience, for even as a boy he had written love-letters for maidservants who were more love-lorn than literate. In the rôle of Cupid he acquired, not only epistolary practice, but an extraordinary understanding of the intricacies of the female heart. This dual training formed the basis of his novels, for he never used any narrative technique but the clumsy epistolary form, and every one of his stories throbs with morality, sentimentality, and lovers' heartbeats.

Richardson's work on his collection of model letters led to his writing the first novel of manners in English literature, *Pamela, or Virtue Rewarded* (1740–2). Although *Pamela* was once considered as an exciting narrative of a heroine's struggle to defend her virtue, the modern tendency is to view it as an extraordinarily slow-moving, long-winded, and minute account of a predatory female's success in making capital of her chastity. The church bells rang when England first heard the glad tidings of Pamela's marriage to Mr. B., but readers today often desert her, many chapters this side of the altar. Yet in his painstaking analysis of the thoughts and feelings of his central character Richardson did make an important contribution to the novel form.

A greater achievement in the same vein is his second novel of middle-class manners, *Clarissa, or The History of a Young Lady* (1747–8). The interminable narrative—almost a million words long—of Clarissa's tragic affair with Lovelace is a sort of sequel to *Pamela,* a sermon on "the Distresses that may attend Misconduct both of Parents and Children in relation to Marriage." But, more than that, it is a pier-glass biography so knowing and penetrating and complete that it is still regarded, by the few who have read it all, as one of the greatest novels in English. The same cannot be said, however, of Richardson's next voluminous novel. In writing *Sir Charles Grandison* (1753–4), he committed the error of making the hero a male Clarissa and learned that, whereas calculating chastity in a woman fascinates, negative virtue in a man repels. Sir Charles is a plaster saint, and the Pamelas among Richardson's lady readers would not take a dozen of his vegetable kind for a dissolute Mr. B. or a dissipated Lovelace.

RITCHIE, Lady Anne Isabella Thackeray (1837–1919), elder daughter of W. M. Thackeray, was a novelist and essayist in her own right. Among her novels are *The Story of Elizabeth* (1863), *The Village on the Cliff* (1867), and *Old Kensington* (1873).

ROBERT OF GLOUCESTER (fl. 1260–1300) was the principal author of the metrical work which is commonly known as *Robert of Gloucester's Chronicle* (1300). The poem is written in long lines marked by a sharp caesura. It begins with the destruction of Troy and carries the story of English history down to the death of Henry III in 1272. The most interesting section of the work comes near the end, where the poet is writing contemporary history. Famous passages are those on the town and gown riot at Oxford in 1263 and the death of Simon de Montfort in 1265.

ROBERTSON, Frederick William (1816–53) was associated with Charles Kingsley and F. D. Maurice in spreading religion among the workers of Victorian London. Although he died at thirty-seven, he was already famous as a preacher, and his *Sermons Preached at Trinity Chapel, Brighton* (1855–63) have been widely read.

ROBERTSON, Thomas William (1829–71). In a series of plays, among which are *Society* (1865), *Ours* (1866), and *Caste* (1867), Robertson tried to introduce naturalism into a theater which had dined for years on farce and melodrama. Although his plays have an air of dull domesticity which earned him the title of head of the "tea-cup and saucer school," he does deserve credit as an early advocate of real dialogue and real doorknobs.

ROBERTSON, William (1721–93) was a Scottish historian whose works, when first published, were more popular than the *History* of his fellow-countryman and contemporary, David Hume. Robertson published a *History of Scotland during the Reigns of Queen Mary and of James VI* (1759), a *History of the Reign of the Emperor Charles V* (1769), and a *History of America* (1777). Dr. Johnson once jokingly blamed his own tendency towards verbiage on reading Robertson, but, on the whole, the histories are well written.

ROBINSON, Henry Crabb (1775–1867) has at least three claims to a place in literary history: as one of England's first foreign correspondents; as one of the early champions of German literature on English soil; as a diarist who left a candid, gossipy record of his famous literary acquaintances, including Blake, Coleridge, Wordsworth, Lamb, and Hazlitt (*Diary, Reminiscences, and Correspondence*, 1869, 1927).

ROBINSON, (Esmé Stuart) Lennox (1886–   ) has been director of the Abbey Theater since 1923. Two of his comedies of

Irish peasant life, *The White-headed Boy* (1916) and *The Far-off Hills* (1931), have been favorites in the repertory of the inimitable Abbey Players and are well known on both sides of the Atlantic.

ROCHESTER, John Wilmot, second earl of (1648-80). When he died at thirty-three, Lord Rochester had already made an ever-lasting reputation as the most depraved libertine in the depraved court of Charles II. But the picture is strangely paradoxical. He could be courageous as well as cowardly, a charming gallant as well as a disgusting debauchee, a singer of tender lyrics and a writer of infamous obscenity. As a lyrist—in such exquisite songs as "Absent from thee I languish still," and "I cannot change, as others do"—Rochester outranks his fellow courtiers, Sir Charles Sedley and Lord Buckhurst. Few satirists have attained the cynicism of his *Satire Against Mankind* (1675) or the finality of his four-line *Epitaph on Charles II* ("Here lies our Sovereign Lord the King.")

ROGERS, Samuel (1763-1855). In the early years of the nineteenth century this affluent banker's son was hailed as a great poet by many who sneered at Wordsworth and Coleridge. By 1850 his popularity had dwindled. When, in that year, he was offered the laureateship out of respect for his grey hairs, he gallantly declined in favor of Tennyson. Today readers of his didactic poem *The Pleasures of Memory* (1792) usually find it pleasant but pedestrian. Many are more grateful for his *Recollections* (1859) of better writers with whom he wined and dined.

ROLLE, Richard, of Hampole (1300?-49) was a mystic who left Oxford at nineteen to become a hermit. Throughout his wandering life, many sought him out for spiritual advice. He wrote verse and prose both in Latin and in English, but so much has been ascribed to him that the canon of his work is far from fixed. Among his prose works in English are a moral epistle called *The Form of Perfect Living* (after 1348) and a commentary on the Psalter. A more celebrated poem, no longer assigned to him by the best authorities, is *The Ayenbite of Inwyt* (*Remorse of Conscience*), a didactic work of some five thousand couplets dealing with the life of man in the here and the hereafter.

ROSCOE, William (1753-1831), M.P. for Liverpool, wrote two popular biographies, *Lorenzo de' Medici* (1795) and *Pope Leo the Tenth* (1805), and one of the most celebrated children's poems of the nineteenth century, *The Butterfly's Ball and the Grasshopper's Feast* (1806).

ROSCOMMON, Wentworth Dillon, fourth earl of (1633?–85) wrote a blank-verse translation of Horace's *Ars Poetica* (1680) and an unoriginal *Essay on Translated Verse* (1684) in limping heroic couplets. Although his verse is dull, he has been congratulated on being an early champion of *Paradise Lost,* on daring to write blank verse, however bad, in an age of rhyme, and on preserving both an "unspotted bays"—the words are Pope's—and a relatively unspotted character in a spotty age.

ROSSETTI, Christina (Georgina) (1830–94) was a talented member of a distinguished family of poets and painters. She was the daughter of Gabriele Rossetti, an Italian scholar and political refugee who escaped to London in 1825, and sister of the artist and poet Dante Gabriel Rossetti. Christina never attended school but was educated by her mother. It is possible that this isolated training may have increased a natural shyness that resulted ultimately in her complete withdrawal from society. With her brothers Dante and William, she was early associated in the Pre-Raphaelite Brotherhood, a group of poets and painters who tried to interpret the spirit of art before the time of Raphael (1483–1520). Her melancholy, anemic features embodied a type which these painters admired, and she often posed for them. She also contributed to their short-lived magazine, the *Germ* (1850), some of the loveliest of her lyrics. She never married. Her love for Charles Cayley, to whose religious liberalism she could not square her more rigid faith, she expressed sadly in *Monna Innominata* (1881). In 1865 she visited Switzerland and Italy. Six years after her return to England she was afflicted with a sickness from which she never fully recovered. Thereafter she became more and more isolated and at the time of her death was seeing almost nobody.

Verses (1847) was published when she was only seventeen. *Goblin Market and Other Poems* appeared in 1862. The title poem, an extraordinarily magic filigree of allegorical narrative, is her most famous single piece. *The Prince's Progress and Other Poems* (1866) reveals the characteristically devotional trend of this secular nun's genius. But in *Sing-Song: A Nursery Rhyme Book* (1872) she is astonishingly lively and simple. These last verses have, in fact, many of the characteristics of Mother Goose rhymes and of Stevenson's *Child's Garden of Verses* (1885).

ROSSETTI, Dante Gabriel (1828–82). If all the English authors who were also painters and musicians could be assembled, one of the chief of the group would be D. G. Rossetti. He was the eldest son of an Italian political refugee who settled in London in

1825 and the brother of Christina and William Rossetti. Rossetti studied art in the Royal Academy in 1846 and three years later founded, with his brother William, Millais, Holman Hunt, and others, the Pre-Raphaelite Brotherhood, a society of poets and painters who sought to follow the artistic technique of the Italian artists before Raphael (1483–1520). In 1850 he contributed to the *Germ,* the short-lived magazine of the P. R. B., twelve poems, of which the best is *The Blessed Damozel.* The living likeness of the dead girl of the poem, who leans over the golden bar of Heaven and yearns toward her earth-bound lover, Rossetti found the same year in Elizabeth Siddall. Like the typical Pre-Raphaelite heroine, who appeared frequently both in poetry and in painting, she was raven-haired, lily-cheeked, ox-eyed, and unhealthy. Although she sat as Rossetti's model, he could not afford to marry her for ten years—and she died two years later. In a stormy passion of grief he buried in her coffin the manuscript of many of his unpublished poems. In 1869, impoverished and neurotic, he consented to having his wife's body disinterred and the poems published. So appeared in 1870 the sensuous sonnet sequence addressed to her, *The House of Life.*

Although plagued by insomnia and enslaved by the chloral which he took to subdue it, Rossetti continued to write, and his *Ballads and Sonnets* were published the year before his death. Among the poems of the 1870 and 1881 volumes are: *Sister Helen, The King's Tragedy, The White Ship, Troy Town, My Sister's Sleep,* and *The Ballad of Dead Ladies.* All of these have a fascinating mixture of realism and romance. Victorian moralists led by Robert Buchanan attacked Rossetti as a member of the "Fleshly School of Poetry." Actually—as the painter-critic Ruskin knew—Rossetti the poet did with words what Rossetti the painter did with pigments. In both forms of art he treated romantic themes in a realistic—sometimes earthy—manner, giving his classical and medieval subjects a turn that had little of the didactic morality of the typical Victorian writer, but was lush with form and color and life.

ROSSETTI, William Michael (1829–1919) was the brother of Christina and Dante Gabriel Rossetti. He was one of the original members of the Pre-Raphaelite Brotherhood and edited its publication, the *Germ.* He published art-criticism (*Fine Art, Chiefly Contemporary,* 1867) and a blank-verse translation of Dante's *Inferno* (1865) and edited the works of Walt Whitman, Shelley, Blake, and his own brother and sister.

ROWE, Nicholas (1674–1718) was a playwright and a scholar. In the days when sentimentality, didacticism, and bombast were the ingredients of a hit, he wrote two highly successful domestic tragedies. In "gay Lothario" of *The Fair Penitent* (1703) he created a character who not only bequeathed himself to the language but who also sat as a model for the most accomplished villain of the century, Lovelace of Richardson's *Clarissa Harlowe*. *Jane Shore* (1714) was written in avowed imitation of Shakespeare. As a scholar, Rowe gave the world the first modern edition of Shakespeare's plays (1709) and a respected translation of Lucan's *Pharsalia* (1718). Between two comparative nobodies, Tate and Eusden, he served a three-year term as poet laureate.

ROWLANDS, Samuel (1570?–1630?) was a resourceful hack who catered to popular taste. His writings in verse include *The Betraying of Christ* (1598); *The Letting of Humours Blood in the Head-Vein* (1600), a series of epigrams and "characters" on London types; and *'Tis Merry When Gossips Meet* (1602), the lively ale-house conversation of a widow, a wife, and a maid. Rowlands' best-known prose-work is *Greene's Ghost Haunting Conie-Catchers* (1602), an attempt to capitalize on Robert Greene's reputation as an authority on the Elizabethan underworld.

ROWLEY, Samuel (d. 1624), an actor in the Admiral's Company, is remembered chiefly as the author of the historical play *When You See Me, You Know Me, or the Famous Chronicle History of King Henry VIII* (1603–5). The work is interesting as a forerunner of Shakespeare's *Henry VIII* (1613).

ROWLEY, William (1585?–1642?). Beyond the fact that he was an actor from about 1607 to 1627, a dramatic collaborator with better playwrights, and a writer of two or three conventional plays of his own, little is known of William Rowley. He wrote *A Shoemaker a Gentleman* (1607–9), *A New Wonder, a Woman Never Vexed* (c. 1607–c. 1625), and *A Match at Midnight* (1621–37), apparently without assistance. But *A Fair Quarrel* (1615–7) and *The Changeling* (1622), in both of which he collaborated with Middleton, are much more distinguished. In the second of these Rowley probably wrote the coarse farce of the attempted cuckolding of a physician which accompanies but has little structural connection with the better dramatist's powerful tragedy.

RUSKIN, John (1819–1900). In *Praeterita*—Past and Gone— (1885–9), Ruskin tells his own story of his unusual upbringing at Herne Hill. He was the only child of a wealthy wine merchant and a stern and unemotional mother who made a profession of educating him. His father contributed to his development by taking him on numerous coaching tours in the British Isles and on the Continent and by buying him paintings and sketches of Turner, the English landscape artist. His Calvinist mother put him through a course in Bible-reading which he declared to have been the "one essential part" of his boyhood training. She was a good deal of a matriarch, however, who kept him almost completely under her thumb, and who seems even to have forced him in 1849 into the unhappy marriage with Euphemia Gray that was annulled five years later.

Ruskin's love of nature and of art he expressed in the first volume of *Modern Painters* (1843) when he was only twenty-four. This amazing volume, "by an Oxford graduate," was designed to be a defense of the painter Turner, then under attack because of his change of technique, but it went beyond an appreciation of one artist and became the first of a five-volume study (the last appearing in 1860). His theories of the relationship of morality and art he expressed further in *The Seven Lamps of Architecture* (1849) and *The Stones of Venice* (3 vols., 1851-53). He believed that great art should be not only technically sound but rooted firmly in individual and national morality. Thus his "seven lamps" or leading principles of art, are Sacrifice, Truth, Power, Beauty, Life, Memory, and Obedience. Gothic architecture he believed to be noble because based on national integrity, and Renaissance architecture ignoble because built on national corruption. These art criticisms brought him such a reputation that his defense in 1851 of the Pre-Raphaelites—a contemporary group of experimenters in poetry and painting—did much to accredit them.

When, in 1862, he published *Unto this Last,* the first of a series of social studies, Ruskin suffered a sharp decline in popularity. It was followed by *Munera Pulveris* (1862-3), *Sesame and Lilies* (1865)—ultimately expanded to three lectures on reading, education, and the duties of women—, *Ethics of the Dust* (1866), *The Crown of Wild Olive* (1866), *Time and Tide* (1867), and finally *Fors Clavigera* (1871-84), a violent and sometimes markedly eccentric series of letters to British workingmen. Ruskin's early injection into his art criticisms of ethical and economic theory had been the beginning of a growing sociological interest that led ultimately to a shift from aesthetics to ethics. Life without industry, he believed, is guilt, and industry without art is brutality. Being a man of considerable wealth, moreover, he did not permit his passion for industrial reform to find an outlet solely in his writing.

He experimented, not too successfully, with "the guild of St. George," "the Hinksey Diggers," "the hand-made linen workers of Langdale," and other social expressions of his ideas; and he fulminated from lecture platforms against the ruin that was coming through the railroad, the telegraph, and other evidences of the growing industrialization of Victorian England. In spite of these manifold activities, however, he served Oxford University from 1870 to 1879 and again in 1883-4 as Slade Professor of Art. He died in his home in Brantwood, on Coniston Lake in Westmoreland, after several years of increasing mental deterioration.

Ruskin's earlier literary style, that of the first volumes of *Modern Painters,* is rhythmic, colorful, and overelaborate, its interminable sentences constructed with self-conscious artistry. The style of his later work is rougher, less controlled, and more furious and impatient in its mood.

RUSSELL, Bertrand (Arthur William), third earl Russell (1872–   ) is one of the most widely publicized of contemporary thinkers and writers. His early reputation as a mathematician and philosopher has been partly obscured by the frequent storms which have greeted his radical pronouncements on politics, marriage, religion, and education. Among his many books are *Roads to Freedom* (1918), *The Prospects of Industrial Civilization* (with Dora Russell, 1923), *Marriage and Morals* (1929), *Education and the Social Order* (1932). He has taught and lectured widely in America.

RUSSELL, George William. See **Æ.**

RUTHERFORD, Mark, is the pseudonym under which **William Hale White** (1831–1913) wrote a number of autobiographical novels. In *The Autobiography of Mark Rutherford, Dissenting Minister* (1881) and its sequel, *Mark Rutherford's Deliverance* (1885), he narrated his own spiritual struggle against the bigoted Calvinism of the dissenting clergy. Like the novels of Anthony Trollope and Mrs. Oliphant, these stories are valuable as studies of ecclesiastical life in Victorian England.

RYMER, Thomas (1641–1713) was appointed historiographer royal in 1693. Before that he had made a name as an arch-classicist in dramatic criticism. In *Tragedies of the Last Age* (1678) and *A Short View of Tragedy* (1692) he damned the Elizabethans for disregarding the unities of time, place, and action. For example, he mocked Shakespeare for moving his characters in *Othello* from Venice to Cyprus without supplying ships.

S

SACKVILLE, Charles, Lord Buckhurst and later sixth earl of Dorset (1638–1706). Although his reputation as a poet and a profligate is not so great as theirs, Lord Buckhurst is traditionally grouped with his fellow-courtiers, Sedley and Rochester. Despite the dissipation of his youth, he lived to become respected as a statesman, a poet, and a patron of literature. The most celebrated of his songs is "To all you ladies now at land," composed at sea during the first Dutch War in 1665. It is a playful plea to the girls the English soldiers left behind them. Buckhurst is also remembered as Eugenius, one of the critics in Dryden's *Essay of Dramatic Poesy* (1668).

SACKVILLE, Thomas, first earl of Dorset and Baron Buckhurst (1536–1608). Before he abandoned literature for affairs of state, Sackville made three important contributions. He collaborated with Thomas Norton, a fellow lawyer, on *Gorboduc* (1562), the first English classical tragedy, probably writing acts IV and V. To the 1563 edition of *A Mirror for Magistrates,* he contributed two long poems in rhyme royal: an *Induction,* in which Sorrow guides the poet to Hell, and *The Complaint of the Duke of Buckingham,* the self-told story of one of Richard III's victims. The *Induction,* for all its archaisms and allegory, breathes a melancholy music which is rare in the poetry between Chaucer and Spenser.

SACKVILLE–WEST, (Hon.) V(ictoria Mary) (1892–   ) was born in spacious, fifteenth-century Knole Castle and bred in the aristocratic manner befitting the daughter of the third baron Sackville. The castle and its environs served as the setting for *The Edwardians* (1930), a witty novel about a duke's vain struggle to free himself from the bondage of the nobility. A more serious novel is her *All Passion Spent* (1931). Her reputation as a poetess rests largely on *The Land* (1926), a poetic tribute to the English countryside. V. Sackville-West is the heroine of *Orlando* (1928), a unique biography by her intimate friend Virginia Woolf. She is the wife of Harold Nicolson, the biographer, and the cousin of **Edward Charles Sackville-West** (1901–   ), the novelist.

SAKI is the name of the cup-bearer in *The Rubáiyát of Omar Khayyám* and the pseudonym under which **H(ector) H(ugh) Munro** (1870–1916) wrote short-stories, novels, and plays. Munro was born in Burma and spent the later years of his life as a foreign correspondent and general contributor to several London periodicals. He was killed in action during the First World War. Saki's short-stories — including such favorites as *Tobermory, The Lumber-Room,* and *The Open Window*—were collected in 1930. In their ingenious plotting and their characteristic blend of fantasy and satire they are remote from the less artificial tradition of recent years, but they are still read by a large cult of idolators.

SANDYS, George (1578–1644) was a traveler and scholar whose translation of the *Metamorphoses* of the Latin poet Ovid (43 B.C.– A.D. 18?) appeared in 1626. The translation, in heroic couplets, is generally faithful and sometimes strikingly literal. Sandys was a pioneer in the use of the closed couplet.

SASSOON, Siegfried (Lorraine) (1886–   ). Although he wrote poetry before the First World War and has written much since, Sassoon's name is permanently linked with that conflict. His first-hand experience at the front led him, not to the more conventional patriotism of Rupert Brooke's *1914,* but to a vigorous pacifism. In such poems as *Aftermath (The War Poems of Siegfried Sassoon,* 1919), he wrote bitterly of the horrors of war. Sassoon's *Memoirs of a Fox-hunting Man* (1928) and *Memoirs of an Infantry Officer* (1930) are significant autobiographies.

SAVAGE, Richard (1697–1743) was a pitiful hack who is remembered chiefly because of his friendship with Dr. Johnson. The two shared penury during Johnson's early years in London, and Johnson told his Grub Street friend's shabbily romantic story in *The Life of Mr. Richard Savage,* published first in 1744 and later incorporated into *Lives of the Poets* (vol. III, 1781). Among Savage's productions in verse are *The Wanderer* (1729), a didactic descriptive poem which Johnson called "a heap of shining materials thrown together by accident"; and *The Bastard* (1728), in which Savage promoted the improbable story of his illegitimate birth to Lady Macclesfield.

SAVILE, George. See **HALIFAX.**

SCHREINER, Olive (Emilie Albertina) (1855–1920) is remembered as the author of *The Story of an African Farm* (1883), published under the pseudonym Ralph Iron. Although set in the author's native South Africa, this novel contains serious discussions of Victorian problems.

SCOTT, Michael (1789–1835) was a Glasgow merchant and manager of Jamaica estates who, when nearing middle age, wove his first-hand knowledge of the sea into two robust novels, *Tom Cringle's Log* (1829–33) and *The Cruise of the Midge* (1834–5).

Both were published anonymously in *Blackwood's Magazine* before appearing in book form under their author's name.

SCOTT, Sir Walter (1771–1832). The most popular of the earlier writers of the Romantic Movement was a poet and novelist who found his inspiration and much of his literary material in his native Scotland. Sir Walter Scott was born in Edinburgh of a good family and spent most of his life in or near this Athens of the North. A sojourn in Kelso when he was a child developed a natural love of romance, and before he was graduated from the University of Edinburgh he had already begun to collect historical facts and string them into tales. Nevertheless, he studied law, was admitted to the bar, and became Sheriff of Selkirkshire in 1799 and Clerk of the Session in 1805. But he found his real delight in his translations of German romantic literature, and in his "Liddesdale raids" through the hills to the south of Edinburgh. Out of the native songs and ballads which he collected on these horseback rides came his first important book, *Minstrelsy of the Scottish Border* (3 vols., 1802–3). Two years later lovers of romance were thrilled by the appearance of Scott's first long tale in verse, *The Lay of the Last Minstrel* (1805). Other romances in rhyme followed rapidly: *Marmion* (1808), *The Lady of the Lake* (1810)—the most widely read of all—, *The Vision of Don Roderick* (1811), *Rokeby* (1813), *The Bridal of Triermain* (1813), and *The Lord of the Isles* (1815). Although the Scottish tales are best, the poet revealed in the others that his historical and romantic interests were not entirely local. Technically Scott is not a great poet, and he wrote too rapidly always to write well. But the stories were fresh and exciting and sold in such quantities that they brought wealth to the author and to his publishers.

The purchase and expansion of Abbotsford on the Tweed absorbed more than Scott earned but helped him to realize his dream of establishing himself as a Scottish laird. This romantic ambition was further realized when he was created a baronet in 1820. Meanwhile his poems had been eclipsed by the more exotic narrative verses of Lord Byron, and in 1814, with the publication of *Waverley*, Scott turned—anonymously at first—to the most famous single series of historical novels in English literature. Writing furiously, tirelessly, and often carelessly, he issued nearly two novels a year in the decade and a half before his death. The stories of the "Great Unknown" were immensely popular. But rich as the novels made their author, they did not save him from financial ruin, and the crash of the publishing house of Constable and Ballantyne (1825), in which Scott was heavily involved, left the novelist with obligations of over a hundred thousand pounds. From that unhappy date his novels were written courageously to pay his debts—but not written as well.

Scott's historical novels, like his poems, may be divided roughly into the Scottish tales and those of England and the Continent. The best are probably those of his own country, including *Waverley* (1814), *Guy Mannering* (1815), *Old Mortality* (1816), *Rob Roy* (1818), and *The Heart of Midlothian* (1818)—considered by many as his masterpiece. But his tales of the Crusades, *Ivanhoe* (1820) and *The Talisman* (1825), are stirring; his revivals of the spacious days of Queen Elizabeth—*Kenilworth* (1821), *The Monastery* (1820), and *The Abbot* (1820)—are vivid, if not always historically accurate; and *Quentin Durward* (1823), the tale of a young Scot at the court of Louis XI of France, is one of his best. In spite of Scott's unhappy inclination to over-document his stories, they have in the narrative parts sweep and rapid tempo. As he himself admitted, he was a master of "the big bow-wow strain," not gifted with "the exquisite touch" with which his contemporary Jane Austen made "ordinary commonplace things and characters interesting." But some of the actors of his "pocket stage" are unforgettable. This is true especially of those of the lower classes of society and those of his own Scotland. Such characters as Dominie Sampson, Jeanie, Effie, and Davie Deans, Andrew Fairservice, and Caleb Balderstone stand out in living flesh and blood in a gallery of lay figures.

SEDLEY, Sir Charles (1639?–1701). To this profligate wit of the court of Charles II literature was a fashionable plaything. He wrote pleasant songs in the Cavalier tradition ("Phyllis is my only joy") and unimportant comedies (*The Mulberry Garden,* 1668). He was a respected dramatic critic. Dryden, in the *Essay of Dramatic Poesy* (1668), introduced him under the name of Lisideius, advocate of the French conventions in drama.

SEELEY, Sir John Robert (1834–95) was professor of Latin in University College, London, when he published anonymously *Ecce Homo* (1866), a widely discussed work on Christ and Christian ethics. He was professor of modern history at Cambridge when he wrote his historical works: *The Life and Times of Stein* (1878), *The Expansion of England* (1883), and *The Growth of British Policy* (1895). Whether or not Seeley carried out his avowed aim to make statesmen with his histories, it is generally agreed that he greatly helped the spread of imperialism.

SELDEN, John (1584–1654). Jurist, politician, philologist, heraldist, orientalist—Selden was appallingly learned. What he wrote in ponderous works like his *Titles of Honour* (1614) and *History of Tithes* (1618) is all but forgotten. What he said is not. His *Table Talk* (1689), collected by a secretary after his death, is a collection of observations on such varied topics as law, literature, politics, religion, and marriage. Selden could be dogmatic and short-sighted, as when he condemned the style of the King James Bible for its Hebraisms or ridiculed the writing of drama in verse as an outworn tradition. But he said much that was salty and sensible and spoken with the crotchety bluntness of Samuel Johnson. And both Johnson and another great table-talker, Coleridge, recommended John Selden.

SETTLE, Elkanah (1648–1724) had his little day in 1673. In that year his heroic tragedy, *The Empress of Morocco,* was produced and was printed with super-elegant engravings. When certain wits asserted that it shamed Dryden, a pamphlet squabble was on, and Settle's fate was sealed. Today the rest of his tragedies are as obsolete as the civic pageants which he staged in the nineties as the last incumbent of the office of City Poet or the puppet shows which he wrote in his declining years. He survives as Doeg, the miserable rhymester and political turncoat of the second part of Dryden's *Absalom and Achitophel* (1682). As John Wilkes said of Settle at the famous dinner with Samuel Johnson, "Who can expect much from that name?"

SEWARD, Anna (1747–1809) has been kept on this side of oblivion partly because she knew important people, including Boswell, Johnson, and Scott, and partly, no doubt, because of her inept epithet "The Swan of Lichfield." *The Poetical Works of Anna Seward,* edited by Scott, appeared in 1810, her *Letters* a year later.

SHADWELL, Thomas (1642?–92) "Sh[adwell] never deviates into sense," jibed Dryden about the hero-dunce of his *Mac Flecknoe* (1682), and posterity has since relegated "the True-Blew-Protestant Poet, T. S." to the footnotes as a nobody who was idiot enough to become an ex-friend of a great satirist. But, although a third-rate bard, Shadwell was not the worst of England's obscure laureates, and as the author or adapter of seventeen plays, he deserves a better fate. His best plays, ungainly specimens of Jonsonian "humors" comedy, are worth more to the student of seventeenth-century society than to the belletrist. *Epsom Wells* (1672), *The Squire of Alsatia* (1688), and *Bury Fair* (1689) present real pictures of actual locales, and *The Virtuoso* (1676), which glorifies that insatiable theorist, Sir Nicholas Gimcrack, is one of the gayest of many satires on the early aberrations of the Royal Society.

SHAFTESBURY, Anthony Ashley Cooper, third earl of (1671–1713), was the grandson of the villain of Dryden's *Absalom and Achitophel* (1681). His *Characteristics of Men, Manners, Opinions, Times* (1711) is a collection of miscellaneous ethical essays. He ·vas a deist and in his earlier days a disciple of Locke. In his optimistic belief in man's perfectability, he looked ahead to Rousseau and many eighteenth-century English sentimentalists. Charles Lamb ridiculed his over-refined "genteel" style.

SHAKESPEARE, William (1564–1616). The first name in English literature is that of an Elizabethan poet and dramatist whose skill in transforming human character and action into art created a world of unforgettable people and phrases. About such a writer traditions are certain to grow up; of these the most astounding is the strange heresy that Shakespeare's dramas were written by Francis Bacon, or the Earl of Oxford, or a syndicate of playwrights using the name Shakespeare. Such theories have no basis in sound evidence; although it is true that no Boswell pursued William Shakespeare to record his acts and his words, there are more documented facts about his life than about the lives of many of his fellow playwrights regarding whose existences and labors no doubts are raised.

Shakespeare was born in Stratford-on-Avon on or about April 23, 1564, of a substantial middle-class family. His father, John Shakespeare, was a tanner and glover by trade, and a property-owner whose solid reputation brought him several civic offices. His mother was Mary Arden, of a family socially above her husband's. Because of his father's financial reverses, William's formal education was scanty; he apparently had to supplement his early grammar school training with much reading and social intercourse. Stratford records show that in 1582 he married Anne Hathaway, daughter of a farmer in the neighboring hamlet of Shottery. Anne was eight years older than her eighteen-year-old husband, and the birth of a daughter, Susanna, six months after the marriage may be significant; there is no sound evidence, however, even in his bequest to his wife of his "second-best bed," that he was unhappy in his marriage. Although he early, and quite naturally, made the metropolis of London the center of his professional activity, he never gave up his connection with his home town. In 1597 he

established his family in New Place, one of the show residences
of the village; he bought other property there; and in 1611 or
1612 he retired to Stratford to spend the last four or five years of
his life under the shadow of the Holy Trinity Church, where his
bones still rest.

London was the city of his professional life. Speculation as to
just why or when he went there is futile; his father's financial
difficulties and the increase in the size of his own family by the
arrival in 1585 of twins—Hamnet and Judith—would be enough
to drive him to a place where he could make a living. At any
rate before the end of the eighties he was getting himself well
established in London as actor and writer; and before ten years
more had passed he had attained the distinction of membership,
with the famous tragedian Richard Burbage and other notable
actors, in the Lord Chamberlain's Company of players. In 1599
he became a stockholder in the company's newly erected Globe
Theater on the Bankside, and in 1608 he shared also in the Black-
friars Theater, within the city limits. These and other sources of
income made him a wealthy man, and there is abundant docu-
mentary evidence that he owned much property, made loans,
participated as a principal in law cases, and appeared as wit-
ness in a dowry suit. With the accession of King James I in
1603 Shakespeare and his fellows of the Lord Chamberlain's Company became the King's Men by royal appointment and so were
the foremost of the adult companies of the city. The remaining
eight or nine years of his professional life form a record of continual success until his retirement to Stratford at the beginning
of the second decade to be with his wife and two married
daughters.

Shakespeare's professional activity is revealed best by the succession of poems and plays that have made him an immortal in
literature. Most of his non-dramatic poems he wrote early in his
career when he was seeking, after the custom of the time, the
patronage of a rich nobleman. His long narrative poems, *Venus
and Adonis* (1593) and *The Rape of Lucrece* (1594), were both
dedicated to the young Earl of Southampton. They are complementary pieces on classical subjects, descriptive rather than
narrative, and rather lush and overloaded with details. They deal
respectively with the themes of male and female chastity. Shakespeare's *Sonnets* were written in the last decade of the sixteenth
and the first of the seventeenth century, but were not collected and
printed until 1609. Of the total of one hundred and fifty-four,
one hundred and twenty-six seem to have been addressed to a

young man who was the poet's patron, and the rest to a "dark lady," a disdainful brunette whom the author courted. The quest to identify these two persons, and also "Mr. W. H., the onlie begetter of these ensuing sonnets" has brought about much spiliing of scholarly ink. The sonnets follow the usual conventions in theme and form; they are of unequal merit, but the best of them are at the top in an age of sonnet-writing. Among the favorites are "When, in disgrace with fortune and men's eyes," "When to the sessions of sweet silent thought," "Full many a glorious morning have I seen," and "Let me not to the marriage of true minds." Shakespeare's greatest lyrics, however, were not his sonnets but the lovely songs that are a part of his plays. These range in mood from rollicking drinking songs and bawdy sailor chanties to the most mournful of dirges; they number nearly a hundred, are woven skillfully into the dramas in which they appear, and form collectively one of the finest bodies of lyric poetry in any literature.

But Shakespeare is best known not as a lyrist but as a dramatic poet. During his professional life he composed an average of about two plays a year, besides collaborating with his fellows on other dramas. The range of these productions is remarkable; with the exception of domestic tragedy and one or two other subordinate forms, he attempted all current types—comedy, tragedy, history. In his own lifetime his reputation was high, and in the past two centuries it has increased steadily. Because Shakespeare was an actor and producer, he had little concern with the printing of his dramas, and fewer than half of those in the "canon" were published before the folio edition of his collected plays that appeared seven years after his death. It is for this reason, in part, that the dates of composition are not always certain; allusions to current events in the plays themselves and references to them in stage and publication records must also be used as evidence of when they first appeared. In these ways, the sequence may be determined approximately. In the following list the division of types in the first folio edition of 1623 has been employed; the dates after each play indicate the years within which, according to the best evidence, it was written. COMEDIES: *Love's Labor's Lost* (1590–2), *The Comedy of Errors* (1592–4), *The Two Gentlemen of Verona* (1592–4), *A Midsummer Night's Dream* (1594–6), *The Merchant of Venice* (1594–6), *The Taming of the Shrew* (1594–7), *The Merry Wives of Windsor* (1597–1600), *Much Ado About Nothing* (1598–1600), *As You Like It* (1599–1600), *Twelfth Night* (1599–1601), *All's Well that Ends Well* (1600–4), *Measure for Measure* (1603–4),

Pericles (1607–8), *Cymbeline* (1609–10), *The Winter's Tale* (1610–11), *The Tempest* (1611–12); HISTORIES: *1, 2, 3 Henry VI* (1590–2), *Richard III* (1593–4), *King John* (1594–6), *Richard II* (1594–6), *1, 2 Henry IV* (1597–8), *Henry V* (1598–9), *Henry VIII* (1612–13); TRAGEDIES: *Titus Andronicus* (1593–4), *Romeo and Juliet* (1594–7), *Julius Caesar* (1598–9), *Hamlet* (1600–1), *Troilus and Cressida* (1601–3), *Othello* (1604–5), *King Lear* (1605–6), *Macbeth* (1605–6), *Antony and Cleopatra* (1607–8), *Timon of Athens* (1607–8), *Coriolanus* (1608–10).

An examination of the dates in this chart will reveal that whereas Shakespeare continued to write comedies throughout his career, his great tragedies are the work of his maturity, and his history plays—with the exception of *Henry VIII*—fall within the last decade of the sixteenth century. The comedies present, naturally, the widest variety, ranging from rollicking farces like *The Comedy of Errors, The Merry Wives of Windsor,* and *The Taming of the Shrew* through lyrical dramas like *A Midsummer Night's Dream* and *The Tempest* to such "dark comedies" as *All's Well that Ends Well* and *Measure for Measure,* which the twentieth century would hardly regard as comic. The tragedies have less range in subject matter and mood; every one, in fact, follows the classical pattern of the tragic downfall of a single titanic figure, or, in the love tragedies, of a pair of tragic lovers. The history plays are the most closely interrelated of all; eight out of the ten (the exceptions are *King John* and *Henry VIII*) present a historical sequence that deals with the war with France and the English civil wars from the last years of Richard II (1377–99) to the accession of Henry VII (1485)—a century of intrigue and armed rebellion.

Regarding Shakespeare's dramatic technique a whole library has been written. In one respect he was not original; except for one or two plays every drama can be traced to a definite source. The dramatist ranged widely for his raw materials: classical legend, history, and biography; Italian tale—comic or tragic—; English and Scottish chronicles; even older plays were all used. But all these were transformed; they came from the mint of Shakespeare's creative genius fresh, entertaining, alive; and in his power to make these dramatic reconstructions Shakespeare is the most original of dramatists. The patterns of his plots are sometimes intricate but always clearly woven. His characters are true to life and consistently developed. He mixed the elements of tragedy and comedy in his plays as they are mixed in life. Essentially he was a romanticist, but with his romanticism he compounded realism. He knew the formulas of the classical critics, and could follow them when he wished; but he was too natural an artist to be bound by rules for composition. He knew life first and knew how to present it in lively action. In his art he followed the advice that he had Hamlet give the players: he held the mirror up to nature; he showed virtue her own feature, scorn her own image, and the very age and body of the time his form and pressure. And thus it was that his friend and fellow dramatist Ben Jonson could write in praise of him: "He was not of an age, but for all time!"

SHARP, William (1855–1905) issued poems, biographies, and fiction under his own name and during the last ten years of his life published, as "Fiona Macleod," a body of strangely different verse and prose permeated with Celtic mysticism. The mystery of his pseudonym was not revealed until his death. In 1909–10 appeared the seven-volume collection of *The Writings of Fiona Macleod,* arranged by Mrs. William Sharp; in 1912 followed the five-volume *Selected Writings of William Sharp.*

SHAW, George Bernard (1856–1950) was born in Dublin, one of a brood of children whose father was a poverty-stricken ne'er-do-well. It is possible that Shaw's persistent abstinence, his hatred of alcohol and tobacco, came from his father's weakness for these indulgences. Whether his inherited reactions also made him a social reformer, vegetarian, anti-vaccinationist, and anti-vivisectionist cannot be proved. Shaw's mother was a gifted musician, who went with her younger children to London to teach music. Her talented son, who had left school at fifteen to work in the office of a Dublin land agent, joined her there in 1876.

Despite a lack of formal education, Shaw had already shown an interest in music, painting, and writing, and he spent his early years in London as a hack writer for various magazines, and published several unsuccessful novels. He was music critic for the *Star* (1885) and later for the *World,* and from 1894 to 1898 he wrote distinguished dramatic criticism for the *Saturday Review.* Out of these interests and activities grew two of his best-known non-dramatic works, *The Quintessence of Ibsenism* (1891) and *The Perfect Wagnerite* (1898).

In the meantime his lifelong absorption in political and social philosophy began to appear. By 1882 he was reading Henry George enthusiastically, and George led him to Karl Marx. In 1884, with Sidney Webb and others, he founded the Fabian Society, so-called because its theory of social revolution was the "delaying" policy of Fabius "Cunctator," and during the eighties and nineties he scribbled tracts and argued from the soapbox in the cause of Fabian Socialism. But his political philosophy was chameleon-like, and it is not at all clear, to illustrate, that his expressed admiration for such dictators as Mussolini and Hitler was genuine or sprang merely from his continuous propensity for showmanship.

From his earliest years as a playwright Shaw wrote in open rebellion against Victorian conventions, both those of the theater and those of the world which it pretended to represent. No admirer of the "well-made" plays of Arthur Wing Pinero and Henry Arthur Jones—although they were regarded in their time as rebels against tradition—he took his cue from Ibsen and Samuel Butler. His first play, *Widowers' Houses,* was begun in 1885 with William Archer, but finished alone and not performed until 1892. It is a drama of social ideas, an attack on the unearned profits from rackrenting in Ireland, and in it Shaw pulled no punches. In *Mrs. Warren's Profession,* written in 1894 but prohibited from appearing on the stage until 1902, he boldly maintained the un-Victorian thesis that "prostitution is caused, not by female depravity and male licentiousness, but simply by underpaying, undervaluing, and overworking women so shamefully that the poorest of them are forced to prostitution to keep body and soul together." In *Arms and the Man* (1894) and *The Devil's Disciple* (1897) he ridiculed military heroism. In *Candida* (1895), considered by many as his greatest play, he presented an emancipated woman who—contrary to the best Victorian tradition—makes two men, her stiff-necked husband Morell and the adolescent poet Marchbanks, dance to her well modulated tune. In *Man and Superman* (1903) he again pointed to the subservient rôle of the male animal. In *Major Barbara* (1905) he exposed the greed of professional charity; and in *Pygmalion* (1912) he demonstrated ironically that a cockney flower girl, if properly tutored in the superficial acquisitions of high society, can pass for a duchess in a matter of weeks.

These representative plays are high comedies shot through with the inimitable "Shavian" wit and marked by Shaw's tendency to use his characters as mouthpieces to spout, sometimes in long, undramatic speeches, his provocative doctrines. Not content with confining his message to the dialogue itself, Shaw commonly talks on into the stage directions and continues talking in compendious prefaces, so that the characteristic Shavian play must be read as well as seen in the theater.

But that Shaw's genius has not been confined to the high comedy o: social satire is revealed in his amazing *Back to Methuselah* (1921), a cycle of five plays that form a philosophic fantasy from Adam and Eve to the year 31920 A.D., and in his *Saint Joan of Arc* (1923), a history play. Those who thought that his receipt of the Nobel prize for literature in 1925, when he was but a year from the psalmist's span, would be the capstone of his career did not reckon with his persistent vitality. After that date he wrote many more plays, including *The Apple Cart* (1929), a political extravaganza, *Too True to be Good* (1932), a drama with almost no plot but with abundant wit, *Geneva* (1938), and *King Charles's Golden Days* (1939). And if these latest fruits were not welcomed with the astonished enthusiasm that greeted his dramas of forty years earlier, they helped to convince the world that he was still the same old Mephistophelean pundit and showman, an incredibly hardy perennial, a satirical Peter Pan who refused to grow old, and—all things considered—the most significant British playwright of the twentieth century.

SHAW, T. E. See **LAWRENCE, T. E.**
SHEFFIELD, John. See **MULGRAVE.**
SHELLEY, Mary Godwin (1797–1851) was the daughter of the brilliant radical reformers, William Godwin and Mary Wollstonecraft. When she was seventeen, she eloped to France with Percy Bysshe Shelley, who was already married to Harriet Westbrook. The poet did not legalize his relationship to Mary Godwin until after the suicide of Harriet in 1816. The resulting scandals and law-suits drove the Shelleys to Italy, where they associated with Byron and other exiles and travelers. Mary Shelley did much to develop her husband's poetic powers. She also produced in the first year of their exile the one novel by which she became known. *Frankenstein* (1818) is a pseudo-scientific, faintly allegorical tale of a young scientist who creates a monster out of the horrid leavings of the dissecting-room and charnel-house and galvanizes the creature into life. The unholy obscenity pursues and destroys its creator. By a common error the name "Frankenstein" has come to be applied not to the young scientist, but—quite incorrectly—to the monster. After Shelley's death by drowning in 1822, Mary returned to London and continued to write. But her *Valperga* (1823) and *The Last Man* (1826) never attained the popularity of her famous first novel.

SHELLEY, Percy Bysshe (1792–1822) has been called the "least embodied" of English poets, and there was about him a luminous and aërial quality that justified the epithet. To use figures from his own poetry, he seems much like a Prometheus bound, a chained west wind, a rebel angel. His short life was one of rebellion against human formulas and dull conventions. He was born, spoiled and proud, of an aristocratic family of Sussex. He was a radical at Eton and was expelled from Oxford for publishing a pamphlet called *The Necessity of Atheism* (1811). In the same year he married a young schoolgirl whom he quixotically thought he was rescuing from the tyranny of home and classroom. Harriet West-brook was not his intellectual equal, and his three years with her were distressing to both. In 1814 he eloped to France with Mary Godwin, the brilliant daughter of the radical reformers, William Godwin and Mary Wollstonecraft. After the unfortunate Harriet had committed suicide in 1816—possibly as the result of a new episode in her life—Shelley married Mary. The couple wandered about Europe meeting many notables; they became acquainted with Byron in Geneva in 1816. In 1818, after Shelley had lost a law-suit for the custody of his children by Harriet West-brook, the Shelleys left England for good. For the remaining four years of the poet's life they lived in Italy, and there in the Gulf of Spezia he met his death by the capsizing of his sailboat, which he handled, according to his friends, with more poetic enthusiasm than nautical skill.

Like most poets Shelley began writing verse in his teens, but only his later fame gave significance to these early poems. His first notable poem was *Queen Mab,* written in 1813 during his first matrimonial adventure. Under the stimulation of his life with Mary Godwin he produced poetry, prose, and poetic dramas that gave him a high rank among English writers. His *Hymn to Intellectual Beauty* (1816) may be regarded as a statement of his creative creed. *Alastor* appeared in the same year, and *The Revolt of Islam*—in Spenserian stanzas—in the year following. In 1819 he wrote the structurally perfect *Ode to the West Wind,* and his famous drama, *The Cenci.* Eighteen-twenty saw *The Cloud,* the *Ode to a Skylark*—perhaps his best-known lyric—and the poetic drama, *Prometheus Unbound,* with its magnificent chorals. *Epipsychidion, Hellas,* and *Adonais*—the fine elegy to the poet Keats—he wrote in the year of Keats' death, 1821. In the same year he issued his best-known prose work, *A Defense of Poetry.*

Matthew Arnold has alluded to Shelley as "a brilliant but ineffectual angel." The epithet is hardly fair. He was undoubtedly impractical, because the dull routine of life irritated his impatient spirit. And he was such a pronounced rebel that he kicked vigorously and persistently against all social and political restraints. But his prose is probably more effectual than that of his father-in-law Godwin. And just what effectuality lyric poetry possesses nobody knows. If to be effectual a poem must move the emotions by beauty of word and phrase, and by melody of rhythm and rhyme, then certainly Shelley's poems are eminently effectual—and often angelic too. He was more sincere and less self-conscious than his friend Byron, and more abstracted and intellectual than the sensuous Keats. With a few exceptions his lyrics have a white radiance of beauty and a rhapsodic quality that appear seldom in English literature. By all measures Shelley is unquestionably one of the great lyric poets of England.

SHENSTONE, William (1714–63). Although he yearned for the literary limelight of London, this shy bachelor spent his days in rural Worcestershire. He wrote verses of all sorts—elegies, songs, ballads, and odes. Despite glimmerings of the new simplicity of the Romantics, they are weighted down by the poetic diction of his time, and have often been compared to the artificial landscaping of Leasowes, the garden in which he religiously puttered. More alive is his best-known work, *The Schoolmistress* (1742), a playful, nostalgic picture of rural education, fashioned in Spenserian stanzas.

SHERIDAN, Richard Brinsley (1751–1816). Like many of the successful comic dramatists of his century, he was born in Ireland. His father, Thomas Sheridan, was an actor and an elocution teacher; his mother was Frances Sheridan, a novelist and a playwright. At twenty-two young Sheridan, not long out of Harrow, made a name for himself in England; he fought two duels over Elizabeth Linley, the celebrated singer, and eloped with her to the Continent. Before he was twenty-four, his first comedy, *The Rivals,* was a famous success at Covent Garden (1775). By the end of the year the same playhouse had also seen his farce, *St. Patrick's Day,* and his comic opera, *The Duenna.* In 1776 he acquired David Garrick's share in Drury Lane Theater, and there the rest of his plays were first produced. *A Trip to Scarborough* (adapted from Vanbrugh's *Relapse,* 1696) and *The School for Scandal* appeared in 1777, *The Critic* in 1779. Finally, after an interval of twenty years, he produced *Pizarro* (1799), an adaptation from the German of the popular Kotzebue.

In the meantime, Sheridan had been successful in another field. He entered Parliament in 1780 and distinguished himself as a member of the Whig opposition under Charles James Fox. In famous speeches against Warren Hastings on the government of

India (1787-8), he gave, according to Edmund Burke himself, "such a display of powers as are unparalleled in the annals of oratory." In 1806 he was made Treasurer of the Navy. Then misfortunes piled up: the death of Fox (1806), the burning of Drury Lane (1809), the loss of his seat in Parliament (1812), his arrest for debt (1813). He died in poverty.

When Sheridan came to the English theater, Comedy, with considerable help from Goldsmith's *Good Natured Man* (1768) and *She Stoops to Conquer* (1773), was just beginning a temporary rally from the sentimental disease which had afflicted it for three-quarters of a century. In three great plays Sheridan resurrected the comic spirit of the Restoration theater. *The Rivals,* except for the sentimental scenes between Julia and Faulkland, is a busy, bustling comedy of situation—reminiscent of Farquhar. *The School for Scandal,* generally considered as Sheridan's masterpiece, is a satire on manners, sparkling with brilliant, epigrammatic dialogue—more in the vein of Congreve's *Way of the World. The Critic* is a classic burlesque of the whole theatrical world—a worthy successor to Buckingham's *Rehearsal* (1671). The three plays are filled with famous rôles. *The Rivals* has Mrs. Malaprop, mistress of the malapropism; Lydia Languish, faithful customer of the circulating library; and "Fighting Bob" Acres, who does not choose to fight. *The School for Scandal* displays Joseph Surface, the "moral" hypocrite; his brother Charles, the good-natured worldling; sharp-tongued Lady Teazle; and scandal-loving Lady Sneerwell. *The Critic* includes Puff, the play-boosting virtuoso turned playwright; Sir Fretful Plagiary, alias contemporary dramatist Richard Cumberland; and the immortal critics, Dangle and Sneer. From time to time, these characters still walk the stage.

SHERWOOD, Mary Martha (1775-1851), who spent much of her life trying to bring Christianity to India, is remembered for a number of nursery classics in which she struggled to save naughty English children from their heathen ways. Mrs. Sherwood's best-known work, *The Fairchild Family* (3 parts, 1818-47), is a collection of moral tales conceived in religious fanaticism and dedicated to the proposition that "all children are by nature evil."

SHIRLEY, James (1596-1666) was a graduate of both Oxford and Cambridge, a convert to Roman Catholicism, a teacher, a soldier, a moralist, and the last of the Elizabethan dramatists. He died of exposure at the Great Fire of London six years after the

Restoration had brought new playwrights and players, and long after he had ceased to be dramatically productive. During his professional lifetime, however, he was very active, and some forty plays have been attributed to him. Of these his tragedies of the reign of Charles I are often pointed to as examples of Jacobean decadence. *The Cardinal* (1641) is better written than *The Traitor* (1631), *The Maid's Revenge* (1626), or *Love's Cruelty* (1631); but even *The Cardinal* is over-complicated in plot and marred by too many exaggerated, if stirring, situations. Shirley's comedies are more important because, as comedies of manners, they anticipated those of the Restoration period. *Hyde Park* (1632), for example, is a satirical representation of high life in London, and *The Gamester* (1633) presents a social group rather than individuals. *The Lady of Pleasure* (1635) seems particularly to foreshadow the comedy of Etherege, Wycherley, and their successors. There is, however, this difference: in spite of occasional coarseness, Shirley is essentially moral; this cannot always be said of Restoration comedy.

SHORTHOUSE, Joseph Henry (1834–1903) wrote *John Inglesant* (1880), a pious "philosophical romance" in which the seventeenth-century hero struggles to find his own faith amid the religious factions of England and Italy. The novel reflects the author's intense interest in the Oxford Movement. Shorthouse achieved his seventeenth-century atmosphere partly by borrowing, without acknowledgment, from seventeenth-century sources.

SIDNEY, Sir Philip (1554–86) was the most complete example in Elizabethan England of the Renaissance type of courtier, scholar, and soldier. As courtier he was verily "the glass of fashion and the mold of form." He was the son of Sir Henry Sidney, nephew of the great Earl of Leicester, and favorite—save for one brief period—of Queen Elizabeth. As scholar he followed the tradition of the court, continued his studies after having graduated from Oxford, became a member of the Areopagus, an exclusive group of writers who defended classical meters in English poetry, and wrote both prose and poetry himself. As soldier he accompanied his uncle Leicester to the Dutch wars and was killed at Zutphen.

Sidney's most important lyrics are not the songs scattered, after the manner of the period, throughout his prose, but his sequence of one hundred and eight sonnets called *Astrophel and Stella* (1591)—the star-lover and the star. These were probably addressed to Penelope Devereux, who married Lord Rich in 1580; there are scholars, however, who insist that they were addressed to Frances Walsingham, whom Sidney himself married in 1583. Whichever lady was honored in them, they form one of the most important of the numerous sonnet groups of the period. Sidney's *Arcadia* (1590) is a pastoral romance dedicated to his sister Mary, Countess of Pembroke, and written for her entertainment. It has the loose structure of the medieval romances and is composed in an elaborate and over-ornamented style, with the prose frequently lapsing into verse. It is notable, however, for its pastoral love episodes and its characterizations of women, and is one of the best examples of the *arcadianism* of the period. The various poems in the *Arcadia* display Sidney's interest in metrical experimentation.

His critical tract *The Defence of Poesy*—also called *Apology for Poetry*—(written about 1580, printed 1595) is, however, his most significant contribution to the literary debates of the times. This was probably a reply to *The School for Abuse,* an attack upon the art written a year earlier by Stephen Gosson. Sidney's tract shows that his literary ideals leaned to the "Ancients" rather than to the "Moderns." To him drama was a form of poetry, the theories expressed in Aristotle's *Poetics* should be followed rigidly, and all literature should teach morality instead of merely entertaining. Outmoded as some of these opinions now are, the *Defence* provides nevertheless a singularly lofty and noble introduction to the long line of English treatises on the art of poetry.

SILURIST, THE. Epithet applied to **Henry Vaughan.**

SINCLAIR, Catherine (1800–64). In addition to a number of forgotten novels for adults, Miss Sinclair wrote several highly popular children's books. Her amusing *Holiday House* (1839), refreshingly free from Victorian moralizing, has been called by Harvey Darton "the first example of modern nursery scepticism."

SINCLAIR, May (1865?–1946) published her first novel, *Audrey Craven,* in 1895 and has written fiction under a number of influences down to the present day. Her first important novel, *The Divine Fire* (1904), has been compared to the work of Meredith, *The Three Sisters* (1914), to that of both Samuel Butler and D. H. Lawrence, *Tasker Jones* (1916), to that of H. G. Wells. In more recent works, notably in *Mary Olivier* (1919), Miss Sinclair has experimented successfully with the impressionistic technique of Dorothy Richardson. Taken as a whole, her novels represent a revolt against the Victorian *mores* and fiction methods, and yet her biographical study, *The Three Brontës* (1912), shows a keen understanding of Victorian characters.

SITWELL, Edith (1887–   ), **Osbert** (1892–   ), and **Sacheverell** (1897–   ). These three talented offspring of Sir George Sitwell, the antiquarian, are inevitably grouped together as eccentrics, both in their poetry and in their personalities. Led by Edith (*Collected Poems,* 1930; *Poems,* 1940; and *Street Songs,* 1942), they have experimented with many of the more radical techniques in modern verse, revolting violently against traditionalism in language and in meter. In addition to their poetry, Edith has published a book on Alexander Pope (1930), Osbert, several novels, and Sacheverell, many studies of art and architecture.

SKELTON, John (1460?–1529) was one of the most conceited poets who ever lived. He never let his readers forget that he held the degree of *Poeta Laureatus* (not to be confused with the laureateship) from Oxford, Cambridge, and Louvain. In his long allegorical dream, *A Goodly Garland of Laurel* (printed 1523), he crowned himself as one of the great poets of all time. He took holy orders in 1498 and at about the same time became tutor to the young prince who was to be Henry VIII. *The Bowge* [free board] *of Court* (written before 1500) is a satire on corruption in the court of Henry VII. *Colin Clout* (written 1519) is a sweeping attack on ecclesiastical graft; *Speak Parrot* (written c. 1521) and *Why Come Ye Not to Court?* (written 1522) are directed specifically against Cardinal Wolsey. As seamy as these satires is *The Tunning* [Brewing] *of Eleanor Rumming* (written c. 1510), the monstrous caricature of an alewife and of those who throng to buy her brew.

Yet Skelton's pen was not always dipped in venom or slime. He wrote *Philip Sparrow* (before 1508), the playful mock-elegy of little Jane Scrope's pet bird, and included in *A Goodly Garland of Laurel* the tender if trifling tributes to Margaret Hussey and Isabel Pennell. He also wrote a complex political morality play, *Magnificence* (1515–23). Although he sometimes used aureate diction and conventional meters, the characteristic "Skeltonic" medium is a racy vernacular poured into fitful doggerel. The short lines and ragged rhymes tumble over one another like the rats in Browning's *Pied Piper.* In both meter and matter Skelton is related to "Hudibras" Butler. But there is really only one John Skelton, *Poeta Laureatus.*

SMART, Christopher (1722–71) paraphrased the Psalms, translated Horace, and published much light satirical verse. But *A Song to David* (1763), written when the poet was at least half mad, is his masterpiece. It is a long poem in biblical language, sometimes strangely confused, sometimes rising into startling beauty.

SMECTYMNUUS. The pseudonym under which five eminent Presbyterian divines of the mid-seventeenth century concealed their identity when they made pamphlet attacks upon the episcopacy in the paper war that preceded the outbreak of military hostilities. The five polemicists were **Stephen Marshall** (1594?–1655), **Edmund Calamy** (1600–66), **Thomas Young** (1587–1655), **Matthew Newcomen** (1610?–69), and **William Spurstow** (1605–66); they constructed their pseudonym from their initials. Their attack was directed principally against Joseph Hall, Bishop of Exeter and Norwich, who replied in 1640 in a violent counter-attack that drew John Milton to the defence of "Smectymnuus." More than two decades after the dust of this wordy battle had settled, Samuel Butler was still satirizing all Presbyterians in the second canto of *Hudibras* under the epithet of "Legion Smec."

SMILES, Samuel (1812–1904) was the author of the popular biographies included in *Lives of the Engineers* (1861–74) and of a series of inspirational works—*Self-help* (1859), *Character* (1871), *Thrift* (1875)—in which he inculcated the Victorian virtues by means of interesting narratives.

SMITH, Adam (1723–90) was both scholar and man of affairs. During the fifties he taught logic and moral philosophy at the University of Glasgow. From 1778 until his death he was Commissioner of Customs for his native Scotland. In his philosophical work, *A Theory of Moral Sentiments* (1759), he stressed the importance of sympathy in human relationships and the social character of morality. In his masterpiece, *An Enquiry into the Nature and Causes of the Wealth of Nations* (1776), he exalted free trade and *laissez-faire,* contending that the individual's untrammeled pursuit of his own interests is most conducive, in the long run, to the public good. This work has been called the foundation stone of political economy. Written in clear expository prose, it has survived to this day as the Bible of the rugged individualist.

SMITH, Alexander (1829–67) was a lace pattern designer in Glasgow. His first volume of poems, *A Life Drama* (1853), was generally popular, but in the following year, W. E. Aytoun in *Firmilian* half-killed it with the laughter of parody. His subsequent volumes, including *City Poems* (1857) and *Edwin of Deira* (1861), were relative failures. Although the "city poem" *Glasgow* and the Poe-like lament *Barbara* have been praised, Smith the poet, like P. J. Bailey and Sydney Dobell, still wears the label which Aytoun stitched upon him—a member of the "Spasmodic School." As a prose writer, however, he is widely admired for the charming informal essays of *Dreamthorp* (1863) and *A Summer in Skye* (1865).

SMITH, Horatio (1779–1849) collaborated with his older brother James (1775–1839) on *Rejected Addresses* (1812), a book of popular parodies. When the committee in charge of the ceremonies at the opening of the new Drury Lane Theater in 1812 advertised for a suitable dedicatory address, the Smith brothers wrote their impressions of what the leading *literati* of the day—including Wordsworth, Byron, Moore, Southey, Scott, Coleridge, and Crabbe —might have said on the occasion.

SMITH, Sydney (1771–1845) became a canon of St. Paul's in 1831, but during most of his life he was a country clergyman. Although an Englishman himself, he helped two Scots, Henry Brougham and Francis Jeffrey, to found the Whig *Edinburgh Review* (1802). In its pages he jested happily, reviewing and reforming without the venom which poisoned the journalism of his day. His best-known long work is *The Letters of Peter Plymley* (1807), a plea for Catholic emancipation. His most popular short work is the *restaurateur's* favorite motto:

> Serenely full, the epicure would say,
> Fate cannot harm me,—I have dined today.

Because of the witty things which he wrote, said, and did not say, Smith ranks with Oscar Wilde as an oft-quoted *bon motist*.

SMOLLETT, Tobias George (1721–71). When this irascible Scot came to London in 1739, he brought along a tragedy intended for the stage. Failing to find a producer, he was forced to fall back on the profession for which he had been trained in Glasgow; he got a job as surgeon's mate on the *Cumberland* and sailed in 1740 on Admiral Vernon's expedition to the West Indies. But his literary aspirations did not die. He saw with open eyes the squalor of navy life and the horrors of the assault on Carthagena, and after his return to London in 1744, he put them into his first novel. *Roderick Random* (1748). Although he took his M.D. in 1750, he eventually abandoned surgery for writing. In addition to writing a popular *History of England* (1757–8) and a farce called *The Reprisal* (1757), he edited two Tory periodicals, the *Critical Review,* from 1756 to 1759, and the *Briton,* in 1762. A short prison term incurred in 1759 for a libel in the *Critical Review* failed to improve his temper. So sour was his *Travels through France and Italy* (1766) that it earned him the rôle of Smelfungus, "the splenetic traveller," in Sterne's *Sentimental Journey* (1768); and his coarse political satire, *The History and Adventures of an Atom* (1769), was one of the bitterest in a bitter age.

Today Smollett is remembered largely for his novels. His first two, *Roderick Random* (1748) and *Peregrine Pickle* (1751), are robust, rambling picaresque romances reflecting their author's own travels. Both contain contemporary figures thinly veiled. The heroes of both—unprincipled rogues, courageous but unchivalrous, witty but dirty-minded—wander aimlessly through pages of violent deeds, practical jokes, and scandalous amours, each with his faithful squire, each finally settling down with a virtuous wife whom he does not deserve. *Ferdinand Count Fathom* (1753) is an even more violent rogue story with a background of Gothic horrors and a really black villain in the title rôle. *Sir Lancelot Greaves* (1760–1), the first English novel published in serial form, is an inferior imitation of Cervantes' mock-heroic *Don Quixote* (1605, 1615), with the scene shifted to eighteenth-century England. Just before his death at Leghorn, Italy, Smollett wrote *Humphry Clinker* (1771); in this, the mellowest of his novels, he depicted, in the popular epistolary form, the follies of an eccentric Welsh family on tour through England, Scotland, and Wales.

Smollett is conventionally classified as one of the four major novelists in the middle of his century. He lacked Richardson's power of character analysis, Fielding's sanity and depth, Sterne's ingenuity and wit. On the whole, he looked backward rather than forward. His work as a pioneer in the field of Gothic horror is of questionable value. He did, however, create the first reasonably authentic scenes from navy life, anticipating such later novelists as Marryat and Conrad. His characters—nautical figures like Lieutenant Bowling and Captain Oakum (*Roderick Random*), Commodore Trunnion and Lieutenant Hatchway (*Peregrine Pickle*), as well as landlubbers like Roderick's faithful Strap and testy Matthew Bramble (*Humphry Clinker*)—tend to be caricatures. But they helped to inspire a lover of Smollett named Charles Dickens.

SOMERVILLE, William (1675–1742) is known best as the author of *The Chace* (1735), a long blank-verse poem on hunting which reveals the influence of Thomson's *Seasons*. Somerville also wrote *Hobbinol* (1740), a blank-verse burlesque of rural games, and *Field Sports* (1742), a short poem on falconry.

SOUTHERNE, Thomas (1659–1746). Although he saw nearly half of the eighteenth century, Southerne is commonly remembered as a Restoration writer. It was during the last years of his friend and collaborator, John Dryden, that he wrote his most popular plays, two tragedies entitled *The Fatal Marriage* (1694) and *Oroonoko* (1695). The former deals with "innocent adultery"; the latter is an early drama on the noble savage theme. Each is based on a novel by the irrepressible Aphra Behn and betrays the wild but fascinating melodrama of its source.

SOUTHEY, Robert (1774–1843). In 1813 Southey became poet laureate. At that time Coleridge, the good-for-nothing young poet with whom in his radical youth Southey had planned a Utopian "Pantisocracy" in Pennsylvania, was wasting his glorious talents in drugs and despair. Today everybody knows the poems of Coleridge, but few can name one by Southey. And posterity has been right. This prolific "Laker" had neither the imaginative power of Coleridge nor the intellectual insight of Wordsworth. His exhaustive project for "exhibiting all the more prominent and poetical forms of mythology which have at any time obtained among mankind, by making each the groundwork of an heroic poem" seems strangely dated now. The fantastic epics which grew out of it—*Thalaba* (1801), *Madoc* (1805), *The Curse of Kehama* (1810), and *Roderick, the Last of the Goths* (1814)— are now studied, if at all, as evidence of the Romantics' fancy for distant climes and varied meters. Two earlier works, the verse play *Wat Tyler* (written in 1794, published without the author's permission in 1817) and the narrative poem *Joan of Arc* (1796), are interesting largely as illustrations of Southey's early radicalism. *A Vision of Judgment* (1821), the laureate's vindication of George III, is not so well known as Byron's bitter travesty of it. Better known than all these are a few short schoolboy favorites, *The Inchcape Rock,* a melodramatic ballad of the sea, *The Battle of Blenheim,* a pacifistic ballad, and *The Cataract of Lodore,* an exercise in metrical virtuosity. Southey was a good prose writer. The radical-turned-Tory contributed for years to the *Quarterly Review;* wrote two substantial histories, *A History of Brazil* (1810–29) and a *History of the Peninsular War* (1823–32); and two readable biographies, *The Life of Nelson* (1813) and *The Life of Wesley* (1820). The *Nelson* is one of the best-known biographies in English.

SOUTHWELL, Robert (1561?–95) was a Jesuit priest who wrote most of his poems during the two and a half years of torture in prison before he was executed for his faith. He dedicated himself to the work of supplanting profane poetry with sacred. *Saint Peter's Complaint* (1595) is a long, conceit-laden poem in which the repentant disciple tells the story of his Master's last days. The most celebrated of Southwell's shorter poems is *The Burning Babe,* first published in the collection called *Maeoniae* (1595). It is a devout lyric about the Christ-child's sufferings for the sins of man.

SPEED, John (1552?–1629), like John Stow, was a tailor turned historian. He was the author of a patriotic *History of Great Britain* (1611), published in the same year as his atlas, *The Theater of the Empire of Great Britain.*

SPENCER, Herbert (1820–1903). Charles Darwin's *Origin of Species* was published in 1859. In 1860 appeared Herbert Spencer's *Program of a System of Synthetic Philosophy.* This was the blueprint for the work of the rest of his life, a Gargantuan attempt to synthesize all knowledge in accordance with the doctrine of evolution. *First Principles* (1862), *Principles of Biology* (1864–7), *Principles of Psychology* (1870–2), *Principles of Sociology* (1876–96), and *Principles of Morality* (1879–93)—these are some of the monuments to his Herculean effort. As an educationist (*Education, Intellectual, Moral, and Physical,* 1861) Spencer upheld the sciences at the expense of the humanities. As a political thinker (*The Man versus the State,* 1884), he helped to spread the dangerous doctrine of *laissez-faire* individualism. Like Thomas Henry Huxley, he was a popularizer of science, particularly of evolution. But since he could not write like Huxley, he has not earned a similar place in the domain of literature.

SPENDER, Stephen (Harold) (1909–   ) belongs—with Auden, MacNeice, and C. Day Lewis—to the remarkable group of younger poets who were at Oxford together in the late twenties. An ardent enemy of fascism and friend of communism, he has advocated the use of literature to promote political action and has poured into eloquent poetry his own yearnings for political justice and international comradeship. Among his works are *Vienna* (1934), a poetic indictment of Nazi Germany; *Trial of a Judge* (1938), a verse drama on the struggle between fascism and communism; *The Destructive Element* (1934), a volume of criticism; and *The Burning Cactus* (1936), a collection of short-stories. *The Backward Son,* a novel, appeared in 1940.

SPENSER, Edmund (1552?–99). "The poets' poet" was the epithet bestowed upon Edmund Spenser by Charles Lamb. It is neat and fitting. In no sense can Spenser be considered "popular"; he is too sophisticated, too scholarly, too classical to be anything but "caviar to the general." On the other hand, no poet has given greater delight to craftsmen in verse; his imagination, his stateliness, his good taste, his richness of line and word, his picturesqueness, his magic rhythms have drawn poets to read and to imitate him. Thomson, Burns, Keats, Tennyson—to name only a few of his followers—have all taken from his storehouse.

Spenser was born in London, the son of a clothier. After having taken two degrees from Cambridge University, where he studied Greek and Latin with enthusiasm, he entered the service of the Earl of Leicester and so became the friend of Leicester's nephew, the popular Sir Philip Sidney, to whom he dedicated *The Shepheardes Calender* (1579). Through this acquaintanceship and that of his scholarly Cambridge friend Gabriel Harvey, Spenser was subjected to the influences of the Areopagus, a select group of classicists who scorned rhyme as barbaric. His admiration for Plato inspired his early hymns in honor of Love and of Beauty, published later with hymns in honor of Heavenly Love and Heavenly Beauty, as *Fowre Hymnes* (1596). In *The Shepheardes Calender* (1579) he imitated the Greek and Latin pastorals. In these twelve eclogues—one for each month of the year—his "shepheardes" are symbols under whose classical names he conceals himself and many of his literary acquaintances. He is Colin Clout, complaining because of his rejection by Rosalind—a Lancastrian charmer of Spenser's early acquaintance—and because his piping no longer finds favor with the patrons of song.

In 1580 "Colin Clout" went to Ireland as secretary to Lord Grey de Wilton, Lord Deputy there. History records Grey as a harsh governor; Spenser praises him not only as Artegall, or Justice, in book five of *The Faerie Queene,* but also in his prose *View of the Present State of Ireland,* a report not published until 1633. In 1586 Spenser was granted Kilcolman Castle in Munster, and here, three years later, Sir Walter Raleigh found him busily at work on *The Faerie Queene,* which he had projected years earlier. Raleigh's urging took Spenser to London with the manuscript of the first three books. They were published in 1590 with a dedication to Queen Elizabeth, the "greatest Gloriana" of the poem. When the dedication brought Spenser no adequate return in patronage, he expressed his disappointment in *The Teares of the Muses,* a lament on the low state of poetry through the neglect of its patrons, and in *Prosopopoia, or Mother Hubberds Tale,* an allegorical satire on the abuses of church and court. Both appeared in 1591 in the collection called *Complaints*. His return to Ireland in 1591 was celebrated in *Colin Clouts Come Home Againe* (1595), which commemorates Raleigh's visit to Kilcolman Castle and gives Spenser's impressions of the Elizabethan court. Three years later he married Elizabeth Boyle, daughter of an Irish nobleman, possibly the Elizabeth whom he courted in his sonnet sequence *Amoretti* (1595). Two marriage hymns, *Epithalamion* (1595) and *Prothalamion* (1596), were written in honor of court nuptials and espousals. In 1596 Spenser returned to London with books four, five, and six of *The Faerie Queene,* and saw them published, together with the first three. He went back to Ireland the next year. It was his last return home; in the savage Tyrone rebellion against the English, Kilcolman Castle was burned to the ground, and Spenser, with his wife and four children, fled to Cork. Disappointed, broken-spirited, and emotionally exhausted, he returned to London only to die there suddenly in 1599.

The most famous of Spenser's poems is, of course, *The Faerie Queene.* Here, turning from the "oaten reeds" of pastoral poetry to the "trumpets sterne" of knightly romance, he planned, as he explained in the dedication to Sir Walter Raleigh, to embody forth twelve virtues in twelve knights of Arthur's court. On each of the twelve days of the annual feast of the Faerie Queene a knight would undertake an adventure; but either the whole poem was not completed, or the last part of the manuscript was burned at Kilcolman. The six books completed deal with the adventures of the following champions: (I) The Red Cross Knight (Holiness); (II) Sir Guyon (Temperance); (III) Britomart and Belphoebe (Chastity); (IV) Triomond and Cambell (Friendship); (V) Artegall (Justice); (VI) Calidore (Courtesy). Two cantos on "Mutability" from an unfinished seventh book appeared in 1609. The poem is complex with interwoven allegory, religious, political, moral. The stanzas are crowded with characters that symbolize contemporary persons at Elizabeth's court. She herself appears not only as the Faerie Queene but also as Una (Truth), Britomart and Belphoebe (Chastity), and other characters. The stories move with the slow tempo of a tapestry in a draft, and the poem is much more descriptive than narrative. The vehicle of expression is the famous "Spenserian stanza," a stately nine-line stanza of which the first eight lines are iambic pentameter and the ninth an iambic hexameter or "Alexandrine." And to give the poem the flavor of the Middle Ages, Spenser used archaic word-forms, not all linguistically accurate but all effective in creating an impression of richness, strangeness, and remoteness in time. It is the attractive weaving of this metrical and verbal pattern that has made Spenser "the poets' poet."

SPRAT, Thomas (1635–1713), Bishop of Rochester, was at one time chaplain to Buckingham and may have had a share in writing the duke's *Rehearsal* (1671). He published his celebrated *History of the Royal Society* in 1667, only five years after that famous body received its charter. In it he announced the aim of the society "to reject all the amplifications and digressions of style" in favor of "a close, naked, natural way of speaking." Bishop Sprat practised what he and his fellow-members preached, and his history is traditionally cited as one of the first steps in the Restoration revolt against ornate prose.

SQUIRE, (Sir) J(ohn) C(ollings) (1884–   ), founder and editor (1919–34) of the *London Mercury,* has written serious poetry, plays, and numerous critical essays, but is best known as the most accomplished contemporary English parodist. His *Collected Parodies* appeared in 1921.

STANLEY, Thomas (1625–78) was the author of *The History of Philosophy* (1655–62), traditionally regarded as the first work of its kind in English. He also edited Aeschylus (1663), translated works of Anacreon, Bion, Moschus, and others, and wrote some excellent love songs, including "When I lie burning in thine eye" and "I prithee let my heart alone." The first of these is strikingly like Lovelace's *To Althea from Prison.*

STEELE, Sir Richard (1672–1729) was born in Dublin but spent most of his life in England. One of the earliest memories of Thackeray's Henry Esmond is of Corporal Dick Steele of the King's Life Guards, fresh out of Oxford without a degree, hiccuping a solemn sermon through his drunkenness, reaching for his sword when his comrades laugh at his religion, and, having fallen flat upon his face, looking up at his young admirer with "Ah, little Papist, I wish Joseph Addison was here!" The same mixture of dignity and buffoonery, moral solemnity and carefree wit permeates Steele's writings. While still in the army, he published a sober tract, *The Christian Hero* (1701), "with a design to fix upon his own mind a strong impression of virtue and religion, in opposition to a stronger propensity towards unwarrantable pleasures." At the same time he set out to second Jeremy Collier in reforming the English stage. His early comedies, *The Funeral, or Grief à-la-Mode* (1701), *The Lying Lover* (1703), *The Tender Husband* (1705), although not without traces of humor, are dripping with the sentimental didacticism which was to characterize eighteenth-century drama; and his last comedy, *The Conscious Lovers* (1722), contained, as Fielding's Parson Adams remarked, "some things almost solemn enough for a sermon."

Steele is best known as the founder of the *Tatler* (April 12, 1709–January 2, 1711) and the *Spectator* (March 1, 1711–December 6, 1712). These unique periodicals, directly through their instant popularity in the London coffee-houses, and indirectly through their prolific progeny, had untold influence on the history of English manners and the course of the English essay. Steele's old schoolfellow Addison collaborated with him on the *Tatler* and was the guiding spirit of the *Spectator*. Their names have become inseparable. Generally speaking, Steele's contributions are marked by warmth often merging into sentimentality and ease sometimes bordering on mere garrulity; those of his fellow-worker by more polish, austerity, and restraint. Steele's later adventures in journalism—including the *Guardian* (1713), the *Englishman* (1713–14), the *Lover* (1714), and the *Theatre* (1720)—were less successful. His political fortunes rose and fell with those of the Whig party. He was made official government gazetteer in 1707 and was removed in 1710; elected to Parliament in 1713 and expelled the next year; made patentee of Drury Lane Theater in 1715 and ousted three years later. He died in poverty in Wales.

STEPHEN, James Kenneth (1859–92) was a master of light verse who followed in the footsteps of C. S. Calverley. His verse is collected in *Lapsus Calami* and *Quo Musa Tendis,* both published in 1891. His parodies of Byron, Wordsworth, and others are intelligent literary criticism.

STEPHEN, Sir Leslie (1832–1904). The father of the novelist Virginia Woolf is well known to students of English literature as the author of lives of Johnson (1878), Pope (1880), Swift (1882), and others in the *English Men of Letters* series, and as the first general editor (1882–91) of the *Dictionary of National Biography*. His varied achievement in other fields includes his *History of English Thought in the Eighteenth Century* (1876), *The Science of Ethics* (1882), and—a defense of his own creed—*An Agnostic's Apology* (1893).

STEPHENS, James (1882–1951) was an Irishman who figured in the modern Irish Renaissance. Like Yeats and Æ, he drew widely on ancient Celtic folklore, both in his simple lyrics and in his fiction. His prose fantasy, *The Crock of Gold* (1912), is a charming compound of mystic beauty and pointed satire; his *Collected Poems* appeared in 1926.

STERN, G(ladys) B(ronwyn) (1890–   ) is one of the wittiest of modern English novelists. She made her reputation with her sixth novel, *Children of No Man's Land* (American edition, *Debatable Ground*), in 1919. More celebrated are *Tents of Israel* (American edition, *The Matriarch: a Chronicle*) (1924), and its sequel, *A Deputy Was King* (1926). The two novels comprise a genealogical chronicle about a Jewish family. Her autobiography she called *Another Part of the Forest* (1941). In 1944 she collaborated with Sheila Kaye-Smith on *Speaking of Jane Austen,* a critical appreciation which reveals her as a devoted "Janeite."

STERNE, Laurence (1713–68) was born in Ireland, where his father was stationed as a subaltern in the army. He took a B.A. from Cambridge in 1736 and an M.A. there four years later. In 1738 he became vicar of Sutton-in-the-Forest, a tiny village near York; this was the first of several church livings. His marriage to Elizabeth Lumley (1741) was unhappy; she became insane in 1758, and in 1767 they separated permanently. The most publicized of his numerous flirtations was with Eliza Draper, to whom he addressed the *Letters from Yorick to Eliza* (1773). When in 1760 Sterne published the first two volumes of nine-volume *Tristram Shandy* (1760–7), he bounded suddenly from such obscurity as is allowed to an eccentric churchman with an eye for the women into the limelight of literary London. And when he came up from York in person, he played the witty, shocking jester—the poor parson Yorick of his book—to perfection. Dodsley immediately rushed into print with the first two volumes of *The Sermons of Mr. Yorick* (1760–9), and two more volumes of *Tristram Shandy* were out in 1761. But Sterne was already threatened by consumption. From 1762 to 1764 he lived on the Continent for his health, and in 1765 he made the famous "sentimental journey through France and Italy." He died in poverty in London.

Sterne was the last of the four major mid-century novelists to enter the field. In his single novel—unless his travel book can be so classified—he outdid Smollett in defying the standards of patient craftsmanship established by Richardson and Fielding. *The Life and Opinions of Tristram Shandy, Gentleman* deals with a period of Tristram's life long before he was old enough to have opinions. The "hero" is conceived in the first book, born in the third, christened in the fourth, given his first breeches in the sixth, and calmly overlooked in the remaining three. In the meantime, his creator is following the whims of a rudderless mind. He wanders in interminable digressions. He flits from mood to mood—from honest tenderness to calculated sentimentality, from indecent innuendo to unblushing bawdry—now exercising his own original wit, now stealing freely from Swift, Montaigne, Erasmus, Burton, "dear Rabelais and dearer Cervantes." The most casual glimpse at the work—with its asterisks, dots and dashes, sentences unfinished, pages blank, black, and marbled—betrays Sterne's random whimsy—or, if the reader is no "Shandean," his belated adolescence. Yet in this medley move some of the timeless characters of fiction: Walter Shandy, the retired business man who reads philosophy and lives in a world of abstract theories; Uncle Toby, the war veteran who projects his narrow world in miniature fortifications on the bowling green, and who, literally, will not hurt a fly; the widow Wadman, his determined pursuer; Corporal Trim, his faithful squire; Dr. Slop, the man-midwife; and last but not least, poor Yorick himself.

The sentimentality which appears in *Tristram Shandy* is given full sway in *A Sentimental Journey Through France and Italy* (1768). In this unfinished travel book (for he never got to his Italian travels) Sterne chose to dwell only on the pleasures of touring, on "gentle passions and affections." His book presents a deliberate contrast with the peevish *Travels* (1766) of Smollett, whom Sterne caricatured as "Smelfungus," "the splenetic traveller." Hence Yorick undergoes the exquisite pleasure—to an eighteenth-century "man of feeling"—of weeping over the corpse of a dead donkey near Boulogne.

STEVENSON, John Hall (1718–85) was the author of several volumes of coarse verse, the most celebrated of which is *Crazy Tales* (1762), a collection of obscene *fabliaux* adapted or imitated from the French. He was the Eugenius of his friend Sterne's *Tristram Shandy* and wrote a continuation (1769) of *A Sentimental Journey*.

STEVENSON, Robert Louis (Balfour) (1850–94) was a hopeless consumptive unable to pursue the ancestral occupation of lighthouse engineer along the misty coasts of Scotland. He travelled far from his native Edinburgh in a lifelong search for health and romance—to America, where he married a California widow, finally to Samoa, where he died at forty-four. The natives there worshipped him as "Tusitala," Teller of Tales. It was a fitting epithet. As a travel-writer in books like *Travels with a Donkey*

(1879) and *Across the Plains* (1892), he is still entertaining; as an essayist (*Virginibus Puerisque*, 1881; *Familiar Studies of Men and Books*, 1882) he is still charming in an age which prefers natural simplicity to elegance wrought by "playing the sedulous ape" to past prose masters; as a verse writer (*A Child's Garden of Verses*, 1885) he is one of the timeless magicians of the nursery. But as a teller of tales—short tales like *A Lodging for the Night* (1882), *The Sire de Malétroit's Door* (1882), and *The Merry Men* (1887), long tales like *Treasure Island* (1883), *Dr. Jekyll and Mr. Hyde* (1886), *Kidnapped* (1888), and the unfinished *Weir of Hermiston* (1896)—he has dwarfed his other achievements. Stevenson reawakened England to the reality of Romance in an age when "Naturalism" and "Realism" were the watchwords of fiction. And he had these arguments for those who mocked him: If his characters were puppets, it was because action is more important than character; if he escaped from life into a never-never land, it was because only in the world of Romance does a man actually begin to live.

STEVENSON, William (fl. 1553–60) is the leading candidate for the authorship of *A Ryght Pithy, Pleasaunt and merie Comedie: Intytuled Gammer gurtons Nedle: Played in Christes Colledge in Cambridge. Made by Mr. S. Mr. of Art.* *Gammer Gurton's Nedle* is the second of the surviving Tudor comedies (the first is *Ralph Roister Doister* by Nicholas Udall) to follow the "regular" act divisions of the Latin dramas of Terence and Plautus. It is a rollicking farce in which Diccon the Bedlam, a mischievous vagrant, puts a village into an uproar by playing a series of practical jokes on the natives. The play may have been composed before the death of Edward VI in 1553. An earlier suggestion for "Mr. S., Master of Art" is John Still, bishop of Bath and Wells, but the evidence in support of his authorship is not so good as that for William Stevenson.

STEWART, Dugald (1753–1828) was professor of moral philosophy at Edinburgh for twenty-five years (1785–1810). Among his works are *Elements of the Philosophy of the Human Mind* (1792–1827), *Outlines of Moral Philosophy* (1793, etc.), and *Philosophical Essays* (1810). In general, Stewart was a believer in the "common sense" philosophy of his fellow-Scotsman, Thomas Reid.

STIRLING, Earl of. See **ALEXANDER, William.**

STOW, John (1525?–1605) was an ambitious tailor with a passion for research. He published an edition of *The Works of Geoffrey Chaucer* (1561) and several straightforward "histories,"

AUTHORS [*Stubbes*

including *The Chronicles of England from Brute until this present year of Christ* (1580). But he is most celebrated as a topographer. His painstaking *Survey of the Cities of London and Westminster* (1598) is an exceedingly valuable source book for study of Elizabethan London.

STRACHEY, (Giles) Lytton (1880–1932) has been called "the father of modern biography." In the short preface to his *Eminent Victorians* (1918) he struck the keynote of his art. He ridiculed the typical two-volume Life-and-Letters of the Victorian biographer, with its formlessness and flattery, and announced his intention of writing brief biography, artistically proportioned, "dispassionately, impartially, and without ulterior intentions." In the four short biographies of *Eminent Victorians*—lives of Cardinal Manning, Florence Nightingale, Thomas Arnold, and General Gordon—and in the more substantial *Queen Victoria* (1921), he put this doctrine to the proof. If his efforts to dispel the fond illusions of the Victorians were not always free from ulterior intentions, they resulted certainly in well-proportioned works of art. Strachey's later works include: *Books and Characters* (1922), a series of essays on literary figures; *Elizabeth and Essex* (1928), a full-length romantic biography which borders on fiction; and *Portraits in Miniature* (1931), a collection of informal biographical sketches. Although Strachey wished nothing for English biography which had not existed in the work of masters long before his time, his followers hailed him as the prophet of a new era. Many tried to imitate his brilliant, if artificial, rhetoric and to catch his subtle irony, only to produce instead pretentious exercises in debunkery.

STRUTT, Joseph (1749–1802) was the author and illustrator of a number of important antiquarian studies, including *A Complete View of the Manners, Customs, Arms, Habits, etc. of the Inhabitants of England, from the Arrival of the Saxons till the Reign of Henry VIII* (1775–6) and *The Sports and Pastimes of the People of England* (1801). His unfinished historical romance, *Queenhoo Hall,* was completed by Scott and published in 1808.

STUBBES, Philip (fl. 1581–91) was the author of a Puritan pamphlet called *The Anatomy of Abuses* (1583), in which he undertook to "discover" the "notable vices and imperfections" which prevailed throughout the world, especially in England. Like Gosson before him and Prynne and Collier in the next century, Stubbes included a fanatical attack on the theater. He was answered by that redoubtable pamphleteer Thomas Nashe in *The Anatomy of Absurdity* (1589).

271

STUBBS, William (1825–1901) was professor of history at Oxford and bishop of Chester and of Oxford. In addition to resurrecting and editing many old charters and chronicles, he wrote *The Constitutional History of England in its Origin and Development* (1874–8), covering the period from the beginnings down to 1485, a three-volume study of comprehensive range.

STUDLEY, John (b. 1547?) made scholarly translations of Seneca's *Agamemnon* (1566), *Medea* (1566), *Hercules Oetaeus* (1567), and *Hippolytus* (1567) into English closet tragedies. In 1581 these translations were included in the comprehensive volume of Seneca's ten tragedies.

SUCKLING, Sir John (1609–42). When Suckling poisoned himself in Paris at thirty-four, he left behind, among other pieces, three bad plays and a sheaf of worldly letters. But, like Lovelace, he is famous for a few poems. His two songs, "Why so pale and wan, fond lover?" (from *Aglaura,* 1638) and *Constancy* (1646), have the carefree cynicism, though not the intellectual subtlety, of the gayer Donne. *A Ballad upon a Wedding* (1646) has touches of charming delicacy in the midst of empty doggerel. But when in *The Sessions of the Poets* (1637) he wrote of himself:

> "He loved not the Muses so well as his sport"

Suckling was not fooling. For he scribbled verse with a careless left hand. He would rather be remembered as gambler and gallant, master of bowls and cribbage, laughing soldier under two kings—the perfect Cavalier.

SURREY, Henry Howard, Earl of (1517?–47). As a boy, Surrey frolicked at Windsor with the Duke of Richmond, illegitimate son of Henry VIII; in his middle teens he married Lady Frances Vere; in his twenties he was wounded in battle in France; and at thirty, condemned by the senile English monarch on a silly charge of treason, he went to the scaffold. In English literature he is inseparable from the older friend whose death he lamented in verse, Sir Thomas Wyatt. They were the pioneer poets of the English Renaissance. The sonnets and short lyrics of both were published for the first time in *Tottel's Miscellany* (1557). At its best Surrey's verse is more graceful than his friend's, although not more original. Good examples are the two sonnets, *Description of the Spring Wherein Each Thing Renews Save Only the Lover* and *Complaint of a Lover Rebuked,* and the simple translation from Martial,

The Means to Attain Happy Life. More important than his poems themselves, however, are Surrey's two portentous contributions to English prosody: the sonnet of four quatrains and a final couplet, later called "Shakespearean"; and his translation of Books II and IV of Vergil's *Aeneid* (1554-7) into the first blank verse in English.

SURTEES, Robert Smith (1803-64) was a popular sports novelist who specialized in stories of hunting. His plotless tales are still useful to the historian of English rural life. He anticipated Dickens in several ways; *Pickwick Papers* (1836-7) is a direct descendant of Surtees' farcical serial, *Jorrocks' Jaunts and Jollities* (1831-4).

SWIFT, Jonathan (1667-1745) was the most sardonic and savage of the major British satirists. These qualities were inherent in him and were developed by his boyhood experiences and later disappointments. He was born in Dublin, the posthumous son of a penniless Englishman, and brought up grudgingly by an Irish uncle. After an erratic career at Trinity College, Dublin, he became—about 1692—half-secretary, half-pensioner in the household of Sir William Temple, the diplomat, essayist, and classicist, who had retired to his beloved gardens at Moor Park near London. Some months later Swift returned to Ireland, where he was ordained in 1694, but he re-entered the Temple household in 1696 and remained there until his employer's death in 1699. At Moor Park he first met Esther Johnson, the daughter of a servant of Temple's sister. He came to love her as Stella in one of the strangest love affairs in the history of English literature.

Five years after having been bluntly rebuffed by Dryden for attempting to write poetry, Swift wrote his first prose satire, *The Battle of the Books* (written 1697, published 1704), a defense of the "Ancients" against the encroachments of the "Moderns" in the literary battle then raging. When he left Moor Park, he obtained a meager church living at Laracor in Ireland, and here Stella joined him. But in 1704 he went far toward wrecking his chances of advancement in the Church of England by publishing *A Tale of a Tub,* an allegorical attack not only on the Roman Catholics and the Calvinists, but also—more mildly—on his own denomination.

Between 1704 and 1713, when he was appointed Dean of St. Patrick's Cathedral (Church of England) in Dublin, Swift visited London periodically and entered actively into the religious and political turmoil of the time. In 1708 he published his mocking *Argument Against Abolishing Christianity,* a classic example of

irony, and the first of his playful *Bickerstaff Papers* (1708–9), a
sustained literary prank in which he so ably predicted the death and
described the funeral of the popular astrologer John Partridge, that
he completely ruined his victim's reputation and business. In the
same year appeared a rival for Stella, Esther Vanhomrigh (pronounced Vanummery), the daughter of an Irish trade commissioner. For some time Swift carried on a curious correspondence
with her, addressing her as "Vanessa" and signing himself "Ca-
denus" (an anagram for Decanus or Dean). But his letters to
Vanessa are in no way as interesting or charming as his pathetic
Journal to Stella, a private love diary composed in London between 1710 and 1713. The *Journal* is written in a sort of baby
talk which Swift called his "little language," and reveals a totally
different person from the self-important dean or the bitter pamphleteer. Vanessa's death in 1723 does not seem to have affected
Swift seriously, but that of Stella five years later marks the beginning of a decline in health and mental power that ended in outright insanity. In spite of the long and close companionship between Swift and Stella, there is no positive evidence that they
ever married.

Much as he seems to have hated Ireland, Swift defended the
Irish on numerous occasions. In the *Drapier's Letters* (1724) he
blasted the plan of a rascal named William Wood to impose a
debased·coinage upon the unhappy country. In *A Modest Proposal*
(1729) he ironically suggested a plan "for preventing the children
of poor people from being a burden to their parents or the
country" by systematically fattening them for the tables of the
rich.

Gulliver's Travels (1726) is Swift's greatest and most famous
satire. Under the fiction of reporting the adventures of Lemuel
Gulliver, Swift vents all his misanthropy in a succession of savage
attacks on human folly and viciousness. The shipwrecked hero
visits Lilliput, where the people are six inches high; Brobdingnag,
a land of giants; the flying island of Laputa and the nearby continent of Lagado; and eventually arrives at the equine Utopia in
which the Houyhnhnms, a nation of gentle and wise horses, are
served by filthy, bestial men called Yahoos. The narrative is so
accurately documented and drawn to such careful scale that Swift
almost forces belief in his fantastic fictions, and *Gulliver's Travels*
—substantially expurgated—is still read in the nursery as an enchanting fairy tale. Many readers are unaware that the unex-
purgated work is a vicious satire which ranges through attacks on
politicians, philosophers, scientists, soldiers, and society women,

until, fairly frothing at the mouth in his savage indignation, the author lashes without restraint the whole wretched race of mankind.

SWINBURNE, Algernon Charles (1837–1909). In 1866 Swinburne fired one of the opening guns in the literary revolt against the conventional *mores* of Victorian England. His *Poems and Ballads,* including such frankly sensual lyrics as *Laus Veneris* and *Anactoria,* appalled his more conservative contemporaries, and he became notorious overnight as a dangerous rebel—"The Victorian Byron." In the twentieth century, with the fires of moral indignation considerably cooled, criticism has centered more often in the riddle of whether Swinburne was a great poet with a rare ear for melody or only a prodigious virtuoso in versification who occasionally rose to real poetry.

He was born in London but divided his boyhood years between the Isle of Wight and Northumberland. After leaving Eton, he went to Balliol College, Oxford, but left without taking a degree. In 1860 appeared his first poetry, two immature closet tragedies in blank verse, *The Queen Mother* and *Rosamond*. They were dedicated to D. G. Rossetti, an Oxford acquaintance who became one of Swinburne's most intimate friends, and whom he later praised as the most distinguished of Victorian poets.

In 1865 appeared *Atalanta in Calydon,* a tragedy in which he succeeded admirably in recapturing the spirit of Greek legend. One of its choruses, the melodious *Hymn to Artemis* ("When the hounds of spring are on winter's traces"), is Swinburne's best-known poem. In the same year appeared *Chastelard,* the first of a series of closet tragedies on Mary, Queen of Scots; *Bothwell* (1874) and *Mary Stuart* (1881) complete the trilogy. *A Song of Italy* (1867) and *Songs before Sunrise* (1871) deal with the cause of Italian freedom. *Songs of the Springtides* (1880) and *Studies in Song* (1880) are lyrics of the sea. With *Tristram of Lyonesse* (1882), his most ambitious narrative poem, Swinburne invaded the rich realm of medieval legend.

During the first two decades of his literary career, he lived part of the time in London, where he associated with Rossetti and the other Pre-Raphaelites, and part of the time on the Continent, where he met Walter Savage Landor and became immersed in French and Italian literatures. In 1879, worn out by continual illness, he became the house-guest of the poet and critic, Theodore Watts-Dunton, at Putney Hill, and there he lived for the last thirty years of his life. These years saw the publication of *Marino*

Faliero (1885), *Astrophel* (1894), *A Tale of Balen* (1896), *A Channel Passage* (1904), and *The Duke of Gandia* (1908)—all inferior to the best of his early poetry.

Swinburne's poetry reveals a variety of themes and qualities: the warm pagan sensuousness which he shared with Rossetti and with his French master Baudelaire; the fondness for the classics which he had in common with Landor; an interest in the Middle Ages like that of another friend, William Morris; a hatred of religious and political tyranny which he caught partly from Shelley and Victor Hugo; a love of the sea which echoed one of the oldest and most dominant notes in English literature. But many readers think of the numberless verse forms, old and new, the flawless manipulation of anapests and dactyls, the infinite monotony of onomatopoeia and alliteration. The reader of Swinburne is in danger of becoming either so bemused by this metrical witchery that the meaning vanishes amid the melody, or so fascinated that he pauses continually in mid-poem for a lesson in prosody.

Despite his absorption in poetry, Swinburne also devoted much time to writing biographical and critical monographs. He was an ardent student of the Elizabethan drama and wrote essays on Shakespeare, Ben Jonson, George Chapman, and other playwrights of the period. Many of his critical sketches appeared in the *Encyclopedia Britannica;* others were collected in *Essays and Studies* (1875) and *Miscellanies* (1886). As an essayist Swinburne was stimulating but over-enthusiastic—a panegyrist rather than an evaluator of literary art.

SWINNERTON, Frank (Arthur) (1884–   ) is a novelist who has concentrated largely on lower-middle-class life in London. Among his novels are *Nocturne* (1917), considered by many as his masterpiece, *Shops and Houses* (1918), *Young Felix* (1923), and *The Elder Sister* (1925). His critical works include *The Georgian Literary Scene* (1935) and studies of George Gissing (1912) and R. L. Stevenson (1914). Swinnerton's novels are sometimes compared to Gissing's.

SYMONDS, John Addington (1840–93) spent much of his life in Italy because of ill-health. His *magnum opus* is his sevenvolume *History of the Renaissance in Italy* (1875–86). Among his other works are *Studies of the Greek Poets* (1873–6), a translation of *The Autobiography of Benvenuto Cellini* (1888), and short biographies of Shelley (1878), Sir Philip Sidney (1878), and Ben Jonson (1886). Symonds was a disciple of John Ruskin, and often his prose is even more ornate than his master's.

SYMONS, Arthur (1865–1945) composed poems and plays and made numerous translations, but he is best known as a critic. A follower of Walter Pater, he was concerned chiefly with measuring the intensity of his own personal response to works of art. His study of *The Symbolist Movement in Literature* (1899) introduced T. S. Eliot to the French symbolists who have so strongly influenced Eliot's poetry. Symons also published studies of Blake (1907), D. G. Rossetti (1910), Hardy (1927), Wilde (1930), and Pater (1932).

SYNGE, John Millington (1871–1909) ranks with Yeats and Lady Gregory among the major figures of the modern renaissance in Irish drama. He was born in Dublin and educated there at Trinity College. After graduation in 1892, he spent some years wandering over Europe. In 1898 he was "discovered" by Yeats in a Paris garret and persuaded to come back to Ireland and write. On his return, he lived for a time among the simple fisher-folk of the Aran Islands off the stormy western coast. Out of this and similar contacts grew his rare plays about the Irish peasantry: *The Shadow of the Glen* (1903), *Riders to the Sea* (1904), *The Well of the Saints* (1905), *The Playboy of the Western World* (1907), *The Tinker's Wedding* (1907). Only in his last play, *Deirdre of the Sorrows* (1910), did Synge go beyond contemporary life to the folklore of his native land. Of the six plays, the one-act tragedy *Riders to the Sea* and the full-length comedy *The Playboy* are often considered as his best.

Because Synge wrote honestly about living people, both *The Shadow of the Glen* and *The Playboy* have aroused fierce resentment in some quarters as slanderous misrepresentations of the Irish. But their author was not a realist in the prosaic sense of the word. He accused the Norwegian master Henrik Ibsen of "dealing with the reality of life in joyless and pallid words." "In a good play," Synge wrote, "every speech should be as fully flavoured as a nut or apple, and such speeches cannot be written by anyone who works among people who have shut their lips on poetry." Synge listened to "herds and fishermen along the coast from Kerry to Mayo," to "beggar-women and ballad-singers nearer Dublin," and, through a chink in the floor, to the musical chatter of servant girls in a County Wicklow kitchen. He caught the joyful and melancholy music of this speech and transferred it to paper, and it has been beautifully conveyed to the stage by the inimitable players of the Abbey Theater. This is Synge's signal contribution to the modern drama.

T

TALFOURD, Sir Thomas Noon (1795–1854) was the jurist whose speeches were instrumental in the passing of the Copyright Act of 1842 and the friend of Charles Lamb who published the humorist's *Letters* (1837) and *Final Memorials* (1848). His once-popular *Ion* (1836), a frigid imitation of Greek tragedy, is now seldom read.

TATE, Nahum (1652–1715) succeeded Shadwell as poet laureate in 1692. He had written a sacrilegious adaptation of Shakespeare's *King Lear* (1680) and, with some help from Dryden, the second part of *Absalom and Achitophel* (1682). After his coronation as laureate he collaborated with Nicholas Brady on a popular verse version of the Psalms (1696), wrote *Panacea: A Poem upon Tea* (1700), and ground out countless periodic poems on less sacred subjects. Tate's *Lear,* in which the Fool is missing, Edgar is in love with Cordelia, and the tragic plot dissolves in sudden bliss —was the standard acting version until the nineteenth century.

TAYLOR, Ann (1782–1866) and **Jane** (1783–1824) were the chief authors of *Original Poems for Infant Minds* (1804–5), a volume of children's verses, both pleasant and forbiddingly moral. It includes that oft-parodied classic, *My Mother,* as well as the cautionary tale about the naughty boy who went fishing and got caught on a meathook himself. The book mothered a moral brood, including the Taylors' own *Rhymes for the Nursery* (1806), with Jane's "Twinkle, twinkle, little star," and *Hymns for Infant Minds* (1808). The sisters Taylor have been been called the inventors of the "awful warning" school of poetry.

TAYLOR, Sir Henry (1800–86) wrote a number of blank-verse dramas in the Elizabethan tradition, including *Isaac Comnenus* (printed 1827), *Philip van Artevelde* (printed 1834), *Edwin the Fair* (1842), and *St. Clement's Eve* (printed 1862). The second of these, a historical drama of fourteenth-century Flanders, reveals Taylor as an intelligent student of character and, in parts, as a real lyric poet. Although it failed on the stage, it has appealed to many readers. Taylor also wrote *The Statesman* (1836), a volume of worldly essays on how to succeed in politics.

TAYLOR, Jeremy (1613–67). During the civil war between Royalists and Puritans in the first half of the seventeenth century, Archbishop Laud was executed by order of Parliament, and many more Royalist clergymen suffered punishment. One of the most famous of these religious servants of the Crown escaped, however, with comparatively mild penalties. Jeremy Taylor was chaplain to Laud and also chaplain-in-ordinary to King Charles I. He accompanied his royal master on the Cavalier campaigns and was ultimately captured at the battle of Cardigan Castle in 1645. On this occasion he was soon released, but in 1654 and 1655 he was imprisoned on three separate occasions. During the reign of Charles I, Taylor was Rector of Uppingham in Rutlandshire (1638) and of Overstone in Northamptonshire (1643). After his series of imprisonments he retired to Golden Grove in Carmarthenshire, Wales, where he served as chaplain and teacher while continuing his writing. A year after the restoration of Charles II to the throne (1660) he became Bishop of Down and of Connor in Ulster.

Taylor's first important treatise was *The Sacred Order and Offices of Episcopacy* (1642). This was followed during the period of Puritan power by *A Discourse of the Liberty of Prophesying* (1647)—a defense of episcopacy—*The Rule and Exercises of Holy Living* (1650), and *The Rule and Exercises of Holy Dying* (1651), two manuals of Christian conduct. *The Golden Grove, or a Manual of daily prayers and litanies* (1655) is his famous guide to Christian devotions. In the two books that have brought Taylor his greatest fame, *Holy Living* and *Holy Dying,* his literary characteristics are best displayed. These pleas for the practice of Christian virtues reveal religious enthusiasm, tempered by deep understanding of human weakness and compassion for mortal man. The style is often spun-out, loose, and florid, with perhaps too many illustrations drawn from classical sources and modern instances. But the lushness of Taylor's exposition is compensated for by harmony, delicacy of phrase, and above all clarity.

TAYLOR, John (1578–1653). This self-confident, irrepressible hack styled himself "The Water Poet" because he was, for some time, a waterman on the Thames. He was appallingly prolific in both doggerel and prose. In 1630 he published *All the Workes of Jon Taylor the Water Poet Beeing 63 in Number Corrected, Revised;* but modern bibliographies list over 160 titles, many of them puckishly alliterative, including pamphlets and broadsides on every imaginable subject. If Taylor had a specialty, it was tall tabloid tales of his own far-flung travels; such a one is *The Pennyles Pilgrimage, or the Moneylesse Perambulation of John Taylor, from London to Edenborough* (1618). Many of his feats of travel were performed, like Will Kemp's morris dance from London to Norwich, to carry out wagers.

TAYLOR, Tom (1817–80) wrote a great number of actable plays, some in collaboration and some adapted from French and German sources. Among his better-known comedies are *Masks and Faces* (1854), written with Charles Reade, and *Our American Cousin* (1858), the play at a performance of which Abraham Lincoln was assassinated. Taylor's serious prose dramas include the melodramatic *Ticket-of-Leave Man* (1863), with its celebrated Detective Hawkshaw. He also wrote historical dramas in verse on Anne Boleyn (1875) and Joan of Arc (1871). He was the editor of *Punch* from 1874 until his death.

TEMPLE, Sir William (1628–99) was the man whom Dorothy Osborne married after she had written him some of the best letters in the language; the conscientious diplomat who effected the triple alliance of England, Holland, and Sweden in 1668 and the match between William and Mary in 1674; the retired gentleman gardener of Moor Park, where his secretary, Jonathan Swift, first met "Stella." Temple wrote graceful, cadenced prose on too many subjects. His political essays, *Upon the Present State of Ireland* (1668) and *Upon the Origin and Nature of Government* (c. 1671), are superficial. In his *Essay Upon the Ancient and Modern Learning and of Poetry* (1692) his all-out argument for the Ancients is not strengthened by his patent ignorance of the Moderns; but his participation in the timeworn academic argument earned him a prominent rôle in Swift's *Battle of the Books* (1704). In less serious essays like *Upon the Gardens of Epicurus* he anticipated the sane familiar essay of Addison and Steele.

TENNYSON, Alfred, Lord (1809–92) was the most English of the poets of the nineteenth century, the voice of Victorian England. For nearly half a century, as poet laureate after the death of Wordsworth in 1850, he was by popular acclaim the king of English poets, his high ideals, nobility of character, and skillful craftsmanship keeping his crown unchallenged. Tennyson was born in a rectory at Somersby in Lincolnshire, not far from the sea that flows and ebbs in so many of his poems. He was the fourth of a family of twelve children. Two of his brothers, Frederick and Charles, were also writers of verse, although they came far from attaining his distinction. The work of all three is represented in *Poems by Two Brothers* (1827). The year after this publication Alfred entered Trinity College, Cambridge, where he led an exceedingly active life as member of the Apostles, a group that included Arthur Henry Hallam, subject of Tennyson's *In Memoriam*. The year before the poet's graduation in

1831, appeared *Poems, Chiefly Lyrical;* it was succeeded by a second volume in 1832 (under date of 1833). These early lyrics of the future laureate are definitely romantic in spirit and technique and reveal the marked influence of Keats. They have at once the merits and the defects of much of Tennyson's poetry, a clear melody that is partly destroyed by self-conscious artificiality and prettiness.

In the same year (1833) Hallam, Tennyson's dearest friend and the fiancé of his sister Emily, died suddenly in Vienna, and the rupture of this David and Jonathan companionship shocked the young poet profoundly. In memory of his friend, Tennyson began the long elegy *In Memoriam* and labored upon it for seventeen years until its publication in 1850. *In Memoriam* ranks with Milton's *Lycidas* and Shelley's *Adonais* as one of the greatest elegies in English. It is more than a tribute to Hallam; it is also the expression of the poet's struggle to find again the faith that was shattered by his friend's death. That he did not succeed entirely in this objective is indicated by Bishop Wilberforce's ironic allusion to Tennyson's "minimum basis of faith" and by Hiram Corson's characterization of *In Memoriam* as "that beautiful poem of nineteenth-century skepticism." But it cannot be denied that some of the loftiest of Tennyson's thinking and feeling are expressed in the quatrains of this greatest of his long poems.

In 1842 his two-volume *Poems* was published, and his reputation and popularity were secure. Even before this publication he had begun work on his *Idylls of the King,* although the first series of these Arthurian poetic romances was not to appear until 1859. The popularity of the poet's retold tales from old Malory came probably from the circumstance that they were Victorian rather than medieval. It has been ironically said, indeed, that Tennyson's knights wore Prince Albert coats, and his ladies crinoline. It is certain that the moral and social patterns of the *Idylls* are those of the nineteenth and not of the fifteenth century. But Tennyson's contemporaries loved their flavor, their color, and their melody. *The Princess* (1847) is a semi-burlesque romance in which the higher education of women is rather grotesquely satirized; although popular enough in an age which thought that woman's place was in the kitchen and nursery, the poem is badly dated in the twentieth century, excepting for the magnificent incidental lyrics, like the famous "Bugle Song."

In 1850, the year of his appointment to the laureateship, Tennyson married Emily Sellwood; three years later he took residence on a farm on the Isle of Wight, where he lived until his final removal to Aldworth in Blackdown, Surrey, in 1867. His formal and rather stiff and pompous *Ode on the Death of the Duke of Wellington* appeared in 1852; three years later came *Maud*, a romance of love and hate, with its popular "Come into the garden" lyric. In 1864 he experimented with Yorkshire dialect in the two *Northern Farmer* poems. In the same year he published *Enoch Arden,* the sentimental tale of a self-sacrificing sailor that is perhaps his most mawkish poem. His love of England led him to write three poetic historical dramas: *Queen Mary* (1875), *Harold* (1876), and *Becket* (1884); of this trilogy only the last was successful in production. In 1884, too, he was raised to the peerage as Baron Tennyson. *Tiresias and Other Poems* (1885), *Locksley Hall Sixty Years After* (1886)—a sequel to *Locksley Hall* (1842)—*Demeter and Other Poems* (1889)—including his requiem *Crossing the Bar*—and *The Death of Oenone* (1892) are evidences that the aging laureate maintained his poetic power and energy to the last.

Tennyson's popularity was firmly rooted in a human sympathy and in a complete understanding of Victorian life and thought. Although by no means erudite, he was scholarly, and the range of his knowledge was wide, covering contemporary science as well as ancient and modern literary art. He was essentially romantic in his inclinations and drew much of his inspiration—as did Keats—from the Middle Ages; but he also made use of classical materials, as he did in *Ulysses, The Lotos-Eaters, Oenone,* and numerous other poems. These raw materials of his workshop he poured into Victorian molds, and so he remained neither medievalist nor Greek but Victorian. He was, moreover, distinctly insular, a poetic "little Englander" whose interests hardly extended beyond the limits of the British Isles. He was a persistent experimenter in verse, and he was the best self-critic of the Victorian poets, seldom rewriting a line without improving it. His consciousness of his high calling as a "bard" and especially as England's bard, kept him from being universal. The ornateness, lushness, sentimentality, didacticism, artificiality, and occasional inanity of his poetry are defects inherent in romantic verse but peculiarly characteristic of his work. They made it impossible for him ever to be high priest of a Tennyson cult, but they did not decrease his popularity.

THACKERAY, Anne Isabella. See **RITCHIE.**

THACKERAY, William Makepeace (1811–63) was born in India, son of a well-to-do civil servant. At public school in Eng-

land he was a "lazy, idle boy," who preferred drawing and reading to fighting. After unsuccessful ventures at law, journalism,
and painting (although he was later a fair illustrator of some
of his own books), he decided to write for a living. His early
work includes facile mimicry of the false notes in contemporary
novels (*Novels by Eminent Hands, Punch,* 1847), satire on the
affectations of the aristocracy and the pretensions of social climb-
ers (*The Memoirs of Mr. C. J. Yellowplush, Fraser's Magazine,*
1837–8; *The Book of Snobs, Punch,* 1846–7), travel books (*The
Paris Sketch Book,* 1840), and light verse. He had published one
full-length novel, picaresque *Barry Lyndon* (1844), before *Vanity
Fair* (1847–8) won him permanent fame in that field. *Vanity
Fair* is a survey of a section of English society in the first half of
his century—centered in the parallel lives of two contrasting
schoolmates—adventuress Becky Sharp and clinging vine Amelia
Sedley. *Pendennis* (1848–50) is a semi-autobiographical study of
a young man's career; *The Newcomes* (1853–5) is Pendennis'
story of the affairs of an upper-middle-class family. The first of
Thackeray's two historical novels, *Henry Esmond* (1852), is a carefully contrived masterpiece breathing the atmosphere of Queen Anne
England and actually written, as if by its chivalrous hero, in the
language of the *Spectator. The Virginians* (1857–59) is its less
successful sequel.

Except in *Henry Esmond,* Thackeray cared little for form;
he spun his novels out serially, projecting as he went, regularly
intruding his bespectacled, broken-nosed face before the reader
to interrupt the story with a gratuitous moral comment, sometimes a whole personal essay. His characters, however, he took
seriously. He specialized in the upper classes and respected the
Victorian taboos. But within these limits he was a master char-
acter-painter, usually avoiding or ridiculing the sentimental and
romantic nonsense of his contemporaries and showing people as
he saw them, beset with vanity and sham. At the height of his
success he gave gossipy lectures in England and America on
The English Humourists of the Eighteenth Century (published
1853) and *The Four Georges* (published 1860). From 1860 to
1863 he edited the *Cornhill Magazine* and contributed to it his
whimsical familiar essays, *Roundabout Papers.*

THEOBALD, Lewis (1688–1744), whose name is pronounced
and sometimes spelled "Tibbald," was crowned "King of Dulness" in the first edition of Pope's *Dunciad* (1728) and held the
throne until he was succeeded by Cibber in the 1743 edition.

Theobald's crime was his *Shakespeare Restored, or a Specimen of the many Errors as well committed as unamended by Mr. Pope, in his late Edition of this Poet* (1726). The objections to Pope's sloppy edition were thoroughly justified, but Theobald did not enhance his dignity as a scholar by the bitter recrimination which he injected into the notes of his own edition of Shakespeare (1733). Among his many intelligent textual emendations, the classic is the line on Falstaff's death (*Henry V*, II, 3): "'A babbled of green fields." Theobald also composed several plays, non-dramatic poems, and translations.

THOMPSON, Francis (1859–1907). Like Coventry Patmore, his literary master, and Alice Meynell, who befriended him in his poverty, Thompson was a devout Roman Catholic. Students have traced in his work the influence of the fervid Catholic poet of the seventeenth century, Richard Crashaw. His only famous poem is *The Hound of Heaven* (*Poems*, 1893), a deeply religious ode on the pursuit of the rebellious Christian by God's love. Here Thompson's gorgeous imagery is profoundly moving. But in his best-known prose work, the essay on Shelley (1909, written 1889), the rich diet of metaphors can quickly spoil the reader's appetite for meaning.

THOMSON, James (1700–48) first came to London from his native Scotland in 1725. In five years he had published all four parts of his first major work, *The Seasons: Winter* (1726), *Summer* (1727), *Spring* (1728), *Autumn* (1730). The work belongs to a transitional stage in the history of English poetry; in his frequent flights of artificial rhetoric and his Latinate diction, Thomson looks backward; in his first-hand observation of Nature and the use of blank verse in place of the traditional heroic couplet, he looks ahead to the Romantics. At the end of his life he published his other major work, *The Castle of Indolence* (1748), a half-playful allegory, in Spenserian stanzas, of his own lazy existence at Richmond. Despite its relative lack of seriousness, it is one of the best of many imitations of *The Faerie Queene*. Thomson probably wrote the patriotic song, *Rule Britannia!* (in *Alfred, a Masque,* published 1740). He certainly wrote *Liberty* (1735–6), a prolix verse salute to the reigning Whigs, and *Sophonisba* (1730), a bombastic tragedy. The latter has been kept from utter oblivion,. with the help of Fielding's *Tom Thumb* (1730), by a single line of magnificent bathos: "O Sophonisba! Sophonisba O!"

THOMSON, James (1834–82). A childhood spent in poverty, the death of the girl he loved, dismissal from the army which he served as schoolmaster, unconquerable insomnia—there were reasons why this introspective Scot did not believe, with most of his fellow Victorians, that God was on his side and progress was inevitable, excuses if not reasons for his eventual resignation to aimlessness, atheism, and alcohol. *The City of Dreadful Night* (1874), by which he is remembered, is a beautiful but desperately pessimistic poem on the miseries of London after dark. Few writers in any language have plumbed the depths of such despair. Although he wrote some cheerful poetry, Thomson is permanently labelled with such epithets as "the poet of pessimism" and "the English Poe."

THRALE, Hester Lynch, later **Piozzi** (1741–1821) and her first husband became acquainted with Dr. Johnson in 1765. During the years that followed, the great man was their constant guest at their home in Streatham, and the acquaintance deepened into intimate friendship. But Thrale died in 1781, and when, in the next year, his widow broke up her household to marry Gabriel Piozzi, an Italian music-teacher, Johnson ended the friendship in a bitter letter. In 1786 Mrs. Piozzi published *Anecdotes of the late Samuel Johnson* and two years later *Letters to and from the late Samuel Johnson*. Both works have proved invaluable to Johnson scholars.

TICKELL, Thomas (1685–1740) was a member of the "little senate" of Whigs who sat at the feet of Joseph Addison. His verse, some of which appeared in the *Spectator* and the *Guardian*, includes a sincere elegy *On the Death of Mr. Addison*. Tickell's translation of the first book of Homer's *Iliad* appeared in 1715, the same year as Pope's, and Pope, convinced that the rivalry had been inspired by Tickell's master, never forgave Addison.

TOMKIS, Thomas (fl. 1607) was the author of two Cambridge University comedies, *Lingua* (1602–7) and *Albumazar* (1615). The first is a spirited anatomical allegory in which the tongue argues against the five senses in defense of his right to qualify as a sixth. It is written in mixed prose and verse and is full of allusions to contemporary plays.

TOMLINSON, H(enry) M(ajor) (1873–1958) was a writer of essays, novels, and travel-books. *London River* (1921) is a collection of essays and sketches, *Gallions Reach* (1927), a romance of adventure at sea, and *All Our Yesterdays* (1930), a novel dealing with the backgrounds of the First World War.

TOTTEL, Richard (d. 1594) collaborated with Nicholas Grimald on *Songs and Sonnets* (1557), popularly known as *Tottel's Miscellany*. In this famous anthology the shorter poems of Wyatt and Surrey appeared for the first time. Among them were the earliest sonnets in English.

TOURNEUR, Cyril (1575?–1626) was a soldier in the Netherlands and spent much of his life there. His cruel experiences in fighting against Spanish tyranny may have given him the taste for brutal situations that emerges in his two blood-chilling plays, *The Revenger's Tragedy* (1606–7) and *The Atheist's Tragedy* (1607–11). In a group of Jacobean tragedies that run riot with incest, rape, and murder none are so terrifying and unrestrained as these two. Tourneur reveled in "horrid" situations. In one such a lecherous duke is poisoned by being tricked into kissing the skull of the girl he has seduced; in another the avengers stamp on their victim. The characters are, of course, grossly exaggerated, flyblown with evil passions. Tourneur's own death was as tragic as those of some of his characters, for he died miserably of wounds received in the Cadiz expedition under Sir Edward Cecil.

TRAHERNE, Thomas (1637?–74). Three of Traherne's works appeared in the seventeenth century, *Roman Forgeries* (1673), *Christian Ethics* (1675), and *A Serious and Pathetical Contemplation of the Mercies of God* (1699). Except for eight poems in the second of these and three in the third, they are in prose, and Traherne was known largely as a prose-writer until Bertram Dobell announced in 1900 his "discovery" of "an unknown seventeenth-century poet." Three volumes of verse followed in the next decade: *The Poetical Works* (1903, 1906), *Centuries of Meditations* (1908), and *Poems of Felicity* (1910). Despite the interest of this discovery, most readers today believe that Traherne's musical prose is superior to his verse. In both prose and verse, he wrote mystically, like Vaughan in *The Retreat,* about the spiritual wisdom of childhood.

TRELAWNY, Edward John (1792–1881) was at Leghorn with Shelley when the poet was drowned and accompanied Byron on his last journey to Greece. He commemorated his two friends— with considerable prejudice against Byron—in *Recollections of the Last Days of Shelley and Byron* (1858). He portrayed his own fabulous career as a Byronic hero in the semi-autobiographical novel, *Adventures of a Younger Son* (1831). In 1940 Margaret Armstrong revived interest in Trelawny with a best-selling biography.

TRENCH, Richard Chenevix (1807–86), Dean of Westminster and Archbishop of Dublin, is best known as the pioneer philologist who wrote *On the Study of Words* (1851). He also published poetry, both religious and profane (*Poems,* 1841; *Alms: and Other Poems,* 1855).

TREVELYAN, Sir George Otto (1838–1928) and **George Macaulay** (1876–   ). The two distinguished historians, father and son, have followed in the footsteps of T. B. Macaulay, who was the uncle of one, great-uncle of the other. The elder Trevelyan's first major work was the classic *Life and Letters of Lord Macaulay* (1876). It was followed by three works on a central theme: *The Early History of Charles James Fox* (1880), *The American Revolution* (1899–1907), and *George the Third and Charles Fox* (1912). G. M. Trevelyan is best known to students of English literature for his readable studies of English history: *England under the Stuarts* (1904), *A History of England* (1926), *England under Queen Anne* (1930–4), and *English Social History . . . Chaucer to Queen Victoria* (1942). He has also written three works on the Italian patriot Garibaldi (1907–11).

TREVISA, John de (1326–1412). This Cornish churchman is celebrated as one of the earliest English translators. His translation of Higden's *Polychronicon* appeared in 1387. Besides rendering Higden's Latin history of the world into pungent colloquial Middle English, Trevisa made several additions, including some comments on the growing importance of the English tongue. The work was printed by William Caxton in 1482.

TROLLOPE, Anthony (1815–82) was the son of the novelist Frances Trollope. He successfully combined two careers. At the General Post Office (1834–67) he rose from an awkward, tardy clerk to a trusted foreign envoy. As a writer he clicked off novels, short-stories, and travel books steadily for thirty-five years (1847–82). How he served both masters—rising at 5:30, scribbling his self-assigned daily stint on trains and steamboats, one eye always on his watch—and still found time for his beloved fox-hunting and lounging at the Garrick Club—he tells in his frank, worldly *Autobiography* (1883). Today his political novels, such as *Phineas Finn* (1869) and *The Prime Minister* (1876), are not so widely read as are two of his "chronicles of Barset," *The Warden* (1855) and *Barchester Towers* (1857). The "Chronicles" are a series of stories of life in a cathedral town. Trollope shunned the calculated surprise and suspense of Wilkie Collins' plots and disliked the caricatures of Dickens. Like his master, Thackeray, he concentrated on "living with" his characters through successive novels, painting them from the life with quiet, indulgent satire. The people of Barchester—conscientious Warden Harding, proper Archdeacon Grantly, ineffectual Bishop Proudie, the bishop's henpecking wife, and his oily, ambitious chaplain, Obadiah Slope—are not easy to forget.

TROLLOPE, Frances (1780–1863). This amazing mother began writing after fifty to support an impoverished, consumption-ridden family and produced 114 volumes before retiring at seventy-six. Neither of her best-known novels (*The Vicar of Wrexhill*, 1837; *The Widow Barnaby*, 1839) is as famous as her *Domestic Manners of Americans* (1832), a bitter travel book which did not improve international relations. One of two literary sons, Anthony, was a novelist equally prolific and more talented.

TUPPER, Martin Farquhar (1810–89) was the author of *Proverbial Philosophy* (1838), a collection of commonplaces in insipid verse. So great is the gulf between the worth of the work and its appalling popularity among the Victorians that it has become trite to laugh at Tupper's triteness. One shudders to reflect that his other works include *Geraldine: a Sequel to Coleridge's Christabel* (1838).

TURBERVILLE, George (1540?–98) did most of his literary work at second-hand. He translated Ovid's *Heroical Epistles* (1567), Mantuan's *Eclogues* (1567), and *Tragical Tales . . . out of sundry Italian* (1587). His only collection of original verse, *Epitaphs, Epigrams, Songs and Sonnets* (1567), reveals the influence of Wyatt and Surrey.

TUSSER, Thomas (1524?–80). His *Five Hundred Points of Good Husbandry* appeared in 1573, an enlargement on the one hundred of 1557. The book is a quaint compendium of doggerel proverbs, particularly on Tusser's specialty, farming. In Tusser one can discover that "Christmas comes but once a year" and that "April showers bring May flowers."

TYNDALE, or TINDALE, William (d. 1536). With the coming of the Protestant Reformation to England in the early sixteenth century came also the need for translating the Bible from "the original tongues" into English. From the reign of Henry VIII (1509–47) to that of James I (1603–25) scores of zealots and scholars, laboring at a dozen great translations, turned the period into a century of Bible-making. The first of all these learned and devoted workers was also the most heroic, for he was the only one who died a martyr to his faith. William Tyndale was well equipped for his task of making it possible for "every plowboy" to read the Bible. Not only did he know Latin, Greek, and Hebrew, but he had the spirit that drove him steadily against strong opposition, and succeeded in his plan in spite of great odds.

The first of his translations, based upon both the ancient texts and the old Wycliffe versioin of the fourteenth century, was printed at Cologne in 1525 or 1526. This was a small octavo printing of a part of the New Testament; only two copies are known to have survived. Tyndale completed his translation of the "Christian Book" and added to it the Pentateuch and the Book of Jonah. His second edition appeared in 1534. At about this time also he seems to have worked with Miles Coverdale on the first complete printed Bible in English. The "Coverdale Bible" came from the presses in October, 1535, just a year before the zealous Tyndale was executed. Tyndale's pioneer labors did not result in a complete Bible that bears his name. But to his scholarship, his industry, his literary skill, and his holy zeal all subsequent translators of the Bible have been indebted; and the greatest of all translations, the "King James" version of 1611, is filled with the felicitous phrasing of the first of the modern translators of the scriptures into English.

TYNDALL, John (1820–93) was a poor Irish boy who grew up to succeed Michael Faraday as Superintendent of the Royal Institution of London. Although he did valuable original research in physics, he was not too proud to talk to the populace. Such books as his *Fragments of Science for Unscientific People* (1871) do not have the literary finish of similar works by his friend and colleague, Thomas Henry Huxley; but Tyndall was a better public speaker than Huxley and did more than his share to spread the gospel of science. His *Belfast Address* (1874) on the relation between science and religion is still widely reprinted.

TYRWHITT, Thomas (1730–86) published *Observations and Conjectures upon Some Passages of Shakespeare* (1766) and, in an appendix to his second edition (1778) of the "Rowley Poems," exposed Chatterton's famous forgeries. But his most important work is *The Canterbury Tales of Chaucer, to which are added an Essay upon his Language and Versification* (1775-8). Tyrwhitt was the first scholar to understand the basic principle of Chaucer's meter. Before his time even such an appreciative critic as Dryden had regarded it as crude and primitive.

U

UDALL, Nicholas (1505–56) was head master of two famous schools, Eton and Westminster. His *Ralph Roister Doister* (written before 1553), a school play, preceded *Gammer Gurton's Needle* (ascribed to William Stevenson, written c. 1553) as the first "regular" English comedy. The farcical tale of the duping of Ralph, the braggart, by Matthew Merygreek, is told in rhyming doggerel. The recipe is from Plautus, but the play is topped with an English sauce.

URQUHART, Sir Thomas (1611–60). The story that this eccentric Scottish royalist died in a fit of laughter on hearing of the Restoration of Charles II is probably apocryphal. But he was certainly "born with the gift of laughter and a sense that the world is mad." In his lesser works—one of which, *Ekskubalauron* (1651), contains a famous account of "the Admirable Crichton"—he often revels in the polysyllabic gibberish of mock-erudition as if he were allergic to plain sense. But this very gusto made his version of the first three books (1653–93) of the French satirist Rabelais one of the best translations in English.

USK, Thomas (d. 1388) was a Londoner who was executed by the Gloucester faction during the reign of Richard II. His *Testament of Love,* a long prose allegory, might well be forgotten had it not once been ascribed to Chaucer.

V

VANBRUGH, Sir John (1664–1726). This son of an expatriate Flemish merchant was a distinguished architect who also constructed a number of successful comedies. *The Relapse, or Virtue in Danger* (1696) was a cynical sequel to Cibber's *Love's Last Shift* (1696), with Loveless, the reformed husband, temporarily relapsing into libertinism and Sir Novelty Fashion metamorphosed into funnier Lord Foppington. *The Provoked Wife* (1697) introduced cowardly Sir John Brute reeling drunk through the streets in a parson's gown. *The Confederacy* (1705) is singular among Restoration comedies for its middle-class background. The half-finished *Journey to London* was completed by Cibber as *The Provoked Husband* (1728). Vanbrugh paints with the broad brushes of farce and caricature, and has more in common with "brawny" Wycherley than with Congreve. Jeremy Collier, the play-damning divine, found his first two comedies happy hunting grounds for "immorality and profaneness."

VAUGHAN, Henry (1621–95). Many of the early poems of this Welsh physician (*Poems,* 1646) are conventional secular lyrics, including playful conceits for "Amoret" and "Etesia." But Vaughan is remembered among the metaphysical poets for a few sacred lyrics from *Silex Scintillans* (two parts, 1650, 1655). In *The Retreat* he anticipated Wordsworth's *Intimations of Immortality* (1807), voicing a wish to "travel back" and relive the "angel-infancy" before his "second race" on earth. In *The World* ("I saw Eternity the other night") he rails at the earth-bound mortals who will not fly towards the Light. In *Departed Friends* ("They are all gone into the world of light") he longs quietly for immortality. Vaughan wrote with a deeper, more mystical insight than his master, Herbert; his poems are less ecstatic, less tangled in conceits than Crashaw's. In his devotion to Nature, he is often compared with Wordsworth. Because of his love for Southern Wales, the land of the ancient Silures, he is called "the Silurist."

VAUX, Thomas, Baron (1510–56). Two of the poems of this courtier appeared in *Tottel's Miscellany* (1557); one of them, *The Aged Lover Renounceth Love,* was the source of the first grave-digger's melancholy chant in *Hamlet* (V, 1). Most of his verse was published in a later anthology, *The Paradise of Dainty Devices* (1576).

VILLIERS, George. See **BUCKINGHAM.**

W

WACE of Jersey (fl. 1160–70) wrote the *Roman de Brut* (c. 1154), a Norman-French paraphrase in rhymed verse of Geoffrey of Monmouth's *Historia Regum Britanniae* (c. 1135). Wace made appreciable additions to King Arthur's rôle. About a half century later Layamon used his poem as a basis for his *Brut,* the earliest English version of the Arthurian legend.

WAKEFIELD MASTER (late fourteenth century). This epithet has been given to the anonymous author of one group of the miracle plays of the Wakefield, or Towneley, cycle of biblical dramas. These scenes from the Old and the New Testaments were played by the craftsmen of the village of Wakefield in Yorkshire in the second half of the fourteenth century during the lifetime of Chaucer; they have been preserved in a fifteenth-century manuscript once owned by the Towneley family but now in the Huntington Library in California. Of the thirty-two playlets in this cycle a group of four seems to have been the work of a single writer who has been characterized by Charles M. Gayley as "our first great comic dramatist, the anonymous Player-Clerk of Wakefield." Attempts have been made without much success to identify him with one Gilbert Pilkington. Whatever his name, the Wakefield Master remains the most realistic, the most comic, the most satirically alive of all the creators of English miracle plays. To him belongs the distinction of having written the most famous of the miracle plays in English, the *Secunda (Pagina) Pastorum,* or *Second Shepherds' Play* of the Wakefield cycle. In this half-farcical production the rascally sheep-thief Mak and his unscrupulous wife Gyll appear on the same stage with the Virgin Mary and the Christ Child of the conventional nativity play.

WALLER, Edmund (1606–87). During a long public career, in Parliament and out, this wealthy, witty courtier revealed himself to his own century as a soft, selfish political opportunist. To ours, he is known chiefly as the author of two perfectly polished love lyrics: *On a Girdle* and "Go, Lovely Rose" (both from *Poems,* 1645). Between his youthful poem in couplets on *His Majesty's Escape at St. Andere* (1625) and the *Divine Poems* (1685) of his old age, Waller wrote numerous occasional verses. He professed his love for Lady Dorothy Sidney ("Saccharissa") and his devotion to Oliver Cromwell (*A Panegyric to My Lord Protector,* 1655); and critics have questioned the sincerity of both professions. He is historically important as an early experimenter with the closed couplet and as a poet who, in a time when lyric grace was often sacrificed to metaphysical brilliance, strove hard for ease and sweetness. Dryden wrote: "He first . . . made writing easily an art" and Pope: "Waller was smooth."

WALPOLE, Horace, fourth earl of Oxford (1717–97) was the youngest son of Sir Robert Walpole, famous prime minister. He himself sat in Parliament from 1741 to 1767. In 1747 he began to live at Strawberry Hill, his "little Gothic Castle" on the Thames at Twickenham. Here he collected curios, played with hidden panels, and established the printing press which turned out two Pindaric odes of his friend, Thomas Gray, and his own *Castle of Otranto* (1764). Walpole's Gothic story, traditionally considered as the first of its type in English literature, was only half serious; but others took it very seriously, and the shadow of Otranto, with its giant ghost, its diabolical usurper, and its poor but princely rightful heir, fell across English fiction for half a century. Half-scholar, half-dilettante, Walpole also wrote verse, history, art criticism, and drama. His most substantial monument, however, is a collection of over three thousand letters. They present a charming picture of a witty cosmopolite and an invaluable record of sixty-five years (1732–97) of English social history.

WALPOLE, (Sir) Hugh (Seymour) (1884–1941) was born in New Zealand, the son of a clergyman who later became Bishop of Edinburgh. He was educated in England, where, after a short career of teaching and preaching, he began to write novels. His understanding of school life is reflected in *Mr. Perrin and Mr. Traill* (1911), a "tragi-comedy" about two schoolmasters, and in the popular boys' books, *Jeremy* (1919) and *Jeremy at Crale* (1927). His experience with the Red Cross in Russia (1914–16) resulted in *The Dark Forest* (1916) and *The Secret City* (1919). He drew on his clerical background in writing *The Cathedral* (1922). This novel and others have been compared to the works of Anthony Trollope, whose biography Walpole wrote for the *English Men of Letters* series (1928). He was also the author of *Rogue Herries* (1930–33), an imposing historical novel in four parts. *The Killer and the Slain* (1942) was published after his death.

WALTON, Izaak (1593–1683) was a London shopkeeper who loved reading, conversation, and fishing, and who retired at fifty-one to devote his whole time to these loves. He has been called the first professional English biographer. He wrote affectionate lives of John Donne (1640), Sir Henry Wotton (1651), Richard Hooker (1665), George Herbert (1670), and Bishop Robert Sanderson (1678). Donne, Wotton, and Sanderson were his close friends. Although Boswell called the collected *Lives* one of Johnson's "most favourite books," many readers remember Walton only as the author of a single little book on fishing. *The Compleat Angler, or the Contemplative Man's Recreation,* first published in abbreviated form in 1653, presents a discussion among Piscator, an angler, Auceps, a fowler, and Venator, a hunter, on the merits of their respective sports. Piscator gives himself an easy first place. It is not only a treatise on how to catch and prepare fish, but also a lesson on how to enjoy a "calm, quiet, innocent recreation." The style is quietly learned, pleasantly witty, simple, unaffected, artful in its artlessness. Izaak Walton was that sort of man.

WARBURTON, William (1698–1779), Bishop of Gloucester from 1759 until his death, was a blustering controversialist in both theological and literary matters. In his most ambitious work, *The Divine Legation of Moses* (1738–41, unfinished), he attempted paradoxically to prove the lawgiver's "divine legation" by the very fact that the Mosaic Law contains no reference to a future life. Warburton was an intimate friend of Pope and as official literary executor, issued the early posthumous editions of the poet's works (1751, etc.). In 1747 he published an ignorant edition of Shakespeare cribbed largely out of Pope and Theobald

WARD, Edward (1667–1731), commonly called "Ned," was a successful tavern-keeper with a talent for tapping the small beer of pamphlet-journalism. He could turn anything into Hudibrastic doggerel and did. Among his more ambitious efforts in the manner of Samuel Butler are *Hudibras Redivivus, or a Burlesque Poem on the Times* (1705–7) and *Vulgus Britannicus, or the British Hudibras* (1710). A contemporary pamphleteer characterized him as "The Hudibrastic Brewer or a Preposterous Union between Malt and Meter." Ned Ward is best known, however, for his prose work, *The London Spy,* which appeared in eighteen monthly numbers between 1698 and 1700. In this authentic guide-book to the city, Ward did for his age what Dekker in *The Gull's Hornbook* (1609) and Pierce Egan in *Tom and Jerry* (1821–3) did for theirs.

WARD, Mrs. Humphry (1851–1920) was an ardent social worker and feminist who enjoyed, at the turn of the century, a considerable reputation as a novelist. Granddaughter of Thomas Arnold and niece of Matthew, she was brought up close to the religious turmoil which seethed in Oxford during the Victorian era. Her most famous novel, *Robert Elsmere* (1888), is the story of a young man's struggle to find his own religion amid that turmoil. Like others of her novels, it reflects the influence of George Eliot.

WARNER, Sylvia Townsend (1893–   ) is a novelist and poetess. Among her novels are *Lolly Willowes* (1926), a fantasy about an old maid who refuses to play the part; *Mr. Fortune's Maggot* (1927), the exotic tale of a missionary on a Pacific isle; and *The True Heart* (1929), the romantic story of an orphan girl's pathetic love. Her poems appeared in *The Espalier* (1925), *Time Importuned* (1928), and *Whether a Dove or a Seagull* (1934).

WARNER, William (1558?–1609). The masterpiece of this literary attorney is *Albion's England,* a patriotic poem in the same general class as Drayton's *Polyolbion* (1612–22) and Daniel's *Civil Wars* (1595–1609). Mixing legend freely with history, Warner began his best-selling chronicle with the Flood and carried it down, in the first edition (1586) to the Norman Conquest, in the sixth (1606) to the reign of James I. He also published a collection of prose tales, *Pan his Syrinx* (1584), and a translation of Plautus' *Menaechmi* (1595), sometimes said to have provided the immediate source for Shakespeare's *Comedy of Errors*.

WARTON, Joseph (1722–1800) and **Thomas** (1728–90). These brothers had much in common. Both were educators, Joseph as head master of Winchester (1766–93), Thomas as professor of poetry at Oxford (1757–67). Both were poets; Joseph's *Enthusiast, or The Lover of Nature* (1744) and Thomas' *Pleasures of Melancholy* (1747) place their authors among the important forerunners of Romanticism. Thomas was poet laureate from 1785 until his death. Finally, both were forward-looking critics. Joseph in his *Essay on the Writings and Genius of Pope* (1756–82) boldly suggested that the work of the most influential poet of the century is generally characterized by "good sense and judgment . . . rather than fancy and invention" and is "not of the most poetic species of poetry." Thomas, like Bishop Percy, Hurd, and Tyrwhitt, was forward in looking backward. In his *Observations on The Fairy Queen* (1754) and his unfinished *History of English Poetry from the Close of the Eleventh to the Commencement of the Eighteenth Century* (1774–81) he did much to destroy the illusion that literate English poetry began with Dryden.

WATER POET, THE. Epithet which **John Taylor** applied to himself.

WATSON, John. See **MACLAREN, Ian.**

WATSON, Thomas (1557?–92) was a scholarly poet who worked almost entirely at second hand. He translated Sophocles' *Antigone* (1581) and Tasso's *Aminta* (1585) into Latin and "Englished" *Italian Madrigals* (1590). His two sonnet sequences, *Hecatompathia, or Passionate Century of Love* (1582) and *The Tears of Fancy* (1592), were largely derived from Italian, French, and classical sources. *Hecatompathia,* if allowance is made for the eighteen-line form of its "sonnets," was the first such cycle to appear after Wyatt and Surrey introduced the sonnet form into England.

WATSON, Sir William (1858–1935) published his first volume of verse in 1880 and wrote much of his best work during the nineteenth century. His verse (*The Poems of Sir William Watson,* 1936) is conventional in form and content; he remained quite untouched by the technical innovations of the new century. Although he was mentioned as a likely candidate for the laureateship on Alfred Austin's death in 1913, he died in relative obscurity.

WATTS, Isaac (1674–1748). A composer of popular didactic verse often attains greater renown than a poet of higher power. This was true of the hymn-writer Isaac Watts, who never wrote a line that did not have a moral or religious purpose. The son of an ardent dissenter of Southampton, Watts had an upbringing that turned his mind early to sacred writing. His first hymns were published in 1706 under the title *Horae Lyricae*. They were followed a decade and a half later by *The Psalms of David Imitated* (1719). The best songs from these two collections still appear in hymn-books of the Protestant churches. The greatest of these is the magnificent song of praise, based on Psalm 90, "Our God, our help in ages past." The ethical trend of Watts' educational theories appears strikingly in his didactic verses for children. The pieces in his *Divine Songs Attempted in Easy Language for the Use of Children* have been reprinted countless times since their first appearance in 1715. Their meter is so simple, and their lessons for the little ones are so direct and clearly expressed that the songs have attained almost to the popularity of nursery rhymes. Thousands of children who never knew the name of the author have been required to memorize and recite the verses about the busy little bee, and the dogs that "delight to bark and bite," and the sluggard who begged to "slumber again." Some of these little moral poems Lewis Carroll parodied charmingly in *Alice in Wonderland* and *Through the Looking Glass*.

WATTS–DUNTON, (Walter) Theodore (1832–1914) was a critic, poet, and novelist. His best-known critical works are the article on poetry first published in the ninth edition of the *Encyclopedia Britannica* (1885) and the essay called *The Renascence of Wonder in Poetry* which appeared in *Chambers' Cyclopædia of English Literature* in 1901. Watts-Dunton's special interest in gypsy life is reflected in the poems collected in *The Coming of Love and Other Poems* (1898) and in his once-popular novel, *Aylwin* (1899). His *Old Familiar Faces* (1916) includes sketches of the Rossettis, Tennyson, Morris, and his fellow gypsy-lover, George Borrow. Many know him best as the faithful friend at whose home Swinburne lived from 1879 until his death in 1909.

WAUGH, Alec (1898–   ) and **Evelyn** (1903–   ). These sons of the critic and publisher, Arthur Waugh, are both novelists. Alec is the author of *The Loom of Youth* (1917) and *The Balliols*

(1934). Evelyn has written *Decline and Fall* (1928), *Vile Bodies* (1930), *Put Out More Flags* (1942), *Brideshead Revisited* (1946), and other smart, satirical novels which reflect the cynicism and disillusionment common among the writers of his generation. Like the early Aldous Huxley he has directed his bitterest attacks against the English upper classes.

WEBBE, William (b. 1552?). His *Discourse of English Poetry* (1586) ranks slightly below Puttenham's *Art of English Poetry* (1589) and far below Sidney's *Defence of Poetry* (written about 1580, printed 1595) among the pioneer efforts of Elizabethan criticism. Webbe's book includes a sadly inadequate historical survey and a number of bizarre original experiments in verse, among them a foolish "translation" of a section from Spenser's *Shepheardes Calender*. But although his judgment is often faulty, he deserves praise for praising Spenser.

WEBSTER, John (1580?–1625) was a London tailor's son who became a great playwright. One of the first of the great Jacobean dramatists, he displayed the power of the Elizabethans without falling into the bathos and gross exaggerations of some of the later playwrights of his period. He wrote an indifferent comedy, *The Devil's Law-Case* (1616–22), and—probably with Thomas Heywood—a classical tragedy, *Appius and Virginia* (c. 1608–30). But his two greatest plays are both dramatizations of Italian crimes in high life. There are differences of opinion as to whether *The White Devil* (1609–13) or *The Duchess of Malfi* (1612–14) is the better, but there is a general agreement that both plays contain scenes that equal those of Shakespeare at his best.

The ability to present intense passion and stirring episodes is the most distinctive element in Webster's genius. In general plot construction he is weak; his dramas lack compression and even consistency in episodes and in characters. He was much better at creating scenes, in other words, than in building acts, and he seems to have been concerned primarily with his effects of terror, even where these delayed the main action and were only feebly related to it. The trial scene of Vittoria Corombona in *The White Devil* and the death of the Duchess in *The Duchess of Malfi* are undeniably splendid. More, perhaps, than any other dramatist of the period Webster has succeeded, moreover, in creating a flesh-tingling atmosphere of impending doom. With this deeply tragical mood such lyrics as the dirge for Marcello in *The White Devil* and the mournful "Hark, now everything is still" in *The Duchess of Malfi* are entirely consistent.

WELLS, Charles Jeremiah (1800–79) is remembered chiefly as the author of *Joseph and his Brethren,* a scriptural drama in verse. This play, originally published in 1824, was resurrected a half-century later and reprinted in 1876 with an appreciative introduction by Swinburne.

WELLS, H(erbert) G(eorge) (1866–1946). "I am a journalist. . . . I refuse to play the artist. If sometimes I am an artist it is a freak of the gods. I am a journalist all the time and what I write *goes now*—and will presently die." These words—spoken by Wells himself when he was arguing with Henry James, Joseph Conrad, and Ford Madox Ford at the turn of the century—are as true today as when they were first uttered. So restless is Wells' elastic mind, so irresistible his desire to unburden it for the world, that he has never been able to linger long within the confines of artistic form. Hence, in many of his novels he admittedly neglects the demands of verisimilitude, habitually creating, instead of living individuals, human broadcasting stations for his favorite social doctrines.

In a general way, his multifarious writing is divisible by types. There are the early romances in which he mingled pseudo-scientific fantasy of the Jules Verne stamp with the knowledge of science which he had gathered under Thomas Henry Huxley at the University of London; among them are *The Time Machine* (1895) and *The Invisible Man* (1897). Halfway between these fantastic fictions and his more realistic novels on contemporary themes are such books as: *When the Sleeper Wakes* (1898), a gloomy picture of capitalism run rampant; *A Modern Utopia* (1905), a political blueprint for the future; and *The War in the Air* (1908), a prophetic prediction of the military tactics of the Second World War. In another group—represented by *Love and Mr. Lewisham* (1900), *Ann Veronica* (1909), and *The New Machiavelli* (1911) —Wells grappled with the problems of the present, placing particular emphasis on the need for greater sexual freedom. Harder to classify are some of his best novels: *Tono-Bungay* (1909), an unrestrained caricature of the methods of big business; *Kipps* (1905) and *The History of Mr. Polly* (1910), two pleasant pictures of the eccentricities of the lower-middle class; and *Mr. Britling Sees It Through* (1916), one of the famous novels of the First World War. In the realm of non-fiction belong his imposing and popular *Outline of History* (1920), his frank *Experiment in Autobiography* (1934), and a host of miscellaneous books and articles on everything from sex to socialism.

One cannot summarize in brief the changing tides of Wells' thinking. In the early 1900's he was a Fabian Socialist. More recently he has been preaching the gospel of a socialist world-state. He is distrustful, however, of the glorification of the masses, suspicious alike of the worship of the American "peepul" and the Russian "proletariat."

WESLEY, Charles (1707–88) and **John** (1703–91). Charles Wesley founded the Methodist Society while an undergraduate at Oxford in 1726; in 1729 his brother became its leader. It was John who, by ordaining ministers in 1784, completed the separation of the Methodist Church from the Church of England. Both left journals and wrote and edited hymns. One of the best of the hymns is Charles Wesley's "Jesus, lover of my Soul."

WEST, Rebecca is the pseudonym of **Cicily Isabel Fairfield** (1892–   ), novelist, critic, and journalist. Her novels include *The Judge* (1922), *Harriet Hume* (1929), and *The Thinking Reed* (1936). In addition to the essays and reviews which have been collected in *The Strange Necessity* (1928) and *Ending in Earnest* (1931), she has published studies of Henry James (1916) and D. H. Lawrence (1930). Her most astonishing creative effort in the thirties went into the making of a stupendous and brilliant super-travel book in two volumes, *Black Lamb and Grey Falcon* (1941); it deals mainly with her experiences in Yugoslavia in 1937.

WHATELY, Richard (1787–1863) was a liberal theologian who taught at Oxford and later became Archbishop of Dublin (1831). He displayed his taste for common sense in his anonymous satire, *Historic Doubts Relative to Napoleon Bonaparte* (1819), a burlesque of the "higher criticism" of the scriptures. He also wrote two popular textbooks, *Elements of Logic* (1826) and *Elements of Rhetoric* (1828).

WHETSTONE, George (1544?–87) wrote non-dramatic verse but is remembered chiefly as the author of *Promos and Cassandra* (printed 1578), a verse tragi-comedy in two five-act parts. The play was based on a story from the *Hecatommithi* of the Italian Geraldi Cinthio (1504–73) and was the immediate source of Shakespeare's *Measure for Measure* (1603–4).

WHITE, Gilbert (1720–93) spent most of his life as a curate in and near his native village of Selborne, Hampshire. The work which made him famous, *The Natural History and Antiquities of Selborne* (1789), belongs among the unclassifiable classics of English prose. Like *The Compleat Angler* (1653), it is not the thorough scientific treatise which the title implies; like Walton's masterpiece it has a quiet unpretentious charm which lifts it from the domain of the specialist into the universal realm of literature. Moreover, it illustrates the growing eighteenth-century tendency towards accurate observation of nature, which reached a climax in the poetry of Wordsworth.

WHITE, Henry Kirke (1785–1806) was a Nottingham butcher's son who published a promising volume of verse when still in his teens—*Clifton Grove . . . with Other Poems* (1803). He died at twenty while a student at Cambridge. In the following year, Southey, who had befriended the young poet, published *The Remains of Henry Kirke White, with an Account of his Life* (1807). Most of White's poems—the best known of which are the hymn "Oft in danger, oft in woe" and a high-sounding blank-verse effort on *Time*—have a borrowed air about them, but because of his sad fate he is a fit subject for sentimental might-have-beens.

WHITE, Joseph Blanco (1775–1841) was a Spaniard, born in Seville and christened originally José Maria Blanco. He came to England in his youth after abandoning the Catholic priesthood. He wrote a number of works on theological subjects but is remembered by students of English literature for a single sonnet, *Night and Death* ("Mysterious Night! when our first parent knew") (1828). Although a remarkably eloquent sonnet for a man who was not primarily a poet, it hardly deserves Coleridge's encomium as "'the finest and most grandly conceived sonnet in our language."

WHITE, William Hale. See **RUTHERFORD, Mark.**

WHITEHEAD, William (1715–85), who succeeded Colley Cibber as poet laureate in 1757, is, like his predecessor, remembered chiefly as a dramatist. He wrote *The Roman Father* (1750), a popular adaptation of Corneille's tragedy *Horace; Crëusa* (1754), another classical tragedy; and *The School for Lovers* (1762), a sentimental comedy.

WHYTE–MELVILLE, George John (1821–78) was the author of *Digby Grand* (1853), *Holmby House* (1860), *Market Harborough* (1861), and other novels. Like R. S. Surtees, he filled his books with hunting scenes. Although he served as a major in the Crimean War, he was killed while riding to hounds.

WILBERFORCE, William (1759–1833) was the leading layman of the "Evangelicals" who figured prominently in English politics at the end of the eighteenth century and the beginning of the nineteenth. He led a long fight for the abolition of slavery and the slave trade. His *Practical View of the Prevailing Religious System of Professed Christians* (1797) had a wide influence. His son **Samuel** (1805–73) was the Bishop Wilberforce who parried words with Thomas Henry Huxley on evolution.

WILDE, Oscar (Fingal O'Flahertie Wills) (1856–1900) was born in Dublin. While at Oxford in the late 1870's, he was inspired by the teachings of John Ruskin and Walter Pater and was already celebrated as the leader of an undergraduate aesthetic cult which sought to effect a renaissance in English art. Soon London was to see his supposed likeness in Postlethwaite, the languid, lily-loving poet of Du Maurier's *Punch* cartoons, and again in Bunthorne, the "aesthetic sham" of Gilbert and Sullivan's *Patience* (1881). In 1882 Wilde was in America—drooping hair, flowing tie, knee-breeches, lily, and all—repeating his favorite *bon mots* to newspaper men and spreading the gospel of art for art's sake to the wide-eyed debutantes of Boston and the suspicious miners of Leadville, Colorado. In 1895, following a notorious trial, he was convicted of sexual immorality and sentenced to two years in jail. Shortly after his release he wrote the *Ballad of Reading Gaol* (published anonymously in 1898), a moving poem of prison life in the shadow of the scaffold, and *De Profundis* (1905), the prose account of his own tragedy. Later he assumed the name of "Sebastian Melmoth,"—the first name suggested by the arrows on his prison garb, the second adopted from Maturin's *Melmoth the Wanderer*. He died in poverty and obscurity in Paris.

For all his showmanship Wilde was hardly an aesthetic sham. If he sometimes took refuge in the aesthetic escapism of Pater, he did see, with Ruskin and William Morris, the oppressive ugliness of Victorian England and the undeniable relation between happy workmen and a pleasant environment. His work was various. In the single year 1891 he published a group of short-stories (*Lord Arthur Savile's Crime, and Other Stories*), a decadent novel (*The Picture of Dorian Gray*), and a collection of paradoxical critical essays (*Intentions*). Except for *Salomé* (printed in Paris, 1893), a sensuous, pagan tragedy originally written in French, Wilde's significant plays are comedies: *Lady Windermere's Fan* (1892), *A Woman of No Importance* (1893), *An Ideal Husband* (1895), and *The Importance of Being Earnest* (1895). All of these are brilliant comedies of manners, their artificial dialogue sparkling with memorable epigrams. The most popular of the four, *The Importance of Being Earnest,* is farcical and superficial, but no writer in the nineteenth century had come as close to reviving the comic spirit of Congreve and Sheridan.

WILKES, John (1727–97). In 1762 John Wilkes, M.P., founded the *North Briton,* a periodical expressly designed to attack Lord Bute, the powerful Scottish minister of George III. For a bitter assault on the throne in No. 45, he was tried for libel. He was expelled from the House of Commons and his *North Briton* was suppressed. After his return in 1768 from a self-imposed exile in Paris, he was four times elected to Parliament from Middlesex and four times prevented from taking his seat. During the struggle the dissolute little reformer sky-rocketed to fame as the "people's hero." He won a temporary victory in 1774 when he was finally allowed to sit in the House. In the same year he was elected Lord Mayor of London, and two years later even Dr. Johnson condescended to converse with him at dinner. But the storm aroused in England by the battle for "Wilkes and liberty" did not subside appreciably until the Reform Bill of 1832.

WILLIAM of Malmesbury (d. 1143?). In two Latin works, *De Gesta Regum Anglorum* and its sequel, *Historia Novella* (both completed 1135–40), William chronicled the history of England from 449 A.D. to 1142. Going back to the Venerable Bede for inspiration, he made some effort to sift historical evidence and impugned the authenticity of Geoffrey of Monmouth's history. His love of anecdote, gossip, and personal comment, if it detracts from the historical objectivity of his work, makes him the most readable of the twelfth-century chroniclers.

WILLIAMS, Isaac (1802–65) was associated with Newman, Keble, Hurrell Froude, and Pusey during the early years of the Oxford Movement. He contributed nine poems to *Lyra Apostolica* (1832) and wrote numbers 80, 86, and 87 of the *Tracts for the Times* (1833–41).

WILSON, John (1627?–96) was a Restoration dramatist who looked backward to the Jacobean era. *The Cheats* (1663) and *The Projectors* (printed 1665), two comedies about the operations of petty criminals, are reminiscent of Jonson's *Alchemist* (1610) and *Bartholomew Fair* (1614). Wilson's unacted tragedy, *Andronicus Comnenius* (printed 1664), is one of the rare blank-verse tragedies in the era of the heroic couplet.

WILSON, John (1785–1854). With Lockhart and Hogg, Wilson was one of the moving spirits of Tory *Blackwood's Magazine*. He and Lockhart concocted the "Chaldee MS." (*Blackwood's*, 1817), the pseudo-biblical satire on the worthies of Edinburgh which first put "Maga" on the map. Later under the pseudonym of "Christopher North" he appeared prominently in *Noctes Ambrosianae* (*Blackwood's*, 1822–35), more than half of which he wrote himself. These glittering dialogues on life, literature, and politics reveal Wilson's catholicity of interests, keen wit, and love of talk and tippling. He also wrote poetry and taught moral philosophy at the University of Edinburgh.

WILSON, Robert, the elder (d. 1600) was an Elizabethan clown actor, famous for his clever extemporizing and—more remarkably —for his authorship of two belated moral interludes, *Three Ladies of London* (1581) and *Three Lords and Three Ladies of London* (1588–90). His son **Robert** (1579–1610) was a play-producer's hack.

WILSON, Thomas (1525?–81) wrote *The Art of Rhetoric for the Use of all such as are Studious of Eloquence set forth in English* (1553). Although based almost entirely on classical sources, the book is noteworthy for Wilson's condemnation of writers who are "counterfeiting the kinges Englishe" by borrowing words from Latin, French, and Italian.

WINCHILSEA, Anne Finch, Countess of (1661–1720). This friend of Pope's is remembered for a handful of simple nature poems containing seeds of Romanticism. *A Nocturnal Reverie* (1713) has some fresh, accurate nature imagery, unusual, as Wordsworth noticed, in an age when poets who had never really observed a bird spouted conventionally about "the feathered folk."

WIREKER, Nigel (fl. 1190) wrote *Speculum Stultorum,* a Latin satire on monastic life allegorically presented in the misadventures of Burnel the Ass. Chaucer refers to the work in his *Nun's Priest's Tale* as "Daun Burnel the Asse."

WITHER, George (1588–1667). In 1613 Wither was jailed for publishing *Abuses Stript and Whipt,* a mild verse satire on corruption in high places. In 1621 he served another term for *Wither's Motto,* a happy poem in praise of George Wither. In 1661 he was still writing verse—and ending up in jail once more for an offensive poem. He also wrote: *The Shepherd's Hunting* (1614), a collection of pastorals composed in jail; *Fidelia* (1615), a verse epistle from a forsaken girl to her lover; and *Fair Virtue* (1622), a semi-autobiographical love poem. With *Hymns and Songs of the Church* in 1623 he threw himself into the Puritan cause. After that, except for some good passages in *Hallelujah* (1641), religious and political zeal smothered his poetry. The few who know many of Wither's early poems have observed that like his friend, William Browne, he sometimes transcended the artificialities of the pastoral tradition and wrote with a genuine feeling for nature. Most readers know only two devil-may-care love lyrics, "Shall I, wasting in despair" (from *Fidelia*) and "I loved a lass, a fair one."

WODEHOUSE, P(elham) G(renville) (1881–   ) is a novelist, short-story writer, and musical comedy librettist with an enormous following on both sides of the Atlantic. By faithfully reduplicating stock farcical formulae and consistently imitating his own inimitable characters, he has turned out popular humor for forty years. He specializes in multiplying comic epithets and similes and in exploiting the traditional eccentricities of the story-book Englishman. His titles include *Leave it to Psmith* (1923), *Carry on, Jeeves* (1925), and *The Luck of the Bodkins* (1935). Jeeves, the super-resourceful butler, has become a household god in some American homes. When the Nazis overran France, they arrested Wodehouse, who had been living with his wife on the Riviera, and interned him in Berlin. From here he broadcast to England and America a praise of his captors that cost him at a stroke much of the popularity that he had earned in both countries. After the liberation of France he was released.

WOLCOT, John. See **PINDAR, Peter.**

WOLFE, Charles (1791–1823) is remembered as the author of *The Burial of Sir John Moore after Corunna,* a poem which first appeared in an obscure Irish newspaper in 1817. The work has survived—perhaps because of the very obviousness of its effect—as one of the most popular war poems in English. Its author was an Irish curate who died of consumption at thirty-two. Only one other poem of his is at all well known—a conventional love elegy entitled *To Mary.*

WOLLSTONECRAFT, Mary. See **GODWIN, Mary Wollstonecraft.**

WOOD, Anthony à (1632–95) was a crabbed antiquarian who spent much of his life burrowing in the Bodleian Library at Oxford. His most celebrated work is *Athenae Oxonienses, An Exact History of all the Writers and Bishops Who have had their Edu-*

cation in The University of Oxford, from 1500 to 1690 (1691–2). Wood's judgments are flavored with gall. For a libel on Clarendon, the historian, he was expelled from the University in 1693, and his book was publicly burned. *Athenae Oxonienses* remains, however, an indispensable authority on many sixteenth- and seventeenth-century notables.

WOOLF, Virginia (Stephen) (1882–1941), novelist, publicist, biographer, and literary critic, was the daughter of the distinguished scholar Sir Leslie Stephen, and the wife of Leonard Woolf, essayist and publisher. Her novels include: *Jacob's Room* (1922), *Mrs. Dalloway* (1925), *To the Lighthouse* (1927), *The Waves* (1931), and *The Years* (1937). In them she displayed her impatience with orthodox linear narrative, as she discerned it in the novels of Arnold Bennett. She used instead a distinctive impressionistic technique, characterized by lyrical intensity and subtle penetration into the stream of consciousness. She was too bold an experimenter to be a popular novelist, but few critics have denied her genius. In addition to her novels, Mrs. Woolf wrote many essays, both in and out of the field of literary criticism. Some of these are brilliant excursions into controversy; others, as in *The Common Reader* (1925, 1932), are sensitive appreciations of her multifarious reading.

WOOLNER, Thomas (1825–92) was one of the original members of the Pre-Raphaelite Brotherhood and contributed verse to its short-lived periodical, the *Germ*. His best-known poem, *My Beautiful Lady,* appeared first in the *Germ* in 1850 and was republished in expanded form in 1863. Parts of it read almost like a parody of Pre-Raphaelite simplicity. Woolner was a better sculptor than a poet.

WORDSWORTH, Dorothy (1771–1855) was the only sister of William Wordsworth. She was the constant companion and inspiration of Wordsworth and Coleridge during the golden era of their collaboration on *Lyrical Ballads* (1798). Her *Letters* and *Journals* are not only invaluable aids to the study of the two poets but also well-written works of art. She was no mere handmaid to genius. Like Jane Welsh Carlyle, she had a share of it herself.

WORDSWORTH, William (1770–1850) was a plodding, egotistical poet, who was devoid of a sense of humor to keep him balanced and of a capacity for self-criticism to keep him selective. Hence in a productive period of over fifty years he wrote a large amount of inferior poetry. But at his best he ranks with the

great poets of English literature. This inequality is so apparent
that even a bootblack of Grasmere, the poet's home, could remark
to an American tourist: "Wordsworth is a great poet, sor, but
sometimes he is domned childish." Poems like *The Idiot Boy*
(1798) are pathetically inane in contrast to *Tintern Abbey* and the
famous *Ode on Intimations of Immortality.*

As Wordsworth himself said, he was fortunate in his birthplace and his boyhood home. He was born in Cockermouth, Cumberland, in the beautiful Lake Country of northern England. After
having prepared at the neighboring Hawkshead Grammar School,
he attended and took a degree at Cambridge University. A tour
of the Continent and a residence in France not long after the fall
of the Bastille brought him what was apparently the one irregular episode in a very regular life—a liaison with a French
girl named Annette Vallon, by whom he had a daughter Caroline. Shortly after the execution of King Louis XVI in 1793,
Wordsworth returned to England, somewhat disillusioned but
still reflecting the glow of a revolutionary dawn when it was
"bliss . . . to be alive."

At Racedown in 1795 he met Coleridge; the two friends moved
to Somersetshire two years later. With Wordsworth's sister,
Dorothy, they tramped the hills and discussed the nature of
poetry. Out of their friendship came *Lyrical Ballads* (1798), a
slender volume of verse which still stands as the most important
landmark in the revolution in English poetry against the artificial
patterns of neo-classicism. The two poets had agreed to divide the
field between them; Wordsworth was to clothe the most ordinary
incidents with the magic of the imagination, Coleridge to treat
the supernatural in such a way as to induce in his readers "that
willing suspension of disbelief for the moment, which constitutes
poetic faith." Of the twenty-three poems in the first edition of
Lyrical Ballads, Wordsworth wrote nineteen, including "We are
Seven," "The Thorn," "The Idiot Boy," and "Lines Written a Few
Miles above Tintern Abbey." One of Coleridge's four poems was
The Rime of the Ancient Mariner. To the second edition (1800)
Wordsworth added seven more poems, including the pastoral
Michael, Coleridge a single lyric, *Love.*

It is doubtful if *Lyrical Ballads* would have caused such a stir
if the second edition had not been prefaced by the famous essay
in which Wordsworth analyzed his poetic faith. In it he defended
his use of humble subjects expressed in "a selection of the real
language of men in a state of vivid sensation"; he attacked the
synthetic "poetic diction" of the eighteenth century, arguing that

"poets do not write for poets alone, but for men"; he hinted at a useful distinction between poetry and prose, and at a theory of poetic inspiration—defining poetry as "the spontaneous overflow of powerful feelings" taking "its origin from emotion recollected in tranquillity"; and he attempted to explain the effectiveness of meter.

From his first poems Wordsworth revealed himself as a democratic liberal who had been influenced by the doctrines of Rousseau and Rousseau's disciple, William Godwin. The poet's conviction that he was "Nature's priest" led to his settling permanently in the Lake Country, first at Dove Cottage, Grasmere, and then —when a legacy from a friend and an appointment as stamp distributor made him independent—at a more pretentious home at Rydal Mount near Lake Windermere, where he lived for the rest of his life. With his sister Dorothy and Coleridge he visited Germany and with Dorothy he took long walking tours in various parts of England and Scotland. In 1802 he married Mary Hutchinson, a friend of his sister. The quiet routine of "plain living and high thinking" was not interrupted until his death at eighty, seven years after he had succeeded Robert Southey as poet laureate. Before his accession to the laurel crown, the political philosophy of his youth had burned out, and to the young Robert Browning he was the "lost leader" of the liberals.

Wordsworth's most pretentious poem is a long account of his development as a poet which he originally planned to call *The Recluse*. But only two of the proposed three parts were ever written, *The Prelude* (1850) and *The Excursion* (1814). As spiritual autobiography these long poems are important, but the prolixity of *The Excursion* led Byron to condemn it as "a drowsy, frowsy poem" and Lord Jeffrey to exclaim bluntly, "This will never do." The stages in Wordsworth's spiritual growth are more compactly expressed in the fine *Lines Written a Few Miles above Tintern Abbey* (1798) and in the *Ode on Intimations of Immortality from Recollections of Early Childhood* (1807), a stately poem in which he interweaves the melancholy melody of the waning of his insight into nature with the Platonic theme of the pre-existence of the human soul.

In these four poems and in such shorter lyrics as the five "Lucy" poems (written in Germany in 1799) and the sonnet "The world is too much with us," Wordsworth justifies the common claim that he is the greatest nature poet in English literature. For the impersonal attachment that is found in much eighteenth-century nature poetry, he substituted a warmth of feeling which grew spontaneously out of intimate association with the goddess; the conventional clichés he replaced with sharp, fresh images drawn from accurate observation.

But Wordsworth was more than a nature poet. In such poems as *Michael* (1800) and *Resolution and Independence* (1807) he reflected the humanitarianism of his time and gave new meaning to the simple emotions of simple people. In his *Character of the Happy Warrior* (1807) and *Ode to Duty* (1807) he treated philosophical themes with dignity. As a writer of sonnets, he ranks close to Sidney, Shakespeare, and Milton. Into this compressed form, which he begged his reader not to scorn, he put much of his best thinking and most felicitous expression. He wrote about five hundred sonnets, including "Milton, thou shouldst be living at this hour," "It is a beauteous evening calm and free," "Earth has not anything to show more fair," and an entire sequence called *Ecclesiastical Sonnets* (1822). The sonnets alone are enough to place him among the major poets of England.

WOTTON, Sir Henry (1568–1639). Secretary to the ill-fated Earl of Essex, Ambassador to Italy under James I, Provost of Eton College, and fishing companion of Izaak Walton—Sir Henry Wotton led a full, exciting life. Walton tells about it with amused respect in the short life appended to *Reliquiae Wottonianae* in 1651. Three of Wotton's shorter poems are still read: *The Character of a Happy Life* (1614), *On His Mistress, the Queen of Bohemia* (1624), and the economical couplet *Upon the Death of Sir Albert Morton's Wife.* The first and most famous of these reflects perfectly the quiet philosophy of a man who knew how to live.

WULFSTAN (d. 1023), Bishop of Worcester and Archbishop of York, is remembered, like his contemporary Aelfric, as a writer of homilies. The most famous is the so-called *Address to the English,* a bitter indictment in which the author ascribes the success of the Danish invasions to the moral degradation of the English people.

WYATT, Sir Thomas (1503?–42). Unlike Surrey, the younger friend with whom his name is always paired, Wyatt died a natural death. This is somewhat strange, for he was twice in the Tower, once when suspected of adultery with Anne Boleyn, whom he may have loved before her marriage to Henry VIII. However, he had served his king well in a number of capacities abroad. Fifteen years after Wyatt's death his shorter poems first appeared in *Tottel's Miscellany* (1557) beside those of Surrey. Both poets exploited two Italian forms new to English literature, *terza rima* and the sonnet. Wyatt had borrowed the sonnet form from Petrarch, sometimes altering the sestet with a final couplet; it was Surrey who introduced the pure "Shakespearean" form. Wyatt's sonnets are more clumsy than his friend's. There is more real poetry in certain of his miscellaneous lyrics—"Forget not yet," "And wilt thou leave me thus!" "They flee from me that sometime did me seek"—than in such sonnets as *The Lover Compareth His State to a Ship* and *Description of the Contrarious Passions in a Lover*. But Wyatt is remembered primarily as an early sonneteer.

WYCHERLEY, William (1640?–1716). The long life of this Restoration dramatist included a gay intrigue with one of Charles II's mistresses, a stormy marriage to a jealous wife, imprisonment for debt, and, in old age, friendship with a fellow-satirist forty-eight years younger, Alexander Pope. He wrote four comedies. *Love in a Wood* (1671), in which he jumbles a foursome of lovers in fashionable St. James' Park, and *The Gentleman Dancing-Master* (1672), in which one character masquerades as a Frenchman, another as a Spaniard, display Wycherley as a master of conventional stage intrigue. But the other two strike deeper. *The Country Wife* (1675) conceals beneath the notorious bawdry of Horner serious satire on two extremes in love, jealousy (Pinchwife) and blind confidence (Sparkish). In *The Plain Dealer* (1676) a misanthropic libertine, Manly, rages for frankness in the world against the conventional hypocrisies represented by his friend Freeman. Both plays are more savage than either their simpler Molière originals or the characteristic comedies of Wycherley's English contemporaries. He displays in them a virile force which has earned him the epithets "Manly" and "Brawny" Wycherley.

WYCLIFFE or WYCLIF, John (1320?–84) has been called "The Morning Star of the Reformation." He was the founder of English Protestantism, leader and inspirer of the Lollards, a group of early reformers, and the moving spirit of the first complete translation of the Bible into English. Of his early life little is known. He was possibly the Wycliffe who served as preacher at Oxford and Master of Balliol College. Later he was Vicar of Fillingham, in Lincolnshire (1361–69), of Ludgershall near Oxford (1369–74), and, finally, of Lutterworth (1374–84). To this last charge he retired after having been condemned by Oxford for heresy. Wycliffe had the strong support of the powerful John of Gaunt but was in constant opposition to the Pope and the ecclesiastical authorities. His arguments that the Bible should be the supreme guide of Christian conduct, and his Latin treatises on the authority of the Church led to his being condemned by an ecclesiastical court in the time of Pope Gregory IX. But he laid the true cornerstone of the English Reformation in his translation of the Latin Vulgate Bible into English. Wycliffe himself translated the gospels of Matthew and Mark and parts of the Old Testament; the rest of the Bible was translated by others, including the scholarly Nicholas of Hereford, and the whole was carefully revised by John Purvey, Wycliffe's vicar at Lutterworth. The early work on the Bible was done in 1382–4, and Purvey's revision in 1389. In spite of the futile gesture of scattering Wycliffe's bones by decree of the Council of Constance nearly fifty years after his death, the seeds that he planted bore fruit a century later in the Tudor Reformation.

WYNTOUN, Andrew of (1350?–1420) succeeded John Barbour as a chronicler of Scottish history. His *Original Chronicle* (not published until 1795) is a verse-history of Scotland from the creation to the accession of James I in 1394. It is of little value as poetry, but in the later sections it is an important source for historians.

Y

YEATS, William Butler (1865–1939) may be thought of as the dean of the Irish literary movement which was so productive at the end of the nineteenth and the beginning of the twentieth centuries. He was Irish to the core, and his poems, pamphlets, and plays have all the Celtic flavor—charm, mysticism, melancholy. He was born in Dublin, the son of a portrait-painter, and he himself studied painting until he abandoned the brush for the pen. He was educated in London and in Dublin, and his first publications appeared in the *Dublin University Review* and in other Irish periodicals. In 1888 he went to London on the invitation of Oscar Wilde and there joined the Rhymers' Club, and so became associated with Lionel Johnson, Arthur Symons, and other writers and critics. In the following year appeared his first volume of verse, *The Wanderings of Oisin and Other Poems*. He studied the poetry of the French symbolists and of William Blake, and edited Blake's poems. He helped to organize the Irish Literary Society of London and of Dublin, and, in collaboration with George Moore and others, he established the Irish Literary Theater, which became the Abbey Theater in 1894. In 1897 he issued a number of

Irish legends under the title of *The Secret Rose*. Another volume of *Poems* appeared in 1895, and still another, under the title *The Wind among the Reeds,* four years later. *The Winding Stair* was published in 1933. Of Yeats' numerous poetic plays—written frequently for the Abbey Theater—the best known are the tragedy *The Countess Kathleen* (1899), the one-act phantasy *The Land of Heart's Desire* (1894), and *Deirdre* (1906), based on an old Irish legend.

In an actively productive period of half a century Yeats underwent an artistic development that revealed him as a genius of many moods and changes. The mountains, woods, and waters of the West Country were to him "a passion," as were those of the English Lake Country to William Wordsworth. But Yeats was more of a nationalist than Wordsworth ever was, and his love for the natural beauty of his own country led him to a consideration of her legends, her history, her traditions. Thus his interest became transformed from the merely factual to that which has been called *trance*. These seemingly contradictory elements he found paralleled in the poetry of D. G. Rossetti and others of the Pre-Raphaelite Brotherhood, who could be almost ritualistically exact in their expression of physical details at the same time that they conveyed a mood that was remote and mystical almost to the point of being apocalyptic. In his poetry Yeats' Ireland became the ancient land of legend, her mountains became symbols of her mighty past, and the Irish melody of his verse suggested moods that are heartbreaking, plaintive, mystic, and remote. His characters speak in fading voices out of a dim land of mists, and there is a timeless quality in the stories.

Yeats' long service to the Irish Nationalist Movement, to the Irish Theater, and to the cultivation of a popular interest in Irish legends and traditions made him a natural leader in the Celtic Renaissance. His preëminence came not alone through his own art but also through what he did to inspire other Irish writers. This was notably true, for example, when, in 1898, he rescued John M. Synge from a garret in Paris and led his feet again into the pathways of creative art.

YONGE, Charlotte Mary (1823–1901) was an industrious Victorian whose hundred-odd novels represent only one aspect of her prodigious literary output. She was a neighbor of John Keble, and her work reflects the influence of the Oxford Movement, in which he was a leader. Her most celebrated novel, *The Heir of Redclyffe* (1853), is an effort to make piety palatable by coating it with romance. She also wrote novels of domestic life (*The Daisy Chain,* 1856) and historical tales (*The Chaplet of Pearls,* 1868).

YOUNG, Edward (1683–1765). In 1742 Young was a melancholy man, saddened by tragedy at home and disappointed in his hopes of preferment in the Church. It is not strange then that his masterpiece, published in that year, was to earn him a place beside Robert Blair, author of *The Grave* (1743), as one of the founders of the "Graveyard School" of English poetry. Young's *Complaint, or Night Thoughts on Life, Death, and Immortality* reveals some of the epigrammatic wit which he had displayed in his series of verse satires, *Love of Fame, or the Universal Passion* (1725–28), and much of the bombast which he had exploited in two successful tragedies, *Busiris* (1719) and *The Revenge* (1721). But the persistent lingering on night, death, and dissolution, although familiar to readers of Elizabethan poetry, heralded a new era in Young's century. Another departure from tradition was his use in *Night Thoughts* of blank verse instead of the heroic couplet. Later in the prose *Conjectures on Original Composition* (1759) he urged such originality as a means to break the stranglehold of the Ancients.

Z

ZANGWILL, Israel (1864–1926) was a Jewish journalist, novelist, and playwright who is remembered as an interpreter of the London Ghetto. His novels include *Children of the Ghetto* (1892), *Ghetto Tragedies* (1893), and *Dreamers of the Ghetto* (1898). Of his plays the most popular and most discussed is *The Melting Pot* (printed 1914).

II
LIST OF ANONYMOUS WORKS

II
LIST OF ANONYMOUS WORKS

ABRAHAM AND ISAAC. The dramatization of the test of Abraham's faith from the account in Genesis 22, 1–15, was done in several miracle plays, as, for example, in those of the Chester and the York cycles. The most effective version, however, is the non-cyclical play that is preserved in a manuscript at Brome Manor in Suffolk. Here the anguish of Abraham, asked by Jehovah to sacrifice his only son Isaac, and the innocence, loyalty, and courage of the boy are painfully pathetic, and the drama has much of the flavor of the medieval child martyrologies. The Brome *Abraham and Isaac* dates from the fifteenth century.

ANCREN RIWLE or ANCHORESSES' RULE. A prose guide to earthly and spiritual conduct written in the first quarter of the thirteenth century for three "sisters" living together as devout recluses, apparently in a house at Tarrant in Dorsetshire. The authorship has been frequently ascribed to Richard Poore, who was Bishop of Salisbury from 1217 to 1229. Whoever the author was, he has displayed in his manual a religious spirit that was tempered by graciousness, tenderness, and good sense.

ANGLO–SAXON CHRONICLE, THE. A famous account written in Old English by monks working in different monasteries of England, of events from the beginning of the seventh century to the middle of the twelfth. It covers the struggles of the Anglo-Saxons against the Danish invaders during the reign of King Alfred (871–901) and contains the poetic recounting of the Battle of Brunanburh, fought by Aethelstan against the Northmen in 937.

ARDEN OF FEVERSHAM. One of the most famous of the Shakespeare apocrypha or plays erroneously ascribed to him. It is a domestic tragedy published anonymously in 1592 and long popular. Shakespeare never based a tragedy on a contemporary murder, but the sordid tale of Arden's death was taken from Raphael Holinshed's account in his *Chronicle* of the actual murder in 1551 of a Kentish gentleman by his wife Alice and her paramour Mosbie. The tragedy has excellent suspense and is almost Senecan in its triangle-plot and in the relentlessness with which Nemesis pursues the victim. But at the same time it is not only Elizabethan but almost vulgar in its demonstration of the moral that the wages of sin is death. In the last act the murderess and her accomplices are sent to their doom with mutual accusations or expressions of repentance somewhat after the manner of the "criminals' good nights" of the broadside ballads. Even the murdered husband is not an altogether innocent victim; his corpse is found—like the blood of the wicked King Ahab in Naboth's vineyard—on a plot of ground "which he by force and violence held from Reede."

AYENBITE OF INWYT or REMORSE OF CONSCIENCE. A moral treatise, composed mainly of homilies on sin, repentance, and confession, which was translated about 1340—not too competently—by Dan (Dominus or Master) Michel of Northgate in Kent from a thirteenth-century French treatise, *Somme des Vices et des Vertus,* by one Friar Lorens. These allegorical guides to righteousness provide dull reading but are of interest to philologists because they furnish good specimens of the southern dialect of the early fourteenth century.

BATTLE OF BRUNANBURH, THE. A stirringly patriotic poem in Old English which glorifies the victory of Aethelstan, King of Wessex, over the Northmen invaders at Brunanburh in 937. The poem is the first of several embedded in the *Anglo-Saxon Chronicle*. It was translated by Alfred Tennyson.

BATTLE OF MALDON, THE. An Old English poem of the tenth century which deals with the heroic death of the ealdorman, or earl, Byrhtnoth, in repelling the invading hosts of Northmen at Maldon in Essex in 991. Byrhtnoth scornfully rejected an offer from Anlaf, leader of the invaders, to withdraw his army on receipt of a tribute, and led his warriors valiantly until slain by a poisoned spear.

BATTLE OF OTTERBURN, THE. See **CHEVY CHASE.**

BEOWULF. The only complete folk-epic in English literature has been preserved in a manuscript once belonging to Sir Robert Cotton, noted antiquary (1571–1631) and now in the British Museum. The manuscript is written in the Wessex dialect and dates from the end of the tenth century; the epic was originally composed, however, about two hundred years earlier. The episodic nature of the poem reveals that it must have been made by combining into one piece several shorter songs, nearly all of which deal with the marvelous deeds of Beowulf. The unity of the epic comes, therefore, from its concern with a central hero. The events narrated are based on a historical event, the raid in the sixth century of Hygelac, king of the Geats—a tribe occupying a district in what is now southern Sweden—against the Frisians. On this expedition one of Hygelac's thanes, Beowulf, greatly distinguished himself. But Beowulf in the flesh never did such mighty deeds as did Beowulf in the poem. In the poem he is a demi-god, slaying monsters with his bare fist or with the aid of a magic sword, swimming for days, fighting with the handgrip of many warriors.

In *Beowulf* four chief episodes have been combined into one long epic: the purging of Heorot, the mead-hall of the Danish king, Hrothgar, of the ravening monster Grendel; the subsequent killing of Grendel's dam in her submarine lair; the triumphant return of the hero to his homeland; and, finally, after a peaceful reign of many decades, the hero-king's saving of his own people by slaying, at the price of his own life, a fire-dragon that had been ravishing the countryside. The epic reveals the pagan philosophy of the ancient Northmen: a grim courage, a fatalistic willingness to yield to Wyrd (or Fate), an eagerness to brag of deeds done, and an admiration for such generosity and spirit of service as the hero constantly displays. In the poem there are occasional traces, however, of Christian influence—introduced, probably, by some Christianized poet or transcriber who had to do with the making of the epic.

The mood of the poem is gloomy, the narratives of the deadly struggles between the hero and his grim adversaries are vigorous and breath-taking, and the language has the rough picturesqueness of primitive poetry, a quality brought out largely through the use of *kennings,* or metaphorical names for more common words, such as *battle-sarks* for *armor, pathway of the whale* for *sea,* and *gold-dispenser* for *king.* The poem is composed in unrhymed alliterative lines of four accents each; every line is divided by a strong caesura into two hemistichs or half-lines that are linked by marked alliteration. To illustrate, the first three lines of the epic, in the original West-Saxon dialect, are given here. The symbol þ is the equivalent of the *th* sound in modern English:

> Hwaet! we Gar-Dena in geardagum,
> þeodcyninga þrym gefrunon,
> hu þa aeþelingas ellen fremedon!

(Lo! we have learned of the glory of the kings of the Spear-Danes in days of yore, how these princes wrought deeds of strength!).

BESTIARY, THE. See **BESTIARY** in *Glossary of Literary Terms.*

BEVIS OF HAMTOUN. A metrical romance of the early four-teenth century. It deals with the usual type of heroic misadventures and ultimate triumph, but has more of the coloring of the Crusades than most of the other medieval tales of knighthood. Bevis, disinherited by treachery, finds his way to the Saracen court of King Ermyn. Here, after suffering because he refuses to renounce his Christianity, he converts Ermyn's daughter Josian to his faith and marries her after having undergone incredible hardships—including the conventional seven-years' imprisonment.

BIBLE, THE ENGLISH. Because of the inherent merit of the Bible and its standing in the history of English culture as a spiritual guidebook, it is the most important single volume read by English speaking peoples. The influence of both its content and its language —as translated into English—has been greater than that of Shakespeare or of any other English writer. And this fact is a paradox, for the original Bible was both ancient and foreign. Even the newest sections in their original form antedate by centuries the beginnings of the English nation. Some of the thirty-nine "books" of the Old Testament were written in Hebrew a thousand years or more before the beginning of the Christian era, and the twenty-seven sections of the New Testament or so-called "Christian Book" were composed before the end of the first century A.D. The translation of the Hebrew Old Testament into Greek —the famous *Septuagint* (*LXX*)—was made by seventy-two scholars in the third century B.C.; St. Jerome's Latin translation of the entire Bible, known as the *Vulgate,* was completed in 405 A.D. and became the standard Christian Bible of the Middle Ages. It was the Vulgate that provided the basis for the various Old English translations and paraphrases of Bede (673–735), Aelfric (c. 955–c. 1020), and other early English clerics. And the first translation of the entire Bible into English by John Wycliffe (1320?–84) and his associates was made also from St. Jerome's Latin text.

The Protestant Reformation in the sixteenth century brought nearly a hundred years of Bible translations, from the New Testament of William Tyndale in 1526 to the famous King James Bible of 1611. The notable contributions of these sixteenth-century "Bible men," William Tyndale, Miles Coverdale, Thomas Cranmer, and others, to the spread of Bible reading in England are explained under their names in the *Dictionary of Authors.* Many of these translations were the work of collaborators. This was true of the Geneva

Bible of 1560, and even more so of the most famous of all, the so-called King James or Authorized version of 1611. This translation was proposed by Dr. Reynolds of Corpus Christi College, Oxford, at a conference called by King James at Hampton Court in 1604. The work was divided among forty-seven scholars of Westminster, Cambridge, and Oxford. The translation was based on the "Bishops' Bible" of 1568 but shows strongly the influence of William Tyndale's earlier version. The "English Revised" version of 1881 (New Testament) and 1884 (Old Testament) was designed to modernize the language of the King James version, but no nineteenth- or twentieth-century translation has replaced in popularity the version of 1611; it is the language of this poetic and spiritual translation that has stamped itself upon the literature of England for over three centuries. For Catholic readers the Douai-Rheims translation—1582 (N. T.) and 1609–10 (O. T.)—and its eighteenth-century and later revisions is the standard; it is based on the Latin version of St. Jerome.

The influence of the Bible—and especially of the so-called King James version—on English thought and English literature may be accounted for largely because it was and is almost universally read as the guide to living; its readers thought of it as inspired, and its philosophy, content, and language became a part of the Englishman's pattern of thinking and speaking. Moreover, it is an anthology that contains all types of literature—legend, history, biography, fable, parable, dream allegory, philosophy, proverbs, poetry in all moods, letters, and even drama, if Job may be thought of as not unlike a Greek tragedy. It was an anthology so universally read that the thoughts and feelings that it contains became among the English a common medium for the exchange of ideas and emotions, and found their way from the spoken into the written word. It is for these reasons that Milton's language, and that of many more English writers, is the language of the Bible, and that Bunyan's *Pilgrim's Progress* reads almost like a detached section from the Book.

BLICKLING HOMILIES. A collection of nineteen homilies—many mere fragments—preserved at Blickling Hall, Norfolk. They date from some time in the tenth century, but it is not apparent that a single date of composition can be assigned to all of them. The homilies vary in theme and in style. Some are downright sermons; others are largely narrative. Many are highly poetic and stirring, as are those containing the various descriptions of doomsday and of visions of Heaven and its glittering hosts.

CASTLE OF PERSEVERANCE, THE. Probably the earliest extant of the morality plays; it dates from the first quarter of the fifteenth century. Together with two other moralities—*Mankind* and *Mind, Will, and Understanding*—it is contained in a manuscript once belonging to Dr. Cox Macro (1688–1767), and is referred to as one of the "Macro Plays." It is a rather tedious dramatic allegory presenting how Mankind, beset during his life by the Seven Deadly Sins and defended by the Seven Cardinal Virtues, ultimately goes to Heaven, is acquitted of his sins in the flesh by the mercy of God, and is given a seat at the right side of the throne. A curious sketch to guide the stage-manager and actors shows that the morality was produced in an open field with the playing-circle protected by a ditch from the possible encroachments of the audience.

CHEVY CHASE. A famous battle-ballad, praised by Sir Philip Sidney, Ben Jonson, Joseph Addison, and others, which recounts how Percy, earl of Northumberland, on a hunting raid across the Scottish border, met and fought a battle with Douglas, the doughty Scots warrior. According to some versions of the song both Percy and Douglas were slain in the skirmish. The ballad is often called *The Hunting of the Cheviot;* and it is probable that events narrated in it are those which appear also in the ballad entitled *The Battle of Otterburn,* which commemorates a conflict between Percy and Douglas at Otterburn in Northumberland on August 19, 1388. Shakespeare alludes to this fight between Northumberland and Scottish noblemen in *Henry IV, Part I.*

CHILDE HORN. See **KING HORN.**

CLEANNESS. See **PEARL POET** in *Dictionary of Authors.*

COURT OF LOVE, THE. An allegorical poem by an unknown who calls himself "Philogenet, of Cambridge, clerk," once ascribed to Chaucer but now admitted to be of uncertain authorship and date. In some fifteen hundred lines, arranged in rhyme royal, the poet tells of his visit to the palace of Citherea, where, under the conduct of Philobone, one of the ladies of the court, he sees the marvels of the place and rehearses the numerous "statutes of love"—which are framed and phrased with apparent satirical purpose. The poem ends with a very charming chorus of birds.

CUCKOO–SONG. See **SUMER IS I–CUMEN IN.**

CURSOR MUNDI or **COURSE OF THE WORLD.** An early fourteenth-century poem in the Northern Middle English dialect, popular in its own century. Its ambitious plan to recount the history of the world, interlarded with saints' legends, homilies, and miscellaneous digressions, carries it to some thirty thousand lines in tetrameter couplets. It was composed by an unknown cleric, possibly of Lincolnshire, and has been preserved in three varying manuscripts.

DAME SIRIZ. A verse fabliau, or folk-tale, of the mid-thirteenth century, which found its way into Middle English after having wandered from the Orient through various European countries. It tells how a "tonsured clerk" named Wilekin bribes the witch, Dame Siriz, to help him seduce Margeri in the absence of her husband. The old woman puts pepper into her dog's eyes to make them run tears and thus convinces the chaste matron that the animal is her daughter who has been bewitched into a dog by a learned clerk whose advances she has refused.

DEBATE OF THE BODY AND THE SOUL, THE. A theological poem composed in the second half of the thirteenth century and extant in several texts. It takes the familiar form of the *débat* or argument between two contestants. In this particular poem the author sees in a vision the contention between the corpse of a knight, who has led a gay life, and his spirit, who accuses the flesh of having brought him to the tortures of Hell. The Body replies that the Soul should have controlled him better during his lifetime. And so the mutual accusations continue until the fiends carry the Soul to their flaming pit, and the author awakens in a cold sweat and with a prayer to Jesus for his own salvation from a similar fate.

DEOR'S LAMENT. A forty-two line Old English poem preserved in the *Exeter Book*. It was composed in the form of stanzas, each of which ends in a refrain. In his complaint the minstrel-poet sorrows over his loss of favor and names the skillful singer who has displaced him. The date of the poem is uncertain; it could hardly have been composed later than the sixth century.

DREAM OF THE ROOD, THE. An Old English Christian poem of one hundred and forty lines preserved in the West-Saxon dialect in the *Vercelli Book;* parts of it have also been carved in runes on the Ruthwell Cross in Dumfriesshire, Scotland. The theme of the poem is a vision of the Holy Cross (Rood) in which the sacred emblem addresses the poet, recounts the story of the crucifixion, and promises to help the dreamer.

EVERYMAN. The finest and most famous of the morality plays was written shortly before the close of the fifteenth century. It was apparently derived from the Dutch morality *Elckerlijk,* but has been as completely anglicized as a production of this general type could be. In tempo, compression, controlled emotional power, and freedom from vulgarity it surpasses all other religious moralities. Like them it deals with the salvation of Everyman's soul, but unlike them it does not follow him from cradle to heaven but presents only the last of his pilgrimage to the grave, after the manner of the popular *Ars Moriendi,* or *Art of Dying,* treatises. Everyman learns that his "Goods" desert him early, and that only his "Good-Deeds" will accompany him into the Valley of Death.

EXODUS. An Old English poem of uncertain date that recounts in rhymed couplets and with considerable life and movement the biblical story of the escape of the Israelites from Egypt and the destruction of Pharaoh's pursuing chariots in the Red Sea. The poem was once attributed to Caedmon.

FINNSBURH FRAGMENT, THE. A fifty-line fragment of an Old English epic that tells of the blood-feud between Finn, king of the Frisians, and Hnaef, leader of the Hocings and brother of Finn's wife Hildeburh. Another episode from the same poem is sung by King Hrothgar's minstrel at the feast in honor of Beowulf in the epic of that name. In the *Beowulf* fragment the feud is at first settled by agreement but breaks out again, Finn is slain by the avengers, and Queen Hildeburh is carried off to Denmark. The events narrated in this fragmentary epic fall between the fourth and the sixth centuries.

FLORES AND BLANCHEFLOUR. A lush and ornate medieval romance of the type made popular in England by the Crusades. The Christian heroine, Blancheflour, is beloved by the Saracen prince, Flores, at whose court she is being brought up as a captive. With the help of a magic ring that will tarnish when she is in danger, the lovers succeed in avoiding or overcoming numerous difficulties and hazards, and are ultimately united after the emir of Egypt, in whose seraglio she has been detained, learns of their suffering and generously surrenders her to Flores.

FLOWER AND THE LEAF, THE. A dream allegory of about six hundred lines in rhyme royal, formerly ascribed to Chaucer but showing characteristics of a century later than his. There is an element of the *débat*—or at least a sharp contrast in the theme—for the poet represents himself as beholding two queens, each with her train of lords and ladies; the first is devoted to the Leaf, and the second to the Flower. The quiet contest is evidently between the chastity and sobriety of the Queen of the Leaf and the irresponsible gaiety of the Queen of the Flower. The poet apparently favors the party of the Leaf, for a sudden squall drives the fair-weather Flower party to take refuge with their less easily tarnished and more permanent opposites.

FOX (or Vox) AND THE WOLF, THE. A three-hundred-line "beast epic" of about 1300, which was borrowed from the French tale of Reynard the Fox. It contains the popular episodes of the unsuccessful attempt of the fox to trick the cock from his perch, and of his being himself trapped in a well with two buckets; from this predicament he escapes very cleverly by inducing Sigrim, the wolf, to draw him up by leaping into the empty bucket and going to the bottom of the well while the tricky fox ascends to the surface in the other bucket, leaving his rescuer to be beaten to death by the friars who come in the morning to get water.

GAMMER GURTON'S NEEDLE. See STEVENSON, William in *Dictionary of Authors*.

GAWAYNE AND THE GRENE KNIGHT. See PEARL POET in *Dictionary of Authors*.

GENESIS. An Old English religious poem of the eighth century which adds to the usual early stories from the Bible much apocryphal material concerning the fall of the angels and other episodes not in Genesis. The poem is written in rhymed couplets, and was formerly attributed to Caedmon.

GUY OF WARWICK. One of the longest—and most popular— of the fourteenth-century verse romances. The hero is the son of a steward in the household of the earl of Warwick. He becomes a great knight, however, and after many brave adventures at home and abroad, he marries the earl's daughter Felice. Of all his deeds of prowess the most famous is his encounter with the Danish giant Colbrand. The last part of the romance takes on the coloring of a saint's legend, for Guy turns hermit, and is supported by his wife, who does not recognize him until he reveals his identity to her just as he is about to die.

HARROWING OF HELL, THE. The subject of a two-hundred-and-fifty-line poem of the thirteenth or fourteenth century and of more than one medieval miracle play is the story of Christ's descent into hell during the interval between his burial and his resurrection to force Satan to release Adam, Eve, Abraham, Moses, and other Old Testament characters who had died before his coming, and who had not therefore been saved. Among the characters in these poems and plays is the Door-Keeper of Hell, whose popularity is apparent from the drunken porter's improvising the rôle in Shakespeare's *Macbeth* (I, 3, ll. 1–23).

HAVELOK THE DANE. A metrical romance of the beginning of the fourteenth century. Its roots are apparently Old English, Havelok being a heroic development of Anlaf Cuaran, who fought against the Anglo-Saxons at Brunanburh (see BATTLE OF BRU-NANBURH). In the romance he is driven from his kingdom of Denmark; he escapes to England, but ultimately, with the aid of a mystical light that gathers about his head and marks his royal birth, he recovers his kingdom and brings his traitorous enemies to justice.

HUNTING OF THE CHEVIOT, THE. See **CHEVY CHASE.**

HUSBAND'S MESSAGE, THE. One of several Old English poems in the *Exeter Book,* a famous tenth-century manuscript which has been preserved in Exeter Cathedral since the eleventh century. The poem is in the form of a love message written by an exile to the wife from whom he has been separated. He wishes to have her join him as soon as Spring makes travel possible. The poem is sometimes interpreted as a sequel to *The Wife's Complaint,* another love lyric in the *Exeter Book.*

HYCKESCORNER. An early Tudor morality play, printed before the beginning of the English Reformation. It is essentially a "conversion play," in which "thre peryllous men"—Frewyll, Imagynacyon, and Hyckescorner (Richard or Dick Scorner)—riotously assault Pyte (Pity) for interfering with their fighting among themselves and leave him trussed up in stolen leg-irons. Pyte is released by his fellows, Contemplacyon and Perseveraunce, who then proceed to preach Frewyll and Imagynacyon out of their sins and into a pious state of complete repentance. Meanwhile Hyckescorner has dropped out of the playlet leaving the reader to wonder why the morality should have been named after a minor clown in the cast.

JACK JUGGLER. A Tudor "school play" printed in 1563 but written five or ten years earlier. The debt of the unknown author to Plautus' *Amphitruo* would have been apparent even if he had not acknowledged it in the prologue. But the interlude is not as fully developed as is the Plautine original. It is little more than a farcical sketch in which the "Vice," Jack Juggler, assumes the guise and identity of the prodigal lackey, Jenkin Careaway, and forces his dupe by insistence and threats himself to believe in the absurd hoax. The play seems purely jocular, but a hint in the epilogue has led many scholars to regard it as a satiric and subtle attack upon the Roman Catholic doctrine of transubstantiation.

JUDITH. An Old English epic fragment, three hundred and fifty lines long, of unknown date and authorship. The poem recounts how the Hebrew heroine of the apocryphal story of Judith, a widow of Bethulia, slew Holofernes, the general of Nebuchadnezzar's army, that was encamped against her people, and carried his head off in a sack. The Old English poem may have been composed as a tribute to Aethelflaed, the queen of Mercia who defended her kingdom against the Danish invaders at the beginning of the tenth century. Certain it is, however, that the Judith of the poem resembles the Christian warrior-queen of Mercia much more than she does the original Jewish heroine of the Apocrypha.

KING HORN. A verse romance of the late thirteenth century. In some fifteen hundred lines it tells of the heroic and amorous adventures of King Horn, who, banished from his kingdom of Suddene, succeeds in overcoming many plots against him and many dangers, and ultimately in marrying the princess Rymenhild, daughter of King Almair of Westernesse. The inferior metrical romance of *Childe Horne* is apparently another version of the same tale.

LOCRINE. One of the most important of the forty-odd plays ascribed to Shakespeare but not written by him. *Locrine* was published in 1595 but may have been written as early as 1591. The tragedy has to do with the love of Locrine, legendary king of Britain, for Estrild, a German maiden, and the murder of the girl by his jealous queen Gwendolen. Although romantic in its treatment and relieved by many low comedy scenes, the tragedy has clinging to it several of the characteristics of the earlier classical tragedies of the *Gorboduc* type (see Thomas Norton and Thomas Sackville in *Dictionary of Authors*). Among these the most conspicuous are the dumb-shows, the symbolical figure of Revenge as chorus, the two ghosts, and the Senecan moralizing. Much scholarly ink has been spilled over the question of authorship, some attributing the play to George Peele and believing that it shows traces of his satirical style. The relationship of *Locrine* and the contemporary tragedy of *Selimus* has also been found puzzling; the consensus of opinion is that the author of *Selimus* cribbed from *Locrine*, and not conversely. The story of Locrine appears in two Elizabethan works, Thomas Lodge's *Complaint of Elstred* and Spenser's *Faerie Queene;* it is also the subject of a poetic tragedy written in 1887 by A. C. Swinburne.

MACRO MORALITIES or PLAYS. See CASTLE OF PER-SEVERANCE and MANKIND.

MANKIND. A morality play of the late fifteenth century. To-gether with *The Castle of Perseverance* and *Mind, Will, and Understanding* it appears in a manuscript once owned by the Reverend Cox Macro (1688–1767), the antiquarian; hence it is often referred to as one of the "Macro Moralities (or Plays)." It is significant in the history of the early drama because it seems to have been one of the first plays produced in an inn-yard by a semi-professional company. Like the later interludes it was de-signed largely to entertain, and it introduces the merry devil Titivillus, who refuses to show his "abhomynabull presens" until New-Gyse and Now-a-Days, his fellow-players, have collected suf-ficient money from the bystanders.

MISOGONUS. A "prodigal son" morality preserved in a muti-lated manuscript in the Duke of Devonshire's library. It may have been written by Thomas Richardes, who signed the Prologue, or by Laurence Johnson, but the author is uncertain. It was ap-parently written in 1560. Like *Nice Wanton,* another wayward child play of a somewhat earlier date, it owes its general theme to the Latin play of *Acolastus* by Gnaphaeus, which had been translated into English in 1540 by Thomas Palsgrave. But it is thoroughly English and very lively in its presentation of Melissa, the courtesan, and the rakehelly companions of the prodigal, who cheerfully assist him down the primrose path until his repentance drives him home to a forgiving father.

MUCEDORUS. An Elizabethan comedy published anonymously in 1598 and at one time ascribed to Shakespeare. It has also been assigned, on quite insufficient evidence, to Robert Greene. The full title is: *A Most pleasant Comedie of Mucedorus, the king's sonne of Valentia and Amadine the kings daughter of Arragon, with the merie conceites of Mouse.* This romantic-pastoral-farcical medley was written for a performance at court but became popular and carried on well into the reign of James I. Like other con-temporary romantic comedies it is filled with disguisings of the pilgrim of love, with lyrical passages between him and his princess, and with the contrasting crudities of Mouse the Clown.

MUNDUS ET INFANS or THE WORLD AND THE CHILD is a typical religious morality play printed by Wynkyn de Worde in 1522 but written about a quarter of a century earlier. Its thou-sand lines present the usual struggle of Mankind in his pilgrimage from childhood to old age, beset by the usual sins but finally converted by Conscience and Perseverance and saved for Heaven.

NICE WANTON. An anonymous morality printed in 1560 but probably written ten or fifteen years earlier. It is called in the original title "a pretty interlude"; like the nearly contemporaneous *Misogonus,* however, it belongs to the wayward child type of Tudor morality, which the translation into English in 1540 of the Latin *Acolastus* of Gnaphaeus had helped to popularize—at least among schoolmasters. *Nice Wanton* reveals in lines of naïve and bleak certainty that if the rod is spared, the child will be spoiled. Ismael and his naughty sister Dalila are the spoiled and undisciplined darlings—the "nice wantons"—who end their wretched lives one on the gallows-tree and the other in a pest-house. Their plaster-saint brother, Barnabas, virtuous but dull, survives to say priggishly "I told you so." It may be significant that the liveliest—and most modern—scene in the interlude depicts a crap game in which Dalila and her lover Iniquitie strip Ismael of the money that he has stolen from his father.

NUT–BROWN MAID, THE. An anonymous poem of the fifteenth century. It is a dramatic lyric that presents a metrical *dèbat* between He and She—the man and the maid—speaking in alternating stanzas. In the refrain that concludes each stanza spoken by the man, he asserts that he

> ". . . must to the grene wode go,
> Alone, a banyshed man."

And in her reply she loyally insists,

> "For in my mynde, of all mankynde
> I love but you alone."

Satisfied at last by this continued assertion of her fidelity to him, he tells her that she has won

> . . . an erlys son
> And not a banyshed man."

Bishop Percy chose *The Nut-Brown Maid* for inclusion in his *Reliques of Ancient English Poetry* (1765).

ORFEO, SIR. A short metrical romance borrowed from a Breton lay. In theme it is a curious medievalizing of the Greek myth of Orpheus and his wife Eurydice. In the romance Orfeo loses his lovely lady to fairyland, and daring to follow her in the guise of a minstrel, he draws her out of her enchantment by his sweet playing. This lay, with its fairy-tale of the rescue of a bewitched lady, was ultimately made into a popular ballad (see Child's *English and Scottish Popular Ballads,* No. 19), in which the kidnaped Lady Isabel is piped away from the "king o Ferrie" by her husband.

OWL AND THE NIGHTINGALE, THE. A Middle English poem of 1,795 lines in octosyllabic couplets. The author may have been either Nicholas of Guilford (fl. 1250) or John of Guildford (fl. 1225), and the date of composition is about 1250. The poem is in the conventional form of a *débat* or disputation between two birds which are the symbols respectively of religion and love. In the course of their argument as to the relative value of their gifts to mankind these allegorical creatures introduce many allusions to the delights of nature and the charms of the English countryside. The anonymous poet is fair to both disputants but seems, quite naturally, to favor the bird of love.

PARNASSUS PLAYS, THE. A trilogy of semi-allegorical plays by an unknown author, presenting and satirizing the university life in the time of Elizabeth and—in the third play—attacking contemporary poets and dramatists. The first of these plays, *The Pilgrimage to Parnassus,* produced at St. John's College, Cambridge, during the Christmas holidays of 1597, is an allegorical representation of the studies and life at the college. The second play, *The Return from Parnassus, Part I,* acted in 1600, satirically represents the students as leaving the halls of learning for London, where they are obliged to live by various menial occupations and ultimately become shepherds (i.e. poets). In this play the allegory tends to wear thin and the realism to wax fat. The last of the trio, *The Return from Parnassus, Part II* (1601), which has the subtitle *The Scourge of Simony,* is the most famous of the three because of its comments on contemporary writers and its definite allusions to Shakespeare, Jonson, and the "war of the theaters." In Act IV, Scene 3, Will Kemp, the famous clown of Shakespeare's company, introduced as a character, is represented as remarking; "Why here's our fellow Shakespeare puts them all down—ay, and Ben Jonson too. O that Ben Jonson is a pestilent fellow; he brought up Horace, giving the poets a pill [an allusion to a scene in Jonson's *Poetaster*]; but our fellow Shakespeare hath given him a purge that made him bewray his credit." Just what "purge" Shakespeare gave Ben Jonson is not clear; the allusion may have been to the attack on the children's company of players, for whom Jonson was writing at the time, put into the mouth of Rosencrantz in Act II, Scene 2 of *Hamlet*.

PASTON LETTERS. See **PASTON** in *Dictionary of Authors*.

PATIENCE. See **PEARL POET** in *Dictionary of Authors*.

PEARL. See **PEARL POET** in *Dictionary of Authors*.

PHILIP QUARLL. One of the most popular of the English imitations of *Robinson Crusoe*. It was published in 1727, or eight years after the more famous tale, and was ascribed by the "editor," one P. L., to Mr. Edward Dorrington, a merchant so fair in his dealings that he could hardly have been dishonest in reporting "the unparalleled sufferings and surprising adventures" of "the English Hermit." The tale is divided into three books; the first contains the account of Dorrington's discovery of the hermit on a South Sea island paradise; the second and third present materials allegedly taken from Philip Quarll's "parchment roll." If it were not for the editor's assertion that "every incident herein related is real matter of fact," it would be necessary for the reader to assign to "the miraculous acts of Providence" such of the hermit's adventures as his making a good man Friday out of a monkey by training little "Beau-fidelle" to fetch wood and water, help with the cooking, and want, in fact, "nothing but speech to complete him for human society."

PHOENIX NEST, THE. One of the most popular of several Elizabethan anthologies of verse. It was issued by "R. S. of the Inner Temple Gentleman" in 1593 and contains, besides many early anonymous pieces, poems by Sidney, Lodge, Breton, and other known writers.

PILGRIMAGE TO PARNASSUS. See **PARNASSUS PLAYS.**

POEMA MORALE or **MORAL ODE.** A metrical homily or sermon dating from the end of the twelfth century. In its almost four hundred lines it deals with the brevity of life, the certainty of death, the pangs of hell, and the joys of heaven. It is significant largely because of its metrical plan; it is the first English poem in "fourteener" lines arranged in couplets. The poem is extant in seven different manuscripts.

QUARLL, PHILIP. See **PHILIP QUARLL.**

REMORSE OF CONSCIENCE. See **AYENBITE OF INWYT.**

RETURN FROM PARNASSUS, THE. See **PARNASSUS PLAYS.**

RUIN, THE. A fragmentary poem which follows *The Husband's Message* in the *Exeter Book* collection of Old English poems. In it the unknown poet laments the ruin of a group of ancient buildings—probably Roman in origin—and reflects on the fate that has overtaken the warriors who in former times banqueted in the now empty halls.

SCOURGE OF SIMONY, THE. See **PARNASSUS PLAYS.**

SEAFARER, THE. An old English lament of about one hundred lines which has as its theme a melancholy description of the discomforts and perils of life on the wintry seas and a final comparison of the uncertain pleasures of earth and the surer rewards of heaven. The poem has been preserved in the *Exeter Book;* its date of composition is uncertain.

SECOND SHEPHERDS' PLAY. See **WAKEFIELD MASTER** in *Dictionary of Authors.*

SECUNDA PASTORUM. See **WAKEFIELD MASTER** in *Dictionary of Authors.*

SELIMUS. See **LOCRINE.**

SQUIRE OF LOW DEGREE, THE. A fourteenth-century metrical romance more charmingly written than most of the longer poems of knighthood. It is conventional, however, in that it presents an inconspicuous youth who, through courage, persistence, and the inspiring love of a fair lady, overcomes his enemies and his hardships—including an imprisonment of seven years— becomes a famous knight, and ultimately marries "the king's daughter of Hungary."

SUMER IS I–CUMEN IN. The first line of a song (Summer has come in) that is also known by the title of *Cuckoo-Song.* It is probably the earliest Spring song in English—a heart-warming praise of all things in nature that are alive and green after the burial of Winter. It was written in the early thirteenth century in rhyme with a refrain on the note of the "cuccu," and is still sung to the original melody and widely parodied.

TALE OF GAMELYN, THE. A verse romance of the mid-fourteenth century, which is significant because of its connection with Chaucer, Lodge, and Shakespeare. It is the Robin Hood-like tale of the abused youngest brother who escapes from the plottings of his oldest brother and becomes chief of a band of outlaws; after many hardships and adventures, he punishes his enemies, makes his peace with the king, and becomes Chief Justice of the Free

Forest. In some manuscripts of Chaucer's *Canterbury Tales, The Tale of Gamelyn* has been put into the mouth of the Cook, although it is not certain that Chaucer wrote it or even intended to make such use of it in his series of stories. In the Elizabethan period Thomas Lodge added a love-interest to the original story and turned it into his prose romance, *Rosalynde.* Then Shakespeare, a decade later, converted Lodge's story into what is probably his best pastoral comedy, *As You Like It.*

THERSITES. An extremely farcical little "school play," acted, apparently, in 1537 and attributed by some scholars to John Heywood (see *Dictionary of Authors*). The theme was taken from Plautus' comedy, *Miles Gloriosus* (or *The Braggart Warrior*), and more directly from a translation of a Latin poem by Ravisius Textor, but the plot is so slight as to be quite negligible. The emphasis is almost entirely on the cowardice of the boy braggart, Thersites, who challenges "King Arthur and the Knights of the Round Table" but quakes with fear at the sight of a snail. There are some irrelevant episodes in the farce, and some of the invective is indecent. But the piece has lively parts, and in spite of its Latin origin is thoroughly English.

TOM TYLER AND HIS WIFE. An anonymous domestic farce of about the middle of the sixteenth century. It is a "shrew" play that looks backward to John Heywood's *Merry Play between John John the Husband, Tyb the Wife, and Sir John the Priest* and forward to Shakespeare's *Taming of the Shrew.* But in *Tom Tyler and his Wife* the victory of the husband over the henpecking spouse is incomplete; although Tom gets a courageous friend to substitute for him and beat her into submission, he is so spiritless from her nagging that he confesses the trick and so comes again under distaff control. The farce has some traces of the earlier morality plays in its allegorical characters of Destiny, Desire, and Patience, and perhaps, too, in the didactic suggestion that man must bear his domestic destiny patiently.

WALDHERE or WALDERE. An Old English heroic poem of the eleventh century which exists only in two short fragments in the Royal Library at Copenhagen. From a Latin poem on the same subject (*Waltharius* by Ekkehard of St. Gall) it is apparent that the tale has to do with the exploits of Waldhere, warrior-hostage to Attila the Hun. The hero escaped from his overlord taking with him the princess Hiltgund and much gold. He successfully fought off Guthhere, king of the Burgundians, and his band of warriors, and ultimately married Hiltgund. But the Old

English fragments cover only the period of the story before Waldhere's successful battle.

WANDERER, THE. An Old English elegy or lament of one hundred and fifteen lines, which has been preserved in the *Exeter Book*. The Wanderer tells of his sufferings and sorrows; he has lost his master and must face the hardships of travel over stormy seas in search of a new lord. In his misfortunes he sees the changes that must come to all mortals. The date of composition of the poem is uncertain.

WARNING FOR FAIR WOMEN, A. An Elizabethan domestic tragedy dealing, like *Arden of Feversham,* with the murder of a husband by his wife's contrivance. The play was printed in 1599 but only after it had been acted by the Lord Chamberlain's Company (Shakespeare's). The full title indicates the content and the flavor of the play: "A Warning for Faire Women, containing The most Tragicall and Lamentable Murther of Master George Sanders, of London, Marchant, nigh Shooters Hill; consented unto by his owne wife, acted by M. Browne, Mistris Drewry and Trusty Roger, agents therein: with their severall ends." The drama was based on a pamphlet account of the murder published immediately after the crime in 1573. As with all of the domestic tragedies of this literary period, the play is didactic, or there is a pretence, at least, that it was created as a deterrent to crime; but with these desires to "warn" the readers, there appears also a considerable enthusiasm for lurid episodes. In *A Warning for Fair Women* the psychological reactions of the criminals to their murder are more penetratingly presented than in most other tragedies of contemporary crime.

WIDSITH. An Old English poem of one hundred and forty-three lines preserved in the *Exeter Book*. The name *Widsith,* or *Far-Traveller,* has apparently been assumed by the minstrel composer of the poem. In it he tells of his journeys to many lands and of the heroes for whom he has strung his harp. The poem dates from not later than the seventh century.

WIFE'S COMPLAINT, THE. One of the several Old English poems preserved in the *Exeter Book*. It is the sometimes obscure lament of a sorrowing wife whose husband has gone on a sea-voyage, leaving her with no friends and with only unsympathetic relatives. Because of its content, it would seem to have some connection with *The Husband's Message,* another *Exeter Book* poem in which a husband separated from his wife urges her to join him.

WORLD AND THE CHILD, THE. See **MUNDUS ET IN-FANS.**

YORKSHIRE TRAGEDY, A. A domestic tragedy published in 1608 with the authorship ascribed—incorrectly—to William Shakespeare. Like *Arden of Feversham* the tragedy is based on a notorious murder case. In 1605 a depraved gamester living at Calverley Hall, Yorkshire, stabbed his long-suffering wife and murdered his two infant children; he was apprehended, tried, condemned, and "pressed to death." The play is a hastily written, catch-penny dramatic sketch composed shortly after the crime. Its brief scenes deal entirely with the murders and the retribution. The emphasis is on the moral that "crime does not pay." There is a strongly stressed moral also in George Wilkins' *Miseries of Enforced Marriage,* another treatment of the same event. Wilkins' drama was produced in 1607 by "his Majesties Servants" (Shakespeare's company). Blame for young Calverley's crime is placed by Wilkins, as the title of his tragedy indicates, upon the murderer's elders, who had pressed him into an alliance with an unloved wife.

III
GLOSSARY OF LITERARY TERMS

III

GLOSSARY OF LITERARY TERMS

ALL THE YEAR AROUND. See MAGAZINES.

ALLEGORY. A form of verbal art in which direct narrative is used to convey through personification and symbolism actions, characters, settings, and ideas which the writer wishes to present indirectly. Thus the reader of an allegory is expected to get not only the apparent or "front" story but the hidden tale or truth that lurks behind it. Allegories are often simple stories which convey metaphorically some spiritual or ethical ideas; such allegories are purposely didactic. In other allegories, however, there may lie behind the "front" story some political, literary, or even personal attack; such allegories are satirical. Allegories may be sustained or short; they may be independent wholes or may be imbedded in non-allegorical matrices; they may appear in the form of prose, poetry, or drama. FABLES and PARABLES are special forms of allegory. In English literature all MORALITY PLAYS, e.g., *Everyman, Mankind, The Castle of Perseverance,* are allegorical. So also are BEAST EPICS, such as *The Fox and the Wolf.* Important examples that are not anonymous are Langland's *Vision of Piers Plowman;* Spenser's *Faerie Queene,* which has a multiple moral-theological-political allegory expressed through tales of knightly deeds; Ben Jonson's *Poetaster,* a dramatic allegory of literary and personal criticism; Bunyan's *Pilgrim's Progress;* Dryden's *The Hind and the Panther,* a theological "beast fable," and his *Absalom and Achitophel,* a political allegory. Occasionally the "front" story in an allegorical satire may be so entertaining as to bury completely, or almost completely, the satire behind it. This is true, for example, of Swift's *Gulliver's Travels,* which children—and most grown-ups—read without realizing that the entrancing tales are the cover of a series of bitter social and political attacks. (See also BEAST EPIC, DREAM ALLEGORY, EXEMPLUM, and PARABLE.)

ALLITERATIVE ROMANCE. See MEDIEVAL ROMANCE.

ANCIENTS AND MODERNS, BATTLE OF THE. A scholarly controversy at the end of the seventeenth and the beginning of the eighteenth century over the relative merits of classical and modern learning. After paper bullets in this warfare had been flying in France for some time, Sir William Temple brought the fight to England by writing a defense of the Ancients in his *Essay Upon the Ancient and Modern Learning* (1690). Later he praised as genuine the *Epistles of Phalaris* (see PHALARIS CONTROVERSY), thus bringing into the battle on the opposite side William Wotton and Richard Bentley, the Cambridge classicist. In the most famous treatise to grow out of this academic warfare, Swift's *Battle of the Books*, the author came weakly to Temple's defense, summed up the controversy in an allegorical tale of a physical struggle between classical and modern books, but left the issue essentially unsettled.

ANTIMASQUE. See MASQUE.

APOCRYPHA. Specifically, the name is given to certain books of the Bible which appeared in the *Septuagint,* or earliest Greek version of the Old Testament, and in St. Jerome's fourth-century translation of the Bible into Latin, but which were rejected by early Protestant reformers as uninspired and unauthentic because they are not part of the Hebrew Bible. Until the beginning of the nineteenth century they were issued in English Protestant Bibles between the Old Testament and the New Testament; nineteenth-century revisers omitted them entirely. Until comparatively recent times, accordingly, the apocryphal books had almost as much influence on literature as did the "canonical" or authentic books. The Old English epic fragment of *Judith* (see *List of Anonymous Works*) was based on the apocryphal book of the same title; and Shakespeare's oft-quoted line from *The Merchant of Venice* (Act IV, 1) "A Daniel come to judgment! yea, a Daniel," alludes to the apocryphal story of *Susanna and the Elders.* (See BIBLE in *List of Anonymous Works* and CANON.) The adjective *apocryphal* is applied also to any work ascribed to an author on insufficient evidence but not definitely established as belonging to the accepted "canon" of his writings. Thus there are some two-score dramas in the "Shakespeare Apocrypha" or group of plays at some time attributed to him but not generally approved as having come from his pen.

ARCADIAN. The adjective form of *Arcadia,* an ancient mountainous district of Greece inhabited, according to long tradition, by simple shepherds who lived an ideal pastoral life. The adjective came to be applied, therefore, to pastoral prose, poetry, and drama written in the mood of rural and idyllic simplicity and peace.

Specifically the term is used of those Elizabethan pastoral tales that have the general content and manner of Sidney's *Arcadia;* of these Greene's *Menaphon* and Lodge's *Rosalynde* are good examples. In drama Fletcher's *Faithful Shepherdess* and, in certain scenes, Shakespeare's *As You Like It* are Arcadian. In lyric poetry of a later date Keats' *On a Grecian Urn* has the same idyllic flavor and mood. (See PASTORAL.)

AREOPAGUS. The term given in literary criticism to an Elizabethan group of poets and critics, including Sir Philip Sidney, Gabriel Harvey, Edmund Spenser, and two or three others, who were associated in an attempt to reform English verse by substituting quantitative for accentual measures and unrhymed classical lines for the more "barbaric" rhymed ones. Their efforts were more academic than practical, and both Sidney and Spenser never expressed their theories to any great extent in their own poetry. The name of the group came—as did that of Milton's *Areopagitica,* or treatise on the freedom of the press—from the *Areopagus,* or "Hill of Ares" (or Mars) in ancient Athens, the seat of the court of highest authority and, incidentally, the natural rostrum from which Saint Paul preached his sermon to the Athenians (Acts 17, 19 ff.).

ARTHURIAN ROMANCE. See MEDIEVAL ROMANCE.

AUGUSTAN AGE. Any period of polished manners, high culture, and great literary attainments which may be favorably compared with the age of the Roman emperor Augustus Caesar (27 B.C.–A.D. 14), during which Vergil, Ovid, Horace, and other great poets lived and wrote. In English literature it is generally applied—somewhat loosely—to the neo-classical period at the beginning of the eighteenth century, when Pope, Addison, Steele, and their literary contemporaries were producing correct and polished satires.

AUTOBIOGRAPHY. See BIOGRAPHY.

BACONIAN THEORY. The absurd hypothesis that Shakespeare's plays were written by Sir Francis Bacon. The Baconians base their assertion partly on specious internal evidence from the works themselves, partly on the assumption that the genius who wrote them would have left posterity a more complete biographical record than did William Shakespeare. See Sir Francis Bacon and William Shakespeare in *Dictionary of Authors.*

BALLAD. The POPULAR BALLAD or FOLK BALLAD is a song of the people in which a story is told. The song was often used to accompany a folk-dance (compare *ballet*) very much as is still done with children's game-songs. Whether the ballad is originally the work of a single author or the product of *communal authorship*—arising spontaneously out of a group—is a timeworn argument among scholars; but all popular ballads undergo considerable change in the process of oral transmission from generation to generation. Ballad-making and ballad-singing are not confined to any literary period; there are ballads in America —*Jesse James* and *Frankie and Johnny,* for example—of comparatively recent origin. But many of the songs which are still sung in the rural regions of America and England today date back to the Middle Ages. The fifteenth century was the golden age of the ballad, and the most fertile field was the border country between England and Scotland. Popular ballads are commonly composed in stanzas, often in the four-line *ballad stanza* with alternate iambic tetrameter and trimeter lines rhyming *abcb.* Some have a refrain; many echo themselves with *incremental repetition* (see *Note on Versification*). However humble their authorship, they usually deal with knights and ladies. The story may be a tabloid murder, as in *Edward* and *The Twa Corbies;* a tale of outlawry, like those in *Johnny Armstrong* and the numerous Robin Hood ballads; a tragedy of love, like *Fair Margaret and Sweet William* and *Bonny Barbara Allen;* a tale of tragedy at sea like *Sir Patrick Spens;* a tale of the supernatural like *Kemp Owyne* or *The Wife of Usher's Well;* or a humorous metrical fabliau like *The Farmer's Curst Wife* or *Get Up and Bar the Door.* The elemental human passions are revealed with masterful compression, no superfluous detail detracting from the dramatic intensity of the story. Conventional figures of speech—*milk-white, red as a rose*—exist side by side with details so perfectly expressed that sophisticated poets have despaired to imitate them.

The efforts of poets to imitate the popular ballads are called LITERARY BALLADS. The author may try faithfully to reproduce the simple charm of his models—as in Keats' *La Belle Dame Sans Merci*—or, like Coleridge in *The Rime of the Ancient Mariner,* he may use the ballad form merely as a framework for a more complex, sophisticated poem. The vogue for literary ballads in England grew up with the eighteenth century revival of the popular ballad under the leadership of Bishop Percy. It continued throughout the next century, influencing, among others, Scott, Coleridge, Keats, Rossetti, and Morris. Many literary ballads take the form of parodies.

The BROADSIDE BALLAD is the term given to narrative songs cheaply printed on one side only of a single sheet, and hawked

in the streets and at fairs and other gatherings for a penny
or two. They were the work of hack poets who strung into
rough jingles events of sensational or current interest, such as a
monstrous birth, the catching of a strange fish, or destruction by
fire or earthquake. Those dealing with murders and executions
were sometimes called *criminals' good nights* because of the practice of putting into the murderer's mouth the account of his
crime—and often, illogically enough, of his execution. These
ballads were designed to be sung to a popular melody indicated
at the top of the sheet on which they were printed. Shakespeare
introduces a ballad-monger—Autolycus—in his *Winter's Tale,*
Act IV, 4, and these popular figures appear also in numerous
other Elizabethan plays. Broadside ballads were sold until displaced by newspapers.

BEAST EPIC. A familiar type of medieval tale in which the adventures and misadventures of animals are told, usually for the
purpose of satirizing the follies and foibles of human beings. The
sly hero of most of the beast epics is Reynard the Fox, whose
tricky deeds are recounted in many German and French tales
as well as in several English ones. The most important beast
epic in English is *The Fox and the Wolf.* (See *List of Anonymous Works.*) Chaucer made use of this type of literature in
The Nun's Priest's Tale, and Spenser drew upon it for the purposes of religious satire in his *Prosopopoia, or Mother Hubberds
Tale.*

BESTIARY, THE. Specifically a collection of curious thirteenth-
century poems in which the alleged habits of animals are used
allegorically to inculcate religious doctrines. The term *bestiary*
is also applied loosely to similar animal tales in prose or verse,
including those that are more properly called *beast epics. The
Bestiary* has its roots in the classical *Physiologus,* and there is also
a fragmentary treatment of the theme in an Old English poem.
The medieval interest in the religious "significance" of animals
sprang also from the stories in Genesis of the creation and the flood.
In the thirteenth-century *Bestiary* the Christian symbolism is
made effective by descriptions of thirteen creatures, all given to
habits that would stretch the eyes of modern zoölogists. Thus
the elephant sleeps by leaning against a tree, and the panther,
symbolizing Christ, has a most wonderfully sweet breath, which
draws all other beasts to him. In the poems of the thirteenth-century
collection the meter varies; most of the lines are arranged in six-
syllable couplets.

BIOGRAPHY. The lives of men, or biographies, come into being under various circumstances. Sometimes they are a record, too often biased, made by a member of the subject's family. One of the earliest of such lives was that of Sir Thomas More (1478–1535) written by his son-in-law, William Roper (1496–1578); another son-in-law who paid a similar tribute to his wife's father was John Lockhart (1794–1854), whose biography of Sir Walter Scott (1771–1832) is standard. Both of these lives were less fulsome than the memoirs of their respective husbands written in the seventeenth century by the Duchess of Newcastle (c. 1624–74) and Lucy Hutchinson (1620–75). Family biographies are likely to be less objective than those written by a friend or acquaintance who has known his subject in the flesh but who has had no family attachment to him. The most famous biography in English was written by an admiring reporter of his subject's every breath and utterance—James Boswell's *Life of Samuel Johnson,* by all odds the best full-length literary portrait written. Few biographers have "Bozzy's" opportunities; most must reconstruct their subject from public and private records, from journals and letters, and from his writings bring him back to life as best they can.

Different periods in English history seem to have occasioned different approaches to biographical writing. Before the beginning of the eighteenth century comparatively little biography was produced; it is astounding that there was no life of Shakespeare until Nicholas Rowe's sketch in 1709, nearly a century after the dramatist's death. But democratic ideals brought interest in men's lives, and the past three centuries have seen much biographical writing. The objectives of biographers, however, varied greatly. Excepting for Boswell's monument to Johnson most biographers of the late eighteenth and early nineteenth centuries glorified their subjects, making them heroic models by which lesser men might make their lives sublime. Later—as the widespread objection to Froude's intimate biography of Carlyle implies—Victorian restraint held biographers to accounts of their subjects' public acts, private lives being regarded as no affair either of writer or reader. Finally, in the twentieth century came the full revelation of the great one's weaknesses, foibles, domestic squabbles, not only his private but his most intimate affairs being ruthlessly exposed. This was Lytton Strachey's formula, but he did it with the careful documentation and literary skill that his imitators failed too often to display.

Closely related to biography are the DIARIES, such as Samuel Pepys' (1633–1703); the JOURNALS, such as Sir Walter Scott's; and

AUTOBIOGRAPHIES or self-portraitures, such as John Stuart Mill's (1873) and John Ruskin's *Praeterita* (1885–9).

BLACKWOOD'S EDINBURGH MAGAZINE. See MAGA–ZINES.

BLUESTOCKING. Originally, a member of one of several mid-eighteenth-century coteries in which London ladies met to discuss literature and escape "the tyranny of cards." The first gathering was at the home of Mrs. Elizabeth Vesey in the fifties; according to Boswell, it was a man, Benjamin Stillingfleet, who wore blue stockings to one of her gatherings and gave the cult its name. (For information about other prominent Bluestockings, see the entries under Carter, Chapone, Montagu, and Hannah More in *Dictionary of Authors*.) Today the term is applied opprobriously to female pedants.

BOWLES CONTROVERSY. See BOWLES, William Lisle in *Dictionary of Authors*.

BRETON LAY. See LAY.

BROADSIDE BALLAD. See BALLAD.

BURLESQUE. A term applied generally to any farcical composition in which a serious subject is treated ludicrously, especially one in which the manner of one or more literary works is held up to ridicule. Although the words *burlesque* and *parody* are often used interchangeably, the word *parody* is more commonly applied to a take-off on a single work and lacks the farcical connotation of *burlesque*. Chaucer's *Rime of Sir Thopas* is a burlesque of the medieval romances; Lewis Carroll's "How doth the little crocodile" is a parody of Isaac Watts' "How doth the little busy bee." English literature is rich in DRAMATIC BURLESQUES, among them Peele's *Old Wives' Tale*, Beaumont and Fletcher's *Knight of the Burning Pestle*, Buckingham's *Rehearsal*, Fielding's *Tom Thumb*, and Sheridan's *Critic*. All contain extravagant ridicule of the drama of their time. In America, the term *burlesque* is applied specifically to a type of musical show in which moss-covered jokes and uncovered women are the chief attractions. See PARODY.

CANON. In biblical criticism the list of books accepted by ecclesiastical councils as inspired and authentic and thus suitable for inclusion in the Holy Bible. In the Protestant Bible there are thirty-nine such books in the Old Testament and twenty-seven in the New. Non-canonical books, or those whose claim for inclusion has not been established, are called APOCRYPHA (q.v.). In general literary criticism the term *canon* is applied also to the authenticated writings of any one author. Thus there are thirty-seven plays in the Shakespeare *canon*—and more than that number, incidentally, in the Shakespeare *apocrypha*.

CAROLINE. A term sometimes applied to the literature of the reign of Charles I (1625–49) from *Carolus,* the Latin for Charles. The epithet is occasionally extended to cover the period of Charles II (1660–85).

CAVALIER. A loyal follower of King Charles I during the Civil Wars between King and Parliament (1642–51). The Cavaliers opposed the "Roundhead" adherents of the Puritan Parliament. Of the major CAVALIER POETS, three—Lovelace, Suckling, and Carew—were courtiers; but a fourth—Herrick—was a clergyman. Although the term of CAVALIER LYRICS has been applied loosely to many of their poems, it is particularly appropriate to those which reflect the easy gaiety and devil-may-care disdain connoted today by the adjective *cavalier.*

CELTIC RENAISSANCE. The term generally applied to a vigorous and productive movement in the late nineteenth and early twentieth centuries to revive interest in the ancient Celtic languages, legends, folk tales, and literatures, and particularly that of southern and western Ireland. Under the stimulation of a notable group of poets, playwrights, and folklorists, the Irish aspect of the renaissance—which was the most important phase—took the direction of much studying of Old Irish (Erse), of searching out and translating the ancient legends of Cuchulain of Muirthemne and other heroes, of collecting of folk tales by the Irish Free State, and, above all, of preserving these characteristic Irish materials in a notable body of Anglo-Irish lyrics, narratives, and dramas. Of all these activities probably the most impressive was the establishment in Dublin of the Irish Literary Theatre and the famous Abbey Theatre Players. Among those active in the Irish phase of the Celtic Renaissance were: W. B. Yeats (1865–1939)—perhaps the dean of the movement; George Moore (1852–1933); G. W. Russell (Æ) (1867–1935); Lady Augusta Gregory (1852–1932); J. M. Synge (1871–1909); Lord Dunsany (1878–   ); James Stephens (1882–1951); and Sean O'Casey (1884–   ). (See the entries in the *Dictionary of Authors.*)

CHAPBOOK. A popular pamphlet or book designed to be sold *cheap,* as the name implies. In the sixteenth, seventeenth, and eighteenth centuries, chapbooks were printed in large quantities and sold

in small bookshops or by itinerant chapmen, or peddlers. They
varied greatly in content; riddles, dream interpretations, accounts
of murders and executions, tales of witchcraft and sorcery, medieval
romances, and condensations of popular thrillers helped to fill
their covers. They were very cheaply made. They were usually
printed on a single printers' sheet so folded as to make one signature of sixteen or thirty-two pages; well-worn wood-cuts provided the only pictures—often unrelated to the text; they were
bound in paper covers, or at best in boards. Although the term
chapbook has gone out of use, the twentieth-century descendant
of the type can be bought in any ten-cent store.

CHARACTER. This term, commonly applied to the personages in
a literary work, is also the name of a literary *genre,* an essay, usually
brief and often didactic, in which a human type is analyzed. The
subject may represent a particular walk of life—*A Courtier*—or a
specific vice or virtue—*A Pedant, A Modest Man.* The term is also
applied to the character sketch of an individual, as in Halifax's
Character of King Charles II. The type flowered in the seventeenth century in the work of Joseph Hall, John Earle, and Sir
Thomas Overbury, a group of CHARACTER WRITERS who took the
Greek philosopher Theophrastus (d. 287? B.C.) as their master.

CHESTER PLAYS. See MIRACLE PLAY.

CHORUS. In Greek drama of the fifth and sixth centuries B.C.
a trained band of dancing singers who in the earlier tragedies of
Aeschylus (525–456 B.C.) carried the burden of the performance.
With the gradual addition to the drama of speaking actors, however, the importance of the Greek chorus diminished until in the
tragedies of Euripides (480–406 B.C.) its rôle was considerably
shrunken. The Roman dramatist Seneca (d. A.D. 65) retained the
chorus to comment on the action of his characters, but his tragedies
were probably presented by one "rhetor" or public speaker, who
recited the choral parts. In English tragedies of the Elizabethan
period the chorus was reduced to a mere shadow of its original
self. In the first English classical tragedy of *Gorboduc* (1561)
by Thomas Norton and Thomas Sackville the chorus consists
of "foure auncient and sage men of Brittaine," who appear at
the end of each act to comment dolefully on the moral. In
Kyd's *Spanish Tragedy* (c. 1589) the spirit of Revenge and the
Ghost of Andrea furnish a "Chorus in this tragedy." Ordinarily,
however, the chorus was reduced to a single speaker, unrelated
to the rest of the characters, who spoke the prologue or uttered
occasional interpretations of the plot. It is in this latter sense that

Ophelia employs the term in *Hamlet,* III, 2, when she tells the prince, who has been explaining the play within the play, that he is "as good as a chorus."

CHRONICLE PLAY. The search in the Elizabethan Age for subject matter for the numerous dramas that were being produced led early to such chronicles as Holinshed's *Chronicles of England and Scotland* (1577). Here the playwrights found legend and factual history for plays made popular by the growing national consciousness of the English. Frequently these chronicle plays, as they are loosely called, were rather crude dramatizations of narrative materials, with unity only in the circumstance that the play dealt in general with the reign of one king. Frequently, too, they were but pseudo-chronicle plays in which the historical materials were used as a framework for a romance; Greene's *James IV,* for example, has more to do with that prince's alleged amours than with the actual facts of his reign. Occasionally the chronicle play was polemical; *The Troublesome Reign of King John* (1588) has some scenes in which the Catholics are attacked with regard neither for historical accuracy nor common decency. But out of these loose-jointed early chronicle plays, which were seldom good tragedy, good comedy, or even good entertainment, there grew such excellent history plays as Shakespeare's tragedies of *Richard II* and *Richard III* and his historical comedy of *1 Henry IV.*

CLASSICISM. In a general sense, the term *classic* denotes any artistic achievement of permanent excellence. More specifically, it refers to the art and literature of ancient Greece and Rome. The word *classicism* is used loosely to summarize the general characteristics of that art and literature—simplicity, restraint, and order—and the adjectives *classic* and *classical* are thus applied to any work which reflects those qualities, whether by direct imitation or not. Thus the restraint and order of *classicism* are often opposed to the enthusiasm and freedom of *romanticism.* Jonson's *Sejanus* and *Catiline,* Milton's *Samson Agonistes,* Dryden's *All for Love,* and Addison's *Cato* may be grouped generally as CLASSICAL TRAGEDIES because they reproduce, in varying degrees, the characteristics of Greek and Roman drama. The Age of Pope, marked by order and dignity—if only in a limited sense of the words—and by a slavish imitation of the ancients, is sometimes called the CLASSIC AGE, sometimes the NEO-CLASSIC (or *new* classic) AGE. *Neo-classic* implies not only *new* but *false* in the sense that the body and the rules but not the essential spirit are reproduced in the imitation. See ROMANTICISM.

CLOSET DRAMA. Drama written to be read and not acted. Milton's dramatic poem, *Samson Agonistes* (1671), written on the model of the Greek tragedy, is an example. The term is sometimes applied also to plays *more suitable* for reading than for production on the stage, even though their author conceived them as acting dramas. Examples are abundant in the nineteenth century; the intellectual tragedies of Robert Browning, to illustrate, are so stuffed with philosophy and psychology that on the stage they seem much more static than mobile; and they are much more enjoyable when read.

CLUB, THE. A supper group organized in London in 1764 by Sir Joshua Reynolds and Dr. Samuel Johnson, which came later to be called The Literary Club and, informally, Dr. Johnson's Circle, from its most dominant member. Many famous contemporaries of the literary dictator belonged to it, including Edmund Burke, Oliver Goldsmith, David Garrick, Edward Gibbon, and James Boswell, Johnson's biographer. The club met at the Turk's Head in Gerrard Street for discussions of classical and contemporary books, and its decisions had considerable influence on literary taste and opinion at the end of the century.

COCKNEY SCHOOL OF POETRY, THE. A derisive epithet applied by Scots reviewers to a group of London writers. The name first appeared as the title of a series of articles in *Blackwood's Magazine* in 1818. Although the magazine also attacked Shelley and the prose writer Hazlitt as "cockney" writers, the main targets of this series were Leigh Hunt and his protégé, Keats. The vague, undemocratic "reasoning" of the reviewer (probably Lockhart) was that men of "low" or "cockney" birth and breeding would inevitably have cockney politics and write cockney poetry. Hence the phrase "Cockney School of Versification, Morality, and Politics," and hence the fact that in the most famous review of the series (August, 1818) the damnation of Keats' poetry is inextricably interwoven with his struggles as a lowly apothecary's apprentice and his friendship with the radical Hunt.

COMEDY. In literary art that form of drama which presents mimetically the lighter, more laughable aspects of human action and character. Generally speaking, it is the opposite of *tragedy*, which presents the serious, sorrowful elements in life. In Elizabethan drama the play that ended happily and with no deaths was a comedy, even though some of the earlier episodes threatened a tragic climax. Because of its content and objective the comedy is ordinarily satirical; it holds up to ridicule either the universal or the contemporary follies and weaknesses of the human animal; thus it aims often to correct society as well as to entertain it. The numerous kinds of comedy are determined by content, action, characters, structure, audience, and other elements. A comedy in which the satirization of life is subtle and in which the appeal is to a sophisticated audience that will smile intelligently but not laugh raucously is a "high" comedy; one directed to "the general" who are capable of appreciating, like Polonius, only "a jig or a tale of bawdry" is a "low" comedy. A comedy in which the action is manipulated to their own ends by one or more of the characters is a "comedy of intrigue." One in which episodes and characters are grotesquely and uproariously exaggerated is a "farce" (q.v.). A comedy written for court production is a "court comedy" (q.v.); one with a background of country life is "pastoral" (q.v.); one that deals with strange, remote, and idealistic element is a "romantic" comedy. And so with dozens of others. Again, comedy that ridicules individual idiosyncrasies is a "comedy of humors" (q.v.); one that presents the foibles of a social pattern is a "comedy of manners" (q.v.). High comedy, says Meredith, appeals to intelligence, and social comedy does not deserve the name if it fails to present both men and women in a constant battle of the sexes. To reduce all good comedy to a common denominator is not easy. Perhaps it may be said that in general, comedy presents a great game of blind man's buff in which most of the characters are playing "it" and getting themselves into difficulties which they cannot avoid and of which they are often unaware. But the audience—and possibly a few wise ones on the stage—know the truth and enjoy the situations that are absurd but not painful. And usually, of course, the climax resolves all misunderstandings and intrigues.

COMEDY OF HUMORS. According to Elizabethan physiology, human health and temperament were governed by the disposition of a number of fluids in the body called "humors." This belief is the basis of the comic theory of Ben Jonson which he defines at length in *Every Man out of his Humor,* in the words of his mouthpiece Asper. In most of his comedies each character—with one or two exceptions—is dominated by a single humor—sometimes a mere whim, sometimes a deeply seated ruling passion. Kitely in *Every Man in His Humor* (1598) is ruled by jealousy, Sir Epicure Mammon in *The Alchemist* (1610) by greed. Jonson did not invent the comedy of humors or the character dominated by a prevailing humor; the tradition goes back to the Roman play wrights, Plautus (c. 254–184 B.C.) and Terence (c. 190–150 B.C.). But Jonson perfected the type in English. The Jonsonian comedy of humors is fundamentally realistic, and its characteristic note is satire rather than wit or—in the common sense of the word— humor. Among the imitators of the type were Nathaniel Field and Thomas Shadwell. See COMEDY OF MANNERS.

COMEDY OF INTRIGUE. See **COMEDY.**

COMEDY OF MANNERS. As superficially distinguished from the *comedy of humors,* the comedy of manners ridicules the social follies of a generation rather than exaggerates the basic traits of character which vary little through the centuries. Thus Etherege's Sir Fopling Flutter (*The Man of Mode,* 1676) is a caricature of the Paris-made Restoration beau rather than a personification of the fundamental humor of vanity. The characters in this type of comedy are often tagged with some superficial mannerism, like the nautical jargon of Ben in Congreve's *Love for Love* (1695) or the malapropisms of Mrs. Malaprop in Sheridan's *Rivals* (1775). In general, the comedy of manners is marked by intellectual wit rather than broad satire; its medium is dialogue rather than stage business; and, although it reflects contemporary manners, it removes them to an airy, unreal realm, where according to Charles Lamb, they should not be tested by the ethics of the mundane world. Lamb called it *artificial comedy.* These generalizations must not be applied too strictly. Even in the Restoration period, the flowering time of the comedy of manners, there was a strong admixture of farce, as in the first two plays of Etherege, and broad satire, as in Wycherley's *Plain Dealer* (1674). The pure *genre* is best represented by Congreve's *Way of the World* (1700). Later plays in the same tradition are Sheridan's *School for Scandal* (1777), Oscar Wilde's *Lady Windermere's Fan* (1892), and Somerset Maugham's *Circle* (1921).

CONCEIT. A fanciful notion or conception, especially in poetry. A conceit may be a brief simile or metaphor or it may be the framework of an entire lyric. Thus in Lyly's "Cupid and My Campaspe," the conventional conceit that a rose grows on Cupid's cheek is but a part of the larger conceit which portrays the god of love as losing to Campaspe at cards the coral of his lips, the rose on his cheek, the crystal of his brow, the dimple of his chin, and, finally, his bright eyes. An excellent burlesque of the Elizabethan conceit appears in Shakespeare's sonnet 130, "My mistress' eyes are nothing like the sun." The unusual conceit was one of the hallmarks of the metaphysical poetry of the seventeenth century. For examples of absurdly extravagant conceits, see Cartwright, Cowley, Crashaw, and Lovelace in *Dictionary of Authors*.

CORNHILL MAGAZINE. See **MAGAZINES.**

CORPUS CHRISTI PLAYS. See **MIRACLE PLAY.**

COURT DRAMA. Queen Elizabeth's love of entertainment was largely responsible for the development at her court of masques and revels, and of a type of comedy that was especially designed to entertain courtiers and royal guests. The court comedy was a highly sophisticated form of entertainment. The plot was usually drawn from classical myth and medieval romance, the chief characters were courtly young gentlemen and ladies, the performance was made colorful and varied with song, dance, costume, and elaborate scenic devices. Almost invariably, moreover, some fulsome compliment to her majesty was woven into the episodes or the speeches. The court comedy was likely to be a "special occasion" drama, suited by its story and its allusions to the noble wedding which it graced or to the royal guests which it entertained. Allegory was frequent in these plays, and thinly veiled allusions to contemporary events or even to court gossip were not missing. Thus the intimate audience had the double pleasure of following the action and interpreting the allusions. Of the court dramatists John Lyly was not only one of the first but one of the best. He pleased her majesty greatly with his complimentary *Campaspe* (1584) and *Endimion* (1588) but lost her fickle favor with his satirical *Woman in the Moon* (1593). George Peele's *Arraignment of Paris* (1584) is a typical court comedy as are also Shakespeare's *Love's Labor's Lost* (1591), *A Midsummer Night's Dream* (1594), and probably *The Tempest* (1611).

COURTESY BOOK. In general any book designed by direct instruction or indirect suggestion to serve as a guide to manners and conduct. Thus *The Babees' Boke* (1475), which instructed young people, among other oddments, not to spit over the table or throw bones on the floor, is a courtesy book. But the term is applied more especially to the books for courtiers which were popular in England in the reign of Elizabeth. These reveal the influence of an Italian book of manners for high society, *Il Cortegiano*, "The Courtier" (1528), by Conte Baldassare Castiglione (1478–1529), which was translated into English by Sir Thomas Hoby in 1561. "Courtesy," or courtliness, was often exemplified in fictitious tales of well-bred courtiers; of these indirect presentations of good manners the most influential Elizabethan examples are John

Lyly's *Euphues, the Anatomy of Wit* (1579) and *Euphues and his England* (1580) two *novelle* that are, in a sense, courtesy books, and that engendered dozens of imitations.

COVENTRY PLAYS. See **MIRACLE PLAY.**

CYCLE. See **MIRACLE PLAY, ROMANCE.**

DÉBAT. A form of literary composition, usually in verse, that presents two persons taking opposite sides in a formal discussion or disputation (cf. *debate*). This species of writing was popular in the Middle Ages. The characters engaged were usually allegorical, the subject discussed was moral or religious, the mood was intellectual and dispassionate. For examples of the pure medieval *débat* and later writing that has some characteristics of it see in the *List of Anonymous Works: The Debate of the Body and the Soul; The Flower and the Leaf; The Nut-Brown Maid;* and *The Owl and the Nightingale.*

DEISM. A philosophical theology based essentially on belief in the transcendency of God; a form of "natural" as against "revealed" faith. The deists were opposed to the Calvinists in that they did not believe in salvation by divine "election" but thought that mankind was capable of ultimate perfectibility. They believed in the existence of a perfect God, but denied the divine inspiration of the Bible, the doctrine of the Trinity, and the possibility of miracles. The "founding" of English deism is usually credited to Lord Edward Herbert, first baron of Cherbury (1583–1648). It spread in the seventeenth and early eighteenth centuries through both England and France. Among the leading deists in England were Anthony Ashley Cooper, third earl of Shaftesbury (1671–1713) and Henry St. John, first viscount of Bolingbroke (1678–1751), to whom Pope dedicated his *Essay on Man* (1732–4). In France the most influential of the deists was Voltaire (1694–1778), who was an exile in England in 1726–9. English deism had a widespread effect upon English literature of the eighteenth century. Pope's *Essay on Man*—with its doctrine that "whatever is, is right"—is deistic; so also are some of the poems of James Thomson (1700–48), an avowed deist. Deism appears also in the poetry of William Wordsworth (1770–1850), but this "priest of Nature" was essentially an adherent to *pantheism* (q.v.).

DOMESTIC TRAGEDY. It might be assumed that this term would be correctly applied to any drama on the theme of a fatal breach between husband and wife. So applied, Shakespeare's *Othello* would be a domestic tragedy. Technically, however, the

term is used only of those tragedies in which the leading characters are of the middle or "citizen" class; the domestic tragedy, in
other words, is not classical, but bourgeois. The type was popular
in the Elizabethan period, although tragic playwrights like
Shakespeare did not depart from the classical formula that dictated the fall of princes as the only proper matter for tragedy.
Elizabethan writers of domestic tragedies usually got their plots
from accounts of contemporary murders of husbands by wives or
conversely; and to avoid trouble with the relatives of murderers
and victims they usually wrote anonymously. For obvious reasons
these tragedies were enthusiastically greeted by playhouse audiences. London citizens who had heard or read of how Alice Arden
of Feversham did in her husband Thomas were thrilled to see his
blood flow again on the boards in *Arden of Feversham* (1585–
92). Similarly Calverley's slaughter of his children and wounding
of his wife appeared on the stage in *The Yorkshire Tragedy*
(1605–8). (For comment on these two domestic tragedies see
List of Anonymous Works.) But not all domestic tragedies were
dramatized realities. One of the most popular of Thomas Heywood's numerous plays was his highly sentimental *Woman Killed
with Kindness* (acted c. 1603). Here is a domestic tragedy with
no bloodshed, for John Frankford, the wronged husband, is such
a Christian gentleman that he leaves remorse of conscience to
punish his adulterous wife—and four scenes later she dies of
grief for her sins.

DRAMA. That form of literary art in which life is copied by
impersonation and mimetic imitation of action. The true drama
requires a plot, or series of related episodes in which the conflict leads to a climax. It requires actors, or impersonators, who
take on the characters of the story. Finally, it requires a setting
or locale in which the action occurs. Of all literary forms the
stage play is the nearest to life; it is, in fact, a direct copy of life
presented not through the artificial medium of the printed page,
but by human beings who unfold the story and the conflict in
lively action and dialogue. Even the reader of the "closet drama"
(q.v.) may be assumed to visualize the characters as acting before him.

Since human experiences and moods are countless, drama takes
many forms, and is classified in terms of its objective, its content,
its mood, its length, and other elements that enter into its construction. Thus in the Elizabethan period a light satirization of
country life with a happy ending was called a "pastoral comedy"

(q.v.); a play in which the plot was drawn from historical facts
was called a "chronicle play" (q.v.); a serious drama in which
the hero and other leading characters were dead at the end was
called a "tragedy" (q.v.). A shadow-like play in which the actors
interpret the action in dumb show is a "pantomime" (q.v.). A
highly-compressed play in which a single act contains the whole
action is called a "one-act play"; classical dramas and their English imitations have five acts, and most full-length modern plays
have three.

DRAMATIC MONOLOGUE. A type of narrative poetry in which
a single character is represented as speaking throughout the poem.
The purpose of a dramatic monologue is to present in brief compass what is essentially a tabloid play. Having selected a single
dramatic moment in the life of the speaker, the poet attempts to
disclose by what this individual says not only his innermost characteristics but the situation, the locale, and the person or persons
addressed. Robert Browning, whether he first created the dramatic
monologue or not, is its greatest exponent. Among his best of this
type are: *My Last Duchess, The Laboratory, The Bishop Orders
his Tomb at Saint Praxed's Church, Fra Lippo Lippi,* and *Andrea del Sarto.* Tennyson's dramatic monologues are not as good
as Browning's, but his *Ulysses* is a noble monologue, and the
pathetic, if horrible, *Rizpah* is very moving. See also SO-
LILOQUY.

DREAM ALLEGORY. A particular type of allegory in which the
author represents himself as getting the materials for his story
from a dream or vision. This device is especially frequent in Old
and Middle English literature, where the cleric authors were
moved often to attempt to see beyond the veil. Langland's *Vision
of Piers Plowman* and the Pearl Poet's *Pearl* are fourteenth-century
examples of the dream allegory. Bunyan's *Pilgrim's Progress,* like
Dante's *Divina Commedia,* is an account of what he saw when he
"dreamed a dream." A brief example of the type is Addison's
Vision of Mirza (*Spectator,* No. 159); here the "dream" is a day
vision of life, death, and eternity, which the author pretended
to get from one of "several Oriental manuscripts." (See AL-
LEGORY.)

DROLL. A short dramatic sketch put on the stage—often on a
temporary platform — during the period of the Commonwealth
and Protectorate to avoid the penalty for violating the Puritan
law of September 2, 1642, against stage plays. These farcical bits

were sometimes scenes taken from full-length plays—*Merry Conceits of Bottom the Weaver* from Shakespeare's *Midsummer Night's Dream* is a good example—were improvised by stage comedians, or consisted of little more than a song and dance, a common monologue, or a "jig"—a short comical "act." The drolls are such an ephemeral form of drama that one need not be surprised at the statement of the best-known manufacturer of them, Francis Kirkman, the bookseller, that he wrote his plays on the backs of tavern-bills. Kirkman's *The Wits, or Sport Upon Sport,* done in collaboration with Richard Cox, was first published in 1662, after the restoration of "legitimate" drama had put drolls into the discard; this is the best collection of these dramatic oddities.

DUMB SHOW. A form of pantomime, or silent acting, employed as part of a regular drama, particularly in plays of the Elizabethan period. It seems to have appeared first in the early English classical tragedies, such as Norton and Sackville's *Gorboduc,* but it was used frequently in later non-Senecan plays. It had a variety of forms and purposes. In *Gorboduc,* the dumb shows provide allegorical interpretations of the political lessons of the five acts; in Lyly's *Endimion* they represent the sleeping hero's dream; in Webster's *Duchess of Malfi,* the dumb show is a "television" of a remote action; in Shakespeare's *Hamlet,* it provides the "induction" for the play within the play. Usually the dumb show is pure pantomime; occasionally, however, its action is interpreted by appropriate song or instrumental music or supplies material upon which the Chorus comments.

ECLOGUE. See PASTORAL.

EDINBURGH REVIEW, THE. See MAGAZINES.

EDWARDIAN. A term sometimes used in criticism to characterize the literature of the reign of Edward VII (1901–10) or, roughly, the period from near the close of the reign of Victoria to the beginning of the First World War in 1914. These two decades present a marked tendency to doubt, to question, and to react against the moods and philosophies of the Victorian Age.

ELEGY. A term loosely applied to any subjective, reflective poem. It is usually, however, a lament, specifically a lament for the dead. Gray's *Elegy in a Country Church Yard* (1751) is a melancholy reflection on the unfulfilled greatness of obscure lives. His *Ode on the Death of a Favorite Cat* (1748) is a MOCK ELEGY. Among the great elegies in English are Milton's *Lycidas* (1637),

Shelley's *Adonais* (1821), Tennyson's *In Memoriam* (1850), and Arnold's *Thyrsis* (1867). Of these, all but *In Memoriam* are PASTORAL ELEGIES because in them the dead are treated, according to classical tradition, as departed shepherds. Other literary terms frequently applied to elegiac verse are MONODY and THRENODY.

ELIZABETHAN. A term applied to the literature produced during the reign of Queen Elizabeth (1558–1603). Because, perhaps, of the importance and continuing influence of this period, the adjective is frequently extended to cover the literary work done also during the reigns of James I (1603–25) and Charles I (1625–49). So Professor Felix E. Schelling adds to the title of his two-volume *Elizabethan Drama* the dates *1558–1642*, his survey extending from the accession of Elizabeth Tudor to the closing of the theaters by edict of the Puritan Parliament at the beginning of the Civil War.

EPIC. A long and dignified narrative poem celebrating the exploits of a central hero. Two general types are usually recognized —the FOLK-EPIC, which is developed from songs about the deeds of a national character, and the LITERARY EPIC, which is composed by a single known author in imitation of the folk-epic. The three great epics of classical antiquity are Homer's *Iliad* and *Odyssey* and Vergil's *Aeneid*—the first centering in the exploits of Achilles in the Trojan War, the other two celebrating the wanderings of Odysseus and Aeneas, respectively, after that conflict. The great medieval epic is Dante's *Divine Comedy.* Among the characteristics of the ancient epic are the division into books and the convention of plunging *in medias res*—into the midst of things— directly after the opening statement of the theme and the invocation to the muse. Because the heroes of epic poetry are commonly depicted on a scale considerably larger than life size and because of the traditional grand style of the poet, the adjective *epic* has become synonymous for the Hollywood favorite *colossal,* and many a movie preview and book blurb shouts the phrases *prose epic, epic sweep, epic grandeur.* Actually there are few outstanding epics in English poetry. The most famous ones are the Anglo-Saxon *Beowulf* and Milton's great "epic without a hero," *Paradise Lost.* Others are Barbour's *Bruce* and the tedious Oriental epics of Robert Southey. See HEROIC, HOMERIC, MOCK–EPIC.

EPIGRAM. A very short poem, usually satirical, that is characterized by wit, pith, pungency, compression, and neat turn of phrase. The term is often applied also to any brief expression in prose or verse which has the characteristics just enumerated. A literary style may be *epigrammatic*. Pope was a master of the epigram in the heroic couplet form; Oscar Wilde of epigrammatic expression in prose.

EPILOGUE. A conclusion or farewell used in several literary types but particularly in the drama, where it corresponds at the end of the play to the Prologue at the beginning. In the medieval miracle and morality plays it frequently took the form of a little exposition or sermonette based on the acted story; often this concluded with a stereotyped prayer for the reigning monarch. The Elizabethan epilogue was borrowed, more likely, not from the miracle play but from the Roman comedies of Plautus and Terence. Like the Latin playwrights the Elizabethan dramatists employed the epilogue to dismiss the audience and to beg applause (the Latin *plaudite*). In the English play the speaker of the epilogue is usually one of the principal members of the cast, like Puck in Shakespeare's *A Midsummer Night's Dream* and Rosalind in his *As You Like It*. The dramatic epilogue carried down to the end of the eighteenth century but is not, on the whole, as important a dramatic device as the Prologue.

EPISTOLARY NOVEL. A novel in which the narrative is carried forward by a series of letters, usually written by one or more of the major characters. Thus in Richardson's *Pamela* (1740), traditionally regarded as the first epistolary novel in English, we learn about the heroine's stern struggle with Mr. B. through the letters which she writes home to her dear parents. Richardson used the formula again in *Clarissa Harlowe* (1747-8) and *Sir Charles Grandison* (1754), and through his vast influence it became the dominant medium in the sentimental novel of the second half of the eighteenth century. Among the best of the later epistolary novels were Smollett's *Humphry Clinker* (1771) and Fanny Burney's *Evelina* (1778).

EPITAPH. An inscription on a tomb or other monument, or, in literature, a brief eulogistic expression, usually in verse. Famous examples of the literary epitaph are William Browne's *On the Countess Dowager of Pembroke* and Robert Louis Stevenson's *Requiem*, the last two lines of which are engraved on his tomb in Samoa.

ESSAY. The name used loosely for a type of prose literature that is essentially expository in mood and usually informative or didactic in objective. As a recognized type in English literature, the essay had its beginning with Francis Bacon (1561–1626), but in the three centuries since his death the form has undergone so many changes as almost to have outgrown its original label. Certain characteristics seem, however, to have clung to it throughout these shifts. First, it must be prose, and the occasional use of the term *essay* for a philosophical or critical poem—such as Pope's *Essay on Man*—does not change this fact. Second, it must be reasonably short, not necessarily as brief as some of Bacon's earlier essays but certainly not as long as a treatise or monograph, even if some of the long "critical" reviews of the early nineteenth century are sometimes called "essays." Third, even if it is "informal" or "personal," it must be basically ideational, informative, or didactic.

The essay has several sub-types which are determined by the content, mood, or structure. The major division is between the "formal" and the "informal" essay. The distinction is not always easy to make. In general, the "informal" essay is a "light" essay, rather loosely written and seasoned with bits of narrative and dashes of humor and whimsy; it must not be thought of, however, as either formless or inconsequential. The "personal" essay is the term given to a bit of easy exposition that has its roots in the individual experiences and moods of the essayist; it represents the autobiographical approach to the essay. In addition such adjectives as "social," "critical," "moral," and the like may be employed to characterize the essay.

Francis Bacon's *Essays* (1597, 1612, 1625) are the first serious body of writing of this type in English. The earliest of these he imitated from the *Essais* (1571–80) of the French courtier Montaigne. Bacon's essays are brief, highly compressed, aphoristic, and dogmatic. In no English essays written since has so much worldly wisdom been packed into such small compass. The "moral essays" of Addison and Steele in their weeklies the *Tatler* (1709–11) and the *Spectator* (1711–12) established the popularity of a kind of delightful social criticism that re-emerged later in the century in the essays of Samuel Johnson (1709–84), Oliver Goldsmith (1730?–74), and others. The romantic movement at the end of the eighteenth century led to a sparkling flood of personal essays from the pens of Charles Lamb (1775–1834), William Hazlitt (1778–1830), Thomas De Quincey (1785–1859), and others, and also to much literary criticism in essay form. The Victorian essay tends to be solid, serious, well-constructed, but heavy. With Stevenson (1850–94) at the end of the nineteenth century came a return of the earlier essay manner of Hazlitt and Lamb that carried over into the first decade of the twentieth century. Since then, however, the personal essay—"the little old lady in lavender," it has been called—has fallen into a decline; and even the formal essays of the nineteenth-century type seem to have been displaced by the heavier "article," in which the expression of ideas has all but given way to the compilation of statistics.

EULOGY. A composition in praise of some person or thing, as in a funeral oration.

EUPHUISM. A prose style which flourished during the reign of Elizabeth. Its chief characteristics are the constant use of balance and antithesis, complex schemes of alliteration, and a profusion of metaphorical comparisons—many of them lifted from the *Natural History* of Pliny the elder (A.D. 23–79). Although the style is apparent in earlier works, notably in Pettie's *Petite Palace of Pettie his Pleasure* (1577), euphuism got its name from its use in Lyly's romances, *Euphues* (1579) and *Euphues and his England* (1580). Later euphuistic romances are Greene's *Mamillia* (1583) and Lodge's *Rosalynde* (1590). Shakespeare parodied the style in a famous scene between Prince Hal and Falstaff (*1 Henry IV*, Act II, Scene 4).

EXEMPLUM. A short tale used by medieval preachers and homilists to illustrate and reënforce their texts. Such moral stories frequently found their way into famous literature. In his *Pardoner's Tale,* for example, Chaucer puts into the mouth of the preacher the story of how Death came to the avaricious "rioters three"—ample demonstration that "radix malorum est cupiditas."

EXETER BOOK, THE. A valuable codex or manuscript book of the tenth century, which was presented to Exeter Cathedral in the next century by Bishop Leofric, and which is still preserved there. Besides riddles and other short verses, it contains some of the most important poems in Old English: *Widsith, Deor's Lament, The Husband's Message, The Wife's Complaint,* and *The Ruin.*

EXPRESSIONISM. A term used in art and literature to indicate that in revealing his ideas and particularly his moods the artist or writer is concerned not with the exact reproduction of obvious details but, through these, with the sensations that lie behind. Since conscientious reproduction of the superficial aspects of the object is of no immediate concern of the author, such details are usually sacrificed to allow the impressions to pass through them. Thus in painting, the conception of country peace would not be expressed by a conventional representation of a herd of cows chewing calm cuds by a silent brook, but by unarticulated details of cows, brooks, trees which collectively would give the idea of a "pastoral." Again "motherhood" might be expressed not by a madonna and child but by an exaggeration of physical details that *suggest* maternity. In a painting, therefore, expressionism might create in pigments apparently unrelated details that look like a scrambled jig-saw puzzle.

Expressionism in literature springs from the same motive. The expressionistic writer is quite ready to sacrifice all conventional forms and practices in composition that there may emerge through his work the intellectual or emotional abstractions which he wishes to express. Paragraphs, sentences, words—even letters, sometimes—are not permitted to intrude between the writer and his purpose. As a result, to the average reader, the expressionistic composition may seem like a mass of "clotted nonsense," with no familiar word orders, and with many strange words, punctuations, exclamations in the medley. Since simple clarity of idea cannot be the objective of the expressionist, his work, like that of the expressionistic painter, frequently demands an interpreter.

Expressionism as a mood and a method has appeared frequently in English literature. There are traces of it, certainly, in the work of John Donne (1573–1631) and the other metaphysical poets who followed him. In general practice, however, it is essentially modern. There is no twentieth century "school" of expressionists, but the theory has had wide practice. Among famous twentieth century expressionists are T. S. Eliot and James Joyce. (See *Dictionary of Authors;* also, in the *Glossary,* IMPRESSIONISM and REALISM.)

FABLE. A short allegorical tale in prose or verse designed to convey a moral lesson. The characters in the fable are usually, but not always, speaking animals or inanimate objects which symbolize human beings. The most famous collection of fables is that attributed to Aesop, a Greek of the sixth century B.C. Many of the Greek fables have become so widely known in English that often a single phrase from one—such as "sour grapes"—suggests the entire story. La Fontaine, a seventeenth-century Frenchman, and Gay, an eighteenth-century Englishman, both wrote famous series of fables after the manner of those of Aesop. (See ALLEGORY.) The term *fable* was also used in literary criticism in the neo-classical period for the *plot* or *action* of a narrative and particularly of an epic poem. Addison so uses it in the first of his series of eighteen *Spectator* papers on Milton's *Paradise Lost* (Jan. 5, 1712).

FABLIAU. Etymologically merely a "short story," but usually a short tale in verse which deals in farcical and often bawdy vein with incidents in the lives of the common people. The form was especially popular in France during the twelfth and thirteenth centuries. There are six fabliaux in Chaucer's *Canterbury Tales:* the stories told by the Miller, Reeve, Cook, Friar, Summoner, and Shipman.

FARCE. A term applied at the end of the seventeenth century to any short humorous play, but now commonly applied to a humorous play in which plot and incident are exaggerated. Many farces are marked by the boisterous stage business which is variously designated as *slapstick* and *horseplay*. Brandon Thomas' *Charley's Aunt* (1892), in which the effect is based almost entirely on comic incidents caused by a female impersonator, is a time-honored farce. In general, farce bears the same relation to high comedy that melodrama bears to high tragedy.

FIN DE SIÈCLE. See **VICTORIAN.**

FLESHLY SCHOOL OF POETRY, THE. The title of a famous review by R. W. Buchanan, published under the pseudonym "Robert Maitland" in the *Contemporary Review* for October, 1871. Although the reviewer took exception, in passing, to the sensuousness in the poetry of Tennyson, Morris, and Swinburne, his main target was D. G. Rossetti, most prominent of the Pre-Raphaelites.

FOLIO. One of several printers' and librarians' terms to describe the various sizes of printed books. The sizes are determined by the number of times the original printers' sheet has been folded; every time it is folded, the number of book sheets is doubled. Thus a single sheet folded *once* at the middle makes *two* sheets, or *four* pages; a book printed on such large pages is called a FOLIO. A printers' sheet folded *twice* makes four sheets or *eight* pages; a book printed on sheets of this size is called a QUARTO. Similarly, one printed on the *eight* sheets that result from folding the original printers' sheet three times is called an OCTAVO; and so on down to such little books as the sixty-fourmo, which has sixty-four leaves to the printers' sheet. Inasmuch as the original printers' sheets are not all of the same size, folios, quartos, and octavos vary within their own group; this fact results in the annoying "elephant" folios which librarians have to lay flat on the book-shelves, and in such differences as that between the cap octavo ($4\frac{1}{4} \times 7$ in.) and the imperial octavo ($8\frac{1}{4} \times 11\frac{1}{2}$ in.).

In modern library practice a growing rebellion against these variations has resulted in some indication of book sizes by inches and centimeters. The earlier terms for book sizes, excepting for *folio,* are usually represented by corresponding numerals: 4to for quarto; 8vo for octavo; 12mo for duodecimo, etc. One other printers' term should be defined. After the original printers' sheet has been folded for printing—no matter how many times folded—it becomes a SIGNATURE. Signatures are usually numbered or lettered to help the binder assemble them in proper sequence. Sometimes the book is trimmed so that there are no folded edges at top and side; but sometimes the task of "opening" or cutting the folds in the book is left to the reader with his paper-knife.

FOLK PLAY. In the Middle Ages popular festivals, such as those of Christmas and May Day, had as one form of entertainment semi-dramatic productions presented by the people themselves on subjects drawn from folklore and legend. These "folk plays," as they are called in the mass, are hardly true drama. Like the ancient singing and dancing games played by children they have action but no unified dramatic conflict, impersonation but no characterization, a stage but no specific locale. They belong, in brief, more to folklore and sociology than to dramatic art. Some of the specific results of this folk instinct for mimetic expression are the SWORD DANCES, such as *The Revesby Sword Play* (as it has been recently renamed) and *The Shetland Sword Dance;* the various Christmas MUMMERS' PLAYS, such as the St. George Plays; and the MAY DAY PLAYS, which include the Maypole dances and the dramatizations of Robin Hood's adventures. In all of these, actions and characters are very much stereotyped. The action is almost completely crude and farcical, with slapstick fights abound-ing. In the Christmas group Saint George and his Dragon, Fathei Christmas, The King, Giant Blunderbore, Old Doctor Ball, and similar figures from folk and fairy tale recur. In the May Day games these are replaced by The Hobby Horse and other nursery favorites and by Maid Marian, Little John, and other characters from Sherwood Forest. The English folk plays had relatively little influence on regular drama. But their amazing persistence is shown by the circumstance that they still appear in folk festivals, corrupted, no doubt, but plainly revealing their ancient origins.

FRASER'S MAGAZINE. See MAGAZINES.

GEORGIAN. A term applied frequently to the period of "the four Georges"—as Thackeray called them—George I (1714-27),

George II (1727–60), George III (1760–1820), and George IV (1820–30). Roughly the characteristics of the "Georgian" period are thought of as being substantially those of the eighteenth century, and especially of the neo-classical phase of that age. Recently the term *Georgian* has been given also to the reign of George V (1910–36), which reveals, it has been claimed, a distinctively new movement in English literature.

GERM, THE. See **MAGAZINES.**

GEST or **GESTE.** (Pronounced, and sometimes spelled, *jest*). In Old French and Middle English a story of brave deeds and high adventures; a romance. The *Gesta Romanorum* (*Deeds of the Romans*) is a Latin collection of heroic tales much used as a source book by writers of medieval verse romances. The word also appears in the popular *Gest of Robyn Hode*, a series of tales of the famous outlaw that is divided into *fyttes* (fitts), or songs.

GOLIARDIC VERSE. Secular lyrics written in Latin by the *goliards,* or wandering students, of the twelfth and thirteenth centuries. The verses deal principally with wine, women, and song; they are youthful, ebullient, fresh, lively, and unrestrained. Their mood is that of "carpe diem,"—"seize the moment"—let us enjoy ourselves while we have youth, health, and opportunity. Probably the best known of these medieval student songs is *Gaudeamus Igitur* ("therefore let us rejoice"), still published occasionally in college song-books.

GOTHIC. The name of a famous style of medieval architecture. The Gothic castle or abbey—or its ruined remains—fully equipped with haunted wings, underground passages, and owl-infested towers, was the customary setting of the GOTHIC ROMANCE. This species of novel—exploited in various ways by Horace Walpole, Clara Reeve, Ann Radcliffe, "Monk" Lewis, Charles Maturin, and Mary Shelley—was dominant in English fiction from 1764 to 1820. In literary criticism, the adjective *Gothic* is applied loosely to prose and poetry in which such elements as horror, violence, death, and the supernatural predominate, whether or not the scene is set in medieval or "Gothic times." There are GOTHIC ELEMENTS, for example, in Edward Young's *Night Thoughts,* Scott's *Bride of Lammermoor,* and Emily Brontë's *Wuthering Heights.* The GOTHIC REVIVAL was one phase of the Romantic Movement.

GRAVEYARD SCHOOL, THE. A term applied to the tendency of certain eighteenth-century forerunners of Romanticism to harp on death and the grave. The pioneer poets of the movement were Edward Young, author of *Night Thoughts* (1742–5), and Robert Blair, the poet of *The Grave* (1743). The reflective melancholy of these poems is echoed in Thomas Warton's *Pleasures of Melancholy* (1747) and Gray's *Elegy in a Country Church Yard* (1751), both of which may be loosely classified as productions of the graveyard school. In its more morbid aspects, the movement was one of the symptoms of the Gothicism which swept English literature—especially fiction—later in the century. See GOTHIC.

GRUB STREET. A street in eighteenth-century London (now Milton street) "much inhabited," according to Samuel Johnson's dictionary (1755), "by writers of small histories, dictionaries, and temporary poems." Because of the inferior work of these impecunious and incompetent scribblers, the name of the street came to be applied as an adjective to all bad writers and, by transfer, also to their wretched productions.

HEROIC or HEROICAL. Of or pertaining to a hero, usually one of rare nobility and strength, as in Homer's epics. Hence epic poetry is HEROIC POETRY. Blank verse, the form of *Paradise Lost* and other English epics, is sometimes called HEROIC VERSE. The HEROIC COUPLET or iambic pentameter couplet was the dominant verse form in England from 1660 to 1800. It was usually the medium of the HEROIC PLAY, an absurd species of drama in which athletic heroes spent their active moments in incredible derring-do and their inactive moments suspended between the horns of a love-and-honor dilemma. The heroic play rose and fell during the Restoration, when such bombastic spectacles as Dryden and Howard's *Indian Queen* (1664), Dryden's *Conquest of Granada* (1670), and Lee's *Sophonisba* (1676) had their day. The absurdities of the form are brilliantly revealed in Buckingham's *Rehearsal* (1672). See EPIC, MOCK–EPIC.

HOMERIC. Relating to the Greek poet, Homer; specifically something on the heroic scale or in the grand manner of his epics, the *Iliad* and the *Odyssey*. A HOMERIC SIMILE is an involved, interminable comparison of the kind found in Homer's epics and imitated in Matthew Arnold's *Sohrab and Rustum*. See HEROIC.

HOMILY. A serious discourse, often a sermon on a biblical text. Anglo-Saxon literature includes homilies by Aelfric and Wulfstan. The two Books of Homilies of the Church of England were published in 1547 and 1563.

HOUSEHOLD WORDS. See **MAGAZINES.**

HUMANISM. The form of intellectual culture which in the fifteenth century gradually took the place of medieval Scholasticism (q.v.) in Christian Europe. With the movement known as the Renaissance (q.v.) there evolved at the close of the Middle Ages a philosophy that was less abstract and speculative than that of the Schoolmen and more concerned with the relationship of human beings and the world in which they lived. The Humanists were anti-Aristotelian, their methods of reasoning were inductive, and they were concerned with the revival of the classical learning of Greece and Rome and with knowledge based on experiment and not on the untested pronouncements of authorities. To the Humanists, as T. H. Huxley said, skepticism was not a sin but a virtue. The attitude of the Humanists became, in brief, that of the modern world, and from the fifteenth century on, the influence of Humanism has been overwhelming. Of the early humanists in the England of the Renaissance the most notable were Desiderius Erasmus (1466–1536), the famous Dutch scholar who taught at Cambridge, John Colet (1467?–1519), Thomas Linacre (1460?–1524), and Sir Thomas More (1478–1535).

IDYLL or IDYL. In Greek literature, a "little picture" in verse, a brief descriptive poem, often dealing with rural life. Hence, loosely, any work of simple charm, whether in verse or prose. Izaak Walton's *Compleat Angler* is often called an *Idyll,* and the same epithet may be applied to Goldsmith's *Deserted Village* and Elizabeth Gaskell's *Cranford.*

IMAGISM. The name given to a twentieth-century experiment in verse which dictates the utmost economy and the most careful possible selection of concrete words to present visual images. The theories of the imagists led them to an almost staccato use of short lines and exact diction and to a complete avoidance of conventional poetic padding. Imagism has had its fullest development in America in the poetry of Amy Lowell (1874–1925), Hilda Doolittle, pseudonym H. D. (1886–   ), and Ezra Pound (1885–   ). In England its chief proponent and most active practitioner is Richard Aldington (1892–   ).

IMPRESSIONISM. A theory in art and literature based upon the conception that objects should be represented not in any great detail but as, at the moment of observation, they have impressed the painter or writer. In painting, impressionism was practiced by a French school founded by Édouard Manet (1832–83) and continued by Claude Monet (1840–1926), Pierre Auguste Renoir

(1841–1919), and others. These artists attempted to present their subjects in terms of the immediate sense impression; in other words, they worked subjectively. To increase the impression that the objects made upon them, they used colored lights and were highly selective in their choice of details. In literature, the same general objectives prevail; in all elements of his composition—episodes, characters, setting, moods—the impressionistic writer attempts to present through a few highly selected details the impression that his materials have made upon him. His elements, in short, become the media through which he transfers his impressions to his reader. Impressionistic literature tends, therefore, to be breathless and sketchy. It does not tend, however, like expressionistic composition, to be distorted. The *impressionist* is concerned with reproducing through essential details, his own immediate impressions; the *expressionist* is concerned with presenting some abstract emotion or idea which lies behind the details and is inherent in the object itself. (See EXPRESSIONISM, REALISM.)

INDUCTION. See PROLOGUE.

INFORMAL ESSAY. See ESSAY.

INNS OF COURT PLAYS. In England of the sixteenth and seventeenth centuries the four residential halls occupied by the legal guilds of London were frequently the scenes of revels, masques, and regular plays that came to be called the "Inns of Court plays." Most of the young lawyers who lived in the fourteenth-century buildings of the Inner Temple, the Middle Temple, Lincoln's Inn, and Gray's Inn had had experiences with amateur theatricals at school and university. It was natural, therefore, for them to turn to this form of art when they wished to entertain themselves and their guests at Christmas or other holiday season. Sometimes they composed and produced their own plays, as when Thomas Norton and Thomas Sackville collaborated on the political tragedy of *Gorboduc* as "furniture of a part of the Grand Christmasse in the Inner Temple" in 1561. Sometimes they brought in a play from outside as when the young gentlemen of Gray's Inn invited the members of the Inner Temple to share their enjoyment of Shakespeare's *Comedy of Errors* on Holy Innocents' Day, December 28, 1594. The four Inns of Court provided one channel, in brief, for the rapid spread of interest in the drama in the days of Elizabeth and James I.

INTERIOR MONOLOGUE. See MONOLOGUE, STREAM-OF-CONSCIOUSNESS.

INTERLUDE. A term applied loosely in the early sixteenth century to all kinds of popular entertainment but specifically to the short, farcical plays which were common in that period. Interludes were often performed at court, at noble houses, and at schools and colleges—sometimes in the intervals between the courses of a banquet. Historically they form a link between the moralities and the more finished comedies of the Elizabethan playwrights. The best-known writers of interludes were Henry Medwall and John Heywood.

IRISH RENAISSANCE. See **CELTIC RENAISSANCE.**

JACOBEAN. A term frequently applied to the characteristics of the reign of James I (1603–25). The adjective is derived from the Latin name for James, *Jacobus,* and should not be confused either with *Jacobite,* an adherent of James II, deposed by the English Revolution of 1688, or of his pretender heirs, or with *Jacobin,* a member of a radical democrat club at the time of the French Revolution a century later. Strictly speaking, in literature the first decade of the reign of James I shows the continuing characteristics of the Elizabethan Age that preceded it; and the second half of his reign begins to merge with that of the Caroline period that followed it.

KAILYARD SCHOOL. A term applied to a group of late nineteenth- and early twentieth-century interpreters of simple Scottish life. *Kailyard* is Scotch for cabbage-patch; the word suggests the realistic simplicity of village life. The writers used lowland vernacular and naïve philosophy in their characters. Sir James M. Barrie (1860–1937) was the best known of the group; he wrote *Auld Licht Idylls* (1888) and *A Window in Thrums* (1889), Scottish sketches, before turning to drama. Other "kailyarders" were "Ian Maclaren" (John Watson, 1850–1907), author of *Beside the Bonnie Brier Bush* (1894), and Samuel R. Crockett (1860–1914), whose *Stickit Minister* (1893) preceded a number of less entertaining religious volumes.

KENNING. See **BEOWULF** in *List of Anonymous Works.*

KIT–CAT CLUB. A Whig club founded near the end of William III's reign to help insure a Protestant succession. Among the members were Addison, Steele, Congreve, Vanbrugh, Tonson, and Walpole. The club met at first at the pastry-shop of one Christopher Cat, whose mutton-pies, Addison says in *Spectator* No. IX, were called *kit-cats.* Later the club met at the house of its secretary, Jacob Tonson, the publisher. Here the forty-two portraits of the members, painted by Sir Godfrey Kneller, had to be made short because of the low ceiling in the dining-room where they were to hang; hence the term *kit-cat* came also to be applied to similar undersized portraits.

LAI. See **LAY.**

LAKE SCHOOL, LAKE POETS, LAKERS. Terms applied loosely to a number of Romantic poets, all of whom lived in the English Lake District (Westmorland and Cumberland). The chief Lake Poets, Wordsworth, Coleridge, and Southey, can hardly be said to form a "school." The term "Lake School" was first used derisively in the *Edinburgh Review*, August, 1817.

LAUREATE. See **POET LAUREATE.**

LAY (LAI). A particular type of short medieval tale of knight-hood in verse form. The French *lais* date back to the twelfth century and may have been based on the songs of Breton min-strels; hence they are often called in English *Breton lays*. The most famous composer of these French romances is Marie de France, who lived in England at the end of the twelfth century under the patronage of Henry II of England. Many of her *lais* and their English imitations deal with material taken from the Arthurian legends. The English *lays* which were popular in the fourteenth-century took themes from many legendary sources, and tended to replace the original rhymed couplets of the Breton lay with "tail-rhyme" stanzas. In more modern romantic periods the term *lay* came to be used loosely of any metrical narrative poem of high adventure, such as Scott's *Lay of the Last Minstrel* (1805) and Macaulay's *Lays of Ancient Rome* (1842).

LITERARY CLUB, THE. See **THE CLUB.**

LITURGICAL PLAY. The name usually given to those brief semi-dramatic parts of the service of the mass which appeared in the Easter liturgy of the Church in the ninth century. They con-sisted of TROPES, or verses chanted in Latin as the officiating priest approached the altar, and were designed to interpret the mystery of the resurrection. The "drama" had as scenery a representation of the empty sepulchre, and as actors priests who took the rôles of the angel at the tomb and the three women seeking the body of Christ that they might anoint it with spices. In the chanted dia-logue the angel challenges the women with "Quem quaeritis in sepulchro, o Christicolae?" ("Whom seek ye in the sepulchre, O Christian women?"); and they reply, "Jesum Nazarenum crucifixum, o caelicolae" ("Jesus of Nazareth, who was crucified, O heavenly one"). The angel tells them that Christ has risen, and begs them to go and announce the event; then follows the jubilation chorus, and the little play is over. From the initial words of the dialogue this dramatic bit came to be called the "quem quaeritis trope." In itself it is not much of a play, being more dramatic liturgy than liturgical drama. But as the seed of the medieval religious plays it is highly important. During the centuries that followed its first appearance in the Easter mass it came to be gradually expanded to cover other scenes from the New Testament—and even the Old Testament; it moved from cathedral to market place; it was played no longer by the clergy but by the laity and no longer in Latin but in the vernacular. The liturgical drama became ultimately, in short, the fully developed religious play of the Middle Ages. (See MIRACLE PLAY.)

LYRIC. Originally *lyric poetry* was intended to be sung, as to the lyre, but the term is now applied loosely to many kinds of poems, whether designed as songs or not. Generally speaking, a *lyric* is a short poem in which a single emotion, usually personal, is expressed. Hence, lyric poetry is commonly distinguished from narrative and dramatic poetry, in which telling a story and analyzing character are primary aims. A lyric may be a simple outburst of sincere feeling, like Tennyson's "Break, break, break," or a ponderous philosophical reflection like Wordsworth's *Ode on Intimations of Immortality*. It may be a love lyric, like Burns' *Highland Mary,* a religious lyric, like Herbert's *Pulley,* or a nature lyric, like Collins' *Ode to Evening*. It may be idealistic, like Lovelace's *To Lucasta,* or cynical, like Housman's *When I Was One-and-Twenty;* gay, like Herrick's *Corinna's Going a-Maying,* or melancholy, like Arnold's *Dover Beach*. It may be written as part of a play or longer poem. Finally, it may be in any one of a number of special stanza forms, such as the sonnet.

MADRIGAL. In general, any melodious song. Specifically, a highly technical and complex form of musical composition which the English borrowed from Italy and the Netherlands in the fifteenth century and popularized during the reign of Queen Elizabeth. The madrigal is sung unaccompanied, by five or six independent voices; and the interweaving of words and melody becomes so intricate that one can hardly follow the singing without copy. Among contemporary collections of Elizabethan madrigals are those of Thomas Morley, Thomas Weelkes, John Wilbye, and John Farmer. In the twentieth century, madrigal singing has been revived by the St. George Singers and the English Singers.

MAGAZINES. In nineteenth-century England one of the most important stimulations to creative writing and criticism came with the establishment and growth of the literary reviews and magazines. These publications had several functions: they issued intelligent judgments on prevailing ideas and current books; they attacked literary fads and fancies; they spread culture and guided reading; they provided a forum for debate and an exchange for literary ideas; above all, perhaps, they established a channel through which young, unknown, and usually impecunious writers could gain a public hearing. In the mid-Victorian period they became less eclectic and more popular and carried into British homes the successive installments of the long novels that were becoming the staple of reading. The famous literary journals of the first half of the century were direct and bitter often to the point of being libelous, and their influence is acknowledged in numerous significant allusions in the great literature of the time.

The journals were divided into two loosely differentiated types, the *Review* and the *Magazine*. The *Review* presumably provided discussions of literature, art, science, politics, and public events and comments on current books; it did not publish original articles. The *Magazine,* as its name implies, was a *miscellany,* a *potpourri,* with original materials and second-hand comments side by side. But the Review and the Magazine did not seriously avoid encroachments on each other's territory. Thus Macaulay's famous "reviews" in the *Edinburgh Review* soon departed from the book under immediate discussion to the broader fields of the subject itself and so became independent essays or monographs.

Only a few of the most influential of these nineteenth-century journals can be listed here; the choice has been determined by the quality of their editors and contributors and by the significance of their place in literature. Names of authors mentioned can be found in the *Dictionary of Authors*.

The *Edinburgh Review* was a Whig quarterly, founded in 1802 and published until 1929. The young and outspoken editors who made it immediately famous were Francis Jeffrey, Sydney Smith, and Henry Brougham. Among its distinguished contributors were Scott, Macaulay, Carlyle, Hazlitt, and Arnold. It is notorious for its biting attack on Wordsworth, Coleridge, and other "Lakers," and for being the particular objective of Byron's assault in his satirical *English Bards and Scotch Reviewers* (1809).

The great rival of the *Edinburgh Review* was the Tory *Quarterly Review,* founded in 1809 and edited until 1824 by William Gifford. Among the contributors were J. G. Lockhart, Robert Southey, the poet laureate, and Sir Walter Scott, who praised Jane Austen's *Emma* in one number of the journal. The savage review of Keats' *Endymion* which appeared in the *Quarterly* in 1818 and drew the indignant fire of Byron and Shelley, was written almost certainly by Croker; but "tartarly" as Byron said it was, it could hardly have "killed John Keats," already dying of consumption. Gifford, the editor, was the object of a bitter epistolary attack by William Hazlitt.

Blackwood's Edinburgh Magazine—familiarly known as *Maga* —was a Tory rival of the *Edinburgh Review.* It was first issued in 1817 under the editorship of John Wilson ("Christopher North"), J. G. Lockhart, and James Hogg ("The Ettrick Shepherd"). Among its numerous contributors were Coleridge, DeQuincey, and the Irish Maginn. Its most sensational achievements were its attack on Edinburgh notabilities in the *Chaldee MS,* its lively discussions at Ambrose's under the caption *Noctes Ambrosianae* (written mainly by "Christopher North"), and, finally, its ceaseless assaults on Leigh Hunt and other members of the "Cockney School of Poetry."

Some of the later journals known principally for their close connections with English literature are:

Fraser's Magazine (1830–82), a monthly which was nearly wrecked early in its career by its courage in publishing Carlyle's *Sartor Resartus.*

Punch, or the London Charivari (1841–   ), the characteristically English comic weekly with such famous humorists and artists on its list of contributors as Jerrold, Thackeray, Hood, Leech, Tenniel, and Du Maurier.

The Germ. Thoughts towards Nature in Poetry, Literature, and Art, continued as *Art and Poetry* for a total of four numbers in 1850. This was the organ of the Pre-Raphaelite Brotherhood; it was edited by W. M. Rossetti and printed contributions by D. G. and Christina Rossetti, William Morris, Coventry Patmore, and others.

Cornhill Magazine (1860–   ), edited by W. M. Thackeray with Ruskin, Arnold, Trollope, and others contributing.

Household Words (1850–59), a weekly edited by Dickens and used as an outlet for his serialized novels; among other contributors were Bulwer-Lytton, Wilkie Collins, and Mrs. Gaskell.

All the Year Around (1859–70), the popular magazine which

Dickens published to replace *Household Words,* and which carried his novels.

The Yellow Book (1894–7), the *fin de siècle* quarterly which published the work of such writers and artists as Henry James, A. C. Benson, Edmund Gosse, Aubrey Beardsley, and Max Beerbohm.

MARTIN MARPRELATE CONTROVERSY. See **MARTIN MARPRELATE** in *Dictionary of Authors.*

MASQUE. Originally a form of amateur and often impromptu masking, mumming, and reveling by young courtiers, who would leave a court ball or other entertainment, assume disguises and masks, ride back like strange guests, and invite the ladies to dance and converse with them. The first masques came to England from Italy in the early part of the fourteenth century and were substantially like the one introduced by Shakespeare in *Love's Labor's Lost* (Act V, 2). But by the beginning of the sixteenth century, in the days of the Tudors, the masque had become much more elaborate, and in the first part of the seventeenth century, at the courts of James I and Charles I, it had evolved into a magnificent pageant, usually allegorical, in which music, dancing, costuming, and scenery had become more important than the framework of episodes and dialogue supplied by its creator. Although these later masques were still produced for private court entertainments, and courtiers frequently played rôles in them, they were never impromptu or casual like the earliest ones. Such prominent poets, playwrights, and musicians as Daniel, Campion, Chapman, Ben Jonson, and Shirley were proud to help create them; and Inigo Jones, the great designer, devoted his best skill to constructing their gorgeous costumes and settings. Ben Jonson was the best of the masque-writers; he developed the ANTIMASQUE, a grotesque and comic foil in characters and situations, to provide a contrast for the delicate and lyrical main theme. One of the last—and best—of the early seventeenth-century masques was Milton's *Comus,* "presented at Ludlow Castle, 1634, before the Earl of Bridgewater, Lord President of Wales." This pastoral type of masque was written at the request of Henry Lawes, the musician, who assisted the poet by composing the music and directing the production. The leading rôles were played by the earl's two sons and daughter.

MEDIEVAL ROMANCE. A type of romantic tale of knighthood popular in western Europe in the Middle Ages. Like the earlier *epic* (q.v.) it deals with the brave deeds of heroes. Unlike the epic, however, the characters and events are not racial but social. The folk-epic expresses national ideals; the knightly romance embodies those of chivalry, the code of the militant aristocracy of the Middle Ages. Furthermore, the folk-epic presents a man's world of feasting and fighting, in which women play but little part; the background of the medieval romance, on the other hand, is, in large part, that of "courtly love," in which both gentle knights and fair ladies play essential rôles. Finally, the epic is more heroic in mold, more direct in expression, more grim in mood than the romance; the tale of knighthood is more sophisticated, more complicated, more colorful.

The medieval romance had a wide distribution in Christian countries, Italy, Germany, France, Spain, and England all having their own knightly heroes and borrowing freely from other nations. Thus there came to be various "matters" or groups of episodes commonly used for the tales. Of these the most widely used were the "matter of France," which dealt with the adventures of Charlemagne (742–814), King of the Franks and Emperor of the West, his chief knight, the noble Roland, and other "peers"; the "matter of Greece and Rome," which retold in chivalric mood and form the fall of Troy and the subsequent conquest of Italy by Aeneas; and—most important in English literature—the "matter of Celtic legend," which presented, among other episodes, the deeds of the great King Arthur and the knights of his "table round." In addition to the major division into "matters," there is a further one into "cycles." A "cycle" of medieval romances is a group of related tales that tell of the adventures of a single hero, such as Arthur, Sir Lancelot, Sir Gawain, or Sir Galahad, for example, or of a single grand adventure in which all knights take part, such as the quest for the Holy Grail.

Most of the medieval romances are anonymous and most are metrical. Of the alliterative poems the finest specimen is *Sir Gawayne and the Grene Knight,* ascribed to the "Pearl Poet" (see *Dictionary of Authors*) in the West-Midland dialect of the late fourteenth century. (For comments on other metrical romances see in the *List of Anonymous Works:* BEVIS OF HAMTOUN, GUY OF WARWICK, HAVELOK THE DANE, KING HORN, and ORFEO, SIR.) But the most widely influential of all the romances of knighthood was neither anonymous nor metrical; it was the *Morte Darthur* written in prose in the fifteenth century by Sir Thomas Malory (fl. 1470), who at the end of the Middle Ages and with an apparent realization that feudalism was decaying, sought to preserve some of the chivalric ideals in a magnificent and well articulated series of tales of King Arthur and his knights.

The end of the Middle Ages meant the end of that form of society which is reflected in the medieval romances. But these heroic and colorful tales lived on because they provided a literary quarry for later romantic poets. Among the many who were drawn to these romantic stories of knights and ladies were Edmund Spenser (1552?–99), in his *Faerie Queene,* and, in more modern times, Alfred Tennyson (1809–92) in *Idylls of the King,* and William Morris (1834–96) in *The Defense of Guenevere.*

MELODRAMA. As the name indicates, the melodrama was originally a popular romantic play in which sentimental, tense, and exaggerated situations were further emotionalized by the employment of interpretative song and instrumental music. The type developed, mainly in France, in the late eighteenth and nineteenth centuries and was widely used in England and America. The term came to be applied also to popular plays in which were introduced such devices as hair-breadth escapes, unjust sufferings, poetic justice, and happy endings. The melodrama tends, in brief, to be lurid rather than quiet; sentimental, emotional, and exaggerated rather than intellectual and restrained. Generally speaking, it bears the same relationship to high tragedy that farce bears to high comedy. The adjective *melodramatic* is applied, finally, not only to characteristic scenes in plays that are not predominantly of the type, but also to short-stories, novels, and, in fact, to all forms of narrative literary art that are marked with the devices and moods which make *melodrama* what it is.

METAPHYSICAL POETS. A term first applied by Samuel Johnson in his *Lives of the Poets* (1779–81) to certain poets of the seventeenth century who formed no conscious "school" but whose work exhibited some common traits. All of the members tended to treat the inward rather than the outward world and to analyze human emotions. Some, like Vaughan and Traherne, were more mystic than others. All made use of startling ideas, strange "conceits," grotesque imagery, and unusual verse and stanza forms. John Donne (1573–1631) was the first of the metaphysical poets and the one who did most to influence the others. Among those who owed a debt to his strangely original mind and art are George Herbert (1593–1633), Richard Crashaw (1612?–49), Abraham Cowley (1618–67), Henry Vaughan (1621–95), and Thomas Traherne (1637?–74). (See *Dictionary of Authors.*)

METRICAL ROMANCE. See **MEDIEVAL ROMANCE.**

MIRACLE PLAY. The name generally, and correctly, given to
the English dramas of the Middle Ages which presented the
miracles of the saints and, more often, scenes from the Bible.
Since the middle of the eighteenth century scholars have attempted to distinguish between the MIRACLE or saints' play, and the
MYSTERY or Bible play, but both terms are still used without much
discrimination for both types. It is not apparent that in the fourteenth and fifteenth centuries when production of these plays was
at its height, they were ever called *mysteries,* although in France
during the same period the equivalent term *mystère* was used.
The English who wrote and produced them called them *miracles,
shows (ludi),* or *pageants (paginae*—see PAGEANT). Saints'
plays were earlier than the biblical plays, were more academic than
popular, and did not survive in great numbers. The Latin plays
of Hilarius that deal with St. Nicholas are perhaps the best known
of these, especially that of *Tres Clerici,* the three schoolboys, slain
in an inn on their way to the university and restored to life by
this patron saint of scholars.

The medieval Bible plays have their roots in the earlier liturgical
plays (q.v.) but are more secular, broader in scope, and more
dramatic than their ecclesiastical ancestors. In England the medieval miracle plays were produced by members of the trade guilds.
They were played out-of-doors usually as part of the Corpus
Christi festival which came two months after Easter; hence they
are often called Corpus Christi Plays. The miracle plays reached
the height of their popularity during the fourteenth, fifteenth, and
early sixteenth centuries; after the Reformation interest in them
naturally declined.

Although there are a few detached miracle plays, like the Brome
Abraham and Isaac, most of them are extant in *cycles.* A cycle of
miracle plays is a related sequence of biblical pageants or scenes
performed regularly by the trade guilds of some one town. The
great cycles are those of Chester, Wakefield, and York, although
one or two plays of the cycles at Coventry and Norwich have
survived. The Wakefield cycle also bears the name of Towneley,
the family who originally owned the fifteenth-century manuscript
now in the Huntington Library, California The number of
separate scenes in a cycle varies; Chester offered twenty-five,
Wakefield thirty, and York forty-eight. Most plays were so short
that they must obviously have been played in a few minutes.
Miracle plays were written in verse of most of the types employed in medieval literature.

The method of production was adjusted to outdoor perform-

ance in a town hilariously celebrating a spring festival. The
members of each guild were assigned a "pageant" or Bible scene
to present. When the great day came, they gave repeated performances on the flat top of a movable wagon or float, also called
a "pageant," which moved from one stated location—like the
town fountain—to another. Since the guilds presented their scenes
in chronological sequence, an enthusiastic playgoer who chose to
remain at one of the established places might, if he could make
a day of it, see a good part of the Bible unrolled before him.

It must be evident that narrative bits taken from the Old and
New Testaments and put into metrical dialogues for amateur
actors would not necessarily make good drama, and structurally
the miracle plays were not good drama. Nevertheless they were
far from being unentertaining, largely because the anonymous
authors, in true holiday spirit, used the Bible tales as frameworks
over which to stretch entirely contemporary realistic comedy. So
treated by the playwrights and so acted by young guildsmen, the
familiar episodes and characters from the Bible took on amazing
color and life. Cain has a fight with his "boy"; Noah beats his
wife for refusing to enter the Ark; and angry king Herod "ragis in
the pagond and in the strete also." Of all the miracle plays the
most famous is the "Second Shepherds' Play" of the Wakefield
Cycle in which the author introduces a completely independent
sheep-stealing scene. (See Wakefield Master in *Dictionary of
Authors*.) The miracle plays were not, therefore, simply religious
plays; they were essentially medieval realistic comedy and thus
were the dramatic ancestors of the comedies of later and less
crude literary periods.

MOCK–EPIC, MOCK–HEROIC. These terms, virtually inter-
changeable, are applied to literary works in which the epic or
heroic tradition is ridiculed or mocked. Sometimes the devices of
Homer's epics are directly burlesqued—as in Pope's *Rape of the
Lock,* the graveyard battle of Molly Seagrim in Fielding's *Tom
Jones,* and Byron's *Don Juan.* In other works the mockery is
aimed at Homer's various literary descendants—as in Chaucer's
Rime of Sir Thopas, a take-off on the medieval romances, Buckingham's *Rehearsal,* a burlesque of the Restoration heroic play,
and John Philips' *Splendid Shilling,* a parody of Milton's grand
manner. See EPIC, HEROIC.

MONODY. See **ELEGY.**

MORALITY PLAY. A type of medieval allegorical church play
designed to furnish a dramatized guide to Christian living and

Christian dying. In the fifteenth and early sixteenth centuries, which were the palmy days of the morality play, the general theme of these dramas was theological; they dealt with the struggle of the forces of good and evil for the soul of man. As this struggle was the greatest conflict which the medieval church could conceive, the moralities, unlike the miracle plays (q.v.) were essentially dramatic. They were not, however, tragic, for despite the seriousness of the warfare between sin and virtue, man's soul was ultimately saved. The characters were, naturally, theological abstractions, the World, the Flesh, and the Devil and their baleful attendants, the Seven Deadly Sins (see *Glossary*) engaging in physical and verbal battle with the Cardinal Virtues. The moralities were not always dull and didactic, however; like the miracle plays they were often seasoned with bits of contemporary realism. The antics of the Vice, a dramatically economical combination of all evils who evolved into a farcical clown, were particularly entertaining.

After the Protestant Reformation of the early sixteenth century the theological moralities yielded to those dealing with ethical conduct, educational problems, and matters of church and state. Some of these early Tudor moralities have lively scenes, but many provide but dull reading with the didactic elements eclipsing the dramatic. The influence of both early and late allegorical moralities appears in Elizabethan drama. Marlowe's *Faustus* (1592) is essentially a belated morality, though one with a tragic ending, and even Shakespeare's *Macbeth* (1606) presents a conflict between good and evil, though evil is presented by the Weird Sisters and Macbeth's remorse of conscience emerges only in his soliloquies. (See in the *List of Anonymous Works*: EVERYMAN, CASTLE OF PERSEVERANCE, NICE WANTON, and HYCKES–CORNER.)

MUMMERS' PLAY. See **FOLK PLAY.**

MYSTERY PLAY. See **MIRACLE PLAY.**

MYSTICISM. The highly abstract term applied to man's efforts to break through the barriers that separate the mundane from the spiritual and to bring about direct intercourse with the divine spirit. The attempt may be philosophical and carried on by intellectual intensity, or religious and brought about by emotional ecstasy. Both gateways to the spiritual world tend to draw the mystic away from himself and his physical surroundings and to elevate him into a remote and glowing realm. He sees natural objects as the garments of the Almighty, or, if he is a pantheist, as divinity itself.

Religion, of course, has produced many mystics from St. Bernard of Clairvaux (1090–1153) through St. Joan of Arc (1412–31) to twentieth-century visionaries. In England George Fox (1624–91) founder of the Society of Friends, may perhaps serve as a typical illustration. In English literature mystics, both religious and philosophical, abound. All of John Bunyan's religious allegories reveal his mystical nature. So also do the poems of the metaphysical poets, Donne, Crashaw, Herbert, Vaughan, and others. The first lines of Vaughan's *The World* are typically mystic:

> I saw Eternity the other night,
> Like a great ring of pure and endless light,
> All calm, as it was bright.

Wordsworth's mysticism took the form of pantheism (q.v.); Cowper's and Francis Thompson's was more ecstatically religious; Shelley's was expressed in his worship of "intellectual beauty." Of all mystics in English literature the most transcendental was William Blake, to whom physical objects were less real than things unseen, and who seems actually to have believed that he could walk to a hill-top and put his finger against the sky. (See PANTHEISM, PLATONISM.)

NATURALISM. A term applied generally to literature which attempts accurately to imitate nature, hence often synonymous with *realism*. More commonly—and in this book—it is used to express a specific kind of realism, the slavish attempt to reproduce details from life without selection, sometimes called *photographic realism*. In French literature, the term *naturalism* applies to a school of nineteenth-century novelists—including Flaubert, Zola, and the brothers Goncourt—who attempted to approach life in a scientific manner, recording external appearances only, but recording them with the all-seeing patience of the chemist and physicist. Hence they revealed aspects of life which Victorian England had been studiously ignoring, and their influence on the English novel—notably on the works of Gissing, Moore, and Hardy—gave rise to violent outcries about the obscenities of naturalism or *Zolaism*. (See REALISM.)

NEO–CLASSICISM. See **CLASSICISM.**

NEO–PLATONISM. See **PLATONISM.**

NOVEL. The general term applied to one of the most popular and significant types of prose fiction. In the two centuries during which this type has flourished it has undergone so many modifications in form, content, and objective that *novel* has not always had a uniform implication. In spite of these variations, however, it may be insisted upon that the novel has remained a form of fiction, because the materials have always been treated imaginatively, and a form of prose in spite of such occasional excursions into verse as William Morris' *The House of the Wolfings* (1889), which is very largely poetry. Beyond these common denominators, however, the novel has undergone such shifts that here little can be done beyond enumerating some of the most important subtypes.

In literary histories the English novel is usually dated from the beginning of the eighteenth century, sometimes with Daniel Defoe's *Robinson Crusoe* (1719) and sometimes with Samuel Richardson's *Pamela* (1740). But the roots of this type go much deeper, thrusting back at least to the Elizabethan "novels" that were copied from the Italian *novelle*. (See NOVELLA.) Since Richardson's time the novel has always been a dominant form and has been used by many important writers as the medium for presenting their conceptions of life.

Richardson's novels have a structure that seems extremely clumsy in the twentieth century; the narratives were carried in a succession of letters and journals, which gave the stories, and those like them, the appellation of "epistolary novels." But before the end of the century other forms appeared, the "Gothic mysteries" of Horace Walpole (1717–97) and Ann Radcliffe (1764–1823), the "picaresque novel" of Tobias Smollett (1721–71), and the "sentimental novel" of Laurence Sterne (1713–68). At the beginning of the nineteenth century the first great woman novelist, Jane Austen (1775–1817), was writing such deft "social novels" that they drew the unstinted praise of Sir Walter Scott (1771–1832), whose media in fiction were the "romantic" and the "historical" novel. The forms used by Scott were also used by the earlier and the later Victorians, Bulwer-Lytton (1803–73), Thackeray (1811–63) and Stevenson (1850–94). Dickens (1812–70) tried his hand at one or two historical novels, but most of his stories reveal the journalist, the humorist, and the social critic at work. The "realistic" novels of Jane Austen re-emerged later in the century in those of Mrs. Gaskell (1810–65), George Eliot (1819–80), and Anthony Trollope (1815–82). The novel of the twentieth century tended at first to be shorter than the ponderous mid-eighteenth-century and mid-Victorian novels, but later came longer novels and novels written in related series, like Galsworthy's *Forsyte Saga* (1906, 1920, 1921, 1922), which presents the epic of a family in successive generations. Among the most sophisticated of modern novels are those that reveal the influence of Sigmund Freud (1856–1939) and other psychiatrists, "autobiographical" and "psychological" novels like those of D. H. Lawrence (1885–1930), and particularly the involute and cryptic "stream-of-consciousness" novel, like James Joyce's *Ulysses* (1922). Excepting for the usual "escape" novel—the love stories and the mystery and detective tales—the mid-twentieth-century novel seems to appeal to serious thinkers who are willing to find their fiction used as a wrapper for social and political theories or to pursue their heroes into the misty regions of the subconscious.

NOVELLA. A term borrowed from the Italian and applied in the Elizabethan period to the brief tale or story which had a compact plot and no special concern with the characters. Boccaccio's *Decameron* (1353), Bandello's *Novelle* (1554, 1573), and Cinthio's *Hecatommithi* (1565) contain good examples of the Italian *novella*. These "merry tales" and other Continental stories like them were translated into English by William Painter (*The Palace of Pleasure*, 1566) and were so popular as to arouse the resentment of Puritan critics like Roger Ascham. Many of them were used by Shakespeare and other playwrights as frames for dramas. The *novella* is of interest because it is the Elizabethan ancestor of the novel (q.v.).

OCTAVO (8vo). See **FOLIO.**

ODE. In ancient literature, a poem written to be sung or chanted by a chorus. The PINDARIC ODE, named for the Greek poet, Pindar (c. 522–442 B.C.), followed a complex stanzaic scheme; it had lines of varying lengths and was divided into three parts, a *strophe,* an *antistrophe,* and an *epode.* The English poet Cowley (1618–67), under the impression that he was writing Pindaric odes, devised instead a looser form; and since his time, there have been few genuine Pindaric odes in English—among them two by Gray, *The Bard* and *The Progress of Poetry.* Prosodists distinguish two other kinds of odes in English: the IRREGULAR or PSEUDO-PINDARIC ODE, characterized by a lack of uniformity in the length of lines and stanzas; and the LESBIAN or HORATIAN ODE, in which a uniform stanzaic pattern is followed. To the first cateogry belong Dryden's *Alexander's Feast* and Wordsworth's *Ode on Intimations of Immortality;* to the second, Shelley's *Ode to the*

West Wind and Keats' *Ode to a Nightingale*. Actually the term *ode* has been used so loosely in English that it has come to signify little more than a poem, usually dignified—except in cases of mock-dignity like Gray's *Ode on the Death of a Favorite Cat*—and usually addressed to some person or object or composed for some special occasion.

OXFORD MOVEMENT. An early nineteenth-century movement for reform in the Church of England which took its name from the circumstance of its origin at Oxford University. It is also called the Tractarian Movement because the leaders carried on their battles in *Tracts for the Times,* a series of ninety pamphlets from 1833 to 1841. The object of the movement was to purge the Church of its growing skepticism and liberalism, restore its discipline, and protect it from losing its dignity and authority through government regulation and control. The movement began with a famous sermon on "national apostasy" preached at Oxford by John Keble (1792–1866) in 1833. The leadership was immediately assumed by John Henry Newman (1801–90), the most able of the reformers and the most vigorous "tractarian." Newman's logical processes led him ultimately to Roman Catholicism; after a final tract (number ninety) had raised a storm against him, he resigned his Oxford position and four years later joined the Roman Catholic Church. His successor as leader of the Oxford Movement was E. B. Pusey (1800–82), who directed the reform away from controversial channels and toward changes that caused less challenge; his followers were called Puseyites. (See Keble, Newman, and Pusey in *Dictionary of English Authors*.)

PAGEANT. In general, any dramatic spectacle in which the appeal is more to the eye than to the ear. In this sense a patriotic or historical pantomime staged out of doors on a national holiday might be called a pageant. In the history of English drama, however, the term has been applied especially both to the different scenes of a cycle of miracle plays, and to the scaffolding or the flat-topped wagon on which they were produced. Thus the fifteenth-century manuscript of the Chester cycle introduces its miracle of the creation and the fall with "Incipit pagina secunda" —"[Here] the second pageant begins." (See MIRACLE PLAY.)

PANEGYRIC. A literary composition, usually highly formal, in praise of some person, object, or event. A eulogy.

PANTHEISM. The theological belief in the immanence, or continued presence, of God is everything in the universe. The theory is opposed to those which present God as a transcendent spirit, superior to and remote from a mechanical universe of his own creation. Once the pantheists thought of God as dwelling in all natural manifestations of his being, the natural world became for them in a sense deified. In English literature the most significant pantheist is William Wordsworth (1770–1850), who thought of nature as a spirit capable of being to man "both law and impulse," and of himself, the poet, as "Nature's priest," at once a worshiper and an intermediary between Nature and man.

PANTOMIME. In general, a form of dramatic art in which the actions and moods are expressed silently by posture, gesture, facial expression, and other non-oral interpretative means. In ancient Rome the mimicry was by body, not by voice. In England in the eighteenth century the term was applied particularly to the silent reproductions of the Italian *commedia dell' arte,* introduced by John Rich (1692–1761), theatrical producer, at the Lincoln's Inn Fields Theater in 1716. In the early pantomimes in England the traditional Italian types, Harlequin, Columbine, Pierrot, Scaramouche, Pantaloon, and others, appeared; later the actions and characters were expanded.

PARABLE. A brief allegorical story in which plot and characters are used to teach a moral. The materials of the parable are usually simple, the action is uncomplicated, and the characters are familiar. Occasionally a brief "moral" expounding the lesson is appended to the story; usually it is allowed to speak for itself. The best-known parables are those from the Bible. Many are used by prophets of the Old Testament; a famous one is Nathan's parable of the ewe lamb (II Samuel 12, 1–6) addressed to the sinning King David. The best, however, are the New Testament parables of Jesus, who "taught them many things by parables" such as those of the prodigal son and the good Samaritan.

PARODY. A work in which the manner of another work, author, or literary type is imitated, usually for purposes of ridicule. Among the prose parodies in English are the opening chapters of Fielding's *Joseph Andrews,* a parody of Richardson's *Pamela,* and Thackeray's *Novels by Eminent Hands,* a series of take-offs on popular nineteenth-century novelists. Among the best verse parodists are Canning and Frere, Lewis Carroll, J. K. Stephen, and J. C. Squire. (See BURLESQUE.)

PASTORAL. A term applied generally to any literary work in a rural setting, more specifically to poems in which shepherds and other rustic swains are the chief characters. Among the forefathers of the English tradition of pastoral poetry are Theocritus, a Greek of the third century B.C., Bion of Smyrna (fl. c. 280 B.C.), Moschus of Syracuse (fl. c. 250 B.C.), Vergil (70–19 B.C.), and two modern poets, Mantuan, an Italian (1448–1516), and Marot, a Frenchman (c. 1495–1544). The earliest example of the type in English is Alexander Barclay's series of pastoral dialogues or ECLOGUES, published in 1515. Later collections of eclogues are Spenser's *Shepheardes Calender* (1579), which contains an eclogue for every month of the year, and Gay's *Shepherd's Week* (1714), six eclogues in which the poet mocks the traditional artificial idealization of pastoral life. Also in the pastoral tradition are PASTORAL ROMANCES in prose, like Sidney's *Arcadia* (1590) and Lodge's *Rosalynde* (1590); PASTORAL PLAYS, like Fletcher's *Faithful Shepherdess* (1610) and Jonson's *Sad Shepherd* (1641); and PASTORAL ELEGIES, like Milton's *Lycidas* (1637), Shelley's *Adonais* (1821), and Arnold's *Thyrsis* (1867).

PERSONAL ESSAY. See ESSAY.

PHALARIS CONTROVERSY, THE. An episode in the literary quarrel of the "Ancients and the Moderns" which had to do with the question of whether or not the *Epistles* of Phalaris, a Greek tyrant of Agrigento in Sicily (sixth century B.C.), were authentic, Sir William Temple believed them to be, but Richard Bentley, classical scholar of Cambridge University, presented in his *Dissertation* of 1699 linguistic evidence that they were spurious. Swift came ineffectively to Sir William's defense in an incidental bit in his *Battle of the Books.* (See ANCIENTS AND MODERNS, BATTLE OF THE.)

PICARESQUE. This term, from the Spanish word *picaro,* rogue, is applied to a type of fiction which was especially popular in eighteenth-century England. The *picaresque novel,* or *picaresque romance* is essentially the reverse of the traditional romance of chivalry—with a rogue or *picaresque hero* replacing the chivalrous hero, and realistic farce replacing romantic adventures. The plot is usually a series of miscellaneous incidents strung on a slender thread; it often ends with the rogue's reform and marriage. Among the Continental sources of the English picaresque novel are two Spanish romances, *Lazarillo de Tormes* (translated, 1576), of uncertain authorship, and Mateo Alemán's *Guzmán de Alfarache* (1599; pt. II, 1604); and a French romance, Le Sage's *Gil Blas* (1715–35). Thomas Nashe's *The Unfortunate Traveller, or the Life of Jack Wilton* (1594) is commonly called the first picaresque novel in English. The eighteenth century produced such examples

as Defoe's *Captain Singleton* (1720) and *Moll Flanders* (1722)—
the story of a female rogue; and Smollett's *Roderick Random*
(1748) and *Peregrine Pickle* (1751). Although there are picaresque
elements in both *Joseph Andrews* (1742) and *Tom Jones* (1749),
Fielding's "comic epics in prose" are avowedly patterned on Cervantes' *Don Quixote* (1605, 15), which is not, strictly speaking, a
picaresque romance. The terms *picaresque* and *picaresque hero*
need not be confined to prose fiction. Byron's *Don Juan* (1819–
24), for example, is picaresque in many respects.

PINDARIC ODE. See **ODE.**

PLATONISM. The philosophy of the Greek thinker Plato (427?–
347 B.C.). Plato was the pupil of Socrates (470?–399 B.C.) and
the teacher of Aristotle (384–322 B.C.); his teaching he carried on
in the Academy, a school of philosophy which he founded in
Athens. His lectures have been preserved in the form of *Dialogues,*
in which he represents his master Socrates as being the chief
speaker. Plato was probably the greatest thinker of all time. Unlike his pupil Aristotle, he did not attempt to formalize or codify
his theories; nevertheless they are so sound and have been presented so brilliantly that their effect on subsequent thinking has
been profound. In the *Republic,* Plato expressed his conceptions
of the ideal state; in *Phaedo* he affirmed his belief in the immortality of the soul; in *Symposium* he talked on ideal love. Reality
he believed to exist not in physical ephemerae but in spiritual
entities; of the two spirits in the universe, the self-moved is
greater than that which is moved from without; beauty, truth,
and virtue are identical; mind rules over matter.

Although Plato's *Dialogues* embody his high theories clearly, his
philosophy came to be reinterpreted and modified by various
groups of later philosophers, or NEO-PLATONISTS. Of these groups
the most important was that of an Alexandrian school of the
early Christian centuries which sought to combine Plato's doctrines, and those of Aristotle, with various Oriental philosophies.
In Italy in the fifteenth century a group of Neo-Platonists at
Florence attempted to merge Plato's philosophy with Christian
doctrines. As a result of the labors of these Neo-Platonists it is
not always possible to separate in English literature Plato's original
ideas from those of his interpreters.

The influence of Platonism on English thought and literature
was extensive. The CAMBRIDGE PLATONISTS—Ralph Cudworth
(1617–88), Henry More (1614–87), Nathanael Culverwel (d.
1651?), and others—followed Plato's essential doctrines when they

rebelled against the materialistic philosophy of Thomas Hobbes (1588–1679). Edmund Spenser's *Hymns in Honor of Love and Beauty* (1596) were derived from Plato's *Symposium* through the *Commentary* of Marsilio Ficino (1433–1499), an Italian Neo-Platonist. Wordsworth's *Ode on Intimations of Immortality from Recollections of Early Childhood* (1807) echoes the concept expressed by Plato in *Phaedo* that knowledge is simply the recollections that the soul has of a previous state of incarnation in human form. And to these few illustrations of what Plato meant to English philosophy and literary art might be added many more.

POET LAUREATE. In general, any poet crowned, or worthy to be crowned, with the laurel wreath symbolic of high poetic achievement. In the history of English literature, a poet appointed by the king or queen to serve in the royal household as official bard. Presumably he will compose all occasional verses that seem called for, such as odes on the birthday of the monarch or on the death of a national hero, but recently the post has become purely honorary. The roster of poet laureates reveals that although a few, such as Dryden, Wordsworth, and Tennyson, have been distinguished, many others are second-rate, like Southey, or mere versifiers, like Tate, Whitehead, and Pye.

The first *acting* poet laureates seem to have been Ben Jonson (died 1637) and his successor William Davenant. The first official one was John Dryden, who was appointed in 1670, two years after Davenant's death, but dismissed in 1689 after the rebellion had brought a Protestant king to the throne. Since then the poet laureates, with the dates of their holding office, have been: Thomas Shadwell (1689–92), Nahum Tate (1692–1715), Nicholas Rowe (1715–18), Laurence Eusden (1718–30), Colley Cibber (1730–57), William Whitehead (1757–85), Thomas Warton (1785–90), Henry James Pye (1790–1813), Robert Southey (1813–43), William Wordsworth (1843–50), Alfred Tennyson (1850–92), Alfred Austin (1896–1913), Robert Bridges (1913–30), John Masefield (1930–   ). Thomas Gray, Sir Walter Scott, and Samuel Rogers have the distinction of having declined the appointment.

PRE-RAPHAELITE BROTHERHOOD. A group of artists and men of letters who organized themselves in 1848 to pursue the general aim of returning to certain standards—simplicity, sincerity, fidelity to nature—which they had discerned in European art before the influence of the Italian painter, Raphael (1483–1520). The group included Dante Gabriel Rossetti and his brother William, Holman Hunt, John Everett Millais, and Thomas Woolner.

Hunt and Millais are best known as painters, Woolner as a sculptor. The brotherhood expressed itself in the *Germ,* a periodical which began on January 1, 1850 and survived for only four numbers. Their poetry is marked by warm personal feeling, the use of symbolism, the conscious adaptation of medieval forms, intentional archaisms, and—notably in D. G. Rossetti—a quality which has been called "fleshly mysticism." There were other poets —including Christina Rossetti, Swinburne, Morris, and Coventry Patmore—who, although they did not belong to the original brotherhood, had strong affinities with the so-called P. R. B. The paintings of the Pre-Raphaelites, first exhibited in 1849, were defended by John Ruskin against numerous attacks. The poetry— especially that of D. G. Rossetti—was ridiculed by R. W. Buchanan in an essay called "The Fleshly School of Poetry," published under a pseudonym in the *Contemporary Review* for October, 1871.

PRIMITIVISM. A philosophical and sociological theory that human virtue has its highest manifestation in the "noble savage" uncorrupted by contact with the evils of civilized society. The theory was expressed by the eccentric French philosopher Jean Jacques Rousseau (1712–1778) in his *Discours sur les Arts et Sciences* (1750) and widely adopted in England. The "noble savage" formula had many ramifications. Of these one of the most significant was the romantic concept that the purest expressions of poetry were to be found in the uncultured countryman whose inspiration was natural and untrammeled by the restraints of formal training. This theory of poetic art found its most complete exposition in William Wordsworth's famous *Preface* to *Lyrical Ballads* (second edition, 1800). It might be added that Wordsworth's various attempts to demonstrate the soundness of this poetic theory in his own writing were often as unsuccessful as were those of the English "primitivists" who transplanted bewildered savages to London and watched them eagerly, but vainly, for manifestations of natural nobility.

PROLOGUE. A preface or introduction. The term applies especially to dramatic writing and the prologue is of frequent occurrence in English drama from the Elizabethan period to the beginning of the nineteenth century. The Elizabethan playwrights probably borrowed the device from the Roman plays, where the speaker of the introduction was also called the prologue. In the Latin comedies of Plautus and Terence the prologue speaker had the function of narrating the antecedent story up to the moment of the play, making preliminary announcements, or even joking the audience into a properly receptive mood. In Elizabethan plays the prologue was variously managed. In Shakespeare's *Romeo and Juliet* a speaker called *Chorus* announces the theme and subject of the tragedy; in his *Henry V* a *Chorus* as prologue apologizes for the physical limitations of the stage. Sometimes the prologue is expanded into an INDUCTION or curtain-raising scene that is more or less related to the main action; Kyd's *Spanish Tragedy,* Greene's *James IV,* and Shakespeare's *Taming of the Shrew* all have such Inductions. In the Restoration and eighteenth-century dramas the prologues were less varied and more formal. Frequently they were written for special occasions, such as a performance at court; and it became customary also, for a playwright to have a literary friend write his prologue for him. A special type of prologue, finally, which had no classical origin, was often used in the medieval miracle play. This dramatic prologue is illustrated in the nativity *Pageant of the Shearmen and Taylors,* where it is appropriately spoken by the prophet Isaiah.

PUNCH. See MAGAZINES.

QUARTERLY REVIEW, THE. See MAGAZINES.

QUARTO (4to). See FOLIO.

QUEM QUAERITIS. See LITURGICAL PLAY.

REALISM. A term used loosely in criticism of art and literature to classify works which depict life as it is. Hence *realism* is commonly opposed to *romanticism, idealism,* and *escapism*—all of which suggest a flight from the world of reality into the world of the imagination. There are, of course, many degrees of realism. Sometimes the word is used to denote an objective literary technique which depicts, in a scientific, unselective manner, only tangible, observable facts. This approach is also called *photographic realism* and *naturalism.* To some readers, particularly those to whom literature and escape are synonymous, realism means the revelation of sordid, unpleasant details which should not besmirch respectable books. These readers fail to see that the "realistic" approach can be used in the service of high ideals just as the "romantic" approach often serves the immoral purposes of distorting the truth and concealing evil. To few authors or books can the term *realistic* be applied without reservation. If Pope wrote *realistic* description in Book II of the *Dunciad,* was he *realistic* when he propounded the doctrine that whatever is, is right? Jane Austen's picture of the Bennet family in *Pride and*

Prejudice may be realistic, but—in another sense—was she realistic in her almost complete obliviousness to the Napoleonic Wars? Scott might be characterized as a realistic romanticist, Dickens as a romantic realist. Historically speaking, the two tendencies have existed side by side in English literature since the beginning, but the modern movement towards realism is a product of the scientific revolution which marked the Victorian period. See EXPRESSIONISM, IMPRESSIONISM, NATURALISM, ROMANTICISM.

RENAISSANCE or **RENASCENCE.** In general, any "rebirth" (which is what the word means) or reawakening. Specifically, it is the term applied to that widespread cultural revival which marks the division between the so-called "Dark Ages" and the modern world. It began in Italy in the fourteenth century and in the fifteenth and sixteenth it spread over western Europe and England, stimulated by geographical discoveries, the invention of printing, and rebellions against the medieval patterns of living and thinking. The Renaissance came to England with the first of the Tudor kings, Henry VII (1485-1509), and in the next century spread its influence over all aspects of culture—scholarship (see HUMANISM), literature, science, art, architecture, and music. The principal channel of this influence was Italian culture, but behind Italian art and letters, lay the Greek and Roman classics, and directly or indirectly Greece and Rome contributed most to the belletristic aspects of the English Renaissance. But the "rebirth" was more than a revival of interest in classical antiquity; it was an intangible but universal spirit of freedom, of novelty, of living, a thirst for seeking out what was new and stimulating either in geographical realms or in those of art and thought. It was, in brief, the dawn of the modern world.

RESTORATION. In English history the return of the exiled Stuart prince, Charles, to the throne in 1660. In English literature the term is applied to the period following the restoration of the king, a period characterized by a reaction against Puritan ideas, evidences of French influence, and growth of interest in social manners, satire, drama, and polished, formal expression.

REVENGE TRAGEDY. See **SENECAN TRAGEDY.**

REVESBY SWORD PLAY. See **FOLK PLAY.**

ROMANCE. See **MEDIEVAL ROMANCE.**

ROMANTICISM. In a loose sense, the tendency in art or literature to represent life as it is not—either, with the help of the imagination, to distort the real world or to escape from it entirely into the shadowy realm of romance. Hence *romanticism* is commonly opposed to *realism*. The term is also applied to a work in which an author expresses his individuality in defiance of established artistic rules. Thus *romanticism* is often regarded as the opposite of *classicism*. One man's distinction between the two terms may be found in the *Postscript* to Walter Pater's *Appreciations* (1889). Although, in Pater's words, "romanticism . . . is . . . rather a spirit which shows itself at all times in various degrees . . . than the peculiarity of a time or a school," the term is often reserved to characterize the literature of the *romantic movement* in Europe during the eighteenth and nineteenth centuries. The limits of the movement in England are often set arbitrarily at 1798, the date of the publication of the *Lyrical Ballads* and 1832, the year of Scott's death—a period which includes Wordsworth, Coleridge, Byron, Shelley, Keats, and Scott. But the movement was gaining headway throughout the eighteenth century, and elements of romanticism are apparent in the works of Thomson, Gray, Collins, Cowper, Beattie, Chatterton, Blake, and Burns—to name but a few. Here are some of the aspects of English romanticism: (1) *Faith in the Imagination:* This meant in poetry a renewed faith in feeling and intuition to challenge the predominance of Reason and the substitution of new forms and techniques for the formal heroic couplet and stylized poetic diction of the age of Pope. (2) *Faith in the Individual:* This went side by side with the spread of democracy which resulted from the American and French revolutions; it is reflected in the literature of the romantic movement by a growing humanitarianism. (3) *Interest in the Past:* The intense curiosity about medieval or "Gothic" times was variously reflected in Mrs. Radcliffe's romances, Scott's novels, Keats' poems, and the Oxford Movement. A renewed interest in past literature resulted in the revival of the folk ballad and the Elizabethan drama. (4) *Interest in Nature:* Specifically, as in the poetry of Wordsworth, the tendency to observe a flower at close range and analyze it as one of the mysteries of the universe, instead of sitting at home embalming it, sight unseen, in a conventional *cliché*. (See CLASSICISM, GOTHIC, REALISM.)

RUNE. A Germanic letter, character, or symbol used by the Anglo-Saxon tribes as early as the second or third centuries and until this form of writing was replaced by the Latin alphabet toward the end of the sixth century. Runes were carved on wood and stone, and appeared in some manuscripts, as in Cynewulf's runic signature in the second part of *Christ*. They are frequently alluded to in later manuscripts; they are described in *The Husband's Message* as being carved on a staff, and in *Beowulf* as being etched on a magic sword, where they tell the story of the Flood. Apparently they were used in communications, but it is also evident that they were regarded as possessing magic powers.

RUTHWELL CROSS. An ancient monument in Dumfriesshire, Scotland, which dates from about the eighth century and is of literary interest because carved upon it are extracts from the fine Old English poem, *The Dream of the Rood*. (See title in *List of Anonymous Works*.)

SAGA. Although the term has come to be applied loosely to any legendary tale of heroic achievement in the remote past, it is more properly applied to the medieval myths and legends of Iceland and Scandinavia. The tales told of Gudrun, the Icelandic heroine, and of Sigurd the Volsung are typical northern sagas, with myth, legend, and epic deeds interwoven. It is from this great body of tales that Richard Wagner, William Morris, and other composers and poets quarried much of their romantic materials.

SAINT GEORGE PLAY. See **FOLK PLAY.**

SATANIC SCHOOL. The term applied by Robert Southey in the preface of his *Vision of Judgment* (1822) to "Immoral writers . . . who . . . have rebelled against the holiest ordinances of human society. . . ." Southey's attack was directed particularly against Byron, but he had in mind also Shelley and other writers who rebelled against moral conventions.

SATIRE. In its pure essence an attitude or mood of ridicule directed against society or individuals. This mood may be light and playful, it may be malicious or merely mischievous, it may be judicious and corrective in purpose, or purely abusive and vindictive. In literary art the satirical mood appears in many forms—prose, verse, or drama—and oftener in some periods than in others. The Restoration period, for example, and the Age of Pope which follows it are more satirical than is the restrained Victorian Age. But even in the great period of satire, the first quarter of the eighteenth century, there are varying degrees of ridicule. Addison, the "parson in the tye-wig," as Thackeray calls him, was gently corrective in his satirical attack on the society belle; Pope, the "wicked wasp of Twickenham," could sting

poisonously with his pen; and Swift, filled with "savage indignation," raged and roared against all humanity. Yet all were satirists—of different degrees of restraint. In literature the term
satire is applied most frequently to poems that ridicule the follies
of society or attack some social institution. Thus Pope's *Rape of
the Lock* derides the empty lives of the beaux and belles of his
time; Dryden's *Hind and the Panther* satirizes the dissenting religious sects while defending the Roman Catholics; Tennyson's
Princess pokes fun at "female" academies. But not all satires are
in verse. Steele's essays and Swift's *Gulliver's Travels* are satires,
and in drama Gilbert and Sullivan made musically merry at the
expense of a score of sacred and smug Victorian institutions.

SCHOLASTICISM. The formal intellectual culture which prevailed in Christian Europe during the Middle Ages from the
twelfth century to the Renaissance in the fifteenth century. It was
promulgated by the "Schoolmen," who were trained in the
studies of the medieval universities (the Trivium—grammar, logic,
and rhetoric, and the Quadrivium—arithmetic, music, geometry,
and astronomy). Of the formal medieval studies logic was the
most practiced. It was employed in the innumerable "disputations" which were designed, in general, to reconcile reason and
the tenets of the Christian faith, but which became highly speculative, narrow, and trivial long before the end of the fifteenth
century. In all their reasoning the Schoolmen employed the de-
ductive methods of Aristotle, arguing from an accepted "thesis"
instead of attempting to establish a hypothesis built on observed
truths. Among the famous Schoolmen of the Middle Ages were
Abélard (1079–1142), Thomas Aquinas (c. 1225–74), and Duns
Scotus (1265?–1308?). The influence of Scholasticism on medieval
literature was, of course, immense.

SCHOOL PLAYS, UNIVERSITY PLAYS. Very live roots for the
growth of English drama in the Tudor period were the schools
and universities. In Eton, Westminster, St. Paul's, and other
grammar schools the Latin comedies of Terence and Plautus were
staple reading, and not infrequently they were acted out by the
boys under the direction of the head master. On special occasions,
moreover, such as Christmas, English comedies, written on the
model of the Latin ones by the head master, were substituted.
Such a practice accounts for the earliest known classical comedy,
Ralph Roister Doister, written for his boys at either Eton or Westminster by Nicholas Udall (1505–56) at about the middle of the
century. This farcical play is copied after the *Miles Gloriosus* or

Braggart Warrior of Plautus, but it is more English than Latin and is well seasoned with such farcical slapstick as small boys would enjoy. It is much better constructed and written than the earlier school plays *Thersites* and *Jack Juggler,* which are hardly more than sketches, and reveals a vigorous advance away from classical models and toward independent comedy.

The young boys who took part in School Plays could continue their dramatic activities after they went up to Oxford or Cambridge. The so-called University Plays were naturally more mature than the earlier type. In contemporary records of the Queen's "progresses" are accounts of her attending at Cambridge and Oxford in the sixties Senecan tragedies and English plays copied from Italian models. They must have been intolerably academic and dull. But it is apparent that when the college boys were allowed more latitude they could write and produce the most entertaining of farces. One such university comedy is *Gammer Gurton's Needle,* probably produced before the death of Edward VI in 1553; it is an extremely lively university satire of a village squabble. Unlike *Ralph Roister Doister* it was not written by a head master but by one of the students, a "Mr. S., Master of Art." It shows some Plautine influences but is much more thoroughly Anglicized than the school farce.

The experiences in these amateur theatricals in school and university sent the young graduates out with a good basis in the drama. Not all of those who took part as undergraduates carried their interests forward, but many must have done so; certainly the young writers who were known as the "University Wits" (see *Glossary*) gained much by their earlier contacts with dramatic art.

SCOTTISH CHAUCERIANS. The name given to a group of fifteenth- and sixteenth-century Scottish poets who reflect, in varying degrees, the influence of Geoffrey Chaucer. In chronological order, the major figures of the group are King James I (1394–1437), Robert Henryson (1425?–1500?), William Dunbar (c. 1460?–c. 1520?), Gavin Douglas (1474?–1522), and Sir David Lindsay (c. 1490–1555).

SCRIBLERUS CLUB. A writers' club organized by Swift in 1714 for the purpose of satirizing literary incompetence. Pope, Gay, Arbuthnot, Congreve, and Atterbury were members. An organ through which the club expressed its ideas of "all the false tastes in learning" was the *Memoirs of the Extraordinary Life, Works, and Discoveries of Martinus Scriblerus,* a satirical fragment written principally by Dr. Arbuthnot but on a plan probably discussed at meetings of the club. The first—and only—book of the *Memoirs* was published in 1741 in the second volume of Pope's prose works.

SENECAN TRAGEDY. The term is applied both to the tragedies (nine and a fragment) attributed to the Roman philosopher and politician Lucius Seneca (d. A.D. 65), and to the Continental and English plays which were modeled after them in the sixteenth and seventeenth centuries. The Senecan plays were probably written to be presented by a "rhetor" or orator, but the Italian, French, and English critics and playwrights of the Renaissance and a little later accepted them as models of what a stage tragedy should be, and their influence was considerable. Among the characteristics of the Senecan plays which found their way into English tragedies, either by direct imitation or through Italy and France, were the five-act division, the use of sententious expressions and formal language, the stock chorus (see *Glossary*), the ghost that urges the blood avenger to action, the epic narratives, the lofty social station of the leading characters, and the sensational nature of the episodes. Although the Senecan tragedies were recast after those of the Greek tragedians of five centuries earlier (seven are from Euripides), they have little of the essential Greek restraint. The Elizabethan playwrights found this trait no drawback; excepting for their early classical tragedies like *Gorboduc* (1561) and strictly academic ones like Jonson's *Sejanus* (1603) the English tragedians had no restraint whatever but introduced physical struggles and much bloodshed on the stage. The fact is that the strong romanticism of the Elizabethan playwrights broke over the boundaries of classical restrictions; the English Senecan plays, while they reveal some Senecan influences, are at the same time vigorously Elizabethan.

One type of Senecan play became very popular on the Elizabethan stage. This was the so-called REVENGE TRAGEDY, the theme of which was retribution for a murder. Usually the revenge tragedy, like most of the Senecan ones, has to do with a father's revenge for the murder of his son, as in Kyd's *Spanish Tragedy* (1587), or a son's revenge for the death of a father, as in Shakespeare's *Hamlet* (1601), or a brother's revenge as in Chapman's *The Revenge of Bussy D'Ambois* (1610). But other revenge tragedies do not involve families; in Ford's *Broken Heart* (1629) the avenger slays the brother of his fiancée, who has forced her into another marriage; and in Cyril Tourneur's *Revenger's Tragedy* (1606) Vendice kills the duke who has murdered his mistress.

Many of the English revenge tragedies have Senecan revenge ghosts, as does *Hamlet*. But not all ghosts in Elizabethan drama are Senecan; "Jack" in Peele's *Old Wives' Tale* (1590) is the very lively little ghost of a dead hobo and by no means stately and awesome.

SENTIMENTALISM. In general, the mood of excessive sentiment, or too-tender susceptibility, of mawkish emotionalism. In literary art the deliberate use of these unrestrained excesses to produce a consciously calculated response from the reader. Sentimentalism is an element that may appear in any form of literature in any period—and does. Shakespeare used it occasionally, as in the scene in *King John* in which little Prince Arthur begs Hubert, his keeper, not to burn out his eyes (Act IV, 1). In the moral age of Queen Victoria Dickens used it often, as in the description of Paul Dombey's death; and so did Thackeray, with more of a smile than his contemporary. Sentimentalism is a staple ingredient in melodrama (q.v.) and in tragic ballads. It is hard, in fact, to find a type of literature or a literary period in which it may not be found.

The period in which sentimentalism flourished most vigorously was, however, the eighteenth century. There were several reasons for this. Before the beginning of the century a reaction had set in against the heartless cynicism of the Restoration period, and reform brought concern for morality, piety, and goodness. Furthermore, among other philosophical concepts that influenced the age was the anti-Calvinistic idea of the perfectibility of man. So *good* men and *good* women came to be stock figures in literature. The SENTIMENTAL NOVEL, popularized by Samuel Richardson with *Pamela* (1740–1), was more absurd in his *Sir Charles Grandison* (1753–4), and impossibly false to human life in Henry Mackenzie's *Man of Feeling* (1771), a series of sketches that drip with insipid humanitarianism. Similarly the SENTIMENTAL COMEDY developed by Sir Richard Steele with *The Funeral* (1701), *The Lying Lover* (1703), and *The Tender Husband* (1705) in a reform movement against the Restoration comedies, soon became completely "genteel," "moral,"—and as dull as a sermon. In poetry sentimentalism appeared, to illustrate, in Goldsmith's *Deserted Village* (1770) and Wordsworth's *Michael* (1800). Reaction against all this lachrymose emotionalism was inevitable. The sentimental novel of the late eighteenth century gave way to Jane Austen's fine social stories; the sentimental comedy was eclipsed by Goldsmith's satirical *She Stoops to Conquer* (1773) and Sheridan's *School for*

Scandal (1777) and *The Critic* (1779). The tear-dropping poetic
idealizations of farm and village, finally, were attacked by George
Crabbe, who in his painfully realistic poem of *The Village* (1783)
tried to

. . . paint the cot
As Truth will paint it, and as bards will not.

SEVEN DEADLY SINS, THE. In medieval theology the cardinal
sins that preyed on the soul of man. Although the roll-call of
these devilish abstractions was not always the same, they were
usually listed as they appeared in the account of their "shriving"
in Langland's *Vision of Piers Plowman:* Pride, Envy, Wrath,
Lechery (or Lust), Avarice (or Covetousness), Gluttony, and
Sloth. These are the sins that Mephistopheles summons from
Hell to entertain Faustus in Marlowe's tragedy of *Dr. Faustus.*
In the morality plays, naturally, they have important rôles; in
The Castle of Perseverance, for example, Covetousness is presented
as the Treasurer of World; Lechery, Gluttony, and Sloth as the
Attendants of Flesh; and Pride, Wrath, and Envy as the Attendants
of Devil. Because it was Pride that released the other sins by
tempting Satan to rebel against God, he is always named first as
the most vicious evil. The Seven Deadly Sins are occasionally opposed in the warfare for Man's soul by the SEVEN CARDINAL VIR-
TUES: Meekness, Charity, Abstinence, Chastity, Industry, Generosity, and Patience—to name them as they are listed in the
Dramatis Personae of *The Castle of Perseverance.* But for some
strange reason the Virtues were never as popular in medieval
literature as their opponents.

SHORT–STORY. A literary term that has come to be applied,
rather loosely, to a prose narrative that has not the brevity of
an anecdote nor the length of a novelette. The type developed in
the mid-nineteenth century, particularly in France and America,
into such a specialized form that Edgar Allan Poe laid down a
formula for its construction, just as he did for that of the lyric.
It was to be so carefully articulated that not a single episode in
the plot could be omitted without destroying the whole; and
mood, characters, plot, and setting were to be perfectly harmonized.
Comparatively few short-stories have been written on such a
rigid prescription, for tellers of tales refuse to be bound by rules.
Thus the label has been retained to cover rather a wide variety of
fictional stories in which emphasis on characters, plot, setting, and
mood varies. It is still true, however, that the short-story seems to
be a fairly modern descendant of a long line of narrative ances-

394

tors, and it seems to insist on retaining its characteristics of comparative brevity and marked suspense. Among the best English short-story writers are R. L. Stevenson (1850-94), Rudyard Kipling (1865-1936), W. W. Jacobs (1863-1944), Katherine Mansfield (1888-1923), and W. Somerset Maugham (1874-   ). (See *Dictionary of Authors*.)

SIGNATURE. See **FOLIO.**

SILVER FORK SCHOOL. A term applied derisively to certain English novelists of the first half of the nineteenth century whose work was thought to be over-genteel and characterized by too much attention to social conventions. Among these writers are: Frances Trollope (1780-1863), Lady Caroline Lamb (1785-1828), Mrs. Catherine Grace Frances Gore (1799-1861), Thomas Henry Lister (1800-42), Benjamin Disraeli (1804-81), and Margaret Oliphant (1828-97). Thackeray satirized the group delightfully in his parody, *Novels by Eminent Hands* (1847).

SOLILOQUY. Etymologically, "a speaking while one is alone (*solus*)." In literary art it is the solitary oral expression of one speaker. The device is employed particularly in drama, where it is used to reveal the innermost thoughts of the soliloquizer, or to convey to the audience information or moods not obtained either from the action or the dialogue. The *soliloquy* should not be confused with the *aside,* a confidential and usually incidental comment to the audience or to a selected individual or group among the actors. It is also to be distinguished from the *dramatic monologue* (q.v.). In drama the soliloquy was used more extensively in the Elizabethan plays. These provide countless examples, such as Mark Antony's lament for Caesar (*Julius Caesar,* III, 1), Juliet's lovelorn sighing (*Romeo and Juliet,* II, 2), and, of course, the numerous soliloquies of the introspective Hamlet.

SPASMODIC SCHOOL OF POETRY, THE. A term of ridicule applied by W. E. Aytoun in *Firmilian* (1854) to a group of Victorian poets, including P. J. Bailey, Sydney Dobell, and Alexander Smith. Their poetry is marked by sentimentality and by a strenuous struggle towards strangeness in subject, language, and thought.

STREAM-OF-CONSCIOUSNESS. A modern literary term applied to that technique of mental and emotional dissection used particularly by writers of the psychological novel. In these highly introverted narratives the external experiences of the chief characters are much less important than the relationship of these events to the consciousness and subsciousness of the actors. The sequence of external happenings is not always chronological or even logical; the "stream" of the narrative is that of the "consciousness" of a leading character. This "stream-of-consciousness," or "interior monologue," is often so full—as in Joyce's *Ulysses*—that the reader must take much longer to cover the author's analysis of it than the character himself did to act and think it out. The stream-of-consciousness novel is, in brief, an excursion from the outer world of events into the Freudian inner world of the character's mind and soul. The outer world is comparatively unimportant; the inner world is all-essential. The most distinguished stream-of-consciousness novelist is James Joyce (1882–1941), and the most famous novel in which this technique is employed is his *Ulysses*. When it appeared in Paris in 1922, it startled—and puzzled—the world, and soon spawned a brood of imitations. Outstanding among the numerous other English fiction writers who have experimented with the technique are Virginia Woolf (1882–1941) and Dorothy M. Richardson (1882–   ). (See James Joyce, Virginia Woolf, and Dorothy M. Richardson in *Dictionary of Authors*.)

SURREALISM or **SUPERREALISM.** The term given to the technique of a small twentieth century group of painters and writers who violate convention by attempting to create reality through eccentric distortions of the object presented. In painting, the leader of the surrealists is the Spaniard, Juan Miró (1893–   ). In literature, surrealism has frequently taken the direction of seeking effective expression by throwing words out of normal and logical sequence.

SYMBOLISM. In general, the presentation of objects, moods, and ideas through the medium of emblems or symbols. In France and Belgium at the end of the nineteenth century the symbolists were members of a school of literature and music that rebelled against realism and sought to express themselves by indirect rather than direct suggestion. They attempted to invest their materials with the suggestion of concealed spiritual and intellectual significance and leaned toward the mysterious and the metaphysical. Their rebellion was not only against realism but against the conventional in form; they took liberties with structure and syntax and wrote much *vers libre*.

The forerunner of the Continental school of symbolism was Charles Baudelaire (1821–1867), whose *Fleurs du Mal* (1857) had the morbid quality that helped give the later group its second name of "poets of decadence." Paul Verlaine (1844–1896),

author of *Poemes Saturniens* (1866), and his disciple Arthur
Rimbaud (1854–1891) were members of the school as was also
Maurice Maeterlinck (1862–   ), the melancholy Belgian author
of *Pelléas et Mélisande* (1892) and *L'Oiseau Bleu* (1909).

In England, symbolism did not have so marked a development
as it did on the Continent. In the work of the Pre-Raphaelite
Brotherhood (q.v.), however, there are marked traces of it, and
in the nineties the members of the Rhymers' Club in London
imitated the French symbolists and contributed symbolistic poems
to the *Yellow Book* (1894–7) and its successor, the *Savoy*. Among
these English symbolists were John Davidson (1857–1900), Lionel
Johnson (1867–1902), Ernest Dowson (1867–1900), Arthur
Symons (1865–1945), and W. B. Yeats (1865–1939).

THRENODY. See ELEGY.

**TOWNELEY PLAYS. See MIRACLE PLAY and WAKE-
FIELD MASTER** (in *Dictionary of Authors*.)

TRACTARIAN MOVEMENT. See OXFORD MOVEMENT.

TRAGEDY. That major form of drama which deals with the serious aspects of life and presents man as blundering blindly toward
an unhappy end. Generally speaking it is the opposite of *comedy*.
Although thinking and feeling are demanded of both the tragic
and the comic audience, it is certainly true that in tragedy the
emotions are more profoundly stirred than in comedy. Tragedy
is, perhaps for this reason, more universal in its appeal, and must
be regarded as the highest aspect of dramatic art. Tragic conflicts
are always deeply serious—never light, as in comedy. They are of
various types, ranging from physical fights to the death to epic
struggles between incarnate social ideals. Perhaps the most tragic
conflict of all is the losing battle of the good in man against the
evil that ultimately triumphs. In comedy satire is a frequent element; in tragedy irony often abounds, like that which leads the
wretched hero to do the wrong thing when in his blindness he
believes that he is doing the right.

Forms of tragedy vary with different literary periods. The Elizabethan "classical" tragedy—romantic in mood though it usually
was—followed the Greek and Roman formula of presenting the
decline and fall of a single great figure, a king, a prince, a famous
general. The "heroic tragedy" of the Restoration period retained
the idea of the lofty hero or villain, but the plays were more epic,
more bombastic, more stylized—and less moving. In the modern
democratic world in which the death of a strutting monarch does
not seem the most tragic event possible, other depressing climaxes

appear; a woman commits suicide because she cannot outlive her evil past, or a strike-leader loses his cause. But whatever the current pattern the basis is the same; the human being, however blindly courageous he may be, is the ultimate victim of fate, the puppet of a laughing god, the mere mortal whose hopes and aspirations are raised only that they may be ironically dashed down and scattered to the winds.

TRAGI–COMEDY. A drama in which the moods and techniques of both tragedy and comedy are blended. Not only does it contain tragic and comic scenes side by side, but while certain episodes threaten the sad climax of a tragedy, the play actually ends happily like a comedy. The tragi-comedy tends, naturally, toward the *melodrama* (q.v.); it permits the audience an indulgence in both tears and laughter. In the Elizabethan period the tragi-comedy was damned by the classical purists like Ben Jonson, but produced freely by the more liberal romantic playwrights like Shakespeare and Beaumont and Fletcher.

TRIBE OF BEN. A contemporary term adopted by the group of young poets who became, in the second quarter of the seventeenth century, the disciples of Ben Jonson, the Jacobean dramatist and critic. Of the lyrists who gathered around Jonson in the Apollo chamber of the Devil Tavern and elsewhere in London, and who came under the rich influence of his classical learning, his abundant wit, and his keen satire, the most famous was Robert Herrick. Among the others were Carew, Suckling, and Lovelace. Herrick's tribute to his master appeared after Jonson's death in 1637 in *An Ode for Ben Jonson,* where the younger poet alludes to "those lyric feasts made at the Sun, the Dog, the Triple Tun" and prays that "my Ben" may send him "thy wit's great overplus."

TROPE. See LITURGICAL PLAY.

TUDOR. A royal house of England which ruled for over a century and gave its name to what is probably the most brilliant period in the history of English literature. The Tudors reigned at the beginning of the modern world, and their dynasty saw the Renaissance, the Protestant Reformation, the growth of trade, and a rich and fruitful development in the literary arts. The first Tudor monarch was Henry VII (1485–1509); he became king by defeating Richard III, the last of the Plantagenets, on Bosworth Field in the final battle of the Wars of the Roses. The succeeding Tudors were Henry VIII (1509–47), Edward VI (1547–53), Mary (1553–

58), and Elizabeth (1558–1603). Of the Tudors Henry VIII and his daughter Elizabeth were the most famous.

UNITIES, THE. The three quasi-classical laws of play-writing are Unity of Action, Unity of Time, and Unity of Place. In the conception of medieval literary critics and French and English neo-classicists of the sixteenth and seventeenth centuries these "rules" were first pronounced in the *Poetics* of Aristotle, a Greek philosopher and critic of the fourth century B.C. Actually Aristotle mentions only two—unity of action and unity of time. "Tragedy," he says, "is an imitation of an action that is complete, and whole, and of a certain magnitude." He writes further that "Tragedy endeavors, as far as possible, to confine itself to a single revolution of the sun, or but slightly to exceed this limit." Aristotle says nothing of the unity of place; Western critics derived this third unity partly from what seemed to have been the practice of Greek and Roman tragedians, and partly, perhaps, from a desire to round out the trio of rules.

The French tragic playwrights followed the unities more consistently than did the English. In England romantic tendencies in literary art were stronger than academic precepts, and although sometimes a neo-classicist like Ben Jonson in *Sejanus* (acted 1603) and *Catiline* (acted 1611) was coldly accurate in his adherence to the rules, most contemporary playwrights, such as Shakespeare, Chapman, Webster, and Ford, violated them freely and with impunity. Even the critics, in fact, could come to no agreement as to whether the prescription for time meant restriction to the period of the action, to twelve hours, or to twenty-four hours; and whether that for place meant one spot the size of the stage, or one street, or a whole city. The neo-classicists of the late seventeenth century were more conscious of the unities than were the Elizabethans; Dryden in his *Essay of Dramatic Poetry* (1668) discusses them objectively, and Rymer in his *Short View of Tragedy* (1692) attacks the Elizabethan tragedians for violating them. A century later, however, Dr. Samuel Johnson in his famous *Preface to Shakespeare* (1765) was defending that romantic playwright for following the laws of Nature rather than those of art as interpreted by the critics.

UNIVERSITY PLAYS. See **SCHOOL PLAYS.**

UNIVERSITY WITS. A name given to a group of Elizabethan writers who shared a common pride in their university training. The group included Lodge and Peele, both Oxford-trained, Nashe, a Cambridge graduate, and Lyly and Greene, who held degrees from both institutions.

UTILITARIANISM. A theory of ethics first outlined in England in the late eighteenth century by Jeremy Bentham (1748–1832) and developed in the nineteenth century by economists James Mill (1773–1836) and his son John Stuart Mill (1806–73); the theory is also called *Benthamism* from its founder. Bentham's belief was based on the social soundness of Utility; what was most useful, he thought, was most good. Utility he defined as the "greatest happiness of the greatest number"; happiness he thought of as equivalent to pleasure. His ethical theories he promulgated in *Fragment on Government* (1776) and *Introduction to the Principles of Morals and Legislation* (1789). Bentham's most ardent disciple was the Scots philosopher James Mill, who expanded the idea of utilitarianism by advocating the search for the maximum enjoyment of the highest pleasures. His son John Stuart Mill, founder of the Utilitarian Society, modified the theory by insisting that happiness must be *qualitative* as well as *quantitative*. Utilitarianism was an influential philosophy of living in the first third of the nineteenth century. But it had its vigorous opponents. Thomas Carlyle attacked it persistently, for example, thundering that no man has an inherent right to *any* pleasure and that duty and not happiness should guide conduct.

UTOPIA. Specifically, the name given by Sir Thomas More to his ideal commonwealth but applied subsequently to all imaginatively perfect countries. The title is from the Greek words meaning "no land." More wrote his *Utopia* in Latin in 1515–6; it was translated into English in 1551. It is a description by an imaginary traveler, Raphael Hythloday, of an ideal, communistic state; it presents More's conception of the perfect government and society. In Greek literature the ideal state appears in the *Republic* of Plato (428–347 B.C.). In modern English literature the most famous Utopia is Samuel Butler's *Erewhon* (an anagram for "Nowhere") written in 1872. A twentieth-century satirical Utopia is Aldous Huxley's novel, *Brave New World* (1932).

VERCELLI BOOK, THE. A significant manuscript book containing several important Old English poems. In some manner it found its way to the chapter house at Vercelli, in the Province of Piedmont, Italy, where it has been preserved for many centuries. It contains: Cynewulf's *Elene* and *The Fates of the Apostles; Andreas*—attributed to him by some scholars; *The Dream of the Rood;* and *The Address of the Lost Soul to the Body.*

VERS DE SOCIÉTÉ. Literally, "society verse." "Occasional" or "light verse" written without too much seriousness in an easy, graceful manner characterized by charm, restrained sentiment, refined playfulness, and epigrammatic wit. Without being vulgar in content, mood, or form, it conveys, nevertheless, the opposite of what Matthew Arnold has called "high seriousness" in literary art.

VICTORIAN. A term applied to the characteristics of one of the richest and most distinctive periods in English literature, that of Queen Victoria (1837–1901). Victoria reigned longer than any other British monarch—sixty-four years. Before her death, accordingly, some very definite reactions had set in, the self-conscious morality and middle-class smugness, which are erroneously regarded as the only essential traits of mid-Victorianism, giving way to greater freedom of thought, feeling, and action. The last decade of Victoria's reign, in which the break with Victorianism was becoming marked, is sometimes called, therefore, *fin de siècle,* or "end of the century," to distinguish it from the earlier decades. The beginning of the Victorian Age is occasionally dated not from 1837, the year of the queen's accession, but from 1832, the date of the First Reform Bill, and of the deaths of Scott and Goethe.

WAKEFIELD PLAYS. See **MIRACLE PLAY** and **WAKEFIELD MASTER** (in *Dictionary of Authors*).

YELLOW BOOK, THE. See **MAGAZINES.**

YORK PLAYS. See **MIRACLE PLAY.**

IV
NOTE ON VERSIFICATION

IV

NOTE ON VERSIFICATION

SCANSION

Here is a line of poetry which has been "scanned" in the traditional way to determine the meter:

$$\overset{x}{\text{And}} \overset{\prime}{\text{nev}}|\overset{x}{\text{er}} \overset{\prime}{\text{lift}}|\overset{x}{\text{ed}} \overset{\prime}{\text{up}} | \overset{x}{\text{a}} \overset{\prime}{\text{sin}}|\overset{x}{\text{gle}} \overset{\prime}{\text{stone}}.$$

—Wordsworth, *Michael*

Although the scansion of that line would be intuitive to anyone who has read much English poetry, the scanning process actually involves four steps:

(1) DIVIDING THE LINE INTO SYLLABLES.
(2) MARKING THE ACCENTED SYLLABLES (′) AND UNACCENTED SYLLABLES (x).
(3) DIVIDING THE LINE INTO FEET.

After the accents have been marked, the above line falls obviously into five similar units, each consisting of an unaccented syllable followed by an accented syllable. These units—separated from each other by vertical lines, like the measures in music—are called **feet.** There are four common feet in English poetry:

Iambus (x ′, forgét): An unaccented syllable followed by an accented syllable—as in the line above.

Trochee (′ x, séldom): An accented syllable followed by an unaccented syllable—the reverse of an iambus:

$$\overset{\prime}{\text{Bub}}\overset{x}{\text{ble}}, | \overset{\prime}{\text{bub}}\overset{x}{\text{ble}}, | \overset{\prime}{\text{toil}} \overset{x}{\text{and}} | \overset{\prime}{\text{trou}}\overset{x}{\text{ble}}.$$

—Shakespeare, *Macbeth*

Anapest (x x ′, understánd): Two unaccented syllables followed by an accented syllable:

$$\overset{x}{\text{And}} \overset{x}{\text{the}} \overset{\prime}{\text{sheen}} | \overset{x}{\text{of}} \overset{x}{\text{their}} \overset{\prime}{\text{spears}} | \overset{x}{\text{was}} \overset{\prime}{\text{like}} \overset{x}{\text{stars}} | \overset{x}{\text{on}} \overset{x}{\text{the}} \overset{\prime}{\text{sea}}.$$

—Byron, *The Destruction of Sennacherib*

Dactyl ($'$ x x, metrical): An accented syllable followed by two unaccented syllables—the reverse of an anapest:

$$\overset{\prime}{\text{Lift}}\ \overset{x}{\text{her}}\ \overset{x}{\text{up}}\ |\ \overset{\prime}{\text{ten}}\overset{x}{\text{der}}\overset{x}{\text{ly.}}$$

—Hood, *The Bridge of Sighs*

Less common feet are the **spondee** ($'\ '$), the **pyrrhic** (x x), and the **amphibrach** (x $'$ x).

(4) NAMING THE METER.

A line of verse which contains one foot is **monometer**; two feet, **dimeter**; three, **trimeter**; four, **tetrameter**; five, **pentameter**; six, **hexameter**; seven, **heptameter**; and eight, **octometer**. The complete name of a line consists of (a) the kind of foot and (b) the number of feet in the line. Thus the line:

And never lifted up a single stone

is **iambic pentameter**—composed of five iambic feet. The other lines quoted above are respectively **trochaic tetrameter, anapestic tetrameter,** and **dactylic dimeter.**

Avoid the common error of regarding the general principles of scansion as mathematical formulae and ascribing every variation from the mechanical norm to "poetic license" or ineptitude. Actually lines as regular as those quoted above are the exception rather than the rule; otherwise English poetry would be as monotonous as a metronome. Common variations are the omission of a syllable or more at the beginning (**truncation**) or end (**catalexis**) of a line; the addition of one or more syllables at the beginning (**anacrusis**) or end (**feminine ending**); and the substitution of one or more feet of a different kind from the dominant foot in the line.

Notice these familiar lines from Shakespeare, scanned as they might be read by an actor:

$$\overset{x}{\text{To}}\ \overset{\prime}{\text{be,}}\ |\ \overset{x}{\text{or}}\ \overset{\prime}{\text{not}}\ |\ \overset{x}{\text{to}}\ \overset{\prime}{\text{be:}}\ ||\ \overset{\prime}{\text{that}}\ \overset{x}{\text{is}}\ \overset{x}{}\ |\ \overset{\prime}{\text{the}}\ \overset{x}{\text{question.}}$$

$$\overset{x}{\text{The}}\ \overset{\prime}{\text{qual}}|\overset{x}{\text{ity}}\ \overset{\prime}{}\ |\ \overset{x}{\text{of}}\ \overset{\prime}{\text{mer}}|\overset{x}{\text{cy}}\ \overset{\prime}{\text{is}}\ |\ \overset{\prime}{\text{not}}\ \overset{\prime}{\text{strained.}}$$

$$\overset{x}{\text{Tomor}}|\overset{\prime}{\text{row}}\ \overset{x}{\text{and}}\ |\ \overset{x}{\text{tomor}}|\overset{x}{\text{row}}\ \overset{\prime}{\text{and}}\ |\ \overset{x}{\text{tomor}}|\overset{x}{\text{row.}}$$

These lines are called *iambic pentameter* because a line takes its name from the prevailing foot. But observe the following variations: the sharp pause or **caesura** in the middle of the first line and the subsequent substitution of a trochee for the dominant iambus; the importance of the word *not* in the second line, resulting in the substitution of a spondee for the final iambus; the unimportance of the two *and's* in line three, both of which would be stressed in a mechanically regular line; and the feminine endings in lines one and three. This does not mean that Shakespeare could not write a "perfect" line when he wanted to; like all real poets he aimed at the mastery of variety within the limits of the line.

RHYME SCHEMES

The **rhyme scheme** of a poem is commonly designated by the letters of the alphabet—*a,* for example, indicating the rhyme at the end of the first line and all subsequent end-words which rhyme with it; *b* indicates the second rhyme, etc. Note the rhymes in the following stanza:

> Morn and noon and night,   (*a*)
> Here I lie in the ground,   (*b*)
> No faintest glimmer of light,   (*a*)
> No lightest whisper of sound.   (*b*)
>   —Anon., *Monologue d'outre Tombe*

Here the rhyme scheme is *abab*. In addition, some lines may contain **internal rhyme** as do one and three in the following passage:

> And through the *drifts* the snowy *clifts*
> Did send a dismal sheen:
> Nor shapes of *men* nor beasts we *ken,*
> The ice was all between.
>
>   —Coleridge, *The Rime of the Ancient Mariner*

Possible rhyme schemes are infinite, and many English poets, John Donne, for example, have freely devised their own. A few of the better-known ones are listed below:

The **couplet** (*aa, bb, cc,* etc.). The iambic pentameter couplet or **heroic couplet** was a dominant verse form in English poetry from 1660 to 1800. If the second line is **end-stopped** with a strong mark of punctuation, and the syntax and thought of the two lines are complete in themselves, it is a **closed couplet.** Here is a closed couplet by the poet who perfected the form:

> Know then thyself, presume not God to scan;
> The proper study of Mankind is Man.
>   —Pope, *Essay on Man*

In the following passage, Dryden uses the **open couplet:**

> A daring pilot in extremity,
> Pleased with the danger when the waves went high
> He sought the storms; but for a calm unfit
> Would steer too nigh the sands to boast his wit.
>
>   —Dryden, *Absalom and Achitophel*

Notice that the syntax and meaning of the first half of the sentence are not complete until the middle of line three; the second line, in other words, is a **run-on line**.

A poem in couplets is usually printed solid. When the couplets are spaced, the poem may be said to be divided into stanzas. A **stanza** is a group of two or more lines arranged according to a definite pattern. It is popularly miscalled a **verse,** a term that should be applied only to a single line. The following stanza—with alternating tetrameter and trimeter lines rhyming *abcb*—is the common form of the **ballad stanza:**

> There lived a wife at Usher's Well,
>   And a wealthy wife was she;
> She had three stout and stalwart sons,
>   And sent them o'er the sea.
>   —Anon., *The Wife of Usher's Well*

Other common rhyme schemes in four-line stanzas or **quatrains** are *abab, abba,* and *aabb.*

The following more complex stanzas also occur in English literature:

Rhyme royal: seven iambic pentameter lines rhyming *ababbcc.* This stanza was named after King James I of Scotland, who used it in his *King's Quair* (1423–4). Chaucer, however, had used it earlier in *The Parliament of Fowls* and other poems, and it is sometimes called the **Chaucerian stanza.** It is also used in Sackville's *Induction,* Shakespeare's *Rape of Lucrece,* and Masefield's *Dauber.*

Ottava rima: eight iambic pentameter lines rhyming *abababcc.* Because Byron made such brilliant use of its recurrent rhymes in *Don Juan,* it is sometimes called the **Don Juan stanza.**

Terza rima: interlocking three-line stanzas (*aba, bcb, cdc,* etc.). It was used by Dante in *The Divine Comedy* and, with a slight variation, by Shelley in *Ode to the West Wind.*

Spenserian stanza: nine lines rhyming *ababbcbcc.* The first eight lines are iambic pentameter; the ninth is an iambic hexameter line or **Alexandrine.** It is the stanza of Spenser's *Faerie Queene* and occurs also in Shenstone's *Schoolmistress,* Thomson's *Castle of Indolence,* Beattie's *Minstrel,* Burns' *Cotter's Saturday Night,* Byron's *Childe Harold,* Keats' *Eve of St. Agnes,* and Shelley's *Adonais.*

In some instances the name of a verse form is applied not to a recurring stanzaic pattern but to the entire poem:

The **sonnet** is a poem of fourteen iambic pentameter lines. Although poets have exercised great liberty within the form, most of the rhyme schemes in English poetry are built on two basic patterns: The **Petrarchan** or **Italian sonnet**—named for the Italian sonneteer Petrarch—in which the fourteen lines are divided into an eight-line **octave** rhyming *abba abba* and a six-line **sestet** rhyming usually *cde cde* or *cd cd cd;* and the **Shakespearean sonnet,** which consists of three quatrains and a couplet: *abab cdcd efef gg.* Much less common is the **Spenserian sonnet,** used by Spenser in *Amoretti*. In this the first eight lines are identical with those of the Spenserian stanza. The complete rhyme scheme is *abab bcbc cdcd ee.*

FRENCH FORMS

A number of verse forms borrowed from the French were especially popular in England towards the close of the Victorian era and occur frequently in the work of Swinburne, Austin Dobson, W. E. Henley, and Andrew Lang. Since these forms are especially attractive to writers of light verse, many of the English poems written in them have been nothing but pretty trifles.

The **ballade**—not to be confused with the ballad—usually consists of three stanzas of eight lines each and a concluding **envoy** of four. The first three stanzas commonly rhyme, like the first eight lines of the Spenserian stanza, *ababbcbc,* the envoy *abab.* The concluding line of the first stanza is repeated—sometimes with significant variations—at the end of each division of the poem. This device is called a **refrain.**

The **rondeau** commonly consists of fifteen lines, divided into three stanzas of five, four, and six. The opening phrase of the first line is repeated as a refrain at the end of the second and third stanzas. The rhyme scheme—with *r* standing for the unrhyming refrain—is *aabba aabr aabbar.* The most popular rondeau in English is probably John McCrae's *In Flanders Fields.*

The **rondel** is a three-stanza form, in which the first two lines of the opening stanza are commonly repeated as the last two in the second and third stanzas. The rhyme scheme is *abba abab abbaa.*

The **triolet,** with its economical two rhymes and its artificial line repetitions, is illustrated in the following characteristically light and saucy example:

> I never say hello to Herman   (*a*)
> Till Herman says hello to me.   (*b*)
> Though Ma delivers such a sermon   (*a*)

> I never say hello to Herman.　*(a)*
> I treat him like the other vermin　*(a)*
> 　　He takes it meekly as a flea.　*(b)*
> I never say hello to Herman　*(a)*
> 　　Till Herman says hello to me.　*(b)*
>
> 　　　　　　　　—Claire Burch, *Romance*

The **villanelle** has five three-line stanzas rhyming *aba* and a con cluding four-line stanza rhyming *abaa*. As in the rondeau, the rondel, and the triolet, only two rhymes are used throughout. The first line of the first stanza is repeated as the third line of the second and fourth. The third line of the first stanza is repeated as the third line of the third and fifth. The first and third lines of the first stanza—which serve as alternating refrains throughout the poem—are repeated as the third and fourth lines of the final stanza.

UNRHYMED VERSE

The popularity of rhymed verse in English literature must not lead the reader to overemphasize the importance of rhyme. Some of the greatest poetry in English does not rhyme. Two kinds of unrhymed verse are commonly confused:

Blank verse is, strictly speaking, *unrhymed iambic pentameter*. It was first introduced into English literature in Surrey's translation of Vergil's *Aeneid* (1554–7). It is the medium of most of the verse in Shakespeare's tragedies and of Milton's *Paradise Lost*. Here is a passage of blank verse:

> The world is all before them, where to choose
> Their place of rest, and Providence their guide:
> They hand in hand with wandering steps and slow,
> Through Eden took their solitary way.
>
> 　　　　　　　　—Milton, *Paradise Lost*

Free verse is a general term for poetry which is unconfined by the traditional patterns of rhyme, rhythm, and length of line. This is not to say that it has no form, but that its rhythms are less regular and often far more subtle than those of traditional verse. Free verse must not be confused with prose arranged typographically to resemble poetry. Although there are examples of what might be called free verse throughout English literature, the movement really belongs to the end of the nineteenth and the beginning of the twentieth centuries. It received its greatest modern impetus from the work of the American poet Walt Whitman, but that it has an ancient origin appears from the following Biblical lyric, which is arranged as prose in the King James version of the Bible, but which has, nevertheless, the pattern, the rhythm, and the other characteristics of free verse.

> Lift up your heads, O ye gates;
> And be ye lift up, ye everlasting doors;
> And the King of glory shall come in.
> Who is this King of glory?
> The Lord strong and mighty,
> The Lord mighty in battle.
> Lift up your heads, O ye gates;
> Even lift them up, ye everlasting doors;
> And the King of glory shall come in.
> Who is this King of glory?
> The Lord of hosts,
> He is the King of glory.
>
> —Psalm 24, 7–10

DEVICES OF POETRY

In addition to such obvious factors as rhyme and meter, there are a number of devices which, although all of them appear in prose, are of particular importance in poetry:

A **simile** expresses a likeness between two things which do not ordinarily belong in the same category.

> O my Luve's like a red, red rose
>   That's newly sprung in June;
> O my Luve's like the melodie
>   That's sweetly played in tune!
>
> —Burns, *A Red, Red Rose*

A **metaphor** can be considered as a compressed simile—a simile with the word *like* (*as,* etc.) omitted.

> Thou still unravished bride of quietness,
>   Thou foster-child of silence and slow time,
> Silvan historian, who canst thus express
>   A flowery tale more sweetly than our rhyme:
>
> —Keats, *On a Grecian Urn*

The foregoing metaphor also illustrates **personification:** treating an inanimate object or abstract idea as if it were endowed with human attributes.

Alliteration, in its simplest form, is the repetition of initial letters, usually consonants.

> The fair breeze blew, the white foam flew,
>   The furrow followed free.
>
> —Coleridge, *The Rime of the Ancient Mariner*

411

Alliteration was the backbone of Anglo-Saxon poetry, as in *Beowulf,* and of such Middle English **alliterative romances** as *Gawayne and the Grene Knight.* Today it survives as an ornament which must be handled with care.

Closely related to alliteration is **onomatopoeia,** the fitting of sound to meaning. It is represented in many single words—in *whirr, buzz, creak,* and such comic strip favorites as *wham, zowie,* and *kerplunk.* Coleridge, in *The Rime of the Ancient Mariner,* has put four onomatopoeic words together in a single classic line:

> It cracked and growled and roared and howled
> Like noises in a swound!

A different kind of onomatopoeia effect is achieved by fitting meter to meaning—as in Browning's *How They Brought the Good News* and Southey's tumbling *Cataract of Lodore.*

Assonance is the repetition of accented vowel sounds in succeeding words with different consonant sounds—or, more rarely, the repetition of consonant sounds where vowel sounds are different. Thus, while *beam* and *stream,* and *mystery* and *history* rhyme, *beach* and *stream,* and *mystery* and *mastery* are assonant.

Repetition is more commonly used for effect in poetry than in prose. It may be the echo of a single word or phrase. It may be, as in the French forms discussed above, a recurring refrain of one line or several. A special kind of repetition is the **incremental repetition** which occurs constantly—although usually not at regular intervals—in the folk ballads; it differs from the simple refrain in that it carries the story slightly forward:

> The first line that Sir Patrick red,
> A loud lauch lauched he;
> The next line that Sir Patrick red,
> The teir blinded his ee.
>
> —Anon., *Sir Patrick Spens*

V

CHRONOLOGICAL CHART

V

CHRONOLOGICAL CHART

In this chart the chronology of the authors has been determined by the dates of their chief literary activities; these dates *precede* the authors' names, and the birth and death dates *follow* the names. Names of English writers in the *Dictionary of Authors* are printed in **bold face.** Titles in the *List of Anonymous Works* are followed by **(A).** Items defined in the *Glossary of Literary Terms* are followed by **(G).**

THE OLD ENGLISH (ANGLO–SAXON) PERIOD (449–1066)

449	Anglo-Saxon invasion and settlement of Britain.
563	Foundation of monastery on Island of Iona in Northern Britain by St. Columba (521–597), Irish missionary.
597	Landing of St. Augustine (d. 604), Italian "Apostle of the English," in Kent.
664	Council of Whitby at which supremacy of Italian (Southern) church over Irish (Northern) was determined.
665?–709	**Aldhelm** (640?–709).
670 ff.	Writings of **Caedmon** and his "School."
731	*Ecclesiastical History of the English Nation* (in Latin) by the Venerable **Bede** (673–735).
c. 750	Composition of *Beowulf* **(A).**
c. 750–c. 800	Writings of **Cynewulf** and his "School."
787	First Danish invasion of Britain.
850 ff.	*Anglo-Saxon Chronicle* **(A).**
800–814	Reign of Charlemagne, Emperor of the West.
871–901	Reign of **Alfred** (849–901), King of the West Saxons.
878	Treaty of Wedmore, which confined the invading Danes to the Danelagh in the north of England.
937	Battle of Brunanburh **(A).**
c. 971	*Blickling Homilies* **(A).**
975?–1020?	**Aelfric** (955?–1020?).

991	Battle of Maldon (A).
c. 1000	Writing of the *Beowulf* manuscript (A).
1000–1025	The *Exeter Book* (G) and *The Vercelli Book* (G).
1017–42	Britain ruled by Danish kings.
1042–66	Reign of Edward the Confessor.
1066	Reign of Harold, "the last of the Saxon kings." Norman invasion under William the Conqueror. Defeat of the Saxons and death of King Harold at Battle of Hastings (Senlac).

THE MIDDLE ENGLISH PERIOD (1066–1500)

1066–87	Reign of William the Conqueror (William I).
1087–1100	Reign of William II (Rufus).
1096–99	The First Crusade.
1100–35	Reign of Henry I.
1135–54	Reign of Stephen.
1147	*History of the Kings of Britain* (in Latin) by **Geoffrey of Monmouth** (1100?–54).
1147–49	The Second Crusade.
c. 1150	Composition of *The Nibelungenlied,* Germanic saga.
1154–89	Reign of Henry II.
1170	Murder of Thomas à Becket, Archbishop of Canterbury.
c. 1175–1200	*Poema Morale* (A).
1189–92	Third Crusade.
1189–99	Reign of Richard I (*Coeur de Lion*).
1199–1216	Reign of John.
c. 1200	Romances of Marie de France; see Lay in *Glossary.*
c. 1200–1225	Composition of *Sumer Is I-Cumen In* (A).
c. 1205	*The Brut* by **Layamon** (fl. 1200).
1215	The Signing of Magna Charta.
1216–72	Reign of Henry III.
c. 1225	*The Bestiary* (G).
c. 1225–30	*The Ancren Riwle* (A).
c. 1250	*The Owl and the Nightingale* (A) and *Dame Siriz* (A).
c. 1250–1300	*The Debate of the Body and the Soul* (A); *King Horn* (A); and *The Fox and the Wolf* (A).
1267–94	**Roger Bacon** (1214?–94).
1272–1307	Reign of Edward I.
c. 1275–1325	*Bevis of Hamtoun* (A); *Havelok the Dane* (A); *The Squire of Low Degree* (A); *Guy of War-*

CHART   [1291–1440

	wick (A); *Flores and Blancheflour* (A); *Cursor Mundi* (A).
1291–1320	Dante (1265–1321), Italian poet.
1307–1327	Reign of Edward II.
1309–77	The "Babylonian Captivity"; schism in Roman Catholic Church.
1314	Battle of Bannockburn.
1327–77	Reign of Edward III.
1337–1453	The Hundred Years' War between England and France.
c. 1340	*Ayenbite of Inwyt (Remorse of Conscience)* (A).
1340–1400	Composition of York, Chester, and Wakefield (Towneley) Cycles of Miracle Plays (G).
1346	Battle of Crécy.
1348–9	The Black Death.
c. 1348–70	Petrarch (1304–74), Italian poet.
c. 1350	The *Decameron* of Boccaccio (1313–1375), Italian writer of *novelle*. *The Tale of Gamelyn* (A).
1350–1400	**The Wakefield Master.** See *Dictionary of Authors.*
1360–70	**The Pearl Poet** (fl. 1350–70). See *Dictionary of Authors.*
1362–96	*Piers Plowman,* attributed to **William Langland** (1330?–1400?).
1369–1400	**Geoffrey Chaucer** (c. 1340–1400).
1377–99	Reign of Richard II.
1381	Wat Tyler's Rebellion.
c. 1382–1388	Translation of Bible (A) of **John Wycliffe** (1320?–84) and others.
1386–90	*Confessio Amantis* by **John Gower** (1330?–1408?).
c. 1387	**Chaucer's** *Prologue* to *Canterbury Tales.*
1388	Battle of Otterburn (Chevy Chase) (A).
1399–1413	Reign of Henry IV.
c. 1400–25	**Thomas Occleve** (1368?–1450?)
c. 1400–38	**John Lydgate** (1370?–1451?).
1400–1450	*The Flower and The Leaf* (A).
1413–1422	Reign of Henry V.
1422–1461	Reign of Henry VI.
c. 1424	*The King's Quair* by King **James I** of Scotland (1394–1437).
c. 1425	*The Castle of Perseverance* (A).
1431	Execution of Joan of Arc, French heroine.
1440–86	*The Paston Letters.* See **John** and **Margaret Paston** in *Dictionary of Authors.*

c. 1450	Printing of Gutenberg Bible by Johann Gutenberg (1400?–1468), German inventor of printing.
1450	Jack Cade's Rebellion.
c. 1450–1500	*Mankind* (A). **Robert Henryson** (1425?–1500?).
1453	Capture of Constantinople by the Turks.
1455–85	The Wars of the Roses.
1461–83	Reign of Edward IV.
1469	*Morte Darthur* by **Sir Thomas Malory** (1394?–1471).
1471	Establishment of Caxton's printing press in England.
1483	Reign of Edward V.
1483–5	Reign of Richard III.
1485	Overthrow and death of Richard III in Battle of Bosworth Field; accession of the victor, Henry Tudor.

THE MODERN ENGLISH PERIOD (1500–   )

1485–1509	Reign of Henry VII. Tudor Period to 1603 **(G)**.
c. 1485–1625	The English Renaissance **(G)**.
1491	Greek first taught at Oxford.
1492	Discovery of the Western Hemisphere by Christopher Columbus (1446?–1506).
c. 1497	*Fulgens and Lucres* by **Henry Medwall** (fl. 1486).
c. 1500	*Everyman* **(A)**. *Hyckescorner* **(A)**.
1502–25	**John Skelton** (1460?–1529).
1509–47	Reign of Henry VIII.
1513	Death of James IV of Scotland in Battle of Flodden Field in war with English. Publication of *The Prince* by Machiavelli (1469–1527), Italian political writer.
1516	*Utopia* by **Sir Thomas More** (1478–1535).
1519	Death of Leonardo da Vinci, Italian scientist and artist.
1521	Martin Luther's refusal to retract at the Diet of Worms.
1522	*Mundus et Infans* **(A)**.
1523	Translation of the New Testament into German by Martin Luther (1483–1546).
1528	*The Book of the Courtier* by Conte Baldassare Castiglione (1478–1529), Italian writer; translated into English by Sir Thomas Hoby (1530–66) in 1561. (See Courtesy Book in *Glossary*).

CHART   [1532–1580

1532–48	*Gargantua* and *Pantagruel* by François Rabelais (1490?–1553), French satirist.
1533–69	Interludes by **John Heywood** (1497?–1580?).
1534	Act of Supremacy to make Henry VIII "supreme head on earth of the Church of England."
c. 1534–41	*Ralph Roister Doister* by **Nicholas Udall** (1505–56).
1535	Complete translation of the Bible **(A)** by **Miles Coverdale** (1488–1568). *Institutes of the Christian Religion* by John Calvin (1509–64), French religious reformer.
1536	Execution of **William Tyndale** (1492?–1536) for heresy.
1537?	*Thersites* **(A)**.
1545–63	Council of Trent.
1545–68	**Roger Ascham** (1515–68).
1547–1553	Reign of Edward VI.
1550?	*Tom Tyler and his Wife* **(A)**.
1553–1558	Reign of Mary Tudor.
1557	*Tottel's Miscellany* by **Richard Tottel** (1525?–1594); miscellany contained poems by **Sir Thomas Wyatt** (1503?–42) and **Earl of Surrey** (1517?–47).
1558–1603	Reign of Elizabeth. Elizabethan Age **(G)**.
1559–63	*The Mirror for Magistrates* with *Induction* by **Thomas Sackville** (1536–1608).
1560	Publication of *Nice Wanton* **(A)**. Completion of the Geneva Bible. See Bible **(A)**.
1560?	*Misogonus* **(A)**.
1561	*Gorboduc* by **Thomas Norton** (1532–84) and **Thomas Sackville** (1536–1608).
1563	Publication of *Jack Juggler* **(A)**.
1566–76	**George Gascoigne** (1525?–77).
1568	Completion of the "Bishops' Bible." See Bible **(A)**.
1572	St. Bartholomew's Day Massacre of French Huguenots.
1576	First London Playhouse—"The Theater."
1577	*Chronicles of England, Scotland, and Ireland* by **Raphael Holinshed** (d. 1580?).
1579–96	**Edmund Spenser** (1552?–99).
1579–1601	**John Lyly** (1554?–1606).
1580–86	**Sir Philip Sidney** (1554–86).
1580–88	The *Essais* of Montaigne (1533–92), French essayist, model for Bacon's essays.

1581	Completion of translation of Seneca's tragedies by **Jasper Heywood** (1535?–98) and others.
1582	The Rheims New Testament. See Bible **(A)**.
1584–96	**George Peele** (1557?–96).
c. 1586	*The Spanish Tragedy* by **Thomas Kyd** (1558–94).
1587–93	**Christopher Marlowe** (1564–93).
1587	Execution of Mary, Queen of Scots.
1588	Defeat of the Spanish Armada.
1588–89	The **"Martin Marprelate"** pamphlets. See *Dictionary of Authors*.
1588–92	**Robert Greene** (1558–92).
1589	*The Principal Navigations, Voyages, Traffics, and Discoveries of the English Nation* by **Richard Hakluyt** (1552?–1616).
1590	*Rosalynde* by **Thomas Lodge** (1558?–1625).
1591–1611	**William Shakespeare** (1564–1616).
1591–1622	**Michael Drayton** (1563–1631).
1592	Publication of *Arden of Feversham* **(A)**.
1592–1614	**Sir Walter Raleigh** (1552?–1618).
1592–1615	**Samuel Daniel** (1562–1619).
1595	Publication of *Locrine* **(A)**.
1597–1601	The "Parnassus Plays" **(A)**.
1597–1625	**Francis Bacon** (1561–1626).
1598	Publication of *Mucedorus* **(A)**.
1598–1634	**Ben Jonson** (1572–1637).
1599	Publication of *A Warning for Fair Women* **(A)**. Erection of the Globe Theater (Shakespeare's) in Southwark, London.
1599–1621	**Thomas Dekker** (1572?–1632).
1599–1633	**Thomas Heywood** (c. 1570–1641).
1600	Founding of the East India Company.
1601–2	Rebellion and execution of the Earl of Essex.
1601–19	**Thomas Campion** (1567–1620).
1602–5	**John Marston** (1575?–1634).
1603–25	Reign of James I. Jacobean Period **(G)**.
1605–15	**George Chapman** (1559?–1634).
1605, 1615	*Don Quixote* by Miguel de Cervantes (1547–1616), Spanish novelist.
1607	English settlement at Jamestown, Virginia.
1608	Publication of *The Yorkshire Tragedy* **(A)**.
1608–21	**Francis Beaumont** (1584–1616) and **John Fletcher** (1579–1625).
1608–23	**John Webster** (1580?–1625).

1608–27	**Thomas Middleton** (1570?–1627).
1610	Completion of Douai Old Testament. See Bible **(A)**.
1611	Completion of King James or "Authorized" translation of the Bible **(A)**.
1618–48	"Thirty Years' War" on the Continent.
1618	Theory of the circulation of the blood expounded by **William Harvey** (1578–1657).
1620	Landing of the Pilgrims at Plymouth, Massachusetts.
1621	*The Anatomy of Melancholy* by **Robert Burton** (1577–1640).
1621–39	**John Ford** (1586–1639).
1622–39	**Philip Massinger** (1583–1640).
1623	First folio of Shakespeare's plays; second folio, 1632; third folio, 1663–4; fourth folio, 1685.
1625–49	Reign of Charles I. Caroline Period **(G)**.
1628	Petition of Rights wrested from the king.
1629–55	**James Shirley** (1596–1666).
1629–71	**John Milton** (1608–74).
1633	Publication of poems by **John Donne** (1573–1631).
1633–63	**Abraham Cowley** (1618–67).
1635	Founding of the French Academy.
1636	*The Cid* by Pierre Corneille (1606–84), French dramatist.
1637–49	Writings of René Descartes (1596–1650), French philosopher.
1638–41	**Sir John Suckling** (1609–42).
1640	First meeting of "The Long Parliament."
1640–1706	*Diary* of **John Evelyn** (1620–1706).
1640–78	**Izaak Walton** (1593–1683).
1641	Execution of the Earl of Strafford.
1642	Beginning of the Civil War between Crown and Parliament. Closing of the theaters by edict of Puritan Parliament.
1642–53	**Richard Lovelace** (1618–57?).
1642–58	**Sir Thomas Browne** (1605–82).
1642–61	**Thomas Fuller** (1608–61).
1645	Execution of Archbishop Laud. Creation by Parliament of "New Model" army under command of Oliver Cromwell (1599–1658).
1645–85	**Edmund Waller** (1606–87).
1646–49	**Richard Crashaw** (1612?–49).

1646–78   **Henry Vaughan** (1621–95).

1648   *Hesperides* and *Noble Numbers* by **Robert Herrick** (1591–1674).

1649   Execution of Charles I by Parliamentary court.

1649–53   The Commonwealth.

1650–51   Political treatises of **Thomas Hobbes** (1588–1679).

1650–55   **Jeremy Taylor** (1613–67).

1650–75   **Andrew Marvell** (1621–78).

1652–54   War between the English and the Dutch.

1653–1659   The Protectorate.

1659–73   Chief plays of Molière (1622–73), French actor and playwright.

1660   Restoration of monarchy in person of Charles II, who reigned until 1685. The Restoration Period **(G)**.

c. 1660   **Thomas Traherne** (1637?–74).

1660–69   *Diary* of **Samuel Pepys** (1633–1703).

1660–97   **John Dryden** (1631–1700).

1662   Founding of the Royal Society.

1663   Building of Drury Lane Theater.

1663–78   *Hudibras* by **Samuel Butler** (1612–80).

1664–76   **Sir George Etherege** (1635?–91).

1665   The Great Plague of London.

1665–86   **John Bunyan** (1628–88).

1666   The Great Fire of London.

1667–90   Chief tragedies of Jean Baptiste Racine (1639–99), French dramatist.

1670   Appointment of **John Dryden** as poet laureate **(G)**; dismissed from office 1689.

1671–76   **William Wycherley** (1640?–1716).

1675–83   **Thomas Otway** (1652–85).

1681–85   Rebellion of the Duke of Monmouth.

1682–1725   Reign of Peter the Great as Czar of Russia.

1685–88   Reign of James II.

1687   *Principia* by **Sir Isaac Newton** (1642–1727).

1687–1721   **Matthew Prior** (1664–1721).

1688–89   The Protestant Revolution which deposed James II and brought William and Mary to the throne.

1688–1702   Reign of William and Mary.

1689–92   **Thomas Shadwell** (1642?–92) poet laureate **(G)**.

1690   Battle of the Boyne in which James II was defeated. *Essay on Human Understanding* by **John Locke** (1632–1704).

CHART   [*1690–1741*

1690–99	Battle of the Ancients and the Moderns (G).
1692–1715	**Nahum Tate** (1652–1715) poet laureate (G).
1693–1701	**William Congreve** (1670–1729).
1696–1729	**Jonathan Swift** (1667–1745).
1697–1726	**Sir John Vanbrugh** (1664–1726).
1698	*A Short View of the Immorality and Profaneness of the English Stage* by **Jeremy Collier** (1650–1726).
1698–1725	**Daniel Defoe** (1659–1731).
1701–14	War of the Spanish Succession.
1701–22	**Sir Richard Steele** (1672–1729).
1702–14	Reign of Anne.
1704	Marlborough's victory at the Battle of Blenheim
1704–14	**Joseph Addison** (1672–1719).
1706–07	**George Farquhar** (1678–1707).
1709–33	**George Berkeley** (1685–1753).
1709–35	**Alexander Pope** (1688–1744).
1713	The Peace of Utrecht.
1713–29	**John Gay** (1685–1732).
1714	Founding of Scriblerus Club (G).
1714–27	Reign of George I.
1714–c. 1800	Georgian Age (G).
1715	First Jacobite Rebellion. See Jacobean in *Glossary*.
1715–18	**Nicholas Rowe** (1674–1718) poet laureate (G).
1718–30	**Laurence Eusden** (1688–1730) poet laureate (G).
1720	The South Sea Bubble panic.
1725–61	**Edward Young** (1683–1765).
1726–48	**James Thomson** (1700–48).
1727–60	Reign of George II.
1729	Beginnings of Methodism under **John Wesley** (1703–91).
1730–51	**Henry Fielding** (1707–54).
1730–57	**Colley Cibber** (1671–1757) poet laureate (G).
1730–93	Industrial and agricultural revolution in England.
1732	Building of Covent Garden Theater.
1734–62	Chief writings of Voltaire (1694–1778), French philosopher and writer.
1737–68	*Letters to his Son* of **Lord Chesterfield** (1694–1773).
1738–81	**Samuel Johnson** (1709–84).
1740–48	The War of the Austrian Succession.
1740–53	**Samuel Richardson** (1689–1761).
1741–75	Acting and playwriting of **David Garrick** (1717–79).

1742–49	**William Collins** (1721–59).
1743	*The Grave* by **Robert Blair** (1699–1746).
1744–46	Second Jacobite Rebellion, ending in the defeat of Charles Stuart, "The Young Pretender," at the Battle of Culloden. See Jacobean in *Glossary*.
1747–69	**Thomas Gray** (1716–71).
1748–71	**Tobias Smollett** (1721–71).
1752	Adoption of the Gregorian Calendar in England.
1753	Founding of the British Museum.
1755	Lisbon earthquake.
1756–60	Expedition in India of Robert Clive (1725–1774).
1756–63	The Seven Years' War between England and France.
1756–97	**Edmund Burke** (1729–97).
1757–73	**Oliver Goldsmith** (1728–74).
1757–85	**William Whitehead** (1715–85) poet laureate **(G)**.
1759–68	**Laurence Sterne** (1713–68).
1760–63	*Poems of "Ossian"* by **James Macpherson** (1736–96).
1760–1820	Reign of George III.
1761–78	Chief writings of Jean Jacques Rousseau (1712–78), French social philosopher.
1764	Founding of "The Club"—"Dr. Johnson's Circle" **(G)**. *The Castle of Otranto* by **Horace Walpole** (1717–97).
1764–70	*The Rowley Poems* by **Thomas Chatterton** (1752–70).
1765–71	**Bishop Thomas Percy** (1729–1811).
1768–1840	**Frances Burney (Mme. D'Arblay)** (1752–1840).
1769	Invention of the steam engine by James Watt (1736–1819).
1769–71	Letters of **Junius**. See *Dictionary of Authors*.
1770–1832	Chief writings of Johann Wolfgang von Goethe (1749–1832), German poet and dramatist.
1775–83	The War of American Independence.
1775–99	**Richard Sheridan** (1751–1816).
1776–88	*The Decline and Fall of the Roman Empire* by **Edward Gibbon** (1737–94).
1779–99	**William Cowper** (1731–1800).
1780–1819	**George Crabbe** (1754–1832).
1781	*Critique of Pure Reason* by Immanuel Kant (1724–1804), German philosopher.
1783–1804	**William Blake** (1757–1827).
1785–90	**Thomas Warton** (1728–90) poet laureate **(G)**.

CHART   [1785–1817

1785–91	**James Boswell** (1740–95).
1786	Impeachment of Warren Hastings.
1786–93	**Robert Burns** (1759–96).
1789	Outbreak of the French Revolution.
1790–1813	**Henry James Pye** (1745–1813) poet laureate **(G)**.
1793	Execution of Louis XVI, king of France.
1793–99	**William Godwin** (1756–1836).
1793–1802	War with France.
1793–1833	**William Wordsworth** (1770–1850).
1794–97	**Ann Radcliffe** (1764–1823).
1794–1825	**Samuel Taylor Coleridge** (1772–1834).
1794–1837	**Robert Southey** (1774–1843).
1795–1848	**Maria Edgeworth** (1767–1849).
1796	*The Monk* by **Matthew Gregory Lewis** (1775–1818).
1796–1833	**Charles Lamb** (1775–1834).
1797–1817	**Jane Austen** (1775–1817).
1798	*Lyrical Ballads* by **William Wordsworth** (1770–1850) and **Samuel Taylor Coleridge** (1772–1834); second edition with Wordsworth's *Preface*, 1800; significant dates in the Romantic Movement.
1798–1863	**Walter Savage Landor** (1775–1864).
1800	Union of Great Britain and Ireland.
1800–32	**Sir Walter Scott** (1771–1832).
1802	First issue of the *Edinburgh Review* **(G)**.
1803–15	The Napoleonic Wars.
1805	Naval battle of Trafalgar; death of Lord Nelson (1758–1805).
1807–17	**Thomas Moore** (1779–1852).
1807–19	**James Hogg** (1770–1835).
1807–22	**Lord Byron** (1788–1824).
1807–50	**Leigh Hunt** (1784–1859).
1809	First issue of the *Quarterly Review* **(G)**.
1811	Establishment of Regency to govern for George III.
1812–15	War between England and the United States.
1812–20	Chief writings of Georg Wilhelm Friedrich Hegel (1770–1831), German philosopher.
1813–22	**Percy Bysshe Shelley** (1792–1822).
1813–43	**Robert Southey** (1774–1843) poet laureate **(G)**.
1815	Defeat of Napoleon by Wellington at Battle of Waterloo.
1816–26	**Mary Godwin Shelley** (1797–1851).
1817	First issue of *Blackwood's Edinburgh Magazine* **(G)**.

425

1817–21	**John Keats** (1795–1821).
1817–26	**William Hazlitt** (1778–1830).
1817	The term "Cockney School of Poetry" **(G)** first applied to London poets by *Blackwood's Magazine* **(G)**. The term "Lake Poets" **(G)** first applied to Wordsworth, Coleridge, and Southey by *Edinburgh Review* **(G)**.
1820–29	Chief writings of Aleksander Pushkin (1799–1837), Russian poet.
1820–30	Reign of George IV.
1820–54	**Thomas DeQuincey** (1785–1859).
1820–73	**Edward Bulwer-Lytton** (1803–73).
1822	The term "Satanic School of Poets" **(G)** used by **Robert Southey** in his *Vision of Judgment* (2nd ed.).
1823–65	**Thomas Carlyle** (1795–1881).
1825–59	**Thomas Babington Macaulay** (1800–59).
1826–45	**Thomas Hood** (1799–1845).
1826–80	**Benjamin Disraeli** (1804–81).
1827–89	**Alfred Lord Tennyson** (1809–92).
1829–42	Chief writings of Honoré de Balzac (1799–1850), French novelist.
1829–63	Chief writings of Charles Augustin Sainte-Beuve (1804–69), French writer and critic.
1830	First issue of *Fraser's Magazine* **(G)**.
1830–37	Reign of William IV.
1830–79	Chief writings of Victor Hugo (1802–85), French romantic poet, dramatist, and novelist.
1832	Passage of First Reform Bill for extending the franchise in England.
1833–42	The Oxford Movement **(G)**.
1833–70	**John Henry Newman** (1801–90).
1833–89	**Robert Browning** (1812–89).
1836–65	**Charles Dickens** (1812–70).
1837–48	Chartist Movement for political reforms.
1837–63	**William Makepeace Thackeray** (1811–63).
1837–1901	Reign of Victoria. For the literary limits of The Victorian Age see *Glossary*.
1838–60	**Elizabeth Barrett Browning** (1806–61).
1839–80	**Charles Darwin** (1809–82).
1841	First issue of *Punch* **(G)**.
1841–75	**Dion Boucicault** (1822–90).
1843–50	**William Wordsworth** (1770–1850) poet laureate **(G)**.

CHART [1843–1866

1843–73	**John Stuart Mill** (1806–73).
1843–89	**John Ruskin** (1819–1900).
1846–8	**Emily Brontë** (1818–48).
1846–71	Chief writings of Fëdor Mikhailovich Dostoevski (1821–81), Russian novelist.
1847–55	**Charlotte Brontë** (1816–55).
1847–81	**Anthony Trollope** (1815–82).
1847–94	**Christina Rossetti** (1830–94).
1848	Founding of the Pre-Raphaelite Brotherhood (G).
1848–60	**Arthur Hugh Clough** (1819–61).
1848–75	**Charles Kingsley** (1819–75).
1849–88	**Matthew Arnold** (1822–88).
1850	Publication of the *Germ* (G).
1850–81	**Dante Gabriel Rossetti** (1828–82).
1850–92	**Alfred Lord Tennyson** (1809–92) poet laureate (G).
1851–1909	**George Meredith** (1828–1909).
1852–70	Reign of Napoleon III (Louis Napoleon) (1808–73) as Emperor of the French.
1852–84	**Charles Reade** (1814–84).
1854	The term "The Spasmodic School of Poetry" used by **W. E. Aytoun** (1813–65) in *Firmilian* (G).
1854–56	The Crimean War.
1856–74	Chief writings of Gustave Flaubert (1821–80), French novelist.
1857–8	Sepoy mutiny against the English, in India.
1857–76	**George Eliot** (1819–80).
1858–96	**William Morris** (1834–96).
1859	The Austro-Italian War. *The Rubáiyát of Omar Khayyám* by **Edward Fitzgerald** (1809–83). *The Origin of Species* by **Charles Darwin** (1809–82). **Tennyson's** *Idylls of the King*.
1859–76	Chief writings of Ivan Sergyeevich Turgenev (1818–1883), Russian novelist.
1860	First issue of the *Cornhill Magazine* (G).
1860–1908	**Algernon Charles Swinburne** (1837–1909).
1861–65	Civil War in the United States of America.
1863–93	**Thomas Henry Huxley** (1825–95).
1863–1900	Chief writings of Henrik Ibsen (1828–1906), Norwegian dramatist and poet.
1865–93	"Lewis Carroll" (1832–98).
1865–99	Chief writings of Lev Nikolaevich, Count Tolstoy (1828–1910), Russian novelist and social reformer.
1866–81	**Gerard Manley Hopkins** (1844–89).

1866–89   **William Schwenck Gilbert** (1836–1911).

1867   Passage of the Second Reform Bill to extend franchise. *Das Kapital* by Karl Marx (1818–83), German socialist.

1867–95   Chief writings of Émile Zola (1840–1902), French novelist.

1869   Opening of the Suez Canal.

1870–71   The Franco-Prussian War.

1871   The term "The Fleshly School of Poetry" **(G)** applied in *Contemporary Review* to D. G. Rossetti and others.

1871–1904   **Henry James** (1843–1916).

1871–1928   **Thomas Hardy** (1840–1928).

1872–98   **Samuel Butler** (1835–1902).

1873–94   **Walter Pater** (1839–94).

1873–1929   **Robert Bridges** (1844–1930).

1874–82   **James Thomson** (1834–82).

1876–91   Chief writings of Friedrich Nietzsche (1844–1900), German philosopher.

1878–94   **Robert Louis Stevenson** (1850–94).

1880–88   Chief writings of Guy de Maupassant (1850–93), French novelist and story writer.

1880–1903   **George Robert Gissing** (1857–1903).

1880–1930   **Arthur Wing Pinero** (1855–1934).

1881–98   **Oscar Wilde** (1856–1900).

1882–1915   **Henry Arthur Jones** (1851–1929).

1883–1922   **George Moore** (1852–1933).

1884   Passage of the Third Reform Bill to extend the franchise.

1884–90   Chief writings of Paul Verlaine (1844–96), French symbolist. See Symbolism in *Glossary*.

1885–1909   **John Davidson** (1857–1909).

1886–1910   **Rudyard Kipling** (1865–1936).

1886–1930   **Arthur Symons** (1865–1945).

1886–1934   **William Butler Yeats** (1865–1939).

1887–1904   Chief writings of Anton Chekhov (1860–1904), Russian novelist and dramatist.

1887–1926   **Sir Arthur Conan Doyle** (1859–1930).

1888–93   **William Ernest Henley** (1849–1903).

1888–1917   **Sir James Barrie** (1860–1937).

1888–1934   **Havelock Ellis** (1859–1939).

1889–1925   Chief writings of Hermann Sudermann (1857–1928), German novelist and dramatist.

CHART [*1890–1913*

1890–1900	*Fin de Siècle* (**G**).
1890–1903	Chief writings of Gerhart Johann Robert Hauptmann (1862–1946), German poet and dramatist.
1890–1930	Celtic Renaissance (**G**).
1890–1935	Writings of Sigmund Freud (1856–1939), Austrian psychoanalyst.
1892–1912	Chief writings of Maurice Maeterlinck (1862–1949), Belgian dramatist and poet.
1892–1940	**George Bernard Shaw** (1856–1950).
1893–97	**Francis Thompson** (1859–1907).
1894–5	Chinese-Japanese War.
1894–7	Publication of the *Yellow Book* (**G**).
1895–1920	**Joseph Conrad** (1857–1924).
1895–1924	Chief writings of Maxim Gorky (1868–1936), Russian novelist.
1895–1933	**Herbert George Wells** (1866–1946).
1896–1913	**Alfred Austin** (1835–1913) poet laureate (**G**).
1896–1931	**Sir Max Beerbohm** (1872–1956).
1896–1934	**Hilaire Belloc** (1870–1953).
1896–1936	**Alfred Edward Housman** (1859–1936).
1897	"Diamond Jubilee" on the occasion of the sixtieth anniversary of Queen Victoria's reign.
1899	The Hague Conference.
1899–1902	The Boer War between Great Britain and the Boer republics of South Africa.
1901–10	Reign of Edward VII. The Edwardian Age (**G**).
1901–30	**Gilbert Keith Chesterton** (1874–1936).
1902–13	**H. H. Munro ("Saki")** (1870–1916).
1902–31	**Arnold Bennett** (1867–1931).
1902–34	**John Masefield** (1878–). **Alfred Noyes** (1880–1958).
1903	Wright brothers make first airplane flight at Kitty Hawk, North Carolina.
1903–07	**John Millington Synge** (1871–1909).
1904–5	Russo-Japanese War.
1904–30	**John Galsworthy** (1867–1933).
1905–	**E. M. Forster** (1879–).
1905–34	**Lord Dunsany** (1878–1958).
1909	Discovery of North Pole by Robert Peary (1856–1920).
1910–36	Reign of George V.
1911–22	**Katherine Mansfield** (1888–1923).
1911–30	**D. H. Lawrence** (1885–1930).
1913–30	**Robert Bridges** (1844–1930) poet laureate (**G**).

1914   Passage of Home Rule Bill for Ireland. Opening of
                  the Panama Canal.

1914–18   The First World War.

1915–41   **Virginia Woolf** (1882–1941).

1916–   **Aldous Huxley** (1894–).

1917–   **T. S. Eliot** (1888–).

1918–31   **Lytton Strachey** (1880–1932).

1919   The Treaty of Versailles.

1919–   **Sean O'Casey** (1884–).

1920–   **Noel Coward** (1899–).

1922   *Ulysses* by **James Joyce** (1882–1941).

1930–   **John Masefield** (1878–), poet laureate **(G).**

1933   Adolf Hitler (1889–1945?), head of National Social-
                  ist Party in Germany, becomes Chancellor and the
                  following year "Führer," or "Leader."

1936   Reign of Edward VIII (Jan. 20–Dec. 11); abdicated.

1936–52   Reign of George VI.

1939   Outbreak of the Second World War.

1941   Outbreak of the Anglo-American and Japanese war.

1945   Final defeat of Germany. Bombardment of Japan
                  with atomic bombs. Capitulation of Japan.

1946   First session United Nations.

1949   North Atlantic Pact.

1950–51   Korean Crisis.

1952   Reign of Elizabeth II begins.

1956   Suez Crisis.

1957   First earth satellite launched.

NOTES

NOTES

NOTES

NOTES

NOTES

NOTES

NOTES